THE WEIMAR YEARS

THE WEIMAR YEARS

RISE AND FALL
1918–1933

FRANK McDONOUGH

Head
of ZEUS

An Apollo Book

First published in 2023 by Head of Zeus Ltd,
part of Bloomsbury Plc

Copyright © Frank McDonough, 2023

A catalogue record for this book is available
from the British Library.

3 5 7 9 10 8 6 4 2

ISBN (HB) 9781803284781
ISBN (E) 9781803284767

Designed by Isambard Thomas, Corvo
Maps by Jeff Edwards
Colour separation by DawkinsColour
Printed and bound in Scotland by Bell & Bain

Head of Zeus Ltd
First Floor East
5–8 Hardwick Street
London ECIR 4RG
WWW.HEADOFZEUS.COM

This book is dedicated
to the memory of
James West (1975–2022)

With love also to his wife Emily
and daughters Martha and Veronica

MAPS

Germany after the Treaty of Versailles

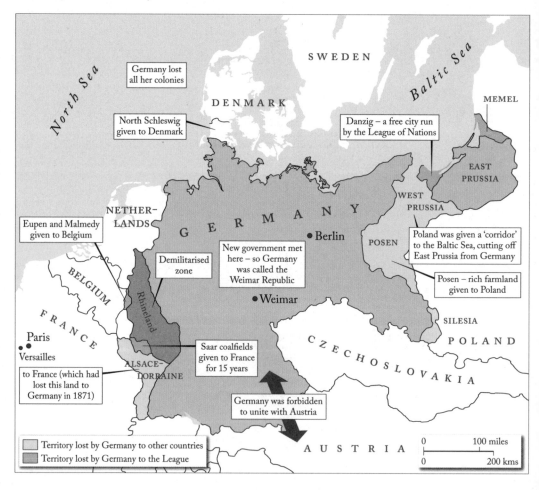

SWEDEN

Baltic Sea

MEMEL

North Sea

DENMARK

Germany lost
all her colonies

North Schleswig
given to Denmark

Danzig – a free city run
by the League of Nations

EAST
PRUSSIA

WEST
PRUSSIA

NETHER-
LANDS

G E R M A N Y

Berlin

POSEN

Poland was given a 'corridor'
to the Baltic Sea, cutting off
East Prussia from Germany

Eupen and Malmedy
given to Belgium

Demilitarised
zone

New government met
here – so Germany
was called the
Weimar Republic

Posen – rich farmland
given to Poland

BELGIUM

Rhineland

Weimar

SILESIA

FRANCE

P O L A N D

Paris

Versailles

C Z E C H O S L O V A K I A

ALSACE-
LORRAINE

Saar coalfields
given to France
for 15 years

to France (which had
lost this land to
Germany in 1871)

Germany was forbidden
to unite with Austria

Territory lost by Germany to other countries

Territory lost by Germany to the League

A U S T R I A

0   100 miles

0   200 kms

States of the Weimar Republic

AUTHOR'S PREFACE

This is the third volume in my comprehensive narrative history of Germany from 1918 to 1945. The first two volumes, *The Hitler Years*, covered the period when Hitler led Germany from 1933 to 1945: the first volume, *Triumph*, began with Hitler coming to power in 1933, and ended shortly after the military conquest of Poland in 1939; the second volume, *Disaster*, covered the period 1940 to 1945, beginning with Hitler's military triumphs in Western Europe in 1940 and concluding with the total defeat of Germany in 1945.

This prequel, *The Weimar Years*, tells the dramatic history of the period from 1918 to 1933. The history of the Weimar Republic cast a tragic shadow over world history as the failure of democracy in Germany led to the rise of Hitler's brutal dictatorship. The book adopts a chronological structure, with each chapter examining a calendar year in detail. Sections in most chapters explore cultural developments to provide further context to the period.

Each book can be read as a separate volume, but taken together this trilogy provides a comprehensive and vivid narrative history of Germany from 1918 to 1945.

INTRODUCTION

The Weimar Republic was born in the smouldering ashes of Germany's catastrophic defeat in the 'Great War' of 1914–18. It held out hope in 1918 for a new era of democracy, but no one can ever forget that its fall led to the appointment of Adolf Hitler on 30 January 1933. He soon created a one-party dictatorship which abandoned the rule of law, democracy, and civil rights, then planned and launched the Second World War. He was primarily responsible for killing untold millions of innocent victims during the Holocaust.

In this new narrative history of the Weimar years, the focus will be on the major personalities and events in political and foreign policy, the economic upheavals that affected political decisions, and the cultural highlights of the period. The book attempts to explain how Weimar democracy developed and why it ended so tragically. It presents a detailed story of a crisis-ridden society that gradually became politically ungovernable.

Despite the loss of 13 per cent of its European territory, under the terms of the 1919 Versailles Treaty, the population of Germany rose from 62.4 million in 1925 to 65.2 million in 1933. The capital city, Berlin, passed the milestone of 4 million inhabitants during the 1920s. But about 36 per cent of the population still lived in small rural communities of fewer than 2,000 inhabitants, and only 27 per cent of the population lived in big cities of more than 100,000 people. Germany's ten biggest cities at the time were Berlin, Hamburg, Cologne, Munich, Leipzig, Dresden, Essen, Breslau, Frankfurt am Main and Düsseldorf. All these cities, apart from Cologne and Munich, had governments with Social Democratic–Centre Party majorities. Hitler's National Socialist German Workers' Party had its poorest election results in these big cities.

The Reichswehr, the reconstituted German Army, remained a powerful force during the Weimar period. It was never fully purged, with most of the officers from the Imperial Army remaining in post. Some officers were hostile to the Republic, and during the Kapp Putsch in 1920 stood on the sidelines. At that time, it was the trade unionists in the big cities who saved the Republic by calling a general strike, which ended the attempted coup. Afterwards, leading officers agreed to tolerate the Republic on condition that there was no interference in its secret rearmament plans. A key army figure was the politically influential Kurt von Schleicher, who became Defence Minister in June 1932, and then Chancellor in December 1932. He emerged as a key behind-the-scenes wire puller in President Hindenburg's inner circle after 1929, and he played a crucial role in the death of the Republic.

The events in Germany during the years from 1918 to 1933 were dramatic and turbulent, including numerous failed coups and uprisings by anti-democratic groups on the Right and Left, most notably the Spartacist Uprising of 1919, the Kapp Revolt of 1920, and Hitler's famous bungled Munich Beer Hall Putsch of 1923. There were also a series of political assassinations, especially between 1919 and 1923, in which over 350 people died. The victims included Walther Rathenau and Matthias Erzberger on the Centre Right and Kurt Eisner, Karl Liebknecht, and Rosa Luxemburg on the Left.

The Weimar years were also characterised by constant economic upheaval, most notably the runaway inflation that impoverished millions of people, and a series of international crises related to German non-payment of reparations to the Allies, which led to the 1923 occupation of the Ruhr by French and Belgian troops. The crisis of 1923 led to the Dawes Plan of 1924, which stabilised the German currency, and greatly assisted in the payment of reparations until 1929, when it was replaced by the Young Plan. The 'great inflation' of 1923 was a deeply traumatic episode in the early years of Weimar, especially among the middle class, who saw their savings wiped out. The onset of the Great Depression after 1929 led to unemployment reaching a staggering 6.6 million. The only period of relative economic and international calm during the Weimar years came between 1924 and 1929, when the German economy underwent a partial recovery, primarily due to American loans, together with a foreign policy under the guidance of Gustav Stresemann, German Foreign Minister, which accepted the territorial settlement in Western Europe, under the Locarno Treaties in 1925, then joined the League of Nations in 1926, and renounced war as an instrument of policy, under the Kellogg–Briand Pact in 1928. Stresemann hoped his policy of reconciliation with the Western Allies would lead the way to a further relaxation of the punitive terms laid down by the Versailles Treaty. His premature death in 1929 was a huge blow to Weimar democracy and Germany's prestige on the international stage.

We must not forget the Weimar years were also a time of far-reaching social and welfare reforms. One of the most beneficial was the Unemployment Insurance Act of 1927, which offered welfare benefits to those out of work. Previously, these benefits had only been offered for unemployment caused by sickness, accident, invalidity and old age. New public housing schemes offered better-off workers and white-collar workers modern rented apartments at reasonable rents, with new kitchens, indoor bathrooms, gas stoves and electricity. Under Article 109 of the Weimar Constitution, women were granted equal rights for the first time and enjoyed more employment opportunities, accounting for 36 per cent of the workforce in 1919. There was also an active feminist movement, and journalists noted the rise of a 'new woman', independent in spirit, who cut her hair short and wore unisex fashions.

The Weimar years also witnessed a free-spirited cultural revolution, which continues to resonate today. New forms of art, design, music, theatre, literature, and architecture flourished; and there was a new and tolerant openness regarding sexuality. The creators of Weimar culture believed they were building a more progressive modern society.

New theatrical forms included those pioneered by Bertolt Brecht and Kurt Weill, while Hannah Hoch produced memorable collages, John Heartfield created radical photomontages, and innovative architects such as Erich Mendelsohn created modernist buildings. Walter Gropius established the deeply influential Bauhaus art school, which included in its faculty great artists like Paul Klee and Wassily Kandinsky. Expressionist and New Realist artists, among them George Grosz and Otto Dix, produced some of the most disturbing and challenging works of the twentieth century during the Weimar years.

A wave of anti-war novels appeared, the most successful being *All Quiet on the Western Front* by Erich Remarque, which became a world-wide best seller. There were many innovative films to rival the products of Hollywood, including Robert Wiene's *The Cabinet of Dr. Caligari*, Fritz Lang's hugely ambitious *Metropolis* and his chilling study of a child killer, *M*, Walter Ruttmann's *Berlin: Symphony of a City* and Josef von Sternberg's *The Blue Angel*.

Perhaps the most well-known popular aspect of Weimar culture was the thriving Cabaret scene, centred on Berlin, which featured in the eponymous 1972 Hollywood film, based on Christopher Isherwood's haunting novel *Goodbye to Berlin*, and more recently in the German TV series *Babylon Berlin*, both of which are set in the later years of the Weimar Republic. Hitler's dictatorship destroyed the creativity of

Weimar, and Germany never regained the cultural dominance it had achieved in the 1920s.

A key feature of Weimar political debate was the so-called 'Jewish question'. The antisemitism of the German Right was long standing. Jews in Weimar Germany had far more opportunities to flourish than ever before, but this did nothing to stem the rise of antisemitism. The Right argued that Jews exercised an influence over political, economic, and cultural life out of all proportion to their small numbers in the population. The Right further associated Jews with the Bolshevik Revolution, control of financial sectors of the economy, and what they saw as the decadence of Weimar culture. Jews were seemingly responsible for every kind of misery.

This explosion of antisemitism was fuelled by the trauma of defeat in the First World War, fear of Bolshevism and a conspiracy theory, published in the form of the (forged) *Protocols of the Elders of Zion*, which claimed that Jews were plotting a world-wide takeover of governments and societies. These ideas not only flourished among Hitler's National Socialists but could be found in groups such as the Pan German League and the Steel Helmet (*Stahlhelm*), the ex-servicemen's movement, and were even popular within the main German conservative party, the German National People's Party.

The failure of Weimar democracy has generated a number of explanations among historians. Some point to unforeseen flaws in the democratic 1919 Constitution, signed in the spa town of Weimar, especially the proportional representation election system, which was undoubtedly democratic, but arguably led to too many political and special interest parties gaining seats in the Reichstag. These all appealed to narrow class or economic interests, but not to the nation as a whole. This led to a succession of unstable coalitions and frequent changes of government from 1918 to 1933, as no one party ever commanded an overall majority in the Reichstag. There were no fewer than 20 different Weimar cabinets, each lasting an average of eight months. The fragility of all these coalitions made the task of each Chancellor ever more difficult, as any contentious measure could put the governing coalition in danger. For a democracy to function effectively all parties need to make compromises, especially if coalition government becomes the norm. The failure to find a parliamentary consensus on the best way forward eventually made Germany ungovernable, and no viable parliamentary coalition was possible after March 1930.

Although the Social Democrats, the greatest defenders of the

Weimar Republic, were the largest Reichstag party from 1919 until July 1932, a member of the SPD only held the post of Reich Chancellor (*Reichsministerpräsident*) four times during the Weimar period. From 1923 to 1928, the Social Democrats stayed outside all the national coalitions, and its reluctance to join governing coalitions made it seem a party that preferred the luxury of opposition to government responsibility. The last coalition in which the SPD participated was the so-called 'Grand Coalition' of 1928–1930. As the representative of the numerically large working class, the SPD stood the best chance, at the outset of the Weimar period, of becoming Germany's 'people's party', but it failed to appeal to voters outside its working-class hard core, and it was in constant conflict with the Communist Party. The two left-wing parties were bitter enemies and refused to join in coalition governments together.

Other historians point to the impact of the Versailles Treaty in weakening support for democracy. The 'war guilt clause' written into the Treaty, which blamed Germany for starting the war, imposed reparations payments that led to economic upheaval, and to Right-wing groups suggesting Germany had not been defeated in the war, but 'stabbed in the back' by Jews, Socialists and treacherous democratic politicians at home, who were dubbed the 'November Criminals' (*Novemberverbrecher*). Defeat in the 'Great War' cast a long shadow and caused bitter debate precisely because too many Germans refused to accept that defeat.

Democracy in the Weimar years looked to a majority of the public like a system imposed by the Allies which had produced no long-term stability. Germany's democratic politicians were mostly dull bureaucrats, with only Gustav Stresemann, Foreign Minister from 1923 to 1929, becoming well known on the world stage. This leadership vacuum greatly assisted the rise of Adolf Hitler as, during the economic depression after 1929, he promised the strong leadership which democracy had failed to deliver, but which a sizeable number of voters desired.

Another historical view is that the inclusion of Article 48 in the Weimar Constitution, which allowed the President to override or dissolve the elected Reichstag, opened the way to destroying democracy. This power was used frequently by the Social Democratic President, Friedrich Ebert, from 1919 to 1925, particularly during the Ruhr crisis and the hyperinflation period, but Ebert used it exactly as it was intended to be used: to 'defend the Republic'. In contrast,

Article 48 was frequently abused by the right-wing President Paul von Hindenburg, who after March 1930 dispensed with parliamentary coalitions and ruled by presidential decree. This 'presidential' system of rule, using his own hand-picked Chancellors, meant that power narrowed to a small, undemocratic, militaristic inner circle who gained undue influence over the ageing Hindenburg, often persuading him to do their bidding. This interpretation of Weimar history places strong emphasis on the weaknesses of the Constitution, which was subverted to serve the needs of reactionary forces. Hitler, it is argued, was given power by Hindenburg under the delusion that he could be controlled.

Then there are those historians who argue that democracy never won the hearts and minds of most of the German people. For example, the Social Democrats never purged the judiciary, the army, and the civil service of reactionaries, who were all deeply hostile to democracy. Parliamentary democracy was viewed by this surviving middle-class conservative elite as 'un-German', suitable for Americans, the French or the British, but not for a nation that desired strong authority and unity. For these people, democracy was an unwelcome foreign importation.

This lack of democratic legitimacy can be seen through the fluctuating electoral support for the three parties who were most loyal to the Weimar Republic: the Social Democratic Party, the German Democratic Party and the Centre Party, who polled between them 76.2 per cent of the vote in the 19 January 1919 national election, but only polled 33.25 per cent in the last fully free Weimar national election on 6 November 1932. At the same time, the two parties that were pledged to destroy democracy, Hitler's National Socialist Party and the Communist Party, polled a collective total of 50 per cent.

1918

·

DEFEAT AND REVOLUTION

·

At the start of the First World War, Imperial Germany was not a parliamentary democracy, but nor was it an autocracy. It had a constitution, a national parliament, and independent states which controlled the local budgets of each region. The national parliament consisted of the Reichstag directly elected by the German people and an upper unelected chamber known as the Federal Council (Bundesrat), with representatives from the 26 individual princely states. Voting in elections for the Reichstag was confined to all males aged 25 and over and based on a constituency-based, first-past-the-post system. Neither the Bundesrat nor the Reichstag had the power to draft legislation but were expected to approve it. Even so, more people were entitled to vote in German parliamentary elections in 1914 than was the case in Britain.[1]

Despite the Reichstag's lack of political power, German national elections were hotly contested. The six leading political parties represented in the Reichstag in 1914 were: the Social Democrats (*Sozialdemokratische Partei Deutschlands*, SPD), which represented the working class but had toned down its Marxist revolutionary rhetoric to advocate gradual social reform through the existing political system; two liberal parties – the National Liberal Party (*Nationalliberale Partei*, NLP) and the Progressive People's Party (*Fortschrittliche Volkspartei*, FVP); the German Conservative Party (*Deutschkonservative Partei*, DKP), which later merged with other right-wing forces and some elements of the NLP to form the German National People's Party (*Deutschnationale Volkspartei*, DNVP); and two special interest parties – the Polish Party (PP), which represented the Polish population in Germany, and the powerful Centre Party (*Deutsche Zentrumpartei*, Zentrum), which represented Catholics.

The power and influence of the military was stronger than that of any of the political parties. It was often described as a 'state within a state'.[2] The Emperor Kaiser Wilhelm II, the eldest grandson of Queen Victoria, had been in power since 1888. He had the final say on policy, controlled the armed forces, appointed the German

previous page   Paul von Hindenburg: field marshal and German national hero during the Great War; President of Weimar Germany from 1925 to 1933.
right   Kaiser Wilhelm II: German Emperor and King of Prussia, 1888–1918.

Chancellor and the cabinet ministers and was able to veto decisions taken by the Bundesrat and the Reichstag.[3] The German Empire's governing system, dominated by the Kaiser, was called an 'autocratic state' (*Obrigkeitsstaat*). On the outbreak of war on 4 August 1914, the German Emperor told the assembled members of the Reichstag: 'I no longer recognise parties. I know only Germans.'[4] He then asked the Reichstag members to endorse an Enabling Act which suspended elections and Reichstag meetings and afforded him unlimited powers. Under Article 68 of the then German constitution, the Army seized wide-ranging executive powers, which included a strict censorship of the press.

Kaiser Wilhelm decided to finance the war not by raising taxation, but by creating Loan Banknotes (*Darlehenskassenscheine*), issuing three-month Treasury Bills and printing money. The idea was for these loans to be paid back in the event of Germany winning the war, capturing territory, and imposing reparations on the defeated powers. It was only in 1916 that new taxes were belatedly introduced on business, but not on incomes. Only 13.9 per cent of Germany's war costs came from direct taxation, compared to 18.2 per cent for Britain. During the war, the amount of money in circulation rose from 7.4 million to 44.4 million marks, which inevitably led to high inflation.[5]

The Germans prided themselves on the superiority of their armed forces and the strength of their economy. In 1914, Germany possessed the most powerful and dynamic economy on the European continent, which had experienced 50 years of uninterrupted growth. Germany produced two-thirds of Europe's output of steel, half its coal production, and 20 per cent more electrical energy than Britain, France and Italy put together. It had a population of 67 million, which had grown from 25 million in 1800. It was also Europe's leader in modern industries such as chemicals and pharmaceuticals. In agriculture, it produced a third of the world's output of potatoes.[6]

Germany's confident hopes of a swift victory were halted in September 1914 by British, Belgian, and French troops on the Marne River in France. From this point onwards, the war on the Western Front became a stalemate, with 8 million troops stretched along a 450-mile front from the North Sea to the Swiss border. Numerous attempts to break the deadlock turned into dogged struggles for mere yards of territory, with millions of lives lost and little ground gained. Barbed wire entanglements impeded the advance of competing armies and machine guns mowed down advancing troops. It was a struggle in which an average of 6,000 troops were killed every day.

The stalemate in the west contrasted sharply with the stunning victories of the German Army on the Eastern Front in 1914 and 1915, masterminded by General Paul von Hindenburg, the chief of the Supreme Army Command (*Oberste Heeresleitung*, OHL), and his brilliant Chief of Staff, the Quartermaster General, Erich Ludendorff. By the end of 1915, the Germans had driven the Russian armies back remorselessly over 250 miles. These stunning victories turned Hindenburg and Ludendorff into national heroes. As the war progressed, Kaiser Wilhelm proved incapable of effective leadership, which resulted in a power vacuum, filled by the military high command. In late August 1916, Germany became a de facto military dictatorship led by Hindenburg and Ludendorff, who were able, until the later stages of the war, to ignore the wishes of the parliamentary parties.

Germany in the period from 1916 to 1918 has been correctly described as a 'Silent Dictatorship'. Censorship over newspapers was tightened; at the same time, Hindenburg ordered the systematic economic exploitation of German-occupied areas in France, Belgium and in East Central Europe, under the Hindenburg Programme of August 1916, which aimed to double industrial production by increasing the output of munitions, explosives, weapons, artillery, and ammunition. On 1 November 1916 Hindenburg and Ludendorff founded the Supreme War Office (*Kriegsamt*), under General Wilhelm Groener, to create a command economy ruled by the army. Compulsory military service was introduced for everyone aged 16 to 60, and businesses not related to the war economy were closed down. More alarmingly, compulsory hard labour was imposed on prisoners of war in labour camps, often under appalling conditions.[7] Under the 'Silent Dictatorship', Germany pursued its war aims in a ruthless manner. At the beginning of 1917, the Imperial Navy (*Kaiserliche Marine*) adopted unrestricted submarine warfare in the Atlantic to disrupt British and French supplies arriving from the USA. This proved counterproductive and provoked the Americans, led by President Woodrow Wilson, to enter the war on the Allied side in April 1917.[8]

As the war dragged on, political tensions on the home front increased. In a remarkable speech to the Reichstag on 6 July 1917, Matthias Erzberger, a leading figure in Zentrum, called on the government led by the increasingly unpopular Chancellor, Theobald von Bethmann Hollweg, to denounce German territorial ambitions and conclude a negotiated end of the war with the Allies.[9]

On 19 July 1917, Erzberger introduced a resolution in the Reichstag for a 'peace without annexations', which was passed by 212 to 126 votes. It was the first major intervention by the Reichstag to oppose the war, but Kaiser Wilhelm refused to be bound by the Reichstag. Hindenburg and Ludendorff considered the resolution a 'scrap of paper' and ignored it. The blame for the political crisis was placed on Bethmann Hollweg, who had rightly been sceptical about unrestricted submarine warfare. He was forced to resign as Chancellor.

His replacement, Georg Michaelis, who took office on 13 July 1917, was the first German Chancellor who was not of noble birth. His background was in business, but his only previous minor political posts were as an undersecretary of state in the Prussian Treasury, and as the head of the Reich Grain Agency (*Reichsgetreidestelle*), the office responsible for the distribution of corn and wheat.[10] The prime movers in the unexpected elevation of this inexperienced bureaucrat to the role of Chancellor were Hindenburg and Ludendorff, who felt he would do their bidding. True to form, Michaelis kept the Reichstag completely in the dark on matters of war and foreign relations. He was forced to resign on 1 November 1917 after his refusal to give support to Erzberger's peace resolution led to the loss of a vote of confidence in the Reichstag.

In Eastern Europe, relentless German military pressure contributed to the abdication of the Russian Tsar Nicholas II in February 1917, which eventually led to the Bolsheviks under Vladimir Ilyich Lenin coming to power in November of that year. Lenin's return to Russia was assisted by his sealed train being given permission to cross German territory – an incident in which Ludendorff played a key role.

After seizing power, Lenin and the Bolsheviks opened negotiations for a peace settlement with Germany. This resulted in the signing of the punitive Treaty of Brest-Litovsk on 3 March 1918, under which Russia lost possession of 34 per cent of its population, 54 per cent of its industry, including 89 per cent of its coalfields, and 26 per cent of its railways, and was also obliged to pay 6 billion marks in compensation for German losses. The Treaty completely contradicted the Peace Resolution of the Reichstag, which had pledged 'peace without annexations', yet the Reichstag deputies ratified the Treaty of Brest-Litovsk without suggesting any amendments.[11]

Victory in Russia gave the German people real hope of victory in the war. On 21 March 1918, Germany launched a spring offensive, better known as the Ludendorff Offensive, on the Western Front. It aimed

Erich Ludendorff, architect with Hindenburg of the German victory at Tannenberg in 1914, would contribute significantly to the rise of Nazism in the 1920s.

to knock Britain and France out of the war before significant numbers of US forces arrived in Europe.[12] Unfortunately, German expectations of victory proved illusory. Scarcely in the annals of military history has there been such a spectacular reversal of military fortune as Germany suffered towards the end of the war. By early June 1918, it was clear that the Ludendorff Offensive had failed. On 8 August, the British Expeditionary Force (BEF), spearheaded by tanks and supported by massive numbers of newly arrived American troops, launched a surprise attack between Amiens and St Quentin in northern France against the German Second Army. It punched a huge hole in the defensive line and captured 15,000 German soldiers. The significance of this decisive British breakthrough in the Battle of Amiens was not lost on Ludendorff, who called it 'the blackest day of the German army in the history of this war'.[13] He knew the Allies were now able to deploy thousands of tanks on the Western Front while the Germans had been able to manufacture only 20.[14] Fritz Nagel, a German officer in the German anti-aircraft artillery, later recalled: 'The German armies were in bad shape. Every soldier and civilian was hungry. Losses in material could not be replaced and the soldiers arriving as replacements were too young, poorly trained and often unwilling to risk their necks because the war looked like a lost cause.'[15]

A two-day military conference on the critical situation on the Western Front was held on 13–14 August 1918 at the headquarters of the Supreme Military Command in Spa, Belgium. Hindenburg chaired it, and Paul von Hintze, the new Foreign Minister, and Ludendorff were present. Ludendorff said Germany now needed to adopt a purely defensive strategy, but he thought it might still be possible to sue for peace with the western Allies on favourable terms. Hindenburg agreed with Ludendorff's judgement about continuing with strategic defence, while Hintze thought the German Army was in no condition to fight a successful strategic defence, and he felt diplomatic steps had to be taken to bring the war to an end.

When Kaiser Wilhelm II was apprised of these discussions in a Grand Council meeting, he seemed blinded by the optimism of Hindenburg and Ludendorff, and instructed Hintze to refrain from making a direct peace offer to the Allies and to wait for a more favourable moment.[16] This proved wishful thinking, as Germany's Central Power allies now began to collapse. On 24 September 1918, the Bulgarian Army was defeated when the Allied armies based in Greece broke through the Macedonian Front. The Bulgarian government, which had previously been under German control, requested an armistice and accepted it five days later. This placed the Austro-Hungarian empire, Germany's principal ally, in a precarious position. Emperor Charles I of Austria, desperate to end the war, sent a circular diplomatic note inviting all the belligerents in the war to send representatives to Vienna to a confidential conference to discuss the basic principles of a peace settlement. On 27 October, Austria-Hungary ended its formal alliance with Germany, and the subject nationalities of the Habsburg Empire all declared their independence. On 30 October, the Ottoman Turks signed a regional armistice. Germany was now left without any allies.

The US government led by President Woodrow Wilson had already outlined a number of principles to be used in peace negotiations in his Fourteen Points, which he had outlined in a speech before the US Congress on 8 January 1918. Among these, Wilson promised no secret diplomacy, free seas, free trade, a reduction in armaments, restoration of Belgian independence, political settlement in the Balkans, the return of Alsace-Lorraine to France, the evacuation of foreign forces from Russia, national self-determination for nationalities – which included home rule for Austria, independence for Poland, Turkey and the subject nations of the Habsburg empire – and the establishment of a League of Nations to prevent further wars.[17]

On 24 September, Georg von Hertling, the 75-year-old German Chancellor, a member of Zentrum and the first leader of a political party to hold the office, appeared before the Reichstag to give a grim report on the military situation. Hertling was seen by his political opponents as another puppet of Hindenburg and Ludendorff. The next day, leading members of the various political parties gave their views on Hertling's speech. Adolf Gröber, of Zentrum, was first to speak. He made it clear his party had no confidence in Hertling. There were equally scathing attacks on the Chancellor from across the political spectrum. Newspaper editorials were soon predicting that Hertling's days in office were numbered.

On 28 September, the Social Democrats and the Progressives launched a new political offensive. They demanded the abolition of two sections of the German imperial constitution. The first was Article 9, which made it impossible for a Reichstag deputy to become a member of the Bundesrat. The second was Article 21, which obliged elected members of the Reichstag to give up their seats if they accepted government cabinet posts. These articles were seen as key impediments to the creation of a truly democratic parliamentary system. Hertling declared these demands for constitutional reform as unacceptable, because he opposed the establishment of a truly parliamentary system.

On 29 September, Hindenburg and Ludendorff informed Kaiser Wilhelm II in Spa in Belgium that Germany must seek an armistice without delay. Hintze, the Foreign Minister, reported that Germany's allies were collapsing, noting: 'Bulgaria lost; the loss of Austria-Hungary imminent; Turkey more a burden than benefit.'[18] Ludendorff insisted the armistice terms must allow German armed forces to evacuate the occupied territories, to leave open the possibility of resuming hostilities. The request by the Supreme Command for an armistice astonished Kaiser Wilhelm who was now faced with the question of whether he could end the war and still keep his throne.[19] It was agreed that the request for an armistice should be submitted to US President Woodrow Wilson, and that Germany would accept a peace settlement based on his Fourteen Points.

Ludendorff warned that the public announcement of Germany seeking an armistice might be the starting point for a socialist revolution in Germany. To ward this off, he suggested a swift 'revolution from above' involving Kaiser Wilhelm democratising his government quickly to broaden its base. A popular democratic government, he continued, stood a much better chance of gaining a favourable peace settlement from the Allies than the Imperial government or the Supreme High Command. Chancellor Hertling was brought in to meet the Kaiser who informed him of this decision. It says much about the nature of German government that the Chancellor took no part in the discussions leading to the decision to request an armistice. Hertling, a committed nationalist to the end, chose to resign along with his cabinet, rather than seek an armistice, but he stressed that time should be allowed for the composition of the new government. The Kaiser decided that the formation of the new government must happen much more quickly. On 30 September, he announced the resignation of Hertling, the third of Germany's war-time Chancellors, and proclaimed: 'It is my wish that the German people should participate more effectively than before in the determination of the fate of the Fatherland. It is therefore my will that men who enjoy the confidence of the nation should take part in the rights and duties of the government.'[20]

On 3 October 1918, Prince Maximilian of Baden (also known as Max von Baden), became the new German Chancellor and the Minister-President of Prussia, at the age of 51. He was the heir to the throne of the Grand Duchy of Baden and belonged to no political party. He was viewed as wise, humane, sensitive and liberal in outlook. If details of Prince Max's private life had been made public, it is unlikely he would ever have been made Chancellor in the first place. A police record in Berlin listed a homosexual offence committed when he was a young army officer, for which he was not prosecuted. Although he had married Princess Marie Louise of Hanover and Cumberland in 1900, it is clear he remained an active homosexual.[21] However, it was felt by Hindenburg and Ludendorff that Prince Max could be relied upon to try and save the Hohenzollern dynasty and form a more broad-based government. He was also acceptable to socialists, liberals, and monarchists, while his work with the Red Cross for better treatment of prisoners of war had earned him widespread international praise.[22]

Prince Max had reservations about approaching Woodrow Wilson for a peace settlement based on his Fourteen Points, partly because he thought the German public were not fully aware of these proposals and partly because a request for an armistice might be interpreted by the Allies as an act of desperation. He also believed that the Americans, though democratic in outlook, knew little about the complexity of European politics.[23] Prince Max decided to form a coalition government based on three roughly centre-left parties in the Reichstag: the Majority Social Democratic Party (MSPD), the largest Marxist inspired party in Germany; the Catholic-orientated Zentrum; and the FVP, a social liberal party known as the Progressives.

Of these parties, the attitude of the Social Democrats was crucial, as it had the largest parliamentary support. The original SPD had been formed in 1863 through the merger of two socialist groups, one

Max von Baden, last Chancellor of the German Empire, October–November 1918.

made up of committed Marxists who wanted revolution, and the other of moderates who preferred a policy of reform. Friedrich Ebert had been elected as the SPD leader in 1913. He came from a working-class background, had trained as a saddle-maker, then became a trade union secretary and a journalist before his election to the Reichstag in 1912. Ebert felt socialism must come in Germany through parliamentary reform.[24]

In 1914, Ebert had voted in favour of war loans and committed the SPD to the Kaiser's political truce (*Burgfrieden*), for the duration of the war. Ebert justified his position by arguing that Germany had entered the war as a defensive action against a ring of hostile states who threatened its existence.[25] His support for the war led to severe criticism from the anti-war left wing of the party. In 1916, Ebert agreed to share the party leadership with another moderate, Philipp Scheidemann, who had been an upholsterer, a printer and a journalist, before being elected to the Reichstag in 1903. Scheidemann was an impressive public speaker who came to favour a compromise peace and tried to mediate between the moderate and left-wing groups in an attempt to keep the Social Democrats together.[26]

On 21 December 1915, a number of Social Democrats voted against authorising further war loans in the Reichstag. The leader of this dissident group was Hugo Haase, a committed pacifist, who came from a Jewish family and had been a lawyer before entering the Reichstag in 1897. Haase functioned as the co-chairman of the SPD Reichstag members, along with Scheidemann, but in March 1916 he and 18 other anti-war SPD members had the party whip withdrawn, for voting against the government's emergency budget in defiance of Ebert.

During 1917, the Social Democrats finally split over the party's stance on the war. Those who opposed the war formed the Independent Social Democratic Party (*Unabhängige Sozialdemokratische Partei Deutschlands*, USPD), led by Haase, on 6 April 1917.[27] To avoid confusion, the pro-war remainder of the SPD became known as the Majority Social Democratic Party (*Mehrheitssozialdemokratische Partei Deutschlands*, MSPD).[28] In 1918 the two Social Democratic groupings decided to suspend their differences and enter Prince Max of Baden's coalition government.

Hindenburg and Ludendorff called the party leaders to a meeting in the Reichstag on 2 October 1918, at which Major Freiherr von dem Bussche gave a gloomy summary on the military situation, on behalf of the German High Command. In his opinion there was no possibility of forcing the enemy to sue for peace, as Allied tanks had already broken through German lines. American supplies of men and armaments were also beginning to tilt the balance further in favour of the Allies. It was therefore sensible to seek an armistice with the Entente powers before the situation grew much worse.[29]

The party leaders in the Reichstag were deeply shocked. They had no idea Germany was hurtling toward certain defeat. Hindenburg and Ludendorff's wartime propaganda had deluded them into believing in an eventual German victory. Ebert was stunned and left speechless. Gustav Stresemann, a patriotic member of the National Liberals, said bluntly: 'We have been lied to and betrayed.'[30]

On 3 October, Hindenburg sent a memorandum to Prince Max making clear a peace offer should be dispatched to the Allies as soon as possible to 'spare the German people and their allies unnecessary sacrifices'.[31] In the early hours of 4 October 1918, Prince Max sent the following brief telegraph message to President Woodrow Wilson requesting an armistice: 'The German Government accepts the programme set forth by the President in his message to Congress of the 8th of January 1918 as the basis for peace negotiation. With a view to avoiding further bloodshed, the German Government requests the immediate conclusion of an armistice on land and water and in the air.'[32]

On the same day, the composition of Prince Max's cabinet was announced. Many of Hertling's cabinet were retained: Friedrich von Payer was the Vice-Chancellor, Wilhelm Solf, the Colonial Minister, took on the additional role of Minister of Foreign Affairs, Siegfried von Rodern remained Finance Minister, and Paul von Krause stayed on as Minister of Justice. The posts of Minister of Food and Post were also retained by Wilhelm von Waldow and Otto Rüdlin, respectively. The new members of the cabinet were the Zentrum figures Adolf Gröber and Matthias Erzberger, both named as Ministers without Portfolio, a title they shared with the progressive Conrad Haussmann. Karl Trimborn, another Zentrum politician, took over as the new Minister of the Interior. The Social Democrat Philipp Scheidemann became Minister without Portfolio, while another Social Democrat, Gustav Bauer, became the head of the newly created Ministry of Labour. The new Navy Minister was Ernst Karl August Klemens von Mann, while Hans Karl von Stein zu Nord-und-Ostheim became the Minister of Economics. Friedrich Ebert was invited to join the cabinet but declined. It was the first German cabinet to include members of the Social Democrats, but the representatives of the Right were completely excluded.

On 5 October, Prince Max gave his first speech as German Chancellor in the Reichstag. He made clear that the German request for an end to hostilities was being made to achieve an 'honourable peace settlement'. He admitted he had only agreed to become Chancellor on the basis that trusted labour figures were included in his cabinet to signal a new direction in German policy. Prince Max also announced that he accepted the peace resolution outlined in July 1917 by the Social Democrats, the Centrists and the Progressives which had urged participation in a League of Nations based on equality for all, a commitment to the restoration of Belgian neutrality, and support for national self-determination and the creation of true democracy. Prince Max then criticised the annexation policy of the German Supreme Command during the war. Never again would a government take key decisions that did not have the confidence of the Reichstag, and did not contain key members of parliament. A fully democratic franchise would soon be implemented. On the same day Prince Max spoke in the Reichstag, Kaiser Wilhelm issued a proclamation to the armed forces of the Reich in which he made clear that Germany would only accept an 'honourable peace'.[33] The USPD issued a manifesto on 5 October addressed to all workers on the proposed peace talks. It was written by Hugo Haase, who suggested that the precarious position Germany now found itself in was entirely due to the catastrophic decisions of German militarists. The USPD had always supported democracy and socialism, while the MSPD had propped up the old ruling class and German militarism. Haase concluded by stating the USPD was still demanding a socialist republic.[34]

On 8 October, Wilson's reply to the German request for an armistice reached Berlin. Wilson had drafted it without consulting America's leading allies, Britain and France. It was courteous and conciliatory in tone. Wilson wanted confirmation from the German government that his Fourteen Points would form the basis of further discussion. He also made clear that an armistice could only be granted if Germany and its allies immediately withdrew troops from occupied areas. Wilson also wanted to know whether Prince Max was speaking as German Chancellor for the 'constitutional authorities of the empire', who had previously been conducting the war.[35] Wilson was criticised by the British and French governments for not discussing his negotiations with the German government beforehand, and on 9 October 1918 the

Supreme Allied War Council made clear that a German evacuation of the occupied areas did not go far enough and demanded the disarming of German forces.

On 10 October 1918, RMS *Leinster*, an Irish ship operated by the City of Dublin Steam Packet Company, was sunk by the German submarine *UB-123* while bound for Holyhead from Dublin. At least 564 people were killed, making it the largest-ever loss of life in the Irish Sea and another blatant example of unrestricted German U-boat warfare.[36] A wave of anger swept through the Allies over the sinking, which came to the attention of Wilson.

Prince Max decided that the best course of action was to accept Wilson's demands without amendment. The German response was sent on 12 October. It confirmed the German government's acceptance that peace negotiations would be based on Wilson's Fourteen Points. Germany further promised to withdraw its troops from occupied areas and proposed the creation of a commission to make the necessary arrangements. It concluded by stating the German Chancellor spoke in the name of the German government and of the German people.[37]

Wilson sent a further response to the German government on 14 October 1918, but this struck a much less conciliatory tone, making clear Allied military leaders would decide the armistice terms. He further demanded the immediate halting of German submarine warfare. Germany, Wilson continued, had been ruled during the war by an 'arbitrary power' which had disturbed the peace of the world and this problem needed addressing by the new German government. Wilson had not directly requested the abdication of Kaiser Wilhelm, but it was clear the 'arbitrary power' he wished to be removed was the German Emperor.[38] On 16 October, Wilson's reply was published in the German press, provoking widespread anger. The whole tone of Wilson's note was seen as an affront to Germany. Many thought the change of tone had been influenced by the British Prime Minister, David Lloyd George, and the French Prime Minister, Georges Clemenceau. Even the Social Democrats admitted there were limits beyond which it was not prepared to go. Some voices on the Right were even calling for the armistice negotiations to be called off.

Prince Max described Wilson's note as a 'terrible document'. On 17 October, he called a meeting of all the leading political and military leaders to discuss three questions: first, should Germany accept Wilson's new conditions? Second, if Wilson's demands were rejected, would the army be able to defend Germany's frontiers? And third, if Germany could hold out for some weeks or months, would more favourable terms be achievable? Admiral Reinhard Scheer, the Chief of the Naval Staff, strongly opposed abandoning unrestricted submarine warfare. Ludendorff thought Wilson's demands must be rejected, although Prince Max reminded him that the idea for an armistice had originated with the German Supreme Command itself. All the political leaders advised Prince Max it was much too late to abandon the armistice negotiations, and insisted the military should stop interfering in political decisions. It was agreed that Prince Max should draft a conciliatory reply to Wilson which agreed to abandon unrestricted submarine warfare.

On 20 October, the German government's reply was sent to Wilson. This caved in completely to all of Wilson's demands and even agreed to the supervision by Allied commanders of the German evacuation of the occupied lands. On Wilson's demand for the destruction of 'arbitrary power', Prince Max pointed out that fundamental constitutional reforms had already been enacted and he reminded Wilson the new German government was composed of elected representatives of the German people, including leaders of the key parties in the Reichstag. No government in Germany could now continue in office without the confidence of the Reichstag and decisions on war and peace would also now be decided in parliament.[39]

Wilson replied on 23 October 1918, expressing satisfaction that the German government had accepted the terms laid down in his Fourteen Points, but stressing that the peace of the world now depended on plain speaking. The terms of the armistice must ensure there was no possibility of a resumption of hostilities by Germany. This safeguard was required because despite the new government and the recent constitutional changes, the German people still did not have the power to control the emperor or the military authorities, and the Allies did not trust those who had been the masters of German policy to uphold the current political changes, nor did they trust the word of those who had been in the saddle of German power since the war began. The American government would not deal with 'military masters' or 'monarchical autocrats', but only with the true representatives of the German people. If these terms were not agreed, the Allies would demand not armistice, but surrender.[40]

While Prince Max deplored the fact that Wilson's reply was pitched in a tone usually addressed to a defeated enemy, he realised the negotiations for an armistice had to continue. He was under no illusion that most of his cabinet now wanted peace, at any price. As Wilson still doubted Germany was committed to democracy, Prince Max felt constitutional changes needed to go much further along the path to democracy.

This was not the view of the German Supreme Command. On 24 October, Hindenburg sent a memorandum to the armed forces, arguing that Wilson was now demanding not an armistice but unconditional surrender: 'Wilson's reply demands military capitulation. It is therefore unacceptable to us soldiers. It proves that the desire of our enemies is to destroy us completely. It also proves that our enemies talk of a "peace of justice" for the sole purpose of deceiving us.'[41]

Hindenburg's memorandum alarmed Prince Max, who was confined to bed with a dose of the highly contagious Spanish flu, which had been spreading throughout Europe since March 1918. In Berlin alone 50,000 people had died of the flu, and 350,000 Germans had perished in the first six months of the pandemic. In his absence, Prince Max arranged for the Vice-Chancellor, Friedrich von Payer, to meet with Ludendorff. During an angry encounter, the latter repeated Hindenburg's view that the Allies were determined to crush Germany militarily and he urged the armistice negotiations should be called off, and the nation be urged to fight to the death. In reply, Payer insisted negotiations for an armistice would continue. When Prince Max was given details about this outburst, he decided Ludendorff had to be sacked. Max wrote to Kaiser Wilhelm stating that Hindenburg should stay as head of the Supreme Command, but Ludendorff must be dismissed, or else Prince Max would resign himself.

On 26 October, Kaiser Wilhelm met Ludendorff and Hindenburg. He immediately asked Ludendorff to submit his resignation, which was duly accepted. Hindenburg then offered his own resignation, but Wilhelm asked him to remain in post by appealing to his sense of duty. As the two military leaders left the palace, Ludendorff refused to accompany Hindenburg back to military headquarters in his coach, saying sharply: 'I refuse to ride with you because you have treated me so shabbily'. Hindenburg knew very well he had been raised to heroic status in Germany mainly because of Ludendorff's military successes. The 'happy marriage' between Hindenburg and Ludendorff was now over.[42]

Ludendorff's replacement as First Quartermaster General was Wilhelm Groener, who was noted for his organisational skills at the War Food Ministry (*Kriegsernährungsministerium*), and then as the head of the War Office (*Kriegsamt*). In both posts, Groener had developed useful links with the leaders of the trade unions. He himself came from a lower middle-class background, but had gained political respect because of his cool judgement and his flair for organisation. Groener increasingly came to see the emperor as an impediment to saving the monarchy and securing a good peace settlement, though he remained loyal to him.[43]

On 26 October, further far-reaching modifications to the constitution were presented to the Reichstag. They were designed to make the Chancellor responsible to both houses of parliament, and to subordinate the military to the civil government authorities. Conservatives, who were in a minority, objected that these proposals would remove the Supreme Command from decision making and reduce the Kaiser to a powerless figurehead, but the constitutional amendments were accepted by both houses of parliament, and, on 28 October, were signed by Kaiser Wilhelm and became law. In a few short weeks, Germany had transformed itself from an authoritarian militaristic dictatorship into a parliamentary democracy on the British model. The German Chancellor was now responsible for all the political actions previously reserved by the emperor. The right of the emperor to appoint, promote or reassign military officers now required the co-signature of the Reich Chancellor or the Minister of War.[44]

On 27 October, the German government sent a further reply to President Wilson which stated:

> The peace negotiations are being conducted by a democratic government whose decisive powers are permanently anchored in the constitution of the German Reich. Accordingly, the German government awaits proposals for an armistice. Only in this way will it be possible for the armistice to pave the way for a peace of justice of the kind indicated by the President in his pronouncements.[45]

Kaiser Wilhelm was fully aware of the growing clamour for his abdication. On 29 October, he suddenly left Berlin for the German military headquarters in Spa in Belgium, stating that his place was now with his soldiers at this crucial moment in the war. Wilhelm's departure was a disastrous error, as it simply increased the popular agitation for his abdication. The German people, previously loyal to the Kaiser, had now lost faith in him.[46]

Prince Max decided to send Wilhelm ('Bill') Drews, the Prussian Minister of the Interior, to Spa in Belgium to discuss the question of abdication with Kaiser Wilhelm. Drews arrived on 1 November, and soon attended a meeting with the Kaiser, Hindenburg and Groener. Drews reported on the growing wave of public support for abdication in the press, business circles, the political parties, and among the public, and informed them that Prince Max now believed the emperor should sacrifice himself by abdicating. Any delay would only lead to the destruction of the monarchy.

In response, Kaiser Wilhelm refused to abdicate, telling Drews bluntly: 'It would be irreconcilable with the duties I have as Prussian king and successor to Frederick the Great before God, the people and my conscience. I cannot and may not leave my post at the most dangerous moment. My abdication would be the beginning of the end of all German monarchies.'[47] Hindenburg then chipped in by saying that if the emperor abdicated the army would become a band of brigands struggling to get back to Germany. Groener offered equally spirited support to the emperor. It was pretty obvious that the Kaiser was not going to go quietly.[48]

On 5 November, President Wilson sent his fourth note to the German government. He confirmed the Allies were prepared to conclude an armistice with Germany based on the Fourteen Points, but added that on the insistence of the French and British governments two qualifications were to be added to this offer. The first required a German acceptance of the freedom of the seas as defined by the Allies. The second obliged Germany to pay compensation 'for all the damage done to the civilian population of the Allies and their property by the aggression of Germany by land, by sea and from the air.' Wilson then informed the German government that the Supreme Allied Commander, Marshal Ferdinand Foch, would lead the negotiations for the armistice.[49]

Up to this point, the 'revolution from above' had been going according to plan, until a spontaneous 'revolution from below' suddenly and dramatically changed the course of events. On 23 October, Karl Liebknecht – who had, on 4 August 1914, co-founded, with Polish-born Rosa Luxemburg, the Marxist-inspired Spartacus League (*Spartakusbund*), a left-wing group attached to the USPD – was released from prison, followed by Luxemburg on 8 November 1918. They had both been imprisoned for organising a public demonstration in Berlin against German involvement in the war on 1 May 1916. Their release was due to an amnesty granted by Prince Max to all political prisoners.[50]

Liebknecht's father had been the co-founder of the Social Democratic Party, but his son was far more radical. Karl studied law and political economy at the universities of Leipzig and Berlin before gaining a doctorate at the University of Würzburg in 1897, and then opening a lawyer's office in Berlin in 1899. His writings consistently opposed German militarism, which got him arrested for dissent in 1907 and jailed for 18 months. In 1912, he was elected to the Reichstag as a member of the SPD. He soon established his revolutionary left-wing credentials by being the only Reichstag member to vote against the granting of war credits to the Imperial Government in December 1914. He repeatedly called for an end to the war and a workers' revolution, being impressed by the workers' and soldiers' councils set up in Russia during the Bolshevik Revolution.[51]

Luxemburg, whose family were Polih Jews, was brought up in Russian-controlled Poland. She studied philosophy, politics, and economics at the University of Zurich, then gained a Doctor of Law degree. She wanted to move to Germany as she believed it was fertile ground for the socialist revolution she desired. In 1897, she married the son of an old friend, Gustav Lübeck, not for love, but to gain German citizenship. The couple never even lived together and were divorced five years later. During the marriage, Luxemburg continued a love affair with Leo Jogisches, a socialist from Vilnius, who financed her education and her formation of the Social Democratic Party of Poland.[52]

Luxemburg was no crude Marxist, but a cool-headed and nuanced thinker, who rightly deserves to be placed at the same level as Marx, Lenin, and Trotsky in the pantheon of socialist intellectuals. She was deeply critical of Lenin's idea of a self-selected vanguard party representing the proletariat in their struggle against the bourgeoisie. Luxemburg believed this would create a bureaucratic elite completely out of touch with the people. What she favoured instead was a 'bourgeois transition' towards revolution: she supported elections and freedom of the press, and felt there should be space for different opinions within the socialist movement.[53]

The release of Karl Liebknecht gave a tremendous boost to popular demands for the abdication of the Kaiser, and the setting up of a socialist republic. Liebknecht spoke at a number of anti-war rallies in Berlin soon after his release and he was greeted by cheering crowds each time. The era of insane mass murder was ending, he said at one rally in Berlin, and a new era was about to begin. The call by the

Karl Liebknecht, socialist and revolutionary: murdered by government troops during the Spartacist Uprising of January 1919.

discredited ruling classes to support the war could only be brought to an end by a dictatorship of the proletariat, the demise of capitalism and the establishment of a workers' republic, he added.

Another group demanding the end of the monarchy and a socialist revolution were the Revolutionary Shop Stewards (*Revolutionäre Obleute*), led by Richard Müller, who belonged to the left wing of the USPD, and had consistently opposed the war policies of the Kaiser. The Revolutionary Shop Stewards had been crucial to the organisation of the January 1918 strike, during which the strikers had demanded the end to the war through a negotiated peace and the introduction of a democratic constitution. The strike was brutally suppressed by troops of the Supreme Command, who put some factories under military protection and forcibly conscripted many of the strikers into military service. This setback did not stop the Revolutionary Shop Stewards from drawing up plans in the autumn of 1918 for an armed uprising.

On 2 November 1918, the leaders of all the revolutionary elements – the Revolutionary Shop Stewards, the Spartacus League, and members of the anti-war USPD – convened a meeting. It had been called at the request of Independent Social Democrat Emil Barth, who told the meeting the time for revolutionary action had now arrived. Only after a 'revolution from below' could Germany gain a fair armistice from the Allies. 'We are the ones who will win peace,' he declared. 'By terminating the war, the revolutionary elements would serve the cause of socialism in Germany and win the goodwill of the Allies.' He proposed the armed revolution should start on 4 November.

Liebknecht then spoke firmly against Barth's plan. He did not care for conspiracies and putsches. Instead, he felt mass demonstrations, strikes, industrial sabotage and inciting soldiers and sailors to desert would bring down the Kaiser, and the compromising government of Max of Baden. A vote was taken at the end of the meeting, in which Barth's proposal was only narrowly rejected, by two votes.[54]

Liebknecht's support for workers' and soldiers' councils on the Bolshevik model attracted Soviet aid to the USPD and to the Spartacist cause, which was channelled through the Russian Embassy in Berlin. On 4 November, evidence of this aid was uncovered by the police when a packing case was captured. Two days later, Adolph Joffe, the head of the Soviet delegation at the Russian Embassy, and his staff were expelled from Germany, on charges of preparing a communist uprising in Germany. After the delegation returned to Moscow, Joffe admitted 1 million marks had been deposited in a bank account and

The Polish-born socialist Rosa Luxemburg: murdered, along with her fellow revolutionary Karl Liebknecht, on 15 January 1919.

placed at the disposal of the USPD to fund revolutionary activities and to purchase weapons.[55]

The anti-war propaganda campaign unleashed by these left-wing socialist groups made a deep impression on sailors in the High Seas Fleet (*Hochseeflotte*), who opposed a German admiralty plan, code-named 'Plan 19', scheduled for 28 October 1918, for one last make-or-break North Sea battle. Hopelessly outnumbered by the Allied navies, which included British, French, and American ships, the plan had little chance of success. Few sailors were interested in sacrificing their lives on such a pointless suicide mission. The Naval Supreme Command had sanctioned Plan 19, on the basis that the British would demand the surrender of the German High Seas Fleet as part of the armistice agreement.

The centre of the agitation against Plan 19 was in the port city of Kiel, on the Baltic coast, which along with Wilhelmshaven formed the anchorage base of the Kaiser's fleet for the duration of the war. Blockaded by Allied ships, it had remained inactive ever since the inconclusive Battle of Jutland in late May 1916. Kiel also contained 50,000 troops stationed in barracks, and many industrial workers were working in armaments factories and shipyards. On 29 October, sailors on two major ships at Kiel failed to return from shore leave. Within hours, the mutiny spread to a number of other battleships and cruisers, forcing the Admiralty to abandon Plan 19.[56]

The mutineers held a meeting on 2 November on a large parade ground in Kiel. They wanted the release of their comrades who had been imprisoned during the rebellion. The key speaker was 27-year-old Karl Artelt, a committed revolutionary and a member of the USPD, who called not only for the release of all the rebel sailors, but for the abolition of German militarism and the overthrow of the ruling classes.[57] The sailors held a further meeting on 3 November 1918, again supported by USPD members, attended by about 6,000 people. They demanded the immediate release of the imprisoned sailors. The demonstrators then moved in the direction of the Waldwiese, a beer hall temporarily acting as a naval prison. The guards fired on the demonstrators, killing seven and wounding 29 others. On the next day, the rebel sailors moved through the town, and soon brought public and naval institutions under their control, detaining their officers, and taking control of their ships. By the end of 4 November, about 40,000 rebels in Kiel had formed councils elected at mass gatherings of sailors, soldiers, and workers. The Revolutionary Shop Stewards announced that a general strike in Kiel factories would begin on 5 November 1918.

Within Prince Max's government, there was concern over the wider implications of the Kiel Mutiny. A sailors' mutiny at a time when armistice negotiations were at a very delicate stage could only weaken the hand of the German government. Scheidemann feared the rebellion in Kiel might ignite a revolution against the old order and he was worried the formation of sailors' and soldiers' councils would turn the naval mutiny into a broader Marxist uprising.

On 6 November, the MSDP leaders held a crisis meeting in Berlin. Scheidemann proposed an ultimatum should be sent to Prince Max stating that the Social Democrats would leave the government unless Kaiser Wilhelm abdicated. Friedrich Ebert, the joint leader of the MSDP, objected to the idea of sending an ultimatum, and suggested he would meet Prince Max to urge a speedy settlement of the abdication question. On the next day, Ebert told Prince Max: 'If the Kaiser does not abdicate, the social revolution is unavoidable. But I do not want it, indeed I hate it like sin.' The German Chancellor agreed to travel to Spa to see Wilhelm II and convince him to abdicate.[58]

In the following days, what had begun as a revolt against suicidal naval orders developed into a fully fledged political revolution. Soldiers and sailors in numerous naval base and coastal towns were disobeying orders. Then the revolution spread through all the regions of Germany. The monarchical federal structure of the country, with its 26 constituent territories each with its own kings, dukes, and princes, dissolved. The course of the German Revolution differed from region to region, but what was remarkably similar in each place was the unwillingness of the local authorities, army and naval personnel and local police forces to intervene to stop it.

The Revolution soon reached the Kingdom of Bavaria in southern Germany. On 2 November 1918, the Bavarian king, Ludwig III, approved a series of democratic reforms, which meant laws in future would be based on a parliamentary majority, not royal consent. This came too late to save the Wittelsbach monarchy, which had ruled Bavaria since the 11th century, from being deposed.

The events of 7 November were a key turning point in Bavarian history. On that day, there was a huge anti-war demonstration attended by 60,000 people. The speakers demanded peace and democracy, but taking the lead was the eloquent Kurt Eisner, a member of the USPD, who had adopted a strong anti-war stance that proved popular with the local population. Eisner was born into a middle-class Jewish family

overleaf Mutinous sailors demonstrate in Kiel, autumn 1918. The revolt by sailors of the German High Seas fleet in November 1918 was a harbinger of revolution.

in Berlin. After studying philosophy and German at university, he became a journalist and had been the editor of the Social Democrat flagship newspaper *Vorwärts* (*Forward*). During the war, he was convicted of treason for inciting a strike of munitions workers in 1918. He served nine months in Munich's Stadelheim Prison before being released during the general amnesty of political prisoners in October 1918.[59] At the end of the huge peace demonstration, Eisner, supported by his followers, liberated the military garrisons, and met with no resistance from the soldiers. By 9 p.m. Eisner had proclaimed Bavaria a republic, and occupied the Bavarian parliament. On the next day, he established a Provisional Government with himself as Minister-President and Foreign Minister. The old order in Bavaria had collapsed with no resistance.

Within days the regional German kings, princes and dukes were all deposed in quick succession. There was no resistance offered anywhere. On the morning of 9 November, only King Wilhelm of Württemberg and Wilhelm II, King of Prussia and Emperor of Germany, remained in office.

On 6 November, the German Ceasefire Commission was despatched to France to agree the terms of the armistice on the orders of Prince Max. The Allies insisted they would not deal with representatives of the German Supreme Command, but only with a Commission selected by the German government. Prince Max chose the anti-war politician Matthias Erzberger to act as the Chairman of the Ceasefire Commission. He was accompanied by Major General Detlof von Winterfeldt for the Army, Captain Ernst Vanselow representing the Navy, and Count Alfred Graf von Oberndorff from the German Foreign Ministry.

Erzberger left Berlin with an authorisation letter from the German Chancellor inside his briefcase. On 7 November, he arrived at Supreme Command Headquarters in Spa to have a brief meeting with Wilhelm II and Hindenburg, who both accepted Erzberger's appointment. Hindenburg praised him for undertaking 'this terrible task for the sacred cause of the country' and told him this was the first time that a politician not a soldier was concluding an armistice.[60] At noon, the German delegation left Spa in a motorcade of five cars, which crossed the German border at 9.20 p.m.

In Berlin, on the same day, the Social Democrat government ministers announced to Prince Max their intention to resign from the government and to lead the German Revolution 'from below' if Kaiser Wilhelm had not resigned by noon on the following day. This ultimatum was forwarded to Wilhelm by telegram, but on the following day, the intransigent Kaiser announced he was determined not to abdicate.[61]

Meanwhile, Wilhelm Groener, who had replaced Ludendorff as the Quartermaster General of the German Army, summoned 50 mid-level front-line army commanders to a meeting at Spa and 39 of them turned up. Hindenburg told them that Kaiser Wilhelm wanted to march on Berlin to put down the revolution, and he asked for their views. Only one officer thought his men would support the Kaiser's hopeless mission to Berlin.

After the meeting, Hindenburg and Groener met with Kaiser Wilhelm to break the news to him that a counter-revolutionary operation was completely out of the question. Wilhelm kept insisting that he would lead the army back to the homeland whatever his officers thought. In reply, Groener told him: 'The army will march home in good order under its generals, but not under the leadership of Your Majesty.' Hindenburg added firm support to Groener's assessment.[62]

Meanwhile, the German Ceasefire Commission had driven for ten hours through the hazardous and devastated war zone of northern France. Erzberger witnessed the extent of the destruction wreaked upon French towns and villages by the German armed forces. The party finally arrived at the headquarters of the French First Army in Homblières, near Saint-Quentin, where they were served dinner by their French hosts. Afterwards, the German delegation was escorted to a train station in the town of Tergnier, where a special train awaited them. They had no idea where it was going.

At 7 a.m. on 8 November 1918, the train finally stopped at a station in a forested area. Soon a second train stopped on a neighbouring track about 100 metres away. They had reached the forest of Compiègne, 40 miles north-east of Paris. At 10 a.m. the German party was led across the railway track to the railway car of Ferdinand Foch, the Supreme Allied Commander. He entered the compartment in the company of Sir Rosslyn Wemyss, the British First Sea Lord, George Hope, a British Rear Admiral, and Foch's Chief of Staff, General Maxime Weygand. Erzberger immediately realised no Americans would be included in the armistice negotiations, and he became immediately concerned about what was about to happen.[63]

Foch greeted the Germans without the faintest hint of friendliness. Erzberger said he had come to receive 'suggestions' on the proposed terms of the armistice. In reply, Foch, who had written up the terms in advance, said he would not be taking any 'suggestions' from the German delegation. Erzberger then added they had come to negotiate on the basis of Wilson's Fourteen Points. Foch responded by saying impatiently: 'Do you wish to ask for an armistice? If so, say so.' In reply, Erzberger asked for an armistice, with no strings attached, and requested an immediate end to hostilities. Foch said it was impossible to consider ending hostilities until the armistice was signed.[64]

Foch then asked Weygand to read out the conditions for an armistice in French. The German Army must evacuate all troops (190 divisions) from France, Belgium, Luxembourg, and Alsace-Lorraine within two weeks. German territory on the left bank of the Rhineland would be occupied by French troops. Three of the key points on the Rhine, Mainz, Koblenz and Cologne, would also be occupied. The Treaties of Brest-Litovsk and Bucharest must be immediately revoked. In addition, Germany was required to surrender substantial amounts of weaponry, railway cars, trucks, and its entire High Seas Fleet, including its submarines. All Allied prisoners of war to be released immediately. To ensure German good behaviour and compliance with these terms, the British naval blockade would continue. Finally, there would be a demand made on Germany for war reparations, the exact amount to be determined later. Foch concluded by stating the Allied terms were non-negotiable. They could only be accepted or refused, and the Germans were given 72 hours to decide.

The meeting lasted just 45 minutes. The terms were severe, amounting to the complete demilitarisation of Germany, with few promises made in return. Erzberger contacted the German High Command in Spa and Prince Max's government in Berlin to ask whether he should sign the armistice, if he was unable to negotiate any improvements.

While he awaited a reply, the German Revolution finally reached Berlin, on the morning of 9 November. The Revolutionary Shop Stewards had organised a general strike in the city. Workers were out on the streets of the city centre demanding a republic. The moderate MSDP realised they needed to place themselves at the head of the revolutionary movement or be swept away on the tidal wave of revolution now flooding Germany.

At 9 a.m. Philipp Scheidemann and Gustav Bauer, two of the leading Social Democratic members in Prince Max's cabinet, announced they had resigned from the government, and they urged all Social Democrats to do the same and join the general strike. Local soldiers refused to put down the strike, left their barracks and joined the street demonstrations. In a meeting with the MSPD's factory leaders, the Berlin leader of the MSDP, Otto Wels, announced the party now supported the general strike.

Prince Max contacted Kaiser Wilhelm at 11 a.m. to explain what was happening in Berlin and implored him to abdicate. Wilhelm said he would abdicate as Emperor, but not as King of Prussia, and he would soon issue a statement on the subject. When it failed to arrive after half an hour, Prince Max, without ever gaining the Kaiser's consent, released the following statement to the press just before noon: 'The Emperor and King has decided to renounce the throne.' Prince Max added that he now intended to propose the appointment of Majority Social Democrat Friedrich Ebert as the new Chancellor and Prime Minister of Prussia and that a new National Assembly (*Nationalversammlung*) would be established, elected on the basis of universal suffrage. [65]

In the afternoon, in Spa, Kaiser Wilhelm received the news that his abdication had been announced and a republic declared in Berlin. Hindenburg was given the task of informing the Emperor that he must now go into exile in the Netherlands, but found Wilhelm in a state of rage about the unilateral announcement of his abdication by Prince Max. Replying, Hindenburg said he could no longer guarantee the safety of Wilhelm, and he warned him that he might soon be arrested by insurgent troops and taken to Berlin as a prisoner, concluding: 'I must advise Your Majesty to abdicate and proceed to Holland.' Wilhelm agreed to abdicate, but he refused to give up the title of King of Prussia, even in exile. At dawn on 10 November, Kaiser Wilhelm departed for the Netherlands on the imperial special train. It was an ignominious end for the Emperor of Imperial Germany. It was not until 28 November 1918 that he formally renounced his throne.[66]

Ebert immediately issued a manifesto urging the country to remain calm and promising that members of the USPD would be involved in the new government. He was even prepared to offer a cabinet post to Karl Liebknecht, but the Spartacist made clear that he was not interested in collaborating with someone he considered an enemy of revolutionary socialism. Ebert realised the MSPD would need to share power initially with the USPD, who demanded that Germany would have to become a 'socialist republic' with representatives chosen from the workers' and soldiers' councils. Ebert further declared that the people of Germany should decide on the form of government in open elections to a new National Assembly. Ebert's chief aims were to create a democratic parliamentary democracy with equal voting rights, improve workers' rights and conditions and introduce social and welfare reforms, but not to form a Bolshevik-style government. To Prince Max he confided: 'I don't want [a communist revolution]. I hate it.'[67]

By now, thousands of people were on the streets of Berlin, enthusiastically celebrating the fall of the Kaiser, and the establishment of a republic. Special editions of newspapers were soon on the streets spreading the news. In the MSPD party newspaper *Vorwärts*, Ebert issued a statement which stated the new government would be 'a people's government' whose chief immediate aim was to bring peace as soon as possible.[68]

Bernard von Bülow, a fervent patriot, who had served as German Chancellor from 1900 to 1909, was staying in a suite in the Adlon Hotel, located near the Brandenburg Gate, on the day the Weimar Republic was proclaimed. He later described what he saw from his hotel window:

> I have seldom witnessed anything so nauseating, so maddeningly revolting and base, as the spectacle of half-grown louts, decked out with the red armlets of social democracy, who in bands of several at a time, came creeping up behind any army officer wearing the Iron Cross or the order Pour le Mérite, to pin down his elbows at his side and tear off his epaulettes.[69]

At 2 p.m. Philipp Scheidemann addressed a huge crowd in Berlin from a first-floor open window in the Reichstag building, proclaiming: 'The German people have been victorious all along the line. The old and rotten has collapsed: militarism is finished! The Hohenzollerns have abdicated! Long live the German Republic! Deputy Ebert has been proclaimed Reich Chancellor. Ebert has been authorised to assemble a new government. All the socialist parties will belong to this government.'[70] The speech was greeted by loud cheers, but Ebert was unhappy with the words his colleague had used. When Scheidemann returned from the window, Ebert told him the form of government would be decided by the elected National Assembly, not by him. Scheidemann later recalled that his enthusiastic speech had been influenced by hearing that Karl Liebknecht was shortly to proclaim a socialist republic.[71]

The Socialist Left was by no means united behind Scheidemann and Ebert's vision of the German future. The minority USPD, the

Revolutionary Shop Stewards and the Spartacus League all wanted a full-blown socialist republic on the Bolshevik model. At 4 p.m. Liebknecht, leader of the Spartacus League, delivered a passionate speech on the balcony of the Berlin City Palace, a former royal residence of the Hohenzollern family. Liebknecht proclaimed the 'Free Socialist Republic of Germany', stressing that the rule of capitalism was over and the goal now was the creation of a 'government of workers and soldiers, a state of the proletariat.' Instead of the imperial flag, Liebknecht promised the red flag should fly from now on. He wanted a Soviet Germany allied to the Soviet Union, but the Spartacists were a small fringe element with about 1,000 supporters, far outnumbered by the USPD to which they were loosely attached, which had 100,000 members.[72]

Ebert formed a Provisional Government on 10 November 1918, composed of members of the two groupings that emerged from the 1917 split of the Social Democrats, the MSPD and USPD. It carried the socialist title: Council of People's Deputies (*Rat der Volksbeauftragten*). The Council derived its power from the hastily assembled workers' and soldiers' councils that had been elected in factories and army barracks in Berlin.

The new German government issued the following proclamation: 'The government created by the revolution, whose political leadership is purely socialist, is setting itself the task of carrying out a socialist programme.' It promised there would be freedom of speech, freedom of the press, and an amnesty for political prisoners. The social insurance laws and an eight-hour day, both suspended at the beginning of the war, would be restored. Work would be found for the unemployed and new affordable houses built. There would be democratic elections in which everyone aged 20 and over would have the right to vote. There was no mention of ending private property or taking industry into state ownership, however. In sum, this was not a socialist manifesto, but

Philipp Scheidemann of the Social Democratic Party: the man who proclaimed the Weimar Republic from a balcony of the Reichstag, 9 November 1918.

primarily reflected the programme of Ebert and the Social Democrats.

The Council of People's Deputies took over the functions of the head of state (Kaiser) and head of government (Chancellor). It had the power to issue decrees replacing the legislation of the Reichstag. The occupants of the existing government cabinet posts stayed in office. There were six members of the Council, three from the MSDP – Friedrich Ebert, Philipp Scheidemann and Otto Landsberg – and three from the USPD – Wilhelm Dittmann, Hugo Haase and Emil Barth. The joint chairs were Ebert and Haase, but Ebert alone was responsible for military and interior affairs.[73]

On the same day, the workers' and soldiers' councils of Berlin met. This assembly was, in theory, Germany's new sovereign body. It served to highlight the deep rifts between the different factions on the Left that had led the German Revolution. It sanctioned the appointment of the Council of the People's Deputies, but to wrest control of the new government from the MSPD, the Spartacists and the Revolutionary Shop Stewards elected an 'Executive Committee' of 12 soldiers and 12 workers, which regarded itself as the real governing power of republican Germany, even though its role in the government machine was not clearly defined. As the Spartacists refused to serve on it, it was controlled by the MSDP.

Late on the evening of 10 November, an exhausted Ebert sat down in a chair in the Reich Chancellery (*Reichskanzlei*). Suddenly the telephone rang. Ebert picked up the receiver. It was Wilhelm Groener, Quartermaster General of the German Army, using a secret hotline, which was unknown to Ebert at the time. Ebert never revealed what was said during this conversation, but Groener said later that he offered Ebert the loyalty and cooperation of the armed forces to suppress revolution, and to maintain law and order, in return for Ebert agreeing to lead the fight against Bolshevik revolution in Germany, put a speedy end to the soldiers' councils and to recognise the sole military authority of the Army and officer corps.

The Ebert–Groener pact, which initially remained secret, meant Ebert recognised the army as one of the pillars of the new democratic republic, and in return Groener agreed to throw the weight of the Army behind the new government. This secret agreement meant the Army would remain a 'state within a state' in the new republic. The Ebert–Groener pact gave the new government the power to suppress the radical Left, but it also made the Republic's survival dependent on the German Army Supreme Command.[74]

Friedrich Ebert, first President of Weimar
Germany, 1919–25.

Meanwhile, in Compiègne, Matthias Erzberger was updated on the dramatic developments in Berlin, and of the flight of Kaiser Wilhelm into exile in the Netherlands. He had been trying desperately to gain some improvements to the harsh armistice terms. On the evening of 10 November, Ebert had sent a radio message to him, stating that the German government authorised him to sign the armistice, even if the Allied conditions could not be improved upon.

The final meeting between the German delegation and the Allies on the armistice began at 2.15 a.m. on 11 November 1918. Foch had offered only some very minor concessions: Germany would hand over 25,000 machine guns, not 30,000, and the number of planes demanded fell from 2,000 to 1,700. Instead of 10,000 trucks, Germany had to give up 5,000. The evacuation of German troops from East Africa was also agreed. The depth of the neutral zone on the right bank of the Rhine was initially set at six miles in depth.

At 5.20 a.m. Erzberger finally signed the armistice. The guns stopped along the Western Front in Europe at 11 a.m. Paris time on 11 November 1918. The Armistice marked a victory for the Allies and a defeat for Germany. Foch had completely ignored Woodrow Wilson's Fourteen Points in drafting the peace terms; the French and British governments were never particularly keen on Wilson's programme anyway.[75]

With the benefit of hindsight, the decision of the Allies to conclude an armistice while all the fighting was being conducted on Allied soil was a huge mistake. It would have been far better if the Allies had invaded Germany. This would have made clear to the German people the full magnitude of their military defeat. Instead, the chaotic ending of the war allowed a myth to develop in Germany that its army had not been defeated and its territory never conquered. This became known as the 'stab-in-the-back myth' (*Dolchstosslegende*), which held that Germany did not lose the First World War on the battlefield, but was instead betrayed by civilian politicians, Jews, and revolutionary socialists on the home front. Advocates of this myth called the leaders who brought down the Kaiser and signed the Armistice the 'November Criminals'. The decision of Wilson to have no dealings with Kaiser Wilhelm II and the Supreme High Command allowed them both to avoid taking full responsibility for their actions. Hindenburg was still regarded as a military hero, and he would remain so for the duration of the Weimar Republic. All the responsibility for the German surrender was placed on Erzberger, and the Social Democratic politicians of the new republic, though the German Supreme Command was in fact the prime mover in advising the German government to sign the armistice.[76]

On 12 November, the Council of People's Deputies issued its first proclamation to the German people, which announced that the state of emergency was lifted, censorship ended, and freedom of religion and expression promised. There would also be an amnesty for all political prisoners, and political trials would be discontinued. All rules for the protection of workers' rights, which had been suspended during the war, were immediately restored. Free elections including that for a constituent assembly would be held, using a proportional representation system, under a franchise open to people aged 20 and above, with the first election taking place on 19 January 1919. A new constitution was promised. On 15 November 1918, Hugo Preuss, the State Secretary of the Interior and a constitutional expert, was commissioned to draft it.

On the same day, a compact was concluded between capital and labour. Negotiations between the two sides began before the November Revolution. The employers recognised the primary role of trade unions in wage bargaining through the creation of the Collective Bargaining Agreement. It was signed by the industry magnate Hugo Stinnes and union leader Carl Legien, and became known as the Stinnes–Legien Agreement, under which both sides agreed to the continuance of a free-market capitalist economy. It also established a set of key workers' rights. In every factory, trade unions were recognised, and in businesses employing more than 50 workers a workers' council was to be elected. The eight-hour day was promised without any reduction in pay, though this part of the agreement was never uniformly implemented. A Central Committee was established composed equally of workers and employers' representatives for the purpose of settling industrial disputes. Trade union leaders hailed the compact as a great victory for workers, but the Spartacists denounced it as a boss's charter imposed on workers and therefore a betrayal of social revolution.[77]

Ebert also created the Socialisation Commission, which met for the first time on 5 December 1918 to examine which areas of the economy would benefit from state control. Ebert's aim was to pacify left-wing demands for the nationalisation of the whole economy. Among its members were leading Social Democrats, most notably Karl Kautsky, the executor of Karl Marx's literary estate, Rudolf Hilferding, the author of the 1910 book *Das Finanzkapital* (*Finance Capital*), and the noted economist Joseph Schumpeter. In a report published a month later, the Commission warned against the nationalisation of the German economy, arguing that taking power from capitalists who could maximise profit and pass it on to the state was likely to make such enterprises less profitable and bring no general benefits to the population. It also proposed that owners of any businesses earmarked for state intervention should be compensated. For the coal industry, nationalisation was recommended, but never uniformly implemented.[78]

There remained considerable disagreement within the Council of the People's Deputies on whether Germany should be a parliamentary democracy or a socialist councils' republic. On 23 November, the Executive Committee issued a call for a National Congress of Workers' and Soldiers' Councils with the aim of electing a Central Council. This body would replace the Executive Committee as the supreme co-ordinating agency of the conciliar system. The meeting of the Congress was set for 16 December 1918.

Ebert countered this move at a cabinet meeting on 29 November by announcing that democratic national elections to a new constituent assembly would take place on 16 February 1919. The Spartacists and the Revolutionary Shop Stewards accused Ebert of jumping the gun and betraying the Revolution. Ebert rejected this charge by stating that sovereignty resided in the people as a whole and not in any one class.

The clash between the rival socialist camps now intensified. Ebert maintained his commitment to the parliamentary road to socialism. The Spartacists and the Revolutionary Shop Stewards stepped up their demands for a Sovietised system and vowed to stop the proposed national elections. The USPD, led by Haase, advocated a system of government combining workers' and soldiers' councils, with parliamentary democracy, but also demanded that national elections should be postponed until the economy had been fully nationalised.

The tension between the Majority Social Democrats and the revolutionary socialists led to bloodshed in Berlin on 6 December. The Spartacists led a march towards the centre of the city. The unarmed demonstrators were confronted by troops attached to the office of Otto Wels, the Social Democrat commander of the capital, on Chausseestrasse. The troops opened fire, killing several demonstrators, and wounding many more. The Spartacists charged Ebert with ordering counterrevolutionary repression.

The showdown between the left-wing factions took place between 16 and 21 December at the Congress of the Workers' and Soldiers' Councils, held at the Prussian House of Deputies in Berlin, with delegates elected from all over Germany in attendance. Of the 500 delegates, two-thirds were members of the MSDP, the rest were members of the USPD, and the Revolutionary Shop Stewards, but less than a dozen were Spartacists. The Majority Social Democrats, derided by the Spartacists as the betrayers of the Revolution, enjoyed the support of most of the delegates. The proposal to give additional power to the Executive Committee was overwhelmingly rejected. A speech on the opening day by Richard Müller, the leader of the Revolutionary Shop Stewards, denounced the USPD for cooperating with Ebert's Social Democrats. Then a Spartacist delegation forced its way into the hall, demanding the immediate removal of the Ebert government, the nationalisation of industry, the transfer of supreme power to workers' and soldiers' councils and the formation of a People's Militia (*Volkswehr*) to replace regular troops.

On the following day (17 December), bitterness between the Social Democrats and the radical Left escalated. Ebert was accused of collaborating with the Army to sustain his bourgeois government. The bitter arguments in the hall grew so heated that the proceedings had to be adjourned early. On 18 December, a number of radical motions were tabled by the revolutionary workers' and soldiers' councils, including demands for the transfer of the power of the Supreme Command to the cabinet and the Executive Committee, and a call for the abolition of the Army and its replacement with a People's Militia. This latter motion was passed by an overwhelming majority, much to the annoyance of Ebert, who had no intention of implementing such a revolutionary proposal.

On 19 December, the Majority Social Democrats took centre stage. The most powerful speech was delivered by Philipp Scheidemann, who said the workers' and soldiers' councils had been a necessity during the early stage of the November Revolution, but now the imperial regime had collapsed, they could not become a permanent feature of the nation's political system. A socialist democracy needed a stable government and economy. Only a National Assembly elected by the people and led by a party able to work across class boundaries could succeed.

The left-wing Independents, Revolutionary Shop Stewards and Spartacists continued to demand a system of workers' and soldiers' councils, the nationalisation of key industries, and the purging of the civil service and judiciary of people still loyal to the old imperial regime. They then tabled another radical motion calling for the new constitution to give supreme legislative and executive power to the councils. This motion was decisively defeated by 344 to 98 votes, a huge victory for Ebert's MSDP.

The radical delegates then declared they would take no part in the election of a Central Council, which ensured that it was composed exclusively of Majority Social Democrats. Ebert was given the green light to move the elections for the Constituent National Assembly from 16 February to 19 January 1919, in a motion passed by a vote of 450 to 50 votes.[79]

The conflict on the Left now spilled out into the streets. On 23 December, three thousand left-wing sailors belonging to the People's Naval Division (*Volksmarinedivision*) imprisoned Berlin's MSDP military commander, Otto Wels, after he withheld their pay. The mutineers had already occupied the former Hohenzollern City Palace. They then marched to the Reich Chancellery, and instructed the guards to stop any calls from inside the Chancellery, but they did not know about Ebert's hotline to Groener.

Ebert now turned to the Army for assistance. Early on the morning of 24 December, in what became known as the Battle of Christmas Eve, a regular army division commanded by General Arnold Lequis opened artillery fire on the City Palace where the rebels were holding out. In the lengthy exchange of fire, 11 rebel sailors and 23 regular troops were killed. A ceasefire and negotiations soon followed. The sailors agreed to withdraw if their back pay was paid and Wels resigned as the city commander.

It was an embarrassing military defeat for the Ebert government's troops. The shooting of socialists by regular army troops on the orders of Ebert was received with bitterness by the USPD, the Spartacists and the Revolutionary Shop Stewards. At the funerals of the fallen sailors, thousands of Spartacists carried placards with slogans such as 'Charged as Murderers of Sailors: Ebert and Scheidemann' and 'Down with Traitors'.[80]

The USPD members on the governing Council of People's Deputies – Haase, Barth and Dittmann – sent a letter to the newly formed Central Council on 27 December asking for answers to a number of questions: Did the Council support the use of the Army to suppress the revolt by the People's Naval Division? Did the Council intend to replace the old army with a people's militia? What did the Council think of the determination of Ebert and Scheidemann to rely on old-line generals of the Imperial Army? In reply, the Council unanimously supported the actions of Ebert and Scheidemann, but gave no answers to the specific questions posed in the letter. On 29 December, Haase, Barth and Dittmann resigned from the Council of the People's Deputies, leaving the government of Germany exclusively in the hands of Ebert and the moderate Social Democrats.

On 30 December 1918, the two-day National Congress of the Spartacist League opened in Berlin. The conference repudiated the USPD, whose leaders it claimed had forfeited their right to be recognised as the leaders of the revolutionary masses. The tie between the Spartacists and USPD was now terminated. In recognition of this new political direction, the Spartacists gave their organisation a new name: the Communist Party of Germany (*Kommunistische Partei Deutschlands*, KPD).

The conference then devoted a great deal of attention to its attitude to the upcoming elections for the Constituent National Assembly, which its extra-parliamentary actions had failed to stop. This brought out differences on strategy. The cool-headed Rosa Luxemburg argued that the victory of socialism would not be won by an armed coup to overthrow the Ebert government. Any such action would undoubtedly end in failure. Only when the bulk of workers were won over to the revolutionary cause could such action be contemplated. In the meantime, the new party should participate in the elections.

Most delegates disagreed with Rosa Luxemburg. They voted instead to boycott the democratic elections and supported a coup to bring down the Ebert government, and they wanted it to start right away.[81]

1919

·

THE JANUARY UPRISING, THE VERSAILLES TREATY AND THE CONSTITUTION

·

The antagonism between the Ebert-led Provisional Government and the revolutionary Left intensified as the New Year dawned. The Left claimed the 1918 November Revolution had changed nothing. It was a mere breakdown in authority of those in command. The Ebert government was, on this view, simply the servant of counterrevolutionary forces. On 3 January 1919, the USPD members of the Prussian government all resigned. On the next day, Paul Hirsch, the Prussian Prime Minister, dismissed Emil Eichhorn, the Berlin chief of police, a Reichstag member of the USPD, who had come to the aid of the People's Navy Division in December 1918 by sending the Berlin Security Guard (*Sicherheitswehr*) to support them. Eichhorn was further accused of giving members of the Revolutionary Shop Stewards key positions in the police.[1]

The dismissal of Eichhorn and his replacement by the moderate Social Democrat Eugen Ernst has been interpreted as either a pretext to begin a pre-planned coup to overthrow the Ebert government or a pre-meditated plan by Ebert to force the Spartacists (now known as the KPD), the Revolutionary Shop Stewards and the USPD to fight an armed revolt before they were ready. On the same day Eichhorn had been forced out, a meeting occurred, attended by the USPD and the Revolutionary Shop Stewards, which invited workers and soldiers to hold a protest demonstration on the following day, and issue a joint proclamation. The KPD decided to attend the demonstration, but warned that an attempted violent overthrow of the Ebert government was unlikely to succeed.[2]

The joint proclamation, calling for a mass demonstration, signed by the Revolutionary Shop Stewards, the Central Berlin Committee of the USPD, and the Central Committee of the KPD, read as follows:

> The Ebert–Scheidemann government has heightened its counterrevolutionary activities with a new contemptible conspiracy directed against the revolutionary workers of Greater Berlin: it tried maliciously to oust Chief of Police Eichhorn with its willing tool, the present Prussian Minister of Police, Ernst. By this action, the Ebert–

previous page   Detail of *The Signing of Peace in the Hall of Mirrors, Versailles, 28 June 1919*, by William Orpen.

Scheidemann government wishes not only to remove the last trusted man of the revolutionary Berlin workers, but primarily it intends to establish in Berlin a despotic rule antagonistic to the revolutionary workers.[3]

On 5 January, 100,000 workers came out on to the streets of Berlin, occupied several newspaper offices, including that of the main Social Democratic newspaper *Vorwärts*. They also seized government food stores, the main Government Printing Office, and the central Railway Office.

Eichhorn refused to leave his post, with the blessing of the leadership of the USPD. At Berlin police headquarters in Alexanderplatz, Karl Liebknecht gave a rousing speech during which he said, 'now is the time for a more determined struggle of the revolutionary proletariat, it must do more than protect the gains of the revolution, it must make this revolution into a socialist one'. Late on the same evening, the left-wing rebels met to discuss what to do next. It was decided to try and overthrow Ebert's Provisional Government. The huge passion generated by the mass demonstration had convinced the radicals an armed revolution could succeed. A Provisional Revolutionary Committee of 53 was established, led by Liebknecht, Georg Ledebour of the USPD, and Paul Scholz of the Revolutionary Shop Stewards. This Committee was given the task of preparing, directing and coordinating the struggle for power.[4] On 6 January, the Revolutionary Committee issued a proclamation, addressed to 'all workers', which read:

It is necessary to stop all counterrevolutionary intrigues! Therefore, come out of your factories! Appear in masses this morning at 11 a.m. in the Siegesallee [a broad boulevard in Berlin]. Our task is to strengthen the revolution and bring it to fulfilment! Forward to the fight for socialism. Forward to the fight for the power of the revolutionary proletariat! Down with the Ebert-Scheidemann government.[5]

In response, 100,000 workers gathered outside the Police Head-quarters on Alexanderplatz, many with rifles in their hands, and waited. Inside the building, the Revolutionary Committee held lengthy discussions, but did not speak to the demonstrators at all. It was becoming obvious that the attempt to overthrow the Ebert government was faltering. Georg Ledebour later recalled: 'The leaders sat the entire evening and the entire night and conferred; they sat during the next morning. When dawn came, they were still conferring. Without any leadership, the crowd went home.'[6]

The Ebert government realised it had no military protection to meet a left-wing revolution in Berlin. On 5 January, a government leaflet had been issued calling on workers to come from all over Germany to help 'protect the Republic against assaults from the armed bandits of the Spartacist League' who 'publicly pronounced today their intention to overthrow the government'.[7] On the next day, thousands of loyal workers heeded the call from Ebert and gathered outside the Reich Chancellery. Philipp Scheidemann addressed them from a window of the building, saying: 'It cannot be tolerated that a small minority rules the people today, that's just as unacceptable as before. The minority must give way to the will of the majority. That's why we are demanding a National Assembly.'[8]

On the same day, Ebert held a meeting of the Central Council of the People's Deputies and said military measures were required if the government was to retain any authority. He gave the task of putting down the left-wing revolt to the SPD politician Gustav Noske, who had played a key role in containing the naval mutiny in Kiel, and had recently been brought into the Council of the People's Deputies as a consultant on defence matters. Noske intended not only to deploy regular troops, but to draft in the paramilitary Free Corps (*Freikorps*), composed of war veterans, with a profound hatred of socialist radicals. The Free Corps were not fighting for the Republic, but against communist revolution.

Realising the Ebert government intended to mount a strong-armed response, the Revolutionary Committee suddenly lost its nerve. On 8 January, it issued its last leaflet, full of empty rhetoric, ending with the fighting words: 'Show those scoundrels your power! Take up arms! Use these weapons against your deadly enemies, Ebert and Scheidemann. Forward to the fight!' On 9 January, the Committee held the last of its futile series of meetings and the KPD withdrew from it.[9]

In contrast, the Ebert government grew in confidence. A Social Democratic Auxiliary Service (*Sozialdemokratischer Helferdienst*) was formed to protect the Reichstag building and many other government buildings in Berlin. On 8 January, the Ebert government issued a proclamation, pledging to fight force with force: 'The government is taking all measures necessary to destroy this rule of terror and to prevent its recurrence once and for all. Decisive action will be forthcoming soon.'[10]

Contrary to an oft-repeated myth, the Free Corps were not the prime movers in suppressing the January Uprising. By the time they became involved, the left-wing revolt had already been put down by regular troops, supported by Social Democrat auxiliary forces. It was 11 January by the time the Free Corps finally arrived in Berlin, in what had become a mopping-up operation. Using artillery fire and machine guns, Free Corps troops forced the occupiers of the *Vorwärts* newspaper building to hoist the white flag. The rebels left the building, arms aloft, begging for mercy. The Free Corps murdered seven of them on the spot and arrested all the others. All the other occupied buildings in Berlin were soon recaptured. Overall, between 130 and 200 left-wing rebels were killed in the January Uprising, and 400 arrested. The Free Corps reported 17 killed during their military engagements.[11] By 12 January 1919, all the military skirmishes had ended, and Gustav Noske led a victory parade of 3,000 troops through the streets of Berlin's city centre.

In an article in *Die Rote Fahne* (*The Red Flag*), entitled 'Order Rules in Berlin', Rosa Luxemburg evaluated the events of what she called 'Spartacus Week'. She explained that the overthrow of the Ebert government and the establishment of a socialist dictatorship had failed due to the 'political immaturity of the German Revolution'. With the government able to draw on the anti-revolutionary Free Corps, supplemented by regular troops, 'a victory was impossible'. Karl Liebknecht, who was directly involved in the revolt, claimed the uprising was defeated because 'the time was not ripe for it.'[12] The January Uprising is often called the 'Spartacist Revolt', but it was really the initiative of the Revolutionary Shop Stewards, supported by the USPD, with the Spartacists only joining in to maintain solidarity with the revolutionary Left.

The putting-down of the January Uprising did not mean the end of violence by the Free Corps. Revolutionary leaders were now hunted down and arrested or killed at a time when they no longer posed any threat. On 15 January, Rosa Luxemburg, Karl Liebknecht and Wilhelm Pieck, the future President of the post-1945 German Democratic Republic, were all captured in the apartment of friends in the affluent Berlin suburb of Wilmersdorf, by members of a local paramilitary 'Citizens Guard', and were then turned over to the notoriously brutal Guard Cavalry Rifle Division (*Garde-Kavallerie-Schützen-Division*), an elite unit of the former Imperial Army, under the command of the nationalist and anti-communist Captain Waldemar Pabst, which had its headquarters at the Hotel Eden. Pabst later admitted he ordered the killings of Liebknecht and Luxemburg.[13]

overleaf Berlin, January 1919: government troops rush to confront the Spartacist rebels.

Liebknecht was interrogated, then brutally clubbed with rifles until he was unconscious. He was then driven to the largest park in Berlin, the Tiergarten, where the car halted. After Liebknecht got out, he was shot three times in the back at close range. The official report claimed that he had been shot while trying to escape. The killers unceremoniously dumped Liebknecht's lifeless corpse outside a local ambulance station, claiming they had found an 'unidentified body'.

Rosa Luxemburg was also held in Pabst's office in the Hotel Eden until a group of soldiers entered. She was brutally struck twice in the face with a rifle butt by a soldier called Otto Runge. Bleeding heavily and unconscious, she was carried downstairs and bundled into a waiting car. On the journey, she was shot once in the head by either Kurt Vogel or Lieutenant Hermann Souchon.[14] On 14 May 1919, Kurt Vogel was sentenced to two years and four months for the removal of her corpse. Otto Runge received a two-year sentence and Hermann Souchon was fined. The court decided Vogel had shot Luxemburg, but Pabst, who ordered the killings, claimed in the 1960s that it was Souchon who had shot her, and a post-war libel court upheld this claim.

Kurt Vogel threw Luxemburg's corpse into the Landwehr Canal, from which a corpse was recovered at the end of May 1919. An autopsy was conducted on it on 13 June, and it was then buried in Friedrichsfelde. Yet it remains unclear whether the corpse recovered was that of Rosa Luxemburg. The report claimed it had what seemed like a bullet hole in the head, but the assistant pathologist questioned whether the corpse was Luxemburg. The autopsy reported no hip damage, even though Luxemburg had a hip birth defect, which left one of her legs shorter than the other. There was also no evidence of injuries to her face consistent with being hit by a rifle butt. In December 2009, a DNA test was performed in Berlin on Luxemburg's exhumed corpse. It was noted it had been headless, handless, and footless when buried. The explanation for this was that the corpse had weights attached to it when it was thrown in the canal. It was therefore impossible to judge how she had died. The new autopsy also concluded that the DNA of the exhumed corpse did not exactly match that of her great-niece. Nevertheless, the report concluded the corpse was 'probably' Luxemburg, but the evidence could not be regarded as 'conclusive'.[15]

Pieck escaped without being harmed by his brutal captors, which has caused much speculation by historians. It has been suggested that he managed to convince his captors that he was someone else. His own explanation was that he escaped while being transferred to a local prison. It seems more likely his release was given in exchange for information of the location of other socialist rebels.[16]

The January Uprising was a pivotal moment in the history of the Weimar Republic with long-lasting repercussions. The Ebert government survived, but only with the help of regular troops and the brutally violent members of the Free Corps. The Republic was now dangerously dependent on the attitude of the army. It also opened an incurable rift on the left of German politics. The left-wing radicals in the KPD and the USPD were now the bitter and sworn enemies of the SPD, and this unresolved conflict became a feature of political life in the Republic. The real victors of the January Uprising were neither the SPD nor the left-wing radicals in the USPD nor the KPD, but the nationalistic and reactionary forces opposed to the Weimar Republic.

Only days after the violent suppression of the left-wing radicals, the democratic elections to the new National Assembly took place. The previous electoral constituencies, which overrepresented rural areas and were based on a first-past-the-post system, were scrapped and replaced by proportional representation, which allocated one seat for every 60,000 votes cast from a nation-wide party list of candidates. The voting age was lowered from 25 to 20, and the previous all-male franchise was expanded to include all women for the first time. Germany was the first major industrialised country to enfranchise all women. Partly due to the deaths of 2 million German men in the war, there were 2.8 million more German women than men eligible to vote in the 1919 election.

Some party names had changed since the last Reich elections in 1912, but their overall structure and ideology had hardly changed at all. The six main political parties who contested the January 1919 elections fitted in to the three pre-1914 political blocs in the Reichstag: social democratic, liberal, and conservative.

The most popular was the Social Democratic Party (*Sozial-demokratische Partei*, SPD), jointly led by Friedrich Ebert and Philipp Scheidemann, both of whom were firm supporters of democracy and social reform. Ebert knew before the elections that if he had to form a coalition government he could only do so with the assistance of the centre-liberal parties.[17] The USPD, who were on the radical socialist left, were led by Hugo Haase and demanded the immediate nationalisation of the economy and the end of the capitalist state. They claimed the SPD had betrayed the German Revolution. The KPD, the former Spartacist League, whose aim was the overthrow of the existing capitalist order, decided to boycott the elections and branded the National constituent assembly a 'counterrevolutionary agency' and would have preferred all power to be in the hands of the workers' and soldiers' councils. Participation in the elections would only have revealed how miniscule was the support for the KPD among the German people.

There were two political parties competing for the votes of the fragmented middle class. The first was the German Democratic Party (*Deutsche Demokratische Partei*, DDP), founded in November 1919 by leaders of the former FVP and the National Liberal Party (NLP) and a new group called the Democrats (*Demokraten*). The DDP was led by Friedrich von Payer, who proclaimed himself a true believer in liberalism. The party sought to rally the middle class to support the new democratic republic, promised economic and social reform, and condemned violence and terror. It drew support from business, academia and among professionals.[18]

The second middle-class party was the liberal-conservative German People's Party (*Deutsche Volkspartei*, DVP), led by Rudolf Heinze, who was well known for his willingness to compromise on key issues for the needs of party unity. Its most famous member was Dr Gustav Stresemann, who would become one of the most distinguished and adaptable politicians of the Weimar era, even though during the wartime period he had been one of the most vociferous supporters of Ludendorff's military adventures. DVP members were primarily drawn from the old NLP and only grudgingly accepted the Weimar republic. The DVP represented the interests of German industrialists and the middle class, regretted the disappearance of the monarchy, stressed the benefits of private property and enterprise, championed Christian family values, opposed welfare spending, and was hostile to radical socialism. The party was only prepared to tolerate the Republic if it managed to keep the radical left under control.[19]

Occupying the centre ground was Zentrum, led by Alfred Gröber. In English, the party was usually called the Centre Party. It was established in 1870 to represent the interests of Germany's Catholic community and lobbied to retain the autonomy of the Catholic Church. Catholic priests functioned as unofficial canvassers for the party. Party members were Catholic first, but could be liberal or conservative on different issues, and this flexibility helped the party become the cement that bound together most Weimar coalitions. Zentrum supported democracy but rejected the idea of a socialist state. Realising the times had changed, the party politely dropped its previous pro-monarchist attitude, and became a broad middle-of-the-road party that could accommodate a progressive liberal politician such as Matthias Erzberger and a conservative pro-monarchist right-winger like Franz von Papen. The party supported the extension of social welfare legislation, and was not opposed to strong trade unions. Due to its adaptability, Zentrum provided four German Chancellors in the Weimar period.[20]

The leading mainstream right-wing conservative political party was the DNVP, led by the former Vice-Chancellor Arthur von Posadowsky-Wehner. It adopted the title 'People's Party' although it was uncompromisingly upper-middle-class orientated. The party was formed from an amalgamation of the old DKP, which had represented the wealthy landowning Prussian nobility (known as the Junkers), and some former members of the German Fatherland Party (*Deutsche Vaterlandspartei*, DVLP), a catch-all far-right group which included pro-monarchists, nationalists, and antisemites. The party favoured the 'stab-in-the-back' myth and opposed socialism in all its forms. The DNVP drew its financial support from industrialists, landowners, and high-ranking bureaucrats. Its electoral support came primarily from middle-class Protestants and independent traders, particularly in rural areas. Most of its supporters looked back nostalgically to pre-1914 Imperial Germany. The party only rarely participated in Weimar coalition governments.[21]

The elections for the National Assembly took place on 19 January 1919. This was the first of nine national elections held during the Weimar era. Weimar politics was characterised by a succession of unstable coalition governments, with each political party wanting to pull Germany in different directions. From 1918 to 1933, there were 20 different coalition governments, with an average life-span of no more than nine months, and none served for the full electoral term of four years.

The voter turnout was 83 per cent, with 30.53 million people casting their votes in Germany's first truly democratic election. The Social Democrats performed best with 37.9 per cent of the vote, a total of 11.51 million votes. This was the highest percentage vote achieved by any Weimar party in any democratic election before 1933. It gave the SPD 165 seats, which was some way below the 212 seats needed for an overall majority. Zentrum came next with 19.7 per cent, representing 5.98 million votes and 91 seats. Those elected included a high proportion of right-wing Catholic Bavarians. Third place went to the DDP, recording 18.6 per cent, with 5.64 million votes, picking up 75 seats. A large number of middle-class voters opted for the DDP, as it had projected a strong anti-socialist stance during the election campaign. Some way behind was the conservative DNVP, with 10.3 per cent, polling 3.12 million votes and gaining 44 seats. The USPD, representing the far left, performed very poorly with just 7.6 per cent, a total of 2.31 million votes and 22 seats. Of the six main Weimar political parties, the DVP performed much the worst, taking a 4.4 per cent vote share, with 1.34 million votes, leaving it with only 19 seats.[22]

The 1919 German election was a victory for the three parties who gave the most enthusiastic support to the new Republic – the SPD, Zentrum and the DDP, who between them polled 76.2 per cent of the votes. The two parties on the conservative Right, the DNVP and the DVP, could only muster 14.7 per cent between them. Their position seemed hopeless. The most revolutionary party on offer to voters, the USPD, registered just 7.6 per cent, showing left-wing radicalism had been resoundingly rejected.

On 3 February, the workers' and soldiers' councils formally handed over their powers to the new National Assembly, expressing a desire for the new constitution to create a unitary state in which the central government was supreme, and the powers of the federal states were done away with. They also expressed a desire for the incorporation of the rights of the workers' and soldiers' councils into the constitutional framework of the new Republic.

Weimar, a city in central Germany, in the state of Thuringia, was chosen as the first meeting place of the new National Assembly, as it was felt Berlin was still in a state of unrest and disorder. Weimar had been a focal point of the German Enlightenment and was an historic shrine of German liberalism.

On 6 February, Friedrich Ebert formally opened the new National Assembly. Most members decided the name of the state should remain the German Empire, rather than the German Republic, even though it became described in Germany and abroad as the Weimar Republic. Ebert delivered a speech to the newly elected body the following day. The 1918 Revolution, he declared, had been launched against an autocratic regime, based on military force. Now the German people had returned to the path of legality through parliamentary democracy. The German people were, he added, free at last and free they would always be. Ebert further claimed the new democratic government was not responsible for the misery caused by the imperial regime and its arrogant militarists. The Allies had fought to destroy 'Kaiserism', and it was now gone. The Allies should not therefore, Ebert continued, impose a peace of hate and violence which made Germans wage-slaves for twenty, forty or sixty years. The path to future peace and stability was international cooperation. The government of the German Republic expected to be treated as equals by the Allies and preferred the most awful privations to dishonour.[23]

On 11 February, the first election to the new office of the President of the Reich (*Reichspräsident*) was held. It was felt that as a new head of state was needed quickly, the first president should be elected by votes cast by the elected members of the National Assembly, rather than by a public vote. This was allowed under paragraph 7 of a law enacted on 10 February 1919, regarding the 'temporary power in the Reich'. The winner in the final parliamentary vote was Friedrich Ebert of the SPD, who took 277 votes (73.1 per cent), over the conservative DNVP leader, Count Arthur von Posadowsky-Wehner, who received only 49 votes (12.9 per cent), with one vote each for Philipp Scheidemann (SPD) and Matthias Erzberger (Zentrum). There were 51 invalid votes (13.5 per cent).[24] It was agreed on 25 October 1922 that the first president could stay in office until 30 June 1925, when the first public election for the office would take place.

In his opening speech to the National Assembly as President, on 11 February 1919, Ebert promised to live up to the responsibilities of his new office. 'As a son of the working class', he would not disavow his socialist convictions, but he would protect the constitution and would not act as the leader of a political party in a partisan manner. He pledged to begin negotiations for the unification between Germany and Austria, although this was unlikely to be allowed by the Allies. He called freedom and law 'twin sisters', insisting that freedom could only exist in Germany if there was order: 'Every tyranny, whoever it may come from, we will fight to the limit.'[25]

The first act of Ebert's term as President was to ask his SPD colleague Philipp Scheidemann to become Chancellor and form a cabinet. It would be regarded as a 'Provisional Government', set up to operate until the new constitution became law later in the year. The USPD members announced they did not want to join a coalition government. The cabinet formed by Scheidemann, therefore, contained the representatives of the three parties which received the most votes in the national elections: the Social Democrats (SPD), the Centre

Party (Zentrum), and the Democrats (DDP). This coalition grouping became known as the 'Weimar Coalition'.[26]

The SPD had seven members in the cabinet including Scheidemann. The other six were Gustav Noske as Defence Minister, Otto Landsberg as Minister of Justice, Rudolf Wissell as Economic Affairs Minister, Gustav Bauer as Labour Minister, Robert Schmidt as Minister for Food, and Eduard David as Minister without Portfolio. The DDP was represented by Eugen Schiffer, the Vice-Chancellor (replaced on 17 April by DDP colleague Bernhard Dernberg), Hugo Preuss, Minister of the Interior, and Georg Gotheim, Minister of the Treasury. Zentrum also contributed three members: Matthias Erzberger, Minister without Portfolio, Johannes Bell, Colonial Minister, and Johannes Giesberts, Postmaster General. Only one member of the new cabinet had no party affiliation, Count Ulrich von Brockdorff-Rantzau, who had been Foreign Minister since December 1918. Despite his aristocratic background, he was widely respected as open-minded and liberal.

The new Scheidemann government announced a comprehensive policy programme. This included gaining a peace treaty in accordance with Wilson's Fourteen Points at the Paris Peace Conference, which began on 18 January, the admission of Germany to the League of Nations, support for disarmament of all nations, and the prevention of war through arbitration. Also promised were educational opportunities for all, the creation of a new army based on democratic principles, freedom of speech, religion, the press, and the arts. Trade union rights would be extended to all.[27]

In his first speech to the National Assembly as Reich Chancellor, Philipp Scheidemann said Germany had finally achieved liberty within its borders. It was important that no form of enslavement was now imposed from abroad. A Germany that was oppressed and punished would become a danger to the world, but a Germany left free to act would reach out and help other nations.

The elections and the creation of the new National Assembly did little to end the bitter political violence engulfing Germany. At 10 a.m. on the morning of 21 February, Kurt Eisner, the 51-year-old Prime Minister of the Free State of Bavaria, who led a coalition of left-wing socialist parties, was assassinated in Munich, shortly after he left his office in the Palais Montgelas (now part of luxury hotel Bayerischer Hof). He was walking with his armed bodyguard, his secretary, Felix Fechenbach, and his colleague Benno Merkle to the Bavarian parliament building in Prannerstrasse (now Kardinal-Faulhaber-

Strasse). Eisner was shot in the head and in the back by Anton Graf von Arco auf Valley, a 22-year-old Munich University law student, and a former lieutenant in the Bavarian Lifeguards regiment. He had close links to conservative right-wing groups and had been waiting near the main entrance of the building for his pre-planned assassination.

Eisner was killed instantly. His assassin was wounded in return fire by soldiers guarding the entrance to the parliament building, but he survived. Arco-Valley was half-Jewish, a fact that had prevented him being allowed to join the right-wing Thule Society, even though he was deeply antisemitic. Arco-Valley assumed that he would be killed in the attack on Eisner and had written a note outlining his motive in advance: 'My reason: I hate Bolshevism. I love my Bavarian people, I am a faithful royalist, a good Catholic. Above all. I respect the honour of Bavaria. Eisner is a Bolshevist. He is a Jew. He is no German. He is betraying the Fatherland.'[28] Arco-Valley was sentenced to death, but this was reduced to life imprisonment, and he was granted a full pardon after five years.[29]

Eisner had been warned several times about the possibility of assassination, and had received numerous death-threat letters, but he observed: 'You cannot evade assassination forever, and, after all, they can only shoot me dead once.'[30] In Eisner's briefcase, as he was gunned down, was the text of a speech announcing his resignation, after his party, the USPD, had performed badly in the 12 January Bavarian state (*Länder*) election, recording only 2.5 per cent of votes, and gaining three seats, a disastrous result for a government that had been in power for just over two months.[31] The SPD had won 33 per cent of the poll, just behind the conservative and newly formed Bavarian People's Party (*Bayerische Volkspartei*, BVP), an offshoot of the Centre Party, on 35 per cent.

Eisner's assassination was greeted with shock and anger when it was announced in the packed Bavarian State Parliament.[32] It triggered a riot inside the parliamentary chamber. One of Eisner's supporters, Alois Lindner, a burly bartender in the Munich central station (*Hauptbahnhof*), who had sneaked into the chamber, fired several shots using a Browning pistol at Erhard Auer, the leader of the Bavarian SPD, who was getting ready to give a speech denouncing Eisner's murder, and was seriously wounded. Auer, a severe critic of Eisner, was suspected by Lindner of ordering Eisner's assassination, though there is no evidence for this claim. Two others were killed during the shooting incident in the parliament: Major Paul Ritter von Jahreiss, a Bavarian

War Ministry official, and Heinrich Osel, a Conservative member of parliament. Lindner escaped and ended up in exile in Hungary.

Munich now descended into chaos and socialist revolution. The Majority Social Democrats declared the 'People's Republic of Bavaria', and promptly suspended parliament. A cabinet led by Johannes Hoffmann was formed, but it was unable to restore order, as a wave of street demonstrations and civil unrest spread throughout the city. Hoffmann and his government fled to Bamberg after receiving assurances of military support from Philipp Scheidemann's central government.

Meanwhile, Kurt Eisner lay in state, wearing a white silk funeral gown, in the eastern cemetery in Ostfriedhof in Geising. Thousands filed past his open coffin to pay their respects. Eisner's funeral on 26 February saw 100,000 people lining the procession route to the crematorium. His death afforded him a posthumous popularity as a martyr of the Bavarian Revolution.

The radical socialist Left saw the chaos in Munich as an ideal opportunity to abolish parliamentary democracy and put power into the hands of Soviet-style workers' and soldiers' councils. On the night of 6–7 April, a group of socialists and anarchists declared the Munich Council (Soviet) Republic (*Münchner Räterepublik*). The men who led this revolution were radical idealists, intellectuals, poets, and dreamers. The poet and playwright Ernst Toller, aged just 25, and a member of the USPD, was designated as the self-styled 'Chair of the "Revolutionary National Council"'. Toller's government was dubbed 'the regime of the "coffee-house anarchists"' or the 'Pseudo-Councils' Republic'. Toller issued a cascade of revolutionary decrees during his brief period in office, including an eight-hour working day, the end of private property, a pension for mothers, the nationalisation of public utilities, a promise that all citizens could withdraw 100 marks from local banks. All prisoners of war would be released. Munich University would be made free for anyone to study, without the need of qualifications, but the study of history was banned as it was deemed 'hostile to civilisation'.[33]

Dr Franz Lipp, who had a long history of psychiatric problems, was appointed by Toller as the People's Delegate on Foreign Affairs. He claimed to be a close friend of Pope Benedict XV, and complained to Toller that Johannes Hoffmann, the head of the SPD government in exile in Bamberg, had taken the key to the toilet in his Ministry with him. In a letter to Gustav Paulukum, who oversaw transport matters, Lipp announced: 'I have just declared war on Württemberg and Switzerland, because the dogs refused to lend me sixty locomotives.

JANUARY UPRISING, VERSAILLES TREATY

I am sure we will win.'[34] Lipp then had all telephone lines cut, as he had a phobia of hearing bells. Instead, he communicated with a stream of bizarre telegrams. When Toller was informed of his bizarre behaviour, he commented: 'Without doubt Lipp has gone mad. We must send him to a [mental] sanitorium. To avoid a sensation, he must resign voluntarily.' A letter of resignation was prepared for him, which Lipp duly signed, saying: 'Even this, I will do for the revolution.'[35]

On 13 April, Toller's chaotic government was replaced, during what became known as the 'Palm Sunday Putsch', by a Second Munich Council (Soviet) Republic, led by the Russian émigré Eugen Leviné, a veteran of the 1905 Russian Revolution. This coup was an attempt to introduce a full-blown Soviet-style system in Bavaria, a move sanctioned by the KPD.[36] Leviné's new communist government made clear it would not be run by coffee-house dreamers, but by resolute revolutionaries. A Red Army, recruited from factory workers, fully armed and commanded by Rudolf Egelhofer, was formed. One of Munich's churches was taken over and turned into a revolutionary temple dedicated to the Goddess of Reason, and a ten-day general strike brought the city to a halt.

The two rival Bavarian governments – Hoffmann's in Bamberg and the Second Munich Council Republic in Munich – clashed violently on 18 April just outside the city. The Munich Council forces, led by Toller and numbering 15,000, defeated Hoffmann's 8,000 poorly equipped soldiers in Dachau. Hoffmann then called on Gustav Noske, the Defence Minister in Berlin, to assist him in putting together an armed force sufficient to defeat the Munich rebellion. A force of 30,000 men was assembled, consisting of Prussian and Württemberg army troops, supported by a large contingent of the Bavarian Free Corps, commanded by Lieutenant General Burghard von Oven, including a brutal local force called 'Free Corps Epp', named after its brutal commander, Franz Ritter von Epp.

On 26 April, Red Army soldiers in Munich captured seven members of the Thule Society, including the society's chair, Countess Hella von Westarp, in the Hotel Vier Jahreszeiten, located at 17 Maximilianstrasse, in the centre of Munich, and held them along with three other hostages in the Luitpold School in Müllerstrasse. The Thule Society (*Thule-Gesellschaft*), named after a mythical northern country in Greek legend, often cited as Iceland, was an exclusive secretive society, led by Baron Rudolf von Sebottendorf. It was anticommunist, antisemitic, and believed in ideas of 'blood purity' and the

overleaf The funeral procession of the assassinated Bavarian socialist Prime Minister Kurt Eisner, 26 February 1919.

'Aryan master race'. It even used a swastika as its symbol. It also had its own newspaper, the *Münchener Beobachter* (*Munich Observer*), which later became the official Nazi Party newspaper, the *Völkischer Beobachter* (*People's Observer*).[37]

On 30 April, all the hostages were executed on the orders of Rudolf Egelhofer, in the courtyard of the Luitpold School. News of the brutal shootings, including claims the men's genitals had been mutilated, horrified the people of Munich. It spurred on the Free Corps to exact swift revenge. Many people, who had nothing whatsoever to do with the communist regime, were summarily executed in a week-long orgy of violence. In one incident a total of 53 Russian prisoners of war were gunned down. Many others living in working-class areas were also summarily killed. On 1 May, the Free Corps led the armed assault to retake Munich from the communist revolutionaries. There was bitter street fighting, with the attackers deploying heavy artillery, machine guns, flame throwers and even aircraft.

On 6 May, Lieutenant General Burghard von Oven, the commander of the counterrevolutionary operation, declared the reign of the Second Munich Council Republic was over. His troops were greeted like victors returning from war. The official death toll following the suppression of the Munich Council Republic was 606 dead – 233 Red Army soldiers, 335 civilians, and 38 members of the Free Corps. In the weeks following, it has been estimated a further 400 communists were killed in a vicious wave of reprisals by the Free Corps.[38]

There followed a series of trials involving about two thousand communists and socialists in the aftermath of the Munich Revolt. Eugen Leviné was condemned to death for treason and shot by a firing squad in Stadelheim Prison. Gustav Landauer and Rudolf Egelhofer were killed by Free Corps troops. Many others were given lengthy prison sentences, most notably Ernst Toller (five years) and Erich Mühsam (15 years).

The major consequence of the revolution in Munich was to move Bavaria in a decidedly right-wing direction. The Munich Council Republic was held up as an object lesson in the chaotic and violent rule of communism. Bavaria now became profoundly anti-communist, anti-republican and anti-democratic, and a haven for all manner of right-wing eccentrics.[39]

As these remarkable events unfolded, Munich also saw the first appearance on the political scene of Adolf Hitler, a soldier attached to the 7th Company of the 1st Replacement Battalion, a Munich-based

Reichswehr regiment. No other German figure is so closely associated with such far-reaching historical changes and monstrous crimes as Adolf Hitler. His own account of his early life, offered in his part-autobiography *Mein Kampf* (*My Struggle*), is inaccurate, but to fully understand the history of Weimar Germany it is important to find out more about this hugely important figure.

For the first 30 years of his life, Hitler was not a politician. Baptised as a Catholic, he was born at about 6.30 p.m. on 20 April 1889 on the second floor of an inn called Gasthof zum Pommer, in the Austrian town of Branau am Inn, close to the Austrian–German border. Adolf was the fourth child of the marriage between Alois Hitler and Klara Poelzl. His mother was 28 and his father 51 years old at the time of his birth. Their first three children – Gustav, Ida, and Otto – all died before the age of three. Two more children were born after Adolf's birth. Edmund (1894), who died in 1900, and Paula (1896), who lived until 1960.

Hitler's father, Alois, was born on 7 June 1837, in the small village of Strones in the Waldviertel, an agricultural region in north-west Lower Austria. He was christened Alois Schicklgruber, the only son of Maria Anna Schicklgruber, who was almost 42 years old at the time of his birth. Alois was deemed an 'illegitimate child', as the space on the birth register allotted to the father was left blank. In 1842, Maria Anna Schicklgruber married Johann Georg Heidler, often spelled 'Hitler' or 'Huttler' in local records.

It is usually assumed that the stepfather of Alois was his real father, but there is a complication in verifying this assertion. After the mother of Alois died in 1847, he went to live with Johann Georg's younger brother, Johann Nepomuk, a wealthy farmer, who raised him as his own foster-son. On 1 January 1877, Alois officially registered Johann Georg as his father and even changed his name to Alois Hitler, as he preferred the name to Schicklgruber. Even so, the identity of Adolf Hitler's paternal grandfather remains uncertain. There was some speculation that Adolf's paternal grandfather was Jewish, but no convincing evidence has been uncovered to support this theory.

There are few eyewitness accounts of Hitler's early years. In *Mein Kampf*, Hitler portrayed his father as a 'lowly customs official', who had brought up his family in a state of hardship, but this was clearly false. Alois had carved out a successful career as a well-paid imperial customs official, who enjoyed a salary of 2,600 crowns per month, on a par with the principal of a fee-paying secondary school, and with generous pension rights. When he retired in 1895, aged 59, he received a monthly pension of 2,200 crowns per month. Adolf Hitler's family were comfortably middle class.

The private life of Hitler's father resembled a soap opera. He had many love affairs and three wives. In 1864, he married Anna Glasl, 14 years his senior and relatively well off, but in poor health. The marriage was childless, and in 1880 the couple were granted a legal separation, but remained married. By this time, Alois was already involved in a love affair with a 19-year-old house-cleaner called Franziska ('Fanni') Matzelberger. His first wife died on 6 April 1883, and on 28 July of the same year Alois married Fanni. They had two children: Alois junior and Angela. Fanni soon contracted tuberculosis, then a terminal illness, and she died in August 1884.

Alois does not seem to have been overcome with grief about the premature death of his young second wife. In fact, while Fanni was seriously ill, he began an affair with Klara Poezl, his second cousin, who was acting as a nurse to Fanni, as her life ebbed away. On 7 January 1885, Alois Hitler, now aged 47, married Klara, then aged 24. She was pregnant on her wedding day and given their close family relationship the couple needed a special dispensation from the Catholic Church to allow the marriage to go ahead.

Alois Hitler was a stern father, but he provided his family with a comfortable lifestyle. The family lived in a number of places during Adolf's childhood. They mostly resided in detached houses, with handmade carpets on the floor, and curtains on the windows. There was a well-stocked fruit and vegetable garden and a beehive, which produced honey. The Hitler household often even included a cook and a maidservant.

At primary school, Adolf received good marks and was popular with his classmates. He enjoyed playing imaginary war games, especially 'cowboys and Indians'. The young Adolf liked to play the (North American Native) Indians (who were the underdogs). His love of such games was inspired by books about the American West by the German writer Karl May, who remained one of Hitler's favourite writers for the rest of his life.[40] It would be wrong, however, to depict Hitler's childhood as completely tension free. He had a strained relationship with his father, for not only was Alois strict, he was also humourless, frugal, domineering and a heavy drinker. Hitler later recalled: 'I never loved my father. I therefore feared him more. He had a terrible temper and often whipped me.'[41]

If Adolf's father was a negative source of anger, his mother was a compensating source of love. Klara Hitler was quiet, submissive, uncomplicated, and kind. She pampered Adolf when his father was not around, and let him do what he liked. In *Mein Kampf*, Hitler writes: 'I honoured my father, but I loved my mother.'[42] Dr Eduard Bloch, the family doctor, claimed that he had never witnessed a closer attachment than the one between Adolf Hitler and his mother.

From 17 September 1900 onwards, Adolf attended the fee-paying *Realschule* in Linz. The transition to secondary school proved difficult, as he was no longer the leader of his class, as he had been in primary school. His marks fluctuated in a range fluctuating between 'average' and 'mediocre'. His teachers viewed the young Adolf as intelligent, but moody, lazy, and stubborn. In *Mein Kampf*, Hitler claimed he liked history because his teacher was a passionate German nationalist, geography because he loved reading maps, and art, his favourite subject, because he liked to sketch and paint in watercolours. Hitler claimed he deliberately failed at academic subjects to avoid becoming the dull civil servant his father wanted him to be.

On 3 January 1903, Alois Hitler, then aged 65, collapsed and died after suffering a fatal lung haemorrhage, while drinking red wine in a local tavern called the Weisinger Inn. He was buried in a local cemetery in Leonding. The death of his father came as something of a relief to young Adolf, who was now free to contemplate his first great impossible dream: to become a renowned artist. In 1905, according to Adolf, his mother allowed him to leave school, aged 16, without any qualifications. Living with his mother in an apartment in Linz – for she had sold the large house in Leonding after her husband died – Hitler could now do what he liked.

In Linz, the provincial capital of Upper Austria, with a population of 60,000, Hitler resembled a Bohemian dilettante, with long hair, a moustache, fashionable clothes, a dark hat, and a black cane with an ivory handle. He looked more like a budding poet rather than the future rabble-rousing dictator he would become. During the day, he visited local cafés, art galleries and libraries. In the evening he went to the local opera house. He particularly loved the works of Richard Wagner, whose operas held him spellbound. Much has subsequently been made of the fact that Wagner was antisemitic, but what attracted the young Hitler to Wagner was the epic scale of his operas.

In the autumn of 1906, Hitler struck up a close friendship with a budding classical musician called August ('Gustl') Kubizek, after meeting him at the Linz opera house. Kubizek, who was a couple of years younger, was Hitler's only close childhood friend. His account of their friendship between 1905 and 1908 was not published until 1954, and though clouded by hindsight and his obvious admiration for Hitler, it contains important insights into Hitler's personality during this period.[43]

Kubizek describes Hitler as a person 'whose eyes dominated his face'. Hitler's blue eyes would always be described as his most extraordinary feature. Kubizek also thought him 'highly strung' and liable to 'fly off the handle', especially when describing schoolteachers and bureaucrats. He poured forth many fantasies, including wanting to be a painter, a playwright, and an architect. His greatest passions at this time were art, architecture and operatic music. He told Kubizek his greatest ambition was to gain entry to the prestigious Academy of Fine Arts in Vienna. Hitler had no friendships with the other sex, but Kubizek does mention a brief 'infatuation' with a young and beautiful middle-class girl called Stefanie Isac, whom he had seen in Linz city centre. Hitler admired her from afar, even wrote several love poems about her, but they were never delivered. In fact, he never even spoke to this fantasy girlfriend.[44]

The most traumatic event of Hitler's youth was undoubtedly the death of his mother. On 18 January 1907, Hitler's mother Klara became seriously ill, with breast cancer, and underwent a life-saving mastectomy in the Barmherzige Schwestern hospital in Linz. In early September 1907, Hitler went to Vienna to sit the entrance exam for the Academy of Fine Arts. He made it past the first round, but failed to go any further, and was rejected. His examiners told him the drawings he had submitted were 'unsatisfactory'. To soften the blow, the Director of the Academy told him a career as an architect would be a much better choice for him. Hitler had over-confidently expected to be admitted, and he claimed this decision hit him 'like a bolt from the blue'. In *Mein Kampf*, Hitler angrily described his examiners as 'fossilised bureaucrats devoid of any understanding of young talent'.[45] Hitler's paintings and drawings do show technical competence in copying other people's works, but no aptitude to create original works of his own. He could paint and draw buildings and landscapes, but not people. History might have been hugely different had the examiners given him a place. Unfortunately, to gain a place on the architecture course Hitler would have needed to return to college to obtain the School Leaving Certificate (*Abitur*), which he was not prepared to do.

While he was away in Vienna, the condition of his mother had deteriorated. He returned to Linz to nurse her, but on the evening of 21 December 1907, Klara Hitler died, aged 47, with her distraught son at her bedside. Dr Bloch, the Jewish family doctor, who had already noticed the close relationship between the two, later commented: 'In all my career I have never seen anyone as prostrate with grief as Adolf Hitler.'[46] In 1938, after Hitler incorporated Austria into the German Reich, he made sure Dr Bloch was given protection from the Gestapo and in 1940 sanctioned a visa that allowed Bloch to move to the USA.

On 12 February 1908, Hitler returned to Vienna, where he was to remain for the next five-and-a-half years. He received a partial inheritance of 1,000 crowns from his mother's will, plus an orphan's pension of 25 crowns per month, with a further 824 crowns due from his father's will when he reached 24, on 20 April 1913. Hitler had enough money to live in Vienna for at least a year without needing to find a job.

At the time, Vienna was one of the great cosmopolitan capitals of Europe, with the magnificent Habsburg buildings dominating the Ringstrasse. It also contained the largest Jewish population of any German or Austrian city. In 1910, 175,318 Jews lived in the city, making up 8.6 per cent of the population. Jewish people were prominent in the legal and medical professions, finance, the press, and the arts. There was a strong strand of antisemitism in the city, with the local Stock Exchange nicknamed 'the Jewish Monte Carlo Casino.'

In March 1908, Hitler was joined in the single room of a house he was renting, at Stumpergasse 29, which was owned by an unmarried mender, Maria Zakery, by his close friend, August Kubizek, who had gained entry to the prestigious Vienna Academy of Music. The rent was 20 crowns per month. For the next four months, they shared a flat together. During these months, Kubizek saw Hitler read books voraciously, not to learn, but to find justification for his own views, write the outline of a play, based on German mythology, and a derivative Wagner-style opera, which he never completed. Hitler continued to visit the Vienna State Opera House regularly and secured standing room on the promenade of the theatre where women were not allowed.[47]

There has been an unwillingness among most of Hitler's biographers to look more closely at the nature of Hitler's very close relationship with Kubizek. They dressed alike and went on long hikes together. After one such lengthy walk, they were caught in a thunderstorm, sought refuge in a barn and decided to spend the night there together. Kubizek later recalled:

I felt sorry for Adolf as he stood in the doorway in his sodden underclothes, shivering with cold and wringing out the sleeves of his jacket. Being susceptible to colds of every kind, he could easily have developed pneumonia. So, I took one of the big cloths, spread it out on the hay, and told Adolf to remove his wet shirt and underpants and wrap himself in the dry cloth. This he did. He lay down naked in the cloth. I folded the ends together and wrapped him up tightly in it. Then I fetched another cloth and draped it over the top… He was highly amused by the whole venture, whose romantic conclusion pleased him greatly.[48]

On Hitler's attraction to women, Kubizek has nothing to report, recalling that women were attracted to Hitler, but they 'had absolutely no sexual attraction for him'. Despite the homoerotic encounter in the barn mentioned above, Kubizek denied Hitler was a homosexual and suggested he lived a life of self-imposed sexual abstinence, mainly because he feared contracting syphilis.[49]

In the summer of 1908, Kubizek returned to Linz for a long vacation with his parents, because the two friends, living in one room, had started to get on each other's nerves. In September 1908, Hitler applied to re-sit the entrance examination for the Vienna Academy of Fine Arts, but he was not judged good enough even to do that. For Hitler, this was another shattering blow. It ended his unrealistic dream of becoming a renowned artist. He descended into a state of deep depression, and when, in November 1908, Kubizek finally returned to Vienna, he found his friend Adolf had disappeared, leaving no forwarding address. Hitler could obviously not bring himself to tell Kubizek of his double failure.

Hitler described his Vienna period as the 'saddest period of my life', but this period is difficult to research, due to a lack of reliable sources.[50] Only a handful of people who knew Hitler during this period recorded their views, and they did so much later, distorting any understanding of what he was really like at this time.

Hitler had no intention of looking for a mundane job, nor did he come forward to undertake his compulsory military training, as he was legally obliged to do. From 18 November 1908 to 20 August 1909, he lived in an apartment at 22 Felberstrasse. It seems his savings were now rapidly running out. On 22 August 1909, he moved to a much cheaper apartment at 58 Sechshauser Strasse, but on 16 September he vacated his room, probably because he had failed to pay the rent. He was homeless for about six weeks, living rough, mostly sleeping on park benches.

In October 1909, Hitler took up residence in the Meidling, a men's homeless hostel (*Asyl für Obdachlose*), funded by a wealthy Jewish family. It offered a bed and soup and bread every night. He undertook a few jobs at this time: he cleared snow, carried baggage for tips at the local railway station, and worked for a few days as a labourer. At the hostel, he was befriended by Reinhold Hanisch, an unemployed former domestic servant, who described Hitler at this time as 'shabbily dressed and incapable of organising his own life'. After hearing Hitler's life story, Hanisch told him to write a letter to one of his well-off relatives for some money to buy some artists' materials, and then set himself up as a commercial artist, painting post cards, with Hanisch acting as his agent. Hitler wrote to his aunt Johanna ('Hanni'), his mother's sister, who sent him a 50 crowns note by return of post.[51]

In December 1909, Hitler moved to the *Männerheim* men's hostel at 27 Meldemannstrasse, in the working-class district of Brigittenau. It was a much smarter hostel, occupied by workers and clerks on limited incomes. The residents of this 'Dormitory for Men' paid three crowns a week for a single room, with a bed, a table and electric light. The room had to be vacated during working hours. Residents also had access to a dining room, a library and a reading room, a writing room, a shower room and a laundry. Hitler was allowed to paint during the day near a window in the writing room.

Those who knew Hitler at the Meldemannstrasse hostel from 1909 to 1913, all describe him as a 'loner' who held dogmatic opinions on every subject. In *Mein Kampf*, Hitler admitted: 'I think the people around me thought I was an oddball'.[52] Residents detected that he disliked Social Democrats, trade unionists and Jesuits, but no one mentioned him declaring pronounced antisemitic views. Hitler did not drink or smoke, and certainly had no interest in seeking out female companionship outside the hostel. There is no conclusive evidence that he engaged in a same-sex relationship with a fellow resident either.

While he lived at the *Männerheim*, Hitler completed somewhere between 400 and 600 paintings, drawings, advertising posters and postcards, most of which were of well-known buildings in Vienna, copied from other people's work, and then sold in shops, taverns, cafés and art shops. By the end of 1910, it has been estimated he was earning 40 to 60 crowns a month from his artwork. His income was further boosted by a gift of 3,800 crowns from his aunt Johanna, which is further evidence of his healthy financial state at this time.

Hitler's partnership with Hanisch ended acrimoniously. Hitler claimed his painting of the Vienna parliament had sold for 50 crowns, not the 10 crowns Hanisch had claimed. Hitler took legal proceedings against Hanisch, and the case was held at the Brigittenau police station on 5 August 1910. A record of the trial has survived. Hitler claimed Hanisch was a 'practised liar' who registered at the Männerheim hostel under the false name of Fritz Walter. Hanisch was found guilty and sentenced to seven days in jail. In the 1930s, Hanisch sold his story to the popular press. In 1936 the Gestapo arrested Hanisch for spreading 'libellous stories about Hitler'. On 4 October 1937, he was found dead in his cell, reportedly of a 'heart attack'. It is likely he was murdered.

In *Mein Kampf*, Hitler claimed that he was keenly interested in political developments in Vienna, but he belonged to no political party, and kept up to date by reading newspapers, periodicals, and cheap pamphlets. Before he came to Vienna, he was already a fervent German nationalist, who identified much more with the German Reich than the multi-national Habsburg Empire. Hitler claimed that the two political figures in Vienna who influenced his political ideas were Georg von Schönerer, the leader of the Pan German Party, and Karl Lueger, leader of the Christian Social Party. Schönerer's party, unlike its German equivalent, was not exclusively preoccupied with German imperial expansion outside Europe, but instead championed the idea of a Greater German Reich containing all German speakers in a single state. Schönerer was deeply antisemitic, regarding Jews as responsible for all the evils of the world. Hitler felt the major weakness of Schönerer as a politician was his inability to arouse the masses, but he borrowed two ideas from Schönerer: the use of the 'Heil' greeting and calling himself Leader (*Führer*).

Dr Karl Lueger, the mayor of Vienna, made a much bigger impression on the young Hitler. It was not Lueger's ideology Hitler admired, as he felt he did not champion nationalist ideas enough, but rather he admired his speaking abilities and his pragmatic and flexible approach to political issues. Lueger was willing to exploit policies he thought would be electorally popular. Hitler was most impressed by Lueger's ability to create powerful slogans such as: 'We must do something for the Little Man.'[53]

Hitler claimed that during his Vienna period he developed a 'great hatred' towards the Social Democratic Party, but there were some aspects of its appeal he admired, such as the SPD's effective use of propaganda, and its ability to rouse the masses to go out on the streets in demonstrations and parades. Hitler believed that only by being challenged on the streets could the socialists be stopped from winning over the masses.

Hitler also claimed, in *Mein Kampf*, that the idea of creating a party that combined the passionate nationalism of Schönerer with the charismatic populism of Lueger, together with the street fighting and propaganda slogans of the socialists, was already forming in his mind. Yet we only have Hitler's word that his ideas were as clear as this so early in his life. It is more plausible to suggest these views about his political views in Vienna were self-serving rhetoric designed to portray himself as a man of unclouded vision at a time when Hitler in fact had no independently thought-out ideas of his own. He was just an interested spectator on politics.

It is important to assess Hitler's views towards the Jews during his Vienna period, given the importance to the later history of the Nazi Party. Surprisingly, there is little evidence during his early years to suggest antisemitism was a dominant preoccupation. In *Mein Kampf*, Hitler claimed he went from being a 'weak kneed cosmopolitan' when he arrived in 1907 to a 'fanatical antisemite' when he left in 1913. What prompted this change was, he said, seeing Jews on the streets of Vienna and noticing they were 'an alien force'. He also claimed he bought and read many antisemitic pamphlets, one of the most notable of which was called *Ostara*, named after a German goddess of spring. The message of the pamphlet was simple: the Aryan is the hero and the Jew the enemy. Yet there is no evidence Hitler had given any thought at this time of how to solve 'the Jewish problem'. Another possibility, and a more plausible one, is that his virulent antisemitism was not a dominant preoccupation during his Vienna period and some of his behaviour adds weight to this view. Hitler regularly attended musical evenings at the home of a Jewish family; most of his closest acquaintances at the *Männerheim* were Jewish and he preferred to sell his paintings through Jewish art dealers. His biographers agree that Hitler's antisemitism emerged after Germany's defeat in the First World War.

In May 1913 Hitler, then aged 24, decided to end his period in Vienna. He was prompted to do this by receiving the last instalment of his father's inheritance on his 24th birthday on 20 April. He moved to the German city of Munich, accompanied by a 20-year-old trainee pharmacist named Rudolf Häusler, with whom he had become friendly at the *Männerheim*. There is no evidence of any sexual relationship between the two men.

During his Vienna period, Hitler had avoided military conscription. In Munich, he registered first as a 'stateless' citizen and then as an 'Austrian citizen'. The documents relating to his failure to enlist show the Austrian authorities were looking for him. Police files in Linz indicate that he had not registered his address in Vienna with them. The Austrian police eventually tracked him down to Munich. In January 1914, the police arrived at his new address, 34 Schleissheimer Strasse. This was located in a poor area of Munich where he had taken lodgings, along with Häusler, with the family of Joseph Popp, a tailor.

The charge of 'draft dodging' was a serious criminal offence in Austria in 1914. Hitler was asked to report to Salzburg on 5 February 1914 to explain why he had avoided military service for so long. In a written statement, he claimed he had not come forward in 1909 because he was 'a very inexperienced man, without any financial aid'. He even claimed that he had submitted his documents in the post. Of course, these explanations were untrue, but they were accepted. In the end, Hitler was declared unfit for military service due to a minor lung condition. Hitler later claimed he was not a draft dodger because he was a coward, but because he did not want to join the Austro-Hungarian Army, as he felt a greater affinity for Germany.[54]

Hitler described the brief time he spent in Munich before the First World War as 'the happiest and by far the most contented of my life.'[55] The members of the Popp family, with whom he lived, recalled Hitler leading a very solitary existence. His friendship with Häusler did not last long, and the latter left the room he shared with Hitler, but for what reason is not known. Hitler painted postcards and watercolours to sell to local art dealers and commanded an income of 120 marks per month, a moderate sum, but one which allowed him to live tolerably.

The event which truly transformed Adolf Hitler's life was the outbreak of the First World War in August 1914. Without the war, and the fact that Germany lost it, it is almost certain Hitler would never have entered politics. According to *Mein Kampf*, Hitler wrote a letter to King Ludwig III of Bavaria on 3 August 1914 volunteering to serve in the German Army, even though he was an Austrian citizen, and on the next day he received written permission to do so. This seems implausible, however. No one had checked Hitler's citizenship status, as he was ineligible to serve in the Bavarian army. Hitler first tried to volunteer on 5 August 1914, but it was not until 16 August that he was finally inducted into the Recruit Depot VI of the Bavarian Infantry Regiment, and on 1 September 1914 he was transferred to the 16th

Reserve Infantry Regiment (known as the 'List Regiment', after its first commander, Colonel Julius List).[56]

Hitler described his time in the German Army during the war as 'the greatest and most unforgettable time of my life'.[57] Hitler spent most of the war on the Western Front as a regimental dispatch runner, carrying messages between the staff at military HQ and the front-line troops. Hitler did not take part in trench warfare, but his job was a hazardous one and many of his comrades were killed by enemy fire while trying to deliver messages.

The war not only gave Hitler the chance of showing his nationalist passion for the German cause, but also allowed him to escape from boredom, frustration, and failure. It gave his life a new purpose and energy. The army became for Hitler a surrogate family, and he followed orders from officers without comment. Photographs taken of Hitler during the war show him usually isolated from the other soldiers, with a dour expression on his face and looking much older than his mid-twenties. All the soldiers who knew 'Adi' thought he was a bit of an eccentric and over-subservient to authority. They noticed he could sit for hours, silently brooding or reading, but occasionally jump to his feet and break into a monologue – usually berating anyone who showed signs of defeatism. One of his fellow soldiers commented: 'There was this white crow among us who wouldn't go along with us when we damned the war.'[58]

Hitler never asked for leave, never received letters nor gave details of his early life to his fellow soldiers. He was not interested in joining in the sexual banter about women and refused to join his comrades on their frequent trips to local bars and brothels. There is no evidence that, as has been suggested, in 1916 and 1917 he had a love affair with a French woman called Charlotte Lobjoie or that he was the father of her son born in March 1918.[59]

Many of the ordinary soldiers who served with him thought Hitler lived a comfortable life away from the front line. The officers under whom Hitler served told a different story, however. Lieutenant Colonel Friedrich Petz, who commanded the regiment until March 1916, later recalled: 'Hitler was an extremely hard-working, willing, conscientious and dutiful soldier who was also completely dependable and obedient towards his superiors'.[60] In truth, Hitler was a decent soldier, not exceptionally brave, but not a coward either. In December 1914 he was awarded the Iron Cross (2nd class) and in August 1918 he gained the Iron Cross (1st class). The latter award was given on the recommendation of a Jewish officer named Hugo Gutmann. It was an award rarely given to a volunteer soldier. The award of the Iron Cross was particularly important in Hitler's later political career as it gave tangible evidence of his bravery.

It is perhaps surprising Hitler was not promoted to the officer rank. Most historians describe Hitler's highest rank as 'corporal' or 'lance corporal', but the highest rank he ever officially achieved, that of *Gefreiter*, did not allow him to give commands to other soldiers, and it is best translated as a 'Senior Private', a rank awarded for experience, not leadership qualities. A senior officer of the List Regiment, giving evidence at the Nuremberg war trials, said the question of promoting Hitler did often crop up, but he was rejected because 'we could discover no leadership qualities in him'.[61]

Hitler's closest friend in his regiment was Ernst Schmidt, who was also a dispatch runner. They were invariably seen together. Hans Mend, another dispatch runner, claimed in an interview in December 1939 that Schmidt and Hitler had a sexual relationship, and he further alleged that other troops in the regiment 'suspected Hitler of homosexuality right away', as he was not interested in women. Mend commented: 'At night, Hitler lay with Schmidt, his male whore.' Mend further alleged it was Hitler's known same-sex activity in the regiment that explains his failure to be promoted. At the end of the war, when Schmidt returned to Munich, the two continued to be close friends. Schmidt always denied there was a same-sex relationship, and Mend has been seen as an unreliable witness. Mend was sentenced to two years' imprisonment for sex offences against women in 1940, and died in custody in Osterstein Castle, near Zwickau, on 13 February 1942.[62]

Hitler also claimed in *Mein Kampf* that he kept his political views to himself during the war and in corroboration, most fellow soldiers could not remember him making political speeches. The only time Hitler became angry was when he heard any soldier questioning whether Germany would win the war. Most soldiers suggested Hitler's closest companion was not Ernst Schmidt, but an adopted fox terrier he called Fuchsl. Hitler was very fond of the animal and taught it a number of tricks. In September 1917, the dog disappeared, prompting Hitler to comment: 'The bastard who took him away doesn't know what he did to me.'[63]

On the evening of 18 October 1918, south of Ypres, Hitler was briefly blinded in a mustard gas attack, and transported to Pasewalk military hospital in Pomerania. On 10 November, a pastor told Hitler a revolution had broken out in Germany, the Kaiser had abdicated, a republic had been declared, and the war was lost. On hearing this news, according to his own account, Hitler began to weep, for the first time since he stood over his mother's grave: 'And everything went black again before my eyes, I tottered and groped my way back to the dormitory, threw myself in my bunk, and dug my burning head into my blanket and pillow. So, it had all been in vain.'[64]

Hitler later claimed this was the exact moment when he decided to enter politics, but this appears to be completely untrue. When he returned to Munich on 21 November 1918, his only firm plan was to stay in the Army for as long as possible. He was assigned to the 7th Company of the 1st Replacement Battalion of the 2nd Infantry Regiment, a demobilisation unit of the List Regiment, which meant he had board and lodgings, food and 40 marks' army pay per month. He soon met up again with Ernst Schmidt, when they were both assigned to act as guards in a camp for prisoners of war in the small, picturesque southern Bavarian town of Traunstein, close to the Alps, in December 1918.[65]

Hitler claimed he returned to Munich in March 1919, after the assassination of Kurt Eisner, but as the camp at Traunstein was dissolved towards the end of January, this is clearly incorrect. He was certainly back in Munich by 12 February at the latest. He was transferred to the 2nd Demobilisation Company, in the barracks of the 2nd Infantry Regiment in Lothstrasse, just north of Oberwiesenfeld. One of Hitler's tasks was to perform guard duty at various locations in the city.[66] It did not seem to matter to Hitler at this time that his local regiment was in the control of a left-wing soldiers' council or that the Bavarian government was led by Jewish intellectuals and pro-Soviet revolutionaries. It would not be the last occasion when Hitler would compromise his so-called 'unshakeable principles' for opportunistic reasons.

What Hitler did in the dramatic weeks between Eisner's assassination and the crushing of the Munich Council Republic is also something of a mystery. In *Mein Kampf*, he devoted less than a page to the communist seizure of power, and the Free Corps counter-attack that ended it so brutally. There is no evidence that Hitler's local regiment lifted a finger for either side. Hitler took no part in crushing the communist-style government in Munich, nor did he pledge loyalty to the exiled Hoffmann government or volunteer to join the right-wing Free Corps. Ernst Schmidt claimed that Hitler did not talk much about his feelings about the revolution in Munich, but thought it was clear 'how bitter he felt'.[67] Hitler claimed soldiers' councils in Munich 'disgusted' him, yet a photograph, taken by Heinrich Hoffmann, who later became Hitler's official photographer, on the day of Kurt Eisner's funeral procession, shows a soldier who looks very much like Hitler. When the photo was deposited by Heinrich Hoffmann's grandson in an archive in 1993, an arrow was pointing to the person believed to be Hitler, and Hoffmann's son confirmed in an interview in the 1980s that the photo is of Adolf Hitler.[68]

Hitler clearly accommodated himself to the new political realities in Munich, without ever becoming committed to the socialist cause. On 3 April he was elected by his fellow soldiers as the liaison representative of his battalion, which is unlikely to have happened had he opposed the revolution. On 13 April, the day of the Palm Sunday Putsch, Hitler told his comrades to keep out of the fighting, saying: 'We're no pack of revolutionary guards for a gang of vagrant Jews'. On 15 April, during the era of the more extreme left-wing Second Munich Council Republic, Hitler put himself up for election as the battalion representative in the 2nd Demobilisation Company (*Battalions Rat*). He came second in the poll with 19 votes, behind the 39 votes recorded for the winner, Georg Dufter, but he was still given the role of Deputy Representative. In this role, he was expected to show total loyalty to the communist rulers. His behaviour at this time is best described as a combination of 'desperation, passivity and opportunistic adaptation'.[69]

Yet as soon as the Second Munich Council government was crushed, Hitler immediately aligned himself with the counterrevolutionary Bayerische Reichswehr Group Commando 4 (*Reichswehrgruppen-kommando-IV*), set up on 11 May 1919 and commanded by General

Arnold von Möhl, which instituted martial rule over Bavaria until the Hoffmann government was able to return to the city from Bamberg on 17 August. Hitler denounced all the soldiers he knew to be 'pro-Soviet' in his regiment in a cold and calculated manner. He even denounced Georg Dufter, the soldier who defeated him in the vote for battalion representative.

On 9 May, Hitler, clearly by now viewed as a reliable informer, was appointed the junior member of a three-person Investigation and Decommissioning Board of the 2nd Infantry Regiment, to investigate the political behaviour of his regiment's soldiers during the period of the two Munich Council Republics. This, apart from any other considerations, helped him to avoid being discharged from the Army. According to Ernst Röhm, Hitler had already been recruited as a Reichswehr informer on the left-wing revolutionary movement in Munich when they first met on 7 March.[70] This might help to explain how Hitler seamlessly moved into intelligence work once the revolution was crushed. While serving on the Decommissioning Board, Hitler created a fictionalised account of his behaviour during the revolutionary period, indicating he was always a bitter opponent of all the socialists he served.

The head of the Information Department (*Nachrichtenabteilung Abt. Ib/P*) of Reichswehr Group Commando 4 was Captain Karl Mayr, who was given considerable army funds to create a group of instructors to indoctrinate soldiers and workers against the dangers of Soviet Bolshevism, and to ignite in them support for patriotic and nationalist ideas. Mayr was a go-getting secret service chief, who wanted communism crushed, and Hitler immediately came to Mayr's attention during his work with the anti-communist investigation committee. Mayr later described Hitler as 'like a tired stray dog looking for a master'. However, Hitler was not an empty shell, but retained the inner belief that he had special qualities.[71] His conformist and submissive manner in front of his military superiors had once more helped Hitler's advancement, but it must be appreciated that it was calculated.

Mayr later recalled that Hitler was 'an individual paid by the month from whom regular (intelligence) information could be expected'.[72] As well as Hitler's role as an Informant (*V-Leute or V-Männer*), Mayr also appointed him as a Propaganda Agent (*Propagandaleute*). But before Hitler began his work, he was sent on a week-long training course in political indoctrination, which took place from 5 to 12 June at Munich

Government troops deployed during the crushing of the Munich Soviet Republic, May 1919.

95

University. Mayr selected all the speakers, who included the nationalist historian Karl von Müller, who gave lectures on post-Reformation German history, and the political history of the First World War; and his brother in-law, Gottfried Feder, a Pan German economic expert, who had become well known in Bavaria for highlighting the dangers of 'interest slavery', which he put down to Jewish dominance of financial markets.

Feder gave his first lecture on 6 June, which was attended by Hitler and up to 400 others. Hitler was totally captivated by Feder, writing: 'For the first time in my life I fundamentally got to grips with the international stock-market and loan capital.' What really attracted Hitler to Feder was the link he made between the dangers of capitalism and the dominance of Jews. This would soon become an integral part of Hitler's own worldview.[73]

At the end of his own lecture, Müller noticed Hitler speaking to a group of fellow students and told Mayr: 'Do you know that one of your trainees is a natural-born public speaker'. Mayr immediately saw the potential in Hitler, and pencilled him in for further training courses, but this time not as a trainee but as a speaker, which was Hitler's greatest skill.[74]

On 7 May, the Allied draft peace terms were presented to the German delegation headed by Count Ulrich von Brockdorff-Rantzau, the German Foreign Minister, at the Trianon Palace Hotel, near to the Palace of Versailles. The Allies had excluded the Germans from the discussions surrounding the drafting of the proposed treaty. No prior discussion of the terms was permitted by the Allies, with the Germans allowed only 15 days to outline objections to specific clauses. Count Brockdorff-Rantzau remained seated as a summary of the terms was read out by the French Prime Minister, Georges Clemenceau. He then protested about the requirement that Germany should accept sole guilt for the war. US President Woodrow Wilson's comment on Brockdorff-Rantzau's speech was: 'The Germans are really a stupid people. They always do the wrong thing.'[75]

It is, of course, an established tradition of war that the loser pays the costs of defeat, but the terms of the proposed Versailles Treaty were severe, to say the least. Alsace and Lorraine were returned to France, something which had been a French aim during the war. German territory west of the Rhine was to be occupied by Allied troops for at least 15 years to ensure German compliance to the treaty – if Germany did comply, the occupation of Cologne would end after five years,

Koblenz after ten years and Mainz after 15 years. The left bank of the Rhine and the right bank to a depth of 31 miles were to be permanently demilitarised. In this region no German arms or soldiers could be stationed. The aim of these clauses was to stop another unprovoked German invasion of Belgium and France.

The Saar, a rich coal mining region, would be governed for 15 years by a commission of the League of Nations. In that time, the Saar coal mines would be given to France, as compensation for the German destruction of French coal mines during the war. At the end of the 15-year period, the people of the Saar would decide, in a referendum, whether they wished to remain under League control, to unite with France or return to Germany. If the people chose the latter option, Germany would be allowed to buy back the mines from France. Belgium received Moresnet, Eupen and Malmédy, but the local populations there would be allowed a referendum to confirm or reject this change. A referendum was also offered to determine the fate of North Schleswig, which voted in favour of being transferred to Denmark.

Germany suffered even greater territorial losses in Eastern Europe. The newly constituted state of Poland included the industrially rich area of Upper Silesia, along with Posen and West Prussia – the latter including the so-called Polish Corridor, which controversially separated East Prussia from the rest of Germany. Poland was also given extensive trading rights in Danzig (Gdansk), which was now designated a Free City under League of Nations authority. Danzig was Poland's natural seaport, but ethnically it was a German city and would remain a source of unrest between Germany and Poland during the inter-war years. In addition, the German port of Memel was detached from the Reich, but was not formally awarded to Lithuania until 1923.

German territorial losses under the Treaty as a whole amounted to 13 per cent of its European lands, together with six million of its people. If Germany had been allowed to unite with Austria, it would have lessened the blow of these European territorial losses. Both countries were favourable to the union, but no referendum was offered. The Allies decided instead to prohibit the union with Austria (*Anschluss*).

Germany's European losses were paralleled by the sacrifices it was forced to make elsewhere. All overseas colonies under German control were redistributed under mandates issued by the League of Nations, but it was stipulated these mandates must not simply serve the interests of their guardians. When the German delegation protested the loss of its colonies, the Allies pointed out the native inhabitants of the German colonies were strongly opposed to being returned to German control.

The Allies were also determined to limit Germany's ability to rearm and wage a war of revenge. Under a series of punitive military clauses, the German Army was limited to 100,000 men, and confined exclusively to keeping order within its own borders. The German General Staff, seen by the Allies as the embodiment of German militarism, was dissolved, and officers were only allowed to serve for a maximum of 25 years. Conscription and the manufacture and import of armaments were also banned, including military airplanes, armoured cars, artillery, tanks and poison gas. An Inter-Allied Control Commission was established to ensure compliance by Germany with all the military disarmament clauses.

German naval power was also drastically reduced. At its disposal would be no more than six small battleships, six light cruisers, twelve destroyers and twelve torpedo boats. Submarines were strictly forbidden. The maximum number of German naval personnel was to be 15,000. The remainder of the German fleet was to be surrendered to the Allies, but on 21 June, in an act of deliberate defiance and sabotage, the German Admiral Ludwig von Reuter, without the permission of the German government or the President, decided to scuttle the entire High Seas Fleet, which was being held at the Royal Navy's base at Scapa Flow in the Orkney Islands of Scotland. A total of 52 out of the 74 vessels sank.[76]

The treaty also terminated all German commercial trade agreements, which effectively froze German exporters out of Allied markets. The Allies also imposed 'most favoured' status on their exports to the German market for a period of five years. To make matters even worse, Germany was deprived of all its foreign financial holdings and its merchant fleet was reduced to one-tenth of its pre-war size. Article 227 gave notice of the Allied intention to ask the Netherlands government to surrender the former Kaiser Wilhelm II to face a war crimes trial. Articles 228 to 230 further promised that other leading German military figures would also face war crimes trials for atrocities committed during the war. If found guilty, they would receive the harshest penalties.

To justify the claim for a huge compensation bill (known as reparations), the Allies insisted the German government must sign Article 231, the infamous 'war-guilt clause' which stated: 'The Allied and Associated Governments affirm and Germany accepts the responsibility of Germany and her allies for causing all the loss and damage to which the Allied and Associated Governments and their nationals have been subjected as a consequence of the war imposed upon them by the aggression of Germany and her allies.' The German delegation at the Paris Peace Conference regarded Article 231 as a forced confession of its exclusive guilt for the war, and Germans bitterly disputed this allegation. They argued war-guilt was not something that could be determined unilaterally by the Allies. Only by consulting all the archives of the participants could an objective assessment be made about who was most responsible for the outbreak of war.

As the Allies had not yet agreed the exact amount the German government should pay in reparations, a definite financial sum was not outlined in Article 253 of the treaty. Instead, the final figure would be decided by the Allied Reparations Commission, which promised to announce its decision on or before 1 May 1921. An immediate down payment of 5 billion gold marks was to be deposited by the German government between 1919 and 1921, along with deliveries of coal, cattle, ships, and other goods in lieu of the later cash payments. Finally, the Allies declined Germany's request to join the League of Nations.[77]

The Allied terms provoked a wave of anger and revulsion throughout Germany, which stretched right across the political spectrum. Every German hated the Treaty of Versailles. The general feeling was that Germany had been deceived and tricked by the Allies. The German government, headed by Social Democrat Chancellor Philipp Scheidemann, instructed the German delegation to inform the Allies that the terms were unbearable and ruinous for Germany.

On 12 May, the National Assembly met in the great hall of the University of Berlin to discuss the proposed peace terms. Scheidemann said, in a rousing speech: 'I ask you, who can, as an honest man, I will not say as German, but only as an honest, straightforward man, accept such terms? What hand would not wither that binds itself in these fetters? The treaty, in the opinion of the government, cannot be accepted.' The speech was greeted with cheers from all sides.[78]

During the following weeks, the German delegation attempted to secure some modifications to what they regarded as the harsh terms of the treaty. Within the German government the SPD and DDP members were opposed to signing the treaty. Zentrum, however, began to move away from this uncompromising stance. One of its most influential members, Matthias Erzberger, argued convincingly that

rejection would mean economic ruin and a probable Allied invasion of Germany.

The Allies were not in the least bit sympathetic to the German outcry over the treaty terms. On 16 June, they conceded only one minor concession by offering a referendum in Upper Silesia, but they reiterated that Germany had been responsible for the outbreak of the war and refused to budge on the other terms embodied in the draft treaty. On 18 June, the German delegation advised the German government to reject the treaty. The nation's military leaders were then consulted. Field Marshal Paul von Hindenburg said he preferred honourable defeat to shame, but he thought if the Allies decided to invade to impose the treaty, 'We can scarcely count on being able to withstand a serious offensive on the part of the enemy.'[79]

On 19 June, Scheidemann's government suggested that if the Allies would drop the war-guilt clause, forget about trying war criminals, and modify the economic clauses, then the treaty would be signed. On the next day, however, Scheidemann decided he could not sign the treaty and promptly resigned. President Ebert wanted to do likewise, but his Social Democrat colleagues convinced him his resignation would produce chaos, and most probably lead to an Allied invasion.

On 21 June, the Social Democrat Minister of Labour, Gustav Bauer, who had previously spoken out against signing the treaty, was appointed as the new Chancellor. On the next day, he formed a new coalition government based only on the SPD and Zentrum, because the DDP refused to agree to signing the Treaty of Versailles. The three DDP members of the cabinet all resigned. Bernhard Dernberg was replaced by Matthias Erzberger, as Vice Chancellor and Minister of Finance; Hugo Preuss, the Minister of the Interior who had drafted the new Weimar constitution, was replaced by Eduard David of the SPD, and Georg Gotheim, the Minister of the Treasury, was replaced by Wilhelm Mayer of Zentrum. Count Ulrich Graf von Brockdorff-Rantzau, the Foreign Minister, also resigned and was replaced by the Social Democrat Hermann Müller.[80]

Bauer informed the National Assembly that the government had no choice but to accept what he called the 'peace of injustice'. A resolution declaring Germany's willingness to sign, but rejecting Articles 227 and 231, was put to a vote of the members of the National Assembly and was passed by 237 to 138 votes, with the former Chancellor, Philipp Scheidemann, refusing to attend. Voting against acceptance of the treaty were the Conservative DNVP, the DDP and the DVP. In

Gustav Bauer, Social Democratic Chancellor of Germany from June 1919 to March 1920.

overleaf *The Signing of Peace in the Hall of Mirrors, Versailles, 28 June 1919,* by the Irish artist William Orpen.

desperation, President Ebert, who still did not want to sign, asked General Groener for his advice regarding the possibility of armed resistance. Groener advised him the military could not resist an Allied invasion, and the treaty had to be signed. Hindenburg handed in his resignation rather than be a party to the signing of the treaty.

On 28 June 1919, the Treaty of Versailles was signed, exactly five years after the assassination of the Archduke Franz Ferdinand, the spark that led to the outbreak of the First World War. It was signed in the Hall of Mirrors of the Palace of Versailles where 48 years before the German Empire had been proclaimed. The treaty was ratified by a vote in the German National Assembly by 209 to 116 on 9 July. The politicians who signed the treaty on behalf of Germany were the Social Democrat Hermann Müller, and Johannes Bell of Zentrum.[81]

The Treaty of Versailles was a staggering blow to the Weimar Republic. Instead of using their power to assist the embryonic democracy in Germany, the Allies treated its leaders as no different from Kaiser Wilhelm. Hatred towards those who had signed the treaty spread widely in the population, especially on the nationalist Right. The myth of the 'stab in the back' now made rapid headway. The leaders of German democracy were depicted by the Right as cowards and traitors under the umbrella term the 'November Criminals' and were blamed by the public for all the misfortunes that followed.

There was a huge contrast between the political and economic distress of the Weimar years and the vibrant culture of the period. Yet what is now routinely called 'Weimar culture' is by no means the posthumous glorification of a world destroyed. Many aspects of Weimar culture really were years ahead of their time. That culture not only encompassed film, literature, modern art, architecture, design, literature, drama, poetry, and cabaret, but also displayed path-breaking attitudes towards sexuality.

One of the Weimar pioneers in this area was undoubtedly the German Jewish sexologist Dr Magnus Hirschfeld, who campaigned for the decriminalisation of abortion, prostitution, and same-sex activity, for the greater availability of contraception, treatment for venereal disease, and for gay, transgender and women's rights. He was author of a three-volume definitive study called *Sexual Pathology: A Textbook for Physicians and Students* (*Sexualpathologie: Ein Lehrbuch für Ärzte and Studierende*). Hirschfeld promoted the right of the individual to control his or her own body. He offered medical and psychological counselling to thousands of individuals each year, including gay people, cross-dressers, and intersex individuals. Hirschfield's radical ideas changed the way Germans thought about sexuality, and he played a significant role in making Germany during the Weimar years a more modern, open, and humane society. Hirschfeld welcomed democracy in Germany, commenting at the beginning of 1919: 'The great revolution of the last weeks can be greeted only with joy. This new time brings in freedom to speak and to write and we assume with certainty the emancipation of those previously oppressed.'[82]

On 6 July, Hirschfeld opened the Institute of Sexual Science (*Institut für Sexualwissenschaft*), a non-profit foundation, based in a villa in Tiergarten Park, Berlin. The Institute became a focal point of scientific and research interest in sexuality. It also maintained teaching and medical facilities, archives, a library, and a museum. According to a published report, the Institute attracted 3,500 visitors in its first year, including 1,500 medical doctors and students. Hirschfeld and his medical colleagues pioneered some of the first hormone treatments and the first sex-reassignment surgery in the world.[83]

Hirschfeld's Institute also sponsored a number of feature-length films, beginning with the silent film *Different from the Others* (*Anders als die Andern*), released on 28 May 1919. It was directed by Richard Oswald, and starred Conrad Veidt and Fritz Schulz, with a screenplay co-written by Oswald and Hirschfeld. It was the first film to explore the social and legal difficulties facing gay people. The film is about the love between a male teacher and gifted violinist (Paul Körner) and his male admirer (Kurt Severs), who wants to become his student. The budding romance between Paul and Kurt is thwarted by a male prostitute who blackmails the musician. The blackmailer goes to prison, but Kurt is also found guilty, under Paragraph 175 of the German Criminal Code, the law that made same-sex activity a criminal offence. Kurt's exposure as a gay person destroys his career, and the film ends with his tragic suicide. Hirschfeld appears in the film as a sympathetic psychiatrist who explains same-sex activity and highlights the injustice of the law. Following the film, Veidt became a gay icon, even though the actor was himself straight. The film was years ahead of its time. The first British film to deal with gay love was *Victim*, released in 1961, which also featured a similar blackmail plot.

Different From the Others provoked protests from Catholic and Protestant church groups. Members of the Free Corps often disrupted lectures by Hirschfeld. In Cologne and Nuremberg he needed police protection at his public lectures. In October 1920, a law was introduced by the German government which gave local authorities powers to ban films that were deemed 'dangerous to youth'. A panel of censors suggested *Different from the Others* presented a one-sided view of Paragraph 175. Public screenings were then banned, but private screenings and for use by medical professionals and students for educational purposes were allowed.[84]

Hirschfeld also undertook research on cross-dressing by completing a detailed study called *The Transvestites: The Erotic Drive to Cross-Dress*, which challenged the prevailing psychiatric orthodoxy which viewed cross-dressing as leading to same-sex attraction. By looking at 16 case studies of cross-dressers, Hirschfeld concluded that transvestism was something distinct from sexual orientation and he showed that cross-dressers were often straight.[85]

Hirschfeld pioneered sex reassignment therapies, including hormone replacement and sex reassignment surgery. He commissioned the first male-to-female sex reassignment surgeries undertaken in two stages, beginning in 1920 at the institute in Berlin, and completed in Dresden in 1921. In addition, Hirschfeld offered a range of counselling services for gay men and women. These therapies included Hirschfeld's Adaptation Therapy, which he explained as follows: 'In the first place we reassure the gay personality, whether male or female, we explain that they have an innocent, inborn orientation, which is not a misfortune.'[86] Hirschfeld felt the best hedge against feelings of depression for gay people was to be involved in a gay social network. Hirschfeld also organised several campaigns for the repeal of Article 175 of the Criminal Code.

The new Bauer government was keen to make an immediate impact in the field of economic policy. On 7 July, Matthias Erzberger, the German Finance Minister, introduced important new taxation reforms

The pioneering sexologist Magnus Hirschfeld, outspoken challenger of prevailing sexual orthodoxies.

in the National Assembly, which became known as the Erzberger Financial Reforms. The first was to give the federal government the supreme authority to tax and spend, thereby ending the dependence of central government on the constituent states, which had bedevilled the former German Empire. This led to the creation of a national Inland Revenue system. The second was to lower the tax burden on low- and moderate-income households and make richer citizens pay more. Measures included the first German inheritance tax and a one-off 'soak the rich' wealth tax. In March 1921, a federal income tax was introduced, with a graduated scale which meant the more a person earned the more they paid. Erzberger also reformed the previously independent state railway companies, amalgamating them into the state-owned German Reich Railway (*Deutsche Reichsbahn*), which became very profitable and provided much needed additional revenue to central government. The proportion of the total tax revenue taken by central government increased from 40.3 per cent in 1913 to 49.6 in 1932, while in the same period, tax collected by the states decreased from 37.3 to 28.3 per cent.[87]

But the biggest political event during the summer of 1919 was the ratification of the new democratic Weimar Constitution, which was adopted by the National Assembly on 31 July by a margin of 262 to 75 votes. It was signed by President Friedrich Ebert on 11 August and came into force on the same day. The Weimar Constitution (*Weimarer Verfassung*) was a compromise worked out between the various political factions represented in the National Assembly. It retained the term *Reich*, with all its imperial associations, to denote the new Republic. The chief author of the Constitution, the liberal Professor Hugo Preuss, decided to retain those features of the Bismarckian Constitution that were likely to function under a democratic system and to incorporate some aspects of the 1848 liberal Frankfurt Constitution which had never been implemented. The federal structure was retained, which was welcomed in the southern German states, and by the dominant state of Prussia, which covered 75 per cent of German territory, even though the power and autonomy of the states was weakened. Between 1919 and 1932, Prussia became a stronghold of the Social Democrats who ruled it in coalitions with the Centre Party (Zentrum) and the German Democratic Party (DDP).

The Weimar Constitution was divided into two main parts. The first, which had 77 articles, laid out the various components of the Reich government. Section 1 (Articles 1–19) defined the German Reich as a Republic whose power derived from the people. The territory of the Reich was defined as the regions covered by the German federal *Länder*.[88] The legislative authority vested in the Reich was extensive, giving the federal government authority over foreign policy, defence, colonial affairs, citizenship, child-welfare, health, freedom of movement, immigration, public order, emigration, banking, taxation, customs, trade, social insurance, currency, postal, telegraph, telephone, railways, and water services. Except for all these, the *Länder*, elected by a secret ballot, could govern their territories as they saw fit. In the event of a conflict, Reich law superseded regional state law, but the adjudication of conflicts would be determined by an independent Supreme Court (*Reichsgericht*).

Section 2 (Articles 20–40) described the functions of the national parliament in Berlin, which retained the title of Reichstag. The Reich Chancellor was given a dominant position over the cabinet, and was required, along with the Reich cabinet, to resign in the event of a defeat in the Reichstag, after a vote of no confidence. In the event of a tie, the President had the deciding vote. The Reichstag also had the power to impeach the Reich President, the Reich Cabinet, or individual Ministers, before the Supreme Judicial Court (*Staatsgerichtshof*).

All Germans – male and female – over the age of 20 were given the right to vote in all elections, which were to be held every four years unless a government lost a vote of no confidence in the Reichstag, in which case an election would be held within 60 days. In place of the former single member constituencies, the country was divided into 35 electoral districts. The voting system was based on an exact proportional representation of the votes cast for each party or independent candidate in elections: one seat was allocated in the Reichstag for every 60,000 votes. This allowed smaller parties to gain representation in parliament, with as little as 1 per cent of the votes. Only candidates on pre-prepared lists drawn up by the leaders of the political parties were allocated seats, which tended to mean only those known to be loyal to the party line made it on to the party list.[89] Any constitutional amendments required a two-thirds majority in the Reichstag.

Section 3 (Articles 41–59) described the duties of the Reich President, who was head of state, and elected by the people for a term of seven years with no restriction on the number of terms served. The powers given to the Reich President were extensive and effectively compromised the power of the Chancellor and the Reichstag. Hugo Preuss wanted to create a strong President as a counterweight to the power of parliament, and he expected the President to perform duties in a non-partisan manner. But in certain circumstances the Constitution afforded the President unlimited power. The President appointed the Chancellor and approved all cabinet posts. He was also made the commander of the armed forces, with the exclusive power to make treaties and alliances. If a local state failed to fulfil its obligations under the Constitution or Reich law, the President could use armed force to compel it to do so. The President was also given extensive subsidiary powers under the notorious Article 48 to appoint and dismiss elected governments, and to use armed force and suspend civil rights during a time defined by the President as a 'national emergency'. This turned out to be a dangerous anti-democratic weapon which allowed the President, in principle, to override the Reichstag, the Reichsrat and the federal states.

It is often assumed President Paul von Hindenburg, who was elected by voters, abused Article 48 most flagrantly between 1925 to 1934, but President Friedrich Ebert, elected by members of the National Assembly, used Article 48 on a staggering 136 separate occasions between 1919 and 1925. The substantial difference was that Ebert did not intend to destroy the Republic when he used this measure, whereas Hindenburg from 1930 onwards used Article 48 to pass legislation in defiance of the will of parliament. In this sense, Article 48 offered little protection against a President who was hostile to the Constitution. It was not the intention of the architects of the Weimar Constitution to smooth the path towards a personal dictatorship, but the dangers of Article 48 offered that possibility from the very beginning.[90]

Section 4 (Articles 60–67) covered the powers of the Reichsrat, which was the upper parliamentary chamber, the successor to the Bundesrat

The Weimar Constitution was signed into law by President Friedrich Ebert on 11 August 1919.

of the German Empire from 1867 to 1918. This was a body in which representatives of the federal *Länder* could participate in the passage of legislation. Members of the Reichsrat represented the individual state governments and parliaments. The previous domination of Prussia was limited to 40 per cent of total votes in this assembly, with the remainder shared between the other states. Government Ministers and individual Reichstag members proposing laws had first to submit them to the Reichsrat which could voice objections and suggest amendments. If a dispute between the Reichstag and Reichsrat could not be resolved, the President could submit the proposed law to a referendum. Laws vetoed by the Reichsrat very rarely became law and the Reichstag retained the power to overrule a vote in the Reichsrat by a majority vote in the Reichstag.

Section 5 (Articles 68–77) outlined the process by which government legislation would become law, and emphasised that supreme legislative power resided in the Reichstag. Laws could be proposed by the federal government or by any individual Reichstag member and were passed by a majority vote in the Reichstag. The Reich President had the power to decree that any proposed law could be presented to voters in a referendum before it became law. Section 6 (Articles 78–101) covered the details of Reich administration and Section 7 (Articles 102–108) outlined the justice system.

Part 2 of the Weimar Constitution covered the basic rights and obligations of the German people. Section 1 (Articles 109–118) set out the rights of Germans citizens, based on the principle of equality. Any privileges based on birth or title were abolished, and the further creation of aristocratic titles was discontinued. The 'national identity' of ethnic minorities was now protected by law. Individuals were given the right not to be arrested without cause or detained without appearing before a court. Citizens were also given the right to privacy of mail, telegraph, and telephone. In return, every citizen had a moral duty to uphold the welfare of the community.

Section 2 (Articles 119–134) dealt with community life and declared the right to free assembly and to form clubs and societies. All citizens were eligible for public office without discrimination, including on grounds of gender. All citizens and civil servants enjoyed freedom of political opinion. Section 3 (Articles 135–141) granted religious rights and freedom of religious belief and conscience. It further promised no state religion or church would be established. Section 4 (Articles 142–150) covered the operation of educational institutions in the Reich.

Both public and private education was regulated by the government. Primary school was compulsory and education was provided free of charge up to the age of 18.

Section 5 (Articles 151–165) covered the economy. It gave the right to own private property and protected inheritance rights, and further promised the expropriation of property by the state must be accompanied by appropriate compensation. The Reich also promised to bring into public ownership suitable private enterprises and to protect labour and the right of trade unions to improve working conditions. The rights of the self-employed were similarly protected. A watered-down version of the workers' council movement was incorporated into Article 165, which created the National Economic Council, in which all important trade and professional groups were to be represented. This would review drafts of government social and economic legislation. In practice, however, the Council became a powerless talking-shop.

The final 16 Articles (166–181) gave details of the orderly implementation of the new constitution. All public servants and members of the armed forces were required to take an oath to uphold the Constitution. The previous constitution, dated 15 April 1871, was suspended, but Reich laws that did not contradict the new constitution remained in force.[91]

The Weimar Constitution was intended to be a charter for an advanced democracy. It claimed to be the most egalitarian and libertarian in the world. The centrepiece of the power structure was the dual power system whereby the Reich President and the Reichstag were elected by direct popular vote. This certainly transformed Germany into a state in which central government was supreme, and where the powers of the federal states were controlled and their autonomy limited, which represented a break from the pre-war *Kaiserreich*. The federal *Länder* were now expected to enforce national laws. The result was the extension of the central government's control over local officials.

The Weimar Constitution of 1919 was, therefore, not a federation of states (*Staatenbund*), as the Holy Roman Empire had been, or a federal state (*Bundesstaat*) as the Wilhelmine Empire had been, but a central unitary state deriving power from the people (*Volksstaat*). Only subsequent legislation and political action would determine the success or failure of the Constitution. It is all too easy in hindsight to point to obvious weaknesses in the Weimar Constitution, but it is impossible to know what other sort of constitution would have prevented the destruction of democracy.

The proportional representation electoral system has been viewed as one of the key weaknesses of the Weimar Constitution. The Social Democrats were the biggest advocates of this system, as they felt the pre-1914 first-past-the-post system had left them grossly underrepresented in the Reichstag; but proportional representation encouraged weak coalition governments and allowed far too many political parties a voice in the Reichstag.

A further interesting feature of the Weimar Constitution was the provision for referenda to be held. A referendum could be called by the President and the Reichsrat, if either were opposed to a piece of legislation passed by the Reichstag. It was also possible for the Reichstag to call a referendum to decide if the President should remain in office. The public was allowed the right to submit a petition either as an ordinary bill or as an amendment to the Constitution and if the number of signatures exceeded 10 per cent of registered voters, a referendum of the whole electorate would be conducted.

One issue the Weimar Constitution avoided was the creation of a national symbol, flag and colours for the new Republic. The young democracy decided to retain the German eagle, the traditional German state symbol, but it modernised its design by removing its imperial symbols. It was also proposed by Social Democrats and liberals that the old black, white, and red flag of the German Empire should be replaced by the black, red, and gold flag of the 1848 failed democratic revolution. It was thought this change would really symbolise the birth of a new democratic republic. The nationalist Right saw the attempt to drop the old imperial flag as sacrilege and protested the change. In two votes in the Reichstag, the proposal by the Right to retain the old black, white, and red flag was defeated, but the vote to introduce the black, red, and gold flag achieved a healthy majority. The flag controversy spilled into the street politics of Weimar, with political and paramilitary groups marching under their own flags, and many still flew the old imperial flag, which was also retained on ships of the merchant marine.

Many of the most fervent supporters of the Weimar Republic suggested 11 August, the day the Constitution became law, should become an annual national holiday. It was commemorated each year as Constitution Day, but a political consensus was never achieved to pass a vote in the Reichstag to make it a public holiday. The first Constitution Day took place on 11 August 1921, with a lavish ceremony in Berlin's Opera House. From 1922 onwards, the ceremony and other festivities centred on the Reichstag building in Berlin, with classical music, poetry readings and children's parades. It has been estimated that this event never attracted more than 100,000 spectators, and even this figure was bolstered by schoolchildren being compelled to attend by their teachers. In general, Constitution Day was ignored by the German public.[92]

Between 21 and 25 August 1919, Adolf Hitler and 25 of his colleagues in Captain Karl Mayr's Education and Propaganda Department delivered lectures on a five-day anti-Bolshevik and nationalist indoctrination course for Reichswehr soldiers in Lechfeld, about 30 miles west of Munich. Hitler gave lectures on the following subjects: Peace Conditions and Reconstruction, Emigration, and Social and Economic Terms. In all these talks antisemitism was a principal component, which grew out of Hitler's personal search for reasons why Germany had lost the war. Hitler also began to realise the effect his exceptional speaking ability could have on an audience. 'I began with enthusiasm and passion,' he wrote in *Mein Kampf*, 'I suddenly had the opportunity to talk to a large audience and what I had always instinctively assumed without knowing: I could "speak well".' It was less what he said than how he said it that set Hitler apart as a public speaker.[93]

On the evening of 12 September, Hitler visited a small beer hall restaurant called the Sterneckerbräu in Munich's old town. Karl Mayr had sent him there to observe a meeting of the German Workers' Party (*Deutsche Arbeiterpartei*, DAP). Mayr knew about the DAP already as he had been invited to attend the meeting and had sent Hitler in his place. It seems Mayr was already thinking of this organisation as one that could be moulded to suit the Reichswehr's propaganda needs.

The DAP was founded on 5 January 1919 in the Fürstenfelder Hof, by Anton Drexler, a railway toolmaker, and Karl Harrer, a journalist and member of the Thule Society. During the war, Drexler had joined the short-lived right-wing and antisemitic DVLP and founded a branch of the equally nationalistic Free Workers Committee for a Good Peace League. Drexler's new party was designed to appeal to workers by supporting social reform alongside strong patriotic ideas. The aim was to turn workers against the communist ideas of the Left, and win them over towards nationalism. It was more a loose political club than a political party at the beginning, and its meetings were held in the dimly lit backrooms of beer halls. With few members and meagre finances, the DAP stood little chance of becoming a major political party.[94] In his speech at the first meeting, Drexler described the DAP as a 'socialist organisation, composed of folk comrades engaged in mental and physical work' and promised it would be 'guided by German leaders who put aside personal goals and allow national needs to be the highest concern of the party programme.' The DAP was fighting against, he continued, interest, inflation and 'the drones in the state, most of whom are Jews' who 'live the good life and reap what they have not sown.' Above all, the DAP 'opposes any threat to the unity of the state.'[95]

The meeting Hitler attended on 12 September 1919 was held in a back room of the Leiberzimmer beer hall and was attended by 41 people. The guest speaker was none other than Gottfried Feder, already a DAP member, who spoke on the subject 'How and By What Means Can Capitalism Be Eliminated?' Hitler had, of course, encountered Feder before on his propaganda course at Munich University in June 1919. At the end of Feder's speech, Adalbert Baumann, a teacher at a local school and the chair of the Citizens Association (*Bürgervereinigung*), a small political club, put forward the view that Bavaria should break away from the Reich. On hearing this, Hitler, according to his own account, stood up and launched a blistering attack against the idea of Bavarian separatism, arguing that only a united Germany could meet the political and economic challenges facing it. Anton Drexler later recalled: 'Hitler made a rousing speech in favour of a greater Germany that was received by me and all who heard him with great enthusiasm.' He told one of his colleagues in the leadership of the DAP: 'He has a mouth on him, he'll come in useful.' Once again, it was Hitler's brilliant speaking that had impressed his listeners.[96] Drexler, who was always on the lookout for new members, then walked up to Hitler and gave him a copy of his autobiographical pamphlet called: 'My Political Awakening', and advised him to read it, as it contained the key ideas of the DAP. He also invited Hitler to come to the next meeting and join the party and he wrote down Hitler's name and address before he left.

Hitler was not impressed by what he saw at the meeting. It seemed little different from the many similar nationalist groups that were springing up in Munich which he had already observed. Hitler was, however, much more attracted by Drexler's pamphlet which, unable to sleep, he read in his bunk in his army barracks, just before dawn on the following morning. It told the story of how the humble Drexler had decided to create a new political party, combining nationalism with anti-capitalist and socialist ideas, with the aim of weakening the appeal of Marxism among the working classes. Hitler identified with Drexler's life as it mirrored his own experiences, including rejection from jobs, anxiety and depression, and a growing conviction of the role of the Jews as the corruptors of the world.

Hitler claimed in *Mein Kampf* that he was already thinking of creating a political party along similar lines, even before he ever attended the meeting of the DAP. Hence, when a postcard arrived a few days later from Drexler inviting him to join the committee of the DAP, he accepted, after mulling it over for a few days. Hitler claimed joining the DAP was the 'most decisive resolution' of his life.[97] He thought this small, poorly organised, and little-known party could be moulded to suit his own purposes. According to Hitler, he was the seventh member of the party, but in fact he was the seventh member of the committee, and was soon made responsible for recruitment and propaganda. Hitler's membership card listed him as number 555, but Drexler admitted later that party membership numbers started at 501 to make the party membership look bigger than it really was. At best, Hitler was the 55th member of the DAP.[98]

Hitler's subjective account of his motivation for joining the DAP must be treated with great caution. His claim about wrestling with nagging doubts before joining the party hardly seems credible. Mayr, his army boss, whose account is far more reliable, claimed that he had 'ordered' Hitler to join the party to use it as a propaganda vehicle for the army. It is clear Hitler was given army funds to book local beer halls for speaking engagements, to place advertisements in local newspapers, to rent a local office above the Sterneckerbräu beer hall, to buy a typewriter, install a telephone, print up party membership cards, and to design party posters. In addition, from September 1919 to April 1920, Hitler also continued to draw his army salary. This suggests the Army had decided to 'plant' Hitler in the DAP to bolster its popularity.

Hitler now had a field of action for his enthusiastic love of Germany, his propaganda skills, his brilliant speaking and organisational abilities. Within weeks, Hitler had transformed the DAP from a lounge-bar ranting club for misfits into a noisy local nationalist party. On 16 October, he organised the first public meeting of the DAP, which was attended by 111 people. Hitler took the stage as the second speaker, rousing the audience by reciting his various hatreds: the Jews, the November Criminals, and the Treaty of Versailles. Hitler's swift take-over of the DAP was not welcomed by the DAP Chairman Karl Harrer, who would have preferred the party to remain a small secret group, and called Hitler a 'megalomaniac'.[99] In December 1919, Hitler persuaded the seven-man DAP committee to strip Harrer of all his powers, and he resigned from his post on 5 January 1921 to be replaced by Anton Drexler.

Hitler's speeches at subsequent public meetings of the DAP helped raise the profile of the party and increase its membership, thereby cementing his position as the rising star of the party. He spent hours practising his gestures and facial expressions while reading his speech aloud. Simplicity and repetition were central to his speeches. He evoked melancholic images of the suffering and despair inflicted by the Versailles Treaty, and his passion touched a nerve in the audience. It was Hitler's public speaking in the beer halls of Munich that rescued him from the graveyard of under-achievers. In his speeches, Hitler cast himself in the role of an alienated, bitter, and resentful outsider in the 'alien' Weimar Republic. He inspired the audience to share his anger, his bitterness and his fears, and promised to rescue Germany from the November Criminals who had 'betrayed the Fatherland'. He built up this idea of a better tomorrow on the feelings of bitterness arising from Germany's defeat in the war. Most of his early rabble-rousing beer-hall speeches were full of antisemitic hatred. For example, in a speech given on 13 November 1919, before an audience of 130 people in the Eberlbräu beer hall, Hitler blamed the Jews in the German government for the signing of the Versailles Treaty, especially Matthias Erzberger, and he promised: 'We will carry on the struggle against the Jews until the last Jew is removed from Germany'.[100]

It was also during the autumn of 1919 that Hitler's growing obsession with antisemitism becomes much clearer. In September, Captain Karl Mayr received a letter from Adolf Gemlisch, in Ulm, who had attended one of Hitler's propaganda courses in the summer. Gemlisch asked Mayr: 'What is the attitude of the governing Social Democrats to Jewry?' Mayr asked Hitler to pen a reply to the letter. On 16 September, Hitler replied to Gemlisch, offering his first written recorded opinion on the so-called Jewish Question. He began by describing antisemitism as a 'political movement', which could be defined not by emotional impulses, but only by a recognition of facts. 'The Jews were a race', wrote Hitler, not a 'religious association', who maintained their racial unity and racial purity by owning their primary allegiance to their own 'race', and not to the country in which they lived. To Hitler, Jews were like a 'racial tuberculosis', a critical barrier to national unity. They sought to manipulate public opinion towards supporting cosmopolitan and international ideologies, through their control of the press. According to Hitler, Jews were happy to promote racial inter-marriage, but they themselves only married people of their own 'race'. For all these reasons, Jews had to be 'removed' from society, not in 'violent pogroms', but through a programme of antisemitic legislation and emigration. He further claimed that only a government of 'national vitality' could achieve this goal. This letter shows that Hitler at this stage favoured legislation and emigration as the 'Final Solution', not genocide.[101]

Political violence, a key feature of German politics during 1919, continued to shock the public. On 8 October, Hugo Haase, the leader of the USPD, was walking towards the entrance of the Reichstag building in Berlin, with the intention of delivering a speech highlighting a secret alliance between President Ebert and Rüdiger von der Goltz, a Free Corps general, who was active in suppressing communism in the Baltic, when an Austrian born right-wing activist called Johann Voss fired three shots which hit him in the stomach, arm, and thigh. Haase was rushed to a local hospital and underwent several operations, but gangrene soon developed in his wounds, and he died on 7 November. A huge crowd gathered for his funeral at the Friedrichsfelde Central Cemetery (*Zentralfriedhof Friedrichsfelde*). His killer Voss was declared 'insane' and committed to a mental hospital and never faced a trial, even though he was suspected of being a 'government paid assassin'.[102]

Meanwhile, in August 1919, the National Assembly had established a Committee of Enquiry to investigate the question of the circumstances leading to the end of the war, with the aim of refuting the Allied claim of Germany's sole guilt for the war. The investigation concentrated primarily on three narrowly defined questions: (1) What was the origin, execution, and collapse of the German offensive in 1918? (2) Were the failures in the direction of operation in 1918 due to adverse conditions within the army? (3) Did economic, social, or moral conditions at home affect the army and navy?

On 18 November, the two key German military commanders, Field Marshal Paul von Hindenburg and General Erich Ludendorff, both gave evidence before the Committee in the central committee room of the Reichstag building. It was agreed Hindenburg would be cross-examined by Reichstag member Eberhard Gothein of the DDP. Before Hindenburg gave his evidence, Ludendorff read out a statement stating that though they both had the right to refuse to give evidence it was the right of the German people 'to hear the truth'.

Hindenburg then proceeded, despite Gothein's repeated objections, to read out a prepared statement, probably written by Ludendorff, saying:

> Our repeated requests for the maintenance of stern discipline and strict application of the law met with no results. Our operations in consequence failed, as they were bound to, and the collapse became inevitable; the Revolution was merely the last straw. As an English General has very honestly said, 'The German Army was stabbed in the back.' It is plain enough upon whom the blame lies. If any further proof were necessary to show it, it is to be found in the utter amazement of our enemies at their victory.'[103]

After Hindenburg finished giving his evidence, he said he felt tired and could not be sure when it would be convenient for him to attend the committee again. In his own evidence, Ludendorff backed up Hindenburg's assessment of why Germany lost the war, but it was Hindenburg's public endorsement of the right-wing 'stab-in-the-back' theory that caused a public sensation. It was only natural that Hindenburg's view would be taken up by the political parties on the Right, who were happy to blame the Republic for all its current misfortunes.[104]

On 12 December, the leading British economist John Maynard Keynes launched a blistering attack on the Treaty of Versailles in his best-selling book *The Economic Consequences of The Peace*. Keynes, who became the most influential economist of the twentieth century, had attended the Paris Peace Conference, as a senior delegate of the British Treasury, but he was so appalled by the injustice the Germans had suffered in the Treaty of Versailles that he had resigned in despair, on 7 June 1919. His book was full of flashing insights and indignation, which laid out clearly the economic crisis facing Europe by explaining what the Treaty had failed to do, and what the consequences would be. Keynes pulled no punches and upset many people. He famously described the Versailles Treaty as a 'Carthaginian Peace' – a peace that has the intention of crushing the defeated enemy.[105]

Keynes further argued that the Allies, blinded by self-interest, were determined to punish rather than to rehabilitate Germany. The Versailles Treaty offered nothing to make Germany a 'good neighbour', and had conceded far too much to the vengeful spirit of the French government, which wanted to keep Germany weak. It imposed impossible terms on Germany which would soon plunge Europe into economic chaos. The demand for reparations was way beyond what Germany could afford to pay. Keynes also warned the territorial provisions of Versailles would lead to future foreign policy disputes. He blamed the 'idealist' US President, Woodrow Wilson, whom he described as a 'blind and deaf Don Quixote', for being unable to produce a peace settlement based on his Fourteen Points, which it had been promised during the Armistice negotiations would give Germany a 'just peace' with no 'punitive damages'.

Keynes predicted the economic demands on Germany would cause high inflation and economic stagnation, which would spread throughout Europe. The Treaty of Versailles had to be modified, not just for the sake of Germany, but for the benefit of the world economy. It would damage the conditions for economic recovery and sow the seeds for another world war. In his persuasively argued and deeply influential book, Keynes laid the foundation for the failure of the American Senate to ratify the Treaty of Versailles, and he also helped to create a climate of public opinion in which Germany's demands for a revision of the terms of the treaty met with a sympathetic response, especially in Britain. Here was sowed the seeds of the policy of appeasement.[106]

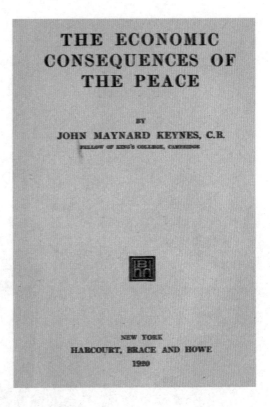

THE ECONOMIC
CONSEQUENCES OF
THE PEACE

BY
JOHN MAYNARD KEYNES, C.B.
FELLOW OF KING'S COLLEGE, CAMBRIDGE

NEW YORK
HARCOURT, BRACE AND HOWE
1920

In *The Economic Consequences of the Peace* (1919), the British economist John Maynard Keynes gave eloquent voice to what he perceived as the injustice done to Germany in the Treaty of Versailles.

1920

·

FAILED REVOLT FROM THE RIGHT

·

The last ceremonial act associated with the Treaty of Versailles took place in Paris on 10 January 1920, in the Clock Room at the Quai d'Orsay, the home of the French Ministry of Foreign Affairs, when at precisely 4.15 p.m. the Peace Treaty was finally ratified. The ceremony was chaired by Georges Clemenceau, the French Prime Minister, who signed on behalf of the French government, followed by the two German delegates, Ernst von Simson, and Baron Kurt von Lersner, then by David Lloyd George, the British Prime Minister, Francesco Nitti, the Italian Prime Minister, Keishiro Matsui, for Japan, and finally by representatives of the various other Allied countries.

At the end, Clemenceau said: 'The Protocol and ratification of the treaty concluded between the Powers of the Entente and Germany are signed. From this moment, the treaty comes into force, and it will be executed in all its clauses.' He then announced the repatriation of German prisoners of war would now take place.[1]

The signing immediately brought to the fore a new area of disagreement between the Allies and the German government concerning the Allied demand for the extradition of German 'war criminals'. The German government announced it would begin legal action against individuals highlighted by the Allies, but stressed these trials would be conducted by the Supreme Court in Leipzig, with German judges presiding.[2]

The Allies wanted to put Kaiser Wilhelm II on trial, who was still living in exile in the Netherlands. On 16 January, the Allies served a formal summons on the Netherlands ambassador demanding the extradition of the Kaiser, who was viewed as the chief culprit for starting the war. It was an unprecedented diplomatic move. Never had a head of state been tried for starting a war before. A week later, the country's monarch, Queen Wilhelmina, and her government announced it would not allow his extradition. This meant Wilhelm II never faced trial, even though the Allies could have tried him in absentia.[3]

Undeterred, on 3 February, the Allies submitted a list of 895 war criminals they wanted to face justice, but they accepted the German government should assume responsibility for the legal proceedings against them. An Inter-Allied Commission was set up to collect evidence regarding the perpetrators of war crimes, and this material was forwarded to the German legal authorities. Hermann Müller, the German Foreign Minister, gave an assurance that everything would be done to ensure impartial trials.

Yet German legal proceedings against the war criminals turned into something of a farce. In May 1920, the Allies handed the Germans a reduced list of just 45 accused. Even all of these could not be traced. Trials were held between 23 May and 16 July 1921, but only 12 individuals were ever brought to trial, and the judges passed lenient sentences on all of them. A typical case was that of Sergeant Karl Heynen, charged with using severe corporal punishment on 200 British and 40 Russian prisoners of war, in a forced labour camp in Herne, Westphalia. For this, Heynen was given a ten-month prison sentence. The Leipzig correspondent of *The Times* of London called the trial 'a scandalous failure of justice'.[4]

Meanwhile, those who supported the peace settlement in Germany were constantly vilified by the nationalist Right. No politician suffered more in this regard than Matthias Erzberger of Zentrum, who was Minister of Finance. In response to frequent right-wing criticism, Erzberger could be blunt and sharp-tongued, which increased the number of his political enemies. His most quarrelsome opponent was the pro-monarchist Karl Helfferich, a prominent member of the conservative DNVP, who strongly opposed the Treaty of Versailles and had been Vice-Chancellor from May 1916 to October 1917. Erzberger blamed Helfferich for the financial difficulties which led to the collapse of the German Empire, describing him as the worst of all the wartime finance ministers.

In response, Helfferich published, in July 1919, a series of articles in the conservative newspaper *Kreuzzeitung* (*Cross Newspaper*), under the headline: 'Get Rid of Erzberger!' (*Fort mit Erzberger!*). These were gathered together and published in pamphlet form. In them, Helfferich charged Erzberger with 'intentional deceits, not twice or three times, but ten and twenty times', further claiming he dishonestly 'mixed political activities with personal commercial interests', and was prepared to sign the 'disgraceful, servile' Treaty of Versailles, concluding that if he was not stopped, Erzberger 'will lead the German nation to total destruction'.[5]

Erzberger, not surprisingly, decided to sue Helfferich for defamation and insult, seeking substantial damages. The case was held at the Berlin Regional Court (*Landgericht-Berlin*), from 19 January to 12 March 1920. As his lawyer, Helfferich appointed Dr Max Alsberg, one of Berlin's best, who conducted Helfferich's defence with consummate skill. His knowledge of detail and cutting rhetoric grabbed newspaper headlines, and often drew loud cheers from the public gallery.

The public excitement aroused by the libel trial found near-tragic expression, however, in the attempted assassination of Erzberger on 26 January 1920, as he was entering the court building. His would-be assassin was a 20-year-old student and former naval officer Cadet, Oltwig von Hirschfeld, who fired two shots, one wounding Erzberger in the shoulder, but not seriously. A second shot aimed at his stomach was miraculously deflected by the chain of his pocket watch.[6] Hirschfeld received many telegrams and letters congratulating him for trying to kill Erzberger. He was put on trial on 22 February 1920, but the jury amazingly acquitted him of charges of manslaughter and attempted murder, despite the evidence, and found him guilty of the much less serious charge of 'inflicting bodily harm', for which he received a sentence of just 18 months in prison.[7] The sentence reflected the fact that German judges of the period were not impartial, but predominantly authoritarian, nationalist, and opposed to democracy. Most of them sympathised with radical right-wing counterrevolutionaries, who were let off with light sentences even for crimes of violence and murder. In contrast, radical left-wingers received lengthy prison sentences and were subjected to brutal treatment.[8]

Erzberger had been subjected to forensic cross-examination during the trial, and he often struggled to recount events in which he had participated several years before. When Erzberger defended his own actions, for example, by declaring that he was proud to be the author of the famous 1917 Peace Resolution in the Reichstag, or saying that he supported the Weimar Republic, he received a chorus of jeers from the public gallery. He was also not assisted, as the trial progressed, by the illegal publication of his tax records by the newspaper *Hamburger Nachrichten* (*Hamburg News*), which accused him of false accounting. He called for an investigation into his tax affairs, which subsequently exonerated him, but that verdict came months after his libel action was long over.

On 12 March, the judge issued a fine of 300 marks and the entire court costs against Helfferich for 'technical libel', but he also ruled that all the financial accusations brought against Erzberger were essentially true, namely, that he had used his public office to serve his private financial ends. The case was generally regarded as a victory for Helfferich and a humiliating defeat for Erzberger, who immediately resigned his post as the Reich Minister of Finance and gave up his seat in the Reichstag.[9]

The Republic was undoubtedly shaken to its roots by the fall of Erzberger, but worse was soon to follow. For weeks, powerful military elements had been plotting to overthrow the Weimar Republic. The attempted coup, which came to be known as the Kapp Putsch, was led by a group of disgruntled members of the officer corps who wanted to set up a military dictatorship, led by General Walther von Lüttwitz, an outspoken critic of the Treaty of Versailles. He felt the government, dominated by the anti-militarist SPD, would be a constant threat to the interests of the Reichswehr. Lüttwitz believed he could lead a coup without any parliamentary or public support. He found support from William Pabst, a veteran cavalry officer, who worked out a plan under which Gustav Noske, the current Defence Minister, would establish a military dictatorship, with the support of the Reichswehr, but Noske rejected the plan, warning any move to rule against the wishes of the people would end in disaster.[10]

Another key figure in the proposed coup was Dr Wolfgang Kapp, the son of a German liberal who had migrated to the USA in 1848. Kapp himself was born in New York City, but became a fanatical Pan German upon his return to Germany, where he carved out a successful career as a Prussian civil servant. He co-founded the wartime right-wing Fatherland Party, with the leading naval figure Alfred von Tirpitz. Kapp was soon chosen as the proposed new head of government if the coup succeeded.

Matthias Erzberger, German Finance
Minister 1919–20.

According to the Allied peace terms, the German Army had to be reduced to 200,000 and naval personnel were not to exceed 15,000 by 10 April 1920. The German government was therefore faced with quickly dismissing up to 60,000 men. Further reductions to an army strength of 100,000 were scheduled to occur in the following months.[11]

Among the units earmarked for immediate disbandment was the naval brigade led by one of the most notorious Free Corps commanders, Captain Hermann Ehrhardt, a unit which had played a key role in the suppression of the Munich Council Republic in the previous year. Ehrhardt went to see Lüttwitz to protest the order to disband his brigade, but Lüttwitz told him not to worry as he intended to stop this. On 29 February, Lüttwitz duly went to see Noske to protest the decision to disband the Ehrhardt brigade, but Noske told him the decision was irreversible. He was clearly suspicious of Lüttwitz's motives, however, and informed General Hans von Seeckt, the head of the Troop Office (*Truppenamt*), the secret Reichswehr agency created to replace the German High Command, that Lüttwitz was planning to defy the order of the German government to institute armed forces cuts. Seeckt immediately went to see Lüttwitz to inform him Allied demands could not be resisted and asked him whether he would uphold the Constitution. The answer Lüttwitz gave was ambiguous.

On 1 March, in a speech at a military review, Lüttwitz said he would not permit the dissolution of the Ehrhardt brigade. The rumours of an impending coup now reached the two leading right-wing political parties, the DNVP, led by Oskar Hergt, and the DVP, led by Gustav Stresemann. These two politicians told Lüttwitz that defying the army reductions required by the Allies was suicidal, and that a coup would have no political or popular support. They decided to stand aloof from

Wolfgang Kapp, nationalist and counter-revolutionary. His eponymous putsch would fail to bring down the Weimar Republic.

the coup and did not see Kapp as a credible German Chancellor, but to ratchet up the political pressure on the Bauer government, the DNVP and DVP introduced a motion in the National Assembly for new elections to take place not later than 1 May, and requested a new law outlining the procedure and date for a presidential election. Both these motions were defeated by votes in the National Assembly.

At 6 p.m. on 10 March, Lüttwitz went to see President Ebert in his office, and made a number of demands: the immediate ending of dismissals of army officers; the creation of a 'cabinet of experts', the removal of Walther Reinhardt, the head of the army command within the Ministry of the Reichswehr, and the return of the Ehrhardt brigade to his command. Ebert told him all these matters were the responsibility not of the political authorities.[12] Noske now realised arrests had to be made to try and head off the coup attempt, and, on 11 March, he dismissed Lüttwitz from his military command, and ordered the arrest of Kapp, Pabst, and several others.

On 12 March, rumours began circulating that Ehrhardt's brigade intended to march on Berlin from its camp in Döberitz to begin the coup. Noske sent emissaries to negotiate with Ehrhardt, who issued more demands, including the reinstatement of Lüttwitz to his former post, and for Noske's own resignation. The Bauer government was given until 7 p.m. to reply. A cabinet meeting was convened on that afternoon at which Eugen Schiffer, the Vice-Chancellor, suggested the cabinet should leave Berlin rather than be taken prisoner by the conspirators. Schiffer offered to stay behind in Berlin, and serve as the government's representative in negotiations with the rebels.

Before departing, Noske called top-ranking military officials to a meeting in his office at the Defence Ministry at 1 a.m. and told them he was considering military action against the rebels, but he wanted to know what the officers thought. Only two of them, Reinhardt and Gilsa, supported him. The chief spokesperson for the rest was Seeckt, who advised that in a pitched street battle the Ehrhardt brigade would win, as they had the support of large sections of the police. German soldiers, Seeckt added, must not be allowed to fire upon each other, which implied that the German government would not be defended by the army in the event of a coup. Reinhardt decided to resign. Seeckt declined either to fight against the Ehrhardt brigade or to take orders from the coup leader. One armed service that did openly support the coup was the Navy. Rear Admiral Adolf von Trotha communicated this decision to Lüttwitz on 13 March 1920.[13]

overleaf The Ehrhardt Marine Brigade on
the streets of Berlin during the Kapp Putsch,
March 1920.

In the light of this lack of army support for the government, President Ebert, Chancellor Bauer, and the rest of the cabinet departed in a convoy of cars to Dresden before moving on to Stuttgart.[14] On the morning of 13 March, the Ehrhardt brigade arrived at the Brandenburg Gate in Berlin, their helmets decorated with the swastika. They occupied government buildings and hoisted the flag of the old Empire. Wolfgang Kapp declared himself the new German Chancellor. In his first proclamation to the nation, Kapp announced that he was establishing a government of 'order, freedom and action,' which promised to suppress strikes, restore the sovereignty of the federal states, protect workers from exploitation by big business and restore the old imperial flag. He ordered army commanders to proceed against all the enemies of the new government.[15]

The Allies at once declared they wanted nothing to do with a German government established by military force, but, in any case, the Kapp government lacked credibility from the very beginning. Key civil servants in the government ministries refused to cooperate with the rebel government. Kapp could not even find a secretary willing to type his proclamations. The Reichsbank would not sanction his requests for money, telling him that his government had no authorisation to sign cheques. Most significantly, the trade unions organised a general strike designed to lock down the entire economy, with Carl Legien, the SPD trade union leader, issuing the following statement 'We are calling on all workers, office employees and civil servants to go on strike immediately. All factories must be brought to a standstill. Victory will be on the side of working people.'[16]

None of the political parties gave any support to Kapp whatsoever, but instead aligned themselves with the Ebert–Bauer government in internal exile, and backed the call for a general strike. Later court trials of the leading conspirators revealed the utter confusion in the Kapp Chancellery during the brief days of the coup. Lord Kilmarnock, a British Embassy official in Berlin, reported to Lord Curzon, the British Foreign Secretary, that the Kapp government had no credibility, and would soon surrender to the legitimate government without conditions and vanish into ignominy.[17]

By the afternoon of 14 March 1920, the largest general strike the world had ever seen brought Germany to a complete standstill. In Berlin, there was no water, gas, telephone, electricity, trains, or trams. The Ebert–Bauer government from its temporary refuge in Dresden issued a proclamation which depicted the Kapp government as being led by a small military clique that had no support at home or abroad.

At 10 a.m. on 16 March, Kapp announced his resignation as self-styled German Chancellor after just four chaotic days in office, realising his position had become untenable. On the next day, he took a taxi to a waiting plane which took him to exile in Sweden. Later on the same day, Lüttwitz resigned, too. The Kapp Putsch had lasted just four chaotic days. The main reason it failed was the impact of the general strike, organised by the trade unions, which made it impossible for the rebel government to function. The Weimar Republic had been saved, not by the Army, but by the workers. The other key factors contributing to the failure of the coup were the loyalty of key civil servants in Berlin, the Reichsbank's refusal to allow the rebel government any money, and the failure of the right-wing parties to support the rebels. After the coup was over, Hans von Seeckt returned to his role as the Chief of the Reichswehr Army Command. His decision not to support the Kapp Putsch militarily did help indirectly to save the Republic; in the circumstances, doing nothing was better than doing something. Seeckt commented later: 'Nobody can carry out a putsch in Germany but me.'[18]

Dr Otto Gessler took over at the Defence Ministry, and set up a committee to investigate the actions of the Army during the Kapp Putsch. When it issued its report, in September 1920, a total of 172 officers were discharged, among them 12 generals. Of the 705 people charged with direct involvement in the Kapp Putsch, only Kapp received a prison sentence and that was only for 18 months. In fact, more officers and soldiers who opposed the Kapp Putsch were purged under the guise of implementing the troop reduction demanded by the Allies. The Reichstag voted an amnesty on 4 August 1920, which allowed supporters of the Kapp Putsch and participants in rebellions in Bavaria and the Ruhr to continue in post. The overall effect of the Kapp Putsch was not the creation of a pro-Republican army, but the strengthening of the nationalist and militaristic forces that opposed it. A major chance to reform the Army had been missed.[19]

On 18 March, the National Assembly met in Stuttgart. Gustav Bauer, the SPD Reich Chancellor, declared that German democracy had won a great victory. He implored the Allies not to assist the enemies of the Republic by making impossible financial demands of the German people. Noske resigned as Defence Minister, mainly because he thought he should have seen the coup coming. The SPD dropped Noske from its Reichstag party list, thus banning him from seeking election to the Reichstag. Even so, he did become the Minister-President of the province of Hanover.

On 27 March, Gustav Bauer and his cabinet resigned. Bauer felt they had been discredited by failing to prevent the Kapp Putsch. The Social Democrats' public standing had plummeted during the rebellion. The trade unions, who had been central to the collapse of the coup, demanded the right to be consulted in the creation of a new, truly socialist government and demanded the punishment of all those who led the coup, the disbandment of paramilitary organisations hostile to the Republic, and the nationalisation of 'appropriate' industries. It was felt by many that the new government needed to include politicians not tainted by having aided the coup. Ebert favoured a workers' government and he even offered Carl Legien, the trade union leader, the opportunity to become Chancellor, but he turned this offer down. The USPD once again refused to join a coalition with the SPD.

In selecting the new cabinet, Ebert turned once again to the members of the outgoing government. The new Chancellor was Hermann Müller, a Social Democrat and the current Foreign Minister, who promised new elections would soon occur. Müller's first cabinet was based on the three centre-left parties in the previous cabinet: the SPD, Zentrum, and the DDP, known as the Weimar Coalition. These parties together accounted for 331 out of the 421 seats in the current National Assembly.

Most members of the previous Bauer cabinet remained in post in the first Müller cabinet, including the former Chancellor, Gustav Bauer, who took the post of Minister of the Treasury immediately, replacing Wilhelm Mayer, and he took on the additional role as Minister of Transport, from 1 May, replacing Johannes Bell of Zentrum. The key cabinet changes were: Erich Koch-Weser (DDP) replacing Eugen Schiffer (DDP) as Vice Chancellor, and he also took on the additional role of Minister of the Interior. Otto Gessler (DDP) replaced the discredited Gustav Noske (SPD) as Defence Minister, and Joseph Wirth (Zentrum) replaced the financially compromised Matthias Erzberger (also Zentrum) as the Minister of Finance.[20]

On 29 March, Müller gave a speech to the National Assembly in Berlin. He suggested that what Germany now required in the aftermath of the Kapp Putsch was some house-cleaning, noting that a republic without democrats could not survive. The Weimar administrative system and economic life now had to be fully democratised. Specific reforms were promised including a new law on industrial disputes,

The Social Democratic politician Hermann Müller would twice serve as German Chancellor (March–June 1920 and 1928–30).

more welfare benefits for the victims of war, and new codes of loyalty for civil servants. He also promised the nationalisation of key public utilities, with that of the electric industry already under way, and he hoped this would be followed by nationalisation of the coal industry. Finally, he promised the Kapp rebels would be punished and the Reichswehr would be reconstructed on 'democratic lines'.[21]

The Kapp Putsch may have been a bungled fiasco, but it made possible a victory of immense importance for right-wing counterrevolutionary elements in Bavaria. On the night of 13–14 March, General Alfred von Möhl, the commander of the armed forces in the Munich area, after hearing news of Kapp's coup in Berlin, decided to launch one of his own, supported by a local paramilitary self-defence militia, known as the Home Guard (*Einwohnerwehr*). Möhl informed Johannes Hoffmann (SPD), the Prime Minister of Bavaria, that he could not guarantee the safety of his government unless it transferred power to the Army. Hoffmann hurriedly assembled his cabinet in the early hours of 14 March, urging the rejection of the general's ultimatum. Most of his ministers shrank from such a course of action. Instead, they supported a proposal by Ernst Müller-Meiningen, the DDP leader, who suggested the right-wing nationalist Dr Gustav Ritter von Kahr, the government president of Upper Bavaria and a member of the pro-monarchist BVP, should take over.

Deprived of political or military support, Hoffmann was unceremoniously driven from office. On 16 March, Kahr was elected as the Prime Minister of Bavaria in a vote in the Bavarian Assembly. The Social Democrats refused to participate in Kahr's right-wing conservative government, and would never again hold power in Bavaria during the Weimar years. Under Kahr, Bavaria became a conspiratorial, anti-Republican 'cell of order' (*Ordnungszelle*). Kahr immediately issued a decree to curtail the immigration of 'Eastern Jews' to Bavaria, and he actively encouraged antisemitism.[22] Captain Hermann Ehrhardt, whose naval brigade had played a key role in the Kapp Putsch, immediately found a safe haven in Munich, where he established a new secret society called Organisation Consul (OC), whose main purpose was to murder leading supporters and politicians in the Weimar Republic.[23]

Adolf Hitler was now in the perfect place to establish a new anti-democratic, nationalistic, antisemitic party. On 20 February, the German Workers' Party (DAP), led by Anton Drexler, changed its name to the National Socialist German Workers' Party (*Nationalsozialistische*

Deutsche Arbeiterpartei, NSDAP). Members of the party, contrary to widespread belief, did not initially call themselves Nazis but rather National Socialists (*Nationalsozialsten*), but their opponents used the term, and the name stuck.

On 24 February, the first large meeting of the newly named NSDAP took place in the first-floor hall of the Hofbräuhaus, before a crowd of 2,000 people. This day was commemorated by the party as Founding Day, and became the location of an annual speech by Adolf Hitler. At the meeting, Hitler was given the task by Drexler of reading out the 25 points of the NSDAP party programme, which he declared 'unalterable'. The main authors of the programme were Hitler and Drexler, with some economic ideas from Gottfried Feder added. They were remarkably like those being advanced by many other nationalist right-wing parties at the time. The party's most notable gimmick was to combine nationalist and antisemitic ideas with anti-capitalist and so-called 'socialist' measures. This novel combination allowed the NSDAP a banner under which workers could shelter along with conservative middle- and upper-class groups, thereby acting as a bulwark against communist revolution at home and offering the possibility of restoring German military power abroad.

The 'national' elements of the party programme included promises to revise the Treaty of Versailles, to unite German-speakers into an expanded Greater German Reich, which would exclude Jews from German citizenship rights, treat them as foreigners and halt future Jewish immigration. The 'socialist' parts of the party platform included pledges to nationalise trusts, abolish land rents, restrict interest on loans, introduce profit-sharing in industry, promised the nationalisation of big business, to open large department stores to small traders, confiscate profits made by industry during the war, and create a People's Army. The anti-capitalist elements of the party programme appeared to spell the end of interest-bearing loans and clearly threatened the existence of banks.[24]

Overall, the NSDAP promised to fight against the 'corrupting parliamentary democracy' and replace it with a strong centralised government under the direction of an all-powerful leader. In *Mein Kampf*, Hitler wrote of the night he presented the party programme: 'A fire was sparked, from whose embers the sword would necessarily come which would restore freedom to the German Siegfried and life to the German nation. The hall gradually emptied. The movement was under way.'[25]

In the Ruhr, a left-wing military uprising was also set off by the Kapp Putsch. The Rhenish-Westphalian industrial region was already a focal point of left-wing radicalism. It was the beating heart of Germany's iron and coal industries. It was also the region where the influence of the Left was at its strongest. The left-wing parties there initially decided to form an alliance to stop the spread of the Kapp Putsch.[26] A regional Red Ruhr Army (RRA) was created on 13 March, numbering an estimated 50,000 armed workers, attached to a coalition involving the USPD, the KPD, the Communist Workers' Party of Germany (*Kommunistische Arbeiter-Partei Deutschlands* – KAPD, a breakaway party from the KPD), and the *Freie Arbeiter Union Deutschlands* (FAUD). The RRA was organised in three centres: Hagen held by the USPD, Essen by the KPD and USPD, and Mülheim by the KAPD. These forces managed to seize rifles, machine guns and ammunition from the local government armaments stores and used them to overcome the understaffed local police, Reichswehr and Free Corps units. The RRA managed to gain control of many localities in the Ruhr, including Essen, Düsseldorf, Duisburg, Dortmund, Hagen, Münster, Arnsberg, Mülheim, Elberfeld, and Oberhausen. In all these areas, Executive Councils were set up with the aim of creating a 'dictatorship of the proletariat'.[27]

After the legitimate German government returned to power in Berlin, on 20 March, the trade unions announced the end of the general strike, and the new government opened negotiations with the Ruhr rebels in an attempt to end the revolt. A conference was held in Bielefeld on 23–24 March 1920. Carl Severing (SPD), the Reich Commissioner for the Ruhr, took a leading role in the negotiations on behalf of the government. A draft agreement promised an amnesty for crimes committed by those opposing the Kapp Putsch, and cooperation between local authorities and the workers' Executive Councils. The rebels explicitly stated they wanted the Reichswehr to stay out of the Ruhr, but government concessions were conditional on the immediate surrender of arms by the rebels. The Ruhr Red Army rejected this settlement, preferring 'honourable downfall' to 'dishonourable surrender'.

The Müller government appointed the Reichswehr regional commander, Oskar von Watter, to suppress the Ruhr rebellion by force. The Ruhr Red Army proved no match for the well-equipped and trained Reichswehr troops, though it performed well in combat with the less-well-organised Free Corps. Once again, the Army showed no reluctance whatsoever about putting down a left-wing revolt by force. On 2 April, Watter's military forces marched into the Ruhr area, designated a demilitarised area under the terms of the Treaty of Versailles. These forces included members of the ruthless Ehrhardt brigade, who had supported the Kapp Putsch only a few weeks before. The fighting was accompanied by summary extra-judicial executions by Watter's forces. On 3 April, President Ebert, the commander of the Reich's armed forces, issued an order prohibiting further extra-judicial killings by the Reichswehr and the Free Corps troops, but, once again, President Ebert had sanctioned the suppression of a revolt by left-wing radicals and workers.[28]

On 5 April, a large part of the Ruhr Red Army fled into the region of the Rhineland occupied by the French Army for protection. In response to the Reichswehr military presence in the Ruhr, on 6 April, French troops occupied a number of cities in the region, including Frankfurt am Main, Hanau, Dieburg, and Darmstadt, thereby cutting off all the economic traffic between northern and southern Germany. The sole purpose of the French troops was to ensure German compliance with the terms of the Versailles Treaty. On 8 April, the German cabinet voted to accede to the French demand for the withdrawal of troops from the Ruhr valley, and this was completed by 26 April.

By 12 April, the Ruhr Uprising was over. It once more revealed the huge gulf between the Social Democrats in the Weimar Coalition and the left-wing radicals on the streets. In the bloody conflict, the Reichswehr lost 208 dead and 123 missing; the Free Corps death toll was placed at 273; but an estimated one thousand members of the Ruhr Red Army and workers were killed.[29]

The Allies were outraged by the use by the German government of Free Corps troops to put down another rebellion. They demanded the immediate disbandment of these paramilitary fighting units who were, they claimed, acting as an unofficial auxiliary reserve army. On 7 April, the Inter-Allied Commission of Control called for the disbandment of all the Home Guard units in Germany. There were loud cries of protest against this order throughout Germany, but especially in Bavaria. Kahr argued Home Guard troops were a valuable bulwark against communist revolution, and he warned Erich Koch, the Interior Minister, that Bavaria would withdraw from the Reich if the Home Guard was disbanded.

The Allies set a date of 31 May 1920 for the dissolution of the Free Corps. The German government did its best to comply, but knew leaders

of the Free Corps would do everything they could to resist the order. Stern penalties were announced for anyone who joined or organised Free Corps associations in future. In the end, the order to disband by 31 May proved impossible to carry out. The Free Corps simply went underground. For years, its members maintained a clandestine existence, specialising in conspiracy and politically motivated assassinations. They had many powerful friends who supported them in their hatred of the Allies and the Republic.[30]

While these key political events were still in progress, on 26 February, the premiere of *The Cabinet of Dr Caligari* (*Das Cabinet des Dr. Caligari*) took place at the Marmorhaus theatre in Berlin. Despite the political upheaval of the early Weimar years, the productivity of the Weimar film industry was astonishing. The film sector was a welcome boon to the struggling economy. German silent films became a world-wide success. Between 1918 and 1930, the number of cinemas grew from 2,300 to 5,000. By the end of the decade, Germany had more cinemas than any other country in Europe. Average cinema attendance for each German adult was about nine times a year.[31] In 1919, 470 films were produced, in 1920 this rose to 510 films. But by 1923, at the height of hyper-inflation, this had dropped to 253 film releases, and by 1932 it was down to just 132. Between 1918 and 1933, German cinema-goers encountered films from a wide variety of settings and genres. It has been estimated that of the ten thousand people working in German cinema in the Weimar period, some two thousand were forced to emigrate after 1933, with the vast majority being Jewish.[32]

The Cabinet of Dr Caligari is regarded as the quintessential work of Weimar Expressionist cinema, breaking new ground technically and artistically. Much of the acting in the film consciously mimics the pantomime style of Weimar Expressionist theatre, and is deliberately over-the-top. The film was directed by Robert Wiene, who was of Jewish descent. It starred the Jewish actor Werner Krauss, in the title role, alongside Conrad Veidt, the biggest male star of Weimar cinema, as his sleepwalking assistant, Cesare. It was shot entirely in a film studio by Willy Hameister, without any exterior sequences, creating a nightmarish dreamworld given added menace by the brilliant use of dark shadowy lighting. It was a technique subsequently used in many other Weimar Expressionist films.

The main narrative highlights a brutal, irrational authority figure, Dr Caligari, satisfying his lust for domination over Cesare, who is conditioned into obedience and becomes a tool of his master's willpower.

A film poster for Robert Wiene's expressionist classic,
The Cabinet of Dr. Caligari (1920).

The co-writers of the screenplay were Hans Janowitz and Carl Mayer, both of whom were pacifists during the First World War. Their war-time experiences left them mistrustful of the authority which had led millions to their deaths on the battlefield.

The complex psychological story is set in a fictitious north German town near the Dutch border, called Holstenwall. Most of the film is a flashback of the story of a student called Francis. One day a fun-fair arrives in town, with a merry-go-round and side shows, including that of the star turn, Dr Caligari, a weird and bespectacled man, performing with his supernatural sleep-walking (somnambulist) assistant, Cesare. To perform in public, Dr Caligari must obtain a licence from the local authorities, but he is treated in an off-hand manner by a rude local town clerk. On the next morning, the same official is found murdered in his bed, the victim of a brutal stabbing. Later on the same day, two students, Francis (Friedrich Fehér) and Alan (Hans von Twardowski), who are both in love with Jane (Lil Dagover), the daughter of Dr Olson, go to the fairground to witness Dr Caligari's show. The highlight comes when Cesare, who only acts at Caligari's command, comes out of his coffin-like box, where he has supposedly slept for many years. Dr Caligari tells the audience the ghostly Cesare will answer any questions they might have about the future. Alan asks Cesare how long he will live, to which the somnambulist replies: 'Until dawn.'

At dawn, Alan is found stabbed to death in his bed. Francis believes Dr Caligari is responsible, and persuades Jane's father to assist him in his own private investigation of the murders, which is authorised by the local police. Cesare is next seen breaking into Jane's bedroom. He lifts a dagger and gazes at her, but instead of killing her he puts his dagger away and abducts her. Carrying her in his arms, he is chased by her father, and a mob. He drops the girl, who is rescued, but Cesare dies at the scene, seemingly of exhaustion.

In the confusion, Dr Caligari escapes, but is followed by Francis, who sees him enter a lunatic asylum. Upon further investigation, he discovers Dr Caligari is the director of the asylum and has been leading a double life. It turns out he became obsessed by the story of a medieval Italian mystic called Dr Caligari, who hypnotised his medium to commit the murders. When a mentally ill somnambulist became a patient at the asylum, Dr Caligari decided to repeat the killings of the original Dr Caligari, using Cesare to commit the crimes. Caligari then becomes insane when he sees Cesare's dead body and is put in a straitjacket, becoming a mental patient in his own asylum.

There is a final bizarre twist in the story when the film returns to the present and we see that Francis himself is a mental patient in the asylum, along with Jane and Cesare. Cesare is quiet and is not a somnambulist at all. The asylum director is Dr Caligari. Francis tries to attack him, but he is restrained. Dr Caligari then announces that he now understands Francis's deluded story, and is confident he can now cure him. The evil authority figure was really a kindly psychiatrist all along. This ending reveals the main body of the film as a delusional flashback of the ill-mind of Francis.[33]

The Cabinet of Dr Caligari is one of the most important films of the Weimar era. Film critics from the time of its release until the present day have probed its inner meanings, with many seeing it as a German unconscious longing for an authority figure they would ultimately find in Adolf Hitler, while others view it as representing the wartime German government conditioning soldiers to kill. Some have argued the revelation at the end of the film that the story is a delusion caused by mental illness devalued its deeper message about the nature of authoritarianism.[34]

It is perhaps more plausible to see *The Cabinet of Dr Caligari* not as a premonition of what was to come, but as a reflection of the mentality in Germany at the time it was released – a time of chaos and confusion. Most of all, it reflected the trauma in war experienced by its writers. This view is reinforced by the recollection of Hans Janowitz, who claimed he and the co-writer of the film Carl Mayer saw Dr Caligari as a representative of 'the great authoritarian power of a [wartime] government we hated' which 'compelled us to murder and be murdered'.[35]

The National Assembly held its last session on 21 May 1920. Few mourned its passing. An election campaign to elect the new Reichstag now followed. Elections did not take place in Schleswig-Holstein, Upper Silesia and East and West Prussia, owing to scheduled referenda due to take place in those areas. The 42 sitting parliamentary members for those areas retained their seats until elections took place.

The Reichstag elections of 6 June, with a voter turnout of 79.2 per cent, proved disastrous for the SPD-led Weimar Coalition, which lost its previous huge overall majority. The most serious reverse was suffered by the SPD itself, which polled 21.9 per cent, securing only 103 seats. The SPD remained the largest party, but had lost 62 seats, dropping from 37.9 per cent of the vote at the last election, from 11.51 to 6.17 million votes. Even heavier losses were suffered by the SPD's partners in government, the liberal DDP, led by Carl Petersen, which polled 2.3 million votes, down from 5.6 million at the previous election, with the number of the party's seats dropping from 75 to 39 and its percentage of votes falling from 18.6 to 8.3 per cent. This marked the beginning of a decline for middle-class liberalism from which it never really recovered. The third party in the Weimar Coalition, Zentrum, led by Karl Trimborn, also fared badly, with its seats falling from 91 to 64, its votes reducing from 5.9 to 3.84 million and its voter percentage moving downward to 13.6 from 19.7 per cent.

By contrast, the two anti-Republican parties: the DVP, led by Gustav Stresemann, and the DNVP, led by Oskar Hergt, both made gains. The DVP increased its seats from 19 to 65, its vote percentage from 4.4 to 13.9 per cent, with its popular vote going up from 1.34 to 3.91 million. The number of votes for the DNVP also rose, from 3.12 to 4.24 million, its number of seats increasing from 44 to 71 and its poll share up from 10.3 to 15.1 per cent. It was now the strongest middle-class party in Germany.

The party furthest to the Left contesting the election, the USPD, led by Arthur Crispien, made the biggest gains, with a large segment of the industrial working class transferring their allegiance from the SPD to the USPD. The party's seats increased in number, from 33 to 83 seats, with its percentage vote increasing, from 7.6 to 17.6 per cent, and its total vote share up from 2.32 to 4.91 million. The USPD was now the second most popular party in Germany. Many working-class voters were clearly outraged by the harsh treatment of left-wing radicals during the recent Ruhr Uprising. The KPD decided to contest the election, but fared badly, only polling 589,454 votes, or 2.09 per cent, and securing four seats.[36]

The new Weimar Republic had clearly disappointed German voters. President Ebert, following the tradition of giving the strongest party the first chance to form a government, asked Hermann Müller, the incumbent SPD Chancellor, to form a new coalition. On 8 June, Müller tried half-heartedly to convince the USPD to join a new coalition, but party leader Arthur Crispien decided he would only take his party into a government if the Independents were the largest party, as part of a purely socialist coalition. As Müller did not want to form a coalition involving the DVP, on 12 June, he declined the opportunity to continue trying to form a government.

Ebert finally turned to Constantin Fehrenbach, one of the leaders of Zentrum, and widely respected as the speaker of the National

Assembly, to form a minority government, after the Social Democrats had refused to join his government. The SPD now played the bizarre role of being crucial in keeping governments in power, but mostly deciding not to participate in them. The Fehrenbach cabinet was based on three parties: Zentrum, the DDP and, for the first time, the centre-right DVP led by Gustav Stresemann. The DDP had only agreed to join a coalition with the DVP, provided that party promised it would accept the Weimar Constitution, which its leader Stresemann duly did. In Fehrenbach's cabinet, apart from himself, there were four other members of Zentrum: Joseph Wirth (Finance), Andreas Hermes (Food), Heinrich Brauns (Labour), and Johannes Gisberts (Mail). There were also three members of the DVP: Rudolph Heinz (Vice Chancellor and Minister of Justice), Ernst Scholz (Economic Affairs), and Hans von Raumer (Treasury). The DDP had two members: Otto Gessler (Defence) and Erich Koch-Weser (Interior). There were also two members with no party affiliation: Walter Simons (Foreign Minister), and Wilhelm Groener (Transport).

Fehrenbach took office as German Chancellor on 25 June 1920, in a minority government whose members held only 168 seats out of a total of 466 seats in the Reichstag. Fehrenbach belonged to the left wing of Zentrum, was forward-looking and pro-Republican, but his coalition could only stay in power if the Social Democrats agreed to tolerate it. Fehrenbach and his cabinet issued a jointly signed statement announcing their resolve to work for the reconstruction of Germany, based on the Weimar Constitution, and to resist any further attempts to overthrow the Republic by force. He further promised to continue the foreign policy of the outgoing government. A comprehensive social insurance system, guaranteeing unemployment benefits, would be carried through, and he declared the chief purpose of the cabinet was to govern with the working classes. On 3 July, the Fehrenbach government won a vote of confidence in the Reichstag by 313 to 64 votes.[37]

Constantin Fehrenbach of the Catholic Centre Party (Zentrum), German Chancellor from June 1920 to May 1921.

Between 5 and 16 July 1920, the Spa Conference took place in Belgium. It was a diplomatic meeting between the Allied Supreme War Council and the German government. It was the first post-war diplomatic conference to include German representatives. The Allies thought it was better to discuss outstanding problems with German representatives face to face, rather than through traditional diplomatic channels. The German government was chiefly represented by the new Chancellor, Constantin Fehrenbach, Foreign Minister, Walter Simons, and Otto Gessler, the Defence Minister. The British and French Prime Ministers David Lloyd George and Alexandre Millerand were also in attendance, along with diplomats from several other Allied countries, including Belgium, Italy, and Japan.

Contrary to German expectations, the conference did not focus on the question of the reparations, but concentrated on the progress of German disarmament and coal deliveries. The Allies adopted a firm and determined stance throughout. The discussion on disarmament focused on the strength of the German Army, the auxiliary paramilitary police units (*Sicherheitspolizei*), and the Home Guard. The Allies thought the armed auxiliary organisations were really disguised secret-reserve army forces that could triple German military power as and when required.

The German military point of view was presented by Gessler and Hans von Seeckt, the Chief of the Reichswehr Command, who demanded German Army strength be fixed at 200,000—100,000 more than the limit set by the Versailles Treaty. They argued it would take 15 months to reduce the army to the desired Allied figure. The Allies greeted this demand with outright rejection, reiterating the figure of 100,000 as non-negotiable. Germany was given until 1 January 1921 to reduce its army to 100,000 or face military occupation, probably of the Ruhr. The Allies also insisted that all the auxiliary German forces had to be completely disarmed and their weapons impounded and surrendered to the Allies. The German government made a promise to meet this obligation but stressed it would be extremely difficult to achieve.

A great deal of time was taken up in Spa by discussions concerning German deliveries of coal, in accordance with the provisions of the Versailles Treaty. Under a further protocol signed on 19 August 1919, Germany had agreed to make these deliveries, but due to the Kapp Putsch, the Ruhr Uprising and the associated strikes in the coal industry they had been unable to comply. Alexandre Millerand, the French Prime Minister, took the lead in these tough negotiations.

The French needed German coal because many of its own mines had been destroyed in the war. This explains why the Allies took such an uncompromising stance, using threats of sanctions and occupation to secure German compliance. The talks almost broke down, but on 16 July 1920 the German government reluctantly signed the Spa Coal Protocol, under which the German government promised to deliver 2 million tons of coal for six months. The Allies warned any missed coal deliveries would be answered by military occupation of the Ruhr.[38]

The Spa Coal Protocol was disastrous for the German economy. The reduction in the supply of coal to the home market damaged the output of the iron and steel industry, disrupted the railways, and led to shortages for the German consumer. In the Reichstag, representatives of the DNVP castigated the German delegation at Spa for failing to uphold German honour by signing the coal agreement.

The discussion of reparations was not even on the agenda at Spa, and was not discussed in any detail. On 12 July, Walter Simons, the German Foreign Minister, handed over a set of proposals which called for 30 annual reparations payments, but avoided outlining any definite sums. There was no mention yet of the total sum the German government would pay, but the share of German payments was fixed on the following percentage scale: France would receive 52 per cent, the UK 22 per cent, Italy 10 per cent and Belgium 8 per cent, with the remaining 8 per cent distributed pro rata among the other Allied nations.

The Spa Conference was seen as a huge anti-climax. On 27 July, in a speech in the Reichstag, Fehrenbach admitted that no advantage had been secured by the German government at the Conference, but he insisted that every effort should be directed towards carrying out the terms of the Treaty of Versailles, in order to prevent an Allied occupation. Foreign Minister Simons, in his speech, said it would have been better if Germany had never signed the Versailles Treaty, but nothing now remained but to carry it out. He praised Lloyd George, who he said had shown some understanding of Germany and its difficulties, but he never mentioned the hard line taken by the French Prime Minister Millerand during the proceedings in Spa.[39]

On 7 August 1920, the swastika was adopted as the official symbol of the Nazi Party flag, during a party conference in Salzburg, Austria. It is an ancient good-will sign used in many cultures for centuries and remains a sacred symbol in Hinduism, Buddhism, Jainism, and Odinism. It is a common sight on temples and houses in India and

Indonesia. Adolf Hitler, who designed the Nazi Party flag, combined the swastika with the three colours used on the German imperial flag from 1871 to 1918, red, black, and white. In *Mein Kampf*, Hitler described the new Nazi flag thus: 'In red we see the social idea of the movement, in white the nationalist idea, in the swastika the mission of the struggle for the victory of the Aryan man, and, for the same reason, the victory of the idea of creative work, as such always has been and always will be antisemitic.' The swastika became the most recognisable symbol of Nazi propaganda, rousing supporters, and striking terror into Jews and other opponents.[40]

During the late summer of 1920, the growth of the National Socialist Party first came to the attention of Robert Smallbones, who had been appointed as the British Consul for the state of Bavaria on 11 January. On 28 September, he sent a letter to Lord Curzon, the British Foreign Secretary, informing him of the recently formed NSDAP, which was 'making itself rather conspicuous in Munich by frequent meetings and lectures', organised by 'Herr Drexler and Herr Hitler'. They were 'extremely violent and usually antisemitic'. Smallbones thought the party, in which socialism was subordinated to the dominant idea of nationalism, 'must have funds at their disposal, as one display of posters cost 10,000 marks'. He speculated that the NSDAP was most probably financed by big business, and concluded that Hitler's brand of so-called socialism was 'of the negative, anti-capitalist kind, which does not frighten the present-day millionaire'.[41]

On the extreme Left of German politics, the USPD had been heartened by its success in the June 1920 national elections. Many members felt there was now a real opportunity for the party to displace the moderate Social Democrats as the main working-class party, but among the party rank-and-file a pro-Soviet group led by Ernst Däumig wanted the party to draw closer to the Comintern, the Third Communist International, founded in March 1919, which preached worldwide revolution, but was really a division of the Foreign Office of the new Soviet Republic. The right wing of the USPD led by Arthur Crispien, including most of its Reichstag members, opposed the party becoming a mere puppet of Moscow's will.[42]

A split in the USPD was inevitable. The showdown came at the party congress, held in Halle in October 1920. The left-wing faction, led by Ernst Däumig, which controlled most delegates, carried the vote to join the Third Communist International by 237 to 156 votes, and the party split in two. On 4 December, the left wing of the USPD, with about 400,000 members, merged with the KPD to form the United Communist Party of Germany (*Vereinigte Kommunistische Partei* Deutschlands, *VKPD*). The right wing of the party continued to function under the name USPD, as a separate political party, with 340,000 members and about 60 of the 81 USPD Reichstag members.[43]

Towards the end of 1920, Lord D'Abernon, the British Ambassador in Berlin, compiled a year-end report for Lord Curzon, the British Foreign Secretary, outlining the current political and economic situation in Germany. D'Abernon felt that after the upheavals of the Kapp Putsch and the Ruhr Uprising, the country had now settled down to a 'considerable extent'. The new German government led by Constantin Fehrenbach was 'not strong' but 'stronger than it was'. The real future danger, D'Abernon thought was the dire condition of the German economy. The plight of the lower middle class, and those on fixed incomes, was deteriorating rapidly, due to rising inflation, which was lowering their standard of living. As for the working class, their wages had increased, with discontent appearing 'less prevalent than earlier in the year'. On the Right, the disarmament of paramilitary organisations had weakened another area of potential future political trouble. On the Left, the break-up of the USPD was likely to marginalise the extreme Left. All this led D'Abernon to conclude the 'chances of disorder during the coming winter months are decidedly less than 12 months ago'.[44]

On 28 December, French Field Marshal Ferdinand Foch, the President of the Allied Military Committee of Versailles, presented his own year-end report to the Allies, which surveyed progress on German implementation of the disarmament agreement laid down in the Treaty of Versailles. Foch struck a decidedly gloomy tone. It was admitted the German government had agreed to reduce its army to 100,000, and was progressing towards meeting this requirement by 1 January 1921, but the German government had not yet fully disarmed the numerous paramilitary groups and auxiliary police units, in particular the *Einwohnerwehr*, which continued to operate and presented a danger to the Allies.[45]

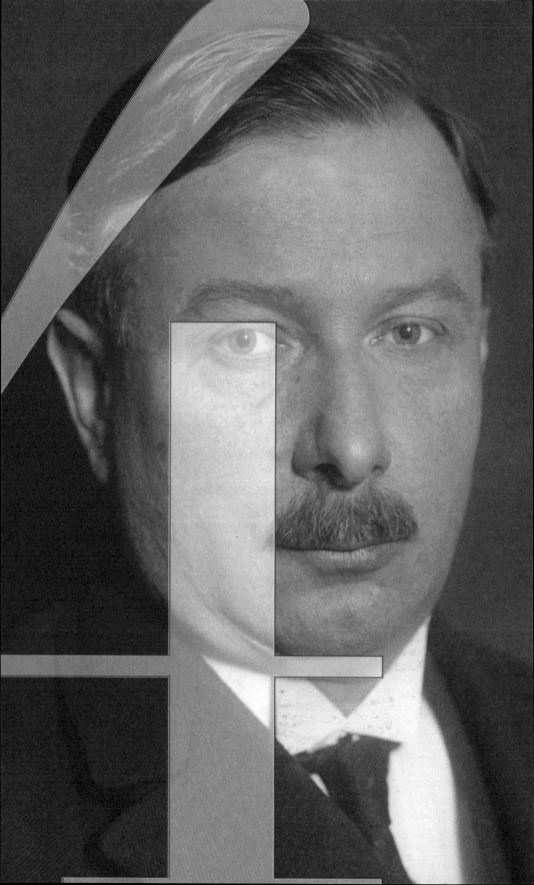

1921

·

MAKE GERMANY PAY

·

On 18 January 1921, the German President, Friedrich Ebert, delivered a speech celebrating the 50th anniversary of the establishment of the German Empire. Ebert said that in spite of its problems, Germany remained a unified state: 'Even if, today, we have to look with sorrow towards our German compatriots who against their will have been separated from the land of their kindred, and towards Austria, who longingly stretches out her arms to us, as we to her, we must be determined to maintain our domestic unity.[1]

Earlier in the month, the German Chancellor, Constantin Fehrenbach, sent a letter to the Allies stating that Germany had done its best to adhere to the terms of the Treaty of Versailles, but that meeting the terms of the Treaty related to the dissolution and disarmament of paramilitary groups had proved impossible.[2] By now, the French government was growing tired of German excuses, and wanted a much stronger stance to be adopted by the Allies against the German government for non-compliance. On 11 January, the French government led by Georges Leygues lost a vote of confidence in the Chamber of Deputies, and fell from power. A new government, led by the moderate socialist Aristide Briand, who had been Prime Minister on three previous occasions, was formed, aiming to take a stronger stance in the upcoming reparations negotiations with the German government.[3]

On 20 January, Briand's new coalition government won a vote of confidence in the French Chamber of Deputies by 462 to 77 votes. On the following day, he delivered an uncompromising speech on foreign policy, saying it was his firm intention to 'make Germany pay' for the devastation it had caused during the First World War. On 24 January, a five-day Conference of the Supreme Council of the Allies opened at the French Foreign Ministry in Paris, with Briand acting as chair. Representing Britain were the Prime Minister, David Lloyd George, and his Foreign Secretary, Lord Curzon, with diplomatic representatives from many other Allied powers present including Belgium, Italy, and Japan. The two key items on the agenda were reparations and disarmament.

previous page Joseph Wirth of the Catholic
Centre Party (Zentrum), German Chancellor
from May 1921 to November 1922.

According to Article 233 of the Versailles Treaty, the German government was required to pay an initial instalment of 20 billion gold marks by 1 May 1921, at which date the Reparations Commission was required to fix the total German reparations debt total.[4] On 28 January, the Supreme War Council of the European Allies in Paris announced that Germany would have to pay 2 billion gold marks per year in reparations, for the first five years, rising to 4 billion from 1926 to 1930, then 6 billion from 1931 to 1963, giving a total of 222 billion gold marks. In addition to the total reparations bill, Germany would be required to pay a 42-year-long tax of 12 per cent on German exports. Reparations payments would be index-linked, allowing Allied creditors to benefit from a future upturn in the German economy. The Allies stressed these figures were, at this stage, only proposals, and would be discussed further with the German government at a Reparations Conference which was due to begin in London on 1 March.[5]

The Allied reparations proposals were greeted with howls of protest throughout Germany. On 1 February, Walter Simons, the German Foreign Minister, said in a speech to the Reichstag that Germany, though willing to make good the damage caused by war, would not accept the Allied War Council bill on reparations, and would soon put forward counter-proposals. More controversially, he raised again the issue of whether Germany was exclusively guilty of starting the First World War.[6] On the same day, Lord Kilmarnock, the Chargé d'Affaires at the British Embassy in Berlin, informed Lord Curzon, the British Foreign Secretary, that the general feeling within the German government was that the proposed reparations bill would be impossible for Germany to pay, and there was a general determination among the Reichstag parties to reject the Paris demands. He further noted that Simons had made it known to his cabinet colleagues that he would rather resign than accept the Allied reparations proposals.[7]

On 11 February, Kaiser Wilhelm II, living in exile in the Netherlands, gave his first press interview since his abdication in November 1918. It was published worldwide by the United Press. He denied he had deliberately started the war and further claimed that Germany would never have lost the war if the home front had stayed loyal. The interview seemed a ringing endorsement of the 'stab-in-the-back myth', during a time of international tension, and delivered when the Allies were still trying to extradite the former German Emperor as a war criminal.[8]

On 24 February, Simons, before departing for London to discuss reparations, gave a speech to the German State Economic Council in which he stated: 'If the Entente [Allies] insist on the execution of the Paris demands and are not prepared to alter them then we shall go in vain to London for I consider them impossible of execution. It is impossible for Germany to pay fixed annuities and it also impossible for her to pay the export levy.'[9]

Between 21 February and 14 March 1921, the London Conference on German Reparations Payments took place. The German government agreed to attend to try and get the Allied reparations bill drastically reduced. On 1 March, Walter Simons made a counter-offer for Germany which offered to pay 30 billion gold marks, under a lengthy instalment plan, but added this offer was dependent on Germany retaining the important industrial area of Upper Silesia in the upcoming referendum. Simons claimed this was a reasonable counter-offer as Germany had already paid 21 billion gold marks in goods deliveries. Simons warned these payments would be serviced by an international loan, which he admitted had not yet been negotiated.[10]

The Reparations Commission responded by stating that only 8 billion gold marks' worth of goods had already been delivered, and that this huge disparity could only be explained by false accounting by the German authorities. The German government had even added as payments items such as the deliberate scuttling of the German High Seas Fleet battle fleet at Scapa Flow for which the Allies had not received any financial gain. David Lloyd George, the British Prime Minister, in a speech on 3 March, admitted that he came to the conference quite willing to be sympathetic to the German objections to the Allied terms, and he had always believed Allied demands must be limited by Germany's capacity to pay, but he felt Simons' derisory offer of 30 billion gold marks did not even warrant discussion, as it fell way short of Germany's treaty obligations, and showed no willingness to make the necessary sacrifices involved, nor to even acknowledge the wanton destruction inflicted by Germany on French and Belgian territory during the war. In these circumstances, Lloyd George declared the German government had to accept the Allied demand of 222 million gold marks, payable over 42 years, or face the immediate Allied occupation of the west German cities of Düsseldorf, Duisburg and Ruhrort.

This Allied occupation began on 8 March 1921. President Ebert complained the Allies were behaving unreasonably, because they had already retained a portion of the purchase price of goods exported to the West, and seized customs and harbour receipts collected in the occupied areas. The German government made a formal protest against these Allied sanctions and then promptly left the conference.[11]

When Simons arrived in Berlin by train, he was greeted as a hero by a large crowd, which indicated the strength of public support for the belligerent position he adopted at the London Conference. Defying the Allies was clearly popular in Germany, but this simply confirmed to the Allies that Germany had no intention of paying reparations. On 12 March, Simons addressed the Reichstag, and received approval by 268 to 49 votes for the position he had adopted during the London Conference. In fact, German intransigence was self-defeating, as it simply led to Allies adopting a much more hostile stance. On 16 March, the Allied Reparations Commission ordered the German government to make an immediate payment of 1 billion gold marks by 23 March, and a further 12 billion by 1 May, as its first instalments of the reparations bill, but on 23 March the German government announced it could not afford to pay the 1 billion demanded, even if it were legitimately owed.[12]

In the midst of this bitter diplomatic crisis, the German government was faced with a fresh wave of violent clashes between the Prussian Security Police (*Schutzpolizei*), and communist revolutionaries allied to the United Communist Workers' Party of Germany (KAPD), and the KPD between 17 March and 1 April. The province of Saxony in central Germany was at the centre of these clashes, which were at their worst in Halle, Leuna, Hamburg, Merseburg, and Mansfeld. They became known as the March Action (*März Aktion*).

The Communists had been buoyed up by performing exceptionally well in elections to the Prussian State Parliament on 20 February 1920, in which the VKPD had performed particularly well in central Germany which led party activists to lead a wave of strikes and street clashes with the police. This prompted Otto Hörsing, the Social Democratic Minister-President of Saxony, and Carl Severing, the Social Democratic Prussian Minister of the Interior, to send in a strong contingent of armed Prussian security police to restore order.

The Communists were led by Max Hölz of the VKPD, who had no coordinated plan for what the left-wing rebels were seeking to achieve. He put together a force of 2,500 armed men, mostly aged between 18 and 45. Hölz was something of a communist folk hero, who had been a leader of a 'Red Army' in Vogtland, near the Czech border, during the aftermath of the Kapp Putsch in the previous year. In his memoirs, Hölz claimed the workers were far from in a revolutionary mood when he arrived. It was the brutality of the police that had forced the workers to take up arms and adopt guerrilla tactics, he added.[13]

On 18 March, the communist daily newspaper *Die Rote Fahne* called on the workers to arm themselves. The Communists were able to equip the rebels with guns and ammunition. The rebels engaged in a wave of arson, looting, bank robberies and bomb attacks on public buildings and factories, during which the VKPD leadership increasingly lost control of the armed workers. The SPD and the USPD both issued a joint appeal to the workers of the industrial region of central Germany. This offered some criticism of the high-handed police action, but claimed the so-called revolutionaries had then behaved like criminals and thugs. They called on workers not to support calls for an insurrection or a general strike.

On 24 March, President Ebert declared a non-military state of emergency for Saxony and Hamburg, using his emergency powers under Article 48 of the Weimar Constitution. Outdoor meetings, demonstrations and Communist newspapers were banned. In an act of desperation, the Communist leadership called for a general strike, but this failed to materialise. By 1 April, the police had successfully put down the revolt without needing to call on the Reichswehr for help. The police confiscated 1,346 rifles, 34 machine guns and 10,000 rounds of ammunition from the rebels. According to the Prussian official figures, 34 police officers were killed and 67 wounded, with 145 rebels and civilians killed, and a further 51 wounded. Some brutal atrocities occured towards the end of the conflict. On 29 March, in Gröbers, near Halle, 11 police officers were brutally tortured, killed and mutilated, while at the Leuna Works, the police maltreated prisoners, and forced rebels to sing 'Deutschland, Deutschland, über Alles'.

The 'March Action' did not remotely threaten even the local Prussian government. It proved to be the final rising of the radical left-wing during the Weimar years. Neither a general strike nor a mass revolt by the working class happened. The immediate consequences for the VKPD and KPD were disastrous. The violent clashes seemed to confirm the 'dictatorial' leadership of the party was out of touch with ordinary working class people. Within weeks, 200,000 members had left the KPD.[14]

Meanwhile, the referendum that would decide the self-determination of the people in Upper Silesia took place on 20 March, as was required by the Treaty of Versailles. The region, in the south-eastern corner of Germany, had a major industrial sector, known as the Industrial Triangle, where the cities of Beuthen, Kattowitz and Gleiwitz contained vast coal, iron and zinc reserves. The German government had made clear reparations would be much easier to pay if it retained these industrial areas.

Upper Silesia was ethnically mixed, with Poles forming 60 per cent, and Germans 40 per cent of the population. At the Paris Peace Conference, the Polish delegation stressed the region was distinctly Polish in character. Before the referendum, the area was occupied by an Inter-Allied Commission of French, Italian and British forces, headed by Henri Le Rond, a French general who wanted to hand over to Poland the entire industrial region. There had already been three Polish uprisings and with Germany militarily weak there was every likelihood Polish rebels would take the law into their own hands if the result failed to go their way.[15]

In the Upper Silesian Referendum, the vote for remaining with Germany polled 59.4 per cent (717,122 votes), with 40.6 per cent (483,513) cast for Poland. The towns and most of the villages recorded German majorities, but in the urban industrial areas the German lead was only very slight. The Polish vote was highest in predominantly rural areas. Even so, the referendum showed that many Polish people had voted to be ruled by Germany. In the light of later events, it should be noted that a large majority of Polish Jews voted to remain in Germany.

The German government claimed the referendum result gave Germany the right to keep all of Upper Silesia, especially the profitable industrial region. This claim was supported by the British government, but the Polish government, supported by the French, contested Germany's demand, as Article 88 of the Treaty of Versailles had made clear the boundaries in the region would be determined by the votes in each electoral district. The French government felt that surrounding Germany with countries that were opposed to German aggression was the best way to guarantee its own security.[16]

The Inter-Allied Commission on Upper Silesia pointed out to the German government that it had not been a winner-takes-all referendum. It decided territory would be allocated by the laborious method of examining the results cast in each individual electoral district. This arduous task was passed to the supposedly impartial Council of the League of Nations Commission, which promised to report on the final Polish–German border allocations later in the year, but in the meantime, there was another Polish uprising in the region, which Allied occupying troops struggled to contain. Due to these disturbances, the League of Nations Commission, made up of four representatives from Brazil, China, Belgium, and Spain, did not begin the challenging task of settling the boundary in Upper Silesia until 1 September, and a parallel commission was put together to hammer out a workable economic division.[17]

On 30 March, Lord D'Abernon, the British Ambassador in Berlin, met with Foreign Minister Simons, who reported that he did not think the German government would re-open negotiations on reparations. Simons added there was no point in Germany making further payment proposals which the French government immediately rejected out of hand. All Germany could now do was settle down to a tough time under sanctions, and wait for the French government to acquire a more correct view of facts and possibilities.[18] On 18 April, Lord D'Abernon had a further meeting with Simons, who told him there had been 'interminable discussions in Cabinet' on the reparations question, but that there was no agreement about making a new offer to the Allies. Simons made it clear there was still no chance of the cabinet agreeing to accept the Paris Allied proposals. D'Abernon concluded Simons had realised that remaining intransigent would only antagonise the Allies, but he had no choice to do otherwise as the cabinet refused to accept the Paris demands.[19]

In a final effort, the German government tried to persuade the US President, William Harding, to act as an impartial mediator in the reparations dispute. In response, the US President was careful to emphasise to the German government that the American government might be willing to join an expert economic commission to determine the amounts of reparations Germany could afford to pay, but only if American involvement in such a commission was agreed beforehand by the Allies, which, of course, the Allies had no intention of doing.[20]

Since no fresh offer to the Allies was made by the German government, the Reparations Commission informed the German government on 27 April that the final non-negotiable reparations bill Germany was required to pay under the Treaty of Versailles amounted to 132 billion German gold marks (£6.6 billion on 1921 values), to be made in annual payments of 2 billion gold marks, plus 26 per cent of the annual value of German exports. All these payments would be in the form of German promissory bonds redeemable for payment in cash and goods. Germany was also required to participate in the reconstruction of the devastated areas in France and Belgium. These figures had been unanimously agreed by the Reparations Commission members based on an expert economic assessment of Germany's ability to pay.[21]

The fixing of the German reparations bill meant a key element of the Treaty of Versailles had now been implemented. The French government had made it clear to the other Allies, through secret diplomatic correspondence, that if the German government refused to accept the reparations bill, French armed forces would occupy the Ruhr, and extract the valuable coal and other industrial revenues generated in this region. The French government was sure the Germans would back down when faced with this possibility. The British government decided that even if British troops did not become directly involved, it would support the French occupation of the Ruhr.[22]

The trickiest problem now was getting the German government to agree to the Allied terms. On 4 May, Constantin Fehrenbach, the German Chancellor, and his cabinet, based on Zentrum, the DDP and the DVP, resigned, unwilling to agree to Germany's capitulation to the Allies on the final reparations. On the next day, The Allied Supreme War Council notified the German government of its default on the first payment of reparations, and issued what became known as the London Ultimatum. Its blunt demand was that, by 11 May, the German government had to agree to pay a total reparations debt of 132 billion gold marks, under what was called the London Schedule of Payments, to comply fully with disarmament, and to start trials against German war criminals. Failure to do all these things would result in an Allied occupation of the whole of the Ruhr, as well as further economic sanctions in the form of a raised levy on German exports.[23]

The grim task of putting together a new German cabinet was given by President Ebert to Dr Joseph Wirth, a respected figure on the left wing of Zentrum, who had previously served as Finance Minister. Wirth was a staunch Republican, an enthusiastic supporter of social reform, and popular in trade union circles. He had been a teacher before entering politics, but a highly trained one, working in the elite *Gymnasium* system. He was known as a fearless political debater, often at loggerheads with right-wingers, but admired on the centre left for making sound decisions as a cabinet minister.

The Wirth Cabinet was dedicated to 'a policy of fulfilment' (*Erfüllungspolitik*) of the Treaty of Versailles. Wirth believed ceaseless German haggling with the Allies over reparations had only made matters worse. Instead, he wanted to convince the Allies of German goodwill, in the hope this would improve relations, and lead to concessions further down the road. Negotiations with members of the Reichstag showed a majority would support a vote to accept the London Ultimatum, with the votes of the left-wing USPD vital in securing the necessary Reichstag majority.

The first Wirth cabinet, which took office on 10 May 1921, was based on the three parties of the Weimar Coalition: Zentrum, the SPD and the DDP. The centre-right German People's Party (DVP), led by Gustav Stresemann, refused to participate, though Stresemann privately felt the Allied terms had to be accepted. The right-wing DNVP insisted the Allied terms should be flatly rejected. Apart from Wirth, the cabinet included three other members of Zentrum: Andreas Hermes (Food), Heinrich Brauns (Labour), and Johannes Gisberts (Mail), all of whom had been members of the Fehrenbach cabinet. There were also three members of the SPD: Gustav Bauer (Vice Chancellor and Treasury), Robert Schmidt (Economic Affairs), and Georg Gradnauer (Interior). The DDP had two members: Otto Gessler (Defence) and a new entrant, Walther Rathenau (Reconstruction). There were also two members with no party affiliation: Wilhelm Groener (Transport) and Friedrich Rosen, who had replaced the intransigent Walter Simons as Foreign Minister.[24]

The first Wirth cabinet was yet another minority government, with only 206 out of 459 Reichstag members. In his first speech to the Reichstag on the evening of 10 May, Wirth urged its members to accept the Allied reparations settlement. Rejection of the Allied ultimatum, he added, would mean the destruction of Germany. The Reichstag voted by a margin of 221 to 175 to accept the reparations payment total demanded by Allies, and to yield to all the other Allied demands. On 11 May, the German government sent an official diplomatic Note to the Allies fully accepting the reparations terms described in the 5 May London Ultimatum. On 30 May 1921, the German government made a payment of 1 billion gold marks to the Allied Reparations Commission, and further deposited Treasury Bonds to the value of 12 billion marks.[25] Once again, the task of making deeply unpopular decisions forced upon the country by the Allies was left to the true defenders of democracy. The opponents of the Republic, who were careful not to support any of these decisions, were thus able to portray themselves as the real German patriots, giving them a huge propaganda advantage.

The most outstanding politician brought into the cabinet for the first time was Walther Rathenau, appointed as Minister of Reconstruction. Rathenau was well known as the writer of best-selling books on economics, sociology, politics, and religion. He was also successful in the business world: his father Emil Rathenau had founded Germany's world-famous General Electric Company (*Allgemeine-Gesellschaft*, or AEG). Walther went into the family business, pioneering many technical innovations, and steering the company through a series of profitable mergers. Rathenau was undoubtedly a German patriot, but he was also a Jew, although not religiously observant. His Jewish identity made him a hate figure for the Right. He summed up his feelings about growing up Jewish in Germany succinctly: 'I am a German of Jewish origin. My people are the German people, my home is Germany, my faith is the German faith, which stands above all denominations.'[26]

Rathenau was initially outraged by the terms of the Treaty of Versailles, but he came to realise a belligerent attitude would get Germany nowhere, and so he became a firm supporter of the policy of fulfilment, believing compliance with the Allied terms, even on reparations, was the only sensible way forward for Germany, He aimed to convince the Allies to accept Germany was in a better position to make payments in goods rather than in cash and foreign currency. In the longer run, he hoped constructive diplomacy would produce further concessions by the Allies.[27]

On 19 May, Lord D'Abernon, the British Ambassador in Berlin, met with the new German Chancellor. Wirth told him the delay in forming a new government was due to his determination only to include members who were prepared to fulfil the Allied terms. He had no use for colleagues who were not as whole-hearted as he was about Germany meeting its obligations under the Treaty of Versailles. D'Abernon thought Wirth was convinced his policy was endorsed by a large majority of Germans, but warned that Wirth was 'engaged upon a task of almost super-human difficulty, without adequate assistance'.[28]

On the question of the disarmament of the paramilitary groups, the Wirth government was also determined to fulfil the Allied demands. The biggest breakthrough came in Bavaria, where on 29 June, the paramilitary group, Citizens Defence (*Einwohnerwehr*), numbering up to 300,000 men, was disarmed and disbanded, under the orders of the Allied Control Commission. For most of the time, Citizens Defence had functioned as an auxiliary police force. Its disbandment seemed to signal that the Bavarian Right was finally coming under the control of the Berlin government. However, the dissolution of paramilitary groups led to a spike in right-wing violence. Many members of Citizens

Defence went on to join other far-right underground paramilitary groups such as the League of Bavaria and Empire (*Bund Bayern und Reich*), and many other Free Corps groups.[29]

During the summer of 1921, there was a bitter struggle over the future direction of the NSDAP, and especially the role Adolf Hitler should play in it. Hitler, the leading speaker of the party, was increasingly at odds with Anton Drexler, the party leader, over strategy. Hitler still supported a revolutionary violent path to power, centred on Munich, while Drexler favoured a parliamentary route, and wanted to create a national party organisation and develop links with other like-minded right-wing nationalist parties. Drexler decided to try and recapture the direction of the party he had co-founded. Without Hitler's agreement, he opened merger talks with the recently established nationalist and antisemitic German Social Party (DSP), led by Richard Kunze, which had support in north Germany. Kunze thought Hitler was 'a fanatical would-be big shot'. Any merger was bound to weaken Hitler's previous dominant position in the NSDAP.[30]

At the same time, Drexler made overtures to Dr Otto Dickel, a schoolteacher who had founded the right-wing People's Work Community (*Völkische Werkgemeinschaft*), an Augsburg-based group, that wanted to create a racially united Greater German Reich, as outlined in Dickel's (1921) book *Die Auferstehung des Abendlandes* (*The Resurgence of the West*).[31] Drexler invited Dickel to give a speech to the NSDAP in the Hofbräuhaus, in Munich, while Hitler was away in Berlin attempting to raise funds for the party. Dickel proved a dynamic and popular speaker, arguing that what Germany needed was a classless racial community that would bring national renewal by ending Jewish domination of banking and culture.

Hitler returned to Bavaria on 10 July to attend a meeting on the merger talks with the DSP and with Dickel's People's Work Community in Augsburg. There were three hours of heated discussions, during which Dickel proceeded to take apart the existing NSDAP party programme, point by point, then criticise the name of the party as being cumbersome and misleading. Hitler became increasingly angry, interrupting Dickel constantly. At the end, he angrily stormed out of the meeting. On the next day, he informed Drexler that he had left the NSDAP with immediate effect. Contrary to popular myth, Hitler's resignation seems to have been an impulsive all-or-nothing decision, not part of a carefully thought-out plan to lead the party.[32] In a letter to the Committee of the NSDAP explaining his resignation,

Adolf Hitler: National Socialist German Workers'
Party (NSDAP) member number 3,680 – and, from
29 July 1921, the party's undisputed leader.

Hitler claimed the ideas of Dickel were incompatible with those of the NSDAP. Drexler and the committee of the NSDAP realised Hitler's resignation would probably spell the end of the party, and in a climb down, on 13 July, asked Hitler what conditions would be required for him to rejoin the party. Hitler's key demands were: to be appointed as chair of the NSDAP with dictatorial power; to fix the party headquarters finally in Munich, to accept the party programme was unalterable, and that all merger talks with other parties ceased.[33]

Drexler and the Committee of the NSDAP accepted all of Hitler's conditions unconditionally. Hitler had turned a situation that seemed to herald his downfall into a triumph, something he would repeat many times in future. On 26 July, Hitler rejoined the party as member number 3,680. An Extraordinary Meeting of the NSDAP took place in the Hofbräuhaus on 29 July, attended by 554 party members who overwhelmingly endorsed Hitler as the new and undisputed leader of the NSDAP. The Führer party under Hitler's absolute leadership was born.

On the day of Hitler's triumph, an anonymously written leaflet, entitled: 'Adolf Hitler – Traitor?', was circulated in Munich. It accused Hitler of being a demagogue whose only talent was a crude propaganda speaking style. It further alleged he was being run 'by sinister men in the shadows in Berlin', even suggesting he was in the hands of 'Jewish conspirators', who had infiltrated into the NSDAP to weaken the party. What is more, the leaflet suggested Hitler was a megalomaniac, incapable of accepting anyone else as an equal. Questions were also raised as to who financed Hitler's 'lavish lifestyle', which supposedly included being chauffeured around Munich in a limousine to his many speaking engagements.[34]

At this stage of his political career, Hitler was still primarily a brilliant public speaker and local Munich celebrity. He was seemingly content to be the 'drummer' for the right-wing nationalist movement in Bavaria and thought he was merely laying the ground for a great leader to emerge. In an interview in May 1921, with the Pan German newspaper *Deutsche Zeitung* (*German News*), Hitler claimed that he was not a leader who would save 'a Fatherland that was sinking into chaos', but only an agitator who understood how to rally the masses.[35]

Soon after taking full control of the NSDAP, Hitler founded his own paramilitary organisation, the Stormtroopers (*Sturmabteilung*, or SA). This group had evolved from the loosely formed security guards that had been deployed in 1920 to protect Hitler from 'Marxist hecklers' during his many speeches in Munich's rowdy beer halls. These security forces soon became formally known as the 'Gymnastics and Sports Division' of the party. A key figure in the transformation of this group into what became, on 10 September, the Stormtroopers was the Reichswehr Captain Ernst Röhm, who had joined the DAP in 1919, as member number 623. This 'tough guy' and bully boy had been wounded several times in the war, and retained the scars of battle on his nose and cheek. He was well known locally as the head of a secret association of army officers known as the Iron Fist, a group that had certainly had a hand in political murders in the early 1920s. Röhm was also the political adviser to Colonel Franz von Epp, who commanded all the German infantry troops stationed in Munich. Through him, Röhm had built up secret stores of arms. It seems likely Röhm, who was an excellent organiser, used army funds to assist the rapid expansion of the SA, and he brought to the Nazi movement a considerable number of officers and men who had seen action with the Free Corps. Hitler greatly admired Röhm, and had no objection to the fact he was a homosexual, which was, of course, illegal at that time. The Stormtroopers not only protected the meetings and rallies of the NSDAP, but started to spread fear and terror at the meetings of their key opponents, especially communists, social democrats and Jews. The SA became an integral part of the party machine and its members were soon called Brownshirts (*Braunhemden*), because of the colour of their uniforms.[36]

In the violent atmosphere of the early years of Weimar there was a noticeable increase in violent crime. On 21 August, the Berlin police arrested the notorious serial killer Karl Grossmann, nicknamed the 'Berlin Butcher', after bursting into his apartment in response to phone calls from neighbours who had heard blood-curdling screams. The police found a young woman prostrate on a bed, recently brutally murdered. After his arrest, Grossmann confessed to killing 20 women, dismembering their corpses, and even selling their flesh in his butcher's shop.[37] The case attracted huge publicity. Grossmann hanged himself in his prison cell on 5 July 1922, before a verdict was reached in what the press had called the 'Trial of the Century'.[38]

Another sensational murder case highlighted by the press was that of the homosexual paedophile Fritz Haarmann, known as the 'Vampire of Hanover', who committed the sexual assault, murder, and body dismemberment of at least 24 young boys and men aged 10–22, between 1918 and 1924. During his sensational trial, which received worldwide press attention, Haarmann admitted that his preferred method of murder was biting the throats of his victims, as he strangled them. He was executed by guillotine in April 1925.[39] The Haarmann case was one of the inspirations, along with another famous Weimar serial killer, Peter Kürten, for the fictional serial child-killer Hans Beckert, played by Peter Lorre in the famous Fritz Lang film *M – Eine Stadt sucht einen Mörder* (*M – A City Searches for a Murderer*) released in 1931, which became the blueprint of the serial-killer film.

Serial killers were seen by the Right as a product of a 'sick' Weimar culture, but the murder rate in Weimar Germany was around the same level as that in Britain and France, and much lower than the USA. The biggest increase in crime in the Weimar years was not in murders, but in thefts, with criminal offences for crimes of this type increasing from 348,247 in 1919 to 823,902 in 1923, a period of severe economic distress.[40]

Due to what was called the 'Weimar crime wave', countless newspaper articles concentrated on what should be done about the repeat offender, known as the 'incorrigible criminal', who was seen as the most likely to commit further offences. Weimar criminologists debated whether such criminals had a genetic or racial propensity to commit crime, an idea greatly influenced by the book *L'Uomo Delinquente* (*The Criminal Man*) by the Italian doctor Cesare Lombroso, who claimed some people were born criminals, and even exhibited similar physical characteristics.[41] On the other hand, there was a growth in psychiatric research on the motivations for criminal behaviour during the Weimar years, which highlighted the social causes of crime. These tended to view criminals as normal people whose criminal behaviour was due to personal circumstances rather than a genetically formed abnormal personality.[42]

It is, perhaps, surprising to realise that most Weimar judges, lawyers, and criminologists favoured prison reform, and a revision of sentencing policy. The 1923 Law on Fines advocated the use of fines in place of short-term prison sentences. First-time offenders also benefited from the increased use of suspended sentences. The worst punishments were reserved for habitual offenders, and those committing the most serious crimes, especially murder. Contrary to popular myth, Weimar judges offered much more lenient sentences in general, not just to political offenders on the Right.[43]

Political violence and murder, however, showed no sign of reducing. Since his messy libel case against Karl Helfferich in the early months of 1920, Matthias Erzberger had gone into semi-retirement. In late August

1921, he was enjoying a summer vacation in Bad Peterstal-Griesbach, a spa town in the Black Forest, in the west of Baden-Württemberg, blissfully unaware an ultra-nationalist death squad called Organisation Consul (OC) was carefully planning his assassination. The operation was masterminded by Manfred von Killinger, a former member of the Ehrhardt Navy Brigade led by Hermann Ehrhardt, which had played a key role in the 1920 Kapp Putsch. The OC, a secret society and death squad, drew up a hit list of political opponents, and had three key aims: (1) to combat the 'anti-national' Weimar Constitution; (2) to set up secret tribunals that would order the execution of defined 'traitors'; (3) to liquidate parliamentarians, Social Democrats and Jews. It is estimated the group was responsible for 354 political murders.[44]

Erzberger, who had signed the Armistice on 11 November 1918, and was a former 'soak the rich' Finance Minister, ticked all the boxes as a key target for assassination. Killinger recruited Heinrich Tillessen and Heinrich Schulz to conduct his cold-blooded murder. Tillessen and Schulz had both been members of the Ehrhardt Naval Brigade, and participated in the Kapp Putsch before finding a safe haven in Bavaria.[45]

On 26 August, despite cloudy weather, Erzberger went for a walk with his Zentrum fellow-member of the Reichstag, Carl Diez, in the Black Forest. They were soon followed by Tillessen and Schulz, who fired two shots at Erzberger's head and back. He fell down an embankment, and the assassins followed him, finishing him off with two head shots. Diez was also shot and seriously injured, but he survived. False passports helped the assassins to flee to Hungary, whose government refused to extradite them back to Germany.[46]

Such was the toxic nature of Weimar politics that the brutal assassination of Erzberger produced a mixed reaction. On the centre left, there was a tremendous outcry. Numerous protest rallies were organised by the Social Democrats, the USPD and the Communists. In Berlin, 100,000 people turned out to express their outrage. Among the other mainstream parties, the murder was also unambiguously condemned. On the Right, however, a substantial minority greeted the murder with shameless glee. Hitler gave a tasteless speech in Munich in September which, identifying Erzberger as a November Criminal, essentially saying he had got what he deserved. The *Magdeburgische Zeitung* (*Magdeburg News*) expressed 'abhorrence' for the murder, but added that Erzberger had been a 'political racketeer and gambler' who had made numerous political enemies.[47]

overleaf The state funeral of the murdered Catholic
Centre Party politician Matthias Erzberger, shot to
death in August 1921 by right-wing assassins of the
ultra-nationalist Organisation Consul.

The murder had a dramatic impact on the attitude of Gustav Stresemann, the leader of the DVP, who had previously been lukewarm towards the Weimar Republic. Stresemann publicly denounced Erzberger's assassination, and repudiated the negative attitude of the extreme Right towards the Republic. Stresemann now declared that the DVP recognised the Weimar Constitution as the legally established basis of German government, and he promised to defend it against all illegal attacks.[48]

On 29 August, President Ebert, realising a stronger response against the violence of the Right was necessary, issued a presidential decree, using his power under Article 48 of the Constitution, which empowered civil authorities to ban any newspaper which incited people to alter the Constitution.[49] Much public wrath was directed against the right-wing Bavarian government, led by Gustav von Kahr, after it became clear the murder had been planned in Munich. Kahr made the situation even worse by refusing to carry out the new presidential decree. On 21 September, Kahr was forced to resign after members of the Bavarian parliament voted to remove him, including members of his own party, the BVP. He was replaced as Minister-President by a moderate conservative, Count Hugo Lerchenfeld-Köfering, who made no secret of his outrage at Erzberger's murder, and displayed a clear willingness to cooperate with the Wirth government in dealing with violence from the Right.[50]

The government crackdown on right-wing violence had little impact on moderating Adolf Hitler's bitter hostility to the Weimar Republic. One incident revealed this very clearly. On 14 September, Hitler, accompanied by Hermann Esser, the editor of the Nazi paper, *Völkischer Beobachter*, and a contingent of Stormtroopers, walked into the Bürgerbräukeller in Munich to violently disrupt a speech being delivered there by Otto Ballerstedt, the leader of the right-wing Bavarian League (*Bayernbund*), which campaigned for the separation of Bavaria from the rest of the Reich. Hitler was bitterly opposed to this and regarded Ballerstedt, a brilliant orator, as 'my most dangerous opponent' on the Munich speaking scene.[51] As he was delivering his speech, Ballerstedt was physically attacked by Hitler, Esser and the Stormtroopers, who dragged him off the stage. He suffered a number of facial injuries. The matter did not end there. Ballerstedt pressed charges against Hitler, who was charged with inciting public violence.[52] On 13 January 1922, Hitler was sentenced to three months in Stadelheim prison. He served his sentence, reduced in length for good behaviour, in Stadelheim from 24 June to 27 July 1922. Instead of the standard tiny cell, the deputy governor, hearing of Hitler's local fame, put him in a spacious former sick-room. He was allowed to conduct party business, writing and receiving letters and visitors twice a week.[53]

On 20 October, the League of Nations Council's 'Committee of Four' issued its report partitioning Upper Silesia between Germany and Poland, but it recommended a division which seemed sharply at odds with the outcome of the referendum. Germany was to receive 70 per cent of the land, and 57 per cent of the population, but Poland was awarded the biggest prize, the major portion of the prosperous Industrial Triangle, which contained Upper Silesia's major industries and 76 per cent of the coal mines, 90 per cent of coal reserves, 97 per cent of iron ore, 82 per cent of zinc ore, 71 per cent of lead ore, half of the steel factories, and all the largest power plants. In all, Poland gained two-thirds of the Industrial Triangle. On 15 May 1922, the German–Polish agreement, which guaranteed the existing territorial settlement for a period of 15 years, was signed in Geneva. Two League of Nations committees – the Mixed Commission and the Tribunal of Arbitration – were to oversee the execution of the complicated settlement, and the many local conflicts that developed out of it.

When the German government was formally informed of the decision of the League of Nations on Upper Silesia, it sent a shockwave through the Weimar Republic. Most Germans viewed it as yet another unfair and dictated settlement by the Allies. On 22 October, the Wirth cabinet resigned, giving expression to the indignation over the portioning of Upper Silesia which was sweeping the country. In his letter of resignation, Wirth pointed out that his government had made a huge effort to improve relations with the Allies. It had demonstrated its genuine willingness to fulfil the terms of the Versailles Treaty. This had been done in the hope of a just solution to the Upper Silesian question. Instead, the Allies had imposed a settlement that robbed Germany of the wealthy industrial areas in Upper Silesia. This would make continuing with the policy of fulfilment and future reparations payments extremely difficult.[54]

Friedrich Rosen met with Lord D'Abernon, British Ambassador to Berlin, a few days after his own resignation as Foreign Minister. Rosen claimed the British government's decision to accept the League of Nations' decision on Upper Silesia was as great a blunder as the one Germany had made over Serbia in 1914, commenting: 'We then thought the Serbian business was a local affair; you think the same over

Upper Silesia, but you are wrong.' The general view in the German government, Rosen added, was that the British had 'deliberately abandoned the German cause' and given in to French demands.[55]

President Friedrich Ebert asked Wirth to stay on as Chancellor and form a new government. Wirth favoured forming a Grand Coalition, but the DDP announced it would not join the new government and the DVP, led by Gustav Stresemann, also refused to join. Wirth therefore decided to call the new government a 'cabinet of individuals' not a coalition. On 26 October, he managed to form a new minority government, primarily composed of members of the SPD and Zentrum. In Wirth's second cabinet, there were four members of Zentrum, including himself, Andreas Hermes (Finance), Heinrich Brauns (Labour), and Johannes Giesberts (Mail), who all had been members of his first cabinet. There were three members of the SPD: Gustav Bauer (Vice Chancellor and Treasury), Robert Schmidt (Economic Affairs), and Adolf Köster (Interior). There was one member from the DDP, Otto Gessler (Defence). Walther Rathenau (Reconstruction) and Eugen Schiffer both left the cabinet, though Rathenau continued to conduct negotiations on reparations with the Allies on behalf of Wirth. Anton Fehr (Food), of the Bavarian Peasants' League (*Bayerischer Bauernbund*, BB), entered the cabinet for the first time. There was only one member with no party affiliation, Wilhelm Groener (Transport). The post of Foreign Minister was left vacant, with Wirth initially taking on the role himself. The new government won a vote of confidence by 232 to 132 in the Reichstag.[56]

In the aftermath of the Upper Silesia settlement, the value of the German mark plunged to a new low of 600 marks to £1 sterling. Inflation, a process in which prices steadily rise, and which results in a steady fall in the value of money, was spiralling ever upwards. This was made worse by the fact that the basis of currency had changed dramatically after 1918. Before the War, currencies were backed up by gold, but this gold standard was being widely abandoned, which meant the strength of currencies was increasingly determined by confidence in financial markets.

Uncertainty over German reparations payments undoubtedly made a major contribution to the fall of the Germany currency. It was already becoming clear it would be difficult for the German government to make the next two reparations payments, due on 15 January and 15 February 1922. The French government thought its German counterpart was doing nothing to deal with inflation, and was using it to deliberately avoid the payment of reparations. The general view of the French public was that Germany's economic problems were self-inflicted.[57]

By December 1921, £1 sterling was worth 1,040 marks. Default on the next reparations payment seemed certain, unless the German government could secure a loan. German industry could not provide the necessary funds, without causing huge cash flow problems, nor could the German banks, which lacked gold and foreign currency reserves. The only two places such a huge loan could be raised were in London or New York. Wall Street bankers were unwilling to get involved in the messy reparations problem at this stage, even though an American 'bail out' remained the dream of the German government. London bankers were also unwilling to offer increased credit to the German government for two reasons. First, the French government was likely to invade the Ruhr if Germany continually defaulted on reparations payments, which would make the German economic situation even worse. Second, the German government was unwilling to embark on drastic austerity measures to balance the books. In these circumstances, a large loan to Germany was viewed as much too high a risk for the City of London.[58]

On 15 December, the German government informed the Allied Reparations Commission that due to its dire economic position, and its failure to raise a foreign loan, it would be unable to make the next two reparations payments.[59] In a speech in Berlin on the same day, Joseph Wirth, the German Chancellor, claimed it was impossible for Germany to balance its budget while the French government was demanding Germany find billions in gold, when the country now lacked credit-worthiness on financial markets. The only cause for hope, he added, was that the British government was gradually beginning to accept the German explanation of why it could not make huge cash payments without access to gold, foreign loans, and currency.[60]

Friedrich Sthamer, the German Ambassador in London, immediately sent a letter to Lord Curzon, the British Foreign Secretary, which claimed the German government had 'left no stone unturned to ensure the payments of the two instalments which are shortly due' under the London Schedule of Payments. It was clear, however, that Germany could only make these payments with a loan raised in the City of London, but this had already been rejected. Accordingly, the German government now wanted a respite from the two payments due in January and February 1922.[61] On 18 December, a conference in London was urgently convened to discuss Germany's reparation payment difficulties. The Allies accepted the German government could not make the German gold mark payments due in January and February 1922, and provisionally agreed to a payment holiday, with the exact terms to be decided at a conference in Cannes in January 1922.[62]

The Weimar Republic would have undoubtedly been helped by having a stable economy, but instead it was fragile, with a rate of growth well below that of its major competitors. German growth from 1913 to 1929 was 0.3 per cent, compared to 1.4 per cent in the UK and 2.2 per cent in the USA. The state of the German budget in 1921 made grim reading. The accumulated government debt was over 400 billion marks. The government had to also bear the cost of food and wage subsidies to deal with rising inflation. The Weimar government refused to cut expenditure or to raise taxes to deal with the deficit. This kept people in jobs. Unemployment in 1921 was at a record low of 0.9 per cent.[63]

In response to rising prices, the German government simply printed money, which only served to push prices up still further. The rising cost of living was already causing industrial unrest in the Ruhr, in the autumn of 1921, and led to bread riots. There were also severe shortages of food in shops. Prices of basic goods rocketed by 40 per cent in the last three months of 1921. Inflation was worst for those on fixed incomes, as it was gradually wiping out their savings and reducing their real spending power. This affected even previously affluent pensioners and those with investments, usually people in solid salaried middle-class occupations such as academics, civil servants, and lawyers. War widows, disabled war veterans and those on welfare on fixed benefits also suffered greatly from the rise in the cost of living.

It would be wrong, however, to think that inflation was bad for everyone. Industrial workers, supported by strong unions, saw their working hours decrease, but their wages increase, often in line with inflation. Big industry also did very well, with industrial production increasing by 20 per cent in 1921–22. The rich industrialists – among them Hugo Stinnes, the richest of them all – grew much richer during the era of high inflation and spent their money on material assets, especially property and new machinery. They also had access to foreign currency loans at low interest rates, and because of inflation interest payments on these were reducing week by week.[64]

1922

·

REPARATIONS
DIFFICULTIES

·

The Allied Supreme Council met in Cannes between 6 and 13 January 1922, to consider the German government's declaration, in December 1921, of its inability to pay the next reparations payments, due in January and February of 1922. The two major Allied leaders, Aristide Briand, the French Prime Minister, and his British counterpart, David Lloyd George, were both in attendance, along with representatives of the Belgian and Italian governments. Lloyd George genuinely wanted a solution to the reparations problem, realising that until it was resolved no permanent peace or economic stability in Europe was possible.[1]

A German delegation attended the Cannes meeting, led by Walther Rathenau, who had stood in for the German Chancellor, Joseph Wirth, in previous diplomatic discussions. Rathenau established a good rapport with the Allied leaders attending the Conference, especially with Lloyd George, who was increasingly coming to the conclusion that the Treaty of Versailles could not be implemented and required revision.

The only definite decisions taken on reparations in Cannes were to postpone the January and February payments due from the German government, on two conditions. First, cash payments of 31 million gold marks (£1.55 million), were to be paid every ten days, beginning on 18 January 1922. Second, within 15 days of 13 January the German government would present a scheme of budgetary and currency reforms. The total reparations bill for 1922 was set at 720 million gold marks (£36 million gold), plus deliveries of goods totalling 1,450 million gold marks (£72.5 million gold), and occupation costs of 220 million gold marks (£11 million gold). The German delegation promised to meet all these conditions.[2]

The other major decision made at Cannes was to accept Lloyd George's recommendation for a major European Conference at Genoa, beginning in April, with the aim of resolving major economic and political issues facing Europe, in particular a strategy to rebuild the German economy and other countries in Central Europe, and to nego-

previous page Walther Rathenau, industrialist and German Foreign Minister, on his way to the World Economic Conference in Genoa, April 1922.

tiate a new diplomatic and economic relationship with the Bolshevik government in Soviet Russia.[3]

The conference in Cannes ended dramatically, when French President Alexandre Millerand recalled his Prime Minister, Aristide Briand, to Paris on 12 January, as a result of widespread criticism within the cabinet concerning his failure to adopt a stronger stance on Germany's inadequate reparations payments in Cannes, and for agreeing to the Genoa Conference without first discussing the matter with the rest of the French government. The general feeling in France was that Briand had fallen prey to the crafty Welshman, Lloyd George, during a widely reported game of golf in Cannes.

Briand decided not to demand a vote of confidence in the Chamber of Deputies and resigned. On 15 January, Raymond Poincaré became the new French Prime Minister. He was well known for his strong anti-German attitude, and his uncompromising stance on French rights under the Treaty of Versailles. This fitted in well with the current state of French public opinion. Poincaré, a former President and a former chair of the Reparations Commission, was frustrated by the continual German failure to pay reparations, and he thought the German government was determined to find any means available to deliberately avoid reparations payments. He believed the German government was deliberately printing money to stoke inflation and engineer a deliberate collapse in the German mark.[4]

Lloyd George described Poincaré as 'cold, reserved, rigid, with a mind of unimaginative and ungovernable legalism. He had neither humour nor good humour. He was not concerned about a just, and least of all a magnanimous peace. He wanted to cripple Germany and render it impotent for future aggression.'[5] This was a harsh assessment, which took little account of legitimate French apprehension about the possibility of a future German military revival. Poincaré feared that once Germany shook off the shackles of Versailles it would once more threaten European peace. He was, in fact, much more far-sighted than his contemporary critics and many later historians give him credit for. He thought the period when France was the dominant military power in Europe would be fleeting, and he had little confidence in the current German government, arguing:

> It may be true that Wirth and Rathenau are honest when they
> talk today about trying to comply with Versailles; but they do not
> speak for the real Germany, which only lets them talk that way
> because, given the political situation, it is expedient to do so. No,

the true voice of Germany sounds from the mouth of Stinnes
and Helfferich, who call the policy of compliance "suicidal mania".
Mark my words: once Germany has recovered from the catastrophe
of 1918, these men will lead again and once again, and once more
Germany will threaten the peace of Europe.[6]

On 1 February, Walther Rathenau assumed the role of German
Foreign Minister. He was a 'confirmed bachelor', who lived with his
mother and insisted Germany should fulfil its obligations under the
Treaty of Versailles. When his mother asked him why he had taken
the job of Foreign Minister, he replied: 'I had to, mama, they had no
one else.' Walter Rathenau's life exemplifies the experience of many
successful Jews in Weimar. Despite dedicating himself to the service of
his country, Rathenau was the subject of vile antisemitic and extremist
attacks from the Right of German politics. When asked why he was so
hated, he said: 'The reason is simply that you're Jewish and conducting
a foreign policy that's good for Germany. You're living proof that the
antisemitic theory about Jews being bad for Germany is nonsense.'[7]

As soon as Rathenau assumed his new responsibilities, he was
called upon to make a foreign policy decision that had far-reaching
consequences. The issue revolved around the advantages of an Eastern
as opposed to a Western European orientation of German foreign
policy. The matter had been the subject of debate in Germany since
the end of the war. The Social Democrats and liberal groups favoured
a Western orientation. Few, except on the extreme Left and among
the Nationalist Right, were looking for a rapprochement with Soviet
Russia, which the Western Allies still regarded as a pariah state.

Within the Army, however, there were some resolute supporters of
closer relations with Soviet Russia. The most important was none other
than Hans von Seeckt, the Chief of the German Army Command.
Seeckt thought French policy was hell-bent on the destruction of
Germany as a major power. Under such circumstances, a future Franco-
German war was, in Seeckt's view, inevitable. In Eastern Europe,
the situation was very different. There, Germany and Russia had a
common enemy in Poland. In a memorandum, written in 1922, entitled
'Germany's Attitude to the Russian Problem', Seeckt wrote: 'Poland is
the nub of our Eastern problem. Poland's existence is intolerable, it is
incompatible with the conditions of Germany's existence. Poland must
disappear and it will disappear thanks to its own internal weakness
and to Russia – with our help. For Poland is even more intolerable to
Russia [than] it is to us.'[8]

Both Russia and Germany were keen to restore their borders to their 1914 positions. This alone made them potential allies. A friendly Russia would enable Germany to avoid fighting a future European war on two fronts, and it would additionally provide a potential freedom of manoeuvre from the unbending policies of the Allies on reparations payments. Seeckt realised that, given Germany's current military weakness, such a policy had to be pursued with extreme caution. He felt economic links should be built up first, then secret military cooperation leading to a full-blown military alliance. In Seeckt's view, Germany and Russia would be an unbeatable combination in a future war. He hated Bolshevism but did not permit his personal political feelings to blur his perception of Russia's usefulness as a military and economic ally.[9]

Seeckt pressed these views on Baron Adolf von Maltzan, the head of the Eastern European division of the German Foreign Ministry. Here he found a willing collaborator, who also saw the logic of a Russo-German rapprochement. Maltzan, a wealthy, pleasure-loving aristocrat, who cultivated political friendships even with communists, thought Germany was in such a weak military position that it was a futile exercise trying to gain concessions from the Western Allies. A Russo-German combination was preferable, as it could function as a counterweight to the power of the Western Allies. Since 1920 Maltzan had already been working quietly but impressively to normalise relations between Soviet Russia and Germany. Joseph Wirth, the Chancellor, was also won over by Maltzan's persuasive arguments.[10]

Rathenau, however, initially expressed little enthusiasm for a Russo-German agreement, but he knew Germany had to find a way to improve its international bargaining position or remain at the mercy of the Western Allies for the near future. As a business magnate, he could also see the economic advantages for German business of closer relations with Soviet Russia. Finally, he thought a Russo-German accord might lead to the diplomatic isolation of the French government, which was already having strained relations with the British government over how to deal with German reparations. The upcoming Genoa Conference seemed a good place for Rathenau to develop these ideas with the Russian delegation.[11]

On 22 March, the Allied Commission on Reparations called on the German government to put severe limitations on the amount of paper money it was printing, declaring that 470 million gold marks and 1.45 billion gold marks worth of goods was still outstanding under the revised payment schedule agreed at the Cannes Conference. The Commission gave the German government until 31 May to make these payments, and to also raise an extra 60 billion German paper marks through taxation measures to meet its further reparations obligations for the rest of 1922. In reply to the Reparations Commission, Joseph Wirth, the German Chancellor, refused to impose the demanded taxes, much to the annoyance of the Reparations Commission.[12]

Between 10 April and 19 May, the European Economic and Financial Conference was held in Genoa, the capital of the Italian region of Liguria. It was the most ambitious international gathering since 1919, with representatives of 34 countries in attendance, including those from Germany and Soviet Russia, who had both been excluded from the Paris Peace Conference. The US government refused to participate, claiming the meeting was a futile talking shop. Raymond Poincaré, the French Prime Minister, also stayed away, leaving Louis Barthou, his deputy Prime Minister, to lead the French delegation.[13] Lloyd George said the primary aim of the conference was to provide for the 'reconstruction of economic Europe', which had been 'broken into the fragments by the desolating agency of war.' The subject of reparations was deliberately left off the agenda, at the request of the French government.[14]

In a major speech at the conference, on 16 April, Walther Rathenau, the German Foreign Minister, who spoke fluent English, French and Italian, made a big impression on the delegates. Rathenau claimed that although there was no fighting 'from the Rhine to the Vistula' in Europe, peace still did not exist. There was also no disarmament as Germany had disarmed, but the rest of Europe had not. As for Germany:

> The barometer of our economic position is the value of the dollar at the Berlin bourse. At present, it hovers around 300 marks to the dollar. Let the needle start to move in the direction of 400, 500, 1,000 to the dollar and we are gone the way of Austria [whose currency had collapsed]. It will be too late to talk of reparations then: we shall have to speak of charity.[15]

After delivering his impressive speech, Rathenau, along with the rest of the German delegation, headed by Chancellor Wirth, surreptitiously slipped away from Genoa. Their destination was Rapallo, on the Italian Riviera, for secret treaty negotiations with the Soviet Russian delegation, headed by the clever and cunning Foreign Minister, Georgy Chicherin, who had earlier telephoned Rathenau in his hotel room to tell him that he would conclude an agreement with the Western Allies unless Germany accepted the Russian offer of an agreement.

Chicherin also let Rathenau know that the Western Allies had dangled the carrot of a share of German reparations payments. This was the deal breaker; Rathenau decided to sign the agreement, which risked severely damaging the already strained relations between Germany and the Western Allies, but seemed worth the risk after hearing the Russians might sign a similar agreement with France and Britain, leaving Germany completely out in the cold.[16]

The Treaty of Rapallo, signed on 16 April, was the first of Germany's major diplomatic surprises of the inter-war period. The agreement was not the result, as is often supposed, of a spur-of-the-moment flight of inspiration by Rathenau, but resulted from painstaking secret diplomacy by the German Foreign Ministry, led by Maltzan, which had already resulted in the signing of a Russo-German trade agreement on 6 May 1921, and had also led to the formal diplomatic recognition of the Soviet government by the German government.[17]

The Treaty of Rapallo was called a 'treaty of friendship', with both signatories agreeing to improve trade relations by offering each other 'most favoured' trading status, re-establishing normal diplomatic relations, and renouncing reparations claims against each other. The German government also agreed to waive indemnities and losses sustained by German citizens due to the abolition of private property in Soviet Russia. The treaty did not contain any secret military provisions, but secret military cooperation did develop in the years following.[18]

The agreement came as a huge surprise to the British and French governments. Their first reactions were a combination of anger and fear. The agreement between Europe's two political outcasts was viewed by the Western Allies as a potential menace to the European balance of power. The French government's response was particularly bitter. Poincaré voiced his objections plainly in a speech on 24 April, in his home town of Bar-le-Duc. He declared the treaty a provocation and reiterated his determination to ensure the complete fulfilment of the provisions of the Treaty of Versailles by Germany. He also warned that if the Allies could not agree how to secure their treaty rights and reparations payments, then the French government would resort to unilateral action against Germany.[19]

The British government was also deeply alarmed. Lloyd George had been trying to create an alliance of the non-socialist countries to force Soviet Russia to recognise the debts incurred by the deposed

overleaf The signing of the Treaty of Rapallo,
April 1922: German Chancellor Joseph Wirth
(second from left) with the Soviet Russian
delegates Leonid Krasin, Georgy Chicherin
(Russian Foreign Minister) and Adolph Joffe.

Tsarist regime before the 1917 Bolshevik Revolution. The release of Soviet Russia from the diplomatic ghetto gave him no pleasure whatsoever. Lloyd George had also been trying to restrain Poincaré from taking unilateral military action by occupying the Ruhr, and he thought the Treaty would only serve to gain support in France for military action.

Even in Germany, opinion on the treaty was sharply divided. Many Germans were positive, thinking it opened the way to strengthen Germany's bargaining position with the Allies. But President Ebert was outraged at the way Wirth and Rathenau had concluded a treaty of such huge significance without his knowledge or consent. Ebert was a firm supporter of a German foreign policy orientated towards Western Europe. He also felt the agreement with Soviet Russia would bolster the extreme Left in Germany. On the Right, many were horrified by the prospect of closer collaboration with Soviet communism, but among those who were anti-Polish the agreement was welcomed.[20]

A belief commonly held among the Allies was that the treaty contained secret military clauses. Both the German and Soviet governments denied this, publishing the treaty in full to pour icy water on this accusation. Yet soon after the signing of the Treaty of Rapallo, Seeckt did conclude a secret agreement with the Russian Army general staff. To conceal secret German military training and rearmament, Seeckt was granted generous funds from the German government to set up the Society for the Encouragement of Commercial Enterprises (GEFU). Under cover of this organisation, he negotiated opportunities for German military training in the use of tanks and aircraft in Soviet Russia. This led to the later creation between 1929 and 1933 of the secret Kama Tank school near Kazan, in the Soviet Union, which trained Germans in the use of modern tanks, and the Lipetsk Fighter-Pilot school, in Lipetsk, also in the Soviet Union which trained German pilots. In return, Russian officers gained valuable training in military strategy from their German counterparts. The Russian military were also commissioned to manufacture artillery ammunition, planes, and poison gas for Germany. These secret military training arrangements and armaments supply deals remained in effect throughout the Weimar years.[21]

It is principally to the credit of the British Prime Minister, David Lloyd George, that the Genoa Conference did not adjourn immediately after news broke of the signing of the Treaty of Rapallo, but nevertheless the conference ended in failure on 19 May, except for a vague commitment to keep currencies tied to gold. In the final session, Rathenau delivered a speech in which he argued Germany wanted reconciliation, stating that his desire was: 'Peace. Peace. Peace'.[22]

By the end of May, the Reichstag had still not passed a levy of 60 billion marks' worth of new taxes, as the Allies had demanded, and was showing few signs of doing so, but the other key Allied condition of releasing the Reichsbank from government control went through on 26 May by the passing of the Reichsbank Autonomy Law. For the Allies, this was seen as a useful step towards Germany getting its financial house in order. On 31 May, the Allied Reparations Commission told the German government that it would not apply additional penalties for non-compliance for the time being.[23] On 12 July, the German government asked the Reparations Commission to agree to the suspension of the remaining payments due in 1922, and gave notice that Germany could not afford to make payments in 1923 and 1924 either.[24] Ten days later, Germany accepted of an economic plan for Allied control of German finances, which involved the Allies supervising all the German government's financial departments.[25]

Meanwhile, political violence had returned to the streets of Germany. On 4 June, Social Democrat Philipp Scheidemann, the first Chancellor of the Weimar Republic, and still a Reichstag member, was walking through the Wilhelmshoehe Park in Kassel, with his daughter and his young grandson, when a man approached him, holding a syringe-like device, usually used for medical enemas, which was filled with liquid cyanide. The would-be assassin lunged towards Scheidemann, attempting to squirt the poison into his mouth and nose from close range. Scheidemann, who had received numerous death threats, always carried a gun with him, and fired two shots at his assailant, who fled the scene. Scheidemann had a very lucky escape. He fell to the ground, briefly unconscious, but had not inhaled enough of the deadly caustic to kill him. The attack was organised by a group of right-wing plotters linked to a small terror squad within Organisation Consul (OC).[26]

A second assassination attempt on a leading German politician was also being meticulously planned by OC for later in the month. The target was Walther Rathenau, the Foreign Minister, who was currently basking in a wave of public acclaim due to the signing of the Treaty of Rapallo. At 10 a.m., on the sunny morning of 24 June, Rathenau set off for work at the Foreign Ministry as usual, from his opulent villa located at 65 Königsallee, in Grunewald, one of Berlin's most beautiful and affluent suburbs. He travelled in the back seat of a chauffeured open-top limousine, without the protection of a body-guard or police motor-cyclists.

As the vehicle slowed down to negotiate a sharp S-curve on Königsallee, leading to Kurfürstendamm Avenue, another car, a large six-seater open-topped tourer, with two men in the back seat, dressed in brand new shiny long grey leather coats, and driving helmets, came out of a side road and then drew level with Rathenau's limousine. One of the passengers lifted a long-barrelled MP submachine gun and opened fire on Rathenau at close range. For good measure, the second passenger threw a hand grenade into the back seat of the vehicle. The car containing the assassins then sped off, but the vehicle broke down close to the murder scene, and they were forced to flee on foot. Rathenau's chauffeur amazingly managed to restart the car, driving the stricken Foreign Minister to a nearby police station, but he died without ever regaining consciousness. A memorial stone in the Königsallee in Grunewald now marks the scene of the crime.[27]

A huge police investigation, led by the Berlin Criminal Police, began a nationwide hunt to find Rathenau's killers. Wanted posters were fly-posted all over the country, and a 4-million-mark reward was offered for information leading to the arrest of the assassins. It soon became clear the murder had been planned by the mysterious

Organisation Consul. The two young men who had carried out the assassination were Hermann Fischer, aged 26, who threw the hand grenade into Rathenau's car, and Erwin Kern, aged 23, who fired the fatal shots. Kern was a Prussian civil servant, a former naval lieutenant, and himself a university graduate in engineering. The driver of the car was 20-year-old Ernst Werner Techow, who also came from a well-connected Berlin family, whose father was a high-ranking Berlin civil servant.[28]

The two assassins made their way to Saaleck Castle in Saxony-Anhalt, but the police soon tracked them there. On 17 July, Kern was killed in a shoot-out with the police, but Fischer shot himself. All through the Weimar years, these men were treated with revulsion by supporters of democracy, but during the Hitler years a monument was erected to the assassins on the spot where they died.[29]

The driver, Techow, was turned in to the police by his parents. In court, he claimed he had acted under duress. He said Kern had told him that Rathenau was a supporter of 'creeping communism', and one of the 'Elders of Zion', the supposed Jewish conspiracy to rule the world outlined in the *Protocols of the Elders of Zion*, a forged

Another victim of the nationalist fanatics of Organisation Consul: police arrive at the scene of the assassination of Walther Rathenau, June 1922.

antisemitic pamphlet popular among the extreme Right.[30] Techow was given a sentence of 15 years. Rathenau's mother wrote a moving letter of forgiveness to Techow's mother, which presumably assisted his defence and his lenient sentence. After his release in 1927, Techow joined the French Foreign Legion and during the Second World War, in Marseilles, he saved some Jews from deportation to Auschwitz.

Police inquiries soon revealed the three men involved in Rathenau's assassination were part of a much larger group of young men, all from affluent middle-class families. In the end, 13 other young men were tried for their involvement in Rathenau's murder. Three were acquitted, but the rest were found guilty, receiving prison sentences ranging from two to eight years; but all were released early due to amnesties. They all belonged to extreme right-wing nationalist organisations, most notably Organisation Consul, the Free Corps, and the Ehrhardt Naval Brigade.[31]

The plan to murder Rathenau was already in motion before the signing of the Treaty of Rapallo, but the conspirators admitted they shared the right-wing condemnation of the treaty and claimed it added to their determination to assassinate its main author. For these young men, using guns to 'silence the traitors' was seen as legitimate, as they did not regard the democratic Weimar Republic as their Fatherland. It is thought the mastermind behind the Rathenau assassination was Hermann Ehrhardt, who had set up Organisation Consul.[32]

The murder of Walther Rathenau sent a shock-wave through the Weimar Republic. It was his political credibility as an accomplished Foreign Minister which made his murder so shocking, not only inside Germany, but around the world. His death was made even more poignant by the realisation that this Republican martyr was deeply proud of his Jewish identity. In the Reichstag debate on the murder on 24 June, Chancellor Wirth gave an eloquent and passionate speech during which he praised Rathenau for his service to Germany, but then pointed to the area where the nationalist right-wing members sat in the Reichstag and said: 'There stands the enemy who drips his poison into the wounds of the people. There stands the enemy, and there is no doubt about it: this enemy stands on the Right!'[33]

On 27 June a state-organised memorial ceremony for Walther Rathenau was held in the Reichstag building in Berlin. It began with Beethoven's *Coriolanus Overture*. President Ebert then bowed to the coffin, and delivered a deeply moving eulogy to Rathenau. To the sound of Wagner's *Götterdämmerung*, the funeral march lamenting the untimely killing of the heroic Siegfried, the doors of the Reichstag swung open and the coffin, draped in the Republican flag, was carried outside, where a huge crowd had gathered to honour the fallen Foreign Minister. The coffin was transported in a hearse to the cemetery. In 1930, a left-wing journalist recalled that Rathenau's funeral was 'one of the few occasions when the German people had been willing to fight for the Republic'.[34]

On 26 June, the day before the funeral, President Ebert, using Article 48 of the Constitution, issued the Law for the Protection of the Republic, which was adopted on 18 July in the Reichstag by a vote of 303 to 102, with the votes against coming from the DNVP, the KPD and the BVP. It laid out heavy penalties for terrorists and their accomplices who glorified, encouraged, or approved of open violence against the republican form of government, including the death penalty for anyone conspiring to kill a member of the government, and it empowered the government to forbid public meetings advocating revolution. The law also set up a Special Court for the Protection of the Republic.[35]

Ebert made clear the new law was directed against political violence on the Right. Not surprisingly, powerful right-wing elements in the Bavarian parliament bitterly opposed the new law. They forced the Bavarian Prime Minister, Count Hugo Lechenfeld, to issue an emergency decree, effectively suspending the law in Bavaria. President Ebert informed Lechenfeld that the Bavarian decree conflicted with the Weimar Constitution, and warned he would use Article 48 to bring Bavaria in line with new federal law. The Bavarian government agreed to withdraw its decree, no later than 18 August, after Ebert had granted some concessions to the Bavarian police and courts in administering the law. Political elements on the Right in Bavaria continued to heap abuse on Lechenfeld for caving in to Ebert, and, on 18 November, Lechenfeld was compelled to resign. He was replaced by Eugen von Knilling, a moderate member of the BVP, who was a mere figurehead for the right-wing Gustav Ritter von Kahr, who had been deposed as Prime Minister in September 1921 but remained the acknowledged leader of the Bavarian monarchists and a key wire-puller in right-wing circles in Bavaria.[36]

Meanwhile, Germany's reparations payment difficulties continued. During July, prices inside Germany rose by 50 per cent, which was then accepted as the beginning of the hyperinflation period.[37] A litre of milk had cost 7 marks in April 1922, but rose to 16 marks in August, and then to 26 marks by mid-September. The prices of other basic goods rose

overleaf The state memorial ceremony
for the murdered Walther Rathenau, held
in the Reichstag.

in a comparable manner. The German government response to rising inflation was to continue printing money, with the number of marks in circulation rising from 35 billion in 1919 to 200 billion in 1922.[38]

Hyperinflation led in turn to a dizzying fall in the value of the German mark, which the Reichsbank, lacking gold and foreign currency reserves, was powerless to stop. On 29 July, the mark hit a new low of 650 to 1 US$. The German government claimed this fall in the value of German currency was linked to the demand by the Allies for cash reparations payments. State and local authorities began to issue money tokens called *Notgeld* to replace payments in worthless paper marks.

Earlier in the month, the German government had declared that its economic problems made it impossible to meet its reparations payments without a foreign loan, and asked the Allied Reparations Commission to extend the moratorium of German reparations payments to all of 1923 and 1924 or there would be financial disaster in Germany.[39] On 1 August, the British government published the Balfour Note, written by acting Foreign Secretary A.J. Balfour, which declared Britain would give up its reparations claims against Germany if the US government would do the same for Britain's war debts, which amounted to £850 million, with added interest.[40] The Balfour Note was universally condemned in the USA as an unworkable solution to Germany's reparations payment difficulties. Andrew Mellon, the US Secretary of State, said the Balfour Note was 'an irritating piece of nonsense', which came perilously close to a British repudiation of its own war debts to the USA.[41]

On 5 August, Joseph Wirth, the German Chancellor, sent a letter to David Lloyd George, explaining that Germany's economic position had deteriorated even further in recent weeks. He admitted the German government's 'policy of fulfilment' was becoming deeply unpopular with the public, and the continued fall in the value of the German mark was not only making cash payments of reparations impossible, but also restricting the payments in goods. He further warned that 'deliveries of coal imposed upon us are excessive and cannot be continued'. In his view, 'German democracy is doomed unless a stop can be put to the further pauperisation of the German people.' Members of the middle classes had become beggars, owing to the rising inflation and currency depreciation. In conclusion, Wirth requested the Allies to revise reparations demands to a level that was affordable for Germany.[42]

The Allies recognised the urgent need to discuss Germany's current payment difficulties. Between 7 and 14 August, the London Allied Conference on Reparations took place in 10 Downing Steet, attended by representatives of Britain, France, Belgium, and Italy. The two major Allied leaders, Raymond Poincaré and David Lloyd George, were present. During the proceedings, a sharp divergence of views between the French and British governments about how to deal with Germany's payment problems became clear. Poincaré made clear the French government felt the German government was not showing much intention of maintaining its reparations payments, or meeting its commitments on disarmament or prosecuting war criminals. On the question of reparations, Poincaré accepted Germany faced economic difficulties, but he pointed out the Germans constantly 'cried aloud' about them, while the German government showed no sign of reining in its public expenditure or reducing the money in circulation. Poincaré felt an occupation of the Ruhr was something that should be undertaken to force Germany to pay. As for a further payment holiday, Poincaré first demanded productive pledges from the German government, including Allied control of forests and mines in the Ruhr.[43]

In response, Lloyd George said there had been significant disarmament in Germany, with the army now reduced to 100,000 men, as called for by the Treaty of Versailles. Germany had also paid £500 million in occupation costs to date. The dramatic fall in the mark did show something was seriously wrong with the German economy, but it was no use applying further economic or military sanctions against Germany, unless the effect was to produce more money to make reparations. As for the proposed occupation of the Ruhr, Lloyd George though this was very risky, as it might lead to a general strike in the region, while the seizure of mines and forests was likely to involve excessive costs of administration. In the view of Lloyd George, Poincaré's proposals would involve serious political trouble with Germany, would produce no cash, and would risk triggering economic catastrophe in the country.[44]

On 14 August, the Conference on Reparations ended without any agreement on Germany's request for a further payment holiday. On the next day, the German government once more defaulted on its reparations payments, claiming it could not afford to pay. The downward tumble of the mark continued. On 24 August, it plummeted to a new all-time low of US$2,000 to 1 mark, or 9,000 to the British pound. On 31 August, the Allied Reparations Commission decided to grant Germany an exceptional six-month moratorium on reparations payments.[45]

On the domestic German political scene, the SPD and the USPD continued to move towards a reunion. A voting arrangement had already been agreed in the Reichstag. The Rathenau assassination had shown the Social Democratic movement that it now needed to be united to defend Weimar democracy. On 6 September, a joint SPD–USPD programme was produced. Socialism, they said, remained the ultimate objective. In the short term, however, there was a more pressing need to defend the Republic. The two parties agreed the Weimar government offered the working class the best opportunity for social reform. Both parties were also pledged to resist all attempts to restore the monarchy. The Reichswehr should be transformed into a bulwark to defend the Republic. The judiciary needed to be purged of all reactionary and anti-republican elements. They also proposed a wealth tax and profit sharing in industry. On foreign policy, they felt the conciliatory policy of Rathenau should be continued.

On 18 September, the annual conference of the SPD took place in Augsburg. President Ebert gave the merger between the SPD and the USPD his personal blessing, and Otto Wels, the SPD party chair, stressed the importance of uniting the two socialist parties. The SPD vote on the merger was passed unanimously. Two days later, the USPD held their own party congress in Gera. There was more heated discussion there over the wisdom of the merger from the extreme Left of the party. Georg Ledebour, their chief spokesperson, was against the merger because he thought the SPD had long ceased to be a socialist party, and he felt the KPD was closer in ideology to the USPD. In the end, the USPD voted by 192 to 9 in favour of the union. The small dissident group, led by Ledebour, broke away to form a small splinter organisation. The newly merged party at first took the name of the United Social Democratic Party but reverted in 1924 to the name SPD. The merged party initially had three joint leaders: Hermann Müller and Otto Wels (SPD) and Wilhelm Dittmann (USPD). A convention of the merged party took place in Nuremberg on 24 September 1922.[46]

During the year there had also been demands for the first popular election of the German President. On 5 October, the Wirth government proposed such an election should take place at the beginning of December. The DDP and the DVP both voiced opposition to this proposal, arguing a presidential contest at this time was bound to add more passion and turmoil to the already complicated economic and political situation. The right-wing conservative DNVP, however, were in favour of a presidential election, and even suggested putting up war hero Paul von Hindenburg as their candidate. The Social Democrats also favoured an election, as they thought President Ebert was certain to win. The matter was settled by a proposal by Zentrum for a constitutional amendment which recommended Ebert's term should be extended by a vote in the Reichstag until the end of June 1925. The Zentrum leadership called attention to Ebert's truly national, non-partisan outlook. On 24 October, the motion to extend Ebert's term of office to 1 July 1925 was passed by 314 to 76 votes in the Reichstag.[47]

There were also significant political changes in Britain and Italy in October 1922. The governing coalition of Conservatives and Liberals, led by David Lloyd George, which had been in power since 1916, dramatically broke down after a meeting of Conservative MPs at London's plush Carlton Club. The most senior Conservative to rebel against Lloyd George was the Foreign Secretary, Lord Curzon, who felt the Liberal Prime Minister had followed his own foreign policy, which had often bypassed the Foreign Office.[48]

On 23 October, Conservative leader Andrew Bonar Law, although already suffering from cancer, became the new British Prime Minister at precisely the moment the reparations problem was reaching its most critical stage. News of Lloyd George's fall was greeted by the German government with some misgivings, as it was felt Lloyd George had accepted that Germany could not pay everything it was liable for under the terms of the Treaty of Versailles, and because he had been a restraining influence on the French government. Poincaré, the French Prime Minister, saw Lloyd George's demise as an ideal opportunity to push the British government to adopt a much stronger line over Germany's tardy payment record on reparations, but Bonar Law, who had a business background, was just as keen to see a restoration of the German economy as Lloyd George had been.

In Italy, on 28 October, Benito Mussolini's right-wing National Fascist Party (PNF) marched into Rome and 'seized power' – or at least that was the myth Mussolini liked to project ever afterwards. In fact, the Italian Army was strong enough to have stopped Mussolini's Blackshirts getting to Rome. It was King Victor Emmanuel III who had decided to depose the democratic government led by Luigi Facta, and invite Mussolini to form a new government. Mussolini, who was supported by the military, big business and the political Right, took office as Prime Minister on 31 October, with the blessing of the head of state. It was a peaceful transfer of power within the terms of the Italian Constitution.[49]

Adolf Hitler strongly identified with the idea of a dynamic right-wing nationalist leader marching to the capital city to rescue a divided nation. On 3 November, the leading Nazi, Hermann Esser, in a speech in the Hofbräuhaus in Munich, said: 'Germany's Mussolini is Adolf Hitler'. This was the moment when the idea of Hitler as Germany's 'saviour' emerged among his followers.[50] On 21 November, he made his first appearance in the pages of the *New York Times*, in a brief profile, with the headline: 'New Popular Idol Rises in Bavaria', though his first name was spelled incorrectly as 'Adolphe'. The article highlighted Hitler's 'extraordinary powers of swaying crowds to his will' through his speeches, and reported him as the leader of the 'well disciplined' National Socialist German Workers' Party whose members, the 'swastika wavers' (*Hakenkreuzler*), 'obey orders implicitly'. The party programme was described as 'half a dozen negative ideas, clothed in generalities'. Hitler was against Jews, communists, Marxist socialists, Bavarian separatists, the Treaty of Versailles, and the prohibitive high cost of living, but the article woefully misjudged the virulence of his antisemitism, claiming: 'He was merely using antisemitic propaganda as a bait to catch followers and keep them aroused.' The article concluded by predicting the party was 'bound to bring Bavaria into a renewed clash with the Berlin government, as long as the German government goes through the motions of trying to live up to the Versailles Treaty.'[51]

Meanwhile, the reparations problem was rapidly approaching a crisis. The German government refused to allow the coal mines and forests in the Ruhr to come under Allied control as security over future payments. The British representative on the Reparations Commission, Sir John Bradbury, warned the British Treasury, on 6 October, that unless the German mark was soon stabilised a breakdown of the German currency would follow and bring about complete economic collapse.[52]

On 2 November, in yet another attempt to break the reparations deadlock, the German government, with the blessing of the Reparations Commission, convened a conference in Berlin of international economic experts, including representatives from Britain, the Netherlands and Belgium, to discuss the country's dire economic problems. On the next day, the German mark hit a new low of 6,156 to 1 US dollar. On 8 November, the economic experts at the Berlin Economic Conference submitted a detailed report to the German government, which outlined government responsibility for the collapse of the mark, by adopting the twin policies of high public expenditure and printing money. They recommended stabilising the mark as the key priority, but also pointed out there could be no monetary stability until a solution to the reparations question had been worked out, as German non-payments and non-delivery of goods in kind had caused the current payment system to break down. The experts suggested a two-year freeze on reparations payments to avoid economic collapse.[53]

On 11 November, Lord D'Abernon, the British Ambassador in Berlin, held a meeting with the German Chancellor. Wirth said the meeting of the committee of experts had produced no positive results, nor had his talks with menbers of the Reparations Commission, who had attended the Conference. Everything had been done in too much of a hurry to produce anything of merit, he added. On 13 November, the German government sent a Note to the Reparations Commission suggesting the stabilisation of the mark was a precondition of financial reform, and proposed to devote a substantial proportion of the Reichsbank's gold reserves to effecting this. The Note further proposed the formation of an international syndicate with the co-operation of the German Reichsbank to secure a loan of 50 million gold marks to help Germany regain financial stability, and finally requested a moratorium on reparations payments for up to four years. The Reparations Commission, in reply, argued these proposals were not detailed enough to grant a lengthy payment holiday.[54]

On 14 November, Joseph Wirth resigned as the German Chancellor, along with his cabinet. His downfall had followed weeks of political crisis. President Ebert had been trying to get Wirth to create a Grand Coalition, and bring into his cabinet the DVP, led by Gustav Stresemann, as the party was supported by many leading industrialists. Wirth submitted this proposal to the leaders of the newly merged United Social Democratic Party, but he found them bitterly opposed, believing the DVP would seek to increase the eight-hour working day and demand public expenditure cuts. Wirth attached such importance to Social Democratic involvement in his government that he decided to resign rather than form another cabinet without them.

On 16 November, President Ebert asked Dr Wilhelm Cuno to form a new government.[55] Cuno was a man of refined manners and considerable charm, who had been a member of the DVP up until the Kapp Putsch, and who afterwards had left the party. He was not even a member of the Reichstag at this point. He had a business background, being head of the Hamburg American Line (HAPAG), a transatlantic shipping enterprise, indeed, the largest German shipping company. He had already represented the German government at several international conferences. Ebert felt Cuno might be able to save Germany from financial ruin and increase Germany's standing on the financial markets. As most Germans were growing tired of the instability of German party politics, the idea of a 'government of economic experts' looked appealing, and Cuno seemed admirably suited to head such a government.

Cuno opened up negotiations with various party leaders and economic experts, with the aim of creating a broad coalition government stretching across the political spectrum, but the Social Democrats refused to join his government, which soon became known either as 'the Cabinet of Personalities' or the 'Business Cabinet', emphasising it was not a coalition of political parties. Cuno became German Chancellor on 22 November 1922 via a presidential decree issued by Ebert under Article 48 of the Weimar Constitution, and without a vote of confidence in the Reichstag. He was the first Chancellor in the Weimar years who was not a member of a political party, and the first from a business background.

The Cuno cabinet was effectively a centre-right coalition, made up of two members of Zentrum, Andreas Hermes (Finance) and Heinrich Brauns (Labour), two members of the DDP, Rudolf Oeser (Interior) and Otto Geisler (Defence); two representatives of the DVP, Johann Becker (Economic Affairs) and Rudolf Heinz (Vice-Chancellor and Justice), and one member of the BVP, Karl Stingl (Post). There were also five Independent members: Wilhelm Cuno himself as Chancellor, Friedrich von Rosenburg as Foreign Minister, Wilhelm Groener at the Ministry of Transport, Hans Luther at Food and Agriculture, and Heinrich Albert as Minister for Reconstruction. The cabinet appointment that caused the greatest controversy was that of Johannes Becker, as Minister of Economics, who belonged to the right-wing DVP and was a member of the board of directors of the Rheinische Steel Corporation (*Rheinische Stahlwerke*) and it was thought by Social Democrats he would seek to water down employment reforms.[56]

There was no written coalition agreement for Cuno's government. The political parties represented in his cabinet provided his core support in the Reichstag, but the survival of his government was heavily dependent on the toleration of the USPD and the DNVP. Cuno was not able to submit the new government to a vote of confidence in the

Reichstag. As a compromise, on 24 November, the Reichstag agreed to 'take notice' of Cuno's government declaration, which included Wirth's motto: 'First bread, then reparations'. Only the Communists voted against Cuno's Reichstag declaration. In his speech to the Reichstag, Cuno promised to secure the proposals contained in the German Reparations Note of 13 November and to do all he could to stabilise the mark.[57]

Cuno hoped for a favourable response from the Allies on the reparations payments problem, but the French government was in no mood to make concessions. If Germany continued to default, an occupation of the Ruhr now seemed certain in a matter of weeks. Poincaré still believed Germany was well able to pay, but was deliberately bankrupting its currency for the purpose of avoiding payment. For this reason, he refused to grant the German government the moratorium on payments it was demanding. Central to Poincaré's policy was the notion that the German government needed to offer 'productive pledges' of goods, a plan that involved the French seizure of German industry in the Ruhr. Poincaré was not bothered about the economic injury to the German economy threatened by the loss of the industrial Ruhr, but this was something that deeply alarmed the British government.[58]

Between 9 and 11 December 1922, the second London Conference on Reparations took place, attended by the four main Allied leaders, Andrew Bonar Law (Britain), Raymond Poincaré (France), Benito Mussolini (Italy), and Georges Theunis (Belgium). Mussolini, attending an international conference as Italian Prime Minister for the first time, was greeted by a large crowd of Fascist supporters at Claridge's Hotel, where he was staying.

A diplomatic Note from the new German Chancellor was read by the Allied leaders. Cuno, who described himself as 'a man with practical experience of economic life', emphasised that what the German government needed from the London Conference was 'a clear, decisive pronouncement' on 'the reparations question which will be satisfactory to all parties'. He also reiterated his intention to carry out the economic conditions laid out in the German Note of 13 November 1922 for the stabilisation of the mark and the final settlement of the reparations problem.[59]

The Allied leaders held three meetings during the Conference. The recommendations incorporated into the German Note of 13 November were unanimously rejected as much too vague even to warrant detailed discussion. Bonar Law said if an agreement could be reached at the conference, which would lead to a full settlement of the reparations question, the British government would be prepared to agree to a remission of Allied debts owed to Britain. Poincaré welcomed this offer, but he stressed the stabilisation of the mark and economic guarantees from the German government had to precede any offer of a suspension on German payments. Mussolini, adopting a particularly pro-German line, proposed a scaling down of total German reparations payments to 50 billion gold marks, a two-year moratorium on payments, and the granting of a loan to Germany for 4 billion gold marks to meet its payments.

In the end, the Allies could not agree on a common policy based on any of these proposals. Poincaré warned that the French government intended to proceed with the occupation of the Ruhr on 15 January 1923, jointly with the Allies if possible, or alone if necessary. Bonar Law refused to accept Poincaré's view that the Ruhr should be occupied to guarantee future German payments of reparations. At this point, the meeting was abruptly adjourned. The sharp differences between the British and French governments were reported in the press during the days following the end of this inconclusive conference.[60]

On 14 December, Bonar Law gave an outline in the House of Commons of the Allied discussions at the London Reparations Conference. He pointed out that Germany was near to economic collapse, with the mark in free fall, and had continued to fail to make the required payments, but he refused to accept the French government's view that the German government was following a deliberate scheme of cheating the Allies by wilfully bankrupting its own currency. At the same time, Bonar Law acknowledged the French government was understandably frustrated about the continued failure of Germany to pay, and he agreed they must take stronger enforcement measures. The British government, Bonar Law added, could not support the occupation of the Ruhr, which would have the effect of jeopardising future reparations payments.[61]

The only thing now standing in the way of a French military occupation of the Ruhr was a legal pretext for such action. The Reparations Commission immediately took care of this, by pointing out that Germany was already in arrears to the tune of 2,254 gold marks (£113 million) in cash payments, and needed to make a payment of 500 gold marks (£25 million) by 15 January 1923. Furthermore, on 2 December 1922, the German government had informed the Reparations Committee it was unable to make full timber deliveries under the existing Schedule of Payments, requesting an extension of these deliveries until 1 April 1923. The Germans had also failed to deliver 140,000 telegraph poles. It was the default on deliveries of timber that was used by the Reparations Commission as the evidence of German default.[62]

On 18 December, Friedrich Sthamer, the German Ambassador in London, met with Sir Eyre Crowe, the Permanent Under-Secretary at the British Foreign Office. Sthamer informed him that the German Chancellor was extremely disappointed his proposals had been summarily rejected at the London Conference. What made the German government despair was to see there was no goodwill on the part of the French government, which found all the proposals put forward by the German government unsatisfactory. This led to a reluctance of the German government to propose anything at all.[63]

On 26 December, by a vote of 3 to 1, the Allied Reparations Committee, meeting in Paris, declared the German government to be in voluntary default of the terms of the Treaty of Versailles, due to the delay in timber deliveries to France. It was Sir John Bradbury, the British government representative, who cast the only dissenting voice, arguing the delay in timber deliveries was due to the desperate state of Germany's finances.[64] On the next day, the German government was informed of the decision of the Reparations Commission. Cuno argued the missed timber deliveries were only temporary, but most Germans now believed a French military occupation of the Ruhr was certain to happen within weeks.[65]

On 31 December Wilhelm Cuno, the German Chancellor, gave a speech in Hamburg, in which he expressed regret that the German proposals to stabilise the mark in the German Note of 13 November had been categorically rejected by the Allies at the London Reparations Conference. He argued it was completely unjustified for the French government to suggest the Ruhr should now be occupied to enforce reparations payments, or as protection against the non-existent warlike intentions of Germany. Cuno then explained that he had made the following offer to the French government: 'Germany is ready in conjunction with France and with other Great Powers interested in the Rhine to enter into an agreement not to make war with one another during a generation unless empowered by a referendum. A Great Power not interested in the Rhine is to be the trustee of this arrangement.' He ended with the admission: 'France has declined this offer to my regret.'[66]

1923
·
RUHR OCCUPATION, HYPER-INFLATION AND REVOLT
·

M ost Germans were glad to see the back of 1922. It had been a year of high inflation, the downward slide of the mark, continuing political instability, and no end in sight to the bitter dispute with the Allies over reparations payments. Yet there seemed little chance things would get any better in the coming year. This was borne out by events in January, when the issue of Germany's reparations payments occupied centre stage once again.

The Allies held a make-or-break reparations conference in Paris between 2 and 4 January, to discuss the question of German defaults on timber and coal deliveries. The proceedings were opened on 2 January by Raymond Poincaré, the French Prime Minister, who was in no mood to compromise, and outlined his firm determination to secure deliveries of coal and timber by occupying the Ruhr. Andrew Bonar Law, the British Prime Minister, submitted a plan suggesting Germany paid nothing for two years, then 2.5 billion gold marks per annum for the two years following this moratorium. After 10 years, payments would increase to 3.5 billion gold marks. In return, the German government would have to stabilise the mark, agree to some financial supervision by the Allies, and accept sanctions for non-compliance. The conference then adjourned so that Allied delegates could consider the British plan.[1]

On the next day Poincaré launched a detailed attack on Bonar Law's proposals, declaring them 'completely unacceptable'.[2] The Belgian government was 'horrified' at British leniency towards Germany. The Italian government also rejected the British plan, which was generally viewed by the Allies as 'misjudged'. This view was even shared by Lord Curzon, the British Foreign Secretary.[3] On 4 January, the Paris Reparations Conference ended in failure, primarily because Poincaré stuck uncompromisingly to his position that the French government would act on its own in relation to extracting reparations payments from Germany while Bonar Law's proposals were seen as too lenient towards Germany.

On 9 January the Reparations Commission agreed, by a majority

previous page 'Limit of the occupied zone':
a sign marking the boundary of
the French occupied zone in the Ruhr.

of 3 to 1, with the British representative, Sir John Bradbury, abstaining, that Germany had now 'voluntarily defaulted on coal deliveries'. The infringement seemed minor as the Germans had delivered 11.7 million tons of coal in 1922, instead of the agreed figure of 13.8 million.[4] On 10 January, the French government informed the German government that due to a breach in Paragraph 18 of the Treaty of Versailles, namely the defaults on coal and timber deliveries, territorial sanctions would now be imposed, with the French and Belgians sending in troops to the Ruhr 'sufficient enough to secure these shipments'.[5]

On 11 January, the French and Belgians sent an Inter-Allied Mission for Control of Factories and Mines (*Interalliée de Contrôle des Usines et des Mines*), composed of 72 engineers, into the Ruhr. Their primary function was to direct the operation of the Rhenish-Westphalian Coal Syndicate, which ran the mines in the region, but this was thwarted by the decision of this body to move its offices and administration from Essen to Hamburg, two days before the occupation began. The Franco-Belgian occupation of the Ruhr was undertaken by between 70,000 and 100,000 French and Belgian combat troops, under the overall command of the French General Jean Degoutte, the commander of the French Army on the Rhine. At the spearhead of the occupying force was the French 32nd Infantry Division, equipped with tanks, artillery, machine guns, armoured lorries, and air support. By 16 January, Franco-Belgian forces were in control of the entire Ruhr area, as far east as the city of Dortmund.

The British government strongly objected to the occupation of the Ruhr but adopted the ambiguous policy of 'benevolent neutrality' to prevent a full diplomatic breach among the Allies. Of course, British disapproval of the French-led action in the Ruhr served to bolster German opposition, even if that was not the intended objective.[6] The British press was also extremely critical of the French government. *The Outlook* suggested that Poincaré would go down in history as 'one of the most colossal idiots, or alternatively the greatest of knaves', while *The Spectator* claimed the French government had committed 'the extremity of human folly', and *The Economist* warned the deployment of troops by France and Belgium in the Ruhr might lead to another European war.[7]

There was also widespread international condemnation. The US government withdrew its own occupying forces from the Ruhr, and the Soviet Union voiced 'indignation and protest' against the measures of what it called the 'imperialist French government'. The Polish and

overleaf French troops enter Essen,
11 January 1923, at the start of the
Franco-Belgian occupation of the Ruhr.

French and Belgian troops occupy the Ruhr
in January 1923.

Czech governments, though allies of France, both voiced opposition to the Ruhr occupation.

The Ruhr was vitally important to the German economy, containing as it did 72 per cent of Germany's coal resources, along with 54 per cent of pig iron and 53 per cent of steel production.[8] But active military resistance was out of the question for disarmed Germany. Instead, on 13 January the Reichstag voted by 283 to 12 in support of a German government policy in favour of passive resistance to the French–Belgian occupation. The Reichstag vote was preceded by an enthusiastic speech by Wilhelm Cuno, the Chancellor, who said the occupation was a 'violation of justice and in clear breach of the Treaty of Versailles'. Cuno believed the French and Belgians would find it impossible to operate the mines without German assistance. Gustav Stresemann, the leader of the DVP, called upon the German people to resist the occupation, writing: 'No menace can give France an excuse for such an attack, such a raid on German soil.'[9] Passive resistance against the Ruhr occupation was not only energetically supported by the German government and the public, but it was financed by paying wages for workers to stay at home, and by giving compensation to business owners. This generous financial package obviously assisted passive resistance. The government help was like the furlough schemes adopted by many governments in Europe to cope with the Covid-19 pandemic in 2020-21. It was not, however, financed by government borrowing, to be paid back later, but by simply printing money. During February 1923 alone, the number of notes increased to 450 billion paper marks per week.

President Ebert said it was the duty of every patriotic German to make things as difficult as possible for the invading force. His comments were greeted with widespread public support. One notable exception to this unified response was Adolf Hitler, who constantly ridiculed the policy of passive resistance, saying it was useless unless it was backed up by active resistance, including terrorist attacks and sabotage. On 11 January, in a speech to his National Socialist followers in Munich's Circus Krone, Hitler said: 'Not Down with France' but 'Down with the November Criminals'. It was they who had 'stabbed Germany in the back' at the end of the war and left Germany defenceless.[10] There was a limit to how much influence Hitler could exert on events in the Ruhr, as his National Socialist Party (NSDAP) was banned in Prussia, Baden and Saxony under the Law for the Protection of the Republic which had declared the party a danger to the state.[11]

On 19 January 1923, the German government ordered all government employees to refuse to obey the French and Belgian occupiers. The bulk of the population in the occupied zone followed the government policy of passive resistance. Economic life in the Ruhr Valley came to a standstill.[12] The Reich Coal Commissioner stopped all coal and coke deliveries to France and Belgium, dramatically reducing the amount of coal the French were getting out of the Ruhr. The German government ban on reparations deliveries was then extended to all commodities. Railway employees refused to operate lines that were not under German control, and sabotage of the railways became commonplace.[13] In a powerful speech, Gustav Stresemann of the DVP claimed the occupation of the Ruhr was an attempt by France to assert its military dominance over Europe, adding: 'There could surely be no government in the world that would tolerate such a violation of its sovereignty, and such brutal maltreatment of its citizens were it not completely defenceless. This weakens all the talk about the pretended German menace to France.'[14]

In response to German passive resistance, the French–Belgian occupying forces adopted much stronger enforcement measures. Poincaré did not hesitate to extend the occupation beyond its original boundary. The French and Belgians took control of the mines, factories, forests, customs, and government offices, with immigrant workers brought in to fill their posts. The export of goods from the Ruhr to unoccupied Germany was prohibited, and a tariff wall was erected at the borders. On 23 January, the French sealed off the Ruhr area from the rest of Germany. Many local German police forces and local civil servants were summarily dismissed. The railways were put under Franco-Belgian management. During the occupation, 147,000 Germans were expelled from the Ruhr to unoccupied Germany on the orders of General Degoutte.[15] French military courts imposed harsh punishments to all Germans who refused to cooperate. On 24 January, French occupying authorities imposed fines totalling 207,000 francs on Ruhr industrialists for failing to deliver coal. The blowing-up of a Rhine bridge in Duisburg which had killed nine people was answered by a French military court in Mainz handing out seven death sentences to the perpetrators.[16]

The worst violence during the Ruhr occupation occurred at the Krupp Works in Essen on 31 March between local workers and French troops. The disturbance began when French soldiers occupied the factory's motor sheds, intending to remove lorries for their own use. When workers blocked their path, the French opened fire indiscriminately with machine guns, killing 13 workers and wounding 40. A French military court, sitting on 8 May 1923 in Werden, sentenced the owner of the factory, Gustav Krupp von Bohlen und Halbach, and nine other directors of the company to prison sentences ranging from six months to 20 years, and fined each defendant 100 million marks, while the French commanding officer went unpunished.[17]

By the beginning of May, the German government was feeling the economic strain of financing passive resistance. The nation's central banks were using 30 huge paper factories and 1,800 printing presses to print bank notes night and day. The highest denomination paper mark bank note eventually reached 100 trillion. On 2 May, the German government sent a diplomatic Note addressed to the signatory powers of the Treaty of Versailles, the Pope and neutral countries, offering to make proposals to settle the Ruhr crisis. This move was prompted by a statement by Lord Curzon, the British Foreign Secretary, in the House of Lords, a few weeks earlier, in which he had urged the German government to try and break the diplomatic deadlock by making an offer of what amount in reparations it could pay. But the German Note offered no concrete guarantees of when reparations payments would be paid, and reaffirmed passive resistance would continue until the Ruhr was evacuated. The only concrete offer made by the German government was a pledge to pay a total of 30 billion gold marks, down from the already agreed 132 billion, of which 20 billion gold marks was promised by 1 July 1927, followed by two further payments of 5 billion gold marks on 1 July in 1929 and 1931. The first payment under this plan would not take place for four years. To expect the French government to accept this plan was completely unrealistic. On 6 May, the Franco-Belgian reply called the German Note 'a hardly concealed expression of a systematic rejection of the Treaty of Versailles'. The British government reply also stressed the German proposals were completely unrealistic.[18]

Meanwhile, acts of terrorism were occurring regularly in the Ruhr crisis, with rebel German dynamite squads blowing up bridges, railway lines and French military trains. One of the most famous members of these terrorist groups was Leo Schlageter, who was shot dead by a firing squad in Düsseldorf by French troops on 26 May, after being sentenced to death by a French military court on 10 May for carrying out a number of bomb attacks on railway lines and bridges in the Ruhr during the occupation. The case generated huge publicity because Schlageter, a former member of the Free Corps, had recently joined Hitler's National Socialist Party. On 10 June, a huge memorial for Schlageter, attended by 40,000, was held on the Königsplatz in Munich. Hitler was the keynote speaker, describing Schlageter as a patriotic, self-sacrificing martyr. Hitler also said he favoured terrorist methods over passive resistance.[19]

The economic consequences of the Ruhr occupation were growing. Hyperinflation escalated to stratospheric levels during 1923, and food prices surged. The market price of a loaf of bread was 700 paper marks in January, 1,200 in May, 100,000 in July, 2 million in September, 670 million in October, and 80 billion in November. In the month following 20 May, the cost of an egg rose from 800 paper marks to 2,400, a litre of milk from 1,800 to 3,800, and a kilo of flour from 2,400 to 6,600. All basic food items rose in a similar manner. Farmers were by now refusing to sell their produce for worthless paper money. Trucks and trains carrying food were frequently stopped and looted. As Germans battled hyperinflation, ridiculous situations became a routine part of daily life: a 5,000-paper-mark cup of coffee in a café could cost 8,000 marks by the time it was drunk. Every German seemed to have a hyperinflation anecdote. One came from a Munich woman who dragged a suitcase full of paper marks to her local grocery store, and left it outside, while she went in to buy shopping. When she came back out, someone had stolen the suitcase, but emptied the worthless money on to the pavement. Many Germans stopped using money altogether and began bartering with goods to get what they wanted. A lump of coal could gain entry to a cinema, a bottle of paraffin bought a shirt, and that shirt could buy some potatoes. Half a pound of butter could pay for a month's rent on a flat.[20]

Germans looked for people to blame for the hyperinflation crisis. For many, the answer was the Jews. Incidents of antisemitic attacks were recorded in Cologne and Breslau, but the worst example of violence during 1923 was the antisemitic riots in the Scheunenviertel, Berlin's Jewish quarter, near Alexanderplatz, between 5 and 6 November. Most of the inhabitants of this area were easily identifiable Eastern European Jews, who had come to Germany after the War.[21] Frederick Voigt, the Berlin correspondent of the *Manchester Guardian*, witnessed the violence, which he claimed was inspired by 'the unbridled antisemitic agitation of the conservative press', and organised by gangs of 'youthful black-shirted German nationalists' who directed their violence at all those who were 'Jewish in appearance'.[22]

Another report on the violence by the Jewish Telegraphic Agency

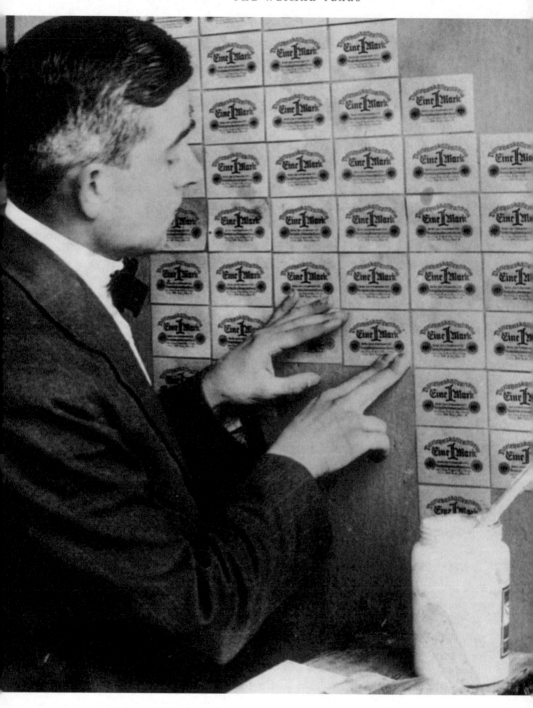

Germany 1923: during the period of hyperinflation,
banknotes lost so much value that they were used as
wallpaper.

(JTA) noted that a 'mob of 30,000' had been involved. No Jew in the area was safe. Homes of Jews were burgled, and food and money was stolen. Shops owned by Jews saw their windows smashed and the goods in them looted. Many Jews suffered public humiliation, some being dragged from their beds and taken on to the streets dressed only in their underclothes. The reporter claimed the riots were 'premeditated and well-organised' and had been whipped up in previous days by 'nationalist speakers' who claimed Germany's economic problems were caused by 'Jewish speculators'. Hundreds of Jews were taken into police custody for their own protection, and tanks were brought in to restore order in the area.[23]

Meanwhile, negotiations on solving the reparations deadlock continued. On 7 June, the German government sent another Note to the Allies, as 'proof of Germany's good will' which made 'improved' proposals to settle the reparations problem. They offered to submit the question of their capacity to pay to an 'impartial Committee' and allow Allied inspection of German industry and financial records, offering further guarantees to ensure reparations payments were made. These guarantees would be backed up by a 10 billion gold-mark mortgage raised on German railways and industry. This German Note was viewed by the British government as a vast improvement on the 2 May Note, but it still made no promise to end the passive resistance. In his reply, Poincaré dismissed the German proposals completely, adding that even if passive resistance were halted, this would not mean an immediate end to the Franco-Belgian occupation of the Ruhr.[24]

This continued intransigence of the French government to resolve the Ruhr was now attracting growing international criticism. On 27 June, Pope Pius XI condemned the French–Belgian occupation of the Ruhr in a letter which claimed it could lead to the final ruin of Europe. He recommended the reparations problem be determined by an 'impartial' panel of international experts. On 29 June, Raymond Poincaré gave a detailed response to the pope's letter in a speech to the French Senate. He said the French government had no desire to permanently annexe the Ruhr, refuted all accusations of imperialism, and promised French troops would stay in the Ruhr until 'Germany has paid its debt'. Finally, he described the German resistance movement in the Ruhr as not passive at all, but 'active, insidious and criminal'.[25]

On 12 July, Stanley Baldwin, the new British Prime Minister, who had replaced the terminally ill Bonar Law on 7 June, made a statement in the House of Commons about the Franco-Belgian occupation of the Ruhr and the problem of German reparations payments. Baldwin began by saying the British government remained determined to ensure Germany paid reparations, but he added the occupation of the Ruhr should end as soon as possible, suggesting the German Note of 7 June seemed a good basis for the opening of fresh negotiations. He also gave support to the German government's suggestion that an impartial body should be allowed to investigate Germany's capacity to pay.[26]

But on 15 July, Poincaré told the French Senate he 'totally rejected' Stanley Baldwin's speech, saying: 'Since the end of the armistice we have done nothing but make concessions. We are at the end of making concessions, because until now we stood all the costs. Instead of helping us to obtain payment, Germany is organizing resistance, forcing us to increase the pressure. We are not responsible for the resulting situation.'[27]

By the end of July 1923, the costly policy of passive resistance was coming under increasing criticism inside Germany. Yet the German Chancellor, Wilhelm Cuno, in a speech in the Reichstag, said: 'No German government could agree to abandon the struggle.' He predicted capitulation to the French government 'would merely be the purchase agreement of the presentation to us of another document for our signature imposing intolerable burdens which will be recognized by the entire world as senseless'.[28] Sympathy for the sorry German economic plight was increasing, especially among British politicians and press. On 2 August, the House of Commons held a debate over the Anglo-French diplomatic deadlock over reparations. Ramsay MacDonald, the leader of the Labour Party, spoke bluntly:

> It is perfectly clear that France is in the Ruhr not for the purpose
> of getting reparations. No sane man can hold to that opinion now.
> Are we not compelled to come to the conclusion that the French
> policy in the Ruhr is a policy that is prompted by war-like feelings,
> feelings that have been handed over from the War, feelings that
> were unsatisfied as a result of the war, and that, in a sentence, it is
> an attempt to continue war after formal peace has been declared?[29]

On 11 August, the British government effectively abandoned its policy of 'benevolent neutrality' over the Ruhr crisis by sending a bluntly worded Note, sharply criticising French government policy, and declaring the occupation of the Ruhr illegal. It even hinted the British government might take 'separate action' to resolve the Ruhr crisis and once again reiterated British support for the idea of an investigation of the German capacity to pay by an impartial committee of international experts. *The Times* commented: 'The Note is strong, but, in our opinion, not too strong. It was high time that such a clear statement of the British case was made.'[30]

When the British Note was received by the French government, it was immediately greeted by a wave of widespread anger. On 20 August, an official reply to the British Note was sent, tenaciously rejecting, point by point over 78 long pages, the idea that the Ruhr occupation was illegal. Poincaré reiterated the French refusal to withdraw from the Ruhr, by stressing the German government would have to give up passive resistance unconditionally, and he flatly rejected the German idea of the creation of an impartial committee of experts to look at the German capacity to pay. He believed the German government would be forced to climb down and raise the white flag.[31]

He was not wrong. Germany's political and economic crisis was deepening. It was becoming quite clear the Cuno government was stuck in the blind alley of passive resistance, but Cuno felt it was his patriotic duty not to try and escape from it. On 9 August, many Berlin stores closed to try and force Cuno from office. On the next day, President Ebert issued a proclamation outlawing the circulation of pamphlets calling for the overthrow of the government, with a penalty of three years' imprisonment or a 500 million marks fine.[32]

On 11 August, a wave of 'Cuno Must Go' strikes, organised by the KPD and involving up to 3 million workers, broke out in a number of German cities, most notably in the socialist strongholds of Hamburg, Saxony and Thuringia. In Berlin, there was a wildcat strike in printing factories that produced paper marks.[33] On the same day, the SPD announced it was withdrawing its support from the Cuno government. In a speech in the Reichstag, Hermann Müller, the co-leader of the SPD, said Cuno's managing of the economic crisis, especially the unlimited printing of money, had created universal bitterness. He urged the Cuno government to step down in favour of a stronger administration which could command widespread support.[34]

Late on the evening of 12 August 1923, Wilhelm Cuno submitted his resignation to President Ebert, along with all his cabinet ministers. At 9.30 p.m. Ebert asked Gustav Stresemann, the leader of the DVP, to form a new broad-based coalition. Public opinion now saw Stresemann as the right leader to navigate Germany out of the current crisis. The key to the formation of the 'Grand Coalition' Stresemann desired was to convince the Social Democrats to put aside party differences in the national interest. They agreed to join Stresemann's government – the first time the Social Democrats and the DVP had served in a Weimar cabinet together since the formation of the Weimar Republic. Some of Stresemann's critics on the Right felt the inclusion of the Social Democrats indicated he was getting ready to give up the policy of passive resistance as soon as possible.

Gustav Stresemann took office on 13 August, forming two cabinets during his 109 momentous days as Chancellor during 1923. Since 1918, Stresemann had moved from a position on the pro-monarchist nationalist Right to become a keen supporter of the Weimar Republic and a firm believer in the policy of conciliation towards the Allies. That the new Chancellor's wife Käthe was the daughter of a Jewish industrialist meant he could never feel comfortable with the antisemitic slogans of the nationalist Right.[35] Stresemann favoured a more realistic attitude towards Germany's weak diplomatic position. Germany's foreign policy, he argued, must be governed by the unhappy fact that it was currently the underdog, and was unable to use force to gain concessions. In his opinion, Germany could only regain its old Great Power position by coming to a rapprochement with the French government to secure a step-by-step revision of the Treaty of Versailles. The centre of his strategy was to convince the French government and people that Germany was not only unable, but also unwilling to attack its powerful neighbour, and to stress the Rhineland and Ruhr must remain part of Germany. To gain good will, Stresemann favoured ending passive resistance as soon as possible, as it was already clear the French were unwilling to budge, no matter how much the British government prodded them.[36]

The first Stresemann cabinet, viewed as a national-emergency cabinet, was formed to deal with passive resistance and hyperinflation. The new government was based on four parties. There were two members of the DVP: Stresemann not only became Chancellor but also replaced the Independent, Hans von Rosenberg, as Foreign Minister, realising it was in foreign affairs where the most important decisions would have to be made, and believing he was best qualified to make them. His DVP party colleague Hans von Raumer became Minister of Economic Affairs. There were four representatives of the SPD: Robert Schmidt as Vice Chancellor and Minister of Reconstruction, Wilhelm Sollmann as Interior Minister, Rudolf Hilferding as Minister of Finance, and Gustav Radbruch as Justice Minister.

Gustav Stresemann, Chancellor of
Germany, August–November 1923.

Zentrum contributed three members: Heinrich Brauns at the Ministry of Labour, Anton Höfle as Post Minister, and Johannes Fuchs as acting head of the yet-to-be-created Ministry of the Occupied Territories. The DDP had two members: Otto Gessler (Defence) and Rudolf Oeser (Transport). There was one independent member: Hans Luther, at Food and Agriculture.

When the Reichstag returned after the summer recess, Stresemann's government won a vote of confidence on 14 August 1923 by 240 to 76, though 13 members of his own party had abstained. The DNVP members explained they were opposing the new government due to the inclusion of the Social Democrats, and suggested the only way out of the current crisis was to create a right-wing dictatorship that did not depend on parliament.[37] In Stresemann's first speech in the Reichstag as Chancellor, he said the upcoming battles in domestic and foreign affairs could only be won with the support of public opinion. On the Ruhr crisis, he pointed out, the British Note to France on 11 August had highlighted the unjust nature of the German occupation. On reparations, he proposed the issue should be submitted to an international court of arbitration.[38]

Stresemann was the eighth different Chancellor since the Weimar Republic had been declared on 9 November 1918. Many on the Right believed it was the Weimar democratic system which produced this political chaos. During the autumn of 1923 there were calls for a 'strong leader' to return Germany to stability. One of the most prophetic and influential books putting forward this idea was published on 24 August 1923. It was called *Das Dritte Reich* (*The Third Reich*), and was written by the German cultural historian Arthur Moeller van den Bruck, who was best known for his eight-volume cultural history of Germany, *Die Deutschen, unsere Menschengeschichte* (*The Germans: Our People's History*), published in 1905. *Das Dritte Reich* was a best-seller, even during the period of the hyperinflation, selling out its first print run of 20,000 copies. By 1933, it had notched up 130,000 sales.

In the book, Moeller van den Bruck claimed Germany's greatest misfortune lay in the democratic political system created by the Weimar Republic, with its multiplicity of parties and ideologies and its unstable and ever-changing coalition governments. To replace this, he suggested a dictatorship, led by a strong authoritarian leader. To further strengthen this thesis, Moeller van den Bruck pointed to the 'glorious history' of the First Reich: the era of the Holy Roman Empire from 800 to 1806, highlighting in particular the achievements of the 'strong leader'

Frederick the Great (1740–1786), especially in building a powerful state and army in Prussia. When looking at the Second Reich, the era of the German Empire from 1871 to 1918, he gave Otto von Bismarck (1815–1898) particular praise for his decisive 'anti-liberal' leadership in bringing about German unification through 'blood and iron'.

In the view of Moeller van den Bruck, Weimar democracy with its powerless coalitions and quarrelling politicians should be replaced by a revolution on the Right that restored order and stability to begin the rule of the Third Reich, which he predicted could rule for a thousand years. This 'Final Reich' was envisaged as a classless society, bringing political, social, and economic unity through one patriotic party, which he called the Party of the Third Reich. This party would be led by a powerful saviour, to be known as the *Führer*, with unlimited power. To achieve this, a new 'movement' must be brought into being, led by radical conservatives, who would borrow from socialism to create a new National Socialism, or better still, a new German Fascism. During the book, Moeller van den Bruck's admiration for Mussolini as the model for the 'strong leader' on the Right is evident, but he also made it clear that Adolf Hitler was not the leader he was envisaging as his *Führer*.

Soon after publication, Moeller van den Bruck started hallucinating, became deeply paranoid and adopted a reclusive lifestyle, suspecting the government was spying on him. He was prescribed various drugs for his condition, including the amphetamines Pervertin and Dexedrine. He also took cocaine, opium and sleeping pills. Doctors eventually diagnosed mental degeneration brought on by syphilis of the brain, and he was committed to the Grunewald Sanitorium in Berlin. On 30 May 1925, Moeller van den Bruck, aged 49, used a revolver to shoot himself with one bullet to the head, leaving a suicide note, stating: 'I die for our cause.'[39]

By September 1923, the British government had realised its diplomatic efforts to persuade the French government to adopt a more conciliatory line towards the German government were fruitless. Stanley Baldwin, the British Prime Minister, decided to meet Poincaré face to face to try to end the damaging divergence of opinion that had developed between the two countries since the Ruhr occupation began. On the afternoon of 19 September, the two men had a two-hour meeting at the British Embassy in Paris. Baldwin asked what would happen if Germany ended passive resistance, but Poincaré said he could not answer that question until the German government had ended the policy. All that emerged from the talks was a joint press release, which stated a 'common agreement of views' had been established, and further stressed that 'on no question is there any difference of purpose or divergence of principle which could impair cooperation between the two countries'.[40]

Upon hearing this news, Stresemann accepted the policy of passive resistance must end unconditionally, as soon as possible, for two reasons. First, he realised there was now little chance of the British government restraining France or siding openly with Germany. Second, the financing of the financial assistance payments to workers and employers in the Ruhr was now costing the mind-boggling total of 40 million gold marks a day. In these circumstances, the liquidation of the Ruhr conflict seemed to be the most sensible domestic policy and the best foreign policy. On 24 September, therefore, Stresemann held two emergency meetings of the Reich cabinet and summoned parliamentary representatives of the occupied Ruhr and leading industrialists to give their views. Stresemann made out the case for ending passive resistance, especially the crippling cost of continuing to finance the occupied area, which was leading to the complete collapse of German currency. Stresemann also promised he would defend any Allied attempts to separate the Ruhr from the rest of the Reich. At the end of the meeting, the majority of those present agreed with the Chancellor's view.[41]

On 26 September, the German government issued an appeal to the German people, announcing the unconditional end of passive resistance in the Ruhr, ending with the following statement:

> In order to maintain the life of the people and the State, we stand
> to-day before the bitter necessity of breaking off the struggle. We
> know that, in so doing, we are claiming from the population of
> the occupied territories even greater spiritual sacrifices than before.
> Your fight was heroic, and heroic was your self-command. We shall
> never forget what was endured by those who went through this
> ordeal.[42]

As soon as passive resistance ended, the Weimar Republic immediately faced three grave threats to its existence: from the Right in Bavaria, from the Left in Saxony, Thuringia and Hamburg, and from a French-sponsored separatist movement in the Rhineland. On the same day as public demonstrations were held against the end of passive resistance, Eugen von Knilling, the right-wing Bavarian Prime

Minister, declared a state of emergency, and appointed the right-wing nationalist Ritter von Kahr as State Commissioner-General (*General-staatskommisar*) for Bavaria, with dictatorial powers. In support of Kahr's rebellion in Bavaria against the Reich government were: General Otto von Lossow, the head of the Bavarian Reichswehr, and Colonel Hans Ritter von Seisser, the chief of the Bavarian State Police.[43] In theory, the dictatorial power Kahr now held was meant to uphold order in Bavaria, but it could also be used to prepare for a national revolution to overthrow the Berlin government.[44]

Knilling telephoned Stresemann on 27 September to explain his actions. Opposition to the end of passive resistance had been so great in Bavaria, he argued, that giving full dictatorial powers to Kahr seemed the best way to keep order to prevent further disturbances.[45] Stresemann, however, saw Kahr's appointment as a provocative move, aimed against the authority of the Reich government. He responded by giving dictatorial powers over the Reich to Otto Gessler, the Defence Minister, who delegated it to General Hans von Seeckt, the chief of the Reichswehr Army Command.

Kahr immediately banned the semi-military formations of the Social Democratic Party and ordered the expulsion from Bavaria of all Jews of foreign nationality. General Seeckt hit back by ordering Kahr to ban the National Socialist daily newspaper, *Völkischer Beobachter*, due to libellous articles it had published on him and President Ebert. Kahr defiantly refused to carry out Gessler's order.[46] General Seeckt sacked Lossow for his refusal to ban Hitler's daily newspaper, and named General Freiherr von Kressenstein as his replacement, but Kahr refused to abide by this order as well.

Behind the scenes, Right-wing elements in Munich had been plotting for months to topple the Berlin government. Deeply involved in these plans and schemes was Adolf Hitler, who had been openly saying in speeches he wanted to emulate Mussolini's 1922 March on Rome, with a copycat March on Berlin, to establish a military dictatorship. During 1923, the National Socialist Party (NSDAP) had gained 47,000 new members, bringing its total membership to 55,000. On 2 September, at a ceremonial German Day in Nuremberg, three paramilitary organisations – the Nazi Stormtroopers, the Oberland League (*Bund Oberland*) and the Imperial War Flag Society (*Bund Reichskriegsflagge*), which had merged to form the German Combat League (*Deutscher Kampfbund*), agreed to make Hitler their 'political leader'.[47] Hitler aimed to use these forces to take control of Bavaria, then march to Berlin and topple the Weimar government. He had already won over the wartime leader General Erich Ludendorff to his plan and was trying to persuade the Bavarian triumvirate of Kahr, Seisser and Lossow to join his treasonous plot. Armed bands under the leadership of the notorious Captain Hermann Ehrhardt, who also supported Hitler's coup, began to assemble on the frontier of Bavaria, awaiting the order to march on Berlin. Taken as a whole, the Bavarian rebels were a powerful coalition, provided they remained united.

Stresemann, realising he needed greater powers to deal with the country's worsening political and economic crisis, promised to introduce a far-reaching Enabling Act (*Ermächtigungsgesetz*), which would transfer power to the cabinet, and weaken parliamentary control, but when Stresemann announced he would use these additional powers to increase the length of the working day, he was met by bitter opposition from the Social Democratic members of his own cabinet. On 3 October, with the matter unresolved, Stresemann and his cabinet all resigned. President Ebert promptly asked Stresemann to form another cabinet. In negotiations with the Social Democrats, Stresemann agreed to maintain the eight-hour day in return for the acceptance of a special Enabling Act, which was passed on 13 October, with 316 votes for acceptance, 24 against, with only 7 abstentions, thereby attaining the necessary two-thirds majority required under Article 78 of the Weimar Constitution. The Enabling Act transferred legislative power from the Reichstag to the government to take 'in financial, economic and social spheres, the measures it deems necessary and urgent, regardless of rights specified in the constitution of the Reich'.[48]

The second Stresemann cabinet, which was another 'Grand Coalition', took office on 6 October 1923. It was almost identical with the previous cabinet, except for three changes: Hans Luther (Independent) replaced Social Democrat Rudolf Hilferding as Finance Minister; Hans von Raumer of the DVP was replaced as Economics Minister by Joseph Koeth (Independent), and Gerhard von Kantz (Independent) replaced Hans Luther as Minister for Food and Agriculture.[49]

The second Stresemann government used the new powers granted to it under the Enabling Act to push through far-reaching currency reform, which paved the way to the end of hyperinflation, and restored confidence in German currency on foreign exchange markets. On 15 October, a government decree was issued announcing the creation of a new reserve bank of issue, called the German Mortgage Bank

(*Rentenbank*), which was empowered to issue a new currency, the Rentenmark, which was subdivided into 100 Rentenpfennig, to replace the old paper mark (*Papiermark*). The highest banknote denomination was 100. The new currency was pegged to the price of gold, using a national mortgage based on all the nation's industrial, commercial, and agricultural land, with twice yearly payments levied on these assets to fund the currency. This was pure bluff, as the mythical mortgage was not intended to ever be redeemed.[50] The new Rentenmarks were redeemable upon demand with interest-bearing gold mortgage certificates. The new currency was the first step in restoring confidence in German currency, and it proved successful. The German government immediately stopped printing paper marks and issuing Treasury Notes to cover public expenditure.

All those who suffered because of public expenditure cuts howled in protest. On 27 October, the Decree for the Reduction of Public Personnel was issued, which allowed for 25 per cent of public-sector workers to be dismissed over the next couple of years.[51] The overall number of unemployed jumped from 180,000 in July 1923 to 1.5 million by December. Most of those who lost their jobs worked in the public sector. Taxes were also raised and the eight-hour day was scrapped, despite Stresemann's promise to the Social Democrats. A brief glance at the frightening exchange rate of the paper mark against the British pound in October 1923 demonstrates the chaotic state of Germany's currency during the period the Rentenmark was being established.[52]

October 9th	£1 = 7,000 million marks
October 10th	£1 = 18,000 million marks
October 18th	£1 = 24,000 million marks
October 21st	£1 = 80,000 million marks
October 23rd	£1 = 250,000 million marks

The date set for the opening of the Rentenbank was 15 November. A few days before the launch, Dr Hjalmar Schacht, the former proprietor of the Darmstadt National Bank, was named as the new National Currency Commissioner (*Reichswährungskommissar*). It was felt Schacht had the necessary competence to push through wide-ranging currency reform. This judgement proved correct. The new Rentenmark duly appeared on 15 November, with 3.2 billion Rentenmark notes issued in the first instance. The key question was the rate at which the new currency should be exchanged for old paper marks. The Rentenmark rate against the old paper mark was initially set at 1 trillion paper marks to one Rentenmark, and the foreign exchange aimed to eventually reach 4.2 Rentenmarks to the dollar.[53]

Civil unrest now took centre stage. During what became known as the 'German October', the Stresemann government faced left-wing revolts in Saxony, Thuringia and Hamburg. The hardships suffered by the working classes due to hyperinflation had set off a new wave of strikes during the previous three months. The Executive Committee of the Communist International (ECCI), based in Moscow, informed the leaders of the KPD, on 15 August 1923, that a 'new and decisive chapter is beginning in the activity of the German Communist Party and Comintern'.[54]

Heinrich Brandler, leader of the KPD, supported by Ernst Thälmann and some other leading communist figures, most notably Ruth Fischer and Arkadi Maslow, decided central Germany was the best place to begin the communist revolt. This began with KPD participation in the state governments in Saxony and Thuringia, as a prerequisite for a full-scale armed revolt, led by the 160,000 strong paramilitary Red Hundreds (*Rote Hundertschaften*).

On 10 October, three members of the KPD were invited to join the SPD-dominated government in the Free State of Saxony, led by Erich Zeigner, who had supported collaboration with the communists as an alternative to the 'Grand Coalition'. In speeches in the Saxon parliament, Zeigner had accused the Reichswehr of being 'politically unreliable' and big business of being corrupt. On 16 October, members of the KPD also joined the cabinet of the SPD-led State government in Thuringia, hoping that by entering these coalition governments they would have access to the weapons needed to conduct an armed revolution. But significantly, the Communists were denied control over the Ministry of the Interior in Saxony and Thuringia, which would have put them in charge of the police.[55]

Otto Gessler, the Reich Defence Minister, gave General Alfred Müller, the commander of the Saxon Reichswehr, unlimited powers to deal with the would-be revolutionaries in Saxony and Thuringia. He also immediately banned the Proletarian Hundreds and all the communist newspapers. Then he removed the power of the Saxony Interior Minister to control the local police. On 19 October, a public statement was issued by the Stresemann government, announcing that military units were being sent to Saxony to defend the state against the advance of right-wing paramilitaries from Bavaria. In cabinet discussions, Stresemann told a different story. Troops were really being sent to 'intimidate radical elements and restore order', with the main purpose being to overthrow the left-wing KPD–SPD coalition government in Saxony.[56]

On 21 October, Brandler, the KPD leader, who had joined the government in Saxony, decided to cancel plans for an armed revolt, but his decision did not reach a group of committed communist rebels in Hamburg, led by Ernst Thälmann, who began an armed revolt on 23 October by storming a number of police stations and seizing weapons. The main Hamburg revolt, which involved 5,000 workers, who believed they were part of a national uprising, was suppressed by the local armed police within a day, leaving 21 rebels, 17 police officers and 61 civilians dead.[57]

On 27 October, a large contingent of armed Reichswehr troops were mobilised under General Müller, to depose the perfectly legal SPD–KPD State government in Saxony. No resistance was offered. In a letter to Zeigner, justifying the move, Stresemann wrote: 'The propaganda of the Communist Party under the leadership of the Communist members of your own cabinet had assumed forms that aimed at the forcible overthrow and destruction of the Reich Constitution.' He also asked Zeigner to offer the resignation of his government, because 'its inclusion of Communist members is inconsistent with Constitutional conditions'.[58] On 30 October, Zeigner resigned as the Prime Minister of Saxony, and, on the next day, a new government was installed in Saxony, composed exclusively of Social Democrats. It was led by Alfred Fellisch, but its powers were limited by the newly installed Reich Commissioner (*Reichskommissar*), Rudolf Heinz of the DVP.

The course of events in Thuringia was less dramatic, but the outcome was the same: the Reichswehr moved in and removed all the Communists from the cabinet. The increased Reichswehr presence in Saxony and Thuringia now made any proposed 'march on Berlin' by right-wing forces in Bavaria much more hazardous, as they would have to move through Saxony and Thuringia. The action of Stresemann's government was unquestionably illegal and unconstitutional. Both of the deposed governments in Saxony and Thuringia had possessed legitimate parliamentary majorities. This once again conformed to the established habit of the German government in Berlin giving lenient treatment to right-wing rebels while dealing ruthlessly with any revolts on the Left.[59]

The SPD in the Reichstag was deeply shocked by the brutal

suppression of the governments in Saxony and Thuringia, contrasting this with the toleration given by Stresemann to Kahr and the other Bavarian government rebels. The Social Democrats declared that unless immediate steps were taken to depose the Bavarian government they would withdraw from the Stresemann cabinet, but Stresemann once again refused to act militarily against Bavaria, as General von Seeckt had already told him the Reichswehr was not strong enough to undertake such an operation.[60]

On 2 November, therefore, the three Social Democrat members of Stresemann's cabinet, Robert Schmidt, Wilhelm Sollmann and Gustav Radbruch, all resigned. Stresemann decided to carry on with a depleted rump cabinet, and he only added Karl Jarres of the DVP to take over from Sollmann as the Minister of the Interior. The other SPD-occupied posts remained vacant. The loss of the Social Democrats from the cabinet meant the special powers offered by the Enabling Act to Stresemann were immediately curtailed.[61] Yet Stresemann's days as Chancellor were now numbered, as it was clear the Social Democrats would bring a motion of no confidence in his government when the Reichstag was next in session, from 20 November onwards.

Meanwhile, in Munich, Kahr and his chief supporters, Colonel Hans Seisser and Otto von Lossow, were losing interest in Hitler's proposed 'March on Berlin'. What Kahr really wanted was a restoration of the Bavarian monarchy and autonomy for Bavaria. Lossow went to Berlin in early November to speak with Seeckt, who told him the Reichswehr would put down any Bavarian armed revolt. Lossow returned to Munich convinced any 'revolution' against the Weimar Republic would have to begin in Berlin, and be led by Reichswehr leaders.[62] On 3 November, Lossow advised Kahr that a march on Berlin was doomed to failure. Three days later, Kahr met with the leading right-wing paramilitary organisations in Munich, and told them bluntly the Bavarian government would not support revolutionary action designed to bring down the Weimar Republic.

After hearing this, Hitler started to panic. He now feared, quite rightly, that the Bavarian triumvirate, instead of supporting a 'national revolution', were secretly scheming to detach Bavaria from the rest of Germany through negotiation with the central government. Hitler sought a personal meeting with Kahr, who refused to see him, as he had already abandoned the project, and wanted to keep Hitler out of the loop. This was a crushing blow to Hitler, who had staked his entire political career on the conspiracy to topple the Weimar Republic going ahead. The trigger-happy alliance of right-wing paramilitary groups he had assiduously nurtured for months also wanted action. In the end, Hitler decided to take matters into his own hands, and begin his own *coup d'état* in Munich, which became known as the Munich Beer Hall Putsch.

On the evening of 8 November, Kahr was due to deliver a speech to prominent Munich government officials, and various local bigwigs in the Bürgerbräukeller in the centre of Munich, the scene of many of Hitler's most famous rabble-rousing speeches. Hitler decided to hijack this meeting to announce the March on Berlin, and he imagined Kahr and the Bavarian establishment would support him.[63]

His armed paramilitary units surrounded the building, and at 8.30 p.m. Hitler, holding a loaded revolver in his hand and accompanied by two armed guards, made a dramatic entry into the beer hall, which was packed to capacity. Kahr was already delivering his speech. Hitler then theatrically jumped on to a chair to make himself heard, fired a single bullet into the ceiling, and announced: 'The National Revolution has begun. The hall is under the control of 600 heavily armed men. No one is allowed to leave.'[64]

Of course, the mention of 'national revolution' was a noticeably big lie. Hitler had only captured a large beer hall, but Kahr was led at gunpoint, accompanied by Seisser, Lossow and Ernst Pöhner, the former Munich Chief of Police, who supported the coup, to an adjoining room to discuss this 'national revolution'. Hitler threatened to kill them and himself, too, if they refused to join his march on Berlin. Kahr and Lossow decided to play along, but it seems they had no intention of actually supporting Hitler.

After he had calmed down, Hitler outlined his plans for a 'provisional national government', offering Kahr the post of Regent of Bavaria, Pöhner the premiership, and Ludendorff the role of commander of the Army.[65] However, realising everything was not going according to plan, Hitler asked one of his aides, Max Erwin von Scheubner-Richter, to go and collect General Ludendorff by car. Then he returned, with Kahr, to the speaking podium in the Bürgerbräukeller where he gave a brief speech, ending with the line 'Tomorrow we will see a German national government, or it will end with us dead.'[66] Hitler gave the impression during his speech that Kahr, Lossow and Seisser all supported him.

In the meantime, Ludendorff had turned up. He told Kahr, Seisser and Lossow that he supported Hitler's plan to do away with the November Criminals, but he was somewhat surprised to hear that

overleaf Crowds listen to a speaker in front of the city hall in Munich's Marienplatz during the Beer Hall Putsch of November 1923. Sixteen Nazis and four policemen died in Hitler's bungled attempt to overthrow Weimar democracy.

in Hitler's proposed new national government he had been given the lesser role of commander of the Army, as Hitler had already appointed himself as the 'dictator of Germany'. What happened next on this farcical evening is a matter of some dispute. Hitler claimed, at his later trial, that Kahr, Seisser and Lossow all agreed to join the conspiracy. Some of those present later testified that Kahr, Lossow, Seisser and Pöhner had announced they would support Hitler's Putsch in their brief speeches. No one present thought they were bluffing. According to Kahr, he only did this because he was forced to do so at gun-point. Ludendorff later claimed that he knew nothing of what Hitler intended to do in the Beer Hall, and he was taken completely by surprise by Hitler's actions.

At 10.30 p.m. Hitler left the Beer Hall to go and defuse a clash between an SA paramilitary unit and Reichswehr troops at the local barracks of the Army Engineers a few miles away. He left Ludendorff to control Kahr, Lossow and Seisser. This proved a huge error of judgement, as Ludendorff immediately allowed them to leave. Once free, Kahr took measures to strangle Hitler's would-be 'national revolution' at birth. The German government was informed of what was going on in Munich, and President Ebert instantly gave full executive power over Bavaria to General von Seeckt, who issued a manifesto warning the army would deal sternly with all conspirators ruthlessly. The Stresemann cabinet issued a proclamation to the German people to the effect that all the resolutions made by Hitler and his co-conspirators were invalid, adding: 'Whoever supports the movement is guilty of treason'.[67]

Kahr now moved the Bavarian government to Regensburg, then issued a government proclamation, which was fly-posted by police throughout Munich. A radio message was broadcast at 2.50 a.m. on 9 November 1923. It maintained that the earlier support given by Kahr to Hitler had been secured at gun-point. Kahr then announced the National Socialist Party (NSDAP) and its associated paramilitary organisations were all banned with immediate effect. The local army and the police expressed total loyalty to Kahr and to the Weimar Republic.

A few minutes before midnight on 8 November, Hitler had accepted his bungled attempt to overthrow Weimar democracy had been a humiliating failure. During the night, he seemed clueless about what to do next. After all, he had planned a coup against the 'despised' Berlin government, not his right-wing friends in the Bavarian

Hitler in Landsberg Fortress where he began writing *Mein Kampf*.

government, and his former paymasters in the Bavarian Army. As a final and futile revolutionary gesture, he agreed to lead a demonstration, numbering about two thousand, through Munich with Ludendorff on 9 November. The aim was to march to the War Ministry and capture it, but as they marched along Residenzstrasse, near to Odeon Platz and the Feldherrnhalle, in the city centre, Hitler and his followers found their path barred by a heavily armed cordon of the Bavarian State Police, under the leadership of Michael von Godin. Several shots were fired on both sides, in an exchange that lasted just two minutes. It left 16 National Socialists and four police officers dead. The 16 National Socialists who were killed were later listed by Hitler in *Mein Kampf*.[68]

Amid the mayhem, Hitler had fallen awkwardly to the ground, breaking the joint in his shoulder and dislocating it.[69] He got to his feet, and was bundled into a car by a young doctor and a medical orderly. In his later account, Hitler claimed he left the scene because he thought Ludendorff had been killed, but Ludendorff was alive and had been arrested.

When it was all over, Hitler turned up at the house of his close friend Ernst 'Putzi' Hanfstaengl, a wealthy landowner, in the Uffing am Staffelsee suburb of Munich. He contemplated suicide or flight to Austria, but did neither. On 11 November, he was arrested by the police, and driven to Landsberg Fortress, a modern prison about 40 miles to the west of Munich, to await trial on a charge of treason. A doctor who examined Hitler in the prison discovered he had a birth defect called cryptorchidism, an undescended right testicle. This defect might explain why Hitler was later reluctant to undress, even in front of a doctor.[70]

The Munich Beer Hall Putsch is the most notorious event in the early history of Hitler and the National Socialist Party (NSDAP). It was hurriedly planned, bungled in execution, and resulted in humiliating failure. Because of what came later it has been elevated to the status of a monumental event, when in fact what occurred was a small, localised revolt, confined to Munich, which lasted a few hours. It failed because Hitler had allowed his party to become a purely paramilitary organisation involved in an ill-defined conspiracy with disparate Bavarian right-wing politicians. Hitler, who had never been brought into the heart of Kahr's conspiracy, had whipped up his own supporters into a frenzy only to find that he had already been deserted by his supposed co-conspirators before he ever arrived at the Bürgerbräukeller.[71]

Gustav Stresemann gave a speech on 11 November 1923 in which he reflected on the recent events in Munich, admitting that 'Germany is now confronted with the demand for a dictatorship', but he stressed that anyone thinking a dictatorship would improve matters was making a 'great mistake'. The recent attempt by Hitler to bring about a dictatorship via a beer hall in Munich would have brought no help to the German people. Stresemann was most 'deeply shaken' by the involvement of Ludendorff in Hitler's attempted coup. Stresemann thought a 'destructive force' such as Hitler's movement represented could never have provided competent government for Germany, even if he had succeeded.[72]

At the same time as the left-wing revolt in central Germany and the right-wing struggle in Bavaria were going on, a much more dangerous threat to the territorial unity of the Weimar Republic had erupted in the Rhineland. In the occupied area, separatist associations and parties flourished, primarily under the patronage of the French occupying authorities. The Reich government was powerless to intervene, as it was prohibited from using the Reichswehr in the demilitarised Rhineland under the terms of the Treaty of Versailles.

The leading figure in the Rhineland separatist movement was Hans Dorten, the wealthy owner of a porcelain company, who created the Rhenish People's Union (*Volksvereinigung*), which demanded a Rhenish republic as an autonomous state within the Reich, but his opponents suspected his real aim was an independent Rhenish republic.[73] In the occupied Ruhr the separatist movement also flourished, with various groups sprouting up, including the Rhenish Republic People's Party and the Rhenish Independence League. Separatists armed themselves, held demonstrations, occupied town halls, and called for the foundation of an autonomous Rhenish republic. Some of their supporters even advocated the full integration of the Rhineland into France. After the end of passive resistance, separatist demonstrations broke out in several Rhineland cities. On 21 October, separatists led by Leo Deckers captured the City Hall in Aachen, and proclaimed a Free and Independent Rhenish Republic. This so-called Rhenish Republic was based in three areas: North (Lower Rhine), South (Upper and Middle Rhine) and the Ruhr, but it received little support from the local population.

The French gave the impression in many places they supported the separatists. The military authorities thought a Rhineland buffer state would offer additional security from a future German invasion, and there is no doubt the French provided arms and offered military security for separatist demonstrations.[74] This was especially true in the Bavarian Palatinate, where the French General Georges de Metz, was in command. He encouraged the local state parliament to proclaim the Palatinate's independence on 24 October. On 26 October, Paul Tirard, the French High Commissioner, announced the separatists were also in effective control of Koblenz, but it had been recaptured with French military support.

On 14 November, there was another separatist revolt in Aegidienberg, a cluster of villages in the eastern part of the Rhineland. It was led by residents in the various small villages, but was bitterly opposed by other patriotic residents. In one incident, a group of locals gunned down 14 separatists. A total of 120 people were killed in all these bloody clashes. To prevent further fighting, the French military authorities installed a force of French Moroccan soldiers to keep order.

The Rhineland separatist movement had been frustrated by popular local resistance. Many locals saw the separatists as French-backed attention seekers. By mid-November, French tactics began to change, with the occupying authorities encouraging the formation of a federal Rhineland state within the German Reich, instead of advocating a completely independent Rhineland. On 28 November, Joseph Matthes, the leader of the Rhenish Independence League, announced that the separatist movement had been dissolved, and then fled to exile in France. On the next day, separatists in Duisburg were disarmed by Belgian troops. On 2 December, separatists hauled down flags from town halls in several Rhineland cities and towns, and the Rhineland separatist movement gradually receded into irrelevance.[75]

On 13 November, a huge turning-point was reached in the reparations crisis when the French and Belgian governments agreed to the appointment of an international committee of financial experts to investigate Germany's capacity to pay. It was a great opportunity to rebuild the shaken structure of European politics. The decision of the American government to underwrite German reparations payments with loans was key to getting the French government on board, as it offered the prospect of Germany making regular payments. It also seems that Poincaré wanted to restore close relations with France's major European ally, Britain, and knew a softening of the French attitude to Germany would prove attractive.

On 30 November, the Reparations Commission appointed two committees. The first and most important would assess Germany's ability to pay reparations. It consisted of ten experts, headed by the respected American banker General Charles Dawes, Chairman of the Central Trust Company, assisted by another American business executive, Owen Young. It became known as the Dawes Committee. There were two representatives from each of the Allies: Sir Robert Kindersley and Sir Josiah Stamp from Britain, Jean Parmentier and Edgar Allix from France, Maurice Houtart and Emile Franqui from Belgium, and Alberto Pirelli and Federico Flora from Italy. The second committee consisted of five financial experts, whose remit was to look at how to balance the German budget, and restore confidence in the German currency. It was chaired by the American financier Henry Robinson, Chairman of the First National Bank of Los Angeles, with one member from each of the four Allied nations: Reginald Mc-Kenna (Britain), Laurent Atthalin (France), Albert Janssen (Belgium), and Mario Alberti (Italy).[76]

Meanwhile, Stresemann's second cabinet fell from power on 23 November, after Stresemann had introduced a motion of confidence in the Reichstag, which he lost by 231 votes to 151, with seven abstentions. President Ebert asked the Stresemann cabinet to remain in office in a caretaker capacity until the formation of a new government was completed. Ebert thought the Social Democrats had made a huge mistake by deposing Stresemann, commenting bitterly: 'Your reason for unseating the Chancellor will be forgotten in six weeks. But you will still be suffering the consequences of your stupidity after ten years have passed.' Stresemann explained to a press conference for the foreign press why he had introduced a vote of confidence that he knew he would lose:

Wilhelm Marx, Chancellor of Germany
from November 1923 to January 1925.

I did it for two reasons. In the first place I had the impression
that my parliamentary majority would not have lasted out for the
important [upcoming] international negotiations and decisions in
the next few weeks. There was a risk that I should not find myself
sufficiently supported, the risk the negotiations might be nullified.
For that reason alone, I had to have the situation cleared up.[77]

There were four failed attempts to form a new government in the
last week of November 1923. The SPD refused to become involved
in a new 'Grand Coalition' and would not return to government
office until 28 June 1928, while the nationalist DNVP wanted to see
a more right-wing cabinet and also refused to participate. President
Ebert finally asked the committed Catholic Wilhelm Marx, leader of
Zentrum, to form a new government. Marx was born on 15 January
1863 in Cologne, then studied Law at the University of Bonn before he
became a respected lawyer, serving as a judge in Prussia. He entered
the Reichstag in 1910, and was known as a centre-ground, flexible
moderate, who aroused neither devotion nor animosity.

On 30 November, Marx became German Chancellor in yet another
minority government, which could remain in power only with the
toleration of the Social Democrats. Marx would remain Chancellor
until 15 January 1925 and served again from 17 May 1926 until 12 June
1928. With a total time in office of three years and 73 days, Marx has
the distinction of being the longest-serving Chancellor during the
Weimar years.

The first Marx cabinet was based on the same three parties as the
outgoing Stresemann second cabinet: the DVP had two members,
Gustav Stresemann, who stayed on as Foreign Minister, and Karl
Jarres, who entered in the dual roles of Vice-Chancellor and Interior
Minister. Zentrum added three members, Wilhelm Marx (Chancellor),
Heinrich Brauns (Labour), and Johannes Fuchs who was appointed to
the newly created cabinet post of Minister of the Occupied Territories.
The DDP had three members: Otto Gessler (Defence), Rudolf Oeser
(Transport), and Eduard Hamm (Economic Affairs). The other
members were Erich Emminger of the BVP, who became Minister of
Justice, and two Independents: Hans Luther, who moved from Food
and Agriculture to become Finance Minister and finally Gerhard von
Kranitz, who took over Luther's vacated post.

In his first speech to the Reichstag as Chancellor on 4 December,
Wilhelm Marx called for the restoration of the Enabling Act, arguing he
needed special powers to restore the country's financial stability, but he

Poster for the Bauhaus Exhibition in Weimar
(July–September 1923), designed by the
typographer Joost Schmidt.

237

also made it clear that he was not sympathetic to any more concessions to the working classes. Social Democrat Philipp Scheidemann said in the Reichstag on 5 December that although he did not agree with the new Chancellor in most respects, he did agree with him on the vital importance of resolving the current dire financial difficulties. On 8 December, the votes of the Social Democrats proved crucial in the passing of another Enabling Act by 313 votes for and only 18 against. It was time-limited to 15 February 1924, but in that brief period, 63 decrees were issued under its authority.[78]

On 24 December, in a Christmas message to the German people at the end of a tumultuous year, Wilhelm Marx said the German government was willing to 'fulfil reparations to the limit of our capacity', but he also made an international appeal to 'give us peace, take away unfair sanctions and oppositions, and give us a chance to work and live, then Germany will save its finances and pay reparations accordingly'.[79]

Even during the frenetic political and economic environment of 1923, path-breaking and free-spirited modernist trends in Weimar culture continued. One of the culture highlights of the year was the first major international Bauhaus exhibition, which opened in Weimar on 23 July and continued until 30 September. The State Bauhaus (*Staatliches Bauhaus* or Building House) in Weimar was founded by the innovative architect Walter Gropius, on 12 April 1919. It moved to Dessau in 1925, then Berlin in 1932, after which it was suppressed when Hitler came to power. The Bauhaus was grounded in the idea of Comprehensive Artwork (*Gesamtkunstwerk*), in which training in all arts would be amalgamated under one roof. Walter Gropius stated in his original manifesto: 'Together let us desire, conceive and create a new structure of the future, which will embrace architecture and sculpture and painting in one unity.'[80]

The Bauhaus style had a profound artistic influence across art, architecture, pottery, graphic design, interior design, and the sans-serif typeface. In architecture, it featured rigid angles of glass, masonry, and steel, creating functional buildings, often with a huge amount of glass, which let in more daylight than conventional buildings. Traditionalists saw Bauhaus buildings as formless symbols of an egalitarian mechanical modern world. The Bauhaus was founded at a time when Expressionism, based on emotional experience and inner turmoil, was giving way to New Objectivity (*Neue Sachlichkeit*), representing a call for a more rational and realistic 'return to order' but also expressing a desire

Walter Gropius, founder of the Bauhaus educational programme.

for a less elitist approach to art that would appeal to the modern human living in an industrial society.

The Bauhaus School developed a craft-based curriculum to train artisans and designers capable of creating useful objects. It proved a magnet for young avant-garde students due to its democratic, cosmopolitan outlook. Students came from a diverse range of social and economic backgrounds, and were selected for admission by talent and enthusiasm, not formal educational qualifications, gender, or background. All students completed a semester-long foundation course (*Vorkurs*), before entering more specialised workshops, which included metal-working, cabinet-making, weaving, pottery, typography, and painting. The *Vorkurs* course was created by the talented Swiss artist and teacher Johannes Itten, who was the most influential figure in the educational development of the early Bauhaus in Weimar. Itten's style of teaching was to prompt objective responses from students, and encourage their creativity to then pursue individual projects in specialist subjects of their own choosing. Itten also encouraged the hiring of talented artists to teach in the Bauhaus, many of whom would soon be among the foremost artists and architects of the twentieth century, most notably Paul Klee, László Moholy-Nagy, Josef Albers, and Wassily Kandinsky. Teachers in the Bauhaus School were given the title of 'master' rather than 'professor', and classes were

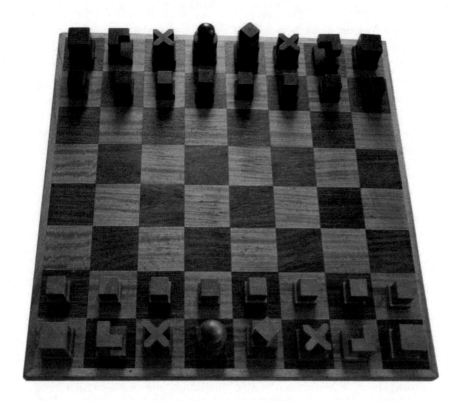

taught by staff jointly. This collaborative, open-form style of teaching made a huge impression on each generation of students. Compared to the socially distant relationship between professors and students at German universities, the close relationship between staff and students was years ahead of its time.

One of the conditions of state funding for the Bauhaus by the Social Democratic-led local government of Saxe-Weimar was for the institution to organise and present a major international exhibition. The 1923 exhibition was called 'Art and Technology – A New Unity' and took place at three separate locations in Weimar. It functioned not only as a showcase for the school's teaching and creative achievements, but also to report to the local government to justify further funding. An impressive array of work was made available, and the exhibition was extensively advertised using specially designed posters, postcards and photos of products.

The centrepiece of the 1923 exhibition was the Haus am Horn, the school's first independent Bauhaus architectural project, designed by

left The Bauhaus model house (*Haus am Horn*),
designed by Georg Muche.
above A chess set designed in minimalist
Bauhaus style by Josef Hartwig.

Georg Muche, a teacher at the school. It was what is now called 'a show home'. It had a single-storey design, with a flat roof, using wood, steel and concrete in its construction. Inside, the atrium-style layout centred on a large living room, with four bedrooms branching off, and a basement for washing and drying clothes. All the furniture and fittings, including a modern fitted kitchen with easy-to-clean worktops, were made by students in Bauhaus workshops. The show house was a huge visitor attraction during the exhibition, and was seen as the house of the future. In 1996, the house became a UNESCO World Heritage Site.

The Bauhaus School also produced numerous iconic household design items. These included: the instantly recognisable Wassily Chair made by Marcel Breuer of tubular steel, with a canvas seat, back and arms; the Bauhaus Chess Set by Josef Hartwig, which removed all religious and monarchical symbols typically used in chess, with the aim of updating the game for a more egalitarian age; the Brno Chair by Mies van der Rohe, with a design based on the idea that a modern chair does not need four legs when it can be constructed in a cantilever style, using a C-shaped metal bar to support the entire seat; the elegant Tea Infuser by Marianne Brandt, which looked ultra-modern in 1923, and was easy to pour; the MT8 Lamp by Wilhelm Wagenfeld, which became known as the Bauhaus Lamp, and had a circular base, cylindrical shaft, and spherical shade, made from glass and metal with an opaque lampshade; and the space-saving Nesting Tables by Josef Albers, each of which was made of solid oak, with a lacquered acrylic glass top of assorted colours.[81]

The innovative furniture designer Marcel Breuer in his Wassily chair.

1924

·

THE DAWES PLAN, HITLER ON TRIAL AND *MEIN KAMPF*

·

In an article in the weekly newspaper *The Time* (*Die Zeit*), Gustav Stresemann, the German Foreign Minister, wrote: 'The New Year will confront us with new and tough decisions affecting foreign affairs. So far as there is any hope of solving the problem of the Ruhr, which for Germany is a question of life and death, such a solution seems only possible in conjunction with the great problem of Reparations.' Stresemann then welcomed the Dawes Committee investigation into Germany's capacity to pay, promising: 'We have nothing to conceal. The accusations that were formerly brought against us, that we had consciously worked for the bankruptcy of German finances, can no longer be maintained. The consequences of Germany's economic collapse are too clear for all to see.'[1]

On 15 January, Charles G. Dawes, chair of the Expert Committee, presided over its first meeting at the Reparations Commission in Paris. Dawes told press reporters the economic experts would approach their task not as politicians, but as people with practical experience, who would investigate Germany's capacity to pay and set out proposals for the German government to ensure Germany's payment obligations could be met in future.[2] The members of the Dawes Committee devoted enormous energy to their task by making lengthy fact-finding trips to Berlin, Paris, London, Rome, and Brussels in the first three months of 1924. The two most important of these trips were to Berlin and Paris.

In Berlin, where Dawes and his team arrived at the end of January, the Committee looked at economic statistics and examined Germany's recent economic policy. Dawes was impressed by the German government's preparation of all the necessary information in advance and by their answering all the questions posed to them. Dawes concluded the German government could increase revenue by 4 billion gold marks by raising the burden of taxation on the German people.[3] He also pointed out that with better management of the national railways, 2.5 billion gold marks in surplus revenue could be raised every year. This could

previous page Charles G. Dawes, US banker, diplomat
and politician – and chair of the Committee that
proposed the plan, agreed in 1924, for a staggered
payment of Germany's war reparations.

be achieved by transferring the railways from government control to a privatised corporation under the controlling influence of the Allied reparations creditors, who would issue interest-bearing debentures to the value of 11 billion gold marks, secured by a mortgage on the property of the railways. Another revenue-raising measure suggested by Dawes was to issue interest-bearing industrial debentures to the value of 5 billion gold marks. Dawes made clear the Franco-Belgian occupation needed to end, and full economic sovereignty restored to Germany for this economic plan to work.[4] The German government readily accepted these preliminary recommendations.

On 19 February, the initial outline of the Dawes Committee financial plan, as it related to Germany, was presented to Raymond Poincaré, the French Prime Minister, in Paris.[5] He raised two objections: first, he opposed the suggestion the railways in occupied Ruhr should return to immediate German control; second, he offered no swift promise to end the Franco-Belgian occupation of the Ruhr. Dawes felt that Poincaré took a 'tough stance,' which obstructed the work of the Committee by refusing to budge on his insistence on delaying the evacuation of the Ruhr.[6] In reality, pressure was mounting on Poincaré to moderate his uncompromising attitude towards Germany, and find some way of disentangling France from the Ruhr, without losing face, as he would soon face national elections against Édouard Herriot, the leader of the Radical-Socialist Party (*Parti Republicain Radical et Radical-Socialiste*), who favoured a withdrawal from the Ruhr at the earliest opportunity, a stance which was likely to prove attractive to voters.

The British government, headed by the first-ever Labour Prime Minister, Ramsay MacDonald, who took office on 22 January, was sympathetic to Germany's plight and favoured a policy of conciliation. MacDonald understood why the French were anxious about a German military revival, but he thought the policy of coercion adopted by the French government had been self-defeating. MacDonald immediately recognised the Dawes proposals offered a way out of Germany's economic problems, and a pathway to end the Ruhr occupation. To ensure his own view prevailed in foreign affairs matters, MacDonald took on the role of Foreign Secretary, and he would make a significant impact during his brief time in office in 1924. One of his first concessions to Germany was to reduce the reparations tax on goods from 26 per cent to 5 per cent.[7]

Meanwhile, Adolf Hitler awaited trial in Munich for high treason. The charge related to the events of the previous November when Hitler and his co-conspirators had attempted a bungled coup to take power in Bavaria. During his first days of imprisonment in Landsberg Fortress, about 40 miles west of Munich, a demoralised Hitler contemplated suicide, and even went on a hunger strike. He told Alois Maria, the prison psychologist: 'I've had enough. I'm done. If I had a revolver, I'd use it.'[8]

The Munich Beer Hall Putsch Trial began on 26 February 1924, in Munich's First District People's Court at 3 Blutenburgstrasse, housed in the former building of the Reichswehr Central Infantry School. The nineteenth-century red-brick building had previously been Bavaria's War School. Mounted guards and two battalions of state police officers patrolled outside. The courtroom itself was a converted former dining hall, 52 feet long and 38 feet wide. A newly installed judicial bench dominated the room. Chairs were packed in tightly and the spectator seats were full of Hitler's supporters. The chief judge, holding the title Supreme Court Director, was 53-year-old Georg Neihardt, a decidedly nationalist member of the notoriously right-wing Bavarian judiciary. He had previously commuted the life sentence of Communist Kurt Eisner's assassin, Count Arco-Valley, from a death sentence to life imprisonment, because of the murderer's 'glowing love of his people and Fatherland'.[9] He was supported by two professional judges, and three 'lay' judges, plus an alternate.

At 8.30 a.m., Hitler entered the court, packed with newspaper reporters from home and abroad, wearing a plain black suit, with his Iron Cross (1st Class) and Iron Cross (2nd Class) pinned to his jacket, emphasising his service in the German Army during the First World War. In addition to Hitler, the nine other defendants were: General Erich Ludendorff, Wilhelm Frick, Ernst Röhm and Friedrich Weber, all charged with high treason; and Robert Wagner, Ernst Pöhner, Heinz Pernet, Wilhelm Brückner and Hermann Kriebel, indicted on the lesser charge of assisting treason. Of the ten, only one (Röhm) was born in Munich and none of the rest was a native of southern Bavaria.[10]

The proceedings began with a lengthy presentation by the prosecuting lawyer, Hans Ehard, who recounted the events leading up to the Munich Beer Hall Putsch, accusing Hitler of attempting to establish a new regime in Bavaria to function as a springboard for a 'March on Berlin' to set up a new Reich government. Then another prosecuting lawyer, Ludwig Stenglein, argued that as many of the details about the preparations for the coup were too sensitive to be made public, the entire trial should be held behind closed doors.

The defence lawyers objected, as they wanted Hitler's story and that of his co-defendants to be widely reported in the press. Hitler saw the trial as an ideal opportunity to establish himself as a leading figure in German politics. In the end, the chief judge, Neihardt, decided some topics would be examined in secret, but others would not. For Hitler, this was an ideal decision as he could now lay out his politics to a worldwide press audience. In a series of speeches, which allowed him to push his nationalist ideas to the German people, he implicated the three key Bavarian figures in the conspiracy: Kahr, Lossow and Seisser.

From the beginning, Hitler was the chief focus of attention in the courtroom, and in the newspaper reports of the proceedings. At 2.30 p.m., Hitler delivered his opening speech, which lasted about three hours. [11] Hitler portrayed the story of his road to the Bürgerbräukeller as the struggle of a genuine patriot trying to save Germany first in war and then against the November Criminals of the Weimar Republic, who had instigated the 'stab in the back' 1918 revolution, an 'unspeakable crime', which had led to a succession of weak democratic coalition governments. Hitler then laid out the key aspects of his own political ideology, declaring himself a 'committed antisemite', a mortal enemy of Marxism and of Weimar democracy. The National Socialists he led had been created with the specific aim of saving Germany. Finally, Hitler rejected the charge of high treason, arguing three key figures in the Bavarian government, Kahr, Lossow and Seisser, had been at the heart of the conspiracy, and should be on trial, too. Hitler ended with the words: 'High treason is the only crime punishable when it fails.'

On 29 February, Erich Ludendorff gave his much-anticipated testimony, wearing a sober dark blue suit. He too spoke for three hours to the packed courtroom, relying on extensive notes. He freely admitted that he wanted a restoration of the monarchy and then went on to attack Weimar democracy and the Catholic Church. He denied any prior knowledge of the coup and assigned himself a passive role in the whole enterprise. Ludendorff said Hitler was a 'sloganeer and an adventurer', who had 'misled and lied to me'. [12]

The key witnesses for the prosecution were the three members of the Bavarian triumvirate, who gave their evidence in closed sessions. The first to give evidence was Otto von Lossow, the German officer who led the Bavarian Reichswehr. He had requested a stand-up lectern to deliver his evidence, and he came prepared, with a large set of notes. Lossow spoke for nearly six hours in a strident and loud tone, denying he was ever interested in a 'March on Berlin', but

overleaf The defendants in Hitler's trial for treason in Munich, February–March 1924, photographed by Heinrich Hoffmann. Left to right: Heinz Pernet, Friedrich Weber, Wilhelm Frick, Hermann Kriebel, Erich Ludendorff, Adolf Hitler, Wilhelm Brückner, Ernst Röhm and Robert Wagner.

ernet   Weber   Frick   Kriebel

dorff   Hitler   Brückner   Wagner

Röhm   phot. Hoffmann Mch

admitted his relationship with Hitler had initially been a good one. He was impressed by Hitler's speeches, but this feeling soon faded, as he gradually realised Hitler's speeches always said the same thing. In his conversations with Hitler, he soon realised that Hitler regarded himself as the German Mussolini, had lost all sense of proportion, and refused to listen. Lossow disputed Hitler's idea that the triumvirate had any intention of becoming involved in a coup to overthrow Weimar democracy or giving any support to the idea of a Hitler–Ludendorff dictatorship. In cross-examination, Hitler angrily asserted that Lossow's testimony was 'untrue and incorrect'.[13]

The next to give evidence was Gustav Ritter von Kahr, who was the 'Bavarian dictator' at the time of the attempted coup, but who had recently resigned from the Bavarian government. Kahr sat at the witness table, facing the judges, but with his back to the courtroom. He denied having any intention of joining a coup with Hitler to topple the Weimar Republic, but admitted having conversations with leading army figures about regime change. He constantly refused to answer defence questions, using the excuse of 'state secrecy' or saying: 'I can give no information on that.' Kahr was also extremely vague on dates. When Hitler asked him why he had given him a warm handshake of support after he had announced the coup in the Bürgerbräukeller, Kahr denied this had ever happened.[14]

The third member of the triumvirate to give evidence was Colonel Hans Ritter von Seisser, the head of the Bavarian State Police at the time of the aborted coup. Seisser admitted that he found Hitler a compelling speaker at first, but soon thought Hitler had given in to megalomania, in the days leading to his attempted coup. Seisser said he had firmly rejected Hitler's idea of a 'March on Berlin'. Seisser also took frequent issue with the testimony of Hitler, and his co-defendants, by constantly saying their evidence was 'invented and untrue'. Seisser's performance strengthened the triumvirate's credibility, and shifted the chief responsibility for the failed coup back on to Hitler. In cross-examination, Hitler grilled Seisser extensively, even suggesting that he had broken his 'word of honour', when promising to support the coup in the Bürgerbräukeller. Seisser, mortified that his honour was being questioned, picked up his briefcase, then dramatically left the courtroom, never to return, for which the judged fined him 60 marks.[15]

On 27 March 1924, after four weeks of worldwide press coverage, Hitler delivered his closing speech, lasting more than an hour in length. He began by saying the Weimar Republic was founded on a 'crime of high treason' in which the German Army had been 'stabbed in the back' by socialists and Jews. As the country suffered one catastrophe after another, the democratic leaders of the republic remained subservient to the Allied powers, and Germany was reduced to a pawn on the international chessboard. The Treaty of Versailles was, according to Hitler, 'immorality in 440 clauses'. As for the League of Nations, it was really a league that guaranteed the 'corrupt peace treaty.' Now the so-called Weimar government was hauling genuine German heroes into court and branding them traitors. Respect for law would only return when the President of Germany was tried for high treason. Looking straight at the judge, Hitler concluded his speech with the following statement: 'Even if you pronounce us guilty a thousand times, the eternal goddess of the eternal court of history will smilingly tear up the verdict of this court and she will acquit us.' Hitler had undoubtedly seized his moment in the international spotlight, and delivered one of his most powerful speeches.[16]

On 1 April, Judge Neihardt delivered the verdicts. Adolf Hitler was found guilty of high treason and sentenced to five years' imprisonment, with a reduction for the four months he had already served, making him eligible for release on parole after six months. Neihardt rejected a demand by the prosecution for Hitler to be deported to Austria after he served his sentence, arguing: 'Hitler sees himself as German'. Hitler also received a fine of 200 gold marks.[17]

The other chief defendant in the trial, General Erich Ludendorff, who arrived to hear the verdicts in full general's regalia, displaying all his medals, was amazingly acquitted of all the charges. Neihardt said Ludendorff had gone to the Munich Beer Hall in November 1923 with the intention of supporting Gustav von Kahr's government, not overthrowing it, and he rejected all the evidence to the contrary.[18] Of the other co-defendants, Kriebel, Weber and Pöhner were found guilty of high treason, and given the same sentences as Hitler. Röhm, Brückner, Pernet, Wagner and Frick were all found guilty of the lesser charge of 'abetting treason', each receiving 15 months' imprisonment plus a fine of 100 gold marks, but they were all immediately released on parole.

News of the verdicts shocked not only the German press, but newspaper editors around the world. The leading SPD newspaper, *Vorwärts*, described the trial as 'a farce and a mockery', suggesting it was such an obvious injustice that the judge should be put on trial himself. *The Times* asked if the crime of high treason was 'worth more than a mere six months in prison?' and the *New York Times* regarded the verdicts as 'an excellent joke for April Fool's Day'.[19]

The high-profile Munich Beer Hall Putsch Trial made Hitler famous. He turned a bungled fiasco into a triumph: no longer was he the buffoon who had botched a coup in a beer hall, but instead a true patriot, who had tried to rescue Germany from democratic chaos. Significantly, on 13 March 1924, Hitler was mentioned in the diary of Joseph Goebbels for the very first time. Goebbels had followed the trial coverage in the newspapers day by day, and by 22 March he was writing 'there was no one like him [Hitler] in Germany'.[20]

On 9 April, Charles Dawes handed his eagerly awaited report to the Reparations Commission in Paris. This document constituted what became known as the Dawes Plan. The report began by stating, 'The standpoint adopted has been that of business and not politics. Political factors have been considered only in so far as they affect the practicality of the plan.' The Dawes Plan, designed to find a practical way for Germany to meet its reparations payments, set no maximum payment figure, recommended the full restoration of full economic and fiscal sovereignty to Germany, and ruled out any further punitive measures.[21]

The major problem the Dawes Committee tried to solve was how to increase the amount of revenue the German government could raise. This led to the chief recommendation, that the financing of the plan was to come from a combination of interest-bearing railway bonds, to the value of 11 billion gold marks, secured by a mortgage on the fixed assets of the railways, along with industrial debentures to the value of 5 billion gold marks, a transport tax, and sales taxes on such items as alcohol, tobacco, beer and sugar. The Dawes Plan was really a revenue-raising package, which laid considerable cost of living burdens on the German public.

All the revenue raised from these various sources would be channelled through a new Gold Note Bank, to be established in Berlin, and administered by the Reichsbank, with a German President and a directorate consisting of a German director, supported by seven German and seven foreign members. This would act as a collection and distribution centre for all the payments. An Agent General of Reparations nominated by the Allies would transfer the payments to the creditor nations. This role was taken by the American S. Parker Gilbert, a graduate of the Harvard Law School, and former Under-Secretary of the US Treasury, who became one of the most powerful economic figures in Germany.[22] His role was designed to settle payment problems without the need of imposing sanctions or resorting to force again. To assist with this, the Reichsbank was made independent of the German government and placed under a supervisory body half of whose members were representatives of the Allies.

A new schedule of payments was established under the Dawes Plan. Reparations payments would begin at 1 billion gold marks in the first year (1924/25), assisted by an 800 million gold mark loan, provided by Wall Street bond issues, and raised by a consortium of American bankers led by J.P. Morgan. These payments would then rise annually to 1.2 billion gold marks for 1925/26, 1.2 billon in 1927/28, 1.75 billion in 1928/29, and then to 2.5 billion in 1929/30. All these figures were subject to fluctuations in the German economy. The payments schedule would begin from the date Germany, the UK, France, Belgium, and Italy signed the Dawes Plan. It was envisaged this would happen at a conference attended by Germany and the Allies later in the year. Dawes concluded the report by stating: 'The Committee is confident it lies within the power of the German people to respond to the burdens imposed by the plan, without impairing a standard of living comparable to that of all the Allied countries.'[23]

On 11 April, the Reparations Commission asked the German government to formulate a reply to the Dawes Plan. On the next day, Gustav Stresemann, the Foreign Minister, gave a positive response during a speech in Schneidemühl, saying: 'The Experts' Report undoubtedly shows an effort to grasp the situation in Germany from the economic point of view and is inspired by reasonable and business-like considerations.'[24] The German cabinet's discussion of the Dawes Plan on 14–15 April was preceded by conversations by Chancellor Wilhelm Marx with the Presidents and Prime Ministers of the various German *Länder*, who all supported acceptance of the plan. The cabinet was also wholeheartedly in favour of sending an affirmative response to the Reparations Commission. The reply was published as an official diplomatic Note on 16 April. It stated the German government regarded the report 'as providing a practical foundation for the speedy settlement'.

On 26 April, the replies of the Allied Powers were all published. The French government reply, in a tone of bitterness, was ambiguous. It offered no promise of a swift end to the occupation of the Ruhr, and warned France needed to see unmistakable evidence of the German government carrying out the financial and legal requirements of the Dawes Plan before giving final confirmation. The British government offered a much more positive response, stressing the restoration of fiscal and economic sovereignty to Germany was vital if the Plan were to work. The Italian and Belgian governments were also prepared to accept the decisions outlined by the Dawes Committee.[25]

Progress towards solving the reparations problem now seemed in sight, but political passions in Germany remained high, as the Dawes Plan was published in the middle of the German national election campaign, with voters set to go to the polls on 4 May 1924. On 13 March, President Ebert had dissolved the Reichstag, after the Social Democrats warned they would not agree to a renewal of the Enabling Act, which had lapsed on 15 February. As a result, the state of emergency was lifted.[26]

Chancellor Marx issued an appeal to the nation. He promised his government would restore law and order, stabilise the currency, bring about a return to a stable economy and implement the Dawes Report. Gustav Stresemann said the foreign policy of the German government was inspired by the belief that what the German people now required was a period of tranquillity, and the implementation of the Dawes Plan would bring this about.[27]

During the campaign, Stresemann agreed to include in the party's election manifesto a commitment to introduce a constitutional People's Monarchy (*Volkskaisertum*). This news gained adverse publicity abroad. Stresemann decided to be interviewed by the Berlin correspondent of the *New York Times* to allay worries that he was moving back towards the agenda of the nationalist Right. Stresemann explained the DVP's commitment to the eventual restoration of the monarchy in no way precluded serving the Weimar Republic loyally. To back up his argument, he pointed out that the monarchist Adolphe Thiers had been the first President of the Third Republic of France.[28]

In the national election of 4 May, in which voter turnout was 77.4 per cent, the German people gave their verdict on the economic chaos of hyperinflation, and the Ruhr occupation. All the parties connected with German government in 1923 suffered heavy losses. The SPD narrowly remained the largest party, with 100 seats, down by three from the June 1920 election, with 20.5 per cent of the vote (6 million votes), down 1.4 per cent previously, but if the USPD deputies, who had joined the SPD parliamentary group since the last election, are added, the Social Democrats actually lost 71 Reichstag seats overall. Voters were clearly unhappy with the party failing to back a more left-wing socialist agenda, and choosing instead to stay mainly in opposition, while holding the fate of each government in its hands. The DVP led by Gustav Stresemann also performed very badly, winning 45 seats, a loss of 20 from the previous election, with a vote share of 9.2 per cent (2.96 million), down from 13.9 per cent in 1920. This was hardly a ringing endorsement by voters for Stresemann's foreign policy. The DDP, which was also part of the Marx government, suffered a similar loss of support, winning 28 seats (down 11 from 1920), with a vote share of 5.65 per cent (1.65 million), down from 8.3 per cent in 1920. Electoral support for the DDP had been gradually collapsing ever since the prominent role played by the party in the creation of the Weimar Constitution in 1919, but the DDP performance in May 1924 represented an all-time low. Only Zentrum remained steady with 65 seats, 1 up from 1920, and 13.4 per cent of votes (3.91 million), down from 13.6 at the previous election.

The clear victors in the May 1924 election were parties on the extreme Left and Right. The right-wing DNVP won 95 seats, a gain of 24, with 19.5 per cent (5.96 million), up from 15.1 in 1920. Thanks to the party's electoral pacts with smaller right-wing parties, the DNVP could rely on the support of ten additional Reichstag members, making it now the strongest grouping in the Reichstag. A further worrying development for the health of Weimar democracy was the electoral performance of the extreme right-wing National Socialist Freedom Party (*Nationalsozialistische Freiheitspartei*, NSFP), led by Erich Ludendorff, which was hastily formed in April 1924, through an electoral pact with the German People's Freedom Party (*Deutschvölkische Freiheitspartei*, DVFP). The NSFP was really a means of carrying on National Socialism, still banned after the Munich Beer Hall Putsch. This new party polled 6.5 per cent of votes (1.91 million), and won 32 seats in the Reichstag, with Ludendorff and Ernst Röhm becoming members of the Reichstag for the first time. Hitler had refused to endorse this new party. On the extreme Left, the KPD also performed very well, gaining 58 seats, up from four in 1920, taking its vote share to 12.6 per cent (3.69 million), up from 2.1 per cent at the previous election. Most former supporters of the USPD had clearly switched their allegiance to the KPD, which once again highlighted the split on the Left of German politics.[29]

The DNVP immediately called for the resignation of the Marx cabinet, and urged the appointment as Chancellor of Admiral Alfred von Tirpitz, the former chief of the Imperial Navy during the First World War, and a firm advocate of unrestricted submarine warfare. The idea of Tirpitz as Chancellor caused great alarm among the Allies, as he was inextricably linked with the worst aspects of the Kaiser's regime. On 26 May, Marx and all his cabinet members resigned. President Ebert immediately asked him to form another coalition government, representing the Centre Right, including if possible the nationalist DNVP. Stresemann thought the DNVP would become far less extreme when faced with the realities of government, but their demands, which included, along with Tirpitz as Chancellor, the removal of Marx as Chancellor, and Stresemann as Foreign Minister, and giving no promise to vote in favour of the Dawes Plan, proved unacceptable. In any case, Marx was reluctant to serve in a cabinet headed by nationalists. On 3 June, Wilhelm Marx became Chancellor of a fragile minority government once again. The second Marx cabinet was based on three centre-ground parties: Zentrum, the DVP and the DDP, who between them commanded only 138 of the 472 seats in the Reichstag. All the cabinet members from the first Marx cabinet remained in post, without any changes.

The Reichstag debates that followed Marx's confirmation as Chancellor showed his government could rely on a parliamentary majority to confirm the Dawes Plan. A no-confidence vote tabled by the nationalist DNVP was easily defeated on 6 June, with the Social Democrats giving vital support to the government, not because they supported the domestic policies of the Marx cabinet, especially his earlier suspension of the eight-hour day, but because they unanimously supported the foreign policy of Gustav Stresemann to implement the Dawes Plan.[30]

The driving force behind the opposition to the Dawes Plan in the Reichstag was Alfred Hugenberg, a leading member and future leader of the DNVP. He had carved out a successful business career, including membership of the board of the mighty Krupp industrial company. He had made huge profits during the hyperinflation from shrewd asset purchases and sales, and he used them to build a media empire. He bought up scores of newspapers, was the owner of the country's leading news agencies, and would go on to acquire a controlling interest in Universum Film (UFA), Germany's leading film company. Hugenberg thus became the most powerful figure in German propaganda during the Weimar years. He hated the Republic and socialism in equal measure. His brand of politics was fervently nationalist. He wanted to see the Hohenzollern monarchy restored, and to further this aim he collaborated with extreme right-wing groups. Hugenberg had a particularly strong dislike of Stresemann's conciliatory foreign policy, and through his various media outlets strove to undermine it.[31]

There was also a national election in France in May 1924, which resulted in victory for the Cartes des Gauches, an alliance of Socialists and Radicals. The architect of the Ruhr occupation, Raymond Poincaré, was replaced as French Prime Minister by the radical Socialist Édouard Herriot, who took office on 15 June 1924, and also took on the additional role of Foreign Minister. The son of an army officer, Herriot had been a noted academic, served as the mayor of Lyon and had been a cabinet minister in Aristide Briand's government during the War. He was a bitter critic of Poincaré, believing the harsh line he adopted towards Germany was misconceived and self-defeating. In his first speech, on 17 June, he adopted a decidedly different policy line from that of his predecessor, by declaring: 'We are the enemies of a policy of isolation and force, which leads to occupation of territory.' He further stressed that the French government now accepted the Dawes Plan 'without reservation'.[32]

On 7 July, the *Völkischer Kurier* (the *People's Courier*), a Munich newspaper, published a statement from Adolf Hitler announcing he had 'stepped down from the leadership of the National Socialist movement', and would now refrain from all political activities for the duration of his imprisonment, because he was 'writing a substantial book'. Hitler saw his proposed book as the new Bible of National Socialism. The book's original title was 'Four and a Half Years of Battle Against Lies, Stupidity and Cowardice: Account Settled.' This was rejected as being too long-winded by Max Amann, Hitler's publishing manager, who shortened it to 'My Struggle'.

Mein Kampf was published by Eher Verlag, the Nazi publishing house, in two volumes, running to 782 pages. The first volume appeared on 18 July 1925 with the second following on 11 December 1926. Amann had edited both books extensively, trying to make them less verbose and repetitive. Despite its literary weaknesses, *Mein Kampf*, which is part autobiography, part ideological manifesto, and part blueprint for political action, remains an important book for understanding the essence of Nazi ideology. Hitler claimed it was aimed at committed followers of National Socialism, not the general reader. One early convert to National Socialism writes:

> My greatest political experience occurred when I bought and read a copy of Hitler's book. I saw therein a confirmation of the very views I had cherished, but which I could not express properly. Now I had

the necessary equipment to take up the quarrel with my political opponents. I had found the cause to which I could devote my life.[33]

The book was not, as is often routinely argued, 'unreadable', though it was poorly structured, consisting primarily of a series of speech scripts, but despite its meandering tone it offers a road map for Hitler's future actions that cannot be so easily dismissed. It was priced in the new currency at 12 Reichsmarks, about twice the price of most books at that time.[34] In 1925, the book sold 9,473 copies, falling to 6,913 in 1926, and even further to 3,015 in 1928, counting sales of both volumes. After 1930, however, sales began to increase, jumping to 90,351 in 1932. By 1945, the book had sold 15 million copies in Germany, making it comparable in sales to the Bible.[35]

Hitler had begun working tentatively on the book in the first weeks of his imprisonment, but only started to labour on it intensively from mid-June 1924. The prison governor gave him permission to buy a typewriter, and provided him with a table and some paper. Hitler later claimed that his time in Landsberg was a 'university education paid by the state', which enabled him to gain 'clarity about a lot of things that I had previously understood only instinctively'.[36] It is often stated that Hitler dictated the book to fellow prisoner Rudolf Hess, his loyal secretary, who then typed up the chapters. This is a myth, repeated uncritically in many biographies, and in some general histories of the rise of Hitler. According to the memoirs of prison guard Otto Lurker, it was Hitler alone who diligently typed up the book each day from handwritten notes, using one or two fingers, on a portable American-made Remington typewriter.[37] The typewriter was a gift from one of his rich benefactors, Helene Bechstein, the wife of Edwin Bechstein of the famous piano manufacturing firm. Hess himself described his own role in the composition of the book in a letter: 'Whenever a chapter is done, he brings it to me. He explains it to me, and we discuss the odd point.'[38]

The first volume of *Mein Kampf* presents a heavily redacted autobiographical story from his early life up to the founding of the National Socialist Party (NSDAP) in February 1920. The book opens with Hitler stating the purpose of his life: 'Today it seems to me providential that Fate should have chosen Braunau on the Inn [Austria] as my birthplace. For this small town lies on the boundary of two German states which we of the younger generation have made it our life's work to reunite by every means at our disposal.' Hitler suggests that many people who become important start out very ordinary. He then goes on to describe his childhood and his time in Vienna, portraying himself as a poor man who constantly faces deprivation and disappointment, but who learns life-changing lessons along the way, especially about his chief enemies: bureaucrats, democrats, Marxists and Jews.

The end of his ambition to be a renowned artist in Vienna is depicted as a 'magnificent failure', destroyed by 'fossilised bureaucrats with no understanding of real talent'. He then explains how German patriotism became embedded in his soul during his time in the German Army in the Great War of 1914–18, relating theatrically how he broke down and cried when he was told of the German defeat. Finally, Hitler relates his post-war activities, especially his realisation that he was a great speaker, and his role in the development of the National Socialist Party, but he does not cover the failed Munich Beer Hall Putsch in any detail, claiming it was pointless to 'reopen wounds that are only just healing'.[39] Most of this potted autobiography is selective amnesia, but for Hitler it acts as the essential prelude to his proposed 'historic mission' to save Germany.

The second volume, written after his release from prison, mostly in his Bavarian mountain retreat in Berchtesgaden, which would become known as the Berghof, was more of a political manifesto, developing many of the ideas he mentioned in the first volume, but in more detail. The autobiographical element is toned down as he comments on all sorts of topics, including culture, education, the theatre, films, comics, art, literature, history, sex, marriage, prostitution and even syphilis – in fact, he devotes ten pages to this latter topic, declaring it his key task 'to eradicate it', as he felt it was weakening the racial purity of the nation.

The dominant theoretical concepts in both volumes are race and space. Hitler depicts human history, not as a class struggle, as Marx would have it, but as a Darwinian struggle for existence between the strong and pure 'Aryan' races over the 'weak and mixed race' ones. In this struggle, he says, war is 'the great purifier': it is how the strong races trample over the weak. Accordingly, the question of how Germans will become the 'strongest race' is given detailed attention. Hitler divided the world into three racial groups: (1) Aryans, defined as those races who created advanced cultures; (2) the bearers of culture, classed as those races who cannot create cultures, but who can copy from Aryans; (3) inferior peoples, categorised as races that have no capacity either to create culture or to copy from others. The Aryan race, on this view, can only maintain its racial dominance by ensuring the 'purity of its blood'. The key objective of Hitler's racial policy was to create a pure Aryan folk community of Germans, which he called *Volksgemeinschaft*. This 'master race' would then become 'the highest species of humanity on this Earth.' Hitler aimed to educate citizens to 'see race in the centre of all life'.

The idea of a popular folk community bound together by 'common blood' is at the core of Hitler's proposed future National Socialist state. This was a romanticised notion, that the 'lost Germany' of the pre-industrial age could be restored through the creation of a simpler, rural society, based on principles of hierarchy, patriotism, order, and obedience. The idea of the urban-dweller being trapped by modernity is evoked frequently in *Mein Kampf*. In Hitler's view, this folk community required an authoritarian *Führer*. There would be no majority decisions, no democratic elections, only a state in which the *Führer* and a small elite decided everything. The Leader would give orders downwards, which would be obeyed without discussion. Hitler envisaged the folk community being a 'classless society', in which individuals would find their own natural level through hard work and will-power. This required removing all 'racial impurities' from German blood, thereby creating a 'blood-pure' community.

The future National Socialist state would not promote equality, only equality of opportunity. Hitler believed an elite group (a *Herrenvolk*), would emerge from this process, providing stronger, taller, fitter and faster males, with women given the role of wives and mothers each producing several children. Those who could not reach the Aryan ideal of perfection would have to content themselves with becoming loyal and patriotic members of the folk community.

Hitler was vague in *Mein Kampf* about where 'socialism' fitted into his proposed folk community. He claimed National Socialism was a 'dictatorship of whole community'. The idea first came to prominence in the 1890s, when the Liberal pastor, Friedrich Naumann, set up the National-Social Association, which aimed to persuade industrial workers, who might be attracted by Marxist-inspired socialism, to give their support to the existing imperial state and to war. In Hitler's view, National Socialism fitted into this tradition by being primarily concerned with strengthening the state, not with the narrow sectional interests of the working class.

As we have seen, intricately connected to the concept of the folk community was the idea of 'racial hygiene'. During his imprisonment Hitler studied several books on the subject. One that greatly influenced him was called *Die Freigabe der Vernichtung Lebensunwerten Lebens* (*Allowing the Destruction of Life Unworthy of Life*), by Karl Binding and Alfred Hoch, which argued brain damaged and severely disabled people had no right to live and should be selected for euthanasia. The idea of compulsory sterilisation and euthanasia for 'inferior people' (*Untermensch*), was given further academic credibility by the Munich professor Fritz Lenz. In *Mein Kampf*, Hitler promised to implement these ideas if he came to power and promised physically and mentally 'defective people' should be prevented from begetting 'defective offspring' by sterilisation, claiming this would be a 'humane act'. Lenz was delighted after reading *Mein Kampf*, describing Hitler as 'the first politician possessing considerable influence who has recognized that racial hygiene is a crucial political task and is prepared to support it'.[40]

If the 'Aryan' possessed all the positive qualities Hitler admired, the opposite was true of the two key enemies he outlined in *Mein Kampf*: Jews and Marxists. A virulent hatred of Marxism is indicated on many pages in the book. Hitler's chief desire, if he gained power, was to 'eliminate' or 'exterminate' Marxism in German politics, and then destroy Bolshevism through a war of conquest against the Soviet Union. A passionate and violent hatred of Jews also runs through the book, but especially in the chapter 'Nation and Race' in the first volume. Hitler defined Jews not as a religious group but as a united race planning a 'world conspiracy', as outlined in the forged book *The Protocols of the Elders of Zion*, which Hitler believed was true.

Hitler represented Jews as stateless people (the State of Israel was not established until 1947), who sought to undermine the 'ethnic unity' and 'racial purity' in every country they lived by promoting 'international' ideas. Hitler ascribed every ill in the world to 'Jewish influence'. They were seemingly responsible for the German defeat in 1918, the German Revolution, hyperinflation and cultural degeneracy. Hitler describes Jews in *Mein Kampf* in the language of parasitology, variously as 'not human', 'a germ carrier of the worst sort', a 'germ of disunion', or as 'vermin', 'bacilli' and 'parasites'.

Antisemitism had two functions in Hitler's thinking: first, it provided a simple scapegoat for all the problems in Weimar society, and second, it suggested the 'solution' to ending them was to 'eliminate' Jews from Germany. Hitler's antisemitism was demonic in its negative passion, but was central to the ideological mindset he displays in *Mein*

Kampf. He uses the words 'removal' and 'elimination' when describing how he will deal with Jews if he comes to power. Hitler writes at one point: 'We shall only succeed in persuading the masses to become nationalists if, in addition to a positive struggle for the soul of our people, their international poisoners [the Jews] are exterminated.' He also suggests it would have been a good thing if the Jews who had 'stabbed Germany in the back' could have been killed by poison gas during the First World War, but he admitted such a policy would not be possible in the context of current times. Instead, Hitler promised to combat the 'Jewish menace' by removing their legal rights, weakening their economic position, and encouraging them to emigrate abroad.

A large amount of space in *Mein Kampf* is devoted to foreign policy. Hitler's key aim is to make Germany the most dominant power in Europe through territorial conquest, and to gain revenge for the German defeat in the Great War. Hitler admitted he had entered politics to demand the end of the Treaty of Versailles, primarily by settling accounts with France, thereby restoring Germany's 1914 borders. This implied a future war concentrated in Western Europe, but Hitler now shifted his emphasis to the idea that Germany, whose population was expanding, needed to have living space (*Lebensraum*), in Eastern Europe. This notion was influenced by the geopolitical ideas of Karl Haushofer, a former Bavarian army general and University of Munich professor – ideas which had already influenced Hess, who passed them on to Hitler. Haushofer visited Hitler in prison, but they failed to get on, the learned professor describing Hitler as 'half-educated'. [41]

Hitler also read works of political geography by the Pan German writer Friedrich Ratzel while in prison, which outline similar ideas to those of Haushofer. The concept of *Lebensraum* was something Hitler was already thinking about, as in early notes for the book he uses the term *Bodenerwerb* (acquisition of land) but he then drops this and substitutes it with *Lebensraum*.[42] Hitler, a lover of slogans, liked *Lebensraum* as an easily explained concept which summed up where his foreign policy would be heading if he came to power. This simple slogan now became an enthusiastically supported cornerstone of Hitler's ideology.

These ideas clearly influenced Hitler to shift the axis of his foreign policy objectives. 'To demand that the 1914 frontiers of Germany be restored,' Hitler wrote in *Mein Kampf*, 'is a political absurdity'. The revision of the Treaty of Versailles would be a mere prelude to gaining living space in Eastern Europe, through a war of conquest against the

Soviet Union, which he thought had been militarily weakened by being under the control of 'Jewish-Bolsheviks' since the 1917 Revolution and was now 'ripe for collapse'. The main aim was to create a 'Greater German Reich' of 250 million 'racially pure' Germans, completely self-sufficient in food and raw materials. The model he was looking to emulate here was, of course, the USA. The desired war against the Soviet Union would be a 'racial crusade' to rid Europe of Hitler's two most hated enemies, the Bolsheviks and Jews.

Hitler's newly proposed foreign policy objectives were concentrated on the entire European continent. He would first aim to revise the Treaty of Versailles by incorporating all German speakers in Austria, Czechoslovakia and Poland into a Greater German Reich. He thought the French government was bound to oppose this, and so a war with France was implicit in Hitler's thinking. As a counterweight to French hostility, Hitler wanted to build close relations with Italy and, especially, the United Kingdom. Hitler believed Anglo-German antagonism was a key cause of the Great War, and he wanted to persuade the British government to abandon its longstanding determination to uphold the balance of power in Europe by offering to guarantee the British Empire in return for a 'free hand' to gain territory in Eastern Europe. Interestingly, Poland, the country that was treated with tremendous harshness during the Second World War, hardly features at all in *Mein Kampf*.

Hitler laid out in *Mein Kampf* everything he intended to do if he was ever given power. The book completed his journey from beer-hall agitator to a contender for the leadership of the extreme Right. Hitler also admitted he had learned one big lesson from the Munich Beer Hall Putsch, namely, that using force to gain power was no longer viable, because the Weimar Republic, supported by the Army and the police, was now too stable and strong. As a result, he would now pursue the parliamentary route to power. At the end of the first volume of *Mein Kampf*, Hitler wrote: 'Parliament is a terrible thing, but we must join it to kill it.'[43]

During the summer of 1924, the final details of the Dawes Plan were agreed. The London Conference on the Application of the Dawes Plan which ran from 16 July to 16 August was convened for this purpose. The leading Allied representatives were: Ramsay MacDonald, the British Prime Minister; Édouard Herriot, the French Prime Minister; Alberto de' Sefani, the Italian Finance Minister, deputising for Italian Prime Minister, Benito Mussolini; Georges Theunis, the

Belgian Prime Minister and Owen Young from the USA. Also present were diplomatic representatives from Japan, Portugal, Romania, and the Kingdom of the Slavs, Croats and Slovenes (later Yugoslavia). It was agreed that once the Allies had agreed on the mechanism for implementing the Dawes Plan during the initial discussions, the representatives from the German government would then be invited to London to join the final deliberations.

Presiding over the Conference was Ramsay MacDonald. In his opening speech, he struck a decidedly conciliatory tone, saying Germany had to be given a chance to get back on its feet. MacDonald's desire for a reconciliation with Germany had a major influence over the mood and tone of the proceedings. Herriot stoutly defended the French point of view, insisting on the need for safeguards to prevent further German defaults, but he accepted another invasion of the Ruhr would not be used to enforce payment in future. The American delegates insisted no agreement would be acceptable unless the German government gave its wholehearted approval.

Foreign Minister Gustav Stresemann and Chancellor Wilhelm Marx in London for the conference on the implementation of the Dawes Plan, August 1924.

Following these initial discussions, it was decided to allow the Reparations Commission to retain the power of determining whether sanctions should be invoked in any given situation, but to ensure fairness an American delegate would be added to the Commission. It was finally agreed that the issue of 'flagrant defaults' by Germany would be decided by a Court of Arbitration, composed of three neutral representatives, with an American presiding. The Conference then worked out a plan for the restoration of Germany's economic unity. It called for the elimination of the administrative and commercial measures which France and Belgium had introduced in the Ruhr since January 1923. On the sensitive issue of the timing of the Franco-Belgian withdrawal from the Ruhr, Herriot said he was personally willing to be cooperative, but he stressed the severe limitations being placed upon him by his cabinet with regard to this matter. MacDonald suggested this question should therefore only be addressed in secret sessions.

On 1 August, members of the German government were invited to the London Conference. On 5 August, Wilhelm Marx (Chancellor), Gustav Stresemann (Foreign Minister) and Hans Luther (Finance Minister) all arrived in London, armed with a grim resolve to agree to the implementation of the Dawes Plan. MacDonald greeted them in 10 Downing Street, and immediately urged them to raise the question of the evacuation of the Ruhr directly with Herriot. In his first speech to the Conference, Marx said: 'The German government has, like the Allied governments, stated on an earlier occasion that it regarded the Experts' Plan as a suitable foundation for the solution of the Reparations question.' Marx concluded his speech by promising that as soon as free economic activity was restored in the Ruhr, the German government would devote all its energy to fulfilling the Dawes Plan.

On 8 August, Stresemann had a private conversation with Herriot, who told him difficulties had arisen within the French cabinet over the question of the timing of the evacuation of the Ruhr, but he agreed the withdrawal of troops should take place 'within a reasonable time'. The divided French Cabinet then recalled Herriot to Paris for an emergency meeting, on the day after his first meeting with Stresemann. After his return to London, Herriot resumed his talks with Stresemann, on 11 August, pointing out that he had always personally opposed the Ruhr occupation, and wanted to move faster towards withdrawal, but he admitted his cabinet colleagues would only agree to withdrawal from the Ruhr within one year. Herriot promised to accelerate this timeframe if he could. As a final concession to Germany, Herriot promised to remove troops from the Dortmund zone once the London agreement on the Dawes Plan was signed.

The failure of Herriot to agree to a swift withdrawal from the Ruhr came as a huge disappointment to the German delegation. For several days, it seemed the deadlock between Germany and France on the timetable for the Ruhr withdrawal might bring the London Conference to an abrupt end, without any agreement. On 13 August, further tense discussions took place between the German, French and Belgian delegates on the Ruhr question. Herriot was in a much more uncompromising mood this time than he had been during his earlier private talks with Stresemann, saying the date for the Ruhr evacuation had to be in a year's time.

MacDonald met Stresemann soon after this meeting ended. Stresemann told him that Herriot's attitude had stiffened, largely due to promptings from his mutinous cabinet back in Paris. MacDonald, though sympathetic to the German position, forlornly accepted the French government could not budge from a one-year withdrawal period, and to avoid a further blow-up on the issue, he advised the Germans to face facts and accept this. On 15 August, Marx's cabinet took the decisive step of giving its full approval of the Dawes plan, and reluctantly agreed to the year-long French-Belgian timetable for withdrawal from the Ruhr. All the participants at the London Conference then accepted the Dawes Plan, pending ratification by the various parliaments.[44]

The spotlight now shifted to the Reichstag. The Dawes Plan legislation was debated in parliament towards the end of August. These laws concerned the creation of the national bank of issue, the interest-bearing debentures on the national railways and industry, the liquidation of the Rentenmark, and its replacement by the Reichsmark, and the acceptance of the new schedule of payments. On 25 August, Wilhelm Marx told Reichstag members he would ratify the London agreement on the Dawes Plan whether the Reichstag approved it or not, with the assistance of President Ebert using his powers under Article 48 of the Constitution.[45]

The most important piece of legislation related to enacting the Dawes Plan was a bill concerning the ownership and finance of the *Reichsbahn*, the German national railway system, which required a two-thirds majority in the Reichstag, as it involved a modification of the Constitution. The Marx government was assured of support from the Social Democrats, Zentrum, the Democrats, and the People's Party, but to reach the required majority it needed two-thirds of the Reichstag members of the DNVP to vote in favour. At the second reading of the bill, the law failed to receive the required majority, with 248 votes in favour and 174 against. President Ebert tried to regain the initiative by threatening to dissolve the Reichstag and call new elections if the *Reichsbahn* measure was not passed, while Marx appealed to the Nationalists by saying there would be no change in his desire to remove the detested Article 231 'war guilt' clause of the Treaty of Versailles.

The key moment in the increasingly bitter Reichstag debate came when the DNVP leader, Oskar Hergt, announced that he would allow his Reichstag party members to vote as they pleased. Most industrial business groups, including the powerful Federation of German Industry (*Reichsverband der Deutschen Industrie*), had declared themselves in favour of the acceptance of the Dawes Plan. Many industrial magnates even lobbied the DNVP members to vote in favour. On 29 August, the Reichstag voted by 314 to 117 votes to accept the railway bill, and the rest of the Dawes legislation, with the votes of 48 Nationalists giving the legislation the required majority.[46] Ludendorff commented bitterly: 'This is a disgrace. Ten years ago, I won at Tannenberg. Today we have witnessed a Jewish Tannenberg'.[47] Marx issued the following statement after the crucial vote:

> The Reichstag, by the decisions taken today, has set its seal to the agreement reached in London, these are measures that will be of supreme importance for the destiny of the German people in the years ahead. The government of the Reich desires to express its thanks to all the members who have contributed to this result. All who participated had to overcome serious misgivings and even set aside their personal convictions.

In a definite concession to the right-wing DNVP, Marx then raised the delicate question of war guilt, stating: 'The government of the Reich hereby states that it does not recognize this assertion [of war-guilt]. It is a just claim on the part of the German people to be freed from the burden of this false accusation.'[48] These words were greeted with disappointment by the French and British governments. To undo some of this self-inflicted diplomatic damage, Marx wrote to Ramsay MacDonald and Édouard Herriot, stating that Germany had no desire to escape its reparations obligations, but he felt the German people regarded themselves as innocent of 'war guilt' and he was merely giving expression to this widely held view.[49]

On 30 August, the Dawes Plan was put into effect by a formal signing ceremony in London, attended by the representatives of the German government, all the Allied governments concerned, and by members of the Reparations Commission. The US government, being an invited and unofficial participant in the negotiations, did not sign the agreement. After the signing, the French government issued instructions for the evacuation of a section of the Ruhr, to be followed in a year's time by complete withdrawal. Two days later, the 20 million gold marks instalment due from the German government in reparations under the Dawes Plan was paid on time, and the process for creating the railway and industrial debentures was set in motion. Offices were provided in Berlin for all the various commissions involved in implementing the agreement.[50]

With the historic Dawes Plan now signed, the idea of Germany joining the League of Nations became favoured by the Allies. On 23 September, President Ebert chaired a meeting with the Marx cabinet at which the matter was discussed. It was agreed that efforts should be made to secure Germany's immediate admission, but with certain conditions attached, most notably that Germany should be given rights equal to the existing members, have permission to participate in the League's Mandate System, which was viewed as a way of regaining control of the German colonies, and to be offered a permanent seat on the League Council. Then there was the delicate issue of Article 16 of the League of Nations, the so-called sanctions clause, which obliged League members to apply sanctions against any country that engaged in aggressive war. The German government argued it was not able to participate in or defend itself against military or economic sanctions, and, therefore, wished to be regarded as neutral. Finally, the German government emphasised entry into the League must not be understood as acceptance of the charge that it alone was responsible for the outbreak of the Great War.

On 29 September, a German Note containing all these demands was presented to the League of Nations. In reply, the League Council accepted Germany's claim to be made a member of the Council, but stressed an application for full membership must not be submitted with conditions, and rejected the desire of Germany to remain neutral, as it was felt this would undermine the basis of the League's commitment to collective security. Germany's desire to join met with opposition from Soviet leaders, who argued it would undermine the Treaty of Rapallo. Given these problems, Stresemann decided the most sensible option for the German government was to postpone applying for membership for the time being, and move step by step towards gaining entry.[51]

Another matter requiring frequent negotiation during 1924 was the question of Allied military control. The Allies had the power, under the terms of the Versailles Treaty, to inspect German armed forces and stocks of armaments. On 9 January, the German government suggested the work of the Inter-Allied Military Control Commission should now end, as Germany had disarmed under the terms of Article 213 of Versailles, and all rearmament supervisory functions should now be transferred to the League of Nations.[52] The French and British governments disagreed, arguing the inspection of German armaments should continue. On 5 March, the Allies sent the German government a statement of its position. Military control, they declared, could not yet be dispensed with. It was important for the Allies to gain conclusive evidence on whether Germany was fulfilling the disarmament clauses of the Treaty of Versailles. They reminded the German government that for almost two years there had been no Allied inspection at all.

On 22 June, Herriot and MacDonald sent a joint confidential Note to Chancellor Marx, challenging him to answer rumours of increased military activity by nationalist paramilitary organisations. In reply, Marx assured the Allies there was no 'secret rearmament' going on in Germany. The Allies remained unconvinced. On 30 June, the German government finally agreed to the Anglo-French demand for a fresh military inspection.[53] The Allied Military Commission of Control Inspection, headed by Marshal Ferdinand Foch, occurred in the autumn, and resulted in an extremely critical report, published on 22 December 1924, which made clear the German government's insistence that the required disarmament had been carried out to the letter was incorrect. The Commission found paramilitary organisations were still engaged in clandestine military training, and also discovered large stores of hidden arms. These worries about secret German military rearmament were enough for the Allies to refuse to withdraw forces from the Cologne Zone in the Rhineland on 10 January 1925, as had been specified in the Treaty of Versailles.[54]

Whilst the Allied Control inspection was in progress in the autumn of 1924, there was a huge shake-up in German currency. On 11 October, the Reichsmark (RM) was introduced, as part of the Dawes Plan, as a permanent replacement for the interim currency, the Rentenmark, which had restored economic stability, and the old Papiermark, which had collapsed under the weight of hyperinflation. The denominations of Reichsmarks came in lower-value coins and banknotes of 5M, 10RM, 20RM, 50RM, 100RM and 1,000RM. Each Reichsmark was divided into 100 Reichspfennigs. Germany finally had a stable currency once again, guaranteed by the independent Reichsbank.[55] The Reichsmark remained the German currency until it was replaced by the Deutsche Mark on 23 June 1948, which itself was succeeded by the Euro in 2002.

During October, negotiations had been undertaken by the beleaguered Chancellor, Wilhelm Marx, to reconstruct his cabinet in order to broaden its voting strength in the Reichstag. Marx wanted what he called a 'National Union' government, to include members from across the political spectrum. He negotiated with the DNVP and the SPD, but neither of these parties wanted to join a coalition with the other. Then the DDP added to Marx's torment by opposing the inclusion of the DNVP in government, due to its right-wing stance. On 20 October, Marx was forced to admit all his efforts had failed and, with the agreement of the cabinet, he asked President Ebert to dissolve the Reichstag, and call a national election, the second during 1924. The hope was that the extremists on the Left and Right would lose support at the polls. During the election campaign the Social Democrats attacked Marx, depicting him as weak, lacking vision and much too tolerant of the nationalist Right. They wanted to put an end to what they called the 'inflation Reichstag'. Stresemann, the leader of the DVP, disagreed, arguing the diplomatic position of Germany would be greatly enhanced if the nation's strongest right-wing party the DNVP was included in the cabinet. Zentrum candidates highlighted the virtues of the Marx government, which they claimed had brought economic stability. The DNVP election manifesto promised to restore the monarchy and terminate the Treaty of Versailles and the Dawes Plan.[56]

The German national election took place on 7 December 1924. Voter turnout was 78.8 per cent. The parties who had supported the Dawes Plan did well. The party gaining the most seats was the SPD, which won 131 seats, a gain of 31 from May 1924, with a popular vote of 26 per cent (7.88 million), up 5.5 per cent. The middle-class parties made smaller gains. The DVP, led by Gustav Stresemann, won 51 seats, up from 45, and polled 3.05 million votes, or 10.1 per cent of the electorate, an increase of 0.99 per cent since May. Zentrum won 69 seats, up from 65, polling 13.6 per cent overall (4.11 million), only up by a narrow 0.22 per cent since May. The DDP improved its position slightly, winning 32 seats, up from 28, taking 6.3 per cent of the popular vote (1.91 million), an increase of 0.6 per cent. The big electoral surprise was the performance of the nationalist DNVP, which improved its position, winning 103 seats, an increase of eight from May, taking 20.5 per cent of the popular vote (6.20 million), an increase of just 1 per cent.

The two other parties who had opposed the Dawes Plan, the Communists and the National Socialists, performed poorly. The KPD won 45 seats, a loss of 17 seats since May, polling 8.9 per cent of votes (2.7 million), down 3.7 per cent. The National Socialist Freedom Party (NSFP), led by Ludendorff, won 14 seats, down 18 on May, polling a total vote of 3 per cent (907, 242), down by 3.55 per cent.[57] The mediocre performance of these extreme parties was proof of the change that had come over the economy since the May election. The gradual consolidation of economic affairs was clearly impacting on voting behaviour. Inflation was now under control and unemployment was falling. This meant the working classes and the lower middle class were much better off than they had been six months earlier. In these circumstances, the parties of the extreme Right and Left seemed much less attractive.

On 15 December, Wilhelm Marx resigned as Chancellor, along with his second cabinet. President Ebert, reluctant to see him depart, asked him to try and form a new cabinet. There were two possibilities: a return of the centre-left 'Grand Coalition', including the Social Democrats, or the formation of a centre-right 'Bourgeois Coalition', including the Nationalist DNVP. Marx tried to put together both types of coalition, but he soon gave up when he could find no agreement. On hearing this, Ebert asked Marx, and his current cabinet, to continue in office, in a caretaker capacity, until a new cabinet could be formed early in the New Year.

The failure of Germany's parliamentary system to generate a stable government was directly related to the fragmentation of Weimar party politics. In confidential remarks to a meeting of government leaders on 19 December 1924, Otto Gessler, the Defence Minister, argued the persistent failure of efforts to form a government capable of commanding a parliamentary majority was not just a government crisis, but a constitutional one that could only be remedied by a reform of the Weimar Constitution. Specifically, Gessler complained the Weimar Constitution had given Germany a parliament that might work if there were two or three parties that could gain a majority in the Reichstag but was unworkable with such a large number of parties who had representation in the Reichstag.[58]

At 12.15 p.m. on 20 December 1924, Adolf Hitler was released from Landsberg Fortress. He was met outside the prison gates by Adolf Müller, the owner of the printing company used by his publisher, Eher Verlag, and by Heinrich Hoffmann, his personal photographer, who took a photo of him standing outside the prison, which was published in many newspapers. Hitler told waiting reporters that he wanted to rest after his spell in prison and finish his book. He refused to discuss whether he would return to politics.[59] The *New York Times* ran an article on Hitler's release, under the headline: 'Hitler Tamed By Prison', which reported the 'demi-god of reactionary extremists' looked much wiser as he left prison, noting his behaviour during imprisonment had convinced the authorities that he was no longer to be feared, and concluded: 'It is believed he will retire to private life and return to Austria, the country of his birth.'[60]

On 23 December, the verdict was declared in the libel and slander trial of the newspaper editor Erwin Rothart, for publishing a letter in the central German newspaper *Mitteldeutsche Zeitung*, earlier in the year, from a Bavarian nationalist, who had accused President Friedrich Ebert of 'treason', for his part in the January 1918 munitions workers' strike. Ebert had faced many similar accusations, but he had always been exonerated in court proceedings related to them. Rothart publicly goaded Ebert to disprove the 'treason' allegation, by writing: 'Come on now, Mr Ebert, prove that you are really not a traitor.'[61] Ebert decided to accept the challenge and clear the stain on his reputation. The trial took place in the regional court in Magdeburg, Saxony, from 9 to 23 December in a blaze of publicity.

On 9 December, in a statement read to the court, Ebert stated that he had opposed the 1918 munitions strike, and had only joined the strike committee to bring the dispute to an end. On 12 December, former Chancellor Philipp Scheidemann corroborated Ebert's statement by saying that he and Ebert had been seen as 'strike breakers' by the union leaders. On 14 December, Ebert's lawyer read out a letter to the court from Paul von Hindenburg, written in December 1918, in which he called Ebert a 'true patriot'. At this time, Ebert was ill, struggling with severe stomach pains, during the period of the trial, but he refused to make his illness public for fear it might be seen as a plea for sympathy. Ebert was told by his doctor that he required hospital treatment to determine what was causing his stomach pains. For the time being, Ebert refused to follow this medical advice.[62]

In delivering his verdict, the judge agreed Erwin Rothart was guilty of 'technical libel' and sentenced him to three months in prison on that charge, but he added that President Ebert, under the criminal law in force at the time, had committed treason by supporting the munitions strike, whatever his reasons had been for doing so. Rothart was therefore judged not guilty of slander. It was yet another mind-boggling verdict, giving favourable treatment to a right-wing defendant. When President Ebert first received news that the court had branded him a traitor, it came as a devastating blow, especially as two of his sons had been killed in the war. On 24 December, the members of the second Marx cabinet took the unusual step of visiting him at the presidential palace, and delivered to him a joint statement, which asserted that his non-partisan actions as Reich president had 'always been designed to advance the interests of the Fatherland'.[63]

1925
·
DIPLOMATIC TRIUMPH AT LOCARNO
·

At the beginning of 1925, Germany was still without a government. On 9 January, President Ebert asked Hans Luther, the Minister of Finance, who was not attached to any political party, to form a government. Luther had been trained in local government, with expertise on economic matters. He had helped guide the German economy out of the hyperinflation period, played a key role in stabilising the German currency, and impressed the Allies at the London Conference during negotiations on the Dawes Plan. Luther decided to form what became known as a 'Bourgeois Cabinet' rather than a traditional party-based government.

The first Luther cabinet, predominantly right-wing and conservative, was formed on 15 January. It consisted of one designated representative (*Vertrauensmann*) of the four parties that had agreed to participate. The right-wing DNVP, taking part in a Weimar government for the very first time, was represented by Martin Schiele, its leader, who took the post of Minister of the Interior. The two other DNVP members in the cabinet were Otto von Schlieben, the Minister of Finance, and Albert Neuhaus, the Minister of Economic Affairs. To the relief of the Allies, Gustav Stresemann remained as Foreign Minister, representing the DVP, and was joined by his DVP colleague Rudolf Krone, the Minister of Transport.

There were two Zentrum members included: Heinrich Braun (Minister of Labour) and Josef Frenken (Minister for the Occupied Territories). Karl Stingl of the BVP entered the cabinet as the Minister of Post. The other members of the cabinet were supposed to be non-party affiliated experts, but only Gerhard von Kanitz, who remained as Minister of Food and Agriculture, was really independent. Otto Gessler, continuing as Defence Minister, still styled himself as 'Independent' even though he was associated with the DDP.[1]

The Luther cabinet was clearly a shift to the Right in German politics. Given the political differences among its members, it seemed unlikely it would last very long. Instead of seeking a vote of confidence, the new government opted for a Reichstag vote on a less controversial

previous page Aristide Briand and Gustav Stresemann: both men strove tirelessly for international reconciliation in the mid-1920s.

'acknowledgement of the government declaration', which was passed on 19 January by a vote of 246 for and 160 against.

On 19 January, Luther gave his first speech as Chancellor to the Reichstag. He declared his government would seek the support of all Germans who were willing to cooperate in a positive and constructive spirit. He admitted his cabinet had discussed changing the form of Weimar government to a monarchy, but had decided to retain a constitutional republic, but promised to look again at relations between the Reich and the German States, with a view to offering them much greater autonomy. On foreign affairs, Luther promised to achieve lasting peace, but denounced the Allies for failing to evacuate the Cologne zone of occupation, as agreed under the terms of the Treaty of Versailles. He was heckled by right-wing nationalists and Communists, as he pledged his wholehearted support for the Dawes Plan, with cries of 'traitor' being heard in the chamber. On domestic policy, he pledged to increase German exports and expand the social insurance scheme for unemployed workers.[2]

In foreign policy, the Dawes Plan had undoubtedly eased tension in Europe, but Stresemann believed permanent peace would not be established until France and Germany settled their differences in a much more comprehensive manner. Back in December 1922, the Cuno government had proposed a Rhineland Security Pact, under which the signatories would guarantee Germany's western frontiers. At that time, the French government rejected the proposal, but towards the end of 1924, Lord D'Abernon, the British Ambassador in Berlin, told Stresemann the new British government, headed by Stanley Baldwin, which had gained a landslide victory in the 1924 British general election, might now be favourably disposed to the idea.[3]

On 20 January, Stresemann addressed a carefully worded 'secret' memorandum to the British government, reviving the Security Pact proposal. Stresemann argued the agreement would settle German differences with France in a spirit of friendly understanding, giving the French a much needed sense of security. Stresemann favoured an agreement in which Germany, France, Belgium, Italy, and Britain undertook to guarantee the western frontier of Germany, with all the signatories further pledging not to wage war against each other. As part of the agreement, Germany would accept indefinitely the continued demilitarisation of the Rhineland. It was German military weakness which guided Stresemann's approach to foreign policy at this point, making him anxious to avoid a conflict with France. Stresemann also made it clear that Germany was willing to enter arbitration treaties with all other interested states, particularly with Poland and Czechoslovakia.[4]

Stresemann's proposal amounted to an acceptance of the frontiers established in Western Europe by the 1919 peace settlement, a renunciation of recourse to war with France, and a promise to agree to arbitration agreements with countries in Eastern Europe. Stresemann hoped the agreement would pave the way to the swift end of Allied occupation of the Rhineland, and of the Inter-Allied Military Control Commission. Austen Chamberlain, the new British Foreign Secretary, initially reacted to Stresemann's bold move without much enthusiasm. This was hardly surprising, as maintenance of close relations with France, and a distrust of German motives, had been part of his political outlook even before 1914. At the same time, Chamberlain had no desire to entangle Britain in Eastern Europe, as he had once famously said 'no British government ever will or ever can risk the bones of one British grenadier in defence of the Polish Corridor'.[5]

In his first response to Stresemann's memorandum, Chamberlain explained that nothing could be done behind the back of the French government, but by mid-February 1925 he had changed his mind, and gave the proposal his full endorsement in a speech in the House of Commons – a move aimed to sway the French government to follow suit. Chamberlain viewed Stresemann's proposal for a Security Pact as much more attractive than the recently proposed Geneva Protocol, concerning the peaceful settlement of international disputes, which was provisionally adopted, by a vote in the League of Nations General Assembly, on 2 October 1924, but which the British government had rejected on 12 March 1925.[6]

Pleased with Chamberlain's support, on 9 February, Stresemann opened negotiations with the French government by sending an almost identical memorandum to Édouard Herriot, the French Prime Minister, who saw two advantages to the proposed Security Pact. First, it would signify German acceptance of the loss of Alsace-Lorraine. Second, it would open the way to greater economic cooperation with German business, which pleased French industrialists who were already busy forming industrial cartels with their German counterparts. However, the French government immediately recognised that Germany was agreeing only to a settlement in Western Europe, but making no similar promises regarding the frontier with Poland and Czechoslovakia. Herriot feared a guarantee of Germany's western frontiers would only encourage the German government to seek a revision of its eastern boundaries later. For this reason, the French government was in no hurry to respond to Stresemann's proposals.

The French government tried to get the British to join in a guarantee of the frontiers in Eastern Europe, but the British government declared it would only guarantee the frontiers in Western Europe, not those of Poland and Czechoslovakia.[7] Stresemann was equally unwilling to guarantee the current boundaries with Poland, since doing so might imply renouncing German claims on Upper Silesia and the Polish Corridor and never would a German government give up its claims on Danzig. In a revealing letter to Wilhelm, the former German Crown Prince, Stresemann admitted the three aims of German foreign policy were (1) the solution of the reparations question; (2) the protection of Germans abroad living under foreign rule; (3) the readjustment of Germany's eastern frontiers, including the recovery of Danzig, Upper Silesia and the Polish Corridor, with a longer term aim of the union of Germany with Austria. These were ambitious aims, concluded Stresemann, but had to be attained by gradual, peaceful means.[8]

On 6 February, Gustav Bauer, the former Social Democrat Chancellor, resigned his seat in the Reichstag in disgrace 'for failing to distinguish politics from business'. His fall was part of the 'Barmat-Kutisker Corruption Scandal' which had erupted after the publication of a letter referring to money paid to him. Bauer was immediately expelled from the SPD.[9] The prelude to this messy corruption scandal came at the end of 1924 when it was alleged in the press that high-ranking members of the Social Democrats and the Centre Party had used their political positions to procure by bribery large loans from the Prussian State Bank (*Preussische Staatsbank*) and the Reich Postal Ministry (*Reichspostministerium*), amounting to 38 million gold marks, which were used by Ivan Kutisker and the Barmat brothers, Julius and Henri, to buy up companies cheaply during the hyperinflation period, and engage in currency speculation.

Shortly before Christmas 1924, Kutisker, a Jewish Lithuanian entrepreneur, was arrested. On 31 December, Julius Barmat, a Russian Jewish wholesale merchant and financier, was also taken into police custody, along with his brother, and other executives. This came after the collapse of their company, Barmat Enterprises, with 10 million Reichsmarks in debts. In the weeks following these initial arrests, further allegations of a complex web of corruption at the heart of Weimar government emerged. It soon became clear that the Barmat brothers and Kutisker had established close relations with Social Democrat and Centre Party leaders. The former Minister of Post Anton Hofle of Zentrum resigned his seat in the Reichstag on 9 February, and was also taken into police custody after being accused of granting loans of 34.6 million gold marks to the Barmat brothers. He took his own life by a drug overdose, while in prison, on 20 April 1925.

The allegation of a number of Jewish businesspeople receiving millions in loans from German government funds was seized on by the Right as proof that the 'Jewish worldwide conspiracy' outlined in the forged *Protocols of the Elders of Zion*, was real. For the Communists, too, here was unmistakable evidence that moderate Social Democrats had been corrupted by their involvement in government. A fact-finding committee in the Reichstag and the Prussian parliament was convened to investigate parliamentary involvement in the scandal. A major target of this investigation was Ernst Hellmann, the leader of the Social Democrats in the Prussian Parliament, but it could not be proved he had profited personally from the scandal. The investigation then focused on determining whether President Friedrich Ebert was involved. It was discovered his son had worked for the Barmat brothers and that, in 1919, Ebert had fast-tracked a visa for Julius Barmat to make his many business trips to Germany, but when the final report on the affair was published, in October 1925, Ebert was cleared of all allegations suggesting bribery. Bauer was reprimanded, but also cleared of accusations that he had profited from the loans advanced to Julius Barmat.

The resulting high-profile public trial on the affair in Berlin lasted over a year. The principal defendants, Julius and Henri Barmat, were found guilty of two acts of bribery, and each was sentenced to 11 months in prison, but acquitted of all other charges. Kutisker was found guilty on more serious charges of fraud and bribery, and sentenced to five years in prison, plus a fine of 4.5 million Reichsmarks. He died in prison on 13 July 1927.[10]

The Barmat-Kutisker Scandal did little to improve the failing health of President Ebert, who had been suffering from undiagnosed severe stomach pain for weeks. He became even more ill in mid-February, and was confined to bed with what was initially diagnosed as a severe bout of influenza. His condition then deteriorated further, and his doctors next thought he was suffering from a recurrence of a severe gall-bladder infection known as cholecystitis. Finally, on 23 February, he was admitted to a hospital in Charlottenburg with appendicitis and

President Friedrich Ebert lying in state before his funeral in 1925. A sequence of early deaths of able politicians of the centre and left inflicted repeated blows on Weimar's fragile body politic.

peritonitis. Ebert underwent an emergency appendectomy, performed by August Bier, one of Germany's most eminent surgeons. At first, he seemed to be recovering, but then his condition suddenly worsened. On 28 February at 10.15 a.m., Ebert died in his sleep, aged just 54, of post-operative septic shock, with his wife and family at the bedside.[11]

Friedrich Ebert was a Social Democrat of humble origins, and a firm supporter of democracy, who had led democratic Germany through six difficult years from the ashes of defeat in 1918 to the threshold of international reconciliation. He considered himself a patriot and a social reformer, not a rabble-rouser. Despite all the hostility he faced from the extreme Left and Right, he remained the Republic's anchor of stability, always showing a willingness to find a consensus among different viewpoints. His departure from the political scene was undoubtedly a bitter blow and a key turning point in the history of the Weimar Republic.[12]

The state funeral of Friedrich Ebert was a huge public event, attended by vast crowds in Berlin and Heidelberg.[13] Ebert's coffin was draped in the flag of the Reich President in which the black-red-gold colours of the Republic were prominent. The black eagle on a yellow background was also displayed. The main ceremony was held in the presidential palace, followed by a sombre funeral procession including

representatives of the police, the Reichswehr, the Reichstag and the German states, which wound a slow passage through Berlin's streets to the Brandenburg Gate, and to the nearby Reichstag building, then proceeded to Potsdam railway station where the coffin remained for a while so that ordinary Germans could pay their respects.

The funeral train journeyed to Ebert's home town of Heidelberg for the service and burial in the Bergfriedhof Cemetery. The memorial service began with the funeral march from Beethoven's Eroica symphony, played by the orchestra of the German State Opera. A moving eulogy was then read by Hans Luther, the German Chancellor, and the ceremony ended movingly with the music of Mozart. A short newsreel film of the funeral, showing scenes from the Berlin and Heidelberg ceremonies, appeared in cinemas throughout Germany.[14]

The various political parties now focused on the task of selecting presidential candidates. The Law for the Election of the German President, enacted on 4 May 1920, contained two key provisions: if no candidate won a two-thirds majority in the first ballot, a second ballot would occur, and new candidates could enter the contents, and the person receiving the most votes in the run off contest would be declared the winner. There were seven major candidates: the Social Democrats picked Otto Braun, the Prime Minister of Prussia; the KPD chose Reichstag member Ernst Thälmann, a charismatic public speaker; Karl Jarres, a conservative member of the DVP, mayor of Duisburg during the Ruhr crisis, and former Minister of the Interior, was selected as the leading candidate of the Reich Bloc (*Reichsblock*) and endorsed by two parties on the Right, the DNVP and the DVP. Zentrum refused to endorse Jarres, and chose instead Wilhelm Marx, the former Chancellor, as their candidate. The BVP picked Heinrich Held, the Prime Minister of Bavaria. The DDP selected Willy Hellpach, the State President of Baden, and the German National Freedom Party (DVFP) endorsed as their candidate Erich Ludendorff, who was supported half-heartedly by Adolf Hitler. There were 10 other minority candidates, none of whom stood much chance of attracting many voters.

In the first ballot, held on 29 March 1925, 68.9 per cent of the eligible German voters turned out.[15] Jarres, the only candidate backed by more than one party, topped the poll with 38.77 per cent (10.4 million), but this was short of the required majority. Braun came in second on 29.04 per cent (7.8 million). In a distant third place was Marx, with 14.47 per cent (3.8 million), followed by Thälmann with 6.97 per cent (1.8

million). Hellpach polled 5.84 per cent (1.58 million), with Held on 3.75 per cent (1 million). Ludendorff, with only 1.06 per cent (285,793), performed very poorly, indicating the far Right was in severe decline. The other ten minor candidates polled only 0.1 per cent between them (25,761 voters).

As no candidate had gained the required majority, a second election now had to take place. The Social Democrats thought Braun had done pretty well, but they doubted he could appeal to the centre-ground voters needed to win the run-off election. The Social Democrats, the Centre Party and the Democrats, calling themselves the People's Bloc (*Volksblock*), decided to select Wilhelm Marx as their joint candidate, even though he had performed poorly in the first ballot and lacked personal magnetism. As he was a committed Catholic, there were also worries he might lose votes in predominantly Protestant areas. The KPD decided not to withdraw their own candidate, Ernst Thälmann. The right-wing parties engaged in a heated discussion in party committee rooms about who should be their candidate. Stresemann argued that Jarres of the DVP was likely to win the run-off election, but the DNVP thought he was not well known enough nationally to prevail over the People's Bloc candidate, Marx. Jarres accepted this gracefully, and he withdrew from the run-off election.

In a dramatic move, the DNVP proposed the legendary hero of the Battle of Tannenberg, Field Marshal Paul von Hindenburg, who was 77 years old, and living in retirement in Hanover, should enter the run-off election. The mere mention of the name Hindenburg provoked passionate reactions. The Right believed he retained huge popularity, but the Left regarded him as the embodiment of 'discredited German militarism', a 'war criminal' and supporter of the 'stab-in-the-back myth'. The thought of a pro-monarchist Field Marshal as German President horrified the western Allies, and the American President, Calvin Coolidge.

Hindenburg was initially unwilling to accept the nomination, suggesting he had never been a party man, and had no intention of becoming one now. After some gentle and flattering persuasion, particularly from the soft-spoken Admiral Alfred von Tirpitz, who told the old general on a visit to his country house that the country needed a national saviour, and he was perfect for this role, Hindenburg suddenly changed his mind, seeing this as an irresistible call to duty, telling Tirpitz: 'If you feel my election is necessary for the sake of the Fatherland, I'll run in God's name.' On 9 April, Hindenburg sensationally announced that he would join the presidential race.[16] Many on the Right thought that once in power Hindenburg would destroy Weimar democracy, and restore the monarchy. Hindenburg's candidature was jointly endorsed by the DNVP, the DVP, and the BVP. Adolf Hitler also offered support by saying that he would prefer to be ruled by a man in a 'steel helmet rather than a top hat'.[17]

Hindenburg did almost no campaigning himself, relying on his supporters to put his case. He also refused to respond to the frequent attacks made on him by supporters of Marx and Thälmann, who mocked and denigrated him in the press. Posters and flags went up that emphasised Hindenburg's military background. His most high-profile personal intervention in the campaign came on 11 April, when he gave a national live radio address to voters, known as the 'Easter Message'. Hindenburg had never seen a radio microphone before, and his voice sounded halting and nervous. He kept banging his fist on a table after making his points, which confused listeners. During his talk, Hindenburg pledged to create a National Community (*Volksgemeinschaft*), and promised to rule in a non-partisan manner. He said his decision to stand for election only came after careful reflection. He was motivated by a feeling of loyalty and duty to the Fatherland. German freedom, he added, was not to be gained by war or internal revolution. What the nation needed now was a sustained period of peace. At the end, not realising the microphone was still on, he commented: 'Well, thank God that's over.' Hindenburg never lost his nerves about appearing live on radio, and his future radio speeches were always recorded on a phonograph before being broadcast.[18]

On the following day, Marx issued his own election manifesto, which expressed his loyalty to democratic principles under the campaign slogan: 'For the Fatherland, for the People's State, for the Republic.' The elected head of state, he remarked, was the symbol and protector of German unity. All individuals and groups in the country were entitled to freedom, but it was also important to realise that they had obligations to society. The Weimar Constitution and the black-red-gold banner of the Republic pointed the way to fulfilling these obligations.[19]

On 26 April 1925, Paul von Hindenburg became the first democratically elected German President by a narrow margin, gaining 48.3 per cent of the votes (14.65 million), with Wilhelm Marx polling 45.3 per cent (13.75 million) in second place, and Ernst Thälmann occupying third spot on a much lower 6.4 per cent (1.93 million) share of the vote.

The turnout was 77.6 per cent, up by 7.7 per cent on the first ballot. The margin of victory for Hindenburg was only 904,036. Marx had picked up 350,000 more than the Centre Right candidates secured in the first round. It is often claimed that Thälmann's decision to stay in the contest tipped the balance in Hindenburg's favour, but this is a myth. It was the 2.66 million new pro-Hindenburg voters who had abstained in the first round, and who mostly voted in the run-off for Hindenburg who tipped the balance.[20]

In Hindenburg middle-class German voters had elected a man whose sympathies lay with the exiled German monarch, Wilhelm II, and the German Army. The Right naturally thought Hindenburg would soon restore the monarchy. The Left felt the Weimar Republic had suffered an irreparable blow, predicting that Hindenburg would be the gravedigger of democracy. The French press, pulling no punches, claimed Hindenburg's victory showed that Germany could not be trusted, and another war was now bound to come. The British press was much less gloomy, generally suggesting Hindenburg should be judged by his actions. Gustav Stresemann, the German Foreign Minister, was confined to bed, suffering from a bout of angina, when he heard the news of Hindenburg's victory, and wrote in his diary:

> The result of the election is psychologically extraordinary. There can be no doubt the personal element won the day. During the turmoil of the election campaign, there was no lack of effort to discredit the significance of Hindenburg's personality, but with little success. Many indeed were doubtful whether the burden of age might not be too heavy for one who aspired to the Presidential office. But in the end the great name produced its effect and brought forth voters who would hardly have been available in such numbers.[21]

On 11 May 1925, Hindenburg arrived in Berlin for his presidential inauguration. He was greeted by large cheering crowds, headed by the right-wing paramilitary veterans' group, Steel Helmet, and supported by many other right-wing organisations, all carrying the black-white-red flags of the defunct German Empire. On the following day, the induction ceremony took place in the hall of the Reichstag. Hindenburg entered the chamber in the company of Paul Loebe, the Social Democrat speaker of the Reichstag. All the members rose, except the Communists, who shouted: 'Down with the monarchists!' Hindenburg took the oath of office, swearing to uphold the Weimar Constitution, and then gave a short acceptance speech. The Reichstag and the President, he said, were the embodiment of that popular sovereignty which was now the foundation of Germany's national life. The duty of the President was to unite all the constructive forces in Germany in a spirit of non-partisanship. The speech surprised everyone, as Hindenburg had pledged to uphold democracy.[22]

On 19 May, Stresemann had his first conversation with Hindenburg on foreign affairs. He found Hindenburg was much better acquainted on such matters than he imagined, but he also noticed the pro-monarchist conservative *Kreuzzeitung* (*Cross Newspaper*), which displayed the Iron Cross as its emblem on each front page, lay open on his desk. When the conversation began, Hindenburg raised no objections to the proposed Security Pact, but was less supportive of the idea of Germany joining the League of Nations. He was pleased, however, that Stresemann was fighting against what he called 'the war-guilt lie'. Overall, Stresemann thought Hindenburg took a 'calm and dispassionate' view on foreign policy, concluding: 'I had the impression of a man who had grown up in conservative traditions and made no concealment of the fact.' But he thought it was important 'to see that irresponsible people do not acquire influence over him'.[23]

Away from the heated events of Weimar politics, new artistic tendencies continued to emerge. Between 14 June and 18 September 1925 a deeply significant German art exhibition called 'New Objectivity: German Painting Since Expressionism' (*Neue Sachlichkeit: Deutsche Malerei seit dem Expressionismus*) was held in the Kunsthalle in Mannheim.

It was organised by Gustav Hartlaub, and brought together a number of artists united by their rejection of the emotionalism of Expressionism, which had dominated art in the early Weimar period. A total of 125 pictures by 32 artists were displayed in the exhibition, which later travelled to Dresden and several other German cities. Other exhibitions under the same title soon followed, most notably in the spring of 1927, at Karl Nierendorf's gallery in Berlin. In his introduction to the exhibition, Hartlaub wrote: 'What we are displaying here is distinguished by the – in itself purely external – characteristic of the objectivity with which the artists express themselves.'[24]

New Objectivity adopted a neutral, detached, unsentimental approach to art, without any decorative frills. For artists attached to the movement, it represented a more realistic approach to the challenges of life in a modern industrial society. The process of representation in the paintings of New Objectivity artists excludes anything that might reflect the artist's intention or brilliance of technique, in favour of

Paul von Hindenburg around the time of his
election as President of Germany in 1925.

concentrating on the subject of the painting itself, a belief stressing the painter should not be imposed on the creative process.[25]

Many of the artists associated with New Objectivity were not attached to any one geographical place and therefore reflected a wide range of life in Weimar Germany. In the north of Germany, there were more left-wing politically committed types, while in the south more conservative-minded artists flourished. Between these two groups stood the independently minded Max Beckmann, who influenced both groups. He was apolitical, saying 'I have never been politically active in any way'.[26] The First World War, in which he had served as a medical orderly, led Beckmann, who previously painted beauty in vivid colours, to switch his focus to modern everyday life and people, depicting them realistically, without emotion. Some of his work reflected the cabaret culture of the Weimar period, while his many self-portraits reflected changes in his own personality.[27]

The most dominant figure of the New Objectivity movement was undoubtedly the left-wing artist Otto Dix, noted for his harshly realistic portrayals of the brutality of war and everyday life. Dix had served in the First World War and had been profoundly affected by the

horrific sights he had witnessed. He represented his harrowing wartime experiences in 50 anti-war etchings for a series called *War* (*Der Krieg*), which included his famous works *The Trench* and *War Cripples*. Dix referred again to war in *The War Triptych* (1929–32). These paintings set out to shock, and they did, making Dix a hate figure among the far Right, who often picketed his exhibitions. His other noted works were *Metropolis*, a graphic depiction of night life in Weimar, and *The Big City*, highlighting a jazz-loving dancing couple in evening dress. Dix was also noted for his idiosyncratic style of portrait painting, most notably his startling and realistic portrait of the monocled feminist journalist Sylvia von Harden, with her cocktail on a table in front of her, holding a cork-tipped cigarette, and his striking portrait of the art dealer Alfred Flechtheim, with his prominent long hands resting possessively on a painting.[28]

The third most famous New Objectivity artist was the left-winger George Grosz, a former member of the Spartacist League, who advocated the idea of a left-wing artistic collective. Grosz was best known for his oil paintings of people, including boxer Max Schmeling and diminutive poet Hermann Karl Hesse, along with his graphic portrayals of the decadence of Berlin life during the Weimar period including his many striking communist propaganda posters. His communist views meant he faced police prosecution on a number of occasions: in 1920 for defaming the German Army, in 1923 for affronting public morality, and, in 1928, for blasphemy. Each time, he received hefty fines.[29]

Alongside the open-minded aspects of Weimar art, there was a significant amount of intolerance against Jews. By the mid-1920s, antisemitism was a fact of life, which led many Jews to contemplate hiding their Jewish appearance. On 16 July, an anonymous article appeared in the Jewish periodical *Israelitisches Familienblatt* (*Israelite Family Paper*), titled 'The Blond and the Brunette', which related the story of two women who meet at a holiday resort without knowledge of the other person's relationship to Jewishness. The brunette is slender, intelligent, modest, and an excellent mother. The blond, with more than a hint of hostility, loudly proclaims to her new friend that she cannot abide the Jewish women at the resort who were always overdressed, over-made-up, and wear the contents of 'jewellery store windows', which was an obvious antisemitic slur.

When the two women meet for breakfast on the following morning, the blond says she's famished, but only orders cheese and bread. The

Winter Landscape, by the Austrian artist Franz Sedlacek, an example of the work of the artistic movement known as *Neue Sachlichkeit* (New Objectivity).

brunette suggests she would be far better off eating meat, to which the blond says: 'Not for anything. My parents are very Orthodox. I was raised strictly. I only eat Kosher.' The blonde's decision to come out openly as Jewish, having carefully withheld this information about her Jewishness on the previous day, was sparked by her Jewish identity

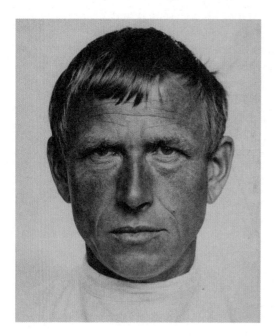

being challenged. The assumption of the brunette was that the hair colour of her holiday companion indicated she was a Gentile.

In fact, blond hair was used by a great many German Jewish women to appear 'less Jewish'. This was typical for the middle-class Jewish women who visited spa vacation towns in southern Germany, Austria, Switzerland, and northern Italy, for fresh air and rejuvenation. In these small spa towns, knowledge that someone was Jewish could spread quickly and lead to unwanted attention, which became known as 'holiday resort antisemitism' (*Bäder-Antisemitismus*), which was fairly common, particularly in Germany and Austria. According to *Israelitisches Familienblatt*, many Jewish women prided themselves on presenting themselves in public as 'not at all Jewish' as a defence mechanism against growing antisemitism.[30]

The second half of 1925 was dominated by negotiations surrounding the Locarno Treaties. It was not until 16 June when the French government finally replied to Stresemann's February Security Pact memorandum. This delay was due to a lengthy crisis in French politics, brought about by a worsening of the French economy, and the alarming fall in the value of the franc. On 17 April, Édouard Herriot was replaced as the French Prime Minister by the left-wing radical Paul Painlevé, who had previously occupied the post for ten weeks from 12 September to 16 November 1917. Painlevé gave the post of Minister of Foreign Affairs to Aristide Briand, who favoured reconciliation with the Germans. Briand remained in office until 12 January 1932. He was

above Otto Dix, photographed *c.*1933.

Otto Dix's *Portrait of the Journalist Sylvia von Harden* (1926).

sure the policy of coercing Germany which led to the Ruhr occupation had failed and he thought the current climate of French public opinion favoured a long-lasting peace settlement with Germany.

The French government's reply promised to engage in an exchange of views with the German government, with a view to establishing a permanent peace, but also insisted that Germany must first agree to become a member of the League of Nations, without requiring any special conditions.[31] Briand thought Stresemann's proposal for a mutual security treaty covering the boundaries of Western Europe was a workable proposal, but he was concerned the German government was offering no similar guarantees for Eastern Europe, where only looser treaties or arbitration agreements were being proposed. Briand wanted these eastern treaties to contain greater security commitments from the German government. It seemed to Briand that Germany was trying to secure its position in the west, while leaving open the possibility of territorial adjustments in the east at a later date.[32]

On 20 July 1925, Stresemann replied to the French government by acknowledging the signing of the Security Pact would not obligate the Allies to alter the Treaty of Versailles. Then he highlighted his misgivings regarding the application of Article 16 of the Covenant of the League of Nations. This was his way of saying Germany did not have the military power to become involved in the League's military actions, especially, giving a promise to go to the aid of Poland in the event of an attack by the Soviet Union. On Eastern Europe, Stresemann emphasised that Germany could not guarantee its eastern frontiers in perpetuity, but was prepared to promise they would not be altered by force. Similarly, he demanded that the Allies evacuate their zones of occupation earlier than anticipated.[33]

The French government thought Stresemann's reply was positive enough to proceed from diplomatic correspondence to direct talks. In the House of Commons, Austen Chamberlain, the British Foreign Secretary, stressed the diplomatic discussions remained at the stage of 'an exchange of opinion', but added that British obligations could only relate to the western frontiers of Germany.[34] In the Reichstag, there was a two-day debate on Stresemann's reply to the French government, on 22 and 23 July, during which the Foreign Minister explained and defended his response to the French government, which was approved by 235 for and 158 against.

The terms of the Western Security Pact now started to take shape through further detailed diplomatic discussions. It was decided

Pillars of Society (1926), George Grosz's nightmarish depiction of members of the German elite who supported fascism.

Germany, France and Belgium would pledge not to go to war with each other, reaffirm the permanence of their existing boundaries in Western Europe, and confirm the demilitarisation of the Rhineland. The British and Italian governments would guarantee these pledges, and all the signatories would assist in the case of a clear violation. It was further agreed that the League of Nations Council would determine whether any violations of the treaties had occurred. In return, the German government promised to join the League of Nations, but in return wanted a permanent seat on the League Council, and to be granted exemption from Article 16, which called for sanctions on potential aggressors. Germany also agreed to conclude arbitration treaties with Poland and Czechoslovakia, but these were not guaranteed by the British government. By the start of September, a meeting of legal experts on the German and Allied sides had ironed out the minute details of the treaties in London.[35]

On 15 September, Pierre de Margerie, the French Ambassador to Berlin, presented Stresemann with the formal Allied invitation to attend the Security Pact Conference, beginning on 5 October 1925 at the small town of Locarno, in southern Switzerland, near the picturesque Lake Maggiore. Invitations were also sent out to Great Britain, France, Italy, Belgium, Poland, and Czechoslovakia. The German government accepted its invitation but let loose an ill-judged broadside about the war-guilt clause, and the continued Allied occupation in the Rhineland. This was due to pressure on Stresemann from the Nationalist DNVP members of the Luther cabinet, who had insisted Stresemann should bring up the question with the Allies before the conference began.

These comments on war-guilt went down very badly with the Allies. The French government fired off a quick reply, which argued the war-guilt question was already settled once and for all and added the Allied military occupation would only end when Germany had fully met its obligation to disarm. The British government issued an equally stern response, stating:

> The question of Germany's responsibility is not raised by the proposed pact. We are at a loss to know why the German government thought it proper to raise it at this moment, and we are obliged to observe that the negotiations of a security pact cannot modify the Treaty of Versailles, nor alter the judgment of the past.[36]

The Soviet Union was deeply alarmed by the proposed Locarno Conference. Georgy Chicherin, the Soviet Foreign Minister, arrived in Berlin on 20 September, to discuss the matter with Gustav Stresemann. He argued that Austen Chamberlain and the British Conservative Party were engaged in a massive attempt to create a united European front against the Soviet Union. Chicherin offered to conclude a 'secret' political pact with the German government to renew and extend the Treaty of Rapallo, but Stresemann told him he did not want to enter into a secret agreement, poured cold water on the idea that there was a British plot for war against the Soviet Union, and reassured Chicherin that the Locarno treaties would not affect the Treaty of Rapallo. He further added that the German government would not be forced into aggressive action against the Soviet Union, and would never recognise the current Polish borders.[37]

The Locarno Conference took place from 5 to 16 October 1925. The prevailing ambiance at the gathering was one of friendliness. Delegates were photographed strolling through the town together, and there was a pleasant boating trip on Lake Maggiore on board a little steamboat, where the champagne and cordiality flowed in equal measure. This contrasted with the tension of previous international gatherings between Germany and the Allies. The chief representatives of each country involved were: Gustav Stresemann, German Foreign Minister, Aristide Briand, French Foreign Minister, Austen Chamberlain, British Foreign Secretary, and Emile Vandervelde, Belgian Minister of Foreign Affairs. During the closing days of the conference, Benito Mussolini, Italy's Prime Minister, Edvard Beneš, the Czech Minister of Foreign Affairs, and Aleksander Skrzyński, the Polish Foreign Minister, also attended.[38]

Chamberlain came to Locarno determined to bring about a Franco-German reconciliation. He had some private worries about Stresemann's real aims, but these preconceptions disappeared once he had talked to him in person, and decided he genuinely wanted a rapprochement with the western Allies. The self-controlled Chamberlain, fluent in French and German, played a key role during the proceedings in ironing out difficulties and points of contention between Stresemann and Briand, and this was something they both acknowledged. Chamberlain also made it clear once again that the British government would not undertake any territorial guarantees in Eastern Europe.[39] Behind the scenes, much hard bargaining went on, with Stresemann repeatedly trying to extract further concessions from the Allies, but all the contentious questions were discussed in a friendly spirit. The extent to which Germany had disarmed figured in these conversations, as did the German demand for equality in armaments. The continued Allied occupation of the Rhineland received a great deal of attention, too. Stresemann gained a notable concession when Briand, who was extremely accommodating to Stresemann's demands throughout the conference, promised to evacuate Cologne at the earliest possible opportunity, which occurred on 1 December 1925.

When the question of Germany's entry to the League of Nations cropped up, Stresemann defended his government's unwillingness to be bound by Article 16 of the Covenant. Germany, he said, could not pledge itself to support Poland in a war involving the Soviet Union. Briand tried to reassure him by saying that as Germany would be given a permanent seat on the League Council it could veto any proposal it disagreed with.[40] A formula was finally worked out whereby each member of the League was obligated to cooperate against military aggression 'to an extent which is compatible with its military situation, and which takes its geographical situation into account'.[41] In return, Stresemann promised Germany would seek entry into the League of Nations as soon as possible.

Mussolini, the Italian Prime Minister, was initially lukewarm on the proposed Locarno agreements. He wanted a guarantee of the Brenner frontier between Italy and Austria to be added to the treaties, but Stresemann said this would only be possible if Germany was allowed to unite with Austria, something the Allies were not willing to accept. However, once it became clear the agreements would be signed, Mussolini turned up, on 14 October, wanting to share in the glory of joining Britain in guaranteeing the peace of Europe.[42]

The 'big day' of the Conference took place in the town hall in Locarno on 16 October 1925. It witnessed the signing of the Treaty of Mutual Guarantee between Germany, France, Belgium, Great Britain, and Italy (the Locarno Pact). Under its terms, Germany recognised its western borders as fixed by the Treaty of Versailles, and the continuance of the Rhineland demilitarised zone in perpetuity. Stresemann emphasised the voluntary affirmation of Germany's western borders was much more acceptable than the dictated terms of the Versailles Treaty. Germany, France and Belgium all agreed not to attack each other ever again, and Britain and Italy agreed to function as the joint guarantors of the agreement. All the parties agreed to settle disputes by peaceful means in future. The Locarno Treaties would only come into force when Germany was finally admitted to the League of Nations. The signatories further agreed to meet in London on 1 December for a formal signing ceremony.[43]

Annexed to the main treaties were the German–Polish, German–Czechoslovak, German–Belgian, and French–German arbitration treaties, which promised all disputes which could not be settled amicably through normal diplomatic channels would be submitted to an Arbitration Panel or to the Permanent Court of International Justice. To add further insurance in Eastern Europe, France signed binding treaties with Poland and Czechoslovakia, pledging mutual assistance, in the event of conflict with Germany. Polish and Czech leaders signed these agreements in fear rather than hope. The agreements reaffirmed existing treaties of alliance concluded by France with Poland on 19 February 1921, and with Czechoslovakia on 25 January 1924. The British government refused to be a party to the arbitration treaties.[44]

The Locarno Treaties were a key turning-point in the international relations of the 1920s. They were the effective diplomatic end of the Great War, and reconciled Germany and France in a way that had previously seemed impossible. Locarno was a much bigger triumph for the appeasement of Germany than Neville Chamberlain ever achieved, and how ironic that his half-brother Austen was one of its chief architects.[45]

It seemed to most contemporary observers that the French government was the big victor at Locarno. Germany had, after all, agreed to the loss of Alsace-Lorraine, the permanent demilitarisation of the Rhineland, and the peaceful settlement of disputes in Eastern Europe. The British government had also agreed to guarantee French borders in the event of a German attack. Yet it was Germany that stood to gain most from the Locarno Treaties. German sacrifices were in name only, as French powers of enforcement against Germany under the Versailles Treaty had already gone. Germany could now default on its reparations payments with no military consequences. No promise by Germany not to revise its eastern frontiers at a future date left a gaping hole in the Locarno settlement.

Stresemann told the German cabinet that the Polish delegation saw Locarno as 'a total defeat'.[46] Stresemann had gained a great diplomatic triumph, restoring Germany to diplomatic respectability by satisfying the French desire for security, and he sold it to the German public as heralding an era when more concessions were likely to come. He also pointed out that he had not renounced Alsace-Lorraine for good, only the possibility of regaining the province by force. Peaceful revision, perhaps through a referendum, was still possible. Stresemann further thought League of Nations membership would give Germany a new weapon to defend its own interests.

On 18 October, the German delegation arrived back in Berlin. Awaiting them in the grand hall of the Anhalt station were the Ambassadors of Britain, France, Belgium, Italy and Czechoslovakia, but not Poland. Lord D'Abernon, the British Ambassador, gave a short impromptu speech, saying to Stresemann: 'I am specially charged by Mr Austen Chamberlain to congratulate you on the success of the conference at Locarno, and to say that Mr Chamberlain will always look back with pleasure on his first meeting with you at Locarno and the spirit of candour and openness which the German delegation have impressed on the discussions.'[47] In a private memorandum, Stresemann admitted he had achieved all he wanted at Locarno, but felt Hans Luther, the Chancellor, had returned home from Locarno a beaten man: 'Even at sessions of the conference we had to keep reminding him not to make a sour, discontented face.'[48]

What most disturbed Luther was that the Nationalist members of his cabinet would soon bring him down. This proved an accurate prediction. Members of the DNVP and other groups on the Right, including the Pan German League, the National Socialists and the Steel Helmet, were all deeply critical of the Locarno agreements. They felt they were a betrayal of the territory already given up under the Treaty of Versailles, particularly the renunciation of Alsace-Lorraine, the acceptance of the demilitarisation of the Rhineland, and the complete failure to make any progress on the removal of the war-guilt clause.[49] The Luther cabinet met on 19 October, during which the DNVP leader, Martin Schiele, who was regarded as a moderate right-winger, refused to give his seal of approval to the Locarno agreements.[50]

A grassroots revolt now developed from the right wing of the DNVP, which pushed for its members to leave the Luther cabinet, and called on its Reichstag members to vote against ratification of the Locarno Treaties. On 22 October, the DNVP's National Racist Committee met in Berlin, then put forward a resolution denouncing the Security Pact, which was rejected at a meeting of the party executive committee on the following day.[51] At a heated meeting of the DNVP Reichstag delegation on 25 October, a majority agreed that Schiele and the other three DNVP members of the Luther cabinet, Oskar Hergt, Minister of Justice, Otto von Schlieben, Minister of Economics, and Albert

Neuhaus, Finance Minister, should all resign from the cabinet on the following day. In justifying this move, Schiele insisted the Locarno accords did not follow the guidelines the cabinet itself had given to the German delegation before it departed, which insisted any initial agreements at Locarno should be non-binding.[52]

Admiral Alfred von Tirpitz, who supported the DNVP revolt over the Locarno agreements, appealed to President Hindenburg in the hope that he could be persuaded to block ratification of the Locarno Treaties, using Article 48 of the Constitution, and appoint an interim government led by the Nationalists. In response, Hindenburg refused to support the non-ratification of the Locarno accords, and castigated the DNVP for 'their unexpectedly premature and brash action' in leaving the Luther cabinet.[53] In Stresemann's opinion most of the credit for Hindenburg's support for ratifying the Locarno Treaties was due to Hans Luther, who had 'performed a great service in keeping the old gentlemen in line'.[54]

Luther decided to press on with the ratification of the Locarno accords. On 23 November, the debate on Locarno in the Reichstag began, with Luther saying that after the Locarno Treaties were signed on 1 December, he would tender his resignation to President Hindenburg. Stresemann then spelled out the government's case, arguing the French demand for security guarantees had to be dealt with. If Germany had failed to agree to the Locarno accords, then a Franco-British alliance against Germany would have soon followed. Instead, the British were now obligated to protect Germany in the event of French military aggression. The German delegation at Locarno had raised the question of war guilt, he added, and the German government would keep on pressing the case for justice in this area.

Count Kuno von Westarp, the key speaker in the debate for the nationalist DNVP, controversially suggested that Britain and France viewed Locarno as part of a cunning plan to gain German support for a war against the Soviet Union. He urged his party colleagues to vote against ratification of the agreements, and declared his party would not accept the Reichstag vote as binding, unless it achieved the two-thirds majority required by Article 76 of the Weimar Constitution. This suggested that if the Nationalists came to power in future, they would not feel themselves bound by treaties negotiated by previous German governments. Constitutional lawyers ruled that ratification did not require a two-thirds majority, and, on 27 November, the Locarno Treaties passed a vote in the Reichstag by 300 for, with 174 against.

overleaf The signing of the Locarno
Treaties, December 1925.

German entry into the League of Nations was further endorsed by 275 for and 183 against. Those voting against included the DNVP, the KPD and the National Socialists. Those voting in favour not only included the loyal coalition parties in the Luther cabinet, but also the Social Democrats and the DDP. Once more, the votes of the Social Democrats proved the decisive factor. On behalf of the party, Otto Wels said the SPD regarded the draft law on Locarno 'as the fulfilment of our own demands'.[55] On 28 November, President Hindenburg signed the Locarno Laws, even though he admitted to having doubts about the wisdom of Germany joining the League of Nations. On the same day, the Upper House, the Reichsrat, also sanctioned the Locarno accords. The whole episode revealed that the Right of German politics was still bitterly opposed to peace and reconciliation.[56]

On the morning of 1 December 1925, in the Reception Suite of the British Foreign Office in London, the formal signing ceremony of the Locarno Treaties took place. The key signatories were: Stanley Baldwin, the British Prime Minister, Austen Chamberlain, British Foreign Secretary; Aristide Briand, who had recently taken over as French Prime Minister in addition to his role as Foreign Minister; Hans Luther, the German Chancellor; Emile Vandervelde, the Belgian Foreign Minister; and Vittorio Scialoja for Italy. Benito Mussolini did not attend after being advised by the Foreign Office that large anti-fascist demonstrations were likely if he turned up.

In the afternoon, the dignitaries visited King George VI at Buckingham Palace. The King said he welcomed the Locarno Treaties with great satisfaction, as he felt they would open a new optimistic era of international relations. He wanted the relations of Britain and Germany to become ever more friendly. In the evening, Austen Chamberlain hosted a grand dinner at Lancaster House. During the meal, a silent newsreel film of the Locarno Conference was shown. Afterwards, Stresemann gave a short speech. He thanked Chamberlain who, he said, had acted as the informal chair during the entire Locarno proceedings with great diplomatic skill, which had contributed greatly to what could be called the 'spirit of Locarno'.[57]

On 5 December, Hans Luther kept the promise he made in the debate on the Locarno Treaties and handed his resignation to President Hindenburg, along with his entire cabinet. Hindenburg asked him and his cabinet to remain in office in a caretaker capacity for the time being, while negotiations on the formation of a new more broadly based government were completed. On 14 December, Hindenburg gave the task of forming a new government to Erich Koch-Weser of the DDP, telling him he personally favoured a 'Great Coalition', involving the SPD, but privately Hindenburg was sure the Social Democrats would reject this offer at which point he hoped to persuade Luther to form another minority bourgeois government, which would have friendly relations with the Nationalist DNVP.

Predictably, the Social Democrats demanded increased unemployment benefits and a reduction in taxes for the low-paid as their condition for joining the government, but this was a price the other potential coalition partners were not prepared to pay. On 17 December, Koch-Weser told Hindenburg his effort to form a government had failed. Hindenburg decided to return to the matter after Christmas.[58]

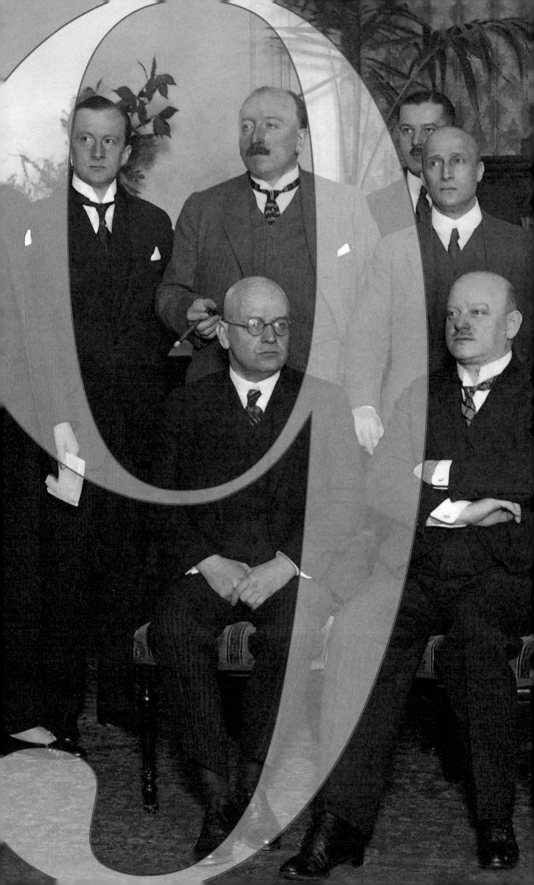

1926
·
GERMANY JOINS THE LEAGUE OF NATIONS

·

Talks on the formation of a new German government dominated political debate at the beginning of 1926. Negotiations resumed on 8 January. Once again, the Social Democrats (SPD) refused to join a 'Great Coalition' after their list of social and economic demands for participation, which included increased unemployment benefits and tax reductions for the low-paid, were rejected by the other prospective coalition partners. Hindenburg asked Hans Luther to stay on as Chancellor, and form another cabinet, which he duly did on 20 January, thereby ending a political crisis that had lasted six weeks, and seemed to confirm right-wing claims that parliamentary government was incapable of producing political consensus or stability.

The second Luther cabinet consisted of the same parties involved in his previous government: the DVP, Zentrum and the DDP. The following continued in their cabinet posts: Hans Luther, Independent (Chancellor), Gustav Stresemann, DVP (Foreign Minister), Karl Stingl, DVP (Post), Rudolf Krohne, DVP (Transport), Otto Gessler, Independent (Defence), and Heinrich Brauns, Zentrum (Labour). The new entrants were DDP members: Wilhelm Külz (Interior) and Peter Reinhold (Finance), Julius Curtius of the DVP (Economics), and for Zentrum, Heinrich Haslinde (Food and Agriculture) and the former Chancellor Wilhelm Marx (Justice, and Occupied Territories).[1]

Luther presented his cabinet to the Reichstag on 27 January, causing much merriment when he shouted at a Nationalist heckler that government had to 'be carried on somehow'. He then sought to appease the Social Democrats by promising legislation favourable to the interests of organised labour. During a heated debate, Major Wilhelm Henning of the DNVP accused the new cabinet of being 'the assassins of their own people', by signing the Locarno Treaties and promising to join the League of Nations. Kuno von Westarp, who became the new DNVP leader on 24 March, pledged the party would adopt an approach of 'ceaseless opposition' to the Luther government.[2]

The Chancellor immediately submitted his government to a vote of confidence. Of the 440 Reichstag members participating in the vote, only 160 chose to support the government, with 150 voting against, made up of the DNVP, the National Socialists and the KPD. Survival for Luther had depended on the 130 Social Democratic members who chose to abstain.[3]

On 10 February, Sir Eric Drummond, Secretary-General of the League of Nations, received a formal application from the German government to join the League of Nations, requesting a permanent seat on the Council, which consisted of four permanent members – Britain, France, Italy and Japan – and six non-permanent members, who were elected by the General Assembly for a three-year term.[4] Stresemann assumed the granting of a permanent seat on the Council would be a formality, given that it had been a condition of the Locarno Treaties. On 2 March, Luther, speaking on national radio, said Germany's entry into the League of Nations was conditional on there being no changes to the League's Council.[5]

A special meeting of the Council and Assembly of the League of Nations began on 8 March to deal specifically with the German application. Stresemann and Luther were present. One by one, Poland, Brazil, Spain and China all raised objections to the German conditions of entry, and they all demanded to be made permanent members, too. This raised a real problem, as the agreement for Germany to join the League with a seat on the Council had to be carried by a unanimous vote.[6] The issue was further complicated by the British government backing Spain's claim, and the French government supporting the Poles. The Polish government argued that because there were serious areas of unresolved territorial disputes remaining between Germany and Poland, Germany should only be given a permanent seat on the Council after these were fully resolved. In response, Stresemann said he would not have supported the signing of the Locarno Treaties if he had thought Germany's election to a permanent seat on the Council would lead to the granting of a similar concession to other powers.[7]

After further heated discussion, a compromise was finally worked out. Only Germany would receive a permanent seat on the Council, but three additional non-permanent seats would be created, and offered to Brazil, Poland and Spain. The Polish government reluctantly accepted this proposal, but Brazil first declared its veto on German admission, and then announced its withdrawal from the League on 11 June.[8] Spain also threatened to leave.

On 17 March, the League of Nations Assembly met. It was finally agreed Germany's admission to the League required further negotiation, and would therefore be stalled, while an Examining Committee was established to discuss the revised constitution of the League. Germany was invited to join it. The Committee would report its recommendations to the League Council later in the year.[9] When Stresemann arrived back in Berlin on 18 March, he was met with howls of derision from the nationalist press, claiming Germany had been humiliated in Geneva. On 22 March, there was a lengthy debate on foreign policy in the Reichstag. In his speech, Stresemann made clear that if the suggestions of the League Committee to look at Germany's request for admission did not 'come up to our expectations' then Germany would reconsider its request to join the organisation. The Nationalist DNVP called for Germany to withdraw its application to join the League altogether, and introduced a motion of censure, which was defeated by 260 to 141 votes. The Luther government then asked for a vote of confidence, which was passed by 262 votes to 139. Once again, the Social Democrats saved the government. On this occasion, they were motivated by their desire to continue with Stresemann's policy of conciliation.[10]

In the early months of 1926, the future of Hitler's NSDAP seemed hopeless. The upturn in the German economy made most Germans think their economic suffering was now over. In such an atmosphere, Hitler's gospel of hate was deeply unattractive. The man himself had kept a low profile since his release from prison at the end of 1924, and settled down to finishing the second volume of *Mein Kampf.* The ban on the party newspaper, *Völkischer Beobachter,* was lifted on 26 February 1925, but Hitler was prohibited from public speaking in most parts of Germany until 1927, and this ban was not lifted in Prussia until 1928.

Hitler had put Alfred Rosenberg and Hermann Esser in charge of the party in his absence, but they proved incapable of establishing any authority, and the party split into two disunited factions – the German Party (DP), which included the nucleus of the pre-Putsch Munich-based National Socialist Party, and the NSFP, which contained new 'socialist' members in north-west Germany. The NSDAP had been formally re-formed on 27 February 1925, and these two groups were reabsorbed into the original party. The only consolation for Hitler was that both factions continued to pledge allegiance to his leadership. Hitler now aimed to turn the NSDAP into an organisation that would seek power by constitutional means in future. The national party was divided into 35 Reichstag electoral districts, each led by a Regional Leader (Gauleiter), appointed by Hitler.

There were also new entrants into the party's inner circle, particularly in north-west Germany, who felt the party needed to develop a modern national organisation and move in a more 'socialist' direction. Of these, the two most dynamic were Gregor Strasser and Dr Joseph Goebbels. Strasser, born in Geisenfeld, Bavaria, was a qualified chemist (and a diabetic), who had been awarded the Iron Cross (1st Class) in the Great War. He was also a superb organiser, troubleshooter and public speaker. On 11 March 1925, Hitler had given him the task of organising the party in north-west Germany, which was a key part of Hitler's plan to build a truly national party. Strasser grew the party branches in north-west Germany from 70 to 262 during the rest of 1925. He believed passionately in the 'socialist' and 'anti-capitalist' parts of the party programme. Strasser found orthodox socialism too internationalist in outlook and believed National Socialism should appeal to the underdogs in German society and be the committed enemy of big business.

Goebbels was born and brought up by a devout Catholic family in Rheydt (now Mönchengladbach), near Düsseldorf. He was short, with a deformed foot, a disability then known as 'club-foot,' which he developed at the age of seven. It made him ineligible for military service during the Great War, and forced him to walk with a noticeable limp. Goebbels aspired to a literary career, which resulted in many rejection letters from publishers. He gained a PhD from Heidelberg University, in 1921, but displayed a much greater flair as a journalist, becoming the editor of the Berlin-based party newspaper, *Der Angriff* (*The Attack*).[11] Goebbels was a peerless sloganeer, and a brilliant speaker, with a mellifluous voice. His propaganda approach was simple: find out what people hate and make them hate it more. He dismissed truth and accuracy as irrelevant to the art of propaganda, and instead made a virtue out of lying. He felt this was a vital asset in political campaigns.

Goebbels also wanted the NSDAP to move to the Left, and demanded the destruction of capitalism. 'National and Socialist,' he wrote in his diary. 'What has priority and what comes second? There is no doubt about the answer amongst us here in the west. First, socialist redemption and then national liberation will arrive like a powerful strong wind.' Goebbels thought he had more in common with Communists than the bourgeoisie.[12]

On 24 January 1926, the north-western party Gauleiters, known as the Working Community (*Arbeitsgemeinschaft*) of the North and West Gau of the NSDAP, met in Hanover to discuss a revised, and more

socialist-orientated, 'draft party programme'. It included proposals for a corporate state in which agricultural peasants would own their own land, and even advocated public control of certain parts of industry.[13] This north-west group were not opposed to Hitler's leadership, but felt the Munich-based faction around the *Führer* were middle-class reactionaries, not real anti-capitalist socialists. When Hitler heard about Strasser's proposals to revise the party programme, he was furious, and called a leaders' conference for 14 February in Bamberg, Upper Franconia. Bamberg was chosen because it was as close to the northern Gau as possible, while remaining firmly on Bavarian soil.

Hitler packed the Bamberg meeting with all his loyal Munich cronies. Strasser and Goebbels were able to attend, but there were precious few others from the north-western branches present. In all, 60 delegates were present. The real issue at stake at the Bamberg meeting was whether the party should remain a '*Führer* party', in which the leader's authority was undisputed, or whether power would derive from the party programme, which could be altered by pressure from party members.

Hitler spoke at the meeting for nearly five hours, brushing aside all the concerns raised by the draft programme of the Working Community.[14] Hitler's speech amounted to a dressing down for Strasser and Goebbels, making clear that he would not tolerate the party going in the direction of 'undiluted socialist principles' or let ideological disputes divert the party from the key aim of gaining political power. On foreign policy, Hitler stressed Germany's arch-enemy was France, while ruling out any alliance with Soviet Russia, which Strasser and Goebbels favoured, as he felt Germany would need to gain future territory at Russia's expense. He also emphasised his support for private property ownership and private enterprise, and opposed the expropriation of land from the former princes and its redistribution to peasants. For Hitler, this proposal was 'pure communism'. Finally, he asserted that the 25-point NSDAP party programme could not be altered.

At the end of the meeting, Hitler gained full acceptance for the principle that he was the undisputed leader and the elimination of any notion the party was in any way a democratic or consensus-based institution. Above all, he had affirmed that nationalism, not socialism, was at the centre of National Socialist ideology. He also gained an important pledge to retain the existing 1920 party programme by arguing it already contained firm commitments to implement a number

Joseph Goebbels, future Nazi propagandist.
By spring 1926, Goebbels had fallen under
Hitler's spell.

of 'socialist' policies. Hitler said: 'The New Testament is also full of contradictions, but that hasn't stopped the spread of Christianity.'[15] Strasser made a short statement, in which he said he accepted the *Führer*'s leadership, which prompted Hitler to put his arm around him, in a very public show of party unity. Strasser then promised Hitler that he would collect all the copies of the draft programme that were previously distributed.[16]

At Bamberg, Hitler had re-established firm control over the NSDAP. But it was a hollow victory, in that all he had really achieved was to remain the leader of a small and insignificant right-wing fringe party. A confidential report by the Reich Ministry of the Interior described the NSDAP as a 'numerically insignificant, radical-revolutionary splinter group, incapable of exerting any noticeable influence on the great mass of the population and the course of political events.'[17]

In the weeks after the Bamberg meeting, Hitler made a concerted effort to woo Goebbels. He invited him to speak in Munich on 8 April, telling his inner circle: 'Once he's here, I'll win him over to our side.'[18] Hitler's personal chauffeur-driven Mercedes met Goebbels at the central railway station on 7 April. At the end of Goebbels' speech at the Bürgerbräukeller, on 9 April, Hitler embraced him, reportedly, with tears in his eyes. Goebbels was smitten: 'I love him, he has thought through everything... Such a sparkling mind can be my leader. I bow to the greater one, the political genius.'[19]

Meanwhile, German foreign policy once again took centre stage. Stresemann had reacted to the delay in Germany's admission to the League of Nations by taking a crucial step in improving relations with the Soviet Union. He wanted to keep friendship with the Soviet Union as a form of insurance policy, which might be used later to alter Germany's eastern borders at the expense of Poland.

The pivot of German foreign policy towards the western Allies at Locarno had filled the Soviet government with feelings of deep anxiety. The delay in Germany joining the League offered the Soviets an ideal opportunity to make a dramatic diplomatic intervention. The Soviet Foreign Minister, Georgy Chicherin, told Stresemann that if the Locarno powers could not push through the entry of Germany to the League, then what could Germany expect of them when more serious matters were discussed? He felt a new Russo-German agreement would weaken the idea of the western Allies developing a common front against the Soviet Union. In response, Stresemann explained that he had always wanted to sign a new agreement with the Soviet Union, and had only delayed this due to a wish not to antagonise the members of the League of Nations during Germany's application process.[20]

On 24 April, the Treaty of Berlin (otherwise known as the German–Soviet Neutrality and Nonaggression Pact), was duly signed in Berlin by Gustav Stresemann for Germany and Nicolai Krestinski, the Soviet Ambassador, for the Soviet Union. It greatly strengthened the relationship between the two powers. The treaty consisted of just four brief articles: (1) The 1922 Treaty of Rapallo remained the basis of Russo-German relations, to which was added a promise by the two governments to maintain friendly relations with each other, and to promote a solution to all outstanding political and economic questions that concerned them both. (2) Germany and the Soviet Union pledged neutrality in the event of an attack on the other by a third party. (3) Neither party would join in any coalition for the purpose of an economic boycott on the other. (4) The duration of the treaty was set at five years. In 1931, it was renewed for three more years. To this, Stresemann added the additional assurance that if the League ever contemplated anti-Soviet sanctions or a military attack then he would do everything in his power to oppose it. The agreement was endorsed by a vote in the Reichstag on 10 June, with only three dissenting votes. On 29 June, the agreement was officially ratified by the German government. On 3 August, it was officially registered in the League of Nations.[21]

In Germany, the Russo-German Treaty was received with universal acclaim. There was much greater public and political unanimity than there had ever been over the Dawes Plan, the Locarno Treaties and Germany's proposed entry into the League of Nations. On 27 April, the Reichstag Committee on Foreign Affairs, usually the scene of bitter party disputes, gave the treaty its unanimous approval. The Nationalist DNVP believed the new agreement with the Soviet government would bring closer the return of Upper Silesia, Danzig and the Polish Corridor, for it was clear that a revision of Germany's eastern frontiers required Soviet support, or at the least benevolent neutrality. Stresemann felt the agreement would quieten Soviet apprehension about the Locarno Treaties, maintain Germany's good relations with Russia and appease the pro-Russian element on the Nationalist Right.[22]

In the rest of Europe, the Treaty of Berlin caused a high degree of anxiety. The reaction in France, Poland, Czechoslovakia and Romania was wholly critical. The French press claimed the Treaty placed Germany's entry into the League in jeopardy, and accused Stresemann of provocatively signing the German–Soviet Treaty to undermine the Geneva negotiations over Germany's entry into the League of Nations.[23] To the French government the treaty represented another Russo-German threat to Eastern Europe, and the French responded in June 1926 by signing an agreement with Romania, to add to its existing security agreements with Poland and Czechoslovakia. Aleksander Skrzyński, the Polish Foreign Minister, urged the Allies to examine what effect the new German–Soviet treaty would have on the obligations Germany would have to assume if it joined the League of Nations.[24] In Britain, *The Times* adopted a surprisingly conciliatory tone, suggesting the agreement was not in conflict with the agreements made at Locarno, but the *Daily Mail* was much less charitable, arguing the Treaty of Berlin had raised suspicions about Germany's true motives in moving closer to the Soviet Union at a time when it was supposedly aiming to become a loyal member of the League of Nations.[25]

In domestic German politics, two other controversial issues predominated in the first half of 1926: first, a bitter dispute over the use of the old Imperial flag; and second, a national referendum to expropriate the property of the former ruling German princes. The German Chancellor, Hans Luther, who had always been indifferent to the Republic and its symbols, decided in late April, without consulting the Reichstag party leaders beforehand, to ask President Hindenburg to issue a Flag Law Decree (*Flaggenordnung Erlass*) on 5 May, which would allow German diplomatic and consular missions abroad to fly the old black-white-gold Imperial flag alongside the post-1918 black-red-gold Republican flag, which was proscribed under Article 1 of the Weimar Constitution as the official German national flag. At the time, the old Imperial flag was allowed to be used at sea, provided it contained an inserted black-red-gold logo in the top right-hand corner.[26] Stresemann raised no objections to the Flag Decree, arguing Germans overseas 'are deeply attached to the old flag, which stood in their eyes as a symbol of the Reich'.[27]

Furious political protests quickly followed, however, led by the Social Democrats, but also supported by the Democrats and Zentrum. They all agreed the old flag could continue to be used at sea, but not flown outside German embassies or consulates abroad. The Social Democrat Reichstag member Rudolf Breitscheid felt Luther's decision to issue the Flag Decree without consulting parliament was ill-judged, commenting: 'We cannot escape the impression that it is the procedure of the government to push parliament more and more into the background and to treat it, intentionally or unintentionally, with contempt.'[28]

Most people assumed the initiative for the Flag Decree had come from Hindenburg, who had never hidden his own sympathy for the old Imperial flag, but in fact the idea had come from Luther, as he later admitted in his memoirs. In a letter sent by Hindenburg to Luther on 9 May, which was published in the press, the president insisted he had no intention of altering the national colours of black-red-gold, as determined by the Constitution, but he felt the widespread debate on the issue showed how divided public opinion was on the matter.[29]

The publication of Hindenburg's letter did little to quieten the criticism of Luther. On 12 May, the Social Democrats tabled a vote of no confidence in his government, which was narrowly defeated. Then Erich Kock-Weser, the leader of the DDP, introduced a vote of censure against Luther personally, on the grounds that his behaviour, especially his lack of prior consultation on the issue of the Flag Decree, had now made a compromise much more difficult. This vote was adopted by 176 to 146 votes, with DNVP members choosing to abstain.[30] On 13 May, Hans Luther resigned as Chancellor, but his cabinet remained in office, led by Otto Gessler, in a caretaker capacity, until a new government could be formed. The irony was that the controversial Flag Decree remained in force.

The DNVP refused to enter the next government, and the Social Democrats were unwilling to tolerate a minority government led by Gessler, which forced President Hindenburg to turn to Wilhelm Marx, of Zentrum, to form a new cabinet, on the basis that the Social Democrats were willing to tolerate a minority government led by him. On 17 May, Wilhelm Marx became the German Chancellor for a third time, with the intention of expanding his coalition as soon as possible to gain a Reich majority, but only in conjunction with parties who supported Germany's foreign policy. This ruled out the DNVP joining, but Marx hoped the Social Democrats would soon join his coalition. However, as the DVP opposed the SPD returning to government, this was a remote possibility.

At a farewell dinner for Luther on 28 May, Stresemann asked the outgoing Chancellor if the press was right in thinking his fall was due to their own personal differences, to which Luther replied: 'On the main lines of foreign policy we were always in agreement. Our differences were not differences on matters of fact but arose out of our differences of temperament.'[31]

The third Marx cabinet retained all the ministers of the second Luther cabinet, with one exception: Johannes Bell (Zentrum) replaced Marx in his dual roles of Minister of Justice and Minister of the Occupied Territories. It was once again a minority government, consisting of members of Zentrum, the DVP, the DDP and the BVP. The Reichstag agreed to accept the new government by a simple majority vote, thereby avoiding a vote of confidence.[32]

At the same time as the Luther cabinet crisis was taking place, a campaign was underway for a referendum on the expropriation of the property of the former German ruling houses without financial compensation, something German governments since 1918 had failed to do. Article 153 of the Weimar Constitution ruled that property could only be expropriated for public welfare, and with appropriate financial compensation, and in the courts, anti-Republican judges usually sided with the property rights of the princes whenever expropriation cases came up, and they mostly received generous compensation settlements.[33]

On 15 March, Hindenburg announced that expropriation without compensation would not serve the public interest, as it represented the seizing of assets for political reasons, and infringed Article 153 of the Constitution. On 24 April Marx, then the Justice Minister, confirmed the President's opinion was legally correct. For that reason, a simple majority in a national referendum would not be sufficient. To pass a law on the matter would require 50 per cent of all those registered to vote.

At the beginning of 1926, the Social Democrats had agreed to pursue a referendum for the purpose of resolving the matter, but they were willing to offer some compensation to the ruling families, as they felt offering limited compensation would give a better chance of gaining enough votes to make the measure a law. The Communist KPD wanted the former ruling families' property taken into public ownership, without any compensation. Under Article 73 of the Constitution, and the Referendum Law of 27 June 1921, a petition for a referendum had to be signed by 10 per cent of all registered voters. Between them, the Social Democrats and Communists managed to obtain 12.5 million signatures in support of a referendum.

On 6 May, Reichstag members rejected the petition for a referendum by 236 for and 142 against, but this rejection automatically triggered a referendum, which was set for 20 June. The SPD and KPD, after protracted negotiations, finally agreed the question on the ballot paper would be: 'Do you agree to the confiscation of the property of the German princes without compensation?'

The referendum was the first in German history. It was preceded by a bitter campaign. Only the Social Democrats and Communists openly supported the referendum proposal. All the non-socialist parties were united in their opposition to expropriation without compensation, and urged their supporters to abstain. They based their stand on the sanctity of property rights, which they claimed should not be disregarded because the owners in question happened to be royal princes. President Hindenburg, who had so far managed to keep out of controversial political and foreign issues, came out firmly against expropriation without compensation. He was horrified at the prospect of the possessions of the former royal princes being seized.[34] In a letter to Friedrich von Löbell, published in the press on 7 June, Hindenburg called the referendum a 'grave injustice', and 'contrary to principles of morality and justice'. The Social Democrats and the Communists were critical of Hindenburg for departing from the path of political impartiality during the hotly contested referendum campaign.[35]

The Social Democrats and the Communists both mounted strong campaigns, using speakers, posters, pamphlets, public rallies, and door-to-door canvassing. The Social Democrats issued a manifesto stating the referendum was 'about whether the political power embodied in the state is supposed to be a tool of domination in the hands of the upper class or a tool of liberation in the hands of the working masses', while the Central Committee of the KPD claimed 'the hatred against the crowned robbers is the class hatred against the system of capitalism and its system of slavery'.[36]

The parties of the Right urged their supporters to abstain from voting to ensure the proposition failed. The DNVP used more money on the referendum campaign than it had spent on the national election campaign of December 1924. A DNVP manifesto distributed to voters described the proposal as 'the cowardly rape of the property of the defenceless princes', and predicted if it was successful it would be followed by 'the expropriation of all private property', while the BVP described the referendum as 'a grave violation of the moral imperative of the protection of private property'.[37]

On 20 June 1926, the German public went to the polls for the referendum. A total of 96.2 per cent of those who voted (14.45 million) supported property expropriation without compensation, with only 3.8 per cent (585,027) voting against. This was an impressive performance, amounting to more votes for the 'Yes' campaign than Hindenburg had achieved during the 1925 presidential election, but with the turnout of registered voters recorded at 39.3 per cent, this fell way short of the required number of voters needed to make the measure a law. The Social Democrats felt the required majority could have been achieved if the Communists had accepted their original suggestion of some minimal compensation for the royal princes. The Communists argued the Social Democrats had mounted a half-hearted campaign and only joined the 'Yes' campaign in order to 'throttle it'.[38]

The question of compensation for the princes was now devolved to the local state governments. The biggest settlement was signed on 29 October 1926 between the deposed House of Hohenzollern and the Prussian government, settling the royal estates of former monarch Wilhelm II, with 20 of the 60 former royal castles deemed private property and financial compensation for the others set at 32 million Reichsmarks.[39]

On 3 September, the report of the Committee on the Reorganisation of the Council of the League of Nations was submitted. It proposed that Germany alone be granted a permanent seat on the League Council, while the number of non-permanent seats was to be increased from six to nine. Holders of these three new seats, chosen by the League Assembly, would be eligible for election again at the end of their initial three-year term, thus making these seats, allotted to Poland, Chile and

Romania, semi-permanent. Colombia, the Netherlands, and China were given two-year seats, and Salvador, Belgium and Czechoslovakia one-year seats. Poland accepted the proposals, but Brazil and Spain were already in the process of withdrawing.[40]

On 8 September, after a unanimous vote in the Assembly, Germany was finally admitted to the League of Nations. The following telegram was sent by the Secretary-General of the League to Gustav Stresemann, the German Foreign Minister. It read: 'On the instruction of the President of the Assembly of the League of Nations, I have the pleasure to inform you that on 8th September, [the Assembly], declared Germany as admitted to the League of Nations and approved the decision of the Council of 4th September granting to Germany a permanent representation on the League Council.'[41] On 10 September, the German delegation, headed by Gustav Stresemann, entered the Grand Hall of the League of Nations, the Salle de la Réformation, to be greeted by spontaneous applause.[42]

Stresemann, in his first speech to the Assembly, said:

> Germany today advances into the company of States, with some
> of whom it has lived in untroubled friendship for many decades,
> others of who were allied against it in the World War. It is of
> historic importance that Germany and these latter states now find
> themselves associated within the League in enduring and peaceful
> cooperation. This fact alone shows more clearly than words and
> platforms can do that the League may be called upon to give a new
> direction to the political development of humanity.[43]

Aristide Briand, the French Foreign Minister, then delivered a memorable speech in response, welcoming the German delegation, by declaring:

> It is a striking scene when a few years after the most terrible war
> that has ever swept over the world, while the battlefields are still
> wet with the blood of the nations, these very nations are present in
> this peaceful assembly to exchange mutual assurances of a common
> will to labour together for the peace of the world.

Briand stirred the audience deeply with his final memorable phrase: 'Away with rifles and machine guns and cannon, make way for arbitration and peace.' On hearing those words, applause erupted throughout the hall. Briand had publicly demonstrated his confidence in Stresemann's peaceful intentions. This moment was the high point of what later became known as 'the spirit of Locarno'.[44]

Gustav Stresemann addresses the League
of Nations, 10 September 1926.

Briand wanted to build immediately on the good feelings generated in Geneva by inviting Stresemann to meet him face to face, to discuss the most critical issues still outstanding in Franco-German relations, and set out a road map to solve them. This historic private meeting between the two, with just Briand's French interpreter present, occurred at a four-hour lunch in a restaurant in Madame Lodge's Hotel, in the village of Thoiry, in eastern France. There are two sources for what occurred at this meeting, and they differ. The first is a detailed memorandum, dictated by Gustav Stresemann on 20 September, from notes he compiled just after the meeting. The second is in the form of much briefer notes taken by Professor Oswald Hesnard, who acted as the interpreter for Briand at the meeting.[45] These two sources differ from each other in that Stresemann ascribes certain suggestions to Briand which Hesnard's notes claim originated with Stresemann.[46]

The two documents, however, do agree that Stresemann and Briand discussed five issues, and agreed on solutions to solve them. First, they discussed the Saar district, then governed by the League of Nations. It was agreed sovereignty would be restored to Germany, not in a referendum in 1935, but as soon as possible. This could be achieved by Germany purchasing the coal mines from their French owners at a cost of 300 million gold Reichsmarks. Second, they talked about the Inter-Allied Military Control Commission. On this matter, Stresemann could not deny Germany had not yet satisfied all the conditions set out for the end of these controls. Briand insisted progress needed to be made on regulating paramilitary organisations, but he admitted this was a trivial matter. The third issue discussed was German possessions ceded to Belgium under the terms of the Treaty of Versailles. Briand promised France would raise no objection to Germany opening negotiations with the Belgians for the return of the Eupen-Malmédy district awarded to Belgium under the terms of the Treaty, provided adequate financial compensation was offered by Germany. The final two issues concerned the continued Allied occupation of the Rhineland, not due to end until 1930, on which Briand promised he would do all he could to ensure the early withdrawal of Allied troops, and the possibility of German economic assistance for the franc. On this final point, Briand suggested diverting a part of German national railway bonds to France, aiming to commercialise these bonds by raising revenue on them on the money markets, using the 52 per cent French stake in them, which was worth a billion gold Reichsmarks. Stresemann pointed out this proposal would be opposed in Germany. However, it says much for the economic revival of Germany in the mid-1920s that Germany was now in a position to assist France financially.

When he returned to France, Briand encountered strong opposition to all the questions discussed at Thoiry from Raymond Poincaré, who had recently returned as the French Prime Minister. Poincaré, wholeheartedly supported by his cabinet colleagues, made clear that he could not commit to any of the solutions discussed at Thoiry. He refused to open negotiations on the early evacuation of the Rhineland, and the purchase of the Saar coal mines failed to materialise, even though Germany would have been able to raise the money required. Poincaré saw the railway bond proposal as unworkable, too, and he argued it was not needed anyway, as his austerity measures had led to a recovery in the value of the franc from 264 to 124 to the pound. In the end, the Briand–Stresemann Thoiry scheme only made progress in ending the Inter-Allied Military Control Commission, which ceased operations in Germany on 31 January 1927. The failure of the French government to move on the early evacuation of the Rhineland, due to occur in 1930, was a huge disappointment to Stresemann.[47]

The German Foreign Minister arrived back in Berlin at 5 p.m. on 23 September 1926. He was greeted at the railway station by the Chancellor, Wilhelm Marx, several cabinet ministers, and various important foreign diplomats. At 6 p.m. Stresemann met President Hindenburg to update him on the negotiations. After the meeting, Hindenburg released the following press statement: 'The President hoped the forthcoming negotiations would lead to a solution of the difficult questions still pending, and to a speedy liberation of the Rhineland and the Saar area.' On the next day, the cabinet met and agreed in principle with Stresemann's effort to bring the questions outstanding between Germany and France to a satisfactory conclusion.[48]

Before meeting Briand at Thoiry, Stresemann had addressed a group of German expatriates in Geneva, at the Gambrinus beer hall, which came to be known as the 'Gambrinus Speech'. In the speech, Stresemann said the continued occupation of the Rhineland and the exclusion of Germany from its colonies could no longer be justified now Germany was a member of the League of Nations. Then he raised the thorny issue of Germany's war guilt, making clear his attitude on this matter had not changed. He remained convinced Germany was not 'morally guilty' of starting the war, as charged by the Allies, and he was equally unwilling to accept that Germany provoked the war by its actions during the 1914 July Crisis. Stresemann even suggested

Germany had only been defeated in the war by having too many powerful enemies: 'I am of the firm conviction that future ages will not ask how it was possible Germany should have been defeated, but how was it possible that the German people held out against a world of enemies for four years and when lowering their colours, could boast that the Fatherland had not been invaded.'[49]

The Gambrinus Speech was greeted with much anger and bitterness in France. In two speeches, on 26 September, in Saint-German and, on 27 September, in Bar-le-Duc, Poincaré repeated the French view that Germany was exclusively responsible for the war, and that a complete Franco-German rapprochement was only possible when the German government and its people accepted this established and irrefutable fact. In a speech in Cologne on 2 October, Stresemann, determined to have the last word, responded to Poincaré's two speeches by insisting Germany had been drawn into the war through no guilt of the German government. Of course, this argument was once again couched in the language of the 'stab in the back myth', which was still being peddled by the nationalist Right, and prevailed not only with Stresemann, but within his party, the DVP.[50]

The drama in foreign affairs was soon followed by a crisis in German domestic politics, with the Reichswehr at its centre. On 27 September, a south German local newspaper reported that Prince Wilhelm of Prussia, the eldest son of the Crown Prince, who was himself the eldest son of the deposed German Emperor, Wilhelm II, had been allowed to attend army manoeuvres of the 9th Infantry Regiment in Württemberg, as a temporary lieutenant, wearing the uniform of the old Imperial First Foot Guards, even though he was not even a member of the Army. This had been sanctioned by Colonel-General Otto von Seeckt, the Commanding Officer of the Reichswehr, following a request by the Crown Prince.[51] It soon became clear that Seeckt had not sought prior approval from Otto Gessler, the Defence Minister. He did not even seem to realise the political significance of allowing this to happen, as it might be taken to mean that the Reichswehr favoured the restoration of the monarchy.[52] The Crown Prince and his family had only recently been allowed to return to Germany from exile in the Netherlands, on the strict understanding none of the members would engage in political activity.

Once the story broke in the press, there was a huge political outcry. The Social Democrats regarded Seeckt's action as an improper gesture of friendliness to the defunct German monarchy. The pro-republican newspapers seized on the crisis to attack Gessler for allowing it, even though he had known nothing about it beforehand. Under pressure, Gessler took the matter up with President Hindenburg, who already had a strained relationship with him. The nub of the dispute between them was Hindenburg's insistence on being recognised, as head of state, as the real Commander-in-Chief of the Reichswehr, and Seeckt's resentment at being downgraded.

On 1 October, Hindenburg met Seeckt, who was wearing his ubiquitous monocle. Seeckt adopted an arrogant tone during their conversation, freely admitting he had invited Prince Wilhelm, and seemingly seeing no reason to regret it.[53] Once Hindenburg was certain Seeckt was the instigator of the crisis, he decided it was time to dismiss him. Seeckt was shocked, as he thought the President would stand by a fellow Prussian officer when faced with a civilian government calling for his head. In reality, Hindenburg was glad to see him go, commenting 'that man corrupts the character of the officer corps with his conceit'.[54]

In a tense meeting with Seeckt, on 1 October, the Defence Minister, Gessler, told him it had been his duty to discuss the matter with him beforehand, and explained the negative effects his irresponsible behaviour would have on foreign policy. He then told the cabinet he had no intention of taking responsibility for Seeckt's actions.[55] On 5 October, Gessler sent a letter to Seeckt, stating that he could see 'no other possibility' of settling the political crisis than through Seeckt's resignation. He refuted Seeckt's view that it was 'notorious enemies of the Army' on the Left who had brought about his downfall, by informing him the political anger against his actions was just as strong among the moderate parties of the Centre.[56]

On 8 October, Seeckt resigned, to be succeeded by General Wilhelm Heye, who had assisted Seeckt in organising the new Reichswehr after the war and was currently the head of the Reichswehr's Personnel Office, and known to be extremely loyal to Hindenburg. He had the added advantage, from the government's point of view, of being pro-republican.[57] Colonel Carl-Heinrich von Stülpnagel, a close colleague of Seeckt, felt it was the latter's arrogant attitude that led to his undoing, later recalling: 'The affair of the prince only played a minor part, although it was the straw that broke the camel's back. If Seeckt had talked it over quietly with Gessler, he would have been willing to cover this, as he had covered so many other things. But Seeckt treated him harshly and Gessler was not willing to accept that.'[58] In Seeckt's own opinion, the cause of his dismissal was the 'clash between the democratic parliamentarian system and a personality that was independent of it, and in the last resort the unbridgeable gulf between the representative of the old Germany and of the commanding position of its army and the power-consciousness of the Republican and parliamentarian civil authorities'.[59]

The DNVP used the crisis to claim that Stresemann had been the hidden hand behind Seeckt's dismissal, calling Seeckt a 'victim of the Franco-German policy of friendship', a charge Stresemann quickly denied. In a statement published by the *Tägliche Rundschau* (*Daily Review*), on 15 October, Stresemann described Seeckt's departure as 'solely a matter of army discipline', decided exclusively between the Minister of Defence and President Hindenburg, without any interference on his part.[60]

On 4 December, about one thousand guests and a hundred journalists gathered in the industrial city of Dessau for the opening ceremony of the new Bauhaus building, the most famous building erected during the Weimar period, with its innovative futuristic glass curtain walls, and asymmetrical pinwheel design. From an aerial view, the layout resembles airplane propellers. The original Bauhaus school, located in Weimar, had moved to Dessau in the spring of 1925, after funding had been withdrawn by the right-wing local Thuringian government. Fritz Hesse, the mayor of Dessau, and his cultural adviser, Ludwig Grote, financed the move to Dessau and the local government financed the construction of the new school building, designed by Walter Gropius, who believed modern buildings should have clean lines and smooth surfaces which reflected their function. Construction began in September 1925 and the topping-out ceremony had been held on 21 March 1926.

General Hans von Seeckt, Commander-in-Chief of the Reichswehr until his resignation in October 1926.

The new building had a light structure, with its load-bearing capacity moved from the exterior walls to the steel skeleton, leaving the external face of the building reduced to a single-pane glass screen to protect the inhabitants from noise, rain and cold. The interior fittings, furniture, lighting, and free-standing central heating radiators were produced in the school's workshops. The roofs were flat, covered with asphalt tiles. The building, which was fully restored in the 1990s, covers 250,600 square feet, and is composed of three building wings, all connected by bridges, with each having different functions: (1) the three-storey glass-fronted workshop wing contains the workshops; (2) the three-storey vocational wing has studios, classrooms, offices and a library; (3) the five-storey main building is composed of staff and student accommodation. The workshop and vocational wings are connected by a two-storey bridge, which also contains administrative offices. A one-storey building, called the festive area, houses the auditorium, the legendary Bauhaus stage, and the canteen. The windows of the building are not small holes in the walls, but a continuous horizontal embedded curtain glass screen, its sections separated only by thin steel frames. The outer walls were painted plain white, but the interior is painted in assorted colours. The delicate glass façade caused problems for climate control: in summer, the building often became too hot, requiring curtains to be closed. In winter, it cooled down very quickly.[61]

For architectural purists, the Dessau building was seen as lacking the beauty and ornamentation of classical architecture. The sharpest criticism came from right-wing architects. Emil Hogg, a Professor of Architecture in Dresden, called the building a prime example of 'nomadic architecture', which would lead to 'uprootedness and proletarianisation'. Similarly, Paul Schultze-Naumburg, who later joined the NSDAP, saw such modern architecture as 'a direct reflection of Jewish blood that had despoiled the German racial stock'. He also felt what Gropius had built represented a 'soulless, godless, mechanical world'.[62]

On 10 December, the Nobel Prize Committee awarded the Peace Prize for 1926 jointly to the Foreign Ministers of Germany and France, Gustav Stresemann and Aristide Briand, for their 'critical roles in bringing about the Locarno Treaty and Franco-German reconciliation', while at the same time awarding the Peace Prize for 1925, retrospectively and jointly, to Austen Chamberlain, the British Foreign Secretary, for his role in the signing of the Locarno Treaties and to the American financier Charles Dawes, for the central part he had played

overleaf The Bauhaus building in Dessau was formally opened on 4 December 1926.

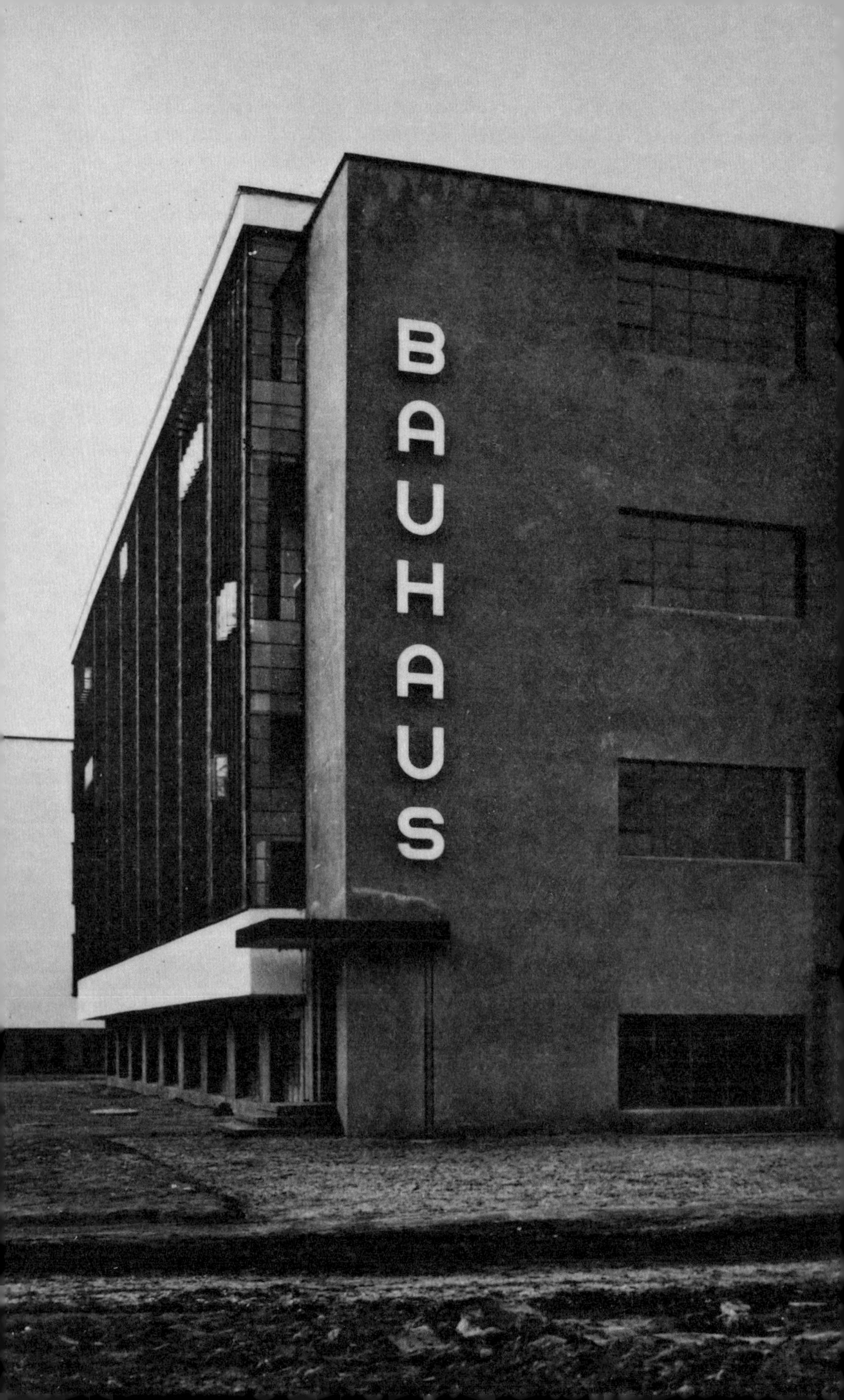
BAUHAUS

in brokering the financial restricting of Germany's reparations under the Dawes Plan.[63]

The year ended dramatically with another domestic political crisis, revolving once again around the activities of the Reichswehr. It began on 3 December, when the *Manchester Guardian* published an article by its Berlin correspondent, Frederick Voigt, on the clandestine connection between the Reichswehr and the Soviet government, headlined 'Cargoes of Munitions from Russia to Germany'. The article gave details of an agreement between the Junkers Company and the Soviet government to build factories for the manufacture of military aircraft. Details of this plan fell into the hands of Voigt, who also discovered plans for the building of chemical plants in the Soviet Union that would manufacture poison gas for both countries. Voigt further revealed that a Soviet cargo ship loaded with ammunition and weapons had sunk in the Baltic, en-route to Germany. A second article by Voigt, published on 6 December, with the headline 'Berlin Military Transactions', gave details about the building of a Junkers plant in Moscow, which was intended to manufacture 100 aeroplanes for German use. It was clear Seeckt had sanctioned these plans, and officers of the Reichswehr had travelled to Russia on false passports to disguise their identities.[64]

On 9 December, the Social Democratic newspaper *Vorwärts* printed these startling revelations, under the headline: 'Soviet Grenades for German Guns'. The Social Democrats were given further damaging information about German secret rearmament: in the harbour of Stettin, local stevedores had observed freighters bringing in artillery shells from Russia for delivery to the Reichswehr. These workers admitted they were given extra money in return for a promise of secrecy.[65] On 16 December, Philipp Scheidemann, a prominent Social Democratic member of the Reichstag, used parliamentary exemption from prosecution to deliver a devastating speech outlining details of the Russo-German secret rearmament, during which he called for the resignation of Otto Gessler, the Defence Minister. Right-wing nationalists called Scheidemann 'a traitor' and walked out of the debating chamber. Of course, the allegations made by Scheidemann were not new, but the effect of revealing them in a Reichstag debate raised the political temperature to boiling point.[66]

The Social Democrats called on the Chancellor, Wilhelm Marx, to immediately remove Gessler as the Defence Minister and reform the Reichswehr. Failure to act would compel them to withdraw their support from the government. On 17 December, the day after Scheidemann's incendiary speech, the Social Democrats tabled a vote of no confidence against the Marx government, which was carried by a vote of 249 to 171, with the DNVP surprisingly voting for the motion because they were determined to join the next government.[67]

The third Marx cabinet resigned on 18 December, but agreed to Hindenburg's request to stay on in a caretaker capacity until a new government was formed. For the third year running, Germans celebrated Christmas with another government crisis. Once again, it would not be resolved until the New Year.

Members of the Bauhaus teaching staff on the roof of the Bauhaus building in Dessau. Bauhaus founder Walter Gropius and the Russian artist Wassily Kandinsky are respectively fourth and fifth from the right.

1927

·

METROPOLIS
AND
MARX'S SOCIAL
REFORMS

·

On 10 January 1927, Fritz Lang's science fiction classic, *Metropolis*, one of the great masterpieces of silent cinema, had its world premiere at the UFA Palast am Zoo in Berlin. Around 1,200 people attended, including the German Chancellor, Wilhelm Marx, and members of his cabinet, along with invited film celebrities, and foreign ambassadors. The Austrian-born director introduced the film himself, with live musical accompaniment performed by a full orchestra, conducted by the film's composer, Gottfried Huppertz. The gala brochure, put together by the UFA publicist, Stefan Lorant, became an instant collector's item.

Metropolis, noted for its elaborate special effects and set designs, is not only the most famous film of the Weimar years, but one of the most important and influential films ever. The Los Angeles of Ridley Scott's *Blade Runner,* and the Gotham City of Tim Burton's *Batman* both owe a great deal to the stunning imagery of *Metropolis*. The idea for the film began after Lang had visited New York City for the first time in late 1924, and was impressed by the Manhattan skyscrapers, later recalling: 'I looked into the streets, the glaring lights and there I conceived Metropolis. The buildings seemed to be a vertical sail, scintillating and very light, suspended in the dark sky to dazzle, distract, and hypnotize.'[1] Lang was also inspired by a number of architectural movements current at the time, ranging from Art Deco and Bauhaus to Futurism. During the New York trip, Lang bought two state-of-the-art Mitchell cameras which were used for the shooting of the film.

Lang's chief aim was to produce a blockbuster film that would appeal to the US market. At the premiere, the film had a running time of 153 minutes, but the American distributor, Paramount, felt the film was much too long and cut it to 116 minutes, and the British distributor released a version 128 minutes in length. The budget was 5.3 million Reichsmarks (equivalent to roughly 19 million Euros now), making it at the time the most expensive German film ever made. The film was loosely based on the 1925 novel *Metropolis*, written by Lang's

previous page Brigitte Helm as the *Maschinenmensch* ('machine human') in Fritz Lang's *Metropolis* (1927).

A poster advertising Fritz Lang's *Metropolis* (1927).

335

wife, Thea von Harbou, who also wrote the screenplay for the film, in collaboration with her husband.[2]

Filming began in the Babelsberg Studios in Berlin on 22 May 1925, and went on until 30 October 1926, clocking up a total of 310 working days. There were 25,000 extras used, who wore 200,000 costumes. The chief cinematographer was Karl Freund, who had worked with Lang previously on many early 1920s Expressionist films, most notably *Der Golem* (*The Golem*) and *Der letzte Mann* (*The Last Laugh*). Freund was a film pioneer who invented a camera, free of the tripod, which could glide freely around the film set. He was ably assisted by Gunther Rittau, a specialist in trick photography – a talent which proved invaluable for some of the innovative special effects on *Metropolis* – and by Eugen Schüfftan, who had developed a special matte-shot device using mirrors to link miniature backgrounds with action foregrounds.[3] The stunning shots of the stadium of the Tower of Babel, several street scenes and the interiors of the Cathedral were all filmed using the Schüfftan Process, which permitted little models to appear as giant structures. The stop-action scenes of cars zipping along roads and airplanes zooming past skyscrapers took weeks to film. Despite subsequent advances in film technology, no other film has ever surpassed *Metropolis* in terms of its impact on special effects.

The film is set in the early twenty-first century, in an ultra-modern city, a sort of dystopian super New York City, in which people travel in cars, monorail trains and air taxis. The story follows the attempt by Freder Fredersen, played melodramatically by Gustav Fröhlich, and the saintly Maria, hero of the workers, played by 17-year-old Brigitte Helm – who also plays the Machine Human (*Maschinenmensch*) – to persuade Joh Fredersen, played by Alfred Abel, the autocratic 'big boss' of Metropolis, and father of Freder, to overcome the vast gulf separating the classes in the city, and bring them together to live in harmony.

In Metropolis, there is no middle class, only the rich and the proletarian masses. It is a place where business magnates and their elite employees live a pampered, carefree, life of luxury, above ground, amid the colossal skyscrapers of the Upper City, where young men join the Club of Sons, surrounded by beautiful scantily clad women in spectacular gardens, and spend their days playing sports and seeking pleasure, while the mass of workers live and toil underground, shut out of daylight, operating the giant steam machines that power the Workers' City.

previous pages   Fritz Lang (right) and the cinematographer Curt Courant (centre) on the set of Lang's 1929 science-fiction film *Frau im Mond* (*Girl in the Moon*).

Maria, a working-class prophet, who lives in the subterranean part of the city, brings a group of children to see the huge pleasure garden used by the pampered elite. She tells them: 'These are your brothers', and then leaves. Freder, captivated by her beauty, decides to visit the underground area to find her. Once there, he witnesses the dreadful conditions of the workers, all wearing identical work uniforms and caps. In the first glimpse of the underground power plant, we see workers straining to move heavy dials of an enormous clock back and forth. Freder then witnesses the explosion of a huge machine that kills and injures hundreds of workers.

Freder returns to the Upper City to tell his father about the horrific conditions of the underground workers, but he is deeply shocked by his father's indifference to their plight. This is because his father has already heard rumours a resistance movement is developing in the underground city. To put a stop to this, Joh Fredersen meets with Rotwang, a demented 'mad scientist' with a false hand, who had invented the killing machine. Rotwang, played theatrically by Rudolf Klein-Rogge, takes Joh to a secret hole in the wall of the underground city, through which he can observe meetings of the workers.

Here Maria is secretly observed by Rotwang and Joh Fredersen giving a speech to the workers, in which she predicts the hands of the workers could be joined to the head of those in power by means of a mediator, who would function as the heart. Freder, now pretending to be an underground worker, thinks he can play such a role, and he talks with Maria at the end of her speech, telling her he is the mediator she wants, and they kiss passionately.

But Joh Fredersen is now determined to stop Maria influencing his workers. In his laboratory, Rotwang shows him a 'Machine Human' he has created from which he says he can create a human clone. Joh asks Rotwang to kidnap Maria for this purpose. Rotwang captures her after a dramatic chase through the underground catacombs, and takes her to his laboratory. In a memorable visual scene, Rotwang transfers the likeness of Maria to the Machine Human, so that the workers can be fooled and controlled. The special effect of the concentric rings of light, which move around the robot, give the illusion they are floating when in reality they were hand-operated.

Rotwang intends to double-cross Joh Fredersen by using the identical clone of Maria to lead a revolt to destroy *Metropolis*, because Joh had married the love of Rotwang's life, Hel, who had died giving birth to Freder. The cloned humanoid Maria, controlled by Rotwang, now urges the workers to destroy the underground machines, saying: 'Let the machines kill the machines'. The workers then lay waste to the underground factory, flooding the Workers' City, then run riot through the Upper City.

When the deluded mob tries to attack the Heart Machine, the engine that keeps the entire city water supply running, its operator, Grot, played by Heinrich George, tells them that if they disable the machine they will destroy Metropolis. At that point, the mob turns on the cloned Maria. Her end is reminiscent of a medieval witch-hunt. She is captured, and tied to a stake, below which a huge bonfire is lit. A horrified Freder watches this, but as the flames take hold, the clone Maria turns back into the Machine Human.

In the meantime, Joh Fredersen has found out that Rotwang was all along behind the plan to use the cloned Maria to destroy Metropolis. The dramatic final scenes of the film feature Rotwang chasing the real Maria, who has escaped from his laboratory, inside the city Cathedral. Maria feverishly grapples with him, until Freder comes to her assistance. There is a protracted struggle between Freder and Rotwang on the roof of the Cathedral, before Rotwang falls spectacularly to his death. The film ends with Freder fulfilling his role as the mediator by persuading his father and Grot, the Heart Machine operator, to shake hands. Without machines we will die, the film suggests, but with them we risk becoming less human.[4]

Upon release, *Metropolis* was a surprising box-office flop, with takings in Germany of only 75,000 Reichsmarks. It had a negative reception from the film critics, too, most suggesting that rather than offering an accurate prediction of the future, it was really a soppy love story, rooted in the industrial relations of present-day Weimar Germany.

The ending seemed to reflect the moderate Social Democratic idea that industry and labour can work in harmony. Willy Haas in *Film Kurier*, the leading German film magazine, claimed that *Metropolis* 'leaves all the American accomplishments in cinematography in the dust and is unique in the history of cinema', but admitted he found the futuristic story ludicrous, consisting of 'a bit of socialism, with its shiny new cult of the machine' mixed with the 'enslavement of the soulless proletariat'. A review by the noted British science fiction writer H.G. Wells called it: 'Quite the silliest film'. He questioned the anti-progress, anti-technology message of the film, which he thought seemed to suggest automation made the lives of workers much worse when it was

Brigitte Helm as the *Maschinenmensch* ('machine human') in Fritz Lang's *Metropolis* (1927).

just the opposite. The noted film critic Mordaunt Hall, writing in the *New York Times*, called the film a 'technical marvel, with feet of clay'.[5]

The film also incensed right-wing nationalists, as it seemed to fuel social tension and even advocated class struggle; but communists also attacked it, with one arguing: 'This film born out of bourgeois-capitalist ideology and produced with the insistently obtrusive intent to propagate the idea of class reconciliation, the better to further capitalist methods of exploitation, only succeeds in unmasking the bourgeois worker-friendly phraseology in all its mendacity.'[6]

In domestic politics, most of January 1927 was taken up with the negotiations to form a new coalition government. Hindenburg favoured a 'Bourgeois Bloc', including the DNVP, with Julius Curtius, a right-wing member of the DVP, as Chancellor. This plan was opposed by Zentrum, who preferred to exclude the DNVP, and have a pro-republican coalition of the Centre Left including the Social Democrats. The DVP wanted the DNVP to join the coalition rather than the Social Democrats, even though Stresemann was worried about foreign reaction to DNVP involvement in government, which he thought might hamper his attempt to get the French government to agree to an early evacuation of the Rhineland. The DDP refused to join a government involving the DNVP, but Otto Gessler resigned from the party on 28 January so that he could continue as the Defence Minister.[7]

Hindenburg was by now thoroughly disgusted by all this horse-trading in party politics. He called all the party leaders to a meeting, telling them bluntly he would resign the presidency and return to peaceful, stress-free retirement, from which he claimed he had been dragged under false pretences, if they would not resolve their differences. 'I have made my sacrifice for Germany,' he said, 'but I find no one willing to follow my example.'[8] In the end, Hindenburg, who wanted a government of the Right and Centre, turned back once more to Wilhelm Marx, asking him to form a coalition of bourgeois parties enjoying a Reichstag majority, but he insisted any DNVP cabinet ministers must accept the legal validity of the Locarno Treaties, Germany's membership of the League of Nations, and the Constitution, and he urged the new government to further the social welfare of the working classes.

What finally tipped Zentrum into joining a government involving the DNVP was the promise of a new School Law, which would authorise the establishment of religiously denominated schools throughout the Reich.[9] The DNVP leadership had come under pressure in the preceding months from industrial and agricultural pressure groups to rejoin the government. Over the next 13 months, the DNVP would be an integral part of the Marx government, providing it with the Reichstag majority it required to secure the passage of its socially reforming legislative agenda.[10]

For the first time, a rising military and political star, General Kurt von Schleicher, acted as a key adviser to Hindenburg during the lengthy coalition negotiations. In the previous year, he had been appointed head of the newly created Armed Forces Department in the Defence Ministry. He was also a close friend of Hindenburg's son, Oskar. Schleicher told Hindenburg that if it proved impossible to form the right-wing coalition the President desired, he should form a cabinet of individuals he had confidence in, without consulting any of the political parties or paying attention to their wishes. In effect, Schleicher had planted a seed in Hindenburg's mind of a presidential authoritarian government, which took no account of the Reichstag or the electorate.[11]

On 29 January, the fourth Marx cabinet was finally formed. It was the first parliamentary coalition of the Right, composed of members from Zentrum, the DVP, the BVP, and the DNVP. Marx moved his government decidedly to the Right, by allocating four cabinet posts to the DNVP members, which reflected their parliamentary strength. These were Oskar Hergt (Vice Chancellor and Minister of Justice), Walter von Keudell (Interior), Martin Schiele (Food and Agriculture) and Wilhelm Koch (Transport). The DVP provided two members: Gustav Stresemann (Foreign Minister) and Julius Curtius (Minister of Economics). Zentrum supplied three members: Wilhelm Marx (Chancellor), Heinrich Brauns (Labour) and Heinrich Köhler (Finance). The BVP was allocated one post: Georg Schätzel (Post); and finally, there was one independent member, Otto Gessler (Defence).[12]

On 3 February, the Marx cabinet was presented to the Reichstag. In his government address, Marx stated: 'The government of the Reich will carry on the present foreign policy in the sense of mutual understanding. This line is clear and is emphasized in the decisions reached during the past year with the concurrence of the constitutional authorities.' He then went out of his way to promise his government would uphold the Weimar Constitution.[13] The new government was given a vote of confidence by a Reichstag vote of 235 for and 174 against, with the Social Democrats, Democrats and Communists all voting against. In the preceding Reichstag debate, Kuno von Westarp, the DNVP party chair, who had personally found the conditions attached to the party's entry into government humiliating, declared his party's officially declared support for the Weimar Republic was 'not the equivalent of an inner conviction supporting the form of government or the system of parliamentary rule', nor did it mean the party had renounced its struggle for a restoration of the monarchy or its determination to see the end of the 'war guilt lie'.[14]

Random antisemitic attacks in Berlin made the news in the early spring. On 20 March, Hitler's paramilitary Stormtroopers assaulted Jews in Berlin. The violence began with a National Socialist attack on communists at Berlin's Lichterfelde-Ost railway station, then continued to the centrally located Kurfürstendamm, where many Jewish shops and businesses were located. It was preceded by an inflammatory speech by Joseph Goebbels to a large crowd in nearby Wittenberger Platz. This was followed by random violent attacks on people who looked Jewish, and the vandalising of shops whose owners had seemingly Jewish names. The German police reportedly stood back while National Socialists attacked anyone 'Jewish-looking'.[15]

For the remainder of 1927, the diplomatic controversies which had dominated politics in the preceding years now retreated into the background, as the focus shifted to domestic reform. It was under the fourth Marx cabinet that the Republic registered some of its most important social advances. Marx believed the inclusion of the DNVP in his government should be compensated for by a number of important measures of social reform.

The first of these reforms was new legislation on the hours of work. The Working Day Decree of 21 December 1923 had maintained the principle of the eight-hour working day, but in practice many possibilities were opened for management–union negotiations to agree to it not being applied. In late February 1927, Heinrich Brauns, the Minister of Labour, who had gained a reputation as a social progressive, decided to introduce the Provisional Work Hours Law, which sought to give a legal right to an eight-hour working day, and to establish new overtime pay rates, offering a 25 per cent increase on hourly rates of pay. On 8 April, the new law narrowly passed by a narrow Reichstag vote of 196 to 184.[16]

The DNVP was also determined to show its commitment to supporting reforms aimed at the agricultural community, which was suffering another economic downturn. On 4 April, Count von Westarp met with his coalition partners to draft a new tariff policy aiming to assist farmers in the domestic economy. In the coming months, several agricultural reforms were introduced, most notably easier access to bank loans, import licences, preferential tariff agreements with France, Spain, Poland and Canada, tariffs to protect agricultural products, and sales tax reductions on sugar and rye. All these measures were designed to give better protection to agricultural interests, and were welcomed by agricultural organisations, but farmers were never given anywhere near the same tariff protection they had enjoyed before the War and agricultural goods had failed to keep pace with the prices of industrial products. Due to a lack of capital, German agriculture was much less mechanised than its British and especially its American counterparts. Rural poverty was a reality in Weimar Germany, as the many photographs of children without shoes in rural areas amply demonstrate. Even at the height of Weimar economic prosperity in 1928, the average per capita income of farmers had fallen 44 per per cent below the national average.[17]

The most important social reform enacted by the Marx government in 1927 was undoubtedly the introduction of a comprehensive scheme of unemployment insurance, under the terms of the German Unemployment Insurance Act of 1927, which was passed by a huge majority in the Reichstag on 7 July, and was made law on 18 July. It was far more comprehensive than the British National Insurance Act of 1911. It granted unemployment benefits to any German citizen who was willing and able to work but had no job and met the conditions of the law. Assistance was provided for a period of 26 weeks. After this, if individuals remained unemployed, they would have to turn to poor relief schemes operated by local authorities.

The scheme was based on the principle of a 3 per cent tax on wages, with equal shares paid by employers and workers. The insurance fund was devised to cope with a maximum of 700,000 unemployed workers. In addition, an 'emergency fund' was created to support a further 400,000 workers during a period of economic crisis, but even this total of 1.1 million was far less than the 1.3 million who were consistently unemployed even during the best economic times. This meant the government would be required to make up any deficit in the fund by public borrowing.

Employers and employees were equally represented on the various boards entrusted with the administration of the insurance programme. At the top was a body called the Reich Institute for Labour Mediation and Unemployment Insurance, while unemployment exchanges to assist those out of work to find new employment were established across the country. The economic burden of National Insurance rose from 259 million Reichsmarks in 1925/26 to 345 million in 1927/28.[18]

The introduction of this measure was complemented by the extension of state arbitration, which created committees to deal with industrial disputes and pay settlements in the regions. They combined the principle of worker–management equality. For its part, the government now had the right to intervene in industrial pay disputes. If negotiations proved fruitless, the matter was referred to a state arbitration body whose decisions had to be accepted by both disputants, with the Minister of Labour given the power to select an arbitrator and impose a pay settlement, if necessary. A hierarchy of Labour Courts rounded out the elaborate arbitration machinery. Over 100,000 arbitration cases were initiated and over 5,000 compulsory settlements were imposed.[19]

All these social reforms enjoyed broad support from all the parties in the Marx-led coalition government, but one issue caused much greater disagreement. This was the renewal of the Law for the Protection of the Republic, which had been introduced following the assassination of Walther Rathenau on 24 June 1922. It gave the state extensive powers to monitor and punish anti-republican individuals and organisations. It also contained the so-called 'Kaiser paragraph' which prohibited the return to Germany of the Emperor or members of the other ruling German dynasties. The law was due to expire in the autumn of 1927. Members of the DNVP hated the law, but as members of the coalition government they were expected to vote in favour of its renewal. Wilhelm Marx had made clear that he was fully prepared to resign as Chancellor if the measure did not receive the required two-thirds majority in the Reichstag. This made the votes of the DNVP members crucial. At a meeting on 11 May between all the coalition parties, strong opposition was uttered by DNVP members about supporting the renewal of the measure.

Stresemann's DVP suggested a compromise, by tabling an amendment permitting an extension of the measure for just two years, and offering the immediate abolition of the Special Courts that had been set up to investigate anti-republican organisations. The DNVP leadership agreed to this compromise, and, on 17 May, all but six members of the DNVP Reichstag delegation voted in favour of it, which meant the measure easily gained the required two-thirds majority.

The former Imperial family protested vigorously against what they saw as the betrayal of the monarchist cause by the DNVP. On 7 June, there was a stormy meeting of the DNVP Executive Committee. Kuno von Westarp made it clear that failure by the DNVP to support the renewal of the law would have led to the fall of the existing government coalition and the formation of a left-wing government led by the Social Democrats.[20]

The entry of the Nationalist DNVP into a government upholding the Weimar Constitution pushed the National Socialists much further to the political periphery. In the spring and summer of 1927, Adolf Hitler decided to remedy this by trying to gain financial support from the business community for the NSDAP. On 5 March, the Bavarian government had lifted its public-speaking ban on Hitler. In April, Hitler spoke to a large group of invited guests from the local business community during which he praised the personalities of individual entrepreneurs.

Present was 80-year-old Emil Kirdorf, the director of the Gelsen-kirchner Bergwerk mining company, who was visibly moved by the speech. On 4 July Elsa Bruckmann, a Munich-based publisher, arranged a meeting between Kirdorf and Hitler at her home. The leader of the NSDAP and the industrialist talked for four hours. Afterwards, Kirdorf was so impressed by what he had heard, he asked Hitler to put down his thoughts in a pamphlet, which he promised to distribute to the most important Ruhr business figures.

In August the Hugo Bruckmann Verlag published Hitler's pamphlet, with the title *Der Weg zum Wiederaufstieg* (*The Road to Resurgence*). Hitler made clear that National Socialism did not intend to attack private industry. On the contrary, he wrote, 'only a strong nationalist state can provide industry with the protection and the freedom to continue to exist and develop'. At the same time, Hitler played down his antisemitism, stressing instead his enthusiastic opposition to Marxism. The pamphlet was greeted with a wave of indifference by the leading industrialists in the Ruhr, who saw no point in financing such a marginal political party. Even Kirdorf, who joined the NSDAP on 1 August, and attended the Nuremberg party rally shortly after as an 'honorary guest', left the party a year later, greatly dismayed by the 'socialist' and 'anti-capitalist' rhetoric that NSDAP activists adopted in the Ruhr valley.[21]

Also in August 1927, Professor Friedrich Wilhelm Förster, a committed pacifist and a strong critic of German militarism, who lived in exile in France, wrote an article, published in his journal *Die Menschheit* (*The Humanity*), which alleged that Gustav Stresemann was playing a duplicitous game in the conduct of his foreign policy – in public emphasising a search for peace and understanding, while in private remaining a committed German nationalist, who had knowledge of secret German rearmament, and desired a war of revenge against France and Poland.[22] This led Stresemann to deny these allegations, vehemently, even threatening legal action for libel and reportedly calling Förster a 'scoundrel'.

Dr Ernst Förster, the uncle of Friedrich, and a retired director of the shipbuilding division of the Hamburg American Line, wrote a letter to Stresemann stating that he regretted his nephew making his 'tactless statement' about Stresemann's 'admirable peace policy', but he asked the German Foreign Minister to apologise for the strong language he had used against his nephew. On 2 November, Stresemann penned a detailed reply to Ernst Förster arguing *Die Menschheit* was playing 'a dishonest and disingenuous game' by continually suggesting German

foreign policy was really inspired by a 'lust for revenge'. Stresemann claimed the recent allegations by Professor Friedrich Förster had made him cut short his holiday, because he knew 'not one word is true'. He felt articles of this type were undermining friendly relations with France and helping to delay the early Allied evacuation of the Rhineland. Stresemann further denied he had called Förster a 'scoundrel' but admitted he had written of the allegations in *Die Menschheit* by stating: 'These scoundrels invent new lies about Germany every day.'[23]

Professor Förster regarded Stresemann's reply as the retraction of his original alleged insult, and he responded by sending a further letter to him pointing out that he did believe there were people in the Reichswehr and on the Right of German politics who favoured a revival of Prussian militarism, and were engaging in 'numerous parades, manifestos, and political manipulations'. These groups 'had been growing stronger' recently. He urged Stresemann to provide evidence to the League of Nations that secret German rearmament was not going on. As this exchange shows, Stresemann was deeply sensitive to charges that he was operating a 'secret agenda' in his foreign policy. Defending himself against such allegations undoubtedly took a heavy toll on his mental and physical health.[24]

On 18 September, an event took place which revealed Germany was still having great difficulty accepting responsibility for starting the Great War. This came during the ceremony at which President Hindenburg dedicated the Tannenberg Memorial (*Tannenberg-Nationaldenkmal*), at the site of Germany's military victory over Tsarist Russia in August 1914, near the town of Hohenstein (now Olsztynek in Poland). The new structure was financed by public donations, and built under the supervision of the Berlin architects Johannes and Walter Krüger. It was a large octagonal structure with towers in each corner, at an average height of 20 metres, surrounding a huge military parade ground.

To avoid passing through Polish territory, Hindenburg travelled by sea from Swinemünde to Königsberg on the cruiser *Berlin*. Members of republican and Jewish ex-service associations were not invited: the only veterans' association taking part was the Steel Helmet. Erich Ludendorff, dressed in a field-grey uniform, attended and gave a flattering speech which praised Hindenburg's war service. A crowd of 100,000 gathered for the ceremony.

The Chancellor and the President had agreed beforehand that the unveiling should be purely commemorative, but the occasion should

President Hindenburg at the dedication
ceremony for the Tannenberg memorial,
East Prussia, 18 September 1927.

be used by Hindenburg to refute once and for all the accusation of war-guilt, which the Treaty of Versailles had made against Germany. For Hindenburg, wearing the Field Marshal's uniform of his Masurian regiment, and holding the baton of his rank in his left hand, it was a matter of national obligation to publicly address this issue. Hindenburg's speech, which was broadcast live on German radio, was co-written by Wilhelm Marx and Gustav Stresemann. In it, Hindenburg boldly declared:

> The accusation that Germany was responsible for this greatest
> of all wars we hereby repudiate. Germans in every walk of life
> unanimously reject it. It was in no spirit of envy, hatred, or lust
> for conquest that we unleashed the sword. With clean hearts, we
> marched out to defend our Fatherland, and with clean hands did
> we wield the sword. Germany is ready to prove this fact before an
> impartial tribunal.[25]

The former Kaiser Wilhelm II, living in exile in Doorn, in the Netherlands, sent Hindenburg a congratulatory telegram on his speech, signing it 'Wilhelm, Emperor and King', and stating: 'Tannenberg showed the world what German power was capable of under strong and definite leadership. May the heroic spirit of Tannenberg penetrate and unite our divided nation.'[26]

Hindenburg's Tannenberg speech was greeted with undisguised horror by the Allied nations. The fact the ex-Kaiser had heartily endorsed what Hindenburg had said made it even worse. Leopold von Hoesch, the German Ambassador in Paris, reported a leading French politician telling him that dredging up the war-guilt issue in such a high-profile manner 'will lead to no positive results, but only to unpleasant antagonism'. King George V had intended to send Hindenburg a congratulatory telegram on his upcoming 80th birthday, but after reading a report of Hindenburg's Tannenberg speech, he categorically declared 'he would send no good wishes'.[27]

Gustav Stresemann was 'not merely surprised', but 'amazed' that Hindenburg's speech had received such a negative reaction among the Allies. What Hindenburg had said in a speech aimed at German war veterans was, Stresemann noted, a 'common conviction of all Germans', who continue to 'resent the allegation that the terrible event of the World War should be imputed to Germany alone, as the grossest of slanders and it is obvious they cannot accept a condemnation passed by judges who are also their accusers'.[28]

In contrast, Hindenburg's speech was greeted with much praise from the German public, especially among the nationalist Right. On 2 October, Hindenburg's 80th birthday celebrations once again demonstrated his huge popularity. Gifts of all kinds were sent to him, varying from a painting on porcelain of Berlin in the Imperial era, a gift from the State of Prussia, to presents from European royalty, and even a live rabbit, sent by a newspaper delivery boy. On the day after his birthday, the Chancellor presented the President with the cash proceeds of the 'Hindenburg Fund', raised by donations from around the country. Hindenburg gave this money to war widows and disabled war veterans. A special postage stamp was also issued, and a marble bust was unveiled, a short while later, in the hall of the Reichstag, by SPD member Paul Löbe, the Reichstag Speaker, who said: 'From the day of his accession to office he has acted as the representative of the whole nation and not as the spokesman of a party, and he always raised his voice on behalf of conciliation and compromise'.[29]

On 23 September, *Berlin: Die Sinfonie der Grosstadt* (*Berlin: Symphony of a City*), one of the groundbreaking works of silent documentary cinema during the Weimar era, premiered in Berlin. Walter Ruttmann directed it.[30] The scriptwriter was Carl Meyer, who was also the co-writer of the Weimar silent classic *The Cabinet of Dr Caligari*. The team of cinematographers on the film was led by Karl Freund, the lead camera operator on Fritz Lang's *Metropolis*, ably assisted by Robert Baberske, Reimar Kuntze and László Schäffer.

The 65-minute film, using double exposure film, and a series of clever jump cuts, presents a montage of memorable images capturing a day in the life of the German capital, starting early in the morning and ending in the deepest night. The account of a single day in Berlin, which took a year to film, is told without characters or plot. Many of the buildings featured in the film, such as the Anhalter Bahnhof train station and the Hotel Excelsior, then the largest hotel in Europe, were both destroyed by Allied bombing during the Second World War. Ruttmann's absorbing film takes the audience through a single day in Berlin, arranged in five acts. The film opens with a train approaching the city, with the viewer feeling as if he or she is peering out of the train window to see trees and bridges whizz by, until finally arriving at the railway station, which bears the name 'Berlin'. Trains are an important theme of the film, and every act of the film contains shots of them.

The first act begins in the calm and empty streets as Berlin wakes up. We see crowds of people going to work, children walking to school and

commuters travelling on trams and trains. Then we glimpse factories springing to life, with images of sheets of metal being cut, molten glass poured into moulds, and smoke spilling out of factory chimneys. The second act shows more images of the general life of the city. By now, the city is bustling with activity. Office workers start their day. Typists set to work on their keyboards, and telephone operators answer calls. Different classes of people are seen travelling to work.

The third act shows a variety of people from different classes going about their daily life. We see industrial and construction workers, shop workers and shoppers. There is a montage of brief images: a bride arriving at a wedding, a coffin inside a hearse, judges entering a court building, the Reich President being saluted by the police, an angry protester addressing a crowd, and a fight between two men being broken up by a police officer.

The fourth act begins with a lunch break. A variety of workers stop work. People are seen eating food. Animals are fed at the Zoo. A paper press turns out newspapers. A man is seen reading the news stories, with headlines such as 'Crisis', 'Murder' and 'Money'. Then there are images of the end of the working and school day. Children play in the park, rowing is seen on the lake, and romantic couples sit on park benches.

The final act is devoted to entertainment in the city at night. People go out to the theatre. Curtains open on a variety of performers, including burlesque dancers, jugglers, trapeze artists and singers. Audiences visit the movies. We also see ice shows, boxing matches and dance contests. There are images of dancing, drinking, and flirting in beer halls, restaurants, and cocktail bars. A vivid firework display ends the film.

Berlin: Symphony of a City is an incredible time-capsule of the 'golden age' of Weimar Germany. The main characters are the city's inhabitants and its industry. The film became a key influence on subsequent documentary film-making. Ruttmann's film, which reduces the human experience to a single day, seems to suggest Berlin offered endless possibilities for enjoyment, but also shows the contradictions of modern life, with individuals often depicted as the wage slaves of business and industry.[31]

Meanwhile, the social reforms of the Marx government continued. One of the key reasons Zentrum and the DNVP had agreed to join the Marx coalition in the first place was the promise of a new School Law, which would authorise the establishment of religious

Stills from *Berlin: Symphony of a City* (1927). Walter Ruttmann's documentary film portrayed the German capital – together with the daily lives of ordinary Berliners – in every aspect.

denominational schools throughout the Reich. Zentrum felt the introduction of a new School Law would be popular among Catholic parents and help increase votes for Zentrum at future elections. The measure also enjoyed widespread support within the DNVP for similar reasons. The drafting of the new School Law was primarily the responsibility of the DNVP's Walter von Keudell, the Minister of the Interior, who presented the first draft to the cabinet on 22 June 1927. Keudell claimed the new measure would give Catholic and Protestant Lutheran churches a direct legal role in the German educational system, at the expense of the non-denominational Christian Common Schools (*Simultanschulen*). Keudell's bill also envisaged that Catholic and Lutheran clergy would in future play a larger part in shaping the curriculum in these schools, with many Common Schools reconverted into religious denominational schools. Schools in the south-western states were potentially the most affected by this provision.

Not surprisingly, there was strong opposition to the School Law from the SPD-led Prussian government and from the DVP, both of whom had grave doubts about the attack it represented on the Common Schools, which they felt had broken down traditional religious barriers. After the Reichsrat rejected the first draft of the School Law by 37 to 31 votes on 14 October, the Marx cabinet submitted the bill to a first and second reading in the Reichstag, which it passed, but the cabinet agreed the measure needed further discussion in the Reichstag Education Committee to see if a compromise could be reached between the parties before it was presented to a further vote in the Reichstag.[32]

Another major reform implemented by the Marx government in the autumn of 1927 was a salary increase for civil servants, under the Salaries Bill, which had followed a pay review instigated by Heinrich Köhler, the Minister of Finance. For years, the pay of civil servants had stagnated in relation to industrial wages. Originally, Köhler had considered an increase of 10 per cent, but by the time the bill was introduced the proposed wage rises being offered were between 21 and 25 per cent. In October, the pay settlement was ratified in the Reichstag by a vote of 333 for and 53 against. Parker Gilbert, the Agent General for Reparations, warned such large pay increases for civil servants would greatly increase government expenditure, and lead industrial workers asking for similar pay rises, which would push up inflation, and endanger Germany's future reparations payments under the Dawes Plan.[33] Hjalmar Schacht, the President of the Reichsbank, had similar misgivings, warning these vastly increased public expenditure commitments were only storing up economic problems for the future.[34]

Just before Christmas 1927, Gustav Stresemann visited Königsberg (now Kaliningrad, Russia). At the time, this East Prussian city was the capital of the Free State of Prussia, and was cut off from the rest of Germany by the Polish Corridor. City officials invited Stresemann there to assess East Prussian public opinion, and then report back to the Foreign Policy Committee of the Reichstag. On 16 December, Stresemann spoke, off the record, to a group of leading officials in the central and local government administration in Königsberg. What he said offers a useful insight into his attitude towards Poland at this time.

Stresemann reported the details of his recent conversations with Marshal Jósef Pilsudski, the Prime Minister of Poland, and August Zaleski, the Polish Foreign Minister, at the League of Nations. He said both had promised that Poland had no wish to annexe East Prussia. Stresemann then told his listeners of his own policy aims towards Eastern Europe. He made clear that the removal of the Polish Corridor by war 'was impossible'. Germany, even if it desired such an outcome, did not have the military strength for such a purpose. The question, therefore, 'must be considered whether a recovery of the Corridor might be possible by peaceful methods'. Stresemann thought such a peaceful settlement might be achievable with the agreement of Poland, and the Locarno powers. Stresemann then moved on to discuss the idea of Germany signing an 'Eastern Locarno', which implied a German promise to respect the Polish frontiers laid down by the Versailles Treaty. Stresemann reiterated this was not something the German government was prepared to do. He thought any settlement in Eastern Europe would only be possible when Germany enjoyed much better relations with France. What Germany wanted, above all, in its foreign policy was to avoid Europe splitting into two camps, which had proved so disastrous in the past and would be again.[35]

1928
·
THE SOCIAL DEMOCRATS RETURN TO POWER
·

The year began with an embarrassing political scandal for the German government. On 14 January, Otto Gessler, the Minister of Defence, resigned, citing 'ill health', but the real reason was his Ministry's involvement in financing secret investment and rearmament in what became known as the 'Phoebus Scandal'. Gessler, who was accused of covering up the scandal, decided to go before he was pushed.

At the heart of all the wrongdoing was Captain Walter Lohmann, head of the Maritime Transport Division, who had been assigned large funds to invest in various projects, including: weapons sales, the development of a modern submarine, building oil tankers, setting up a marine intelligence service, and investing huge sums in aircraft companies, banks, property and ore mining. During 1926 and 1927, large sums were poured into the Phoebus Film Corporation, which had the task of overseeing a propaganda campaign to support secret rearmament.[1] In the first instance, Lohmann bought shares in the company to the value of 1.75 million Reichsmarks. In March 1926, Lohmann and Gessler then signed a joint loan guarantee for 3 million Reichsmarks, and in January 1927, a further loan guarantee for 3.5 million Reichsmarks was sanctioned. In all, 10 million Reichsmarks had been swallowed up by this company alone.[2]

The aim of this clandestine investment was to generate further funds for secret armaments projects, but Lohmann's various investments lost 200 million Reichsmarks. Gessler had secretly ordered Lohmann to take full responsibility if his secret activities were publicly exposed.[3] It was during the messy bankruptcy proceedings of the Phoebus Film Company, which began in the late autumn of 1927, that the full details of the loans sanctioned to Lohmann by the German government were revealed. By 19 January 1928, Lohmann's position became untenable, and he promptly resigned in disgrace. He was followed on 30 September by Hans Zenker, the head of the German Navy (*Reichsmarine*), whose continued denials of any knowledge about the secret loans became unconvincing.

previous page Detail of a group photograph
of the cabinet of Chancellor Hermann
Müller (front row, centre), June 1928.

Gessler had served as Defence Minister continuously for almost eight years and was seen as an indispensable member of the ever-changing Weimar governments, but he had made many enemies along the way. He was most heavily criticised by the Social Democrats and the communist Left, who highlighted what they called his 'unconstitutional behaviour' in not informing the Reichstag of Lohmann's shady investments during the annual defence budget discussions.[4] On the advice of Kurt von Schleicher, Hindenburg picked as Gessler's successor as Defence Minister Wilhelm Groener, who had been the First Quartermaster General of Imperial Germany towards the end of the Great War of 1914–18. He had also served as the Minister of Transport from 1920 to 1923. After his appointment, Groener, who was basically democratic in outlook, wound up most of the Lohmann shady enterprises.[5]

The political commotion over Gessler's fall had hardly subsided when the fragile fourth Marx cabinet collapsed, after it became clear no agreement could be reached over the controversial Schools Act. The end came on 15 February 1928 when Theodor von Guérard of Zentrum announced that his party was leaving the Marx coalition, as it was then clear the Schools Act would fail to pass a vote in the Reichstag. The real reason for the cabinet's fall was the determination of Stresemann's DVP to block the passage of the bill. The DVP saw the proposed Schools Act as an infringement of Articles 146 and 174 of the Weimar Constitution, which had provided for non-denominational Common Schools. Outside parliament, the public had been bitterly divided on the measure.[6] With the agreement of President Hindenburg, Marx and his cabinet remained in office in a caretaker capacity, and came to an agreement with all the democratic parties in the Reichstag to deal with a number of pressing issues in an 'emergency programme', announced on 27 February.

One of these concerned a controversial naval measure. The Treaty of Versailles had left Germany with only six capital ships, which could only be replaced by ships of not more than 10,000 long or imperial tons (a long ton is equivalent to 1.016 metric tonnes). This still left open the possibility of building 'armoured ships' (*Panzerschiffe*), a form of heavily armed cruisers combining heavy armament and high speed, later known in Britain as Pocket Battleships, due to their six 11-inch guns. The design for these ships also included all-diesel propulsion. The plan envisaged four would be built in the coming years, at a total cost estimated at 100 million Reichsmarks.[7]

The Social Democrats, supported by the DDP and the far-left KPD, all saw the new cruiser as nothing more than an expensive toy, with the cost of the first instalment for its building put at 9 million Reichsmarks, which they argued would be better spent on much needed social reforms. On 25 March, a majority in the Reichstag agreed to build *Panzerkreuzer A*, but six days later, the Upper House, the Reichsrat, called on the Reich government not to begin building the first ship before 1 September 1928, thereby leaving open the possibility of a new government abandoning the project. On 31 March, President Hindenburg dissolved the Reichstag, and the campaign for the 20 May 1928 national elections began.

The most noticeable feature of the election campaign was the emergence of numerous special-interest parties, mainly representing groups who felt excluded from the benefits of Germany's late-1920s economic prosperity. The most prominent of these parties were the conservative Reich Party of the German Middle Class (*Wirtschaftspartei des deutschen Mittlestandes*, WP), the Christian National Peasants' and Farmers' Party (*Christlich-Nationale Bauern- und Landvolkpartei*, CNBL – a breakaway group from the DNVP), and the People's Justice Party (*Volksrechtspartei*, VPR), which campaigned for justice for members of the middle class hit by hyperinflation. In all, 41 different political parties contested the 1928 elections and most of these were middle-class splinter groups located on the Right.[8]

The Nationalist DNVP campaign highlighted the reforms it had brokered as a member of the recently deposed Marx government, particularly in the area of agricultural reform, but its candidates tried to distance themselves from Stresemann's foreign policy. Zentrum blamed the DVP for the failure of the Schools Act, and the collapse of the Marx government, while the DVP highlighted its defence of Common Schools, and pointed to the success of Stresemann's foreign policy. The DDP, which had not been part of the Marx coalition, concentrated its campaign on promising to defend the Republic and gaining a quick evacuation of the Rhineland.[9] On the Left, the SPD focused its campaign on its working-class strongholds in the industrial cities, promising further social and labour reforms, supporting Stresemann's foreign policy, and stridently opposing the building of the Panzerkreuzers. The KPD also directed its campaign at working-class areas of the big cities. Under the leadership of Ernst Thälmann the party now adopted a decidedly pro-Stalinist line, and even received generous funds from the Comintern in Moscow.[10] The KPD continued to brand the SPD as 'social fascists', who had betrayed the working class too many times to ever be trusted again.

Adolf Hitler had been in prison during the December 1924 election campaign, and he was fighting his first national election campaign as NSDAP party leader. His campaign was hampered by a continuing public-speaking ban in Prussia, which was not lifted until September 1928, and also by the general mood of optimism brought about by economic prosperity. In 1928, for the first time since the war, unemployment had fallen below 1 million, retail spending was up 20 per cent on 1927, and real wages were 10 per cent higher.

The north German 'socialist' elements of the party had persuaded a sceptical Hitler to adopt a policy called the Urban Plan, which concentrated on trying to increase electoral support in the big industrial cities where the citadels of working-class support for the Social Democrats and the Communists were located. To this end, the NSDAP adopted a strident anti-capitalist tone in its electioneering, persistently attacking 'Jewish finance capitalists', and the middle-class parties for propping up the 'decadent' Weimar Republic. Yet in working-class areas the National Socialists had little success. The percentage of workers in heavy industrial areas joining the NSDAP in 1927 and 1928 was ridiculously small. In contrast, the party had more success in attracting new members in rural areas.[11]

Hitler's speeches during the campaign were primarily directed against Stresemann's foreign policy. In a speech in Munich on 17 April, he described Stresemann's policy of reconciliation with France as 'pure madness' and called the Locarno Pact a 'monstrous deed', because 'for the first time in world history we, as a people, accepted treaties without being forced to do so, which meant our death. Stresemann gave up the last bit of national sovereignty so we could at last join the League of Nations.'[12]

On 25 April, Gustav Stresemann gave an election speech in Munich, in the Bürgerbräukeller, telling the audience: 'The resuscitation of the Reich is not to be solved by catch-phrases.' This was greeted by catcalls from the many National Socialists who had crowded into the hall. They constantly interrupted the Foreign Minister, loudly singing 'Deutschland-Deutschland', and some National Socialist songs. After an hour of this, Stresemann gave up, pointing out that the 'Deutschland song is too sacred to be used as a means of creating disturbance'. The local newspaper, the *Bayerische Kurier*, wrote of the incident: 'How long are Hitler's men to be allowed to do this sort of thing?'[13]

This was Stresemann's last major intervention during the election campaign. On 9 May, he collapsed with a thyroid infection, which seriously affected the function of his kidneys. He went to the Bühlerhöhe spa health resort in Baden-Baden for a prolonged period of recuperation, and then moved for further treatment to Karlsbad in mid-July and on to Oberhof, near Gotha. He also suffered a mild stroke during the summer, which temporarily deprived him of the power of speech, but he quickly recovered from this.[14] The Committee of the DVP issued a press statement announcing Stresemann's withdrawal from further speaking engagements during the campaign, stating: 'The temporary absence of our champion must be made good by the resolute will to bring the election campaign to a successful conclusion for our cause.'[15]

The German national elections took place on 20 May 1928. Voter turnout was 75.6 per cent, down from 78.8 per cent in December 1924.[16] The big election winner was the SPD, which polled 29.76 per cent of the vote (9.15 million), and took 153 seats, an increase of 22 from the previous election. It was the greatest electoral triumph for the Social Democrats since the elections of January 1919. The only other party to increase its share of the vote was the Communist KPD, which polled 10.62 per cent (3.26 million), and won 54 seats, up from 45 in the previous election. It was a surprising result as economic prosperity had previously led to a loss of electoral support for the Communists. The strength of the two left-wing parties was heavily concentrated in large-scale industrial working-class areas. In contrast, the SPD and KPD performed poorly in Catholic and rural areas.[17]

The right-wing DNVP was the biggest loser in the 1928 elections. Their popular vote fell from 20.5 per cent (6.20 million) in December 1924 to 14.3 per cent (4.38 million), with a fall in seats from 103 to 73. The party's losses extended to all but one of Germany's 35 electoral districts. The worst results were in central and western Germany, areas where independent farmers constituted the most important voting bloc. The decision of the DNVP to join the Marx government had clearly alienated many of these traditional voters.[18]

The 1928 election defeat was unprecedented for the traditional German conservative Right. But all the other non-socialist parties performed badly. Zentrum polled 12.1 per cent of the popular vote (3.71 million), down from 13.6 per cent at the previous election, with a fall in seats from 69 to 61. Party disunity over the schools bill was clearly a major factor in explaining this loss of votes. The DVP recorded 8.7

per cent of the popular vote (2.67 million), which was down from 10.1 per cent from December 1924, with the seat total down from 51 to 45. This surprised political commentators in the press who had predicted Stresemann's foreign policy successes would translate into electoral gains for the DVP. The DDP, which had not been part of the fourth Marx cabinet, still lost electoral support, polling 4.8 per cent of the popular vote (1.47 million), down from 6.3 per cent at the previous election, with its seats dropping from 32 to 25. Ever since its impressive performance in the elections of January 1919 the DDP had suffered a progressive loss of voter support.

The losses by all the traditional middle-class parties was primarily due to the growth of support for the many special-interest parties, particularly the WP, the CNBL and the VPR, who captured 12 per cent of the popular vote between them, securing 34 Reichstag seats. These parties represented disenchantment with the traditional middle-class parties, especially in rural areas. Farmers had recently suffered a fall in income, and a decline in the availability of cheap credit. They also found themselves unable to compete on price against imports such as Belgian dairy products, Danish beef, bacon and butter, and a flood of cheap Polish pork.[19]

The 1928 election outcome was also a major setback for Hitler's NSDAP. The party polled just 2.37 per cent of the popular vote (810,127), winning 12 Reichstag seats, down by two from December 1924. The new Reichstag members included: Joseph Goebbels, Gregor Strasser, and Hermann Göring. The NSDAP had not performed badly everywhere, but its weakness in urban industrial areas was marked. In Berlin, where Joseph Goebbels led the campaign, the party polled just 1.57 per cent of the votes.[20] In contrast, the NSDAP had performed much better in north German Protestant rural areas afflicted by a fall in agricultural prices, but it did best in its traditional strongholds of Franconia (8.1 per cent), Upper Bavaria/Swabia (6.23 per cent) and the Palatinate (5.7 per cent).

Hitler had also suffered a loss of support in certain areas close to Austria due to his support for Mussolini's claim over South Tyrol, which had been ceded to Italy at the end of the Great War, but whose inhabitants were German. Hitler, eager to appease Mussolini, was willing to leave South Tyrol to Italy, but during the election campaign his political opponents, particularly in the DNVP and the DVP, claimed his stance was the 'betrayal of German interest to a foreign power'. Some newspapers even claimed he had received campaign funds from Mussolini. This was a charge Hitler vehemently denied, and launched several libel actions to refute.[21]

On the evidence of the 1928 elections, the attempt by the National Socialists to gain support from the working class under the Urban Plan had been a total failure. The *Völkischer Beobachter*, reviewing the party's election results, concluded: 'Clearly, our success in rural areas has proved that with the expenditure of a little work, money and greater time greater success can be expected here than in the big cities.'[22] The party had also made progress during the campaign in establishing a centrally directed organisation and had improved its propaganda, but the NSDAP remained a party on the far-right fringe of the political scene, with only 100,000 members.[23]

Chancellor Wilhelm Marx and his entire cabinet resigned on 12 June 1928. Hindenburg asked Hermann Müller, the leader of the SPD in the Reichstag, who had been Chancellor for three months in 1920, to form a new government on 'the broadest possible basis'. Müller had a particularly good reputation in the Reichstag, known as a clever, thoughtful, and experienced politician, who was able to manage differences of opinion. Hindenburg was impressed by Müller, later describing him as 'the best Chancellor I ever had'. It was unfortunate, he added, that 'he was also a Social Democrat'.[24]

The balance of forces in the Reichstag pointed to a 'Grand Coalition' of the pro-republican parties, the SPD, Zentrum, DVP and DDP, being formed, but finding agreement between them proved extremely difficult. The DVP issued a declaration making clear it would enter a coalition only if it were offered additional representation in the SPD-led Prussian government, something Otto Braun, the Prussian Prime Minister, was unwilling to accept. Zentrum held the balance of parliamentary power, as its 61 Reichstag seats were crucial to attain an overall majority for any prospective coalition of the Centre Left, but the party was reluctant to participate. The Zentrum leadership asked for Joseph Wirth to be made Vice-Chancellor, but Müller rejected this demand. At the outset, Zentrum only had one member in the cabinet, but demanded the right to negotiate further cabinet portfolios soon. The DDP and the BVP proved more accommodating and agreed to participate.

Müller's biggest problem was that his prospective coalition partners could not guarantee their parties would support the new government in key votes in the Reichstag. In the end, he had to abandon the Grand Coalition idea, and opted for a more fragile 'cabinet of personalities',

Chancellor Hermann Müller (second from the left, front row), photographed with his coalition colleagues, 28 June 1928.

with members from various political parties. The prime mover in this arrangement was Gustav Stresemann, who was issued with a 'motion of censure' by his own party for unilaterally agreeing to a deal with Müller, in telegrams and by telephone while in his sick bed at a health sanitorium in Baden-Baden, without consulting his party.[25]

The second Müller cabinet, which finally took office on 28 June 1928, included ministers from five different political parties. It was the first time since 1923 the Social Democrats participated in a Weimar government. Three experienced and able Social Democratic politicians entered the new cabinet: Carl Severing (Interior and Occupied Territories), Rudolf Wissell (Labour), and Rudolf Hilferding (Finance). There were two members of the DVP: Gustav Stresemann (Foreign Minister), and Julius Curtius (Minister of Economics). Müller had placed immense importance on retaining Stresemann, despite his continuing illness, but on 28 June, Stresemann gave Müller a gloomy health update: 'I must give up the idea of resuming my full activities for some time to come.'[26] The DDP also had two members: Erich Koch-Weser (Justice), and Hermann Dietrich (Food). Zentrum initially provided just one member, Theodor von Guérard (Transport),

while the single BVP member was Georg Schätzel (Postal Minister). Wilhelm Groener (Independent) stayed on as the Defence Minister.[27]

On 3 July, Müller presented his new cabinet to the Reichstag. His opening government declaration as Chancellor struck a decidedly optimistic tone, though it was necessarily bland in order to avoid bringing political differences between his half-hearted partners to the surface. Müller said the country had entered a 'tranquil period' of economic stability. The foundations of the Republic, he declared, 'stand firm and unshakable'. He then promised a continuation of the foreign policy of conciliation championed by Gustav Stresemann, and demanded three things of Germany's former enemies: the complete evacuation of the Rhineland, disarmament, and a definitive settlement of the reparations problem. He also promised his government would safeguard the interests of workers, farmers, and the middle class. Müller then told the Reichstag that he would not ask for a vote of confidence, but instead request parliament to approve a list of policies on which the government ministers were agreed, and which he thought the Reichstag would not oppose. On 5 July, the 'vote of approval' was passed by a large margin of 261 to 134 votes, with only 28 abstentions, none of which came from the various parties involved in the Müller cabinet.[28]

The Müller government was soon faced with making a decision about whether to build the controversial armoured ship, *Panzerkreuzer A*, which had been approved in principle by the Reichstag at the end of March. On 10 August, Wilhelm Groener told his cabinet colleagues the building of the vessel was affordable within the current Reich budget, and his request for the building of the cruiser was approved. This decision led to an outcry among the Social Democrat and Communist members of the Reichstag, however. On 15 August, the SPD Reichstag delegation, unhappy with Müller's embarrassing U-turn on the issue, tabled a resolution which criticised Social Democratic cabinet ministers for failing to oppose the construction of the cruiser. The KPD went further and began a campaign for a referendum on the matter, but their referendum petition to voters in October only attracted 1.2 million signatures, way below the constitutional requirement of 4 million to trigger a national referendum.

In November, the SPD Reichstag delegation moved a resolution demanding the building of the armoured cruiser should be halted. Groener made clear that if this resolution were passed, he would resign as Defence Minister, and on 17 November the Reichstag approved the building of the ship by 257 votes for and 202 against, with only eight abstentions. Chancellor Müller had survived his first government crisis, but only at the price of causing deep divisions in his own party. The whole affair was deeply embarrassing for the Social Democrats, a party which was overwhelmingly committed to disarmament.[29]

In the summer of 1928, Hitler had retreated to Berchtesgaden in the Bavarian Alps to draft a new book, primarily on foreign policy, which he dictated to Rudolf Hess, his loyal secretary. Hitler hoped to draw all the strands of his foreign policy into a more coherent ideology than he had managed in *Mein Kampf.* He wanted to make clear that Germany's need for living space and the danger from the Jews were entwined. What was produced, over a period of 18 months, was a 239-page typed manuscript which was never published during his lifetime. It became known as 'Hitler's Second Book' (*Zweites Buch*), and was only published in English in 1961 as *Hitler's Secret Book.* It seems Hitler decided outlining his murderous blueprint for the future at this point might damage his immediate electoral prospects.[30]

In the Second Book, Hitler reiterated the key aim of his foreign policy, which was to secure for the German people its *Lebensraum*, and he repeated his view that Jews remained the most dangerous opponents of the German people, but he then outlined what has been defined by historians as his 'stage-by-stage' plan on foreign policy (*Stufenplan*), though he never actually uses that term in the book. Hitler's foreign-policy plan, which amounted to a single road to global war, had four essential stages. During the first, there would be huge rearmament, the revision of the Treaty of Versailles, and the formation of alliances with the British Empire and Fascist Italy. The second stage would involve a series of 'lightning wars' against France and its allies in Eastern and Southern Europe, such as Czechoslovakia, Poland, Romania and the countries of the later Yugoslavia. The third stage envisaged a war to obliterate the Soviet Union, as he remained convinced Eastern Europe was the only part of the European continent where territorial expansion was possible.

These three stages had all been mentioned in *Mein Kampf*, but in the 'Second Book' Hitler added a new fourth stage, involving a future struggle for world domination against the USA. Hitler had come to recognise the huge economic power of the USA would inevitably translate into a military power. For Hitler, the American 'Aryan' settlers had high 'racial value' and could be seen as one of the 'master' races. He also believed territorial expansion in the west of America during

overleaf A Communist demonstration in Berlin, on May Day 1928, against the government programme of building armoured cruisers (*Panzerkreuzer*) for the German Navy (*Kriegsmarine*).

the late nineteenth century at the expense of the Native Americans was a successful drive for living space, which he wanted to emulate in Eastern Europe, and he was impressed by the introduction of eugenic laws in many American states to maintain the 'racial stock'. What Hitler did not like about America was its 'decadent culture', which encouraged jazz music, along with gangster crime, the influence of 'Jewish speculators' and the proliferation of department stores, which he thought killed off small shopkeepers. In the Second Book, Hitler also expressed a contradictory attitude to war. On the one hand, he saw it as essential to the life and survival of a people, and central to his own foreign policy aims, but on the other hand he suggested war killed the best and the bravest, and spared the weakest and most cowardly. The wars Hitler wanted to wage, therefore, were 'lightning wars' bringing about quick victories.[31]

At the same time as Hitler was planning a future world war, the world's major powers were gathering in the Clock Room (*Salon de l'Horloge*) inside the French Foreign Office on the Quai d'Orsay, Paris, on 27 August, for an elaborate ceremony to sign the General Treaty for Renunciation of War as an Instrument of National Policy. The pact had evolved from negotiations begun in 1927 by Frank Kellogg, the US Secretary of State, and Aristide Briand, the French Foreign Minister. On 6 April 1927, Briand announced his country's intention to enter into a bilateral agreement with the USA, stipulating that neither country would resort to war with each other, and that any dispute between them would be settled by peaceful means. Two months later, Briand submitted to the American government a draft of the proposed treaty. The American reply came in December 1927. Kellogg suggested the proposed Franco-American agreement should be expanded into a multilateral treaty to be signed by other countries, to which Briand readily agreed. In recognition of their joint diplomatic efforts, the agreement became known as the Kellogg–Briand Pact, and was greatly welcomed by the public.[32]

At the signature ceremony in Paris, Briand gave an inspiring speech, saying at one point: 'Can the world present a nobler lesson than the spectacle of this assemblage, where Germany appears for the signature of a pact against war, of its own free will, and without reserve, among the other signatories, its former enemies?' Briand also spoke in glowing terms of Stresemann: 'One can believe me particularly happy, to render homage to the highness of mind and to the courage of this eminent politician who, during more than three years, has not hesitated to assume full responsibility in the work of European co-operation for the maintenance of peace.'[33]

The main text of the Kellogg–Briand Pact consisted of two brief articles. Under Article 1, the signatories condemned the 'recourse to war for the solution of international controversies', and further promised to 'renounce it as an instrument of national policy in their relationship with one another'. Article 2 required the contracting parties to solve all disputes or conflicts by peaceful means. The original 15 signatories were the United Kingdom, Germany, USA, France, Italy, Japan, Australia, Belgium, Canada, Czechoslovakia, India, Ireland, New Zealand, Poland, and South Africa. Eventually, a further 47 nations followed suit. Elements of the pact were later incorporated into the League of Nations charter.

The Kellogg–Briand agreement, which was seen at the time as a milestone in international relations, gave the public around the world the false illusion that perpetual peace had arrived, but did not limit in any way the right of a nation to self-defence against the attack of any other nation, or alter the military obligations arising from the Covenant of the League of Nations or already agreed binding treaties.[34] The pact contained no legal mechanism for enforcement and was, for some, a 'worthless piece of paper', which proved completely ineffective as a means of preventing war. It did provide, however, a legal basis for the concept of a 'crime against peace', the crime for which the Nuremberg Tribunal and the Tokyo Tribunal tried and executed the senior leaders judged responsible for starting the Second World War.[35]

Stresemann thought the agreement would serve to strengthen the League of Nations and the Rhineland Pact, and he decided to rise from his sick bed to attend the signing ceremony, accompanied by his personal doctor, Dr Hermann Zondek, who had advised him not to travel, but was on hand for treatment if necessary, and he also laid down strict time limits on Stresemann's conversations. The arrival of a German Foreign Minister in the French capital was regarded as an important event by the world's press. It was the first time Stresemann had visited Paris as German Foreign Minister. A large crowd assembled at the Paris Gare du Nord railway station, to greet him with cries of 'Vive Stresemann'. The reporter from the *Frankfurter Zeitung* noted: 'Hats were waved, and children held on shoulders; French and German voices mingled in a mighty shout of welcome.'[36]

During the visit, Stresemann met his old adversary Raymond Poincaré, the French Prime Minister, for talks, which were limited to

45 minutes on doctor's orders. It was the first time they had ever met face to face. Poincaré told Stresemann that he had heard all about the friendly and enthusiastic reception he had received from the French public on his arrival. He then emphasised friendly relations between the two countries were not just in the interest of France and Germany but of Europe as a whole. In response, Stresemann pulled no punches by telling Poincaré he had noticed his speeches constantly accused Germany of wanting revenge against France. Poincaré claimed the source of this accusation was not him personally, but Wickham Steed, the former editor of *The Times* of London, who had told him a desire for revenge was a commonly held view among German university professors who wanted to indoctrinate students with the idea of regaining Alsace-Lorraine. Stresemann responded by saying such a view was held neither by the German government nor by most of the German public.

The conversation then turned to economic matters, with Stresemann describing Germany's current financial position. Contrary to what people thought, he said, German industry was stagnating, and the German public had lost their savings during the hyperinflation period, which meant raising revenue internally from banks was extremely difficult. Germany now relied for credit on American loans, but if Germany's economic position suddenly worsened these short-term loans would be called in, and at that moment, the German economy would collapse. Poincaré seemed alarmed by this admission, and he promised that a full and final settlement of German reparations payments would be set soon. Stresemann reiterated that Germany wanted an early end to the occupation of the Rhineland. In reply, Poincaré said the occupation was the sole guarantee of future German reparations payments, and could only be settled in a final settlement of German reparations and Inter-Allied debts to the USA. At this point, Dr Zondek stopped the conversation, but Stresemann felt this came before he had said everything that was on his mind.[37]

Meanwhile, Weimar culture continued to provide new innovations. On 31 August, *Die Dreigroschenoper* (*The Threepenny Opera*) opened at the Theater am Schiffbauerdamm in the Mitte district of Berlin, near the Spree River. It was called 'a play with music', and was adapted from a German translation by Elisabeth Hauptmann of John Gay's eighteenth-century satirical English ballad opera, *The Beggar's Opera*. To this was added four translated songs by the French poet François Villon. The musical play was the product of a creative collaboration

A publicity poster for Brecht's *Dreigroschenoper*
(*The Threepenny Opera*), first performed in
Berlin on 31 August 1928.

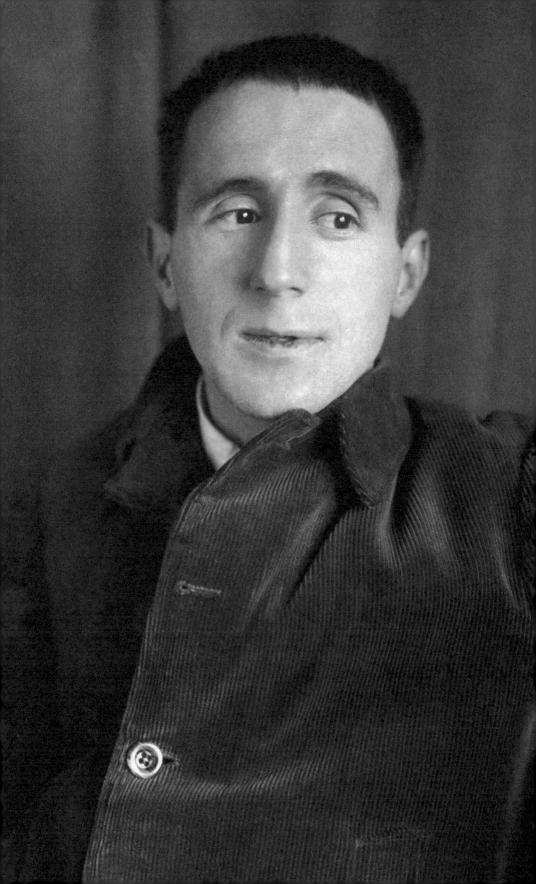

between Bertolt Brecht and Kurt Weill. Brecht came from a middle-class background and was a committed socialist. Weill was from a middle-class Jewish family, and had enjoyed a classical music training, but was greatly influenced by modern American jazz and German dance music. Brecht and Weill wanted to create a new theatrical experience that was entertaining and thought-provoking at the same time. They used the operatic form, as they saw it as the epitome of uncritical elitist culture. Brecht's hard-hitting, unsentimental, and often darkly comic lyrics were fused brilliantly with Weill's musical parodies of traditional opera and modern jazz to create the most popular and influential musical theatre production of the entire Weimar period. Songs from the musical have become standards, with the best known being *Die Moritat von Mack Messer* ('The Ballad of Mack the Knife'), which opens the production.

The Threepenny Opera, which consists of three acts, is set in the poverty-stricken back alleys of Victorian London, but is really a sharply critical satire on the exploitative, corrupt and hypocritical nature of 1920s German capitalism. The story follows the complicated and depraved life of Macheath, 'London's most notorious criminal', better known as Mackie Messer ('Mack the Knife'), who oversees a gang of burglars and thieves with repellent sexual leanings, including rape. He marries Polly Peachum, and collaborates with the corrupt London sheriff, Jackie 'Tiger' Brown, who receives a portion of Macheath's ill-gotten gains, and whose daughter Lucy becomes his bigamous second wife.

All the disreputable characters in *The Threepenny Opera* are united by their breathtaking hypocrisy. The police are corrupt, and indistinguishable from the criminals; sex becomes a business transaction, and no one has any principles or scruples. Polly's father Jonathan is portrayed as the epitome of the 'exploitative capitalist', making his money by owning a shop that outfits and trains beggars in return for a cut of their takings. Jonathan then embarks on a series of plots to have his son-in-law, Macheath, ruined and hanged, including bribing prostitutes and police officers. At the end, the murderous rogue Macheath is captured and sentenced to death, but on his way to the gallows he is suddenly spared death by being pardoned by the Queen herself, who ennobles him with a baronetcy, granting him a castle and a generous pension of £10,000 per year.

The Threepenny Opera proved hugely successful, with 350 performances in Berlin during its first year. It was performed in over 120

Bertolt Brecht: socialist playwright, poet
and theoretician of 'epic threatre'.

theatres in Germany over the next four years. By 1932, it had been translated into 18 languages, and performed more than 10,000 times in European theatres. A film version, directed by Georg Pabst, was released in 1931. The songs became hugely popular with cabaret entertainers, most notably Lotte Lenya, who was married to Kurt Weill.[38]

In early September, Gustav Stresemann was too ill to travel to the League of Nations. The Chancellor, Hermann Müller, stood in for him. He immediately entered into conversations with the French Foreign Minister, Aristide Briand, on the question of the immediate Allied evacuation of the Rhineland, but Briand insisted the question could not be settled until a final reparations settlement was agreed. In a speech to the League of Nations Assembly, on 7 September, Müller claimed that Germany had disarmed, but bemoaned the fact that 'not one of the barriers that have arisen because of the War has been wholly removed', and he suggested such a policy was 'double-faced', with the clear implication these words referred to French government policy. At the League meeting, on 10 September, Briand responded to Müller's outburst by saying that he was ready to go as far as possible on the matter of disarmament, but added that no responsible French government could advocate total disarmament. He also questioned Müller's claim that Germany had fully disarmed, even arguing the German economy could be quickly re-converted to manufacture weapons of war.[39]

This bitter verbal exchange between Briand and Müller in Geneva caused a diplomatic sensation, but behind the scenes efforts to reach an understanding at the League of Nations continued, with Seymour Parker Gilbert, the Agent General for Reparations to Germany, playing a key role by travelling from country to country trying to win Allied governments over to his idea of a fresh examination of Germany's capacity to pay. Parker Gilbert felt the Dawes Plan was a transitional stage during which the German economy was being rebuilt, and confidence restored. With this mission now largely achieved, the time had now come for a final reparations settlement.

On 16 September, at the League of Nations, the representatives of France, Germany, Britain, Belgium, Italy and Japan agreed on the following compromise: a new reparations commission would be appointed to discuss an early date for the evacuation of the Rhineland, and a new committee of 'financial experts' representing the six powers would tackle the reparations problem by updating Germany's capacity to pay, and making fresh recommendations for a 'final and comprehensive settlement'. Müller regarded this agreement as a key step forward.[40]

On 17 September, Müller travelled to see Stresemann to update him on the recent developments at the League of Nations. He told him the results of the negotiations in Geneva should be regarded in optimistic terms, with the reparations question now set in motion, and that he had insisted the expert members of the new committee must be drawn from industrial and banking backgrounds, with American involvement critical. He was much less optimistic about progress on the early evacuation of the Rhineland due to continued French government intransigence.[41]

On 28 September, the ban on Hitler's public speaking in the giant state of Prussia was finally lifted. Soon afterwards, Hitler rented a chalet, Haus Wachenfeld, which overlooked the picturesque Bavarian Alps, near Berchtesgaden, Bavaria. This small holiday home had been built in 1916, under the supervision of Otto Winter, a local entrepreneur. After his death, the property was owned by his widow, Magarete, who rented it to Hitler for 100 Reichsmarks a month.[42] In 1933, Hitler bought the property with the royalties he had received for *Mein Kampf*. It was then expanded during 1935 and 1936 into the huge administrative and government complex that became known as the *Berghof* (Mountain Farm).

Hitler brought his widowed half-sister Angela Raubal from Vienna to become his cook and housekeeper. As Hitler later recalled: 'I told her, "I've rented a house. Do you want to come and run the household?" She came and we moved in straightaway. It was wonderful.'[43] Angela brought her two daughters with her – Angela ('Geli') and Friedl. Geli was an attractive 20-year-old when she came to live at the chalet. Hitler's personal photographer, Heinrich Hoffmann, described her as a 'lovely young woman who, with her artless and carefree manner, captivated everybody'. The relationship between Hitler and Geli seemed to observers much more than just the usual uncle–niece relationship. They soon went everywhere together, on long walks, to the theatre, restaurants, and cafes, and even to party gatherings. Helene Hanfstaengl, who knew Geli, later recalled that 'I always had the feeling he [Hitler] was trying to run her life and tyrannizing her.'[44] When Hitler began renting a luxurious nine-room apartment in the Prinzregentstrasse in Munich, in 1929, Geli was given her own bedroom in it. Everyone in Hitler's entourage knew he took a rather unhealthy interest in his young niece, and most suggested he was deeply in love with her, but whether their relationship was sexual is by no means certain.[45]

On 20 October, Alfred Hugenberg was unanimously elected as the new leader of the Nationalist DNVP, replacing the hapless Count Kuno von Westarp, who had resigned on 8 July in the wake of the party's poor showing in the May elections. Hugenberg had consistently aligned himself with the right wing of the Nationalists, and opposed the party's collaboration in the recent Marx government. He also had a fanatical hatred of everyone connected with the Weimar Republic. Above all, he bitterly opposed Stresemann's conciliatory foreign policy and called him 'a hollow man of no convictions'. Under Hugenberg's leadership the DNVP moved towards an extreme right-wing position.[46]

On 26 October, the chair of the Düsseldorf Board of Arbitration (*Schlichterkammer*) awarded a wage increase of 6 pfennigs per hour to workers in the iron and steel industry in the Ruhr. The employers of the Northwest Group of the Association of the Iron and Steel Industrialists, in a clear act of rebellion, refused to accept the wage settlement, even though it was legally binding, arguing it was the sole decision of the chair, not reflecting the views of most of the arbitration board. On 1 November, the employers closed their factories and locked out 220,000 workers without pay, in what became known as the Ruhr Iron Dispute (*Ruhreisenstreit*). Robert Wissell, the Labour Minister, declared the employers in breach of a legal court settlement, but the lockout continued for five weeks. The Weimar government did not have the power to break the lockout by force, but, on 14 November, the Reichstag voted by 267 to 59 to allow the German and Prussian governments to grant the affected workers the right to unemployment

Alfred Hugenberg, leader of the right-wing nationalist DNVP (German National People's Party) from October 1928.

benefits, which greatly weakened the impact of the lockout.

Chancellor Müller met with the representatives of the employers and the unions to try and end the dispute. He proposed the government appoint a special arbitrator to conduct the negotiations. Social Democrat Carl Severing, the Minister of the Interior, a former metal worker and an astute political operator, was appointed to the role of mediator. On 3 December, the employers' lockout was finally lifted, and employees returned to work.

Severing's report on the dispute recognised the export difficulties of the industry, but he still announced a pay increase, even though it was slightly lower than the arbitration chair had originally recommended. The employers were disappointed with the outcome, which once again revealed the power of organised labour in the Weimar Republic.[47] The National Association of Industry produced a memorandum called 'Progress or Decline', which called for a reduction in business taxes and also in welfare spending. The industrialists took the view that the German economy could not be put on a sound footing unless the power of organised labour was weakened.[48]

On 3 November, Gustav Stresemann finally felt well enough to return to his duties as Foreign Minister. On 13 November, he met the Reparations Agent, Seymour Parker Gilbert, who told him there was no definite understanding on what was expected from the new Committee of Experts. He also warned Stresemann a final reparations settlement would be costly for Germany, but would be even worse if negotiated during a time of economic crisis. In response, Stresemann said that it was not certain a settlement during a severe economic crisis would be worse than one negotiated right now. Stresemann thought everyone abroad overestimated Germany's current economic prosperity. In Stresemann's view, Germany was 'dancing on a volcano'. The economy was flourishing, but only on the surface. Agriculture was already in a serious condition, and industrial growth very sluggish. German prosperity was really based on American short-term loans. If these were called in, large sections of the economy would immediately collapse.[49]

Towards the end of the year, another of Germany's major political parties changed its leader. On 8 December, Monsignor Ludwig Kaas was elected by the party convention in Cologne as the new leader of Zentrum, replacing Wilhelm Marx, who had led the party since 17 January 1922.[50] Kaas, who was on the Right of the party, was an experienced church diplomat, and a distinguished academic,

overleaf Workers locked out of a mine during the *Ruhreisenstreit* (Ruhr Iron Dispute), November 1928.

with doctoral degrees in canon law and theology. He was also an acknowledged constitutional expert. In the party discussions that followed the May 1928 elections, a group on the Right of the party had argued their poor electoral performance was due to the dissatisfaction of Catholic voters with the party moving closer to the Left's social reform agenda, and by neglecting sectional Catholic interests. It seems Kaas was elected as a compromise candidate to mediate between the party's Left, which favoured social reform, and its Right, which wanted to strengthen party ties with the bishops and the Vatican. His rivals in the leadership election, Adam Stegerwald and Joseph Loos, were both on the Left of the party, and much closer to the Roman Catholic labour movement than Kaas.[51]

The election of Kaas reaffirmed Catholic principles would remain at the core of Zentrum's appeal to voters. In his acceptance speech, he said: 'The solidarity of all those who believe in Christ must be greater than that which separates us from one another.' It was felt Kaas stood the best chance of winning back disaffected Catholic voters, but his victory signalled a shift to the Right in the party.[52]

From 9 to 15 December, the League of Nations Council met at Lugano, Switzerland. Stresemann was well enough to attend in person this time, without medical restraints. The chief aim of these discussions was to agree on the appointment of a committee of experts to examine Germany's future reparations payments. The American government had already promised to participate. Stresemann voiced his fear that the experts would not be free to do as they pleased. There was a danger, he said, that they might have to comply with directives issued by their respective governments. Briand tried to reassure Stresemann. The experts, he replied, would be allowed to make up their own minds, and none of the governments would ignore their findings. It was finally agreed the Committee of Experts would first examine the economic aspects of the reparation question and the governments would then make the necessary political decisions.[53]

On 22 December, an official press statement was issued by the Reparations Commission which announced the Allied creditors had agreed with the German government's proposal for the establishment of a Committee of Experts to examine Germany's current capacity to pay reparations and map out a final schedule of payments. Committee members would consist of independent experts who enjoyed an international reputation and had authority in their own country. The number of members would be restricted to two experts per country.

Germany would participate on the committee as an equal partner.[54]

The Committee was headed by the American Owen D. Young, founder of the Radio Corporation of America (RCA), and a current member of the board of trustees of the Rockefeller Foundation. He had previously been a member of the 1924 Dawes Committee. He was supported by the famous American banker John Morgan, who had inherited the family fortune, after his father J.P. Morgan died in 1913.[55] The two German experts appointed were Dr Hjalmar Schacht, President of the Reichsbank, and the industrialist, Albert Vögler. Representing Britain were Sir Josiah Stamp, a director of the Bank of England, and Lord Revelstoke, a senior partner in Barings Bank. France was represented by Émile Moreau, the Governor of the Bank of France, and Jean Parmentier, a former Secretary in the French Finance Ministry. The two Belgian members were Émile Francqui, a former Finance Minister, and the banking expert Camille Gutt, who later became the first Managing Director of the International Monetary Fund (IMF). Italy's two representatives were the tyre manufacturer Giovanni Pirelli and economic expert Professor Fulvio Suvich. Finally, Japan was represented by Kengo Mori, formerly the financial attaché at the Japanese Embassy in London, and Takashi Aoki, the Governor of the Bank of Japan.[56]

1929
·
THE END OF THE STRESEMANN ERA
·

The German President, Paul von Hindenburg, and Chancellor, Hermann Müller, spoke at a New Year's Day reception of foreign diplomats. Hindenburg told them that he wanted the occupation of the Rhineland to end in the coming year 'because a great part of the country still lacks liberty which we claim by divine and human right'. In his speech, Müller supported the President, by saying strained relations between Germany and the Allies remaining from the Great War would only end once the 'foreign yoke of occupation had been removed'.[1]

During the early part of the year, Müller resumed negotiations with the various parliamentary groups in the Reichstag, with the aim of turning his 'cabinet of personalities' into a 'Great Coalition'. These talks dragged on for just over three months. On 6 February, Theodor von Guérard, Minister of Transport and Occupied Territories, and the only Zentrum member in the cabinet, resigned. On 15 February, Zentrum issued an ultimatum demanding three cabinet ministers in return for joining a coalition government. On 13 April, three members of Zentrum did finally join the Müller cabinet, with Theodor von Guérard appointed Minister of Justice, Adam Stegerwald becoming Transport Minister, and Joseph Wirth given the post of Minister for the Occupied Territories.[2]

The Weimar years witnessed the publication of many novels concerned with the 'Great War of 1914–18'. The most famous of all, however, was the anti-war classic *Im Westen nichts Neues* (published in English under the title *All Quiet on the Western Front*), by Erich Maria Remarque, and published in book form on 29 January 1929. Prior to publication, the book had been serialised between 10 November and 9 December 1928 in *Vossische Zeitung* (*Voss's Newspaper*).[3]

Remarque was born in Osnabrück, in the German Empire, on 22 June 1898, to a family that had emigrated from France. He was conscripted into the Imperial German Army at the age of 18. On 12 June 1917, he was posted to the Western Front, but on 31 July the same year he was gravely wounded by shell shrapnel in the left leg, right arm

previous page   Erich Maria Remarque,
photographed in 1929.

and neck, and evacuated from the battlefield to a military hospital in Germany, where he spent the rest of the war, before being demobilised.[4]

The novel tells the story of Paul Bäumer, who is part of a group of German soldiers on the Western Front. It was patriotic nationalistic speeches made by his teacher Kantorek in his local grammar school (*Gymnasium*) which inspired his whole school class to volunteer to fight for the German Army in the Great War. Paul blames his teacher's generation for the war, commenting: 'There were thousands of Kantoreks, all of whom were convinced that they were acting for the best.' In the novel, Paul does not focus on the outbreak of the war or the eagerness of volunteers to enlist. Instead, he vividly describes a bloody war that is already under way. The monotony of trench life, the constant threat of artillery fire, and the random nature of death are all described in detail, though the battles fought are given no names. Only small pieces of land are ever captured, but at a huge cost in lives. At one point, Paul observes: 'I am young, I am 20 years of age, but I know nothing of life except despair, death, fear, and the combination of completely mindless superficiality, with an abyss of suffering. I see people being driven against one another, and silently, uncomprehendingly, foolishly, obediently, and innocently killing one another.'

The main enemy Paul and his comrades face each day is death itself. There are references to artillery guns, but not enemy soldiers, except for a French soldier called Gérard Duval, whom Paul encounters in a shell crater. He watches the man die slowly, and in pain, for hours. Paul then stands over the corpse asking forgiveness from the lifeless body. Towards the end of the war, when the German Army is retreating, Paul watches as his comrades die one by one. In the concluding chapter,

Erich Maria Remarque's anti-war novel *All Quiet on the Western Front* was an instant worldwide bestseller. After 1933, the Nazis would ban it and burn it.

Paul predicts that peace is coming soon, but he does not see a bright future, and, in October 1918, he is killed. The situation report records his death, in a matter-of-fact way, followed by the words: 'All quiet on the western front'.

The publication of *Im Westen nichts Neues* was a major and highly publicised literary event. The book became an instant worldwide best-seller, with 2.5 million sales in 22 languages in its first 18 months alone, going on to sell over 20 million copies. In 1930, the book was adapted into an Academy Award-winning film, directed by Lewis Milestone. It immediately struck a chord and provoked debate among the war's survivors. The anti-war Left welcomed the book as a true indictment of the futility of war, but the novel did not find favour with the nationalist Right, who derided it as the epitome of left-wing defeatism, devoid of any heroic aspects, exaggerating the horrors of war to push a pacifist agenda.[5]

During the spring of 1929, another deeply influential book, *So ist die neue Frau* (*This is the New Woman*), by the Jewish feminist writer Elsa Herrmann, was published. Herrmann suggested the 'new woman' of the Weimar period 'refuses to be regarded as a physically weak being in need of assistance', and will not 'lead the life of a lady and a stay-at-home spouse, preferring to depart from the ordained path and go her own way.' Her chief task was 'to clear the way for equal rights in all areas of life'.[6]

The 'new woman' was the most-talked-about symbol of the sexual revolution during the Weimar years. The image appeared in films, newspapers, magazines, advertisements, and political posters. They all depicted a woman who was independent in spirit and action, gender-fluid, slim, athletic, with short hair – adopting the famous masculine Bubikopf page-boy bob hairstyle. She smoked cigarettes, drank cocktails, wore unisex trouser-suits, worked typically in an office or in the arts, and lived for today. She was the antithesis of the 'old woman', depicted as a mother of several children, and usually a stay-at-home spouse.[7]

A closer look at women's employment in the Weimar Republic sheds light on whether the 'new woman' was more of a myth than a reality. Census data from 1925 and 1933 shows working women not only made up a third of the workforce but also a third of the total female population. Women between 18 and 20 were more likely to work than any other age group, with 77.4 per cent of them employed in 1925, and 78.6 per cent by 1933. Half of these were single women, most of whom lived at home with their parents. In a survey conducted in 1928/29, 97 per cent of female manual workers were still living at home with their parents. In contrast, 70 per cent of married women were stay-at-home spouses, dependent on the earnings of their husbands.

Agriculture was dominated by family-owned farms, and women were the mainstay of the agricultural workforce. There were no independent 'new women' on farms. In 1925, only 23 per cent of agricultural workers were not members of farming families. Women's work on farms consisted of milking cows, looking after poultry, tending gardens, sowing seeds, picking fruit and various other housework duties. One survey revealed that a paid agricultural employee worked 3,554 hours a year, but the wife of a famer worked for 3,933 hours. Few women studied for a high-ranking qualification in agriculture. In 1925, there were only 33 women, out of a total of 2,203 students, enrolled at the three forestry and four agricultural colleges in Germany.

There were more opportunities for women in industry. They were numerically over-represented in textile, clothing, and food production. In 1925, 65.2 per cent of women factory-workers were employed in these three traditional female occupations. Female textile workers, who tended to be older, with higher-grade skills, could reach supervisory positions, but their pay was always lower than that of men. Women did find opportunities in the Weimar period in more modern industries. Between 1926 and 1930, there was a marked increase in women employed in electrical engineering, precision and optical instruments, metal goods and the toy industry. In the chemical industry, women increased from 21.9 per cent of the workforce in 1925 to 23.6 per cent in 1933.

During the Weimar period, the typical female manual worker was young, single, unskilled, and had fewer opportunities for training than the men. In German industry, only 2.2 per cent of women had attained the role of supervisor by 1925, though in the textile industry it was slightly higher, at 5 per cent. The disparity in industrial wages between men and women was wide, with women receiving on average only 70 per cent of men's wages in similar occupations. Local authorities paid unskilled women 75 per cent of the wage of an equivalent male worker. These poor wages were justified on the grounds that most single women did not have a family to support.

The area of the economy where 'new women' were thought to exist in the largest numbers was in white-collar occupations. Around 30 per cent of Berlin's female workforce had white-collar jobs, such as telephonists, civil servants, office workers, typists, and as shop sales staff. From 1925 to 1933, women employed in white-collar roles increased from 27.3 to 30.7 per cent. In these areas, single women predominated, with 90.6 per cent in this category in 1925, and 89.2 per cent by 1933. Youth and good looks were essential to women gaining such jobs. The male manager of a Berlin department store reported his main criterion for employing a woman was a 'pleasant appearance'. Yet women were mainly on the bottom rung even of the white-collar employment ladder. A survey conducted in 1929 by the Trade Union of White-Collar Workers (*Gewerkschaftsbund der Angestellten*, or GDA), showed that 32.2 per cent of men were in the lowest positions, 47.4 per cent in middle-ranking roles, and 20.3 per cent in the most senior positions. In comparison, 72 per cent of women were in low-ranked roles, 25.5 per cent in middle placed positions, with just 2.5 per cent in senior roles. On average, women in white-collar jobs received 10 per cent less pay than men.

The Weimar Republic did open up greater opportunity for women to advance in the professions, however. Women with higher education qualifications were the main beneficiaries. In 1914, women made up 6.7 per cent of university students, but in 1918 this had increased to 10 per cent, and by 1931 rose to 18.8 per cent. The number of young women taking the school-leaving certificate (*Abitur*), the essential requirement for university entrance, increased from 9.1 in 1925 to 23.5 per cent in 1931. The most popular university subjects for women were in the arts and humanities. Most female students came from upper- or middle-class families, with only 1.1 per cent in 1928 defined as 'working class'.

Medicine was a key area of upward mobility for women in Weimar Germany. By 1925, there were 2,572 female doctors, making up 5.4 per cent of the total. By 1933, this rose to 4,367, or 8.6 per cent of the total. Most women doctors worked in big cities with populations of over 100,000 people, and in general practice. There was also an increase in women qualifying as chemists, with women making up 20.4 per cent of all chemists by 1933. In comparison, women's advancement was much slower in the legal profession. By 1933, there were only 251 female lawyers, and just 36 female judges. A career in law was open to women in theory, but it was closed to them in practice. By 1930, not a single woman had been appointed as a public prosecutor in Prussia, and women were still excluded from a career in the judiciary in Bavaria.

The progress of women in academia was similarly slow. Women had the right to appointment to full professorships at German universities after they were granted the 'right to habilitate', meaning to take the second doctorate necessary for appointment to full university academic posts. It was not until 1923, however, that Dr Margarethe Wrangell became the first female full professor, after taking up a post in Botany at the Agricultural University of Hohenheim. By 1932, however, there were still only 74 women on the full-time lecturing staff at all the German universities.

It was in the teaching profession that women advanced at the fastest rate. Teaching was a profession in which women had prospered even before the War. In 1925, a third of women teachers were under the age of 30, a third between 30 and 40 years, and a further third aged between 40 and 60. In all, women made up a third of all teachers. In 1927, 72 per cent of teachers had their own household rather than living with parents. Women could climb the career ladder. In 1933, women made up 14.4 per cent of the most senior positions in German schools.

Overall, very few women in Weimar Germany could attain the glamour and financial independence required to qualify as a 'new woman'. Only a determined young woman, with a university education, could build a career, and attain the necessary financial independence. But the best-paid women in the Weimar era, such as teachers, doctors and lawyers, hardly had time to live the carefree lifestyle of the 'new woman'. As with the later 'summer of love', in 1967, the 'new woman' was more a media-created myth than a reality.[8]

On 7 June 1929, the Committee of Experts, headed by American Owen D. Young, presented its eagerly awaited report in Paris, outlining a solution to Germany's future reparations payments. Its deliberations had been going on since 9 February 1929. Under the terms of what became known as the Young Plan, Germany was required to continue making reparations payments until 1988. A total of 1.7 billion Reichsmarks was due in the first two years, gradually increasing to a maximum of 2.4 billion Reichsmarks by 1966, and then falling to 1.7 billion Reichsmarks in the last twenty years. Annual German payments were divided into two parts: one was an unconditional payment of one-third of the total, with the second part, equal to two-thirds, having the potential for postponement. The plan also removed the 'prosperity index', which held that if the German economy grew so would payments. Now, even if the German economy boomed, German payments would not be raised.[9] In all, Germany would pay a total of 112 billion Reichsmarks under the Young Plan. All the remaining foreign controls on the German economy, including the Reparations

Agent, Transfer Committee, and foreign trustees involvement with the Reichsbahn and Reichsbank, were removed.[10] An additional clause was inserted, authorising the revision of the plan in the event of a serious financial emergency in Germany. The creditor states also promised to further reduce Germany's payments if the US government consented to a reduction of inter-Allied debts. Upon acceptance of the agreement by the German government, the Allied occupation of the Rhineland would end, the date for which was set for 1 July 1930.[11]

To collect all the payments due and to conduct the necessary transfers under the plan, the Bank for International Settlements was established, in Basel, Switzerland, with the issue of 600,000 shares, raising a capital of 1.5 billion gold francs. It opened on 17 May 1930, and was controlled by representatives of all the countries involved (USA, Britain, France, Belgium, Italy, Japan and Germany). It was hoped the bank would function as a safeguard for German currency.[12]

The Young Plan was viewed outside Germany as fair and lenient, as it offered a reduction of payments by 700 million Reichsmarks

per year, removed foreign controls on the German economy, gave protection against possible payment difficulties, and promised an early end to the occupation of the Rhineland. But its critics inside Germany argued that it burdened Germany with reparations payments until 1988, and removed the assurance of American loans, which had previously guaranteed payments. However, on 21 June 1929, the German cabinet unanimously accepted the Young Plan, releasing the following statement: 'The Reich government is prepared to accept the Plan signed by the Experts in Paris on 7 June for the settlement of the Reparations as the basis for the international inter-governmental Conference.'[13]

On 24 June, the Reichstag debated the Young Plan. Alfred Hugenberg, leader of the Nationalist DNVP, gave Kuno von Westarp the task of speaking on behalf of the party. Westarp argued the financial toll of signing the Treaty of Versailles had left the German people in a condition of 'slavery and humiliation'. The German people, he continued, were now being asked to saddle themselves with more crushing financial burdens, which would not end until 1988. The Young Plan, he concluded, was designed to further the interests of the creditor nations, and was therefore unacceptable.[14] Gustav Stresemann, the German Foreign Minister, responded to this attack with moderation and restraint. The central issue, he said, was whether a revision of the Dawes Plan would benefit Germany. The Nationalists were insisting on outright rejection of the Young Plan, but adopting such a rash course would plunge the country into an economic crisis of such proportions that the entire middle class would be wiped out. The main question, Stresemann concluded, was whether the Young Plan would bring an improvement to Germany's economic position and the answer to that question was undoubtedly affirmative.[15]

During the debate, Stresemann received support from the Social Democrats. Rudolf Breitscheid, speaking on behalf of the SPD Reichstag delegation, defended the Young Plan, emphasising it was a significant improvement on the Dawes Plan. He did, however, point out that the financial obligations it imposed would be more difficult to maintain unless the Allied occupation of the Rhineland was soon ended. The Communists attacked Westarp's speech as hypocritical, pointing out the DNVP had voted in favour of the Dawes Plan.

On 28 June, the 10th anniversary of the signing of the Treaty of Versailles, Germany observed a 'day of mourning', with government buildings flying flags at half-mast. The Nationalists, the Steel Helmet

Opening session of the Second Reparations
Conference, Paris, February 1929. Owen D. Young's
plan would cut German payments in half and extend
the schedule for reparations payments to 1988.

and the National Socialists all staged large demonstrations. A proclamation, signed by President Hindenburg and the entire Reich cabinet, was published, which read as follows:

> This is a day of sorrow. Ten years have passed since
> Germany's peace delegates were forced to sign at Versailles
> a document which was a bitter disappointment to all friends
> of justice. For ten years, the treaty has been a burden upon
> all sections of the German people, upon the life of the
> spirit of the national economy, upon the labour of peasants.
> Germany signed the treaty without thereby acknowledging
> that the German nation started the war. This charge makes it
> impossible for our people to regain their tranquillity.[16]

In the weeks following the announcement of the Young Plan a concerted campaign to obstruct it began, led by Alfred Hugenberg, the leader of the DNVP. On 9 July, Hugenberg announced the formation of the Reich Committee for the German Referendum against the Young Plan.[17] The chief participants in the referendum campaign were the DNVP, the Pan German League led by Heinrich Class, the National Socialists led by Adolf Hitler, the Steel Helmet led by Fritz Seldt and Theodor Duesterberg, the United Fatherland Associations under Count Rüdiger von der Golz, and the Christian National Farmers' Party under Albrecht Windhausen. Their aim was to prevent the adoption of the Young plan through a national referendum.

The fragmentation of the Right clearly influenced the formation of the anti-Young Plan referendum coalition. Leaders on the Right had been looking for policies that could unite voters. In late September 1928, the Steel Helmet Executive Committee decided to initiate a referendum on revising the Weimar Constitution to give more dictatorial powers to the Reich President, and weaken the power of the Chancellor and the Reichstag. The Steel Helmet launched a national committee for a referendum on this issue on 19 January 1929.[18] In late April 1929, Hitler sent the Steel Helmet a lengthy position paper on the referendum proposal on the powers of the President, in which he outlined the reasons why he opposed it. Hitler primarily doubted a referendum on the Constitution would generate the emotional power required for success, and he also pointed out to the supporters of the proposal that they had not thought the implications of a Social Democrat winning the next presidential election and using such powers to push Germany further to the Left.[19]

What the creation of the Reich Committee against the Young Plan demonstrated was the growing radicalisation of the German Right, which had been looking for an issue to rally around since the 1928 elections. For the first time, Hitler found he was in possession of substantial funds for propaganda, as well as the prospect of attaining respectability in middle-class circles. The money came from Hugenberg, who was happy to use Hitler and the NSDAP as the rabble-rousers during the drive for a referendum. For his part, Hitler used the campaign against the Young Plan to raise his profile on the national stage.[20]

Between 6 and 31 August 1929, the grandly named Conference on the Final Liquidation of the War took place in The Hague, Netherlands. It was convened to discuss the Young Plan and the evacuation of the Rhineland by the Allies. The gathering was opened at 11 a.m. on 6 August by Pieter Beelaerts von Blokland, the Dutch Foreign Minister, who welcomed the delegates in the name of the Queen of the Netherlands.[21]

At the first session, Gustav Stresemann, the Foreign Minister, and Rudolf Hilferding, the Finance Minister, represented Germany, while France sent Aristide Briand, who was now Prime Minister, having replaced Raymond Poincaré who had resigned due to ill health on 29 July. Briand was accompanied by Louis Loucheur, the French Minister of Labour. Britain was represented by two members of the recently formed minority Labour government led by Ramsay MacDonald: Arthur Henderson, the Foreign Secretary, and Philip Snowden, the Chancellor of the Exchequer, who was known for his sharp mind and blunt way of speaking. It was once said Snowden 'combined a demagogue's fire, with a Yorkshireman's hard head'.[22] The Belgian representatives were Henri Jasper, the Prime Minister, and Paul Hymans, the Foreign Minister, while the two Italian representatives were Antonio Mosconi, the Finance Minister, and Alberto Pirelli, the latter a well-known industrialist. Finally, Japan was represented by Mineichirō Adachi, the Japanese Ambassador to Paris. During the proceedings, delegates from Greece, Poland, Portugal, Romania, Czechoslovakia and the Kingdom of the Serbs, Croats and Slovenes (shortly to be rechristened 'Yugoslavia') also attended. The US did not participate in the conference.[23]

The First Hague Conference, as it was more commonly called, proved a stormy affair. From the beginning, Stresemann insisted the evacuation of the Rhineland and the terms of the financial settlement concerning Germany should be discussed in tandem. No one pushed for any increase in German payments above the sums mentioned in the Young Plan, but most of the proceedings were taken up by an argument between the Allied creditors over the allocation of Germany's payments. Philip Snowden demanded, in a hectoring tone that irritated the other delegates, that Britain should receive a greater percentage of the receipts than had been allocated under the Young Plan. At one point, Snowden even threatened to leave the conference unless British demands were met.[24] Stresemann kept out of this row, saying it was up to the creditor nations to resolve their own differences. There was initially strong resistance to Snowdon's proposals, but, on 28 August, the British demands were met in full, with Britain receiving an additional 40 million Reichsmarks for 37 years.

Stresemann's main aim was to gain agreement on the swift evacuation of the Rhineland. The British government fully supported him, offering to withdraw their own troops by the end of 1929. The French government took a much more negative stance, wanting a staged withdrawal, further evidence of the demilitarisation of the Rhineland, and the sight of Germany's first payment under the Young Plan before agreeing to end the occupation. Eventually, Stresemann got his way on the evacuation issue, after he dropped his demand that the Saar coal mining region be returned before the agreed date of 1935. Behind the scenes, some in the British Foreign Office shared Briand's worries about whether the German government would keep the Rhineland demilitarised once Allied troops had left. One such sceptic was Harold Nicolson, who was *chargé d'affaires* in the British Embassy in Berlin. Nicolson predicted gloomily that Germany would not accept any form of military inspection after Allied troops had left German soil. There were, he continued, good grounds to believe that French suspicions of German future military intentions were justified. After the departure of Allied troops 'we may find the whole attitude of the German government changing, and may be faced not with the stubborn and shifty obstruction of the past, but by an aggressive and almost menacing determination to revise the [Versailles] Treaty'.[25]

During the Hague Conference, Stresemann was often on the verge of complete physical collapse. Some delegates sitting near him noticed him breathing heavily, often removing sweat from his forehead with his handkerchief. In his memoirs Julius Curtius, the Minister of Economic Affairs, who was part of the German delegation at The Hague, remembered that on one day, towards the end of the conference, after an exhausting session during the negotiations over the evacuation of the Rhineland, Stresemann suddenly collapsed, saying: 'I can't go on.'[26]

It was finally decided, on 30 August, under the terms of the Evacuation Agreement, that the withdrawal of Allied troops from the Rhineland would begin on 15 September 1929, and would be completed not later than 30 June 1930. This was the moment Stresemann had yearned for ever since he became German Foreign Minister. Decisions on all the minute details discussed at The Hague would be finalised at a second Hague Conference early in 1930. On 31 August 1929, the conference closed with the signing of the Protocol, which approved the Young Plan and the Evacuation Agreement on the Rhineland. The German delegation were relieved the Young Plan schedule of payments had been accepted with no revisions, and euphoric that a final end date had been placed on the Allied occupation of the Rhineland. Austen Chamberlain wrote a letter to Stresemann expressing his pleasure at the successful conclusion of the Hague Conference, and assuring him that 'it was to him and his policies that Germany owed its success'.[27]

On 9 September, Stresemann attended the Plenary Session of the League of Nations in Geneva to deliver what turned out to be his last public speech. He expressed the hope that Aristide Briand's desire for European unity would be achieved, and the promise that war would be outlawed, as expressed in the Kellogg–Briand Pact, would be fulfilled, saying:

> The German government has always adopted the stand that the starting-point of all efforts for securing peace must be the extension of the methods for the peaceful solution of every kind of conflict between States. War will not be avoided by preparing a war against war, but only by removing its causes. The more we succeed in finding a practical way of settling existing and future differences between our States the more we can realise the idea behind the model treaty for the avoidance of war, drawn up at a German suggestion.[28]

Antonina Vallentin, a Polish-born biographer, and translator, watched as Stresemann delivered his speech, observing: 'A marked man stood there in the shadow of death. His suit flapped about his shrunken figure. His breathing came so hard that his sudden coughing often drowned out his words. One could almost hear the fevered beating of his heart.'[29]

On 11 September Stresemann gave an interview in Geneva to Theodor Wolff, the editor-in-chief of the *Berliner Tageblatt* (*Berlin Daily Newspaper*). He criticised the anti-Young Plan referendum campaign in Germany, saying:

> The enemies of the Young Plan operate with their favourite catchword, namely, that the Young Plan is going to enslave the German people for two generations. Instead of speaking always of the next generation, which will probably live under quite different conditions, one should first remember that the Young Plan will bring much relief to the present generation. In the next ten years, the German people will pay about seven billion less than under the Dawes Plan – is that nothing?[30]

By now, the referendum campaign against the Young Plan was already in full swing. On 1 September, Hugenberg held a highly publicised launch event, concluding with a speech at the monument in the Teutoburg forest, constructed in the 1840s to commemorate the German hero Arminius's defeat of the Roman legions. Hugenberg pointed at the sword Arminius was holding in his hand and claimed Germany's sword would soon be returned. It was now the task of the German people, he concluded, to take up the struggle against foreign domination by rejecting the Young Plan. Adolf Hitler was not present at the launch event, claiming he had a sore throat and high fever.[31] On 12 September, Alfred Hugenberg presented the text of the proposed Law Against the Enslavement of the German People (*Gesetz gegen die Versklavung des deutschen Volkes*), which became more commonly known as the Freedom Law. It contained four paragraphs: (1) rejection of war-guilt; (2) removal of Article 231 of the Treaty of Versailles; (3) rejection of new reparations demands; (4) Reich Chancellors and Reich Ministers and their authorised signatories to treaties to be subject to a criminal charge of treason, punishable by not less than two years in prison.

The last paragraph, which became known as the 'imprisonment paragraph', proved highly controversial. Most members of the National Referendum Committee wanted it removed. Hugenberg had revised an earlier draft which had made even the Reich President subject to prosecution. On 21 September, Hitler made the continued participation of the NSDAP in the referendum campaign conditional on the 'imprisonment paragraph' being retained, and this was reluctantly accepted by the National Referendum Committee, largely because Hugenberg felt Hitler's propaganda and speaking skills were vital in the referendum crusade.[32]

For the proposed law to go forward to a national referendum, it required the signatures of at least 10 per cent of all registered voters, who had to attach their signatures to the referendum petition, between 16 and 29 October 1929. If successful, there would be a Reichstag debate, and a vote on this 'Freedom Law'. If the Reichstag rejected the law, a national referendum would be held. President Hindenburg hampered the anti-Young Plan campaign by issuing a public statement disassociating himself from the National Referendum Committee and asserting his neutrality in the conflict.

On 25 September, Gustav Stresemann returned to Berlin at a time when the Müller government was embroiled in a political crisis over the proposals of Rudolf Wissell, the Minister of Labour, to increase employer contributions from 3.5 to 4 per cent, in order to fund the unemployment insurance scheme. Stresemann's own party, the DVP, was divided over whether to give support to these proposals. On 2 October, there was a heated meeting of the DVP Reichstag delegation, with the party finally agreeing by a narrow margin to abstain when the matter came to a vote on the next day. Stresemann was relieved with this outcome, but he felt unwell towards the end of the meeting, and decided to return to his Berlin residence to recuperate.

At 7.00 p.m. his close party colleague Julius Curtius, the Minister of Economics, went to visit him. They talked for an hour, with Stresemann expressing his pleasure that his party had decided not to use the unemployment insurance question to bring down the 'Great Coalition'. He soon retired to bed. About 10.30 p.m. Stresemann suffered a massive stroke, which left him unconscious and partially paralysed. His doctors were summoned, and remained at his bedside, but a few hours later, at 5.25 a.m., on 3 October, there was a second stroke, which this time proved fatal. At the age of 51, Germany's leading politician was dead.[33]

Gustav Stresemann's death was not a surprise to those close to him. He had never been in good health, having been exempted from compulsory military service on health grounds as a young man. In 1919 he had suffered a heart attack, which exacerbated long-term damage to his kidneys, now believed to be a result of Graves' disease, a thyroid condition which damages the immune system. Stresemann's hectic and stressful lifestyle as Foreign Minister was hardly conducive to recovery. In an ordinary job, he would probably have been retired with a pension on health grounds many years before.

As news spread of Stresemann's death, there was a flood of tributes. The *Deutsche Allgemeine Zeitung* (*German General Newspaper*) wrote,

'It seemed necessary for this man to die for his real greatness to be appreciated by his compatriots.'[34] There were glowing tributes from leading world leaders, including Ramsay MacDonald, the British Prime Minister, who commented: 'His memory is secure, and I cannot believe the great service he has given to pacification with such patience and faith can now be undone.' Aristide Briand, the French Prime Minister, sent a telegram to Stresemann's widow Käte, which read: 'I will always retain the deepest respect for his memory. In pursuit of our common ideal, Dr Stresemann caused me to appreciate his lofty outlook and fine loyalty.'[35]

Stresemann lay in state in the German parliament. Thousands of people filed past the open coffin to pay their respects before his state funeral on 6 October. Hermann Müller, the Reich Chancellor, bowed to the coffin in the Plenary Hall of the Reichstag, where the memorial service was held, before delivering a moving eulogy, describing Stresemann as a towering figure in world politics. There was then a solemn funeral procession through Berlin, pausing for several minutes outside the Foreign Ministry, before proceeding to burial in the Luisenstädtischer Friedhof in Kreuzberg, Berlin. It was estimated that a crowd of 200,000 had lined the route. Film newsreels of the event appeared in cinemas around the world.[36]

Gustav Stresemann's record entitles him to be seen not only as the Weimar Republic's most successful Foreign Minister, but undoubtedly its most dominant political figure. It is impossible to see German history in the 1920s taking the same course without him. Some politicians make an enormous difference, and he was one of those who did. He was a member of every German cabinet from 1923 to 1929, and the Social Democrats were his most consistent supporters. Stresemann raised Germany from a humiliated and disgruntled foe in 1923 into a diplomatic equal and Great Power again at the time of his death. His achievements as Foreign Minister ended the Ruhr occupation of 1923, contributed to the stabilisation of the Republic, finalised the Locarno and Rapallo Treaties and the Kellogg–Briand Pact, took Germany into the League of Nations, eased Germany's reparations burdens through the Dawes and Young Plans, and brought the foreign occupation of Germany to an end. Never has the Nobel Peace Prize had a more justified recipient.

Stresemann's death left a huge void in German political life. He had been a force of stability within a deeply unstable political system, and had gained admiration around the world. There was no speech at the League of Nations in the months following his death that did not begin with a homage to his memory. There was simply no one in Germany or outside it capable of stepping into his shoes.

It is difficult to calculate the exact part his tragic death played in the destruction of German democracy, and the souring of international relations, but he was probably the one Weimar politician who, through the sheer force of his personality, might have saved it, though Stresemann himself thought everything in politics was determined by the state of the economy. Critics of Stresemann have depicted him as an opportunistic and deceitful power-politician with a hidden militaristic agenda, with some even trying to depict him as Hitler in a morning suit.[37] Between the extremes of Dr Jekyll and Mr Hyde, Stresemann was predominantly Dr Jekyll, whereas Hitler was always Mr Hyde. But there is truly little evidence in his private papers or his

Gustav Stresemann lies in state in the
Reichstag, October 1929.

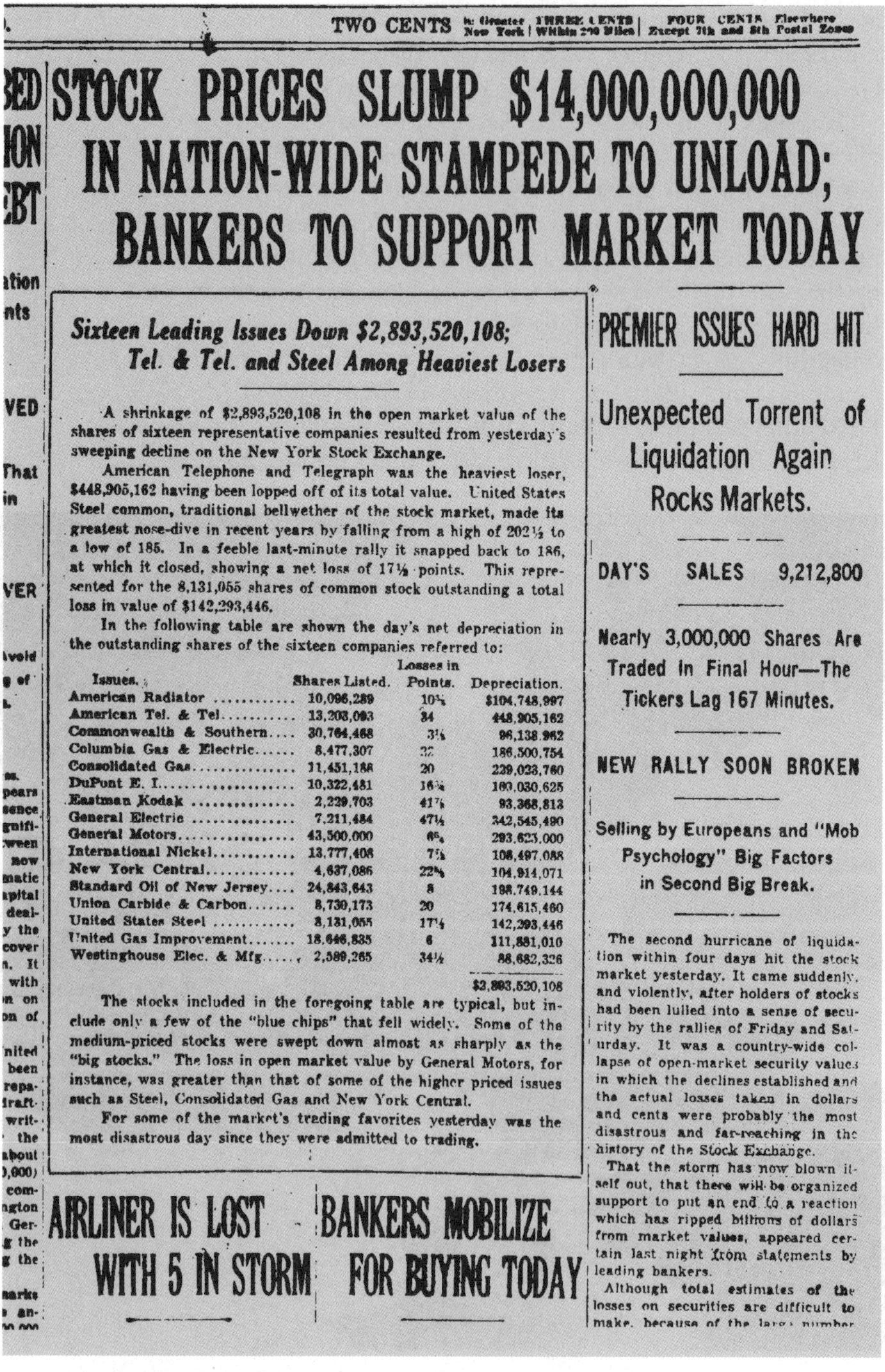

TWO CENTS In Greater New York | THREE CENTS Within 200 Miles | FOUR CENTS Elsewhere Except 7th and 8th Postal Zones

STOCK PRICES SLUMP $14,000,000,000 IN NATION-WIDE STAMPEDE TO UNLOAD; BANKERS TO SUPPORT MARKET TODAY

Sixteen Leading Issues Down $2,893,520,108; Tel. & Tel. and Steel Among Heaviest Losers

A shrinkage of $2,893,520,108 in the open market value of the shares of sixteen representative companies resulted from yesterday's sweeping decline on the New York Stock Exchange.

American Telephone and Telegraph was the heaviest loser, $448,905,162 having been lopped off of its total value. United States Steel common, traditional bellwether of the stock market, made its greatest nose-dive in recent years by falling from a high of 202½ to a low of 185. In a feeble last-minute rally it snapped back to 186, at which it closed, showing a net loss of 17½ points. This represented for the 8,131,055 shares of common stock outstanding a total loss in value of $142,293,446.

In the following table are shown the day's net depreciation in the outstanding shares of the sixteen companies referred to:

Issues.	Shares Listed.	Losses in Points.	Depreciation.
American Radiator	10,096,289	10⅜	$104,748,997
American Tel. & Tel	13,203,093	34	448,905,162
Commonwealth & Southern	30,764,468	3⅛	96,138,962
Columbia Gas & Electric	8,477,307	22	186,500,754
Consolidated Gas	11,451,188	20	229,023,760
DuPont E. I.	10,322,481	16⅜	169,030,625
Eastman Kodak	2,229,703	41⅞	93,368,813
General Electric	7,211,484	47½	342,545,490
General Motors	43,500,000	6⅝	293,625,000
International Nickel	13,777,408	7⅞	108,497,088
New York Central	4,637,086	22⅝	104,914,071
Standard Oil of New Jersey	24,843,643	8	198,749,144
Union Carbide & Carbon	8,730,173	20	174,615,460
United States Steel	8,131,055	17½	142,293,446
United Gas Improvement	18,646,835	6	111,881,010
Westinghouse Elec. & Mfg.	2,589,265	34½	88,682,326
			$2,893,520,108

The stocks included in the foregoing table are typical, but include only a few of the "blue chips" that fell widely. Some of the medium-priced stocks were swept down almost as sharply as the "big stocks." The loss in open market value by General Motors, for instance, was greater than that of some of the higher priced issues such as Steel, Consolidated Gas and New York Central.

For some of the market's trading favorites yesterday was the most disastrous day since they were admitted to trading.

PREMIER ISSUES HARD HIT

Unexpected Torrent of Liquidation Again Rocks Markets.

DAY'S SALES 9,212,800

Nearly 3,000,000 Shares Are Traded In Final Hour—The Tickers Lag 167 Minutes.

NEW RALLY SOON BROKEN

Selling by Europeans and "Mob Psychology" Big Factors in Second Big Break.

The second hurricane of liquidation within four days hit the stock market yesterday. It came suddenly, and violently, after holders of stocks had been lulled into a sense of security by the rallies of Friday and Saturday. It was a country-wide collapse of open-market security values in which the declines established and the actual losses taken in dollars and cents were probably the most disastrous and far-reaching in the history of the Stock Exchange.

That the storm has now blown itself out, that there will be organized support to put an end to a reaction which has ripped billions of dollars from market values, appeared certain last night from statements by leading bankers.

Although total estimates of the losses on securities are difficult to make, because of the large number

AIRLINER IS LOST WITH 5 IN STORM

BANKERS MOBILIZE FOR BUYING TODAY

The *New York Times* reports the progress of the Wall Street Crash, 'Black Tuesday', 29 October 1929.

diaries of Stresemann desiring a war of revenge or territorial expansion beyond restoring the territory lost by Germany under the terms of the Treaty of Versailles, and putting an end to reparations.

Stresemann realised that even a militarily strong Germany could not face a military conflict with the Western Powers, including the USA. With his supreme diplomatic skill, a peaceful revision of the 1919 Peace settlement was achievable. His transformation from an opponent to a pragmatic defender of the Weimar Republic was a genuine conversion, not an exercise in clever opportunism. Stresemann believed that in a world of peace and international cooperation Germany would prosper. Recent studies have suggested the goal of Stresemann's foreign policy was the peaceful revision of the Treaty of Versailles, along with international cooperation and the restoration of Germany as a sovereign Great Power with equal rights on the world stage.[38] Stresemann was always more concerned with Germany's huge economic potential, not its military potential to wage war for territorial gain. Stresemann's readiness to accept unpleasant realities and compromise when required was perhaps his most praiseworthy trait. Stresemann was replaced as Foreign Minister by a fellow-member of the DVP, Julius Curtius.

On 24 October, known as 'Black Thursday', there was a sudden outburst of panic selling of shares on the New York Stock Exchange on Wall Street, New York City. The market lost 11 per cent of its value in a single day. Five days later, on 29 October, 'Black Tuesday', the crisis deepened, with $16.4 billion shares sold. The Wall Street Crash, as it became commonly known, soon plunged the world into the Great Depression. The dramatic falls in share prices in the USA were followed by huge falls in all financial markets, with the sole exception of those in Japan. Between 1929 and 1932 the New York Dow Jones share index fell from 452 to 68 points.[39]

It had been widely believed by speculators that the US stock market would continue to rise indefinitely, which produced a speculative boom, as profits from manufacturing companies skyrocketed beyond their real worth. Even ordinary people began using their savings to invest in shares, hoping for quick profits. As Albert Wiggin, the President of the Chase National Bank, put it: 'We are reaping the natural fruit of the orgy of speculation in which people have indulged.'[40]

There is an unchallenged myth that the Wall Street Crash led to the rise of Hitler and doomed Weimar democracy. In reality, many of the factors that assisted Hitler's rise and the collapse of democracy were present before the full impact of the Depression ever hit the German economy. The instability of Weimar governments had already led to the fragmentation of German politics, and was already turning millions of voters against the traditional German parties, especially in rural areas. Another problem in the German economy that predated the economic downturn was the reliance of German government and industry on short-term loans, mainly from American banks. When these loans eventually dried up in the wake of the Crash, and repayments on the old ones became due, the finances of the German government were deeply affected; but in 1930 more American loans actually flowed into Germany than in 1929.

During the period 1929 to 1932, German industrial production fell by 50 per cent, but a great deal of this decrease can be attributed to the growth of industrial cartels and monopolies inside Germany from 1924 onwards, which produced a glut in industrial production and induced an over-reliance on increasing exports. When world trade collapsed after 1929, and the major capitalist governments – the USA, Britain and France – introduced protective tariffs, German industry had to close factories or reduce the workforce, resulting in millions being thrown out of work. German unemployment grew from 1.6 million in 1929 to 6 million by 1932.

On 3 November 1929, the right-wing campaign against the Young Plan narrowly secured the 10.02 per cent of eligible registered voters required for the 'Freedom Law' to be sent to the Reichstag for a vote. Only 4,137,164 people had signed the petition, a mere 9,925 voters above the minimum threshold, and support for the measure was narrowly confined to traditional DNVP strongholds, particularly Pomerania, East Prussia and Mecklenburg. These three east German states accounted for 75 per cent of all the signatures on the petition. It was obvious that in these areas the DNVP was strong enough to put social and economic pressure on even reluctant signers.[41]

The Freedom Law was debated in the Reichstag on 29–30 November 1929, with a recommendation that the measure was either accepted or rejected. The debate was opened by Julius Curtius, delivering his first speech as the new German Foreign Minister. He denounced the Freedom Law as a mischievous attack on the authority of the State, and affirmed the determination of the Müller cabinet to oppose it. Curtius confirmed it was his task to defend the foreign policy inaugurated by his predecessor. The principle of strong leadership which Hugenberg and his associates constantly eulogised would be destroyed if basic questions of foreign policy were constantly referred to the masses, Curtius added. If the referendum were successful, Germany would be plunged into economic chaos. The Young Plan was not an ideal arrangement, but once enacted it would end foreign occupation and financial control.[42]

Hugenberg did not rise to answer the attack by Curtius in the Reichstag. He delegated that task to Ernst Oberfohren, who trotted out the familiar right-wing objections to the Young Plan, primarily that it contained a schedule for the payment of reparations that would saddle future generations with a debt they could not afford to pay. By rejecting the Young Plan, the German people would be taking the first step to restoring their freedom. Thomas Esser, speaking on behalf of Zentrum, said the supporters of the referendum wanted to replace a policy of negotiation and understanding with one of sabotage and provocation, thinking Germany by mere protest could throw off the burden of reparations.[43]

On the next day, the Reichstag voted. It was a foregone conclusion the Freedom Law would be defeated, but the margin was much larger than expected. Reichstag members voted on each clause. The first paragraph was defeated by 318 to 82, the next two paragraphs were rejected by similar margins, while paragraph 4, the infamous 'imprisonment paragraph', was also overwhelmingly rejected, with only 55 of even the 78 DNVP Reichstag members voting in favour. On 10 December, 12 rebellious DNVP members, led by Gottfried Treviranus and Hans Schlange-Schöningen, announced they were breaking away from the party to form the more moderate KVP. Count von Westarp stayed in the party, but he resigned as the leader of the DNVP Reichstag delegation. The DNVP rebels did not oppose agitating against the Young Plan, but were opposed to Hugenberg's decision to move the DNVP to the extreme Right and ally with the National Socialists.[44]

The rejection of the Freedom Law by the Reichstag meant, under the rules of the Constitution, the measure would now be submitted to the people in a national referendum. The Müller government deliberately set polling day for 22 December 1929, the last Sunday before Christmas, to keep the voter turnout as low as possible. On 6 December, Dr Hjalmar Schacht, President of the Reichsbank, who had been a leading German delegate on the Young Plan Committee, released a memorandum to the press in which he criticised the German and Allied governments for permitting concessions to the

creditor nations at the First Hague Conference, which he felt were to Germany's financial disadvantage, stating: 'I find myself most resolutely obliged to decline responsibility for the execution of the Young Plan.' The fact that Germany's expert on the Young Plan Committee had effectively expressed his opposition to it was interpreted as a boost to the Freedom Law referendum.

Schacht also blamed Dr Rudolf Hilferding, the Minister of Finance, and Joseph Popitz, the state secretary of the Minister of Finance, for delaying much needed fiscal reforms which he thought would deal with the growing government deficit, and he castigated them for general fiscal mismanagement. He particularly denounced the 'feebleness' of Hilferding's budget plans for 1930, which involved using savings from the Young Plan, along with increased revenue from sales tax increases, to achieve reductions of 910 million Reichsmarks in taxes on property and for high earners.[45] Schacht felt these plans would not reduce the government spending deficit. The right-wing papers were jubilant, viewing Schacht's memorandum as a timely boost to the referendum campaign against the Young Plan. The left-wing press were appalled at what was seen as a blatant attempt to embarrass the government, and felt Schacht was motivated by personal hostility.[46]

In a Reichstag debate on 12 December, Müller repudiated Schacht's claims and asked the Reichstag to endorse Hilferding's emergency measures, which were passed by a margin of 222 to 156 votes.[47] This outcome did not satisfy the DVP, who threatened to leave the Müller cabinet unless some modifications were made to the emergency programme. Hindenburg met with the DVP leaders, and begged them not to endanger political stability during a time of economic crisis, and before the Young Plan had been ratified, and they responded to this patriotic appeal.[48]

The pressure on Hilferding continued to increase, however. The final straw was his failed attempt to cover short-term government debt by means of a bridging loan from the American banking markets. This forced him to go cap in hand to Schacht, as the head of a consortium of German banks, for a loan, but the latter imposed harsh terms, most notably the creation of a 450 million 'sinking fund' to cope with future budget shortfalls. On 21 December, Hilferding sensationally resigned as German Finance Minister, shortly after his state secretary Popitz had stepped down.[49] He was replaced by Paul Moldenhauer of the DVP, who was seen as more likely to take a harsher approach to the government deficit.

Dr Hjalmar Schacht, economist, centre-right
politician and President of the Reichsbank.

The messy fall of Hilferding indicated the Müller government was incapable of getting to grips with the deteriorating economic crisis. Müller's position was not helped by severe illness, later diagnosed as gall-bladder disease, which had incapacitated him so much that he had been unable to chair cabinet meetings for much of 1929, and with Stresemann also ill, central government had virtually ground to a halt.[50] The 'December Crisis' left Hindenburg determined to oust Müller's government, once the Young Plan had been ratified, early in 1930, and to replace it with an 'anti-democratic and anti-Socialist' government. Hindenburg's plan was to 'send the Reichstag home for a while', and to rule using the extensive emergency powers granted to him under Article 48 of the Weimar Constitution.[51] The idea for a 'presidential cabinet' had long been championed by Major-General Kurt von Schleicher, who felt the multiplicity of political parties in the Reichstag had made stable democratic government impossible, and that a 'presidential cabinet' was the best way out of the never-ending political chaos.

In January 1928, when Wilhelm Groener was appointed as Defence Minister, he had named Schleicher as the chief of his 'ministerial office', with the task of being the Army's chief political representative and political lobbyist. This role allowed Schleicher to build up his influence, not just within the Reichswehr and the Defence Ministry, but also over President Hindenburg. He came to be seen as the 'true face of the Army', and he mixed effortlessly in military and political circles. In the opinion of Theodor Eschenburg, Schleicher was 'able to interact with anyone and everyone, he had the psychological knack of getting on the emotional wavelength of the most diverse individuals'.[52]

By the end of 1929, Schleicher was the leading political wire-puller, manipulator, and intriguer in a small group around the ageing President, which also included Otto Meissner, the head of the Presidential Chancellery, and Hindenburg's son, Oskar, whom Schleicher had known for twenty years. Schleicher owed his rise to his flair for organisation, his charm, his emotional intelligence, and most of all his ability to convince Hindenburg and many other leading politicians that his advice was invaluable. Hindenburg got into the habit of consulting Schleicher on all critical issues before taking action, even when choosing Chancellors.

The politician Schleicher recommended to Hindenburg as the ideal head of a 'presidential cabinet' was Heinrich Brüning, who had recently been appointed by Ludwig Kaas as the head of the Reichstag delegation of Zentrum. Brüning was a devout Catholic who had

Heinrich Brüning, the reluctant Chancellor.

gained a doctorate in Political Economics before serving as an officer during the War, and being awarded the Iron Cross (1st Class) for his coolness under fire. Because he preferred a constitutional monarchy to a republic, he had opposed the November Revolution of 1918. After the war, he received his formative political experience as the director of the League of Christian Trade Unions, before his election to the Reichstag in 1924, as a member of Zentrum, where he soon established himself as an expert on financial and economic matters. He was known for being serious, cautious, conscientious, in favour of the doctrine of a balanced budget, unmarried, and with no political enemies.

Brüning was first approached by Schleicher in the spring of 1929, but was unenthusiastic about the idea of heading up a 'presidential cabinet', and astounded by how Article 48 would be used under the proposal. Brüning pointed out that making full use of presidential powers under Article 48 would effectively mean the Reichstag was completely dispensed with. Under the Constitution, if presidential decrees failed to gain a majority in the Reichstag, the President could dissolve parliament, but new elections had to be held within 60 days, and a new Reichstag would need to convene within 30 days of the election. In other words, it was a possible recipe for a permanent state of political crisis.[53]

On 26 December 1929, Schleicher arranged a meeting on the subject at the Berlin home of a close associate, Baron Friedrich Wilhelm von Willisen. According to the memoirs of Gottfried Treviranus, who was present, Otto Meissner was also there, Wilhelm Groener had been invited, but was unable to attend. Schleicher once again pressed the case for a 'presidential cabinet', but Brüning repeated his reservations about such a radical departure from established parliamentary procedure, and insisted Müller should stay in office, at least until the evacuation of the Rhineland at the end of June 1930. Brüning later admitted he thought Schleicher's plan for a 'presidential cabinet' was really designed as a prelude to a military dictatorship.[54]

The German Referendum on the Freedom Law took place on 22 December 1929. It proved a humiliating defeat for the right-wing opponents of the Young Plan. A total of 5,838,890 (94.5 per cent) votes were cast in favour, with 338,195 (5.5 per cent) voting against, and 131,494 voters submitting invalid or blank voting slips. To pass the measure had required 50 per cent of the 42,323,473 currently registered voters. The referendum had proved a ringing endorsement of Stresemann's foreign policy.

A poster issued by right-wing opponents of the Young Plan depicts the plan as keeping Germans in chains. 'Until the third generation you will be enslaved,' it proclaims.

Hugenberg was the big loser of the referendum campaign, as he not only failed to unite the Right under his leadership, but also split his own party. The big winner was Adolf Hitler and the National Socialists. The referendum made Adolf Hitler a household name, due to the extensive press coverage he received during the campaign. For the first time, Hitler enjoyed the political credibility he had lacked before. In addition, the huge propaganda campaign organised by the NSDAP for the referendum functioned as a recruitment agency for increased party members and voters.

The early signs of a National Socialist breakthrough really began during the referendum campaign. The changes Hitler had made to party organisation after the 1928 national elections were starting to pay off. He said the referendum campaign created a 'propaganda wave the like of which had never been seen in Germany before'.[55] This helped to increase electoral support for the National Socialists in local elections in the autumn of 1929. In the Baden state elections on 27 October, the NSDAP won 7 per cent of the vote. In the Lübeck city elections, a fortnight later, 8.1 per cent. In Prussia, the party polled 5.3 per cent in the Prussian municipal elections.[56] On 8 December, in the Thuringia state elections, the NSDAP trebled its 1928 vote, recording 11.3 per cent, the highest it had ever recorded. These votes were gained mainly at the expense of the DNVP and the DVP. What these elections showed is that the NSDAP was already emerging as a party of middle-class protest before the full impact of the world economic crisis had hit Germany.[57]

Diplomats at the British Embassy in Berlin alerted the Foreign Office in London to the recent electoral gains of Hitler's National Socialists. On 17 December, Horace Rumbold, the British Ambassador in Berlin, sent a lengthy dispatch to Arthur Henderson, the Foreign Secretary, about what he called the 'unexpected successes' of the National Socialists. Until a few weeks before, Rumbold wrote, the German public outside Bavaria had paid very little attention to Adolf Hitler, but it was becoming clear that Hitler 'has proved more than the leader of a spasmodic movement'. Based on recent results, Rumbold predicted that Hitler could double the seats of the NSDAP from 12 to 24 at the next national elections. His greatest ability, Rumbold observed, was to jumble together slogans from the extreme Right and the extreme Left and mix them, with the promise of a war on capitalism, hatred of liberalism, hostility to parliamentary government, and, above all, the loathing for Jews. These were the principal ingredients of the party programme, which Rumbold thought was full of contradictions.

There was no doubt, Rumbold added, that the National Socialists were gaining ground in elections, and owed their success to the vigour and youthfulness of their followers. Their language was addressed to a German youth deprived of opportunity. They denounced pacifism and praised personal courage. They castigated internationalism and praised xenophobia. They preached against democratic government and praised individuality. 'To my mind,' Rumbold concluded, 'it is the incessant propaganda activity, combined with the ruthless programme of the newcomers, which is impressing the electors at the moment. Among the more sober party orchestras they have the magnetic attraction of a jazz band.'[58]

1930

·

HINDENBURG'S PRESIDENTIAL RULE AND HITLER'S ELECTION BREAK-THROUGH

·

The final details of the Young Plan were reviewed at the Second Hague Conference from 3 to 20 January 1930. All the participants at the first meeting were present once again, plus representatives from the USA, Austria, Bulgaria, and Hungary. The German delegation was led by Julius Curtius, successor to Gustav Stresemann as German Foreign Minister, supported by three other cabinet ministers: Paul Moldenhauer, the Finance Minister, Joseph Wirth, the Minister for the Occupied Territories, and Robert Schmidt, the Economics Minister. One of the key issues discussed was possible sanctions if Germany defaulted on the payment schedule outlined in the Young Plan. Article 430 of the Versailles Treaty already gave the Allies the right to reoccupy the evacuated areas of the Rhineland should Germany fail to meet its obligations. Curtius suggested the issue of German payments should now be left to the Permanent Court of Justice in The Hague. This was accepted, thereby rendering Article 430 invalid.

The next topic to arouse heated discussion was the creation of the International Bank of Settlement, which underpinned all the payments under the Young Plan. On 13 January, Hjalmar Schacht, in typically provocative fashion, declared that the Reichsbank was unwilling to participate in the new bank, unless certain political requirements were met, including the abolition of Allied powers to levy sanctions against Germany. As Schacht had not discussed this matter beforehand, there was deep embarrassment among the German delegation concerning his unwelcome intervention. There followed a meeting between Schacht and the German representatives at the conference. Paul Moldenhauer suggested the Reichsbank should be forced by German law to participate in the new bank. After further discussion, Schacht agreed to this, but this did not end his rebellion On 7 March, Schacht resigned as the President of the Reichsbank, and. was replaced by Hans Luther, the former German Chancellor.[1]

On 20 January 1930, the Second Hague Conference ended with the signing of a protocol in which all the parties fully accepted the terms of the Young Plan. This agreement formally cancelled the

previpous page   President Hindenburg arrives at
Speyer in the Rhineland, July 1930, flanked by State
Secretary Otto Meissner (left), Lieutenant-Colonel
Oskar von Hindenburg and Bavarian prime minister
Heinrich Held (right).

reparations clauses of the Versailles Treaty, scheduled the evacuation of the Rhineland for 30 June 1930, and finally settled all the non-German reparations issues.[2] All that remained was for each government to ratify the plan in their various parliaments. The German Reichsrat, the Upper House of the German parliament, endorsed the plan on 5 February by a vote of 48 to 6. On 12 March, the Young Plan was ratified in the Reichstag by 266 to 193 votes. A no-confidence motion in the Müller government, introduced in the Reichstag by the KPD, was rejected by 277 to 169.

On 13 March, President Hindenburg signed the Young Plan into law. At the same time, he issued a public statement, giving reasons for his actions:

> After thorough and conscientious examination of the Young Plan
> laws, I have, with a heavy, but resolute heart, put my signature to the
> Agreement. Having listened to all the arguments for and against the
> Plan, and having carefully considered both points of view, I have come
> to the conclusion that, in spite of the heavy burdens which the new
> Plan will lay upon Germany's shoulders for many years to come, and in
> spite of the serious objections which may be raised against some of its
> provisions, the Young Plan represents, in comparison with the Dawes
> Plan, an improvement and a relief and a step forward economically
> along the path of Germany's re-establishment and liberation.[3]

With the Young Plan finally agreed, the need for domestic financial reform moved centre stage. Germany was now in the midst of an economic crisis not seen since the dark days of the hyperinflation of 1923, with unemployment exceeding 1.5 million of insured workers. The higher-rank civil servants in the Ministries of Labour and Finance warned that in a few months Germany would be unable to pay unemployment insurance payments.[4]

The financial struggle came to a head on 24 March when Paul Moldenhauer, the Finance Minister, introduced a bill to the Reichstag authorising the Reich Institute of Labour Mediation and Unemployment Insurance to increase the premiums for employers and employees from 3.5 per cent to 4 per cent. Heinrich Brüning, leader of the Zentrum delegation in the Reichstag, suggested a compromise, with premiums frozen for the moment, and the Insurance Fund bolstered by a 150 million Reichsmark loan, but with the proviso that premiums would need to increase later if the economic situation worsened.

Müller supported Brüning's compromise proposal as a means of keeping his government together. He also gained support from Zentrum, the DDP and the DVP, but the SPD Reichstag delegation refused to accept the future possibility of a cut in unemployment benefits. They rejected it, and they were wholeheartedly supported by the trade unions. A further compromise was offered by the Müller government to raise only the rates of worker and employer contributions, to 3.75 per cent. Most of Müller's cabinet were willing to accept this, but Rudolf Wissell, the Minister of Labour, strongly opposed it, suggesting the matter should be referred to the Social Democrat delegation in the Reichstag.

On 27 March, SPD members in the Reichstag rejected the compromise unanimously, and were again supported by the trade unions. Müller summoned his cabinet, telling them he intended to ask President Hindenburg to make use of his emergency powers under Article 48 to push through the national insurance measures, despite the opposition in his own party. The answer came quickly, as Otto Meissner, who represented Hindenburg at cabinet meetings, told Müller the President was not prepared to grant the 'current government' emergency powers. At Müller's suggestion, his cabinet unanimously decided to resign.[5]

The fall of the SPD-led 'Great Coalition' was a deeply significant moment in the history of the Weimar Republic, as it marked the end of truly democratic government. The *Frankfurter Allgemeine Zeitung* (*Frankfurt General Newspaper*) commented: 'Has the Social Democratic Party considered the effects this crisis may have on our entire domestic developments and the prospects of German democracy? Their decision has suddenly made the future dark and unclear. Will we have a dictated budget under Article 48?'[6]

Within an hour of Müller's resignation, Otto Meissner, Chief of the Presidential Chancellery, phoned Heinrich Brüning of Zentrum to tell him the President wanted him to form a new cabinet 'without any fixed ties to parties'. He also invited him to meet with Hindenburg that very evening, but Brüning said he wanted to consult the Zentrum Reichstag delegation beforehand.[7] Hindenburg's plan for a 'presidential cabinet' was now set in motion. The aim was to deprive parliament and the electorate of power, to completely exclude the Social Democrats from government, and to greatly strengthen the power of the President, the Reichswehr, the government bureaucracy and big business. After March 1930, power in the German state was concentrated in the powers of the President under Article 8 of the Constitution, and a Chancellor and cabinet that depended, not on voters or political parties, but on the President's confidence. Power in Weimar Germany now devolved to a small circle of anti-democratic individuals, surrounding the ageing President.[8]

On the morning of 28 March, Hindenburg met Brüning. He told him that he did not think it was wise to construct a government based on a Reichstag coalition. There could no longer be a parliamentary solution. Instead, Hindenburg advised him to create a 'cabinet of personalities', with the support of presidential powers under Article 48 of the Constitution, when necessary. Hindenburg believed this solution would put an end to the endless squabbling of the political parties in the Reichstag, and bring political stability. He promised Brüning: 'You will be my last Chancellor and I will never give you up, but you must make those fellows in the Reichstag come to heel.'[9] Brüning later admitted he took the post because 'I could not resist the President's appeal to my soldier's sense of duty'.[10]

Hindenburg insisted that Brüning retain Wilhelm Groener as Defence Minister, and Georg Schätzel of the BVP as Postal Minister, then bring into the cabinet Martin Schiele (DNVP), who could be relied upon to introduce an emergency programme of relief for German agriculture in the hard-hit provinces east of the Elbe. Schiele resigned his seat as a DNVP member of the Reichstag upon entering the cabinet. Hindenburg also wanted another DNVP rebel, Gottfried Treviranus, a member of the newly formed Conservative People's Party (Konservative Volkspartei, KVP), to join the cabinet.[11]

Heinrich Brüning became German Chancellor on 30 March 1930, and the first presidential cabinet was officially announced to the public as a 'cabinet of personalities' on the same day.[12] Brüning retained seven ministers of the Müller cabinet: Hermann Dietrich (DDP, Vice-Chancellor and Minister of Economics), Julius Curtius (DVP, Foreign Minister), Paul Moldenhauer (DVP, Finance Minister), Georg Schätzel (BVP, Postal Minister), Wilhelm Groener (Independent, Defence Minister), Adam Stegerwald (Zentrum, Minister of Labour), and Theodor von Guérard (Zentrum, Transport Minister). The new cabinet members, all on the Right, were Johann Bredt of the WP as Minister of Justice, Martin Schiele (DNVP but Independent) at Food and Agriculture, and Gottfried Treviranus (KVP) as Minister of the Occupied Territories.[13]

On 1 April, Brüning presented the new government to the Reichstag. As was traditional, he read out the government statement. He referred to President Hindenburg's request for the new cabinet to 'be identified with no party coalition'. This raised immediate doubt from opposition parties as to whether Brüning's government conformed to Article 54 of the Weimar Constitution, which required the Chancellor and his ministers to have the confidence of the Reichstag. Brüning then made clear there would be no change in foreign policy, which would loyally fulfil the existing terms of the Young Plan, and encourage international cooperation, particularly on economic matters. He also promised to introduce measures to deal with the nation's dire economic problems, which required cuts in public expenditure, help for agricultural areas, and the continued subsidisation of unemployment insurance payments. The new Chancellor next warned that he would dissolve the Reichstag and immediately call national elections if its members refused to offer him support, commenting bluntly: 'This cabinet has been formed for the purpose of solving as quickly as possible those problems of vital importance for our nation's existence in the shortest possible time. This will be the last attempt to arrive at a solution with this Reichstag.'[14]

The Social Democrats immediately answered Brüning's blunt government statement by tabling a vote of no confidence, in which they were supported by the KPD. Rudolf Breitscheid, speaking for the SPD, said that if Brüning really wanted to work with the Reichstag he would not have resorted to bullying threats. The Social Democrats had no fear of Brüning's threat to call new elections, but thought an election during an economic crisis was a recipe for chaos. A government against or without the Social Democrats could not survive, he added. Breitscheid then warned Brüning against freely using Article 48 to defy the Reichstag.

The survival of Brüning's government initially depended on the attitude of the DNVP. Most DNVP Reichstag members were inclined to support a government promising agricultural financial aid, though Alfred Hugenberg insisted the DNVP felt no sense of responsibility to keep the Brüning government in power.[15] On 3 April, the no-confidence motion was defeated by 253 votes to 187. The votes of the DNVP proved crucial. At the Nuremberg war crimes trial after the Second World War, Hugenberg claimed he had 'rescued Brüning's government' on this day. The National Socialists were furious with Hugenberg, with Hitler announcing his withdrawal from the National Committee which had been formed to combat the Young Plan.[16]

Brüning and his presidential cabinet urgently needed to take measures to deal with rising unemployment, agricultural depression, and the huge public spending deficit. Brüning was committed to a policy of austerity, wanting to reduce public spending, and achieve a balanced budget, but he also saw the deepening economic crisis as an opportunity to convince the Allies that Germany lacked the financial resources to fulfil the reparations payments demanded by the Young Plan.[17] On 12 April, the Reichstag by a vote of 217 to 206 approved an interim package of tax increases to help balance the budget, consisting of increased sales taxes, including a 50 per cent tax increase on beer, a profit tax of 13.5 per cent on department stores and cooperative stores with a turnover over 1 million Reichsmarks, and an increase in income tax for those earning over 8,400 Reichsmarks per year. But Brüning knew these measures were wholly inadequate to reduce the huge government deficit, which was projected at 436 million Reichsmarks in the coming year.[18]

On 5 June, the cabinet adopted a new financial programme to replace the one adopted on 12 April. The key aim of the revised plan, put together by Paul Moldenhauer, the Finance Minister, was to deal with the government spending deficit. To this end, Moldenhauer announced on 6 June there were now 1.6 million recipients of unemployment benefit and a further 400,000 claiming poor relief, which had raised the deficit on the unemployment insurance fund to 450 million Reichsmarks, with a further 150 million required to bolster the poor relief fund. To deal with these funding shortfalls, Moldenhauer proposed a bleak set of austerity measures including a special 10 per cent tax on unmarried men, extra taxes on fixed salaries, and on fees earned by company directors. It was further proposed to raise national insurance contributions to 4.5 per cent for employers and employees contributing to the unemployment insurance scheme.[19]

Heated political debate ensued on Moldenhauer's new grim austerity measures. There was particularly strong cross-party opposition to the special tax increases on unmarried men, those on fixed incomes, and on company directors. Business leaders and the trade unions bitterly opposed fresh increases in contributions to the unemployment insurance fund. The DVP immediately announced that it would vote against the financial package. This put Moldenhauer, himself a member of the DVP, in a very difficult position. On 18 June, he decided to resign from his post, despite a plea from his cabinet colleagues to defy his party.[20] Hermann Dietrich, the Vice Chancellor, a member of the DDP, replaced him. This did not prevent the battle over the government's financial proposals from escalating. Adam Stegerwald, the Minister of Labour, denied that it was the cost of the unemployment fund that was the cause of the current economic crisis. Hugenberg, the DNVP leader, disagreed, arguing the position of the unemployment insurance fund was hopeless, as the Reich government could not continue to underwrite a scheme that was financially unsustainable.

On 22 June, with the government's budget crisis still unresolved, there came the startling news that the NSDAP had polled 14.43 per cent in the eastern German Free State of Saxony state elections, the highest total recorded by the party in any election and an increase of 9 per cent on the previous state election. The NSDAP vote was some way behind the Social Democrats, who polled 33.4 per cent, but slightly ahead of the KPD, on 13.6 per cent. The NSDAP gains came mainly at the expense of the DNVP, the DVP and the DDP. The result offered solid evidence that Hitler's party was on the verge of a major electoral breakthrough.[21]

On 30 June, the Allies finally completed the evacuation of the Rhineland. President Hindenburg issued a proclamation, signed by all the members of Brüning's cabinet, to mark what he called the 'Day of Liberation', but it failed to mention Gustav Stresemann's pivotal role in negotiating the early evacuation. Instead, Hindenburg stressed the obligation he still felt for Germany's war dead, and he even called for an early return of the Saar coal mining region to German hands.[22] Sir Horace Rumbold, the British Ambassador, commented to Arthur Henderson, the British Foreign Secretary: 'The [Hindenburg] manifesto appears to me to exemplify two of the besetting weaknesses of the German character, ingratitude, and tactlessness.'[23]

The cabinet agreed, on 9 July, to Hermann Dietrich's idea of imposing a new additional tax on all government employees of 2.5 per cent, and a uniform 'citizen tax' commonly known as a poll tax on every person, regardless of income.[24] On 15 July, Dietrich's financial package was debated in the Reichstag. Brüning, speaking forcefully, said the nation wanted action on the budget deficit, and he urged Reichstag members to pass the measures. He then emphasised that if parliament should fail in this duty, then the government would have to make use of all constitutional means to cover the budgetary deficit, implying Article 48 would be invoked by the President.[25]

On the next day, the Reichstag voted on Article 2 of Dietrich's budget programme, concerning the special tax on government employees and the poll tax. Both measures were defeated by a vote of 256 to 193, with the Social Democrats, Communists, National Socialists, and a majority of Nationalists all voting against. Brüning immediately declared that no useful purpose would be served by further parliamentary discussion on the matter.[26] During the evening, the cabinet passed the two emergency decrees the Reichstag had rejected, using presidential authority under Article 48. As soon as the Social Democrats heard this news, they tabled a motion in the Reichstag under Paragraph 3 of Article 48, to nullify the two emergency decrees, arguing public order was not endangered, which was stipulated as the key criterion for the use of Article 48 in such a manner.

Brüning now entered negotiations with Hugenberg in the hope the DNVP leader would support him, rather than face national elections which were likely to result in a loss of voter support, given the party's recent heavy losses to the National Socialists in Saxony. On 17 July, Hugenberg offered to support an adjournment of the Reichstag until the autumn, in return for a promise that Brüning would topple Otto Braun's SPD-led state government in Prussia. In reply, Brüning told him he had no power to depose a democratically elected government.[27]

On 18 July, the vote on the SPD motion to reject Brüning's emergency decrees was passed by the narrow margin of 236 to 221. Brüning then rose to announce the President had given him the power to order a dissolution of the Reichstag, and new national elections. In his memoirs, Julius Curtius recalled: 'In those decisive hours I implored the Chancellor not to take the fateful step of dissolution.' In response, Brüning told Curtius that he felt obligated to protect the President's authority using Article 48, after it was threatened by the nullification of the emergency decrees in the Reichstag.[28]

The Reichstag was thus dissolved, with new national elections set for 14 September 1930. The Social Democratic motion demanding the revocation of the emergency decrees had prevailed narrowly, thanks to those DNVP member who swung enough votes to defeat Brüning. Only a primitive death-wish can explain why Hugenberg supported new elections, at which it seemed his party faced huge losses. On 26 July Hindenburg issued, as emergency decrees, all the measures that had been rejected by the Reichstag, in the form of a law 'For the Relief of Financial, Economic and Social Distress'. This was the first instance of a bill rejected by the Reichstag being made law in this way. It was a procedure German constitutional experts at the time declared dictatorial and unconstitutional.

As Weimar descended yet again into political crisis, innovations in popular culture were continuing. On 1 April, *Der blaue Engel* (*The Blue Angel*), directed by Austrian-born Hollywood director Josef von

overleaf Marlene Dietrich as Lola
in *The Blue Angel* (1930).

Sternberg and produced by UFA, premiered in Berlin. It was the first full-length German 'talking' film, shot simultaneously in German and English language versions. The German version is longer and superior, and not marred by the actors struggling with English pronunciation.[29]

The film, shot between November 1929 and January 1930, was based on Heinrich Mann's 1905 novel, *Professor Unrat* (*Professor Filth*), which tells the story of the downfall of a respectable middle-aged school-teacher, who falls in love with a young cabaret singer. The setting of the film in a cabaret nightclub made musical performances an integral part of the story. A running motif in the film is a church clock, which chimes a popular German song, '*Üb immer Treu und Redlichkeit*' (Always Be True and Faithful), which is also played at the very end of the film.[30]

The film featured the goatee-bearded Professor Immanuel Rath, a 57-year-old grammar-school teacher, played by Emil Jannings, and a travelling nightclub cabaret singer, Rosa Fröhlich, better known by her stage name, Lola Lola, who is played by Marlene Dietrich. During the 1930s Dietrich starred in several more films directed by Sternberg, which made her, for a time, the highest paid actor in Hollywood.[31] In *The Blue Angel*, Dietrich performs her classic song 'Falling in Love Again (Can't Help It)', with music by Friedrich Hollaender, English lyrics by Sammy Lerner, and German lyrics by Robert Liebmann (under the title '*Ich bin von Kopf bis Fuss auf Liebe eingestellt*' (literally, 'I am from head to toe ready for love'). All the other songs Dietrich sings in the film, such as '*Ich bin die fesche Lola*' ('They Call Me Naughty Lola') and '*Nimm Dich in Acht vor blonden Frauen*' ('Beware Blond Women'), reveal Lola's primary interest is in sex, not in a long-term relationship. Dietrich's own private life immediately attracted great attention, with one newspaper dubbing her 'perhaps the busiest and most passionate bisexual person in theatrical Berlin'.[32]

Mann's novel was adapted for the screen by novelist Carl Zuckmayer and the screenwriters Karl Vollmöller and Robert Liebmann, with some input from Sternberg. In the film, Rath follows his students through nocturnal streets to a seedy nightclub, the Blue Angel, located in an unnamed port town, to put a stop to their frequent visits to the club. Once inside, Rath sees the charismatic and sexually exciting star of the cabaret show, Lola Lola, singing '*Kinder heut abend da such ich mir was aus*' (in the English lyrics, 'A Man, just a Regular Man').

After the show, Rath makes his way through the crowded club to Lola's dressing room, and asks her if she will help him to stop his students visiting the club. On the next night, now besotted, Rath returns to see Lola again, but this time he gives her a gift of a pair of panties. They then have a lengthy conversation in her dressing-room. She compliments him by saying 'You're a fine-looking man' and playfully calls him 'Mama's little pet'. They share a bottle of champagne, then he watches her seductive cabaret performance, and he ends up staying the night with her in her apartment. After returning to school on the next morning, the principal, who has heard about Rath's antics at the Blue Angel from his students, requests his immediate resignation. Rath returns to the Blue Angel, presents Lola with flowers, gives her a wedding ring, and asks her to marry him. Lola accepts. Rath then becomes completely dependent on her. His final humiliation comes when he appears as a clown in her travelling cabaret show, and even sells pornographic postcards of his wife during intervals. He becomes increasingly possessive and jealous of Lola, who gradually loses all respect for him.

The travelling cabaret show finally returns to the Blue Angel, in his home town, at the end of a tour. His old students turn out to see their former teacher, now reduced to playing a hapless clown, being humiliated by a magician, who insults him and cracks eggs on his bald head. Rath then gives a shrieking rendition of a cock crowing 'cock-a-doodle-doo'. He looks behind the stage curtain to see Lola kissing and embracing Mazeppa, the show's strongman, played by Hans Albers, who is now her new love interest. In a jealous rage, Rath tries to strangle Lola, but is subdued by Mazeppa, and other members of the show, who put him in a straitjacket. Later on the same night, Rath is released. He leaves the nightclub, as Lola is singing 'Falling in Love Again (Can't Help It)', and walks through dark, snow-covered streets, back to his old school. Humiliated, rejected, broken-hearted, and alone, he dies, seemingly of a heart attack, slumped on the desk at which he once taught.

The Blue Angel was a huge box office success, breaking all previous records in German cinema. It received rave reviews, hailed as 'the first artistic sound film'. The performances of Dietrich and Jannings earned unanimous acclaim, as did all the popular songs featured. All the critics highlighted Dietrich's brilliant portrayal of Lola as a charismatic, sexually empowered, liberated woman, a filmic representation of the Weimar 'new woman'. Jannings was praised for his undoubted skill at playing tragic characters, as he had previously done in F.W. Murnau's *The Last Laugh* (1924), and Victor Fleming's *The Way of the Flesh* (1927).

Leading German critic Wolf Zucker claimed that due to its use of sound and its overall technical quality, he was ready to name *The Blue Angel* as 'the best German film'. In his 1965 autobiography, Sternberg, the director, claimed that when Adolf Hitler became German Chancellor he ordered the destruction of all copies of *The Blue Angel*, except for one copy, which he viewed repeatedly, and he often told members of his inner circle that it was his favourite film.[33]

The cabaret club portrayed in *The Blue Angel* was later copied in the famous 1972 Hollywood film musical *Cabaret*, set in the Weimar period, in which Liza Minnelli played a young American called Sally Bowles, who was also clearly inspired by Lola Lola. The key addition to *Cabaret* was the demonic master of ceremonies played by Joel Gray. In fact, a master of ceremonies in the Weimar period was known as the Conférencier, and was much more than simply a presenter between the acts, but rather a good-natured host, who talked to the audience, and commented on current events and personalities. One of the most famous Weimar Conférenciers was Werner Finck, who became known for his impudent remarks against the National Socialists. He was the Conférencier at the Catacomb Club (Die Katakombe), in Bellevuestrasse, Berlin. Finck would often raise his hand in the Hitler salute and say: 'That's how deep we are in this shit'; and if there were National Socialists in the audience he would say: 'No, I'm not Jewish. I only look intelligent.'[34]

Cabaret venues in Berlin during the Weimar years were diverse and abundant, with 899 venues registered in 1930. In 1931, Curt Moreck published his famous and racy *Guide to Depraved Berlin*, which offered tourists a guide to the numerous sexual pleasures on offer in the various clubs in the city. The socialist-led city authorities were proud Berlin was seen as the most open, tolerant, and decadent city in the world. Some Berlin cabaret clubs gave their customers drugs such as cocaine and morphine upon entry. Prostitution flourished, with performers in the show often soliciting customers after performances. Cross-dressing was perfectly legal in Berlin, which explains why in many of the clubs the most popular acts were often male and female impersonators, with women in top hats and tails and men in cocktail dresses.

Most Berlin clubs featured brash and provocative nude dancing. The most famous and uninhibited nude dancer on the Berlin cabaret scene was the pioneering Anita Berber, who was the subject of a famous Otto Dix painting, and appeared in 27 silent films. She was openly bisexual, and had torrid affairs with both men and women,

The cabaret dance star Anita Berber poses for a fashion magazine.

overleaf A costumed singing group of six perform with mandolins in a Berlin revue, *c.*1928.

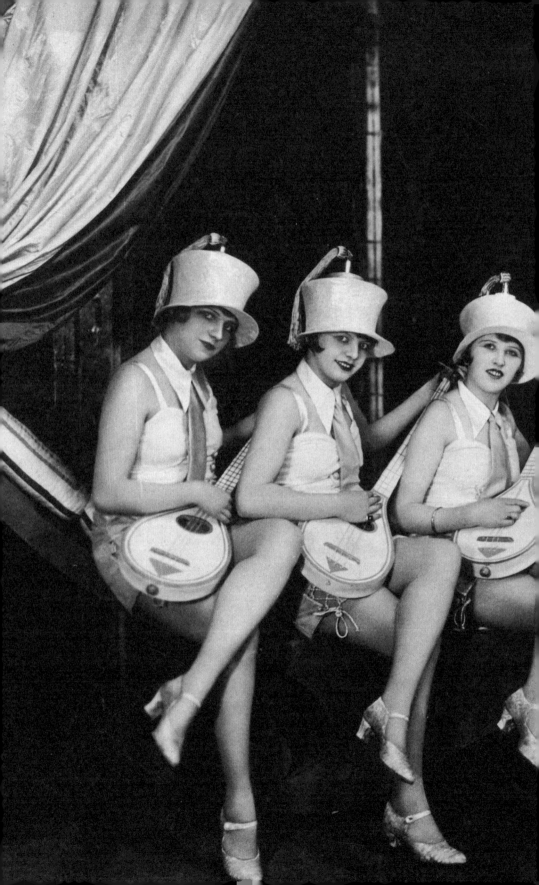

including Marlene Dietrich. She wore heavy make-up, including jet black lipstick, and cut her hair in the classic short bob style, often dyed red. She came on stage wearing a tuxedo and a monocle, but not for long. Her expressionist solo nude dances broke all the boundaries of permissible eroticism. She behaved outrageously, often dancing naked on customers' tables, and smashing bottles of champagne on the heads of hecklers. Off stage, her addictions to alcohol, cocaine and morphine attracted newspaper gossip columns. She died on 10 November 1928 from severe tuberculosis, but it was drug abuse that was the real cause of her premature death.[35] Another popular Berlin cabaret performer, Gerda Redlich, later recalled: 'In cabaret you could see your audience sitting and drinking at tables. It was a good atmosphere. A literary Cabaret would have a Conférencier, introducing each musical act with a lot of satire added. There would be a series of songs, comedy sketches, poetry, and some particularly good dancing. It was always topical and political.'[36]

The dissolution of the Reichstag in July 1930 once again revealed the paralysis of Germany's parliamentary system. It also marked the beginning of a bitter election campaign, fought against the background of a deepening economic crisis. The campaign was far more turbulent than any that had preceded it, with no less than 37 different political parties seeking votes.

The Zentrum election campaign was opened on 29 July, with a speech by the party leader, Ludwig Kaas, who denied the oft-repeated charge that Brüning had deliberately engineered the fall of the Müller government. Kaas emphasised the Centre Party did not want to overthrow democracy, but to save it. A speech by Brüning followed, arguing that after the election the new Reichstag needed to decide whether it wanted to support a balanced budget or not.[37]

On 19 July, the DNVP opened its election campaign, with a strongly worded proclamation issued by Hugenberg under the slogan 'Make the Right-wing Strong', which urged all patriotic Germans to rally in defence of the Fatherland. On 24 July, in a speech at a party strategy conference in Berlin, Hugenberg defended his decision to force Brüning to dissolve the Reichstag, and suggested the party would be more united now all the 'conservative rebels' had departed. Hugenberg decided the DNVP election campaign would concentrate on denouncing Brüning's government, along with the Social Democrats, and all the other parties who were responsible for the current political and economic crisis. In Hugenberg's view this could only be ended by a radical change of the existing political system, and an end of the financially disastrous Young Plan.[38] Interestingly, the DNVP campaign decided not to attack the National Socialist Party, as Hugenberg thought Hitler would gain support at the expense of the Social Democrats. Even so, the DNVP entered the election campaign a bitterly divided party. Of the 78 DNVP Reichstag members elected in 1928, only 37 still supported the party at the time of the election. A recently formed breakaway group, the KVP, led by Gottfried Treviranus, aimed to gain votes at the expense of the DNVP, and several other party dissidents had joined the CNBL. Added to this, the party struggled to secure enough funding for the election campaign from industrialists who had previously bank-rolled the party.[39]

The middle-class parties all sensed a merging of their forces was necessary if democracy were to survive. Early in the election campaign, the middle-class liberal parties decided to regroup their forces, at the instigation of the DDP, which had been in electoral decline for most of the 1920s. On 28 July, the DDP merged with the Young People's Reich Association to form the German State Party (Deutsche Staatspartei, DStP). This new party promptly issued an election manifesto, in which it declared that many German people were demanding a right-wing dictatorship, while others were calling for a proletarian regime, but the new party stood for both private enterprise and social justice. It did not believe Germans wanted lawlessness and violence, but it admitted the Reichstag had failed to create a sense of national unity and had become a disunited collection of special interest groups. The DStP stood firmly behind the Weimar Constitution. Ernst Scholz, the leader of the DVP, proposed a merger of his own party with all the other middle-class parties to form a single State Party, but this initiative failed to attract support.[40]

The SPD was clearly on the defensive, after being in government for the previous two years. The party promised not to place the interests of the state above the interests of the working class. SPD election leaflets defended the record of the Müller governments, and claimed the use of Article 48 by Brüning's 'anti-democratic' government signalled the end of parliamentary democracy. The SPD further promised to use their strength in the Reichstag and in state governments to safeguard democracy and unemployment insurance benefits, and oppose wage and public spending cuts.[41]

The KPD campaign was based on the theory of 'social fascism', which was adopted at the party congress in 1929. The priority was to brand the SPD as part of the 'capitalist enemy'. The KPD called Social Democrat support for the Young Plan as 'high treason against the interests of Germany's working class'. Ernst Thälmann, the KPD leader, argued that his party had 'led the struggle against the Versailles Treaty of shame at a time when no one had even heard of the National Socialists.'[42]

The unknown quantity in the 1930 election campaign was the NSDAP, led by Adolf Hitler. At the May 1928 national elections, the party had polled only 2.37 per cent of votes (810,127), gaining just 12 Reichstag members, but the involvement of the party in the campaign against the Young Plan during the latter part of 1929 had led to noticeable increases in vote share in recent state and local elections.[43]

In the spring of 1930, Hitler had appointed Joseph Goebbels to lead party propaganda. Goebbels created a modern and sophisticated election propaganda machine for the NSDAP, which was centrally controlled from Munich. He introduced opinion surveys to see what the voters wanted in every electoral district, then sent out direct mail-shots tailored to specific occupational groups, culled from local address books, and distributed thousands of leaflets. There were also party postcards, stickers, brochures, films, slide shows, brass bands,

and torchlight parades, but most of all there were numerous election meetings, heavily advertised, with 1,500 specially selected speakers, all trained in newly created National Socialist Speaker Schools. As Goebbels put it: 'We want to create a campaign such as the corrupt parliamentary parties have never seen before.' On 18 August, the *Völkischer Beobachter* announced that 34,000 rallies were planned in the last four weeks of the campaign.[44] Door to door canvassers pushed the National Socialist message with a passion that rivalled even that of the Communists. Goebbels' greatest strength was to recognise that national elections in Weimar Germany were often in effect local and regional contests, with local issues often predominating.

The National Socialist campaign now shifted its focus away from attracting working-class votes in the big cities towards winning over rural voters. In rural areas, the NSDAP promised a new deal for farmers and agricultural workers; security of tenure to restore the farmer's independent status was a key pledge. In the big cities, Jewish financial exploitation was highlighted. The left-wing press suggested big business was behind the sudden NSDAP election propaganda blitz, but this was incorrect. There was some limited support from big business, but the bulk of the finance for the election campaign came from party members' subscriptions, donations and ticket sales from meetings and speeches.[45]

On 19 July, Hitler laid out the broad parameters of the party's election campaign at a meeting in Munich. The big theme of campaign was a frontal attack on all the Weimar pro-Republican parties, under the slogan: 'Fight the Young Plan Parties'. The NSDAP campaign avoided discussions of specific policies, but instead concentrated on promising to destroy the 'corrupt, ineffectual Weimar system' which had led to political fragmentation and the growth of a plethora of 'rotten and fragile' political parties. Hitler's appeal to voters was not the usual promise to improve material conditions, but an emotional appeal to the idea of national unity.

Hitler went on a nationwide speaking tour during the campaign. Between 3 August and 14 September he delivered 20 speeches before huge audiences, mainly in big cities. In all these, Hitler denounced 'the Weimar system', run by the 'November Criminals', which he claimed was the key reason for Germany's political paralysis,[46] and he promised to replace 'the sham of party politics' with strong leadership and then create a new 'racially pure' national community, which would revive and then liberate the German people.[47]

'Let's make the right wing strong!': a German National People's Party (DNVP) poster for the September 1930 German national elections. It would in fact be Hitler's Nazi Party, not the DNVP, that saw an impressive surge in support.

On 14 September 1930, the German national elections took place. Voter turnout was 82 per cent, up by 6.4 per cent from the previous election. The big election winner was undoubtedly Hitler's NSDAP, which polled 18.3 per cent of votes (6.37 million), up 15.7 per cent from the previous election. It was the biggest surge of support by any party in a single election during the Weimar years. The NSDAP won 107 seats, up from 12 in May 1928, and was now the second most popular party in Germany, behind the Social Democrats. Those Germans who voted for Hitler sent a tremor of amazement and fear around the world. Hitler had astonishingly surged into the mainstream of German politics. His promise to come to power legally through the ballot box no longer seemed the rantings of a rabble-rousing extremist. Joseph Goebbels noted in his diary: 'Joy for us and despair for our enemies. In one fell swoop, 107 seats. Hitler is beside himself with joy.'[48]

Only four of the other main parties in the election managed to increase their number of seats. The first was the far-left KPD, which polled 13.1 per cent (4.59 million), up 2.5 per cent from 1928, winning 77 seats, an increase of 23 from the previous election. The party gained support in the areas suffering from the highest levels of unemployment, mainly in industrial areas of the big cities.[49]

The second party resisting the National Socialist voting surge was Zentrum, which won 68 seats, up from 61 in the previous election, polling 11.8 per cent (4.12 million), which was slightly down, by 0.3 per cent on the previous election. The third party to hold its own was the BVP, which was also linked to Catholicism. The BVP polled 1.10 million (3.03 per cent), a slight reduction of 0.04 per cent, but with 19 seats, an increase of two. In general, Catholic regions viewed the NSDAP as a 'pagan party' and Catholics demonstrated a firm loyalty to Zentrum. Hitler believed Catholic resistance to his party was due to the strong opposition of Catholic priests to National Socialism. In the small rural village of Waldsee, for example, the local priest had warned parishioners 'whoever votes for Hitler will have to justify themselves on the Judgement Day. There is no bigger sin than voting for Hitler.'[50]

The fourth party to hold its own in direct competition with the NSDAP was the CNBL, a small rural-focused party, which took 3.03 per cent of votes (1.10 million), up 1.31 per cent from 1928, with an increase of seats from 9 to 19. Overall, small special interest parties such as this held their ground, with their total vote share unchanged at 13.8 per cent.

The SPD lost some ground in the 1930 elections, but was not as heavily hit by the remarkable NSDAP surge in voter support as other parties. It remained the largest party in the Reichstag, with 143 seats, a loss of just 10 from the previous election, polling 24.5 per cent of the vote (8.57 million), down by 5.3 per cent. SPD losses were mainly at the expense of the KPD.

The biggest election loser was the DNVP, led by Alfred Hugenberg. Indeed, Hugenberg's attempt to unite the Right of German politics during the election campaign had paved the way for Hitler's breakthrough. The DNVP popular vote fell from 14.2 per cent in 1928 to 7.2 per cent (2.45 million), with a drop in seats from 73 to 32. One in every three people who voted for the DNVP in 1928 had switched their allegiance to Hitler in 1930. The bitter divisions in the party in the run-up to the election had clearly alienated many of these traditional voters.[51]

The middle-class liberal parties also performed badly in the election. The DVP continued its decline, recording 4.5 per cent of the popular vote (1.57 million), down by 4.2 per cent from May 1928, with its seats down from 45 to 30. The newly formed DStP polled 3.78 per cent (1.32 million), and took 20 seats, which was five less than the DDP had won at the 1928 election. The other breakaway party from the DNVP, the newly formed KVP, gained a miserable 0.83 per cent (290,579), and won just four seats. The swing voters of these traditional middle-class parties had all moved to the NSDAP.[52]

Given the horrors that followed, it now seems impossible to understand why German people of their own free will could vote in such large numbers for a party pledged to destroy democracy. In Dresden, Victor Klemperer, an academic at Dresden University, wrote in his diary: '107 National Socialists. What a humiliation! How close are we to civil war!'[53] In contrast, the Nobel Prize-winning physicist Albert Einstein told the Jewish Telegraphic Agency there was no reason for despair over Hitler's strong showing in the national elections because 'it was only a symptom, not necessarily of anti-Jewish hatred, but was caused by unemployment and economic misery within the ranks of misguided youth'.[54]

It seems 24 per cent of NSDAP voters were voting in an election for the first time, many of them young people and pensioners, 22 per cent of new NSDAP voters had previously voted for the DNVP, with 18 per cent moving from the middle-class liberal parties, and 14 per cent from the Social Democrats. In sum, the biggest movement of voters to the NSDAP came from the middle-class conservative and liberal parties, and the party received the least swing votes from the KPD and Zentrum. There was also a strong reluctance to vote NSDAP in the big cities with large working-class industrial workers.[55]

The most impressive gains for the NSDAP were in Protestant rural areas, especially those of northern and eastern Germany stretching from Schleswig-Holstein to East Prussia. The party performed very well in large northern states such as Pomerania, Mecklenburg, Hanover, Brunswick and Oldenburg, and achieved comparable results in predominantly Protestant Franconia and Hesse-Nassau.[56] Voting support in these areas came primarily from elements of the lower middle class: small shopkeepers, farmers, self-employed tradespeople such as builders, plumbers, electricians and joiners, but there was also an upswing of support from middle-class white-collar workers, lower civil servants, teachers and university students. It was these who would represent the party's core voters during its rise to power, but the NSDAP was not simply a 'middle-class protest party,' as was once thought. It is now clear Hitler's party was able to gain support from all sections of society in a way the other political parties could not.[57]

It was not, as is often supposed, primarily economic misery that drove voters to the NSDAP. Hitler's campaign had focused on the failure of the Weimar political system to solve Germany's problems, and this issue seems to have struck a far stronger chord with voters than the state of the economy. There was a growing loss of confidence in the Weimar political system, which made the decision to vote for a party that was not tainted by involvement in that system much easier.[58] An editorial in the *Frankfurter Zeitung* spoke of an 'election of embitterment' in which voters expressed deep disaffection with 'the methods of governing or rather non-governing' of parliamentary government.[59]

Hitler's dramatic election breakthrough had a devastating impact abroad. There was a large withdrawal of gold and foreign currency from the Reichsbank, and a sharp fall in German stocks on international markets. Even larger German banks were shaken by the wave of panic selling. Julius Curtius, the Foreign Minister, who was in Geneva while the League of Nations was in session, reported when he heard the results: 'the mood was one of the greatest alarm'.[60] The world now started taking much greater interest in Adolf Hitler. *The Times*, on 16 September, observed:

Though their tactics certainly embody violence and their respect for the ordinary decencies of law has been scant, the Nazis have scored their overwhelming success because they have appealed to something more fundamental and more respectable. Like the Italian Fascists they stand for some national ideal, however nebulous, and poorly expressed, to which personal and class interests shall be subordinate.[61]

After the election, Hitler gave many interviews to the foreign press, presenting himself as a patriotic politician whose goal was to relieve Germany of the financial burdens placed upon it by the Treaty of Versailles and the Young Plan. Rothay Reynolds, a journalist with the British *Daily Mail*, interviewed the NSDAP leader, and wrote approvingly:

Hitler speaks with great simplicity and great earnestness. There was not a trace in his manner of those arts which political leaders are apt to employ when they wish to impress. I was conscious that I was talking to a man whose power lies not, as many still think, in his eloquence and in his ability to hold the attention of the crowd, but in his convictions.[62]

Another consequence of Hitler's success at the polls was a genuine fear of a National Socialist revolution, supported by the Army. It soon became clear such anxiety was not ill-founded. From 23 September to 4 October 1930, the Supreme Court in Leipzig heard a case in which Richard Scheringer, Hans Wendt and Hanns Ludin were charged with 'Preparing to Commit High Treason'. The three Reichswehr lieutenants from a garrison in Ulm, Baden-Württemberg, were charged with illegally being members of the NSDAP, which was prohibited for army members, of travelling around Germany trying to persuade other young German officers to join the NSDAP, and of planning revolution.

The high point of the trial came on 25 September when Adolf Hitler, who was called by the National Socialist defence lawyer, Hans Frank, to give evidence, entered the witness box. He denied any involvement in the activities of the three young officers, and declared his wish 'to acquire the power of the state by legal means', but he then promised, menacingly: 'When our party emerges victorious by legal means, a new Supreme Court will replace this one, and the criminals of November 1918 will find their reward. Then heads will roll.'[63] The court found the three accused officers guilty of treason. Each was sentenced to 18 months in prison and dismissed from the Reichswehr.

German Chancellor Heinrich Brüning met Adolf Hitler for the very first time on 5 October, to discuss whether the NSDAP would offer 'loyal opposition' to his government. Brüning made clear to Hitler beforehand that he wanted the meeting to remain confidential. It took place in the Berlin apartment of Brüning's close cabinet colleague, Gottfried Treviranus. Hitler was accompanied by Gregor Strasser and Wilhelm Frick. Brüning told Hitler his economic austerity programme was an attempt to get the Allies to reduce, and then to cancel, Germany's reparations payments under the Young Plan. He made no promise of bringing Hitler into the cabinet, but did offer him the prospect of Zentrum later forming coalitions in State parliaments with the NSDAP, wherever the two parties had a combined majority.[64]

Though clearly nervous, Hitler answered with a monologue that went on for over an hour. It amounted to a denunciation of all the enemies of National Socialism at home and abroad. 'Ever more frequently', Brüning later recalled, he used the word 'annihilating', first directed at the SPD, then against the 'reactionaries', and finally against France as our 'arch-enemy' and Russia as 'the hot-bed of Bolshevism'. When he was part of the government, Hitler said, he would insist Germany put down all these enemies.' At the end of the meeting, Brüning decided Hitler was a fanatic, a 'cheap imitation of Mussolini, interested in nothing but power', and he ruled out involving the NSDAP in the government.[65]

At first Hitler boasted to Goebbels that he had made a tremendous impression on Brüning, but a few weeks later he admitted Brüning had not really taken him seriously as a politician, and he developed a strong animosity towards the German Chancellor.[66] Gregor Strasser felt that Hitler had been impressed by the Chancellor, and his subsequent animosity was a result of the feelings of inferiority he had felt in his presence.[67]

President Hindenburg decided after the election that Brüning and his cabinet must remain in power. Brüning had already announced on 30 September that if the Reichstag rejected his financial programme he would resort once again to Article 48. He had little choice, as the parties supporting his government had been reduced to 193 out of 577 Reichstag members following the September election. The dramatic surge of voter support for Hitler presented the Social Democrats with an uncomfortable dilemma. They detested Brüning's austerity programme, but they also feared the NSDAP joining the Brüning government to create a full-blown right-wing dictatorship. The SPD therefore decided to tolerate the Brüning cabinet and prevent it losing any vote of confidence in the Reichstag. In return, Brüning secretly promised the SPD would be allowed to introduce amendments to his financial measures.[68]

On the opening day of the new Reichstag, on 13 October, a large cohort of National Socialists, dressed in their brown Stormtrooper uniforms, were in a rowdy mood. Since the wearing of uniforms was forbidden under Prussian law, the NSDAP Reichstag members had smuggled their uniforms into the parliament building and changed their clothes there. They chanted National Socialist slogans, shouted down cabinet ministers, and repeatedly baited the Social Democrats and the Communists. They created so much disorder and pandemonium that the proceedings were repeatedly suspended.[69]

On 16 October, Brüning appeared before the Reichstag to request support for his financial programme. Brüning called for prompt action to deal with the worsening economic situation. In essence, Brüning wanted the Reichstag to continue with the existing emergency decrees issued on 26 July, but to cut public expenditure even further, and raise more taxes to raise government revenue, Brüning said these new measures were necessary to continue the social insurance scheme for the unemployed, and to offer financial support to agriculture in the eastern provinces. He announced contributions for employers and employees in the social insurance scheme would rise from 4.5 to 6.5 per cent. There would also be a 6 per cent pay cut for all federal, state and municipal employees, and a reduction in federal subsidies to state governments, plus an increase in the tobacco tax.[70]

On 17 October, Hermann Müller rose to speak for the Social Democrats, at which point the National Socialist members rose as one and noisily left the chamber. Müller made it clear the Social Democrats would not support the various no-confidence motions tabled by the Communists, the DNVP and the National Socialists. The actions of the SPD, he added, were a recognition of the current political realities and motivated by a desire to protect the Constitution.

The prolonged and bitter Reichstag debate on the new financial measures ended on 18 October. The motion to prevent Brüning's emergency decrees proceeding to the Reichstag committee was defeated by 339 to 220. The various motions of no confidence vote were all defeated by 318 to 236. The Reichstag next proceeded to vote itself a recess until 3 December. Thanks to the votes of the Social

overleaf Police outside the Berlin cinema showing the premiere of the Hollywood film adaptation of *All Quiet on the Western Front*, 5 December 1930. The screening was cancelled following violent disruption by Nazi Stormtroopers, and the film would soon be banned across Germany.

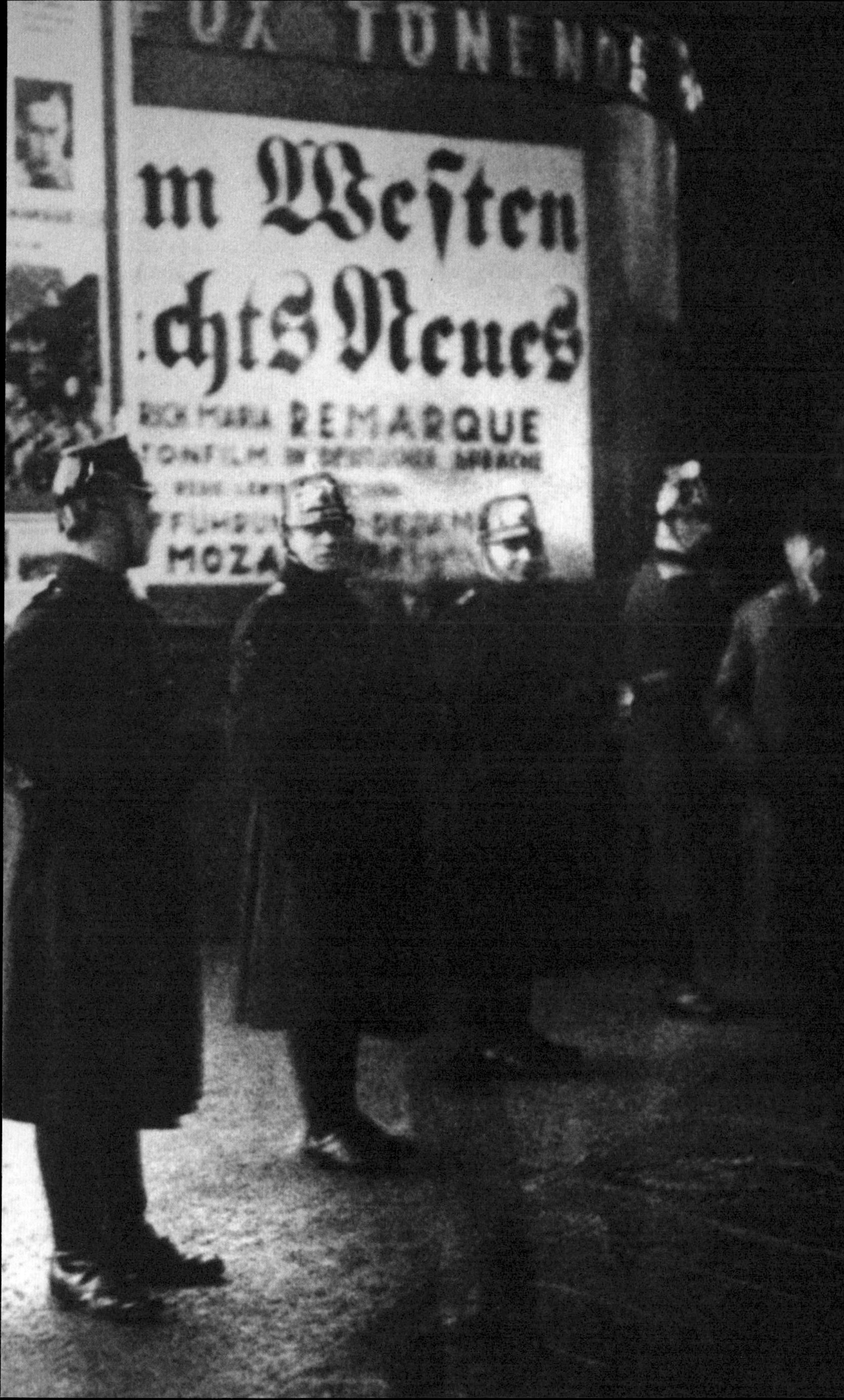
OX TÖNENDE
m Westen
chts Neues
REMARQUE

Democrats, the Brüning government had survived its first battle with the Reichstag.[71]

On 3 December, the Reich budget for 1931/32 was presented to the Reichstag by Hermann Dietrich, the Minister of Finance. He declared that the government, while discussing proposals to reduce the government spending deficit, had decided not to overburden industry since increased production was vital to the nation's economic recovery. Gottfried Feder, speaking for the National Socialists, claimed the government had no right to stay in office, as it had not yet received a vote of confidence from the Reichstag. To clarify the position, he added, the NSDAP would introduce such a motion. The Communists claimed a Fascist dictatorship was already in place, with Germany ruled by the President using Article 48 to throttle parliament and the Social Democrats now propping up this undemocratic system. On 6 December, all the no-confidence resolutions were defeated by 291 to 256 votes. The Reichstag also rejected a motion calling for the suspension of the First Emergency Decree to Secure the Economy and Public Finances, signed by Hindenburg on 1 December, which put into effect the measures Brüning had announced on 16 October, by a margin of 293 to 253.[72]

After six more days of rowdy incidents, mostly involving the National Socialists, the Reichstag finally adjourned for its Christmas holidays. The practice of convening the Reichstag only for brief discussions and to pass laws, then suspending it for long intervals, now became the central way that Brüning governed Germany, with the blessing of President Hindenburg.[73] From 1920 to 1930, the Reichstag had sat for an average of 100 days a year. Between the September 1930 elections and March 1931, it met 50 times. Between March 1931 and July 1932, it was convened on only 24 days. After that, the Reichstag only met three times. In its place came emergency decrees, signed by President Hindenburg, using Article 48, with five in 1930, 43 in 1931 and 57 in 1932.[74]

Inside parliament, the National Socialists had so far achieved extraordinarily little by their obstructive tactics. Outside, it was a different story. On 5 December, the Hollywood film *All Quiet on the Western Front*, an adaption of Erich Remarque's anti-war novel, premiered at the Mozartsaal cinema on Nollendorfplatz in Berlin. A demonstration by National Socialist Stormtroopers, led by Joseph Goebbels, disrupted the event, by smashing windows and forcing their way into the theatre, throwing stink bombs, releasing white mice, and attacking members of the audience. Goebbels argued the film was anti-German, and deeply insulting to soldiers who had fought in the Great War. In his diary, Goebbels noted: 'After 10 minutes the cinema resembled a madhouse… The police sympathized with us. The screening was cancelled, as was a second one. We've won.'[75]

During the following week, the demonstrations spread to countless movie theatres showing the film throughout Germany. On 11 December, Germany's Board of Censors meekly capitulated to National Socialist pressure by banning screenings of *All Quiet on the Western Front*, but insisted the ban had not been implemented due to recent public protests, but because the Board had decided the film was detrimental to German's prestige, dwelled too much on Germany's defeat in the Great War, and gave an unfair depiction of the German military as brutal and cruel.[76] The *Manchester Guardian* described the decision to ban the film, which was endorsed by Wilhelm Groener, the Minister of Defence, as 'a capitulation before the organised mob', and predicted the consequences for Germany would be far-reaching, 'for a German crowd only has to make a great deal of noise and get any film, play, book or picture suppressed. In his diary, Goebbels noted: 'The National Socialist street is dictating the behaviour of the government.'[77]

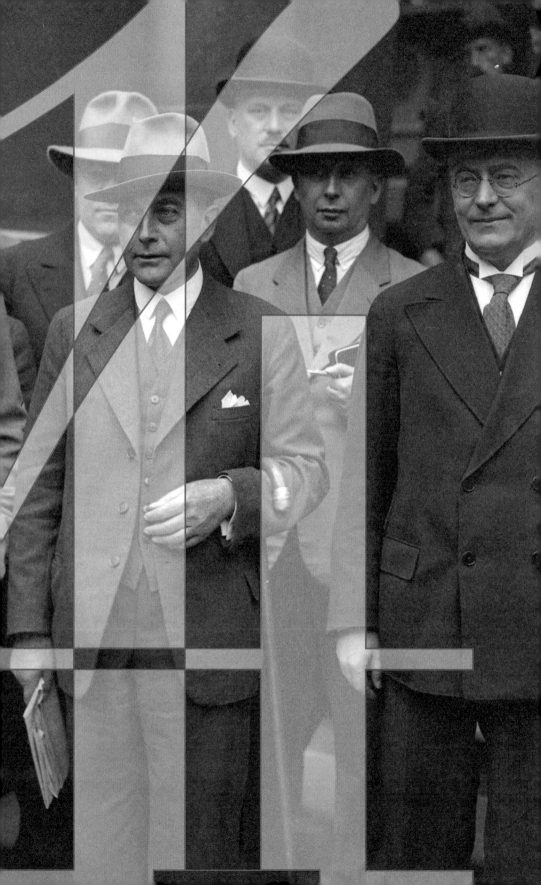

1931

·

BRÜNING'S
AGE
OF
AUSTERITY

·

The year of 1931 was one of deepening economic crisis. The small-business sector suffered greatly, with a fall of 30 per cent in retail sales, while bankruptcies grew by 20 per cent. On 8 January, the number of unemployed rose to 4.5 million, and would rise further to 6 million by the end of the year, forcing the government to adopt ever more drastic austerity measures.[1] Heinrich Brüning, the German Chancellor, took little account of public opinion in pursuing his economic policies, believing public spending cuts, and a lower standard of living, were the necessary medicine to achieve a balanced budget. He even thought the economic crisis could be used to force the Allies to abandon reparations altogether.[2]

One politician who benefited from Brüning's self-inflicted economic misery was Adolf Hitler. The election breakthrough of the NSDAP in September 1930 had brought a flood of new members. At the end of 1930, the party had 389,000 members but by the end of 1931 this had risen to 806,294.[3] The budget of the NSDAP has been estimated at an average of 70 million Reichsmarks per annum between 1931 and 1933, while business donations only amounted to 12 million Reichsmarks at most.[4]

On 1 January 1931, Hitler opened the new NSDAP party headquarters in central Munich, which became known as the Brown House (*Braunes Haus*), located on 45 Brienner Strasse.[5] This grand neo-classical stone building, originally designed by Jean Métivier, and built in 1828, was previously known as the Palais Barlow. It was purchased by the NSDAP for 805,864 Reichsmarks, a sum raised by a one-off payment from party members, together with a loan guarantee of 300,000 Reichsmarks from the German steel-making industrialist Fritz Thyssen. The building had to be substantially renovated. For this task, Hitler hired the architect Paul Troost, who was also an interior designer, noted for refurbishing luxury ocean liners. The grand entrance area on the ground floor became known as the Hall of Banners. Hitler's spacious 'work-room' was on the first floor, containing a bust of Mussolini, a photograph of Henry Ford, a portrait of Frederick the

previous page   German Chancellor Heinrich Brüning and Foreign Minister Julius Curtius, London, 1931.

The Brown House (*Braunes Haus*), 45 Brienner Strasse, Munich, headquarters of the Nazi Party (NSDAP) from January 1931.

Great, and a painting depicting an assault by Hitler's List Regiment at the first Battle of Flanders in 1914. Hitler, who hated day-to-day bureaucracy, spent extraordinarily little time there, but the Brown House became the well-organised administrative nerve centre of the NSDAP, in which all the leading party figures had offices.[6]

On 5 January, Hitler met Dr Hjalmar Schacht, who had resigned as the President of the Reichsbank in March 1930, in Hermann Göring's opulent apartment in Munich. Schacht wrote about his first meeting with Hitler in his memoirs, noting: 'His skill in exposition was most striking. Everything he said he demonstrated as incontrovertible truth. Nevertheless, his ideas were not unreasonable, and were certainly free from propagandist pathos.' Schacht also noticed that Hitler spoke with moderation. 'Even at this first meeting,' Schacht wrote, 'it was obvious to me that Hitler's power of propaganda would have tremendous

pull with the German people if we did not succeed in overcoming the economic crisis.' Hitler was pleased to have the endorsement of such a notable economic expert, and he was already thinking of giving Schacht a major economic role if he came to power. Schacht admitted that following the meeting, he tried to persuade Brüning and other leading German politicians 'to incorporate the National Socialists in a coalition government as soon as possible'.[7]

On the same day as his meeting with Schacht, Hitler appointed Ernst Röhm as the Chief of Staff of the National Socialist Storm-troopers. Röhm's appointment came after a bitter revolt in the organisation, which had broken out during the 1930 election campaign. It was led by Walter Stennes, the Berlin SA commander, and revolved around the proper role and function of the Stormtroopers in the party. Hitler saw the SA as an 'auxiliary troop' (*Hilfstruppe*), serving purely political and security functions, including protecting party meetings, marching on the streets, distributing propaganda, and intimidating political opponents, especially if they were Communists. Hitler did not want the SA to become a paramilitary organisation again, as he was now committed to the party coming to power legally.[8]

Stennes, firmly on the 'socialist' wing of the party, took a different view, seeing the SA as the basis of a future People's Army. He had contempt for the party 'big-wigs', opposed Hitler's law-abiding approach, wanted a more anti-capitalist stance in NSDAP propaganda, and wished to overthrow the Weimar Republic by force. At the end of August 1930, the conflict in the SA came to a head when three Berlin SA leaders were not placed on the list of Reichstag candidates. In response, the Stennes group occupied and trashed the Berlin Gau office of Joseph Goebbels.[9] In an attempt to defuse the revolt, Hitler removed Franz von Salomon, the then leader of the SA. On 2 September, Hitler assumed the supreme command of the organisation, promising increased funding, but warned the rebels they had to accept his leadership or face expulsion. The rebels accepted. Hitler had quelled the rebellion, for the time being at least, but the tensions remained.[10]

As Hitler had no desire to run the SA personally, he asked his old comrade and friend Ernst Röhm to take on the role. After the bungled Munich Beer Hall Putsch of 1923, Röhm had gradually retreated from active involvement in the party. Between 1928 and 1930, he was a military adviser to the Bolivian Army, and published an unrepentant memoir called *A Traitor's Story*. Hitler took a huge political risk in bringing Röhm back to the centre of the NSDAP leadership elite.

Röhm's political views were decidedly on the 'socialist' wing of the party, and he immediately shifted the stress in the SA back to a military command structure, issuing a service manual to each member. But his private life soon became the subject of scandal as Röhm had made no secret of the fact he was a homosexual, something which was then illegal under Article 175 of the German Criminal Code. Stennes immediately objected to Röhm's appointment, citing his same-sex activity, but Hitler rejected attacks on Röhm's private life, stressing the SA was not a 'moral establishment', but an association of 'rough men for a political purpose'.[11]

During January 1931, Chancellor Brüning toured the eastern German provinces, with the aim of assuring East Elbian farmers the government's Eastern Aid agricultural aid package would be expanded. He soon discovered the cost of living and debt crisis faced by farmers in the region was far worse than he had previously imagined. Hostile crowds greeted him in Silesia. In Breslau, a mob of 40,000 National Socialists turned out to jeer him. On 23 January another angry mob, this time of unemployed workers, threw stones at his motorcade as it arrived in Chemnitz. After Brüning returned to Berlin, he told his cabinet colleagues that all moderates must join together to stem the rising tide of extremism he had witnessed during his tour.[12]

On 25 January, Brüning gave a speech to the leaders of Christian unions in Cologne. Democracy and parliamentarianism, he said, were undergoing a severe crisis. In the pre-depression days, when there was prosperity, people found it easy to praise democracy, but since the good times had ceased, opposition to the cause of parliamentarianism had sharply increased. As a result, many previous supporters of democracy now stood on the Right. The present government, Brüning added, was fighting to save democracy by trying to instil a sense of responsibility in members of the Reichstag.[13] In a national radio broadcast to the German people on the same day, Brüning said people should forget about reparations revisions, and concentrate on putting the public finances in order, adding: 'It is not only through reparations burdens that we have fallen into financial misfortune, but to a very large measure by letting ourselves imagine that despite a lost war, despite huge sacrifices in the blood and treasure, both state and individuals could live better than in pre-war times.'[14]

When the Reichstag met on 3 February, it was clear Brüning's call for national unity had been largely ignored by the political parties. The National Socialists resumed their campaign of disruption and

overleaf 'Give us work!' reads a placard wielded by demonstrators, 1931. Mounting levels of unemployment did little to boost the standing of the embattled Chancellor Brüning.

obstruction to impede the smooth running of the Reichstag. The NSDAP joined the KPD in tabling no-confidence motions against the government. NSDAP members also hurled a barrage of boos, heckles and insulting remarks at all the cabinet members when they spoke in parliament, while the Communist members attacked the government's handling of the growing unemployment crisis.

On 7 February, the main opposition no-confidence motion was rejected by a vote of 293 to 221. The support of the Social Democrats for the government was once again vital. To deal with the unruly behaviour of National Socialist and Communist members in the Reichstag, Brüning proposed a new law prohibiting opportunistic multiple no-confidence motions, if the first one was defeated, and to require any proposal for new expenditure by Reichstag members to spell out exactly how it was going to be financed. After these two measures were passed by the Reichstag on 9 February, the NSDAP members walked out of the debating chamber in protest, and they were followed by the DNVP. After the Reichstag had completed all its remaining legislative business on 26 March, it was adjourned until October 1931. Brüning told the cabinet that he intended to pass legislation until then by using emergency decrees signed by President Hindenburg, using Article 48 of the Constitution.[15]

The first of these decrees, drafted by Joseph Wirth, the Minister of the Interior, and Carl Severing, who occupied the same position in the SPD-led Prussian government, was issued on 28 March. It authorised the police to ban the wearing outdoors of uniforms by political associations, and to dissolve rallies where speakers urged illegal actions or maliciously insulted government leaders and religious leaders. This decree was enforced most vigorously in Prussia and Bavaria. In the next three months, 1,105 individuals were convicted of violating the decree, but twice as many were Communists as National Socialists.[16]

On 30 March, Alfred Hugenberg, the DNVP leader, protested against the emergency decree, saying it was being enforced to impede the campaign the Steel Helmet had launched in February, demanding a referendum to dissolve the SPD-led Prussian parliament so as to force new elections. Brüning responded to Hugenberg with a statement accusing the DNVP of 'seeking to undermine the public's confidence in President von Hindenburg', adding: 'To demand a repeal of the decree is a personal attack on the President.'[17]

By now deeply unpopular, Brüning decided to look for a foreign policy issue that would allow him to strike a more active pose on the world stage, and hopefully improve Germany's dire economic position. One area immediately came to mind: German–Austrian relations. The two countries had much in common, including a shared language, and in both, support for the union between the two nations remained strong, even though it was prohibited by the Treaty of Versailles, the Treaty of St Germain, and a financial assistance treaty made between the Allies and Austria, signed in Geneva on 4 October 1922, which promised the maintenance of Austrian independence. Brüning knew a political union was unlikely to be accepted by the Western Allies, but he thought a German–Austrian customs union might be, if it was presented as a purely economic union which did not infringe on the independence and political sovereignty of either nation.

The Brüning cabinet agreed to the proposal on 18 March, fully aware that it might provoke a major diplomatic confrontation. Foreign Minister Julius Curtius promised to take sole responsibility for the initiative, even to the point of denying he had even informed Brüning about it, so the Chancellor would not be compromised if the proposal failed.[18]

Instead of discussing these plans with the Western Allies beforehand, and proceeding step by step, the two countries decided to announce them unilaterally. Accordingly, on 21 March, the German and Austrian governments announced their intention to set up a German–Austrian Customs Union, after Curtius and Johannes Schober, the Austrian Foreign Minister, had finalised the agreement during talks in Vienna between 3 and 5 March 1931. German and Austrian legal experts had carefully drafted the principles of the agreement to stress its purely commercial character.[19]

The reaction abroad was wholly negative. The governments of France, Italy and Czechoslovakia strongly objected, arguing the proposed customs union was really a precursor to full political union between Germany and Austria. The British government informed the German government the proposal should have been circulated for discussion, and not presented as a *fait accompli*.[20] The Austrian-German Customs Union had to be humiliatingly abandoned in the face of Allied hostility. The French government mobilised all its considerable financial strength to block the plan. On 3 September, Curtius, in an embarrassing climb-down, announced the controversial project had been dropped. Two days later, the Permanent Court of International Justice at The Hague, Netherlands, condemned the German–Austrian scheme and declared it illegal by a single vote – 8 to 7.[21]

The bungled fiasco of the German–Austrian Customs Union led directly to the Austrian banking crisis. On 13 May, the Creditanstalt, the largest and most respected Austrian bank, suddenly declared bankruptcy, sending shock-waves through world financial markets. Jittery creditors everywhere withdrew funds. The bank's initial losses amounted to 828 million Austrian schillings. During May, Austria's foreign-currency reserves fell by 850 million schillings. Otto Ender, the Austrian Chancellor, was forced to put together a government-backed financial rescue plan by buying up 100 million schillings' worth of Creditanstalt stock. Support in this rescue package was given by the powerful Rothschild banking family of Austria, and on 16 June the Bank of England provided a sizeable loan to the Austrian government to assist with the plan.[22]

The Austrian banking crisis had a domino effect, with the panic-selling of the stock of German banks soon following. In early June, the Reichsbank announced it had suffered the withdrawal of 1 billion Reichsmarks since the Creditanstalt collapse, with foreign deposits falling by 25 per cent. The German government was now having great difficulty in raising foreign loans to service its huge public-spending deficit, and the Reichsmark was falling on currency markets. On 5 June, Brüning issued the Second Emergency Decree for the Protection of the Economy and Finances, which brought in reductions in welfare benefits, wage cuts for all public-sector employees, plus a 'crisis' tax, levied on better-paid white-collar workers, and increases in sales taxes on sugar and imported oil. The one concession to organised labour was a promise of 200 million Reichsmarks for the funding of public works.[23] This new decree was accompanied by a blunt declaration from Brüning that 'the limit of privations which we can impose on the German people had been reached', and he further warned that Germany could not make the reparations payments due in 1931 under the Young Plan.[24]

On 7 June, Heinrich Brüning, accompanied by Julius Curtius, the German Foreign Minister, met with Ramsay MacDonald, at Chequers, the British Prime Minister's picturesque country retreat. The purpose of the visit was for a 'mutual exchange of views'. Also present was Montagu Norman, the Governor of the Bank of England, who expressed dissatisfaction with Brüning's announcement of his intention to suspend reparations payments. In response, Brüning explained his declaration was really a warning of what would happen if the issue of Germany's payments for 1931 was not urgently addressed. The friendly

Johannes Schober, the Austrian Foreign Minister. The scheme for a German–Austrian Customs Union he agreed with his German counterpart Julius Curtius in March 1931 would be vehemently opposed by the Allies.

meeting only yielded the release of a joint statement, which laid stress on 'the difficulties of the existing position in Germany and the need for alleviation'.[25]

The US President, Herbert Hoover, was following European economic affairs closely, and he fully appreciated the impact the financial collapse of German banks would have on American creditors. The magnanimous proposal by Hoover of a payments moratorium was initially opposed by the French government, Germany's principal reparations creditor, but was finally accepted, on 6 July, with the condition that the German government spent the one-year saving on reparations for domestic rather than military purposes. The Hoover Moratorium really marked the beginning of the end of German reparations payments, which were never resumed.[26]

Germany now suffered its own banking crisis. On 23 June, the North German Wool Combing and Spinning Mills in Bremen, established in 1884, one of Germany's largest textile companies, made public its dire financial situation, announcing its total collapse was imminent. The outstanding bank debts of Northern Wool (*Nordwolle*), amounted to a whopping 100 million Reichsmarks. The collapse was due to mismanagement by the textile company, which had taken on huge loans from the Danat-Bank in Berlin (*Darmstädter und Nationalbank*), which were used to gamble on the price of wool going up in the risky futures market. Instead, the market price fell, and the Berlin Danat-Bank, one of the four largest German banks, lost 40 million Reichsmarks.[27]

On hearing news of the Nordwolle collapse, the public frantically withdrew deposits from the Danat-Bank and its stock-market price plummeted. On 8 July, the bank's directors informed the Reichsbank and the Ministry of Finance that within a few days it would not be able to honour the demands of depositors to withdraw money. On 11 July, the Danat-Bank announced it would not open for business two days later.

The failure of one of Germany's major banks sent shock-waves across the country's entire banking and financial sector. The Reichsbank's reserves of gold and foreign currency dropped below 40 per cent of money in circulation, the level defined as the minimum necessary to defend the gold standard.[28] In a dramatic intervention, Brüning's government issued an emergency decree, signed by President Hindenburg, to guarantee the deposits of the customers of Danat-Bank, as a measure of public safety, and appointed a consortium of industrialists to supervise the bank's affairs in future. Foreign-exchange controls were also introduced to try and reduce the flight of foreign capital. With panic deposit withdrawals from all the other German banks continuing, Brüning announced two bank holidays for 13 and 14 July. The large Dresdner Bank announced on 14 July it too was threatened with insolvency. It was quickly bailed out by the government, which guaranteed its customer deposits, and took a 75 per cent shareholding.[29]

On 15 July, the Reichsbank raised its discount interest rate from 7 to 10 per cent, and then to 15 per cent two weeks later, and also took over all trading in foreign currency, and suspended trading on the stock market for the time being. It was not until 5 August that normal bank payments resumed. On 19 September, Brüning issued yet another emergency decree, appointing a Reich Commissar for Banking, with extensive powers, to inspect the balance sheets of banks, and creating special tribunals that could issue instant punishments.[30]

Between 20 and 23 July, a hastily convened International Conference took place in London, with the aim of funding international assistance to Germany. It was attended by representatives of Britain, France, Italy, Belgium, Japan and the USA. Top of Brüning's list of demands were a request for assurance that the withdrawal of foreign funds from Germany would cease, and a demand for a new international loan. It soon became clear the latter would have to come from France, which had a high level of gold reserves, but the French government wanted to tie the loan to a German promise not to demand any revision of the Treaty of Versailles with regard to its eastern border dispute with Poland. On this point, the negotiations for the German loan collapsed. The only tangible gain for Germany from the London Conference was the Standstill Agreement (*Stillhalteabkommen*), which agreed that all German creditors would not demand payment on current loans, initially for a six-month period, with the proviso to convert them into long-term loans in future. This hardly helped the German government to raise further credit on foreign markets, as there now seemed little prospect of any loans being repaid by Germany. Brüning later described the London Conference as a 'tragic failure' with the leaders of the industrialised world failing to cooperate in the face of a world economic crisis.[31]

On 27 July, Brüning issued another emergency decree, this time authorising the creation of the Bank of Guarantees and Acceptances (*Akzept- und Garantiebank*), with a capital of 200 million Reichsmarks,

overleaf Crowds gather to withdraw savings from a Berlin bank during the crisis that followed the failure of the Danat-Bank, July 1921.

which was designed to underwrite all the deposits held by German banks. Throughout the banking crisis, Brüning had resisted demands from the National Socialists and Communists to recall parliament by persuading the Reichstag's Council of Elders to block the move.[32]

In early August 1931, there was a referendum over the future of the Prussian state, the largest and most powerful in Germany. The Prussian coalition government, between the Social Democrats, Zentrum, and the German Democratic Party, had been in power for most of the period from 1920 onwards, was committed to the Weimar Constitution, and showed a centre-left coalition could function effectively. It was accordingly hated by all the parties on the Right.[33] In February 1931, the Steel Helmet, led by Franz Seldte and Theodor Duesterberg, had launched a campaign to dissolve the Prussian Landtag, and the required 6 million signatures necessary for the referendum to take place were secured. The referendum campaign was supported by the NSDAP, the DNVP, the DVP, the WP, the CNBL and the KPD. Hitler only gave half-hearted support, because he thought the referendum would fail, and Hugenberg, the DNVP leader, was no more enthusiastic, giving only limited financial support.[34]

On 9 August, the Prussian Landtag Referendum results showed 37.1 per cent (9.8 million) of voters had supported the measure, but this was short of the 50 per cent (13.2 million) required to succeed. Yet the fact so many voters had supported such an anti-democratic measure was a bad omen for the next Prussian Landtag elections, which were due in the spring of 1932.[35]

During the summer of 1931, Hitler's relationship with his 23-year-old half-niece, Geli Raubal, was rapidly deteriorating. Geli had lived in a single room in Hitler's eight-room luxury apartment, located at 16 Prinzregentenplatz, Munich, since November 1929. The domestic household staff at the apartment consisted of Anni Winter, his chief housekeeper, her husband Georg, Maria Reichert, Hitler's domestic assistant, and a cleaner, Anna Kirmair. Of these, only Reichert and her elderly deaf mother lived in the apartment. Gossip circulated within Hitler's inner circle about the exact nature of Geli's relationship with 'Uncle Alf', as she called him. Was it a normal uncle–niece relationship or something sexual? Geli had supposedly once told Ernst 'Putzi' Hanfstaengl, one of Hitler's close friends at the time: 'My uncle is a monster, no one can imagine what he demands of me.' Anni Winter, Hitler's housekeeper, on the other hand, was convinced Hitler had no sexual relations with Geli.[36]

It does seem Geli came to view life with her uncle as stifling. He watched over her every step. There were also arguments over her desire to go to Vienna for opera-singing lessons, which Hitler seemingly opposed. Hitler told Heinrich Hoffmann, his personal photographer, that he was over-protective of Geli, but merely as a concerned uncle, saying: 'I reserve to myself the right to watch over her male acquaintances, until such time as the right man comes along. What Geli now regards as restraint is in reality a wise precaution.'[37]

At 2.45 p.m., on 18 September, Hitler departed for a campaign speaking tour of north Germany, driven by his chauffeur, Julius Schreck, and accompanied by Hoffmann, who said he was with Hitler continuously in the period after he left the apartment on 18 September, until 26 September. Anni Winter told the police she saw Geli go into Hitler's room, on the afternoon of 18 September, then hurry back to her own room. This was about 15 minutes after Hitler had left the apartment. Maria Reichert, in her police statement, claimed that at 'around 3 p.m.' she heard the door of Geli's room being locked. At 10 p.m., Reichert knocked on Geli's door, but got no answer. During the 'early part of the night', Reichert heard a 'dull sound and a cry' but did not get out of bed to investigate.

On the morning of 19 September, when Geli failed to appear for breakfast, Reichert became deeply concerned. At 9.30 a.m., Anni Winter knocked loudly on Geli's door, which was locked from inside, but got no answer. At 10.00 a.m., her husband Georg forced open the double-door to her room, with a large screwdriver. All Hitler's domestic staff were present as the door was opened. Inside, Geli was lying on the floor, with her nightdress drenched in blood, and her face downwards. A single bullet had been fired from a 6.35-millimetre Walther pistol. It missed her heart, pierced her lung, and lodged inside her body, just above her left hip. The pistol that fired the fatal shot was owned by Hitler.[38] After finding Geli, Anni Winter phoned Rudolf Hess, Hitler's personal secretary, to tell him the news, and he hurriedly came to the apartment, accompanied by Franz Schwarz, the party treasurer, before the police were called.

At 10.30 a.m., Georg Winter finally called the police. A police doctor and two detectives were sent to investigate the matter. They found a partially written letter by Geli to a female friend on her bedroom table, but it was not a suicide note, and struck a decidedly optimistic tone, stating: 'When I come to Vienna – I hope very soon – we'll drive together to Semmering' (a health resort outside Vienna).[39]

The police report, presented to the Bavarian Ministry of the Interior on 28 September 1931, concluded there were no wounds to her face or body and that Geli had died during the 'evening' of 18 September of a single gunshot wound, with all the evidence pointing to it being self-inflicted.

Hitler had spent the night in the Deutscher Hof Hotel in Nuremberg, before departing for Hamburg for a speaking engagement, after breakfast. Hess phoned the hotel at 11.45 a.m., but Hitler had just departed. Hess asked a bell boy to get a taxi to find Hitler's car and deliver a message, saying he needed 'to call a Herr Hess urgently'. The taxi duly tracked down Hitler's limousine, and Hitler, who was in the car with Hoffmann and Schreck, hurried to the nearest public telephone. Hoffmann later recalled seeing Hitler shouting down the line to Hess: 'Give me a clear answer – yes or no – is she still alive?' When Hess told him she was dead, Hitler was stunned and stood motionless.

On his way back to Munich on the early afternoon of 19 September, Hitler told Schreck to drive as fast as he could. The car was stopped by the police, on the outskirts of Munich, for speeding, and a speeding ticket was issued, which has survived. It records the car was going at twice the speed limit. Hitler finally arrived back at Prinzregentstrasse at about 2.45 p.m. He was able to see Geli's corpse before she was taken away to the mortuary in Munich's Eastern Cemetery. Hitler seemed 'composed' when the police interviewed him at 3 p.m. He admitted quarrelling with his niece about her future and forbidding her to go to Vienna for singing lessons on her own: 'She must have been very angry about it, but she did not get particularly upset and said goodbye to me quite calmly when I left on Friday afternoon.' Hitler told the police he was remarkably close to his niece and her death had hit him very badly.[40]

Hitler's political enemies tried to suggest foul play, with the aim of wrecking his political career. In an article called 'A Mysterious Affair' in the *Münchener Post* (*Munich Post*), a Social Democratic-supporting newspaper, it was reported that Hitler had a 'massive row' with his niece on 18 September, after she had announced her intention to marry a boyfriend in Vienna. The article also claimed Geli had been found with a broken nose and other injuries, concluding her death was certainly not suicide, and was possibly murder. The article prompted the State Prosecutor to have her body re-examined by another doctor, who confirmed there were no signs of violence on the body. The two women who had prepared the body for burial confirmed this finding.[41]

Hitler complained to the *Münchener Post* about the article, claiming it was defamatory and demanding a correction be printed. On 22 September, the newspaper published a statement, by Hitler, making four points:

> (1) It is untrue that I had 'recurrent disagreements' or a violent quarrel with my niece Angela on 18 September or previously. (2) It is untrue that I was 'strongly opposed' to my niece travelling to Vienna. The truth is that I was never against the trip my niece planned to Vienna. (3) It is untrue that my niece wanted to become engaged in Vienna or that I had some objection to my niece's engagement. The truth is that my niece, tortured by anxiety about whether she had the talent necessary for a public appearance, wanted to go to Vienna in order to have a new assessment of her voice by a qualified voice specialist. (4) It is untrue that I left my apartment on 18 September 1931 'after a violent scene'. The truth is that there was no kind of scene and no agitation of any kind when I left my apartment on that day.[42]

The cause of the death of Geli Raubal can never be conclusively solved, but all the surviving evidence points to suicide, even though an inquest on her death was never held. This meant there was no confirmation of the trajectory of the bullet or whether the gun had been fired at close quarters. Hitler's alibi on the day of her death is watertight. Geli was alive when he left the apartment on 18 September. Two witnesses – Heinrich Hoffmann and Julius Schreck – were with him from the time he left the apartment until he returned on the next day. Two witnesses inside the apartment – Anni Winter and Maria Reichert – both confirmed Geli was alive until at least 3 p.m. on 18 September, which was 15 minutes after Hitler had left. The most likely conclusion is that Geli was being psychologically ground down by Hitler's desire to control her life and, feeling trapped, decided suicide was her only way out. In that sense Hitler did play a key part in her decision to end her life.

At her mother's request, Geli's body was taken to Vienna for burial, on 23 September, in the city's Central Cemetery. The Catholic priest, Father Johann Pant, knew the Hitler family well, granted the funeral, and presided at the Requiem Mass, something usually denied to suicide victims. He decided to accept her mother's view that Geli's death was 'an accident', putting forward the theory she had been playing with the gun, which accidentally went off. Hitler did not attend Geli's funeral, feeling his presence would attract too much unwelcome media attention, but he did visit the grave a few days later and placed flowers. There is little doubt that Geli's premature death was a shattering personal blow to Hitler. Heinrich Hoffmann recalled Hitler sinking into a deep depression after her death. Hitler later declared that Geli was the only woman, apart from his mother, whom he had ever loved. He kept her room in Prinzregentstrasse unchanged. His domestic servants placed a fresh vase of flowers in there every day. Hitler also commissioned the sculptor Ferdinand Liebermann to create a bronze bust of her, but after her death the members of his inner circle were told never to bring up the subject of her death in conversations with him.[43]

Meanwhile, the devastating effects of the economic and banking crisis during the summer of 1931 had caused Brüning's popularity to plummet to new depths. Hindenburg was becoming deeply frustrated by how frequently Brüning was issuing controversial emergency decrees. He now wanted a reshuffle of Brüning's government to make it more 'national minded'. This meant gaining parliamentary support from the two Nationalist parties, the DVNP and NSDAP, which Brüning had assiduously avoided up to this point.

On 1 August, Hindenburg met with Hugenberg, the DNVP leader, whom he had refused to see in the previous 18 months. He asked Hugenberg to support the government in Reichstag votes. In response, Hugenberg said this would only be possible if the SPD-led Prussian government was deposed. Hugenberg also assured Hindenburg that Hitler was not, in his opinion, a 'dangerous socialist', but a committed patriot. Hindenburg told the DNVP leader that summarily deposing the SPD-led government from office in Prussia was not constitutionally possible, but he did promise he would try and persuade Brüning to form a new cabinet which included the self-styled 'National Opposition'.[44]

Kurt von Schleicher, the President's key behind-the-scenes adviser, was also becoming frustrated with Brüning, branding him a 'procrastinator' (*Zauderer*). By the end of August, Hindenburg was reportedly on the verge of summarily sacking Brüning. In his memoirs, Brüning recalls being stunned on hearing this news, and could not understand why Hindenburg had suddenly lost faith in him, unaware that Schleicher was secretly undermining him.[45]

On 6 September, Schleicher advised Brüning to reshuffle his cabinet in the direction of 'an extreme German nationalist tendency'. Schleicher had come to the view that Hitler could no longer be discounted as a serious politician. He therefore put forward a strategy

Kurt von Schleicher: his intrigues against Chancellor Brüning would accelerate the demise of Weimar democracy.

for 'taming Hitler' by offering him a place in the cabinet. Schleicher also thought an alliance between the conservative elite and Hitler would give popular legitimacy to a far-reaching revision of Germany's constitution in a more authoritarian direction. In reply, Brüning told Schleicher it would be a 'crime' to violate the Constitution when, via

his secret pact of toleration with the Social Democrats, he enjoyed a Reichstag majority in the event of no-confidence votes.[46]

Schleicher's 'taming strategy', in regard to Hitler, did gain support from Franz von Papen, a member of the Catholic nobility of Westphalia. Papen was a vain, ambitious, self-assured, and natural intriguer. By marriage to Martha von Boch-Gathau he had acquired huge wealth, to add to his own substantial fortune. Before the Great War of 1914–18, he had been an officer in the Imperial Army. At the War Academy in Berlin, he formed a close friendship with Schleicher, and Oskar von Hindenburg, the son of the President. During the War, he served as a military attaché in Washington DC, engaged in illegal espionage activity and was expelled from the USA on a charge of sabotage. The US press called him a 'Devil in a Top Hat'. For the remainder of the War, Papen commanded troops first on the Western Front and then in Ottoman Turkey.[47]

After the War, Papen became a member of the Prussian parliament, and the part-owner of *Germania*, the Zentrum newspaper. He adopted a strong anti-republican, anti-socialist stance in his speeches in the Prussian Landtag, and even favoured a restoration of the monarchy. Schleicher came to think that the pliable Papen, who did not even have a seat in the Reichstag, might be the ideal replacement for Brüning as Chancellor. Schleicher therefore brought Papen into the small

Franz von Papen: Schleicher's favoured choice as a malleable replacement for Chancellor Brüning.

inner circle surrounding Hindenburg. As André François-Ponçet, the French Ambassador, commented: 'Papen is to some extent the butt of others' jokes, they rib him mercilessly, though he takes it all in good part. He is a favourite of the Field Marshal [Hindenburg], his vivacity and cheerfulness help distract the old man; he flatters him with his deference and devotion.'[48]

Papen's first mission was to lobby Brüning to buy into Schleicher's 'taming strategy' concerning Hitler. In September 1931, Papen took Peter Klöckner, the Centre Party's wealthiest donor, to meet Brüning. They both urged Brüning to make a deal with Hitler to prolong the term of the President, and avoid the upcoming election, which was due in the spring of 1932. Brüning showed little enthusiasm for bringing Hitler into his government at the meeting. On 2 October, in a widely reported speech, Papen demanded that Brüning establish a 'dictatorship on a nationalist basis' that would break with parliamentarism completely, and achieve the sensible incorporation of the Nationalist Right with the National Socialists into his government.[49]

On 3 October, Schleicher met Hitler, asking him first whether the NSDAP would tolerate Brüning's government in Reichstag votes, but he firmly said no. Hitler did say he would enter the government on condition fresh elections were called, and the NSDAP formed a government on its own. Schleicher came away from the meeting convinced Hitler was sincere about his goal of pursuing the conquest of power by legal means, and he convinced Hindenburg to meet with Hitler on 10 October for further talks.[50]

On 24 September, Schleicher advised Brüning the best way to govern, if he could not find a viable majority, was to dissolve the Reichstag indefinitely. In the end, Brüning decided to undertake a minor reshuffle of his cabinet to placate Hindenburg. Before then, on 6 October, he issued the Third Emergency Decree for the Protection of the Economy and Finances, which increased police powers to control riots, shortened the period of entitlement to unemployment insurance payments and lowered the percentage of the final-salary pension for government employees from 80 to 75 per cent.[51]

On 6 October 1931, Brüning and his entire cabinet resigned. Hindenburg immediately asked him to form another government, on the understanding he made 'no political commitments to any party'.[52] On 9 October, the second Brüning cabinet was formed. It was another 'presidential cabinet', lacking a formal coalition agreement between the participating parties, and remained reliant on Hindenburg issuing decrees using Article 48 of the Constitution. There were very few changes. Julius Curtius was dismissed as Foreign Minister, due to the humiliating failure of the German–Austrian Customs Union proposal, and Brüning decided to take on the additional role of Foreign Minister himself. Wilhelm Groener (Independent) replaced Joseph Wirth (Zentrum), as the Minister of the Interior, but he also retained his post of Defence Minister, thus concentrating both the Army and the police force under his control. Conservative Hermann Warmbold (Independent) took over the post of Minister of Economics from Ernest Trendenburg (DStP), a former permanent secretary at the Economics Ministry, who had himself replaced Hermann Dietrich in the post on 18 June 1930. Gottfried Treviranus (KVP) replaced Theodor von Guérard (Zentrum) as the Minister of Transport, while retaining his additional role as Minister of Occupied Territories. Finally, on 9 November, Hans Schlange-Schöningen of the CNBL took on the special agricultural role of Reich Commissioner for Eastern Aid. These changes reduced the cabinet's base of support in the Reichstag, as a member of the DVP was no longer involved. Hugenberg and Hitler declared that the new government was as unrepresentative of the popular will as its predecessor.[53]

On the morning of 10 October, Brüning held a meeting with Hitler, immediately noticing the NSDAP leader now had more self-confidence than when they had last met. Brüning asked Hitler whether he would support a constitutional amendment, allowing Hindenburg to continue in office and avoid a presidential election. Hitler rejected the plan. Later on the same day, Hitler met President Hindenburg for the first time, accompanied by Hermann Göring. During the encounter, Hitler stressed his own reverence for the President before offering a monologue on the bankruptcy of the Weimar political system. It was reported that Hindenburg was not overly impressed by the 'Bohemian Corporal' at this meeting, telling Schleicher that he found Hitler uncouth and unsuited to the role of Chancellor.[54] This is not, however, the whole story. Hindenburg informed Kurt von Einen, one of his old army comrades, that he found Hitler 'very appealing' during this meeting. In a letter to his daughter on 14 October, Hindenburg also did not rule out bringing Hitler into government if he moderated his behaviour.[55]

Brüning thought Hindenburg's meeting with Hitler was a mistake, because it encouraged many army officers to regard Hitler as a legit-imate contender for power, and thereby greatly increased his political credibility. Joseph Wirth, who had been dismissed in Brüning's recent cabinet reshuffle, warned the German Chancellor that Hindenburg's 'reactionary friends' would interfere more and more with government policy until he had no choice but to resign.[56]

On 11 October, the so-called 'National Opposition' gathered in the spa town of Bad Harzburg in the Free State of Brunswick. Represented at this huge rally were the National Socialists, the DNVP, the Steel Helmet, the Pan German League and many other smaller right-wing associations. Topping the list of famous personalities present were Adolf Hitler, Alfred Hugenberg, Fritz Thyssen, Franz Seldte and Hjalmar Schacht. The purpose of the meeting, which established the so-called Harzburg Front, was to unite all the right-wing elements together in a drive to oust the Brüning cabinet and set up a 'truly National government'.

The Harzburg meeting, which included grand military parades by the Stormtroopers and the Steel Helmet, was opened by Hugenberg, who declared Germany had to be saved from the 'Red peril'. To halt the 'bloody terror of Marxism', and the spread of 'cultural Bolshevism', the 'National Opposition' was prepared to take over political power in Prussia and in the Reich. Hitler spoke in a comparable manner, predicting that either Marxism or nationalism would triumph in Germany. The political structure of Germany, he added, had to be completely overhauled. The 'National Opposition' did not want war, because its leaders were former soldiers who knew what war meant, but no people could surrender the right to fight.[57]

Hjalmar Schacht, a pillar of the conservative establishment, also delivered a speech. He introduced himself to the audience as a 'concerned patriot', who was a member of no party. He then proceeded to attack the present 'Weimar system', accusing it of 'dishonesty, disorder and indecision'. Schacht described Hitler as Germany's 'last hope' for a return to 'decency and order'. Schacht also suggested the Reichsbank was deliberately obscuring how serious the economic position really was in order to prop up the current Brüning government.[58]

By now, Hitler was predicting to his inner circle that he would soon win power. To prepare for this, Hitler had continuously instituted changes in the organisation of the NSDAP during the year. In June, he set up the Imperial Leaders' School in Munich to prepare National Socialist leaders for their role in national and regional government. On 1 August, he appointed Otto Dietrich as his press chief, and at the end of October, he made Baldur von Schirach head of the expanding

overleaf Nazis gather at Bad Harzburg to found the anti-Brüning 'Harzburg Front', October 1931. The SS chief Heinrich Himmler is in the foreground, wearing a black cap, with the SA leader Ernst Röhm to his right.

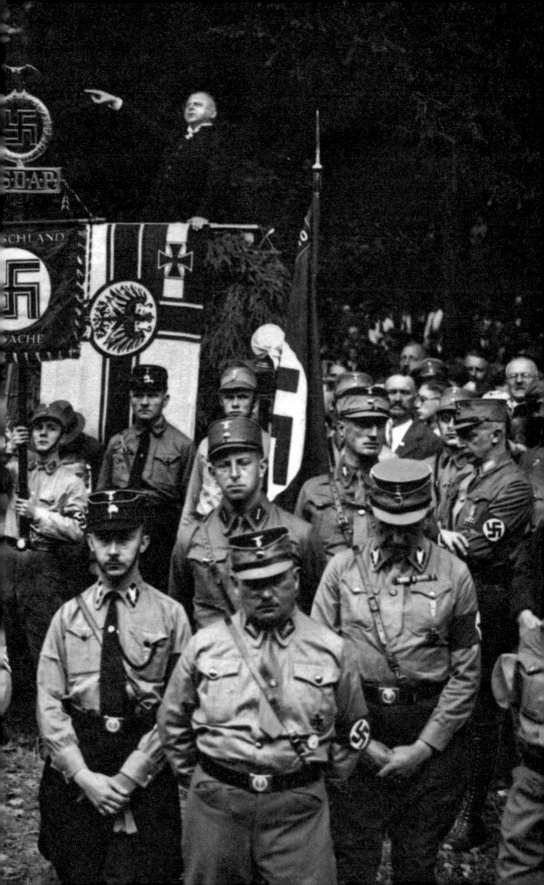

Hitler Youth. He also established the Economic Council, under the leadership of Gottfried Feder, which was given the task of advising the party on economic policy, and established the Race and Settlement Office, under Walter Darré, to advise on racial policy.[59]

On 13 October, the first session of the Reichstag since the end of March began. Immediately, the NSDAP and DNVP Reichstag delegations presented a joint resolution requesting 'the Reichstag withdraw its confidence from the government' and tabled several other motions, including the revocation of Brüning's emergency decrees, and a demand for fresh elections. After three days of heated debate, the motion of no confidence was rejected on 16 October by 295 to 270 votes, and the other motions against the government were all defeated. The Reichstag then voted to adjourn until February 1932. Until then, Brüning pledged to rule by issuing presidential decrees, but he promised to restore parliamentary government once the economic crisis had passed. The DNVP and NSDAP leaders announced they would now resume their boycott of the German parliament.[60] There was a certain logic to the exodus of National Socialists from the Reichstag, as it was no longer the centre of political decision-making.

Out on the streets, there was an alarming increase in violence between the National Socialists and the Communists. Yet the idea Germany was nearing civil war after 1929 has been greatly exaggerated. On 12 October, the Liberal-left newspaper *Die Welt am Montag* (*The World on Monday*) published statistics, based on official sources and newspaper reports, on those killed and injured during political clashes since the beginning of 1923 to July 1931. These revealed that 457 people had been killed, and 1,154 had been injured in the period. However, just over half of those fatalities (236), and one-third of those injured (462), had occurred in 1923 alone. Between 1924 and 1928, the period of economic stability, there had been 66 fatalities and 266 injured. From 1929 to July 1931, the number of deaths increased to 155, with 426 injured. Violence was certainly on the rise after 1930; but it never reached the levels of the 1919 to 1923 period. A closer look at the post-1929 statistics reveals which side suffered more victims. The Communists and Left radicals suffered 108 deaths since 1929, while in the same period, right-wing organisations, including the National Socialists, suffered 31 dead. There were only eight fatalities among pro-republican groups such as the SPD-led Reichsbanner. There were also 10 police officers killed. Most violent clashes resulting in death involved the National Socialists and Communists.[61]

This picture can be confirmed in greater detail with the help of statistical surveys, and police reports in the German state of Saxony. In 1929, there were 51 recorded Communist–NSDAP clashes, in 1929, this jumped to 172, and then hit 229 in 1931. The most violent clashes happened during indoor meetings. There was, however, a noticeable difference in how the police dealt with these violent confrontations. The police acted against Communist 'troublemakers' far more often than against National Socialists. In 1929, the ratio of police interventions was 30 KPD to 11 NSDAP; in 1930, it was 121 KPD to 32 NSDAP, and, in 1931, it was 140 KPD to 63 NSDAP. It was only during 1932 that political violence really escalated, with the Prussian Ministry of the Interior recording 155 deaths; of these 55 belonged to the NSDAP and 54 to the KPD.

The information on weapons seized by police during NSDAP–KPD clashes shows that in 1929 the police confiscated only two guns and eight knives, a figure that rose to 17 guns and 181 other weapons in 1930, but in 1931 this fell to 5 guns and 78 other weapons. This is in stark contrast to the earlier Weimar era, from 1918 to 1923, when firearms featured heavily in clashes between Left and Right. As bad as violence was after 1929, it would be totally misleading to suggest the police could not contain it or that Germany was nearing civil war. In rural areas, there were hardly any violent clashes which resulted in fatalities at all.[62]

The front line of Left–Right violent confrontations after 1929 was primarily in the big cities. Communists felt they ruled the working-class urban streets. Any place that was home to large numbers of industrial workers was prepared to violently resist the advance of the National Socialists on the streets. Communists rarely took action to break up Social Democratic political meetings, except for a few large-scale events, mainly organised by the Reichsbanner. In contrast, Communists adopted a proactive approach whenever the National Socialists held rallies and meetings in the big cities. Most of these violent confrontations occurred during and after indoor meetings. Communists initiated most of them, keen to emphasise National Socialists were not welcome in working-class areas. Well-organised Communist gangs arrived in force at NSDAP meetings, hell bent on violence. The police authorities, however, had a broad spectrum of special powers to break up or ban demonstrations.

As violence escalated, a culture of political martyrdom emerged, with those killed on both sides receiving elaborate funerals attended by thousands of activists. The most famous National Socialist martyr was Horst Wessel, a 22-year-old Stormtrooper, who was shot when he opened the door of his Berlin apartment on 14 February 1930 by Albrecht Höhler, a member of the Communist Red Front Fighters' League (*Roter Frontkämpferbund*). Wessel initially survived the attack, but died on 23 February 1930 of blood poisoning contracted in hospital.[63] Wessel was well known in Berlin as a bitter enemy of the Communists, who objected to his swift elevation to the status of political sainthood, pointing out his death was not politically motivated at all but, they argued, resulted from a private dispute. Wessel was seemingly a common pimp, living off the 'immoral earnings' of Erna Jänicke, a 23-year-old prostitute. According to the Communist version of events, Wessel was killed during an argument over his prolonged refusal to pay his rent, not his political convictions.

Yet propaganda myth was more important than such inconvenient truths. Joseph Goebbels cleverly elevated Wessel into a posthumous National Socialist hero when it became known that the young Stormtrooper had composed several political songs. One was called *Die Fahne Hoch (Raise the Banner)*, generally known as the Horst Wessel Song (*Horst Wessel-Lied*). It became the unofficial NSDAP anthem.

Goebbels organised an elaborate funeral for Horst Wessel on 1 March 1930, at the St Nicholas and St Mary Cemetery in Berlin. His funeral procession, numbering 30,000 people, was followed by columns of Stormtroopers. Goebbels delivered the funeral oration, claiming this 'common man' had now ascended the Valhalla of National Socialist heroes.[64]

The self-sacrificing determination of Storm Troopers to fight Communists for control of the streets can be glimpsed in a letter sent by a 34-year-old SA standard leader to Gregor Strasser:

> In my work for the NSDAP I have faced a court more than thirty times and have been convicted eight times for assault and battery, resistance to a police officer and other such misdemeanours that are natural for a National Socialist. To this day, I am still paying instalments on my fines, and, in addition, have other trials coming up. Furthermore, I have been more or less severely wounded at least twenty times. I have knife scars on the back of my head, on my left shoulder, on my lower lip, on my right cheek, on the left side of my lower lip and on my right arm. I have never yet claimed or received a penny of party money, but I have sacrificed my time to our movement at the expense of the good business I inherited from my father. Today I am facing financial ruin.[65]

The advance of the National Socialists in local elections continued uninterrupted throughout 1931. In elections in Schaumburg-Lippe on 3 May, the NSDAP gained 26.9 per cent of votes. In state elections in Oldenburg on 17 May, the party polled 37.2 per cent. This was the first time the NSDAP had been the largest party in any German state parliament. On 15 November, in the state elections in Hesse, the party captured 37.1 per cent of the vote, with the NSDAP becoming the leading party in the parliament. It was clear that if national elections were called the NSDAP looked set for huge gains, greatly strengthening Hitler's case to be made German Chancellor.[66]

On 25 November, Carl Severing, the Prussian Interior Minister, suddenly announced that a National Socialist member of the Hessian parliament – named as 'Dr Schäfer' – who had been forced to step down due to revelations that he had falsely claimed to hold a doctorate, had handed over sensitive National Socialist documents to the local police. The papers, prepared by an ambitious lawyer, Dr Werner Best, the leader-designate of the NSDAP Landtag delegation, contained the minutes of a National Socialist meeting of regional leaders held in Boxheimer Hof, near the town of Lampertheim. They detailed, with frightening clarity, the party's contingency plans in the event of a Communist coup in Hesse. After crushing the Communists, the Stormtroopers would take ruthless and drastic measures using armed force in revenge. Every order would have to be obeyed, and anyone resisting would be 'shot on the spot, without trial'. The National Socialist authorities would control all food supplies, with Jews receiving no food at all.[67]

The shocking Boxheim Papers, as they became known, seemed to indicate the sort of brutal dictatorship that would engulf Germany should Hitler come to power. The revelations were deeply embarrassing for Hitler, who had made numerous promises that the NSDAP would keep within the bounds of legality once in power. On 26 November, Hermann Göring hurriedly issued a press statement on the Boxheim Papers, insisting the party leadership had nothing to do with their creation, and he also personally assured President Hindenburg that the documents did not represent the views of the party leadership.

To give further reassurance, Hitler gave a series of deliberately soothing interviews during December 1931. On 4 December, Hitler held an international press conference at the Hotel Kaiserhof in Berlin, saying: 'It will not be necessary for me to seize power in a coup d'état. It will be mine within a short time anyway, since every election brings my party closer to power.' In an interview with the *The Times* of London, he played down the revelations in the Boxheim Papers, and reaffirmed his commitment to the legal route to power. 'The National Socialist Movement,' he told the *New York Times*, 'will win power in Germany by methods permitted by the present Constitution in a purely legal way.'[68] Hitler continued his media charm offensive by publishing a two-part 'Message to the American People', which appeared in the party newspaper, *Völkischer Beobachter*, on 13–14 December. He claimed his movement wanted peace for Germany and for Europe, but he refused to accept the legitimacy of burdening Germany with reparations debts stretching years into the future. His movement, he concluded, was not a 'movement of desperation, but a movement of hope.'[69]

Meanwhile, on 8 December in a rare national radio broadcast, Heinrich Brüning announced the introduction of the Fourth Decree for Securing the Economy and Finances and for the purposes of Political Riot Control. It ran to 48 pages, including promising to lower salaries of government employees by 9 per cent, reducing the prices of cartels by 10 per cent, decrease interest rates by 1 per cent to 7 per cent, increase sales taxes from 1 to 2 per cent, and to put an end to government aid for residential building. There was also action on the rise of consumer prices with the appointment of Carl Goerdeler as Commissioner of Price Control. Finally, a 25 per cent 'national deserters tax' was levied, aimed at German citizens who had sold their German assets to escape German taxes.[70]

Brüning then launched into a surprisingly strong attack on Adolf Hitler, saying:

> Although the leader of the National Socialists has emphasized the legal methods and goals of his political intentions, nevertheless one cannot ignore the sharp contrast to these assurances provided by the violent assertions of no less responsible leaders of this same party who continue to incite Germans to senseless civil war and diplomatic follies. When one declares that one intends to break down legal barriers once one has come to power in legal ways, then one is no longer observing legality, particularly if clandestine plans are simultaneously being made for revenge.[71]

On New Year's Eve 1931, President Hindenburg delivered a national radio broadcast to the German people, in which he said 'Germans deserve thanks and praise for the sacrifices they have made and the patience with which they have borne their sufferings and burdens. The greatness of their sacrifice justifies Germany's demand that foreign countries should not seek to oppose Germany's recovery through the imposition of impossible conditions.' At one point, a group of Communists suddenly burst into the studio, interrupting the broadcast, with one shouting: 'Attention Germany! Red fighters are here.'[72]

1932
·
DIGGING WEIMAR'S GRAVE
·

As the New Year dawned, the question of the next presidential election came to the forefront of political debate. Hindenburg's term of office was due to expire in May 1932. In the opinion of Brüning, an election could be avoided by prolonging the 84-year-old President's term of office. To implement this amendment of Article 43 of the Weimar Constitution required a two-thirds majority in the Reichstag. On 5 January, Hindenburg told Brüning he thought this was the best solution, as he did not want to fight another election campaign.[1] To reach the required majority needed the support of both NSDAP and DNVP members in the Reichstag. On 7 January, Brüning asked Hitler to support a one-year extension to the presidential term, and promised that, if he did so, his path to the office of Chancellor would not be opposed by Hindenburg. In response, Hitler demanded the Reichstag be dissolved and new national elections called, while Hugenberg, the leader of the DNVP, made it clear that he strongly opposed extending Hindenburg's term of office.[2]

On 12 January, Hitler informed Brüning by letter that despite his own 'great personal respect for the Reich President', he had decided to reject extension of his office, due to 'constitutional concerns', making it clear that he thought it was Brüning who had pressurised the President to violate the constitution. Hitler's real reason for not postponing the presidential election was that he was contemplating running for the office himself.[3] To run for the office, Hitler needed first to become a German citizen. He had renounced his Austrian citizenship in 1925 and was classed in legal terms as 'stateless'; but due to a German legal technicality, an appointment to a government post, either at Reich or State level, brought with it automatic entitlement to German citizenship.

On 25 February 1932, Dietrich Klagges, the NSDAP Interior Minister of Braunschweig, appointed Hitler to the government council (*Regierungsrat*) in the Office of State Culture and Measurement, and as the State's consul in Berlin. These posts made Hitler a German citizen and eligible to assume public office.[4]

previous page   Adolf Hitler giving a campaign speech during the German presidential election of April 1932.

Before the start of the presidential campaign, Hitler tried to gain financial support from big business. At the invitation of the steel magnate Fritz Thyssen, Hitler gave a lengthy speech on 26 January to 800 members of the Industry Club in the grand ballroom of the Park Hotel in Düsseldorf, the heart of the industrial Ruhr. Industrialists had previously been reluctant to fund the NSDAP, due to the constant anti-capitalist slant of many of the speeches made by members of the 'socialist' wing of the party. Hitler now wanted to prove that big business had nothing to fear from National Socialism.[5] Hitler told his listeners in Düsseldorf that any political system which subjected the talented few in business to the will of the majority could not be called the rule of the people. A nation, he argued, must be ruled by the ablest men, and businesspeople were among that group. Private property could be justified morally and ethically on the grounds that the economic achievements of individuals were not equal. In fact, Hitler felt the principle of inequality that prevailed in business should be extended to politics. The crisis Germany was currently enduring, he went on, stemmed not only from external causes, but from the internal political collapse of parliament. Emergency decrees issued by Brüning could not avert economic catastrophe. Only a strong 'power-state' could create for business the conditions for future prosperity. What was required was a 'new mental outlook' which was only to be found in National Socialism, which stood for nationalism and strong leadership, and repudiated internationalism and democracy, promising in its place a state built on the principles of responsibility, command, and obedience.[6]

Hitler's Düsseldorf speech was an astute performance. It assured big business that freedom of enterprise would be an integral part of his government, and further promised the 'communist menace' would be dealt with ruthlessly if he was given power. Hitler was offering business the opportunity to be partners in the National Socialist future. Above all, it raised Hitler's profile in respectable business circles.

While Hitler's political credibility was growing stronger, Brüning's political prospects were looking decidedly bleak, with the influential behind-the-scenes wire-puller, Kurt von Schleicher, now questioning, in conversations with Hindenburg, his effectiveness as Chancellor. A triumph in foreign affairs seemed the only opportunity to provide Brüning with a much-needed boost. Two international issues offered opportunities in this direction. The first was the German demand for international parity in armaments, which would give a green light to German rearmament. The second was to bring about an end to reparations altogether. Both issues were due for discussion at international conferences in 1932. The first in Geneva concerned the Reduction and Limitation of Armaments, beginning on 1 February 1932, and the second was reparations payments, due for debate, in Lausanne, from 16 June to 9 July.[7]

In Geneva, on 6 February, Brüning pressed the case for recognition of Germany's right to equality in armaments. Not surprisingly, the French government objected, claiming it was really a subtle attempt by Germany to end the arms-limitations clauses of the Treaty of Versailles. A deadlock in the negotiations then ensued, leaving Brüning returning to Germany empty-handed. Brüning defended his position at Geneva in a speech to the Reichstag: 'I shall never let myself be seduced into pursuing a foreign policy which is designed to win prestige at home among voters misled by agitation which would endanger the vital interests of the German people in the longer run.'[8]

On 23 February, the Reichstag convened to set the dates for the two rounds of the upcoming presidential election. The date for the first round was set as 13 March, with 10 April pencilled in for the run-off. During the debate, Joseph Goebbels spoke on behalf of the National Socialists. He pointed out that Hindenburg, elected in 1925 as the candidate of the Nationalists, was now the candidate of the Social Democrats, a 'party of deserters' from the Great War. The Social Democrats exploded in rage against this accusation. Paul Löbe, the Speaker of the Reichstag, expelled Goebbels from the chamber for 'grossly insulting the President of Germany'.[9] On 26 February, the NSDAP and DNVP made yet another attempt to bring down the Brüning government by bringing a motion of no confidence before the Reichstag, but it was defeated narrowly by 289 to 264 votes. Once again, the Social Democrats had kept Brüning in power.[10]

The contest for the 1932 German presidential election created tremendous excitement.[11] On 16 February, Hindenburg told the German nation, in a radio broadcast, that running for re-election was his 'patriotic duty', portraying himself as the guardian of the Weimar Constitution, even though he had spent most of the previous two years undermining it. Hindenburg had been persuaded to accept the candidacy after a non-partisan committee headed by Heinrich Sahm, the Lord Mayor of Berlin, had collected 3 million signatures in support of his candidature.[12]

Hindenburg was primarily supported by the parties on the Centre

Left, including the SPD, Zentrum, the BVP, the DVP and the DStP, who all decided not to run candidates against the incumbent President. The Social Democrats campaigned energetically for Hindenburg under the slogan 'Smash Hitler, Vote Hindenburg'. Otto Braun, the SPD Prime Minister of Prussia, told party colleagues: 'The Presidential Election, which is a crucial prelude to the Prussia [State] Elections will decide whether Germany's future will continue along the peaceful pathways of Republican State life of whether the German people will have to wade through a Fascist valley of misery.'[13]

The official Hindenburg campaign was led by the supposedly 'non-partisan' United Hindenburg Committee (UHC), headed by Gunther Gereke of the CNBL and the conservative Kuno von Westarp. The UHC insisted all party-political supporters of Hindenburg should conduct their own separate campaigns, with the official campaign focusing on the President's charismatic persona, particularly his role in the Great War of 1914–18. The campaign stressed that Hindenburg was the only person who could heal the bitter divisions of German society, and prevent Hitler establishing a one-party dictatorship. The President's campaign spent 7.5 million Reichsmarks, which was 1 million more than Hitler's campaign. Most of Hindenburg's funding, which was brokered by Carl Duisburg of chemical company IG Farben, came from big business, but 1.8 million of it was secretly provided from the funds of the Prussian Ministry of the Interior.[14]

Heinrich Brüning, the Chancellor, was the most energetic campaigner on Hindenburg's behalf. Brüning spoke at a number of rallies, which attracted large crowds, declaring repeatedly that Hindenburg was the nation's saviour, and every vote against him was a vote against national unity. Hindenburg's only personal contributions to the campaign were two short films and a radio broadcast. In one of the films, he discussed why he had entered the race, but he read from notes that he held nervously in his hands, and stared at constantly. In the second, an actor narrated a list of Hindenburg's achievements over a selection of film clips.[15] On 10 March, in a pre-recorded radio broadcast, Hindenburg told listeners that he had only decided to run after careful reflection, and in the belief it was his patriotic duty to do so. He called on German voters to unite behind his candidacy. He also made clear that he did not consider himself the candidate of the Left, noting the first requests for him to run had come from the Right. Significantly, he distanced himself from Brüning, saying some of his emergency decrees 'could be improved'.[16]

HİTLER

The DNVP selected Theodor Duesterberg, the deputy leader of the war veteran's association Steel Helmet, as its presidential candidate. He had a good war record, gaining the Iron Cross (1st and 2nd Class). The National Socialists immediately tried to undermine his campaign by revealing his grandfather had been born a Jew, leaving Goebbels to brand Duesterberg as 'racially inferior'. It was a great irony that Duesterberg, who was well known for his antisemitic views, had Jewish roots.[17]

The Communists chose as their candidate the KPD leader, Ernst Thälmann, whose ill-judged decision to contest the second round of voting in the 1925 presidential election had helped to tip the vote in favour of Hindenburg. The KPD's election slogan in 1932 was: 'A Vote for Hindenburg is a vote for Hitler, and a vote for Hitler is a vote for war'. It seemed certain that Thälmann would not drop out after the first round, and might possibly play a pivotal role again.[18]

The presidential campaign only got into full swing, however, when Adolf Hitler entered the contest. On 22 February, Goebbels publicly announced Hitler's candidature at a huge rally in the Sport Palace in Berlin. The cheering went on for 20 minutes after the announcement. The National Socialists fought an ultra-modern campaign, with propaganda masterminded by Goebbels, who led the Propaganda Directorship of the NSDAP (*Reichspropagandaleitung*) in Berlin's Hedemannstrasse. Hitler's campaign was depicted as a struggle between the Weimar system and National Socialism. It was the first time a National Socialist campaign had been built entirely around the image of the *Führer*. Hitler did not think he could beat such an established national figure as Hindenburg, but he thought he could secure about 12 million votes, and emerge as the most popular leader of any German political party.[19]

During the campaign, Goebbels distributed 50,000 small phonographic records of a Hitler speech, and circulated a ten-minute promotional campaign film featuring Hitler, which was designed to be shown to large crowds on screens erected in city centres.[20] Eight million leaflets were also sent out to voters, accompanied by thousands of posters displayed on billboards in every town and city centre. Loudspeaker vans drove through the streets promoting Hitler's message. A market research team targeted specific voters, with mail-shots culled from each area Address Book (*Addressbuch*).

At the centre of the campaign was a speaking tour by Hitler, who travelled by motorcade to each venue. In a frenetic period between 1 and

A poster for the 1932 presidential election.

11 March, Hitler addressed big crowds in Hamburg, Stettin (Szczecin), Breslau (Wrocław), Leipzig, Bad Blankenburg, Weimar, Frankfurt am Main, Nuremberg, Stuttgart, Cologne, Dortmund, and Hanover. Each of his speeches resembled a modern rock concert, and it was estimated he spoke to a total of 500,000 people during his speaking tour.[21] The key theme of Hitler's speeches was the '13 wasted years' of the Weimar Republic, which he defined as a time of 'unmitigated political and economic chaos', orchestrated by the 'November Criminals'. Hitler skilfully avoided a direct attack on Hindenburg. Instead, he expressed some admiration for the 'Old Gentleman', stressing his service to the Fatherland, but pointing out that he was now essentially a man of the past, who was a puppet of the Social Democrats and Republicans, and he asked him to 'stand aside so that we can destroy those standing behind you'. In place of the current 'democratic chaos', Hitler promised a united National Community under his strong leadership.[22]

Hitler's attitude towards women came under the media spotlight for the first time during the presidential campaign. It was not a subject he felt the least bit comfortable talking about. He was forced to refute claims that he wanted to deprive women of equal rights and jobs if he came to power. Hitler defined women as 'the most valuable unit in the structure of the state' due to their role as mothers. But in fact Hitler, if he came to power, intended to reverse the equality granted to women under the Weimar Constitution, and consign them to the role of increasing the number of 'racially valuable births' in his National Community.[23]

On 13 March 1932, the first round of voting in the presidential election took place. Hindenburg (Independent) topped the poll, with 49.54 per cent (18.65 million), failing by just 0.4 per cent (170,000), to gain an outright majority, which meant a run-off election was now required. Hitler (NSDAP) came second with 30.12 per cent (11.33 million). If Hindenburg had not stood, Hitler would almost certainly have won. In a distant third place was Ernst Thälmann (KPD), polling 13.24 per cent (4.98 million), and below him came Theodor Duesterberg (Steel Helmet) on 6.79 per cent (2.55 million). At the very bottom was Gustav Winter (Inflation Victims), with 0.3 per cent (111,423). The bottom two, Duesterberg and Winter, dropped out of the run-off election. The turnout in the first ballot was 86.21 per cent, which was well up on the 68.87 who had voted in the first round of the 1925 presidential election.[24] Despite his clear triumph, Hindenburg was disappointed, as he had expected a first-round outright victory. He was especially upset by the fact Hitler had won in Hindenburg's home province of East Prussia. Since the 1930 national elections, Hitler had almost doubled the vote of the NSDAP.[25]

The campaign for the run-off election on 10 April was impeded by Hindenburg's issue of an emergency decree imposing an 'Easter truce' on election campaigning, which ran from 20 March to 3 April, prohibiting all political meetings and rallies during this period. This left only a week of campaigning before the voters went to the polls again.[26] Hitler's propaganda machine now moved into top gear, promising a campaign 'the likes of which the world had never seen'. His campaign received a timely boost, on 3 April, when Friedrich Wilhelm, the former German Crown Prince, announced his intention to vote for Hitler in the belief the National Socialist leader would restore the monarchy.

Hitler's major innovation during the run-off campaign was to charter a Junkers D-1720 aeroplane. On 3 April, he began his first 'Hitler over Germany' (*'Hitler über Deutschland'*) air tour. Flying from city to city, making up to five stops a day, Hitler spoke at 23 rallies to an estimated 1 million people. This modern style of campaigning had only previously been seen in the USA. The powerful image of Hitler descending from the clouds like a Messiah was made into a film, and later published as a best-selling photo-book, which sold 500,000 copies.

In his speeches, Hitler attacked the Marxists, the November Criminals, and the Weimar system, promising that he alone could make Germany great again by toppling Weimar's corrupt and chaotic party system to create a classless National Community. Each day, there were bitter and violent street clashes between the Stormtroopers and the Communist Red Front League, which the police found difficult to control.[27]

Hindenburg's campaign for the run-off election was extensive and effective, arguing that Hitler had portrayed himself as an anti-Marxist candidate when his party could not hide its dislike of private property and free enterprise. An impressive election propaganda film called *The Life and Deeds of Hindenburg* was shown in cinemas throughout Germany. The United Hindenburg Campaign knew the President would win, but wanted to pile up as big a vote as possible to demoralise Hitler's supporters. The Social Democrats assisted the campaign by getting its members to canvass tirelessly door to door, especially in working-class areas of the big cities, while a Lufthansa aircraft dropped 20 million pro-Hindenburg leaflets all over the country.[28]

A poster promoting the 'Hitler over Germany'
(*Hitler über Deutschland*) air tour during the
presidential election of April 1932.

When Germans returned to the polls on 10 April, the outcome, as expected, was a clear victory for Hindenburg, with 53.05 per cent (19.35 million) of the votes, an increase of 3.45 per cent (708,486) on the first election. Hitler came second with 36.77 per cent (13.41 million), up 6.65 per cent (2.07 million). In third place was Ernst Thälmann (KPD), on 10.16 per cent (3.70 million), down by 3.08 per cent (1.27 million) on the first contest. The turnout was 83.45 per cent, down slightly, by 2.76 per cent, on the first ballot.[29]

Hitler had emerged from the contest not as the winner, but as the most popular party politician in Germany. About 60 per cent of those who had voted for Hindenburg in 1925 voted for Hitler in 1932. Hindenburg, who received the highest proportion of votes ever cast in a German democratic election, refused to accept that the election proved most voters wanted a broad-based coalition to keep Hitler out of power. Instead, Hindenburg felt the wrong people had voted for him. He would have preferred to have been the leader of the Right, who wanted to destroy democracy, not of the moderate Centre Left, who wanted to save it. He ungratefully told Otto Braun, the SPD Prime Minister of Prussia, that he did not feel bound to support the policies of the parties that had supported him during the presidential campaign.[30]

A few days earlier, Carl Severing, the Prussian Interior Minister, had approached Wilhelm Groener, Reich Minister of the Interior, asking for something to be done about the continuing violence of Hitler's Stormtroopers. The conversation took place during a conference attended by the Interior Ministers of all the German states, who were in agreement that a ban on the SA was necessary. Severing made it clear that if the Reich government did not act to ban the SA, then the Prussian state government, and many other German states, most notably Bavaria and Saxony, would.[31]

On 10 April, Groener sent a memo to Brüning, arguing that Hindenburg's re-election presented an ideal opportunity to rein in the power of Hitler by banning the Stormtroopers. He pointed out the SA had systematically disturbed the political meetings of its political opponents during the presidential campaign. Brüning later recalled that he told Groener a ban on the SA was 'premature'. The decision to ban the SA gained unanimous approval from within the cabinet, but Hindenburg was reluctant to sign the emergency banning decree, when it was presented to him on 13 April. He only agreed to do so after Groener and Brüning threatened to resign.[32]

On 13 April, the Emergency Decree on the Protection of the Authority of the State was issued, banning the SA and SS throughout Germany, and prohibiting members of both organisations from wearing their uniforms. Groener instructed the police to confiscate all SA equipment, including banners, tents, field stoves and trucks. In most states, the police acted vigorously to enforce the ban. The decree stressed the SA and SS constituted a private army and were therefore a danger to public order. Oskar von Hindenburg warned his father the ban on the SA would be seen by the Right as part of an election deal with the Social Democrats.[33]

Kurt von Schleicher felt Hindenburg had signed the decree against his better judgement and he immediately began a behind-the-scenes campaign to undermine it. He let Hitler and other senior NSDAP leaders know that he personally opposed the ban. He then persuaded General Kurt von Hammerstein-Equord, the Chief of the German Army Command, to present Hindenburg with a dossier on whether the Reichsbanner (Black-Red-Gold, a paramilitary organisation, funded primarily by the Social Democrats, which was pledged to defend the Weimar Republic), should also be banned.

The ban on the SA and SS worsened Hindenburg's already strained relations with Brüning and Groener. Hindenburg instructed Groener on 16 April to investigate whether the SA ban should be extended to other organisations. Groener rejected the banning of the Reichsbanner. On 3 May, Hindenburg issued another emergency decree, which set out new guidelines that applied equally to all paramilitary associations. The Reichsbanner then voluntarily disbanded all its semi-military formations, and placed its remaining units under the control of the Reich Minister of the Interior.[34]

Hitler saw the ban on the SA as part of a remorseless campaign by the Brüning government to suppress his party. The SA figurehead, Ernst Röhm, contemplated resisting the decree, saying to Hitler that the Stormtroopers now numbered 400,000. Hitler urged patience on the SA, pointing out that power through elections was getting really close. 'I understand your feelings', he wrote in an address to Stormtroopers. 'For years you have been true to my directives about winning power by legal means. You are horribly persecuted and harassed. Yet despite all the gruesome agony perpetrated against you by today's momentarily ruling parties, you have remained upright and honourable.'[35]

The ban on the SA came only days before important elections for a number of State parliaments in Prussia, Bavaria, Württemberg and

Wilhelm Groener, Brüning's Defence Minister until he was brought down by Schleicher's intrigues in May 1932.

Anhalt, and voters in Hamburg selecting a new Mayor. With 80 per cent of German voters across the country taking part, the elections would give a good indication of the current electoral strength of all the political parties. Between 16 and 24 April, Hitler undertook his second 'flight over Germany', delivering 25 major speeches, not only in big cities but in rural areas, too. The main concentration of the NSDAP campaign was in the giant state of Prussia. In his speeches, Hitler promised to topple the SPD-led government in Prussia, the last bastion of the Social Democrats, which had held power there since the creation of the Weimar Republic.[36]

The NSDAP achieved outstanding success in the State elections of 24 April 1932. In Prussia, which made up 57 per cent of the population of Germany, the NSDAP improved its share of the vote from 1.8 per cent in 1928 to 36.3 per cent, increasing its seats from 9 to 162 seats, and becoming the largest party in the Prussian parliament in the process, though unable to form a government without the support of Zentrum. The SPD vote share fell from 29 to 21 per cent, with its seats falling in number from 137 to 94.

Just before the election, the Prussian government had altered the parliamentary rules of order to require an absolute majority for

the election of a new Prime Minister. Until a new government was formed, therefore, a caretaker administration led by the current SPD Prime Minister, Otto Braun, would remain in office. Reich Chancellor Brüning further insisted no member of the NSDAP should be offered the post of Prime Minister, and he drafted contingency plans for the control of the Prussian police, and the court system passing to Reich government control. On 28 April, Hitler broke off coalition talks with the Centre Party in Prussia.

In Bavaria, the NSDAP vote rose from 6.1 per cent in 1928 to 32.6 per cent, becoming the second largest party in the state parliament, behind the BVP. In Württtemberg, the NSDAP polled 26.4 per cent of the poll, and became the largest party. In the SPD stronghold of Hamburg, the NSDAP vote of 31.2 per cent was narrowly ahead of the 30.2 per cent total secured by the SPD. The best result of all was in Anhalt, where the NSDAP received 40.9 per cent of all the votes, and formed a government.[37] In May, the electoral march of NSDAP continued. In Oldenburg, the party took 48 per cent of the vote, winning 24 out of 48 seats, thereby gaining the first overall majority in a German state by the party. In the SPD stronghold of Hesse, the NSDAP recorded 44 per cent of the votes.[38]

With electoral support for Hitler's party growing spectacularly, Hindenburg's disenchantment with Brüning escalated. Big business was unhappy with Brüning's failure to dismantle the costly social welfare system, while powerful agrarian interests successfully lobbied Hindenburg to overturn Brüning's plan to resettle unemployed workers in foreclosed East Elbian estates. A further reflection of the general unease with the so-called 'socialist' direction of Brüning's economic policy was the resignation of Hermann Warmbold, the Economics Minister, on 6 May. Above all, it was Brüning's unwillingness to reach an understanding with Hitler's National Socialists which had turned him into a political liability, from the point of view of Schleicher and Hindenburg. At the end of April, Schleicher was actively plotting on behalf of the Army to bring down the Brüning government, and install a more right-wing authoritarian one, hopefully involving the NSDAP, backed up by the Army. As Schleicher put it: 'If the National Socialists didn't exist, we should have to invent them.'[39]

On 28 April, with Hindenburg's blessing, Schleicher secretly met with Hitler to discuss the conditions under which the NSDAP would join a coalition government, or at least tolerate one. Schleicher told Hitler that Brüning was on the way out, and a new government was in the offing. On 7 May, Hitler met Schleicher again, with Otto Meissner, Hindenburg's Permanent Secretary, and Oskar von Hindenburg also present. At this meeting, Hitler struck a secret deal with Schleicher under which Hitler promised he would not join a new right-wing presidential cabinet, unless the bans on the SA and SS were lifted beforehand, and new Reichstag elections were called.[40] Goebbels commented on this Schleicher–Hitler meeting in his diary: 'The old man [Hindenburg] will withdraw his support [from Brüning]. Schleicher is pressing for it. Then there will be a Presidential Cabinet. Reichstag dissolved. The [SA and SS] laws hemming us in will go. We will have freedom to agitate and produce our tour de force.'[41]

On 10 May, the Reichstag reconvened, with Wilhelm Groener delivering a hesitant speech defending the emergency decree banning the SA and SS. During his speech, Groener called the SA a 'private army' which had grown into a danger to the state. He was then continually interrupted and heckled by the National Socialist Reichstag members, and seemed to lose his train of thought. The speech was generally reported in the press as an unmitigated disaster. Schleicher advised Groener to go on leave. Hindenburg urged him to resign, but Brüning felt that with the Lausanne Conference on Reparations due to begin on 16 June sacking his Defence Minister should be delayed until then, for the sake of foreign public opinion.[42]

On 11 May, Brüning delivered a confident speech in the Reichstag, mainly concentrating on foreign policy. He said he now pinned his hopes on a diplomatic breakthrough at the Lausanne Conference, and the on-going World Disarmament Conference, depicting himself as a long-distance runner who was now in 'the last hundred metres before the finishing line'. The official stenographic report of the Reichstag proceedings on this day records that at the end of Brüning's speech there was 'long-lasting, stormy approval and applause'.[43]

On 12 May, Brüning's government easily survived a no-confidence vote tabled by the opposition parties in the Reichstag by a margin of 287 to 257, proving the toleration by the Social Democrats was still functioning effectively. Later on that same day, Groener announced his resignation as Defence Minister, but promised to continue as Minister of the Interior for the time being. Groener's humiliating fall was, of course, a huge victory for Schleicher's behind-the-scenes intrigues. It was also a triumph for Hitler, who had been calling for Groener's resignation ever since he had introduced the ban on the SA and SS. Brüning offered the post of Defence Minister to Schleicher, who turned it down, a move that was interpreted as marking the beginning of the end for Brüning.[44]

The downfall of Heinrich Brüning as German Chancellor now came with dramatic suddenness. On 29 May, Hindenburg held a showdown meeting with him. The Chancellor said his cabinet would soon regain popularity after diplomatic victories, but in the meantime, he demanded Hindenburg put an end to his 'shadow government' of the President's inner circle and rely on his cabinet ministers instead. Hindenburg then read from a prepared statement, making it clear that he would not allow Brüning or any of his cabinet members to issue any more emergency decrees, nor would he allow Brüning to carry out a cabinet reshuffle. In response, Brüning said the President obviously wanted him to resign, and Hindenburg agreed, saying: 'I must turn to the Right at long last, the newspapers and the whole nation demand it. But you have always refused to do so.'[45] On the next day, 30 May 1932, at noon, Brüning and his entire cabinet left office. Brüning turned down Hindenburg's offer to stay on as Foreign Minister. As a parting shot, Hindenburg said: 'Now I can have a cabinet of my friends.'

Brüning was the first German Chancellor of the Weimar Republic to resign because he had lost the confidence of the President. All other holders of the office left office when a majority of Reichstag members refused to support them or when it was clear a parliamentary majority was unattainable. Brüning, often a derided figure, deserves some rehabilitation, as he was trying to sustain some semblance of democracy, but was hounded out of office by anti-democratic forces led by Hindenburg and his small inner circle.

Schleicher personally selected the person who succeeded Brüning as German Chancellor. On 28 June, two days before Brüning had even resigned, Schleicher had offered the post to Franz von Papen, a 53-year-old right-wing, well-connected, wealthy member of the Catholic nobility of Westphalia, who was not even a member of the Reichstag, and had recently lost his seat on the Prussian parliament, but whom Hindenburg had met socially many times, expressing admiration for his charming, superficial, light-hearted, self-deprecating personality. Schleicher regarded Papen as a political lightweight, but thought he would be a willing puppet of the President, and his inner circle, in their own desire for a right-wing authoritarian regime.

Papen was spectacularly unqualified for the role of Chancellor at a time of deep political crisis. He thought Germany had failed to develop a viable democratic system since 1918 because votes were split between too many political parties, making a stable coalition impossible. In place of this, Papen favoured creating a 'New State' that would stand above party interests, and provide order so that business could thrive. It was a theory that had been advanced by two of his closest advisers, Walther Schotte, a journalist and historian, and Edgar Jung, a lawyer. They favoured an authoritarian presidential regime, with the Reichstag severely restricted in its rights, a set-up very reminiscent of the constitution of the German Empire. Papen's long-term aim was the restoration of the Hohenzollern monarchy.[46]

Papen later gave a detailed account of how he became German Chancellor.[47] On 26 May, he had received a telephone call from Schleicher, urging him to come to Berlin to discuss 'an urgent matter', but giving no details. Papen finally arrived in Schleicher's office on 28 June, seemingly 'without any idea of what was going on'. Schleicher then told Papen that he had already convinced Hindenburg to replace Brüning with a presidential 'cabinet of experts', completely independent of the political parties, as it had now become impossible to form a cabinet that could command a majority in the Reichstag. Schleicher explained Brüning's unwillingness to cooperate with the National Socialists, particularly his ban on the SA, had caused Hindenburg deep embarrassment. Schleicher felt it was no longer possible to keep a party as strong as the NSDAP out of power, and drive them further to the fringes of power and possibly to armed civil war.

Schleicher then offered Papen the post of German Chancellor. In response, Papen said: 'This offer takes me completely by surprise. I very much doubt I am the right man.' Schleicher responded by revealing that he had already discussed the matter with Hindenburg and 'he is most insistent you should accept the post'. Schleicher next revealed that he had already drawn up a provisional list of cabinet members, which 'I am sure you will approve', as they were all 'respectable men of Conservative tendencies'. Schleicher went on to give details of his secret discussions with Hitler, assuring him the National Socialists would give 'tacit support' for his government, even though they would not be represented in it. He also mentioned the price of this collaboration with Hitler would be to lift the ban on the SA, and call fresh national elections. At the end of the talk, Papen told Schleicher that he would 'think the matter over during the week-end'.

On Monday 30 May, Papen met with Schleicher once again, informing him that having mulled over his offer, he felt he must decline the offer, as he thought the whole Centre Party would turn against him, and the Social Democrats would also offer firm opposition to his appointment, as they regarded him as a right-wing conservative opposed to social welfare policies and trade unions. In reply, Schleicher told Papen that if his government put forward a comprehensive programme to reduce unemployment then his popularity would soon soar, adding that President Hindenburg was 'depending on you not leaving him in the lurch'. This appeal to his sense of duty impressed Papen. He ended the conversation by telling Schleicher he would give a definitive answer after meeting with Ludwig Kaas, the leader of Zentrum.

On the next day, 31 May, Papen met Kaas, who told him bluntly that if he accepted the Chancellorship, he would be immediately expelled from Zentrum. He also reminded Papen of a visit he had personally made to Papen's estate in the Saarland in mid-May when he had reprimanded him for 'intriguing against Brüning'. This account by Kaas indicates that Papen knew all about Schleicher's plan to depose Brüning.[48] Papen's flawed version of events is further undermined by an entry in the diary of Joseph Goebbels, dated 25 May, in which he notes that Schleicher told him that Brüning would be sacked and replaced by Papen. This was three days before Schleicher had offered the post of German Chancellor to Papen.[49]

On 31 May, Papen went to see President Hindenburg, who told him that he now wanted a cabinet of people in whom he had confidence. Replying, Papen told him that if he took on the role, he would not have the support of Zentrum. Hindenburg then placed his hands on Papen's shoulders, looked him in the eyes, and said:

> It is immaterial to me if you earn the disapproval or even the enmity of your party. I intend to have people round me who are independent of political parties, men of good will and expert knowledge, who will surmount the crisis of our country, You have been a soldier and did your duty in the war. When the Fatherland calls, Prussia knows only one response – obedience.[50]

Papen later claimed that it was this emotional appeal by Hindenburg which finally persuaded him to become the German Chancellor.

Papen duly accepted Schleicher's list of cabinet ministers, without suggesting any amendments. The Papen cabinet formally took office on 1 June 1932. It was the second presidential cabinet whose legitimacy was derived exclusively from presidential decrees, and which did not require parliamentary support, provided the cabinet approved of them. The Papen cabinet had an almost completely new set of members. It was, in theory, a non-party cabinet, but did contain three members of the DNVP – Wilhelm von Gayl (Interior), Franz Gürtner (Justice), and Magnus von Braun (Agriculture and Reich Commissioner for Eastern Aid). The remaining members had no party affiliations, but had at one time or another been associated with parties of the nationalist Right. They consisted of: Konstantin von Neurath (Foreign Affairs), Lutz von Krosigk (Finance), Hugo Schäffer (Labour) and Paul von Eltz-Rübenach (Transport and Post). Hermann Warmbold (Independent), who had recently resigned from Brüning's cabinet, returned as the Minister of Economics. Finally, Kurt von Schleicher appointed himself as the new Minister of Defence. He enjoyed a special position in Papen's cabinet as he had been its chief creator and was best placed to engineer its downfall. The Papen government did not contain a single member associated with organised labour or with the parties on the Centre Left.[51]

Germany now had the right-wing nationalist government Hindenburg desired, which the left-wing press called 'the cabinet of barons', due to the aristocratic landowning and military backgrounds of most of its members. The Papen cabinet represented a return to the ruling classes who had dominated German society before the Great War of 1914–18. It was an attempt to create a right-wing National Front, which excluded Centrists, Liberals, Socialists and Communists. Hitler described it as a 'transitional government' which would be soon replaced by a National Socialist government. Papen preferred to call it a 'cabinet of gentlemen', based on a group who 'by virtue of family background and social position, enjoyed the qualifications for membership of an exclusive club'.[52]

On 4 June, Papen issued a proclamation on national radio declaring his government was seeking to unite all 'the patriotic forces of the country'. He then claimed Germany had been brought to its knees by the Versailles Treaty, the economic crisis and by 'mismanagement of parliamentary democracy'. Successive governments had attempted to convert the state into a 'kind of welfare institute' and undermined the nation's 'moral strength'. Papen now promised to put an end to the 'moral disintegration of the people, aggravated by class warfare and cultural Bolshevism'. He was clearly trying to appease Hitler by speaking his language. In truth, Papen's chance of long-term survival was hugely dependent on Hitler's party making big gains in the upcoming national elections, and providing him with a majority in the Reichstag.

To this end, Papen immediately introduced a number of measures favourable to Hitler's NSDAP. The Reichstag was dissolved on 4 June, thus making good on the secret promise Schleicher had made to Hitler, with the new national elections set for 31 July. On 15 June, Hindenburg signed a decree lifting the ban on the SA and SS, which expressed the hope that 'the conflict in political opinion will henceforth assume an orderly form'.[53] On 28 June, the ban on wearing party uniforms was also lifted. Other emergency decrees ended financial help for impoverished East Elbian agricultural workers, and brought in a new rigid means test for unemployment benefits, which lowered entitlement and payments. None of these measures had been debated or voted on in the Reichstag.

Papen was briefly able to escape the bitter conflict surrounding his government by leading the German delegation to the International Reparations Conference, which opened in Lausanne on 16 June 1932. One of his key aims was to achieve a final settlement of the reparations problem, which had haunted German political life since the start of the Weimar Republic. Papen argued that Germany's current economic difficulties demanded a complete end to the payment of reparations. He even offered the French a bilateral military alliance in return for ending reparations, which no one took seriously, least of all the British government, who saw it as an attempt to undermine British–French cooperation. Papen also tried to have Article 231 of the Versailles Treaty (the war-guilt clause) removed, but this was overwhelmingly rejected.

Negotiations on the size of Germany's remaining reparations payments occupied most of the remaining deliberations. On 9 July, the creditor nations and Germany agreed the Young Plan would be abandoned, thereby renouncing over 90 per cent of all future German payments. In the final settlement, Germany was only required to make a promise to pay a final instalment of 3 billion Reichsmarks, paid into a general fund, by the end of June 1935, for European reconstruction, which would be financed by special bonds, only payable when economic stability had been restored in Germany.[54] No further reparations were ever paid by the German government.

The weeks preceding the German national elections of July 1932 were hectic and violent. The lifting of the SA ban led to a wave of violence not seen since the early days of the Weimar Republic. In six weeks, there were 103 deaths in violent clashes between National Socialists and Communists.[55] The worst incident occurred on 17 July in the industrial area of Altona, which at the time belonged to the Prussian province of Schleswig-Holstein. Eighteen people were killed in what became known as 'Altona Bloody Sunday' (*Altonaer Blutsonntag*). The National Socialists claimed the police in Prussia had lost control. The violent clash came during a parade by 7,000 Stormtroopers through the Communist areas of Altona in the western part of Hamburg. Otto Eggerstedt, the Social Democrat police chief of Altona, had allowed the march to go ahead, leaving the local Communists deeply infuriated. A pitched battle raged in the streets that left two SA men and 16 local residents dead. At the time, it was reported that Communist snipers were exclusively responsible for all the killings, but after an extensive recent re-evaluation of all the surviving documents related to the incident, it has been conclusively proved that trigger-happy local police were responsible for all the killings.[56]

On 18 July, the Papen government issued another emergency decree prohibiting all outdoor rallies and marches. The Altona riots provided Papen with a spurious justification to bring the country's largest state of Prussia under Reich control. On 20 July, Papen met the members of the Prussian cabinet in the Reich Chancellery, telling them he had invoked Article 48 of the Weimar Constitution, was removing them from office, and declaring himself as the acting and all-powerful 'Reich Commissioner'. Civil servants were issued with an order demanding 'unconditional obedience' to the new Reich Commissioner. A second decree, issued on the same day, transferred executive power in Prussia to the Defence Minister, Kurt von Schleicher. All this amounted to a *coup d'état* against Prussia, the last bastion of democracy in the Weimar Republic. No general strike or mass protests occurred in response.[57]

Papen justified his Prussian coup by claiming the 1932 Prussian Landtag election had left a divided parliament with no viable coalition. This had left a caretaker government in power, he claimed, that no longer had democratic legitimacy, and was unable to control violent street violence. In these circumstances, public safety in Prussia could no longer be guaranteed. Papen appointed Franz Bracht, former mayor of Essen and a member of Zentrum, as the new Prussian Interior Minister, in control of the police.[58]

The Papen takeover in Prussia was a body blow to Weimar democracy. Otto Braun and the deposed ministers of the Prussian government claimed the seizure of power in Prussia infringed the Weimar Constitution, and they launched an appeal to the German Supreme Court on 21 July, for the granting of an injunction to stop Papen governing in Prussia. On 25 July, the Supreme Court refused to issue an injunction, ruling the matter had to be settled in a final court

overleaf Funeral of a Stormtrooper shot
during the violent clashes between Nazis
and Communists that followed 'Altona
Bloody Sunday', 17 July 1932.

hearing later in the year. The German Supreme Court in Leipzig eventually ruled, on 25 October 1932, in the case of 'Prussia versus Reich' that Papen's action in declaring himself Reich Commissioner to maintain order was only 'partially legal' but decided his deposing of the Braun government was 'not justified'.[59] The Papen government simply ignored the provisions of the Supreme Court ruling, and Papen's 'Commissar government' continued to rule. Braun's so-called 'sovereign government' was allowed to continue in office, but had been deprived of any real power to govern. The Prussian coup showed how easily a State government, seemingly protected by the Weimar Constitution, could be overthrown by an authoritarian regime.

During July 1932, the NSDAP conducted yet another whirlwind election campaign. The campaign was once again conducted by Goebbels with the smooth efficiency of a well-oiled machine. The key campaign slogans were 'Germany Awaken!' and 'Give Hitler Power!' On 15 July, Hitler began his third 'flight over Germany'. In a frantic fortnight he addressed 53 meetings. Thousands waited to see him at each stop. The theme of Hitler's speeches remained the same. He began by describing the economic and political decay of the 'Weimar system'. This was followed by a promise to get rid of all the numerous political parties who had failed the farmer, the worker, the artisan, and the shopkeeper for the past '13 wasted years'. Hitler promised these 'corrupt parties' would be replaced by his genuine 'party of the people'.[60]

The outcome of the national elections of 31 July 1932 was spectacular. Voter turnout was 84.1 per cent, up by 2.1 per cent from the previous election in September 1930. The biggest sensation was the showing of the NSDAP, which polled 37.3 per cent of votes (13.74 million), up by 19 per cent from the previous election. It was the biggest surge of support for any party in a single election since the Weimar period began, and one of the greatest voting advances in democratic political history. The NSDAP won 230 seats, up by 123 seats in 1930, and was now the most popular political party in Germany.[61]

The voter gains by the NSDAP in July 1932 came from 12 per cent of previous non-voters, 6 per cent of former voters for the DNVP, 10 per cent from the Social Democrats, 8 per cent from the two middle-class parties, the DVP and DStP, and 18 per cent from all the special-interest splinter parties. As in the September 1930 election, NSDAP voters were disproportionately male and Protestant, with a hard core of middle-class voters, but with larger numbers of voters from all the social classes than any other party.[62]

A Nazi Party poster for the national
elections of July 1932, which saw a surge in
voter support for the NSDAP.

The election showed the NSDAP had persuaded previous support-ers of middle-class and special-interest parties to switch their votes. The National Socialists had united all the middle-class protest voters towards its crusade to destroy the Weimar political system. Although the NSDAP is often seen as a party that appealed to young people, it has been estimated that 53 per cent of voters for the NSDAP in July 1932 were middle-class and over 53. Voter support for the party was 10 per cent below the national average in cities with over 100,000 people, and highest in small villages with under 5,000 inhabitants.

The core of electoral support for the NSDAP in September 1930 was in the old middle class (*Mittelstand*) of small farmers, skilled workers, self-employed traders and shopkeepers, but this support expanded in July 1932 to encompass the new middle class of teachers, engineers, doctors, lawyers, university students, civil servants, pensioners, white-collar workers, and even included members of the upper classes in the wealthy districts of big cities. The NSDAP was also attracting up to 40 per cent of working-class support, not from industrial manual workers in big cities, but from those who worked for small-scale manufacturing firms and rural labourers, especially in small rural towns. There was also the German equivalent of British 'working class conservatives', working people who always had a tradition of voting for non-socialist parties, and many of these switched to the NSDAP in July 1932. Overall, support for the NSDAP was concentrated disproportionally in occupational groups that harboured the greatest reservations about modern industrial society, and it was weakest among the industrial working class in the urban areas.[63]

In July 1932, there were still 5.4 million unemployed, but the idea that rising unemployment explains the increase in votes for Hitler is a myth. Unemployment was concentrated in areas where support for Hitler was at its lowest. Only 13 per cent of the insured unemployed workers, who comprised 30 per cent of the manual working class, voted NSDAP. The unemployed were most likely to vote for the KPD.[64]

Only three of the other main parties managed to increase their number of seats. The best performance was by the far-left KPD, which polled 14.3 per cent (5.28 million), up from 13.1 per cent, winning 89 seats, up by 12 seats since 1930. The combined votes of the KPD and the NSDAP, who both wanted to destroy democracy, now totalled 51.6 per cent of German voters, indicating a significant disillusionment with the Weimar democratic system.[65]

Catholic voters once again resisted the appeal of the National

previous pages   Hitler on the stump, Berlin 1932. With him
are, from left to right, his adjutant Wilhelm Brückner, SA
Oberführer Wolf-Heinrich Graf von Helldorff, and – in an
overcoat behind Hitler – Joseph Goebbels.

Socialists, with Zentrum winning 68 seats, up from 61 in the previous election, and polling 12.4 per cent (4.58 million), up 0.6 per cent on the previous election. The Bavarian People's Party (BVP), which like Zentrum was linked to Catholicism, also held its own, polling 3.2 per cent (1.92 million), up by 0.2 per cent, with 19 seats, up by 3 seats from 1930.[66]

The two traditional conservative and socialist parties were not hit too heavily by the remarkable surge of support for the NSDAP. The SPD was now the second largest party in the Reichstag, with 133 seats, a loss of just 10 from the previous election, polling 21.6 per cent of the vote (7.95 million), down by 2.9 per cent from 1930. The Nationalist DNVP, which fought a campaign defending the Papen government, saw its popular vote fall to 5.9 per cent (2.17 million), down by 1.1 per cent, and with a drop in seats from 41 to 37 since 1930. It was the poorest performance by the DNVP in any national election since 1920.

The fate of the two traditional middle-class liberal parties was more disastrous. The DVP recorded 1.18 per cent of the popular vote (436,002), down by 3.3 per cent from 1930, with a fall in seats from 30 to only 7. The DStP polled 1.01 per cent (371, 800), down by 2.77 per cent from 1930, with its seat total falling from 20 to just 4 seats. In one fell swoop, two of the biggest defenders of Weimar democracy had been reduced to splinter parties. The two liberal parties put together only attracted 2.19 per cent of voters between them. The moderate liberal and conservative middle-class parties also saw their seat totals fall from 122 in 1930 to 22 in 1932, and the vast majority of their traditional supporters had switched their votes to the NSDAP. Similarly, the vote-share for the specialist-interest parties, which remained strong in 1930 at 14 per cent, totally collapsed to just 3 per cent in 1932, with the biggest losses sustained by Reich Party of the Middle Class, with its seat total falling from 23 in 1930 to just 2 in 1932, and the Christian-Social People's Service (*Christlich-Sozialer Volksdienst*, CSVD) whose seat total fell from 14 in 1930 to just 3 in 1932. All these voters had also defected to the NSDAP. [67]

The July 1932 national elections placed Hitler on the threshold of power. On 6 August, Schleicher met Hitler at Fürstenberg, fifty miles north of Berlin. Hitler demanded to be made Chancellor, and Prussian Commissioner, in a presidential cabinet, with additional cabinet posts for Gregor Strasser (Labour), Wilhelm Frick (Interior), Hermann Göring (Aviation), and Joseph Goebbels (Popular Education). After gaining power, Hitler promised to put through an Enabling Act, which would suspend the Reichstag indefinitely.[68] At the end of the meeting, Hitler said a plaque should be placed on the house where they met to mark their historic meeting.[69] But when Schleicher's proposals were put to Hindenburg on 10 August, he responded by saying he had no intention of removing Papen as Chancellor, as he had grown fond of him, and was determined to retain a cabinet completely independent from all the political parties.[70] In taking this stand, Hindenburg had been influenced by Papen, who had effectively scuppered Schleicher's détente with Hitler.[71] On the same day, Papen met his cabinet, informing them of the details of his meeting with Hindenburg. Schleicher mentioned his meeting with Hitler to cabinet members, but now claimed he had opposed making Hitler Chancellor, and suggested negotiations should now be undertaken with him about involving some National Socialists in his government.[72]

On 13 August, Hitler met Schleicher and Papen in the morning, and then Hindenburg in the afternoon. Schleicher reiterated his support for a more authoritarian government, but advised Hitler to accept a subordinate role to the post of Chancellor. Papen spoke even more bluntly, telling Hitler that Hindenburg felt a party leader could not be made Chancellor at this time. Papen then offered Hitler the post of Vice-Chancellor, even promising to hand over the post of Chancellor to Hitler after he had reformed the Weimar Constitution.[73] In reply, Hitler said he wanted full power. Nothing else would satisfy him. Papen said if that was the case then he needed to talk to Hindenburg.[74] After the meeting, Papen called on Hindenburg to tell him what had happened. Papen later recalled that Hindenburg agreed with 'the attitude I had adopted and made it clear that he did not intend to appoint a man of Hitler's type to the responsible post of Chancellor'.[75]

At 4.15 p.m. on the afternoon of 13 August, Hitler arrived at the presidential palace to meet with President Hindenburg. A large crowd had gathered outside, assuming Hitler was about to be appointed Chancellor. Hitler was accompanied by his party colleagues Wilhelm Frick and Ernst Röhm. Otto Meissner, Hindenburg's Secretary, was also in attendance. This Hindenburg–Hitler encounter only lasted about 20 minutes. Hindenburg began by reminding Hitler he had not kept his pre-election promise to 'tolerate' the Papen government, and then asked if he would enter a cabinet headed by Papen. Hitler said no, reiterating his demand to be made Chancellor, with the same presidential emergency powers Papen currently enjoyed. In response, Hindenburg declared that his conscience could not allow him to give the power of the state to a single party leader who intended to use it in a one-sided partisan manner. Hindenburg closed the meeting in a friendly manner, by attempting to appeal to Hitler's sense of patriotism: 'We are old [war] comrades and want to remain so. The road ahead may bring us together again. So, I extend my hand to you as a comrade.'[76]

Hitler left the meeting feeling it had been deliberately set up by Papen to humiliate him. In the corridor outside Hindenburg's office, Hitler angrily confronted Papen, and asked him how he intended to govern without the Reichstag. In reply, Papen said, dismissively: 'The Reichstag? I'm surprised that you of all people think the Reichstag is important.'[77] Papen, keen to consolidate his own position as Chancellor, added to Hitler's loss of face by publishing a full account of the Hindenburg–Hitler interview, which claimed Hitler had 'demanded the same sort of position for himself as Mussolini had possessed after the march on Rome'. Hitler, for his part, placed the blame for his humiliation equally on Papen and Hindenburg, but he was less angry with Schleicher, crediting him with trying to broker a working agreement between the NSDAP and the Papen government. Schleicher let Hitler know that there was nothing final about his rebuff by Hindenburg.[78]

Hitler's 'all or nothing' strategy over the Chancellorship was now the subject of heated discussion in the NSDAP. Many party members were disappointed by Hitler's refusal to enter government on anything other than his own terms. Gregor Strasser, the party's organisational leader, felt National Socialist electoral support had probably peaked in the July 1932 elections. The time was therefore right now to enter a coalition government, even if Hitler had to accept the post of Vice-Chancellor in the first instance. If the party remained in opposition, then Strasser predicted Hitler would find it difficult to hold it together.[79]

Meanwhile, to stop the rising tide of bombings, shootings and arson attacks initiated by Stormtroopers, mainly against Communists, which had followed the July elections, Papen issued an emergency decree on 9 August, making the killing of a 'political opponent' punishable by death. The decree also established 'Special Courts' to quickly decide on such cases.[80] On 10 August, five uniformed members of Hitler's Stormtroopers broke into the home of Konrad Pietzuch, a Communist mineworker, in the Upper Silesian village of Potempa. They brutally beat him to death right in front of his horrified family. They also severely injured his brother. The police quickly apprehended the five murderers.

The highly publicised trial of the 'Potempa Five' started on 19 August in Beuthen (now Bytom, in Poland). On 22 August, the perpetrators were all sentenced to death, under the terms of Papen's recent decree on political terrorism. The judge pointed to the extreme barbarity of the crime, which led to the victim's carotid artery being severed, leaving him to bleed to death. The courtroom was packed with Stormtroopers, who exploded with rage when the verdicts were announced.[81]

The case generated enormous media coverage all over Germany. Hitler was furious with the death sentences, and sent the five murderers a supportive telegram, stating: 'My comrades I am bound to you in unlimited loyalty in the face of this most hideous blood sentence. You have my picture hanging in your cells. How could I forsake you? Anyone who struggles, lives, fights, and, if need be, dies for Germany has right on his side.'[82] A statement by Hitler, printed in the *Völkischer Beobachter*, also glorified the murderers: 'With this verdict Herr von Papen has used the blood of national heroes to inscribe his name in the book of German history. He has sown the dragon's teeth. And the growth which rises from them will not be restrained through fear of punishment. The battle of the lives of our five comrades has begun.'[83] Papen gave in to Hitler's threat of unleashing further violence, and the 'Potempa Five' had their death sentences commuted to life imprisonment, on 2 September, on the grounds the new emergency decree issued on 9 July on politically motivated murder by Papen was unknown to the defendants at the time they committed the murder.[84]

On 30 August, the newly elected Reichstag met for the first time. No one doubted the huge National Socialist delegation intended to make life as uncomfortable as possible for Papen's 'cabinet of barons'. Following the normal rules of procedure, the opening speech was delivered by the oldest member, who was Clara Zetkin, a member of the Communist Party. Zetkin used her speech to launch a strong attack on the Papen government, which she described as a 'servile tool' of capitalism.[85]

The next procedural step was for the Reichstag to elect a new speaker. It was a longstanding tradition that the speaker was drawn from the party with the largest number of members. On this basis, Hermann Göring was proposed by the NSDAP, and supported in his candidature by Zentrum and the BVP. Göring was duly elected with 367 votes, replacing the Social Democrat Paul Löbe, who had been the Reichstag Speaker since 1920. In his speech accepting the role, Göring reminded Papen's government that there was no reason to dissolve the new Reichstag or bypass it with emergency decrees. The first formal session was thus ended.[86]

Papen had already made up his mind to dissolve the new Reichstag at its first formal meeting on 12 September, and call new national elections. Hitler soon got wind of Papen's plan, and decided to counter it with a speech on 1 September in the Sport Palace in Berlin, in which he derided the idea his party was worried about serial dissolutions of the Reichstag. 'For all we care,' he declared, 'do it a hundred times. We'll emerge as the victors. I'm not going to lose my nerve. My will is unshakeable, and I can outwit my adversaries.'[87]

On 4 September, in open defiance of Göring, Papen issued a new emergency decree, signed by President Hindenburg, promising new measures for a revival of the economy by creating jobs and curbing the power of the trade unions. The key new measure, designed to stimulate business, was the issue of tax vouchers (*Steuergutscheine*), which offered a generous 40 per cent reduction in sales and land taxes to employers who took on new workers. Each new worker employed ensured a 400-Reichsmark employer tax reduction. In a second decree, issued on 5 September, employers were allowed to reduce wages by 20 per cent if they increased their workforces. This latter measure greatly angered the trade unions who felt it breached the provisions for compulsory wage arbitration.[88]

On 12 September, the Reichstag convened for its first full session. On the agenda was a government declaration by Papen, which was to be followed by several days of debate. At the start of the first working session, Communist member Ernst Torgler proposed the agenda be altered to include a vote repealing Papen's emergency decrees issued on 4 and 5 September, and a declaration of no confidence against the Papen government. These motions were only admissible if no member objected. Göring asked if anyone objected, but there was no reply. Göring therefore allowed Torgler's motions to go ahead to a vote.

Papen then arrived in the Reichstag for the very first time, with the intention of dissolving it before any no-confidence motions could be passed, but he had forgotten to bring with him the required dissolution order, which had already been signed by Hindenburg. There was a half-hour gap in proceedings while it was hurriedly fetched from the Reich Chancellery by one of his staff. Once it arrived, Papen lifted the red briefcase in which it was contained, and brazenly showed it to the Reichstag members.

Papen then theatrically placed the dissolution order on Göring's

overleaf The trial of the 'Potempa Five', SA killers of a Communist mineworker in Upper Silesia in August 1932. The death sentences passed by the court in Beuthen would later be commuted to life imprisonment.

desk, but the latter brushed the document aside, and explained, amid loud cheering, that it could not be accepted, as the chamber was already in the process of voting on Torgler's motions, which were passed by 512 to 42, with only 5 abstentions. Papen and the members of his cabinet who were present all walked out of the Reichstag, with the boos of its members ringing in their ears. The 512 votes against Papen's government represented the greatest parliamentary defeat inflicted on any German Chancellor. Papen also went down in history as the first German Chancellor never to give a speech in the Reichstag. The Reichstag was dissolved after sitting for only two days since the 31 July election. Papen gave a speech on national radio on the same evening during which he promised economic reconstruction, and called on the nation to stand behind the President in his attempts to secure national unity.[89]

Papen and Hindenburg completely ignored the Reichstag censure motions. The 4 and 5 September emergency decrees remained in force, and the Reichstag remained dissolved, with new elections set for 6 November, the last possible date allowed under the 60-day limit specified in the Constitution. In effect, Germany was becoming ungovernable. No one thought Papen's government had any parliamentary legitimacy at all, but Hindenburg believed Hitler was too totalitarian to be offered the Chancellorship. Papen felt that he could weaken Hitler's NSDAP by subjecting it to constant national elections, which he thought would wreck its finances, and lead to a loss of voter support.

After a total of four elections during 1932, the National Socialists were pessimistic as the campaign for the fifth began. Constant electioneering had greatly depleted NSDAP finances. In a speech to the Reich Propaganda Conference on 6 October, Hitler tried to mobilise party workers for the coming election, saying: 'We National Socialists will give the nation an unprecedented display of our strength of will. I head this struggle with absolute confidence. Let the battle commence. In four weeks, we'll emerge victorious.'[90]

On 11 October, Hitler began his fourth 'flight over Germany', under the election campaign slogan: 'Down with the Reactionaries'. The tour took him to fifty towns and cities, all over the country, sometimes giving three speeches per day, but the crowds were much smaller than previously. In many rural areas, party activists were bussed in to artificially swell the crowds. The NSDAP campaign struck a far more anti-capitalist tone, focusing on Papen, who was dubbed a 'Chancellor without a people'. Hitler also gave prominence in all his speeches to providing a justification for his decision not to join Papen's government on 13 August, saying that he did not want to get on a train he knew he would get off a few months later because 'I could not support the actions of the reactionaries who drove the train'. He was not a typical bourgeois politician who joins one coalition after another, he added. What he wanted was full power, and he would accept nothing less.[91]

If the electoral prospects for Hitler looked bleak, the hopes of Papen's 'cabinet of barons' looked even worse. In a highly publicised campaign speech on 12 October, Papen promised far-reaching constitutional reform, saying he wanted to diminish the power of the Reichstag, and create a new powerful authoritarian non-partisan state authority, arguing the Reich government needed to be independent of parliament and the political parties: 'To counterbalance one-sided decisions by the Reichstag based on party interests, Germany needs a special First Chamber, with clearly defined authority and strong legislative powers.' In essence, Papen was calling for the legal destruction of parliamentary democracy.[92]

One of the most dramatic events in the days leading up to the election came on 3 November, when transport workers in Berlin, faced with wage cuts imposed by the municipally owned Berlin Transport Company (*Berliner Verkehrsgesellschaft*), went on strike. The action brought the German capital to a complete standstill. It was led by the Revolutionary Trade Union Opposition (*Revolutionäre Gewerkschafts-Opposition*) and supported by the Communist Party (KPD), but not by the Social Democrats (SPD) or the official trade unions, who had asked the workers to accept a legally binding arbitration agreement and return to work. To everyone's surprise, Hitler announced that the NSDAP was supporting the striking workers, in the hope of displaying the party's 'socialist' credentials. It was quite something to see Communists and National Socialists sharing the same picket lines. But Hitler's decision to support the transport workers risked losing middle-class voters in the upcoming election.[93]

In the German national elections of 6 November 1932, the last fully free election in the Weimar Republic, voter turnout fell by 3.5 per cent, from 84.1 to 80.6 per cent. The results were a major setback for the NSDAP, which saw its vote-share fall by 4.2 per cent from 37.3 per cent to 33.1 per cent (11.37 million), with a fall in seats from 230 to 196 seats, a loss of 34 seats and 2 million votes since the 31 July election. The seemingly irresistible rise of Hitler in elections since 1930 had finally been halted. Joseph Goebbels thought Hitler's decision not to enter Papen's government was the chief reason for the loss of middle-class support. Local party reports confirmed this assessment, with one concluding the party leader 'does not know what he wants and has no programme'.[94]

There was a swing of voters in the November 1932 elections from the NSDAP back to the two traditional middle-class parties. The DNVP gained 14 seats, raising its total to 51, with its popular vote up by 2.4 per cent to 8.3 per cent (2.95 million). The DVP gained 4 seats, winning 11 in total, with an increase of 0.68 per cent, taking its vote total to 1.86 (660,889). These increases suggested middle-class voters were returning to their traditional party allegiances. The two left-wing parties had mixed fortunes. The SPD lost 12 seats to end up on a total of 121, with its popular vote dropping slightly by 1.2 per cent to 20.4 (7.24 million), but it remained the second largest party in the Reichstag. The rise of the Communist KPD continued, with the party gaining 11 seats, bringing its seat total to 100, and its voter percentage to 16.9 (5.98 million), up by 2.6 per cent since July 1932. The Communist gains were largely at the expense of the Social Democrats, whose timid leadership had alienated many traditional working-class voters. The two Catholic parties suffered small falls in voter support. Zentrum lost 5 seats, reducing its total to 70, with a loss of 0.5 per cent of voters, leaving it with a percentage of 11.9 per cent (4.23 million). The BVP lost just 2 seats, leaving a total of 20, the BVP vote share fell by 0.1 per cent, to 3.1 per cent (1.09 million).[95]

After yet another inconclusive election, the country awaited the next instalment of the fast-moving political drama. Papen emerged from the election full of confidence, even though only 63 Reichstag members out of a total of 585 supported him, but with President Hindenburg's backing, Papen felt secure in his position.[96] However, this proved an illusion. On 17 November, Schleicher proposed the resignation of the entire Papen cabinet, to allow Hindenburg time to engage in talks with all potential alternative Chancellors. Papen told Hindenburg of his intention to resign as Chancellor, pointing out he had failed to weld the various right-wing parties into a viable coalition government of 'national concentration', and that when the Reichstag met, the opposition would introduce a motion of censure, which was bound to pass, resulting in another dissolution of parliament, and yet another national election. Hindenburg reluctantly accepted Papen's resignation, but he assured him that he retained his full confidence and asked him and his cabinet to stay on in a caretaker capacity to assist in forming a new government. Papen advised Hindenburg to ask Hitler to form a government of 'national concentration', which could command a majority in the Reichstag, fully realising this would be impossible.

Hindenburg held direct talks with Hitler on 19 and 21 November, as part of his discussions with all the party leaders, except for the Social Democrats and the Communists, who had made clear they would not participate in a coalition government. Hindenburg asked Hitler to explore the possibility of heading a coalition government involving the centre-right parties. Letters were then exchanged between Hitler and Hindenburg. During this interchange, Hindenburg insisted that if Hitler formed a government he must retain Schleicher as the Defence Minister, Neurath as Foreign Minister, and that Reich control of Prussia should be made permanent, and the President would retain final approval of all Hitler's cabinet appointments.[97]

Hitler accepted the President's demands at this meeting, but he reported in a letter on 23 November 1932 that a majority government based on members of the Reichstag had proved impossible to form, and so he asked Hindenburg to appoint him as Chancellor, with full presidential powers, and also allow him to pass an Enabling Act which would allow him to rule without the approval of the Reichstag or the President. In response, Hindenburg, in a letter sent by Meissner on 24 November, informed Hitler that he could not grant 'comprehensive presidential powers to the leader of a party that had always stressed its desire to rule exclusively', as he feared a Hitler-led government would inevitably become a one-party dictatorship. This was almost identical to what Hindenburg had told Hitler during their meeting on 13 August.[98] Hitler claimed, with some justification, that Hindenburg's negotiations with him were a total sham, as he had been determined to retain Papen as Chancellor all along. On 30 November, Hitler turned down a request by Hindenburg for a further meeting.

Everything now seemed set for Papen to return to power as German Chancellor. The only other option was Kurt von Schleicher, who had asked Hitler on 23 November whether he would join a cabinet led by him, but received a definite No.[99] Hindenburg then called Schleicher and Papen to a crunch meeting at the presidential palace on 1 December, at which a final decision on the Chancellorship would be taken.

Hindenburg first asked Papen what they should do. Papen told him Hitler had refused all possible parliamentary combinations, meaning the only way to bring him into government was to offer him the post of

Chancellor, supported by full presidential powers, but he felt this was too risky. Papen now offered a drastic solution, suggesting he should remain Chancellor for the time being under a 'state of emergency'. He would then carry through a dictatorial 'fighting programme' that would involve eliminating the Reichstag, using the Army to suppress the Communist and National Socialist parties, and force through a new constitution which would be put to the German people in a referendum or submitted to a new National Assembly. Papen also made clear that refusing or postponing an election for any length of time would mean Hindenburg was violating the current constitution. In essence, Papen was asking Hindenburg to create a full-blown dictatorship, backed up by the Reichswehr.[100]

Then Schleicher spoke, saying it was an extremely dangerous step for the President to violate the Weimar Constitution by proclaiming a military state of emergency. If Hindenburg took this step, Schleicher warned him that he ran the real risk of impeachment, and removal from office by a two-thirds majority in the Reichstag. Given the current parliamentary arithmetic, this seemed a real possibility and it worried Hindenburg.[101] Schleicher then suggested that if Hindenburg made him Chancellor, he could put together a majority in the Reichstag by attracting Hitler critic Gregor Strasser to lead a breakaway group of disgruntled left-wing National Socialists, alienated by Hitler's 'all or nothing' strategy, and by reaching out to other parties across the political spectrum to create a 'cross-front', with a programme designed to stimulate the economy and reduce unemployment.[102]

In response, Papen argued that Schleicher was now proposing a return to the parliamentary system, whereas it was Papen's understanding that it was Hindenburg's aim to create a more powerful and independent presidential regime, independent of the Reichstag. Hindenburg had listened to the proposals by Papen and Schleicher in silence, but then suddenly stood up and said: 'My decision is Herr von Papen's solution.' He added that Papen should now begin negotiations to form a new government.[103]

This was not the end of the matter. Schleicher took some beating at the subtle game of political intrigue. On 2 December, a cabinet meeting took place at which Papen gave a full account of his interview with Hindenburg on the previous day. Schleicher had come to the meeting armed with a report on a war-game conducted by Lieutenant Colonel Eugen Ott on behalf of the Defence Ministry. Ott read out the findings of 'War-game Ott' to the cabinet. The scenario was: could the

Reichswehr cope with a joint civil uprising by the National Socialists and the Communists, and simultaneously defend the Polish border? Ott concluded the Reichswehr could not preserve order in such an eventuality. Schleicher pointed out the Army could face just such a situation if a state of emergency were introduced, as Papen desired, and pointed out the recent collaboration by Communists and National Socialists in the Berlin transport strike showed such collaboration in a civil war situation could not be ruled out.

The impact of Ott's report and Schleicher's follow-up argument proved decisive. A clear majority of the cabinet felt Schleicher was right, and that he should be given the chance to rule in agreement with the Reichstag rather than going down the unconstitutional road of declaring a state of emergency. Papen felt Schleicher had stabbed him in the back, but he was wrong: Schleicher had stabbed him in the front. After the meeting, Papen went straight to the presidential palace to report on the cabinet meeting. Papen said the President could keep him in office, but in that case he wanted to sack Schleicher as Defence Minister, as he could not work with him any longer. The alternative was for Hindenburg to call on Schleicher to become the new German Chancellor. There was a lengthy silence, before Hindenburg said: 'You will think me a scoundrel, my dear Papen, if I change my mind now. But I am too old to take on the responsibility for a civil war at the end of my life. So, in God's name we must let Herr von Schleicher try his luck.'[104]

Papen immediately resigned as Chancellor and as Reich Commissioner for Prussia. As a parting gift, Hindenburg sent Papen a signed portrait of himself, with the following line added: 'I had a loyal comrade' (*Ich hatt' einen Kameraden*). Even after Papen stepped down, the President retained him as a 'personal adviser', even allowing him to retain his government apartment in Wilhelmstrasse, as he wanted his favourite in close proximity. This placed him in a particularly advantageous position to undermine Schleicher.[105]

On 3 December 1932, Kurt von Schleicher, the expert in backstairs intrigue, though virtually unknown to the public, stepped into the limelight through the front door of the Reich Chancellery, as the new German Chancellor and Reich Commissioner for Prussia. He was the third German Chancellor of 1932, with even less parliamentary backing than Papen. The Schleicher cabinet was the third presidential cabinet of the Weimar Republic. All the members of Papen's 'cabinet of barons' remained in their posts, apart from Hugo Schäffer, who was

overleaf Members of Hindenburg's inner circle gather for tea, September 1932. From left to right: Franz von Papen, Otto Meissner, Wilhelm von Gayl, Paul von Hindenburg and Kurt von Schleicher.

replaced by Friedrich Syrup (Independent) as Minister of Labour, and Wilhelm von Gayl, who was succeeded by Franz Bracht (Independent) as Minister of the Interior. There were two other new additions: Günther Gereke (CNBL), who assumed the new cabinet post of Reich Commissioner for Employment, and Johannes Popitz (Independent), who was given the role of Minister without Portfolio.[106]

On 5 December, the leading NSDAP leaders held a meeting in Berlin's Kaiserhof Hotel to discuss their attitude to the new Schleicher government. Hitler stressed there would be no compromise or collaboration with the new government.[107] Goebbels noted: 'Strasser takes the position that Schleicher must be tolerated. The Führer had fierce clashes with him. Strasser as always in recent times, portrays the situation of the party in the blackest colours... Strasser tries to draw those present at the Führer conference over to his side. All, however, stand firmly on the side of the Führer.'[108]

The new Reichstag met for the first time on 6 December 1932. Göring was once again elected as Speaker, but he immediately questioned in his opening speech whether Schleicher, a military figure, with no parliamentary support, should have been given the role of Chancellor in the first place. The Army, Göring added, should remain above party controversies. The National Socialist Reichstag members then opposed two motions that were immediately presented. The first, sponsored by the Social Democrats, called upon the government to make its traditional declaration of policy. The second, tabled by the Communists, was a no-confidence resolution. Göring ensured neither was put to a parliamentary vote.[109] A National Socialist bill making the President of the Supreme Court acting President in the event of the death of the current incumbent was passed. This was directed against Schleicher, as under the existing law it was the Chancellor who would assume the functions of President in such an eventuality. The Reichstag also voted to revoke the emergency decree of 5 September which authorised tax reductions for companies that took on new workers, and passed a wide-ranging amnesty for political prisoners.

On 9 December, after sitting for just three days, the Reichstag was adjourned until the date of the next meeting, which was determined by standing procedure, but likely to be in mid-January 1933. Schleicher did not speak during the session, thereby becoming the second German Chancellor never to have addressed the Reichstag. Schleicher hoped the short adjournment would allow him to gain support for his economic programme.

On the previous day, Gregor Strasser had resigned from all his posts in the NSDAP. In his letter of resignation to Hitler, Strasser made clear Hitler's decision to remain outside government unless he was offered the Chancellorship would lead the party towards decline and irrelevance. He also stressed he had no intention of becoming head of an opposition movement within the party.[110] It now seems likely that Strasser never seriously contemplated taking a post in Schleicher's cabinet or splitting the NSDAP. Minutes of the supposed discussions between Schleicher and Strasser have been shown to have been contemporary forgeries, while passages related to Strasser's resignation in an edition of Goebbels' diaries published in 1934, which indicate Strasser was offered the post of Vice Chancellor by Schleicher early in December 1932, also appear to have been fabricated. The true story is that Schleicher realised that Strasser was not the right person to split the National Socialists, and his total inability to mount serious opposition to Hitler revealed that assessment to be true.[111]

Meanwhile, Schleicher gained a totally unexpected diplomatic success. On 11 December, a five-power declaration by Britain, the USA, Italy, France, and Germany recognised Germany's right to equality in armaments in a system that provided security for all nations, accompanied by a declaration that under no circumstances would any of the signatories make demands using force. Schleicher tried to capitalise on this unexpected good news by delivering an address about his government programme on national radio on 15 December 1932. The radio speech was designed to appeal to political parties in the Reichstag to tolerate his government when the Reichstag resumed its deliberations in January 1933. Schleicher asked the nation to forget that he was a soldier and think of him as 'the impartial trustee of the interests of all in an emergency'.

Schleicher further claimed that he was neither a socialist or a capitalist, with concepts such as 'private enterprise' and 'state control' holding no terrors for him. He admitted no government could carry on unless it had the backing of the masses of the population. The chief aim of his new government was to provide work for the unemployed. For this purpose, he had appointed a Reich Commissioner for Employment, whose chief task would be to achieve this aim. The job-creation scheme would be achieved without resort to inflation. Schleicher also outlined a number of other policies. Millions of Reichsmarks would be allocated for the distribution of land for agricultural settlements in East Prussia, Pomerania and Mecklenburg. To help with the cost-of-living crisis, there would be statutory price reductions on necessities such as bread, milk, meat, and coal. There would also be greater freedom of speech and assembly, a lowering of sentences for breaches of public order, and the Special Courts created to deal with 'political terrorism' would be suspended.[112]

What Schleicher did not know was that Franz von Papen was about to begin plotting his downfall. On 16 December, Papen gave a speech at the Gentlemen's Club (*Herrenklub*) in Berlin, a private members' club whose purpose was to allow the aristocratic elite to network. During his speech, Papen suggested any viable coalition government must include the National Socialists, and he further demanded that Hitler be brought into the cabinet. Listening to the speech was the financier Kurt von Schröder, a keen supporter of Hitler, and the co-founder of a group called Friends of the Economy (*Freundeskreis der Wirtschaft*), whose main aim was to raise business funds for the NSDAP.

Schröder met Papen after his speech. Papen told him that Hindenburg had no confidence at all in Schleicher. Schröder then asked Papen if he would be willing to open a fresh dialogue with Hitler about forming a government. In response, Papen said he had tried this before and failed, but he was willing to try again. Schröder recalled: 'When I saw Papen he said, "I think we can perhaps now have a meeting together to clear these different points that have kept us apart."'[113]

Schröder reported to Wilhelm Keppler, one of Hitler's key financial backers and economic advisers, that Papen was willing to meet Hitler, and Keppler in turn conveyed this news to Hitler, offering his services to set up the meeting. Hitler gave the go-ahead for talks. The location suggested was Schröder's house in Cologne. On 26 December, Hitler told Keppler he would arrive there early on 4 January 1933.[114]

Papen left Berlin at Christmas-time to return to his palatial estate at Wallerfangen, in the Saar in south-west Germany. On 28 December, the phone rang in Papen's home. On the other end of the line was Kurt von Schröder, who asked whether he would be free to meet with Hitler in the next few days at his home in Cologne. 'I told him,' Papen recalled, 'that I was going to Berlin via Düsseldorf on 4 January, but could stop at Cologne on the way.' In his memoirs, Papen unconvincingly presents himself as not conspiring with Hitler to bring down Schleicher. Instead, Papen offered the following explanation of his decision to meet Hitler secretly: 'The answer is simple. The NSDAP had 196 Reichstag seats, and remained a major political factor under the Schleicher government. I still had serious doubts whether Schleicher would ever succeed in splitting the [NSDAP] party.... I thought there was still a possibility of persuading Hitler to join the Schleicher government.'[115] If this were true, then why did Papen not inform Schleicher of his intention to meet Hitler?

In reality, Papen saw his upcoming meeting with Hitler in January 1933 as a means of gaining revenge over Schleicher for bringing about his own downfall. Hitler's own reason for accepting the invitation to meet Papen was his reluctant acceptance that the party was going down a blind alley if it could not gain power. A meeting with Papen offered him a real chance to finally gain the Chancellorship, as he thought Papen was the best person to break down Hindenburg's reluctance to offer him the role.

POSTSCRIPT
·
THE MONTH OF
OF
JANUARY 1933
·

This story must end with the chain of events that brought Adolf Hitler to power in the month of January 1933. These began on 4 January at Kurt von Schröder's home in Cologne. Hitler and Papen arrived separately, but each was photographed entering. In his memoirs, Papen claimed the photographer was not from the press, but was a policeman tipped off by Schleicher.[1]

The meeting began just before noon. Hitler started by criticising Papen for preventing him from becoming Chancellor during August 1932. In response, Papen claimed it was Schleicher who blocked his appointment and he mentioned Schleicher's role in his own dismissal as Chancellor. Hitler then made it clear that he would only join a coalition cabinet if he was made Chancellor, but added a willingness to give a prominent role to Papen and some of his conservative allies, provided they accepted the need to remove Social Democrats, Communists, and Jews from leading positions in German life.[2] Schröder recalled that during the two-hour conversation, Papen had proposed a conservative-nationalist coalition involving Hitler and the National Socialists. Papen later claimed the question of Hitler becoming Chancellor was never discussed at the meeting, but Schröder's account is much more reliable, and he was supported by Goebbels in his diary, where he noted that Hitler had told him Papen was 'dead set against Schleicher. Wants to topple and eradicate him. Has the old man's [Hindenburg's] ear. Even stays with him'.[3]

Newspapers at the time suggested the meeting was designed to use Papen to persuade Hindenburg to appoint Hitler as Chancellor. When Schleicher saw these reports, he went to see Hindenburg. He insisted Papen should be told not to meet with Hitler in future, without his agreement. Instead of acceding to this request, Hindenburg secretly authorised Papen to continue his dialogue with the NSDAP leader.[4] On 6 January, Papen and Hitler issued a joint press statement, printed in full in the *Frankfurter Zeitung*, denying they were plotting to bring down the Schleicher government. On 9 January, Papen visited Schleicher and tried to convince him that he was trying to persuade

previous page   Adolf Hitler, newly appointed
German Chancellor, greets President Hindenburg
at a memorial service, 1933.

Hitler to join the current government, but Schleicher found this extremely unconvincing.[5]

After his meeting with Papen, Hitler gave a speech in Detmold, claiming he wanted power 'not through the back door, but rather through the main gate'.[6] This speech was the starting point of a brief election campaign in the tiny German state of Lippe-Detmold, which had a correspondingly tiny electorate of 117,000. During the next 11 days, Hitler spoke in 16 small towns in the region. He had targeted this small local election to refute the view of the NSDAP being in electoral decline, after the disappointing results in the November 1932 elections. On 15 January, the NSDAP vote increased in the Lippe-Detmold election from 34.7 to 39.5 per cent, which was 6,000 votes up on November 1932, though 3,000 votes lower than the heady days of July 1932. In private, Hitler felt this success had an importance 'it is impossible to underestimate', as it represented evidence of a resurgence of popular support for the party.[7]

On 18 January, Hitler met Papen again. This encounter took place at the plush home of Joachim von Ribbentrop, in the affluent Berlin suburb of Dahlem. Ribbentrop had served in the Great War of 1914–18, but after being wounded in action was sent to Turkey where he met and got to know Franz von Papen.[8] Ribbentrop was now a wealthy wine merchant, who had only recently joined the NSDAP. Care was taken over the security arrangements for the second Hitler–Papen meeting. Ribbentrop's chauffeur picked up Papen from his home while Hitler's limousine was driven into the garage of the house, allowing him to enter the house through the back garden, without being seen.[9] Ribbentrop noted the main issue discussed at the meeting in his diary: 'Hitler insists on being Chancellor. Papen again considers this impossible. His influence with Hindenburg was not strong enough to affect this.' Hitler then told Papen of his reluctance to engage in further talks unless his demand to be made Chancellor was met in full. Papen prevaricated for the time being, because he still thought Hitler could still be persuaded to take the post of Vice-Chancellor.[10]

The pivotal day in these clandestine discussions was undoubtedly 22 January 1933. The day began with Hitler unveiling a memorial at the Nikolai Cemetery in Prenzlauer Berg, Berlin, dedicated to SA martyr Horst Wessel. In the evening, Hitler gave another rabble-rousing speech at the Sport Palace, also dedicated to the memory of Wessel. Hitler then left the Sport Palace just before 10 p.m., travelling by limousine with Wilhelm Frick and Hermann Göring for another secret meeting with Papen. Once again, the venue was Ribbentrop's home. Papen later recalled Hitler had requested this meeting, but it was most probably mutually agreed. Hindenburg had been informed by Papen beforehand, and he gave his consent for Papen to attend. Accompanying Papen this time was Hindenburg's son, Oskar, and Otto Meissner, Hindenburg's State Secretary, both invited by Papen. Meissner later told the Nuremberg war trial that the key reason why Hitler was being brought into secret discussions about a future coalition was because Schleicher had failed to gain National Socialist support or create a viable coalition government.[11]

It seems Oskar Hindenburg had other worries at this time. The Social Democrats and Zentrum had set up a Reichstag enquiry into dodgy property deals related to the so-called Eastern Aid programme set up to bail out ailing Junker farming estates. Serious allegations had emerged indicating government funds had been diverted from the scheme to buy property, racehorses, cars and even luxury goods. Some of those under investigation were friends and relatives of Hindenburg, and Oskar's likely involvement in this scandal might have come to light during further parliamentary scrutiny. This raises the possibility that Hitler promised to shelve the Reichstag investigation on the Eastern Aid affair if he became Chancellor.[12]

Elaborate arrangements were put in place to ensure the secrecy of the meeting on 22 January. Oskar and Meissner, accompanied by their wives, began the evening by attending a performance of Richard Wagner's two-act opera *Das Liebesverbot* (*The Ban on Love*), at the Prussian State Opera House on the Unter den Linden. During the interval, they were seen talking to guests, but once the lights went down for the final act, they collected their overcoats from the cloakroom, and quietly slipped away by a side entrance, taking a taxi to Ribbentrop's house.[13]

At the meeting, Papen stressed that Hindenburg remained unconvinced of Hitler's suitability as Chancellor. Hitler said he would not join Schleicher's cabinet, nor would the NSDAP give his government support when the Reichstag met. He then told Papen he would only cooperate in a coalition government in which he was appointed as Chancellor.[14] Once this brief exchange of views was over, Hitler invited Oskar to have a private discussion with him in another room. This meeting reportedly lasted for just over an hour. Hitler kept no record of what was said, but Oskar later gave evidence at the Nuremburg war trials about what happened. He said Hitler had stressed that he alone could save Germany from civil war, and reiterated that no government could survive without his support.[15]

A one-pot dinner accompanied by champagne followed, though Hitler stuck to mineral water. Oskar and Meissner were the first to leave. 'In the taxi on the way back', recalled Meissner, 'Oskar von Hindenburg was very silent; the only remark he made was that there was no help for it, the Nazis had to be taken into the government. My impression was that Hitler had succeeded in getting him under his spell.' Papen later made the following comment on the meeting: 'I want to make it clear the actual question of forming a cabinet with Hitler as chancellor was not discussed by Oskar Hindenburg, Meissner or myself.' Ribbentrop's diary entry of the meeting contradicts Papen's account, and is far more reliable: 'Papen will now press for Hitler as Chancellor', he wrote, 'but tells Hitler he will withdraw from these negotiations forthwith if Hitler has no confidence in him'.[16]

In Papen's report of the meeting, submitted to Hindenburg, he suggested Schleicher should be given more time to secure support in the Reichstag, but ruled out taking over as Chancellor himself. Significantly, Papen did not recommend Hitler being made Chancellor at this stage. Meissner later recalled that despite all of Papen's persuasion, Hindenburg still remained 'extremely hesitant' to make Hitler Chancellor. He still wanted Papen to assume that role again.[17]

On 23 January, Schleicher met President Hindenburg, informing him his negotiations to put together a coalition, which could pass a vote of no confidence in the Reichstag, had failed.[18] The only alternative to a Hitler-led government, Schleicher told the President, was a 'military dictatorship'. He requested a permanent suspension of the Reichstag through the issue of a state of emergency, an indefinite delay in elections, and a ban on both the NSDAP and the KPD. Schleicher's proposed dictatorship would be kept in power by the Army.[19] Hindenburg rejected Schleicher's proposals. Even worse, Schleicher's plan for a military dictatorship was leaked to the press, leading to a general outcry from all of his political opponents.

On 27 January, the Reichstag Steering Committee announced the Reichstag would meet again on 31 January.[20] Hermann Göring met Meissner at the presidential palace, reassuring him that if Hitler was offered the Chancellorship he had no intention of violating the Weimar Constitution, but he warned that the NSDAP would oppose any attempt by Schleicher to govern without parliamentary support. On the same day, Ribbentrop met Papen, who told him that after a long talk with Hindenburg he considered Hitler being appointed Chancellor was now possible.[21]

On 28 January, Schleicher called an emergency cabinet meeting, informing his colleagues that he would make one further attempt to ask Hindenburg to dissolve the Reichstag, delay elections and allow him to govern in a 'presidential cabinet', under a state of emergency. If Hindenburg refused, he would resign.[22] Schleicher communicated this news to the President. 'No,' was Hindenburg's blunt reply, reminding him that on 2 December 1932 Schleicher himself had said that taking such a course of action would breach the Weimar Constitution, and lead to civil war. Hindenburg told Schleicher that he now needed to find a majority government which could stabilise Germany. 'Whether what I am doing now is right, my dear Schleicher,' Hindenburg added, 'I do not know, but I shall know soon enough when I am up there [pointing heavenward].' Schleicher pondered the statement and then replied: 'After this breach of trust, sir, I am not sure that you will go to heaven.'[23]

Hindenburg now summoned Papen, urging him, in the presence of his son Oskar and Meissner, to take on the post of Chancellor once again. But after a brief discussion they all agreed that Hitler was now the only logical choice for the post of Chancellor. It seems Hindenburg was most deeply influenced by Papen in finally agreeing to appoint Hitler as the German Chancellor. As Otto Meissner put it, 'Papen finally won him over to Hitler, with the argument that the representatives of the other right-wing parties, which would belong to the government, would restrict Hitler's freedom of action.' 'It is my unpleasant duty,' concluded Hindenburg, 'to appoint this fellow Hitler as Chancellor.' Following Papen's suggestion, Hindenburg insisted that if Hitler became Chancellor, it must be in a coalition government under which he could be contained by reliable conservatives, and his new cabinet must include General Werner von Blomberg as the Minister of Defence.[24]

On 29 January, Hitler met Papen once more. They agreed on Hitler becoming the Chancellor of a national coalition, containing only two other Nazis, Wilhelm Frick as Interior Minister and Hermann Göring as Minister without Portfolio. Papen would assume the role of Vice-Chancellor. After coming to power, Hitler wanted to call an immediate general election and pass an Enabling Act to legally dispense with the Reichstag. Papen relayed these proposals to Hindenburg, who was surprised how moderate they were. 'Don't worry, we've hired him,' Papen reassuringly told the president.[25]

At 11.15 a.m. on 30 January 1933 Hitler and his cabinet ministers finally walked into Hindenburg's office. The President gave a short speech, emphasising the need for cooperation by the members of the new government.[26] At 11.30 a.m. Hitler took the oath of office to become German Chancellor. He gave an impromptu speech, vowing to uphold the Weimar Constitution. He awaited a response, but all President Hindenburg said was: 'And now gentlemen, *forward with God.*'[27]

CONCLUSION

·

WHO KILLED WEIMAR DEMOCRACY?

·

G iven all the cumulative problems it faced, it is surprising Weimar democracy lasted as long as it did, but we need to remember that it endured longer than Hitler's Third Reich. The period from 1918 to 1923 was politically and economically turbulent, but democracy survived. Between 1924 and 1929, the economy stabilised, Germany regained international respectability, and democratic rule was never threatened. Even in the period of deep political and economic crisis between 1930 and 1933, during the time of authoritarian 'presidential rule', there was no attempt to overthrow the Republic.

The commonly held view is that the 'Great Depression' led to the collapse of Weimar democracy, and brought Hitler to power, is not credible. The USA and Britain suffered economic problems often as difficult as those of Germany, but democracy did not collapse in either of those countries. This suggests there was something specific about the nature of the political and economic crisis that was peculiar to Germany at this time.

The two decisive ingredients in the period from 1930 to 1933 were the supreme indifference of President Hindenburg, and his inner circle, to sustain democratic government, and the dramatic rise in electoral support for Adolf Hitler and the NSDAP. It was a toxic mixture of these two factors, operating at a time of deep economic depression, which ensured Germany's experiment with democracy failed.

Yet the seeds of the Weimar's democratic tragedy were planted by the type of democratic system established after the November Revolution of 1918, and embedded into the Weimar Constitution of 1919. The November Revolution was a very strange one indeed, which left Germany's judicial, bureaucratic, and military elite largely intact. Weimar judges punished those on the Left with harsh sentences, while treating radicals on the Right very leniently, and the Reichswehr remained a law unto itself, being more preoccupied with shaking off the military restrictions placed upon it by the Treaty of Versailles than defending democracy.

One of the essential ingredients for the successful transition from an authoritarian to a democratic form of government is the existence of a strong, resilient party of the moderate Right, committed to the ideals of democracy. In Britain, the Conservative Party fulfilled this role, evolving from the late 19th century into a mainstay of the British party system. In Germany, no such party was able to take on that stabilising role. The leading conservative party in Germany was the DNVP. Between 1919 and 1930, its voter support reached a high point of 20.5 per cent and 103 seats in the December 1924 election, but then fell to a low point of 7 per cent at the September 1930 election, when it gained just 41 seats. During the Weimar era, the DNVP was a bitter opponent of Weimar democracy, with a leader in Alfred Hugenberg who moved the party to the extreme Right.

Germany's military defeat in the Great War also cast a giant shadow over the Weimar Republic. The 'stab-in-the-back' myth, which held that Germany was not defeated on the battlefield, but betrayed by Liberals, Jews and Socialists on the home front, remained a powerful one. Some of these negative feelings fed into the general hatred of the terms of the Treaty of Versailles. The inclusion of Article 231, known as the 'war-guilt clause', seemed particularly vindictive. Add in the bill for reparations and you have a perfect recipe for deeply held animosity towards democracy. Any government forced to sign such a treaty would have been unpopular, but the fact this task fell to the SPD-led coalition government was deeply damaging for the stability of democracy. The tag 'November Criminals' was hung around the necks of those politicians who had instigated the fall of the Kaiser and were responsible for the establishment of democracy.

There were also two aspects of the Weimar Constitution which undoubtedly contributed to the failure of democracy. The first was the voting system, based on proportional representation, which gave Reichstag seats in exact proportion to the votes cast in elections. In Germany, this system did not work. In July 1932, 27 different political parties contested the election, ranging across the political spectrum, with each representing one class or interest group. These differing parties reflected the bitter divisions in German society and made the task of creating stable coalition governments extremely difficult, and eventually impossible. Some coalitions took weeks to form, but could fall apart in days. The last functioning Weimar coalitions were those led by SPD Chancellor Herman Müller between 1928 and 1930, involving the SPD, Zentrum, the DDP, the DVP, but they finally broke apart over the increasing payments of unemployment benefits.

The Weimar Republic also lacked the one key factor that made democracy stable in the USA and Britain – that is, a two-party system, with one left-wing liberal democratic and one conservative party, alternating in periods of power, with each loyal to the democratic system. If there had been a first-past-the-post electoral constituency system, as operated in Britain, then probably a small number of parties would have ruled, and there would have been a better chance of stable government, although given the deep differences between the Weimar political parties that is by no means certain.

Those who drafted the Weimar Constitution were unwittingly culpable in offering a means of destroying democracy. This was the special powers the Weimar Constitution invested in the role of the President. No one realised when drafting the Constitution how an anti-democratic holder of the post could subvert the power of the President. Article 48 gave the German President extensive subsidiary powers in a 'state of emergency' to appoint and dismiss Chancellors and cabinets, to dissolve the Reichstag, call elections and suspend civil rights.

The two German presidents of the Weimar years were quite different. Social Democrat Friedrich Ebert was an enthusiastic supporter of Weimar democracy. He used Article 48 on 136 occasions during the period 1918 to 1925, but always with the intention of sustaining the Republic by preventing coup attempts, not with the aim of undermining or threatening its existence. Paul von Hindenburg, elected in 1925, was a great contrast. He was a right-wing figure, who had led Germany's militaristic armed forces during the Great War of 1914–1918. Up until March 1930, Hindenburg never used Article 48 at all. Henceforth, influenced by a small inner circle of advisers, all militaristic and authoritarian in outlook, he appointed Chancellors of his own choosing, who remained in power using emergency powers granted under Article 48.

It was President Hindenburg, therefore, who mortally damaged the infant democratic structure in Germany more than anyone else. It was not the Constitution or the voting system that was the fundamental problem, but the culpable actions of Hindenburg, who chose to deliberately subvert the power it had invested in him. Hindenburg appointed three Chancellors between 1930 and 1933: Heinrich Brüning, Franz von Papen, and Kurt von Schleicher, all of whom governed using emergency decrees granted by the President.

The political crisis after 1930 was deliberately manufactured by Hindenburg, who refused to involve Social Democrats in government, who were the strongest supporters of democracy. It must not be forgotten, however, that from 1930 onwards Adolf Hitler was the single most dynamic and popular politician in Germany. He united the voters on the Right of German politics in a way no other politician had been able to do so since the beginning of the Weimar years. The NSDAP managed to be anti-elitist and anti-capitalist while at the same time being patriotic and nationalist. The spectacular voting rise of the NSDAP from 2.63 per cent of voters in national elections in 1928, to 18.3 per cent in 1930, then to a high point of 37.3 in July 1932, was on a scale never seen in a democratic election before.

It was not by elections that Hitler finally came to power, however, but he would not have even been considered as a potential German Chancellor without his huge electoral support. A total of 13.74 million people voted for Hitler of their own free will in July 1932. Solid middle-class groups, usually the cement that holds together democratic governments, decided to support a party openly promising to destroy democracy. This mass electoral support was the decisive factor that propelled Hitler to a position where he could be offered power. Hitler's party grew because millions of Germans felt democratic government had been a monumental failed experiment. To these voters, Hitler offered the utopian vision of creating an authoritarian 'national community' that would sweep away the seeming chaos and instability of democratic government, and provide strong leadership.

Yet Hindenburg needed a great deal of persuading before he finally made Hitler the Chancellor of a 'national coalition'. It was former Chancellor Franz von Papen who played the most decisive role in convincing Hindenburg that Hitler could be 'tamed' by being invited to lead a cabinet of conservatives. By then, the only alternative to Hitler taking on the role was for Hindenburg to grant Schleicher, the current Chancellor, the power to declare a 'state of emergency', ban the Communists and National Socialists, suspend the Reichstag indefinitely and rule with the support of the Reichswehr. Behind-the-scenes intrigues and the personal rivalry between Franz von Papen and Kurt von Schleicher were also factors that played a crucial role in bringing Hitler to power. But it was Hindenburg's decision in March 1930 to create a presidential authoritarian right-wing regime that was the most decisive step that opened a path towards this solution.

The real problem Hindenburg faced was that the three previous Chancellors, Brüning, Papen and Schleicher, had no popular legitimacy, and no parliamentary support. Hindenburg's presidential rule had taken Germany down a blind alley. The only politician who could add popularity to Hindenburg's faltering presidential regime was Adolf Hitler. It was the decision to appoint the NSDAP leader as Chancellor which put the final nail in the coffin of Weimar democracy, and opened the path to catastrophe for Germany and the world. Hindenburg had been the gravedigger and the undertaker.

The history of the Weimar Years is therefore a warning sign of how a democracy under poor leadership can drift towards a form of authoritarian rule that ultimately destroys it, under the pressure of economic crisis and unrelenting political instability. This is a question that continues to engage us today.

·

ACKNOWLEDGEMENTS
NOTES
BIBLIOGRAPHY
INDEX

·

ACKNOWLEDGEMENTS

This book could not have been completed without the advice and support of so many people. I must first thank my fantastic literary agent, Georgina Capel, for her support during the whole project, and also her team, particularly Irene Baldoni and Rachel Conway. Many thanks to Anthony Cheetham, whose idea it was to bring out the two volumes of *The Hitler Years*, and then have a prequel on *The Weimar Years*.

Thanks are also due to the tremendous editorial team at Head of Zeus, headed by Richard Milbank, and for the copy-editing, picture research, and the original eye-catching design of the books. I would also like to thank my good friend Paul McGann for narrating the audiobook, to follow up his wonderful narrations for the two volumes of *The Hitler Years*.

My greatest thanks must go to my wife Ann, who has been a great support throughout the period of writing.

Finally, I must mention the unexpected and sudden death of my son-in-law, James West, aged 46, on 26 March 2022. He leaves behind his loving wife, Emily, and two beautiful daughters, Martha and Veronica. It is fitting, therefore, that I dedicate this book to James, with love.

NOTES

SOURCE ABBREVIATIONS

AP-IMT
Avalon Project, Yale University
(online archive of the Nuremberg
Trial proceedings)

BA-MA
Bundesarchiv, Marburg

BAB
Bundesarchiv, Berlin-Lichterfelde

BBP
British Parliamentary Papers

DBFP
Documents on British Foreign
Policy

FRUS
Foreign Relations of USA

GHDI
German History in Documents
and Images

HCD
House of Commons Debates

HLD
House of Lords Debates

HMSO
His (Her) Majesty's Stationery
Office

NA
National Archives, London

SPD
Stresemann Papers and Diaries

USNA
United States National Archives

POLITICAL PARTY
ABBREVIATIONS

BVP
Bavarian People's Party (*Bayerische
Volkspartei*)

CNBL
Christian National Peasants' and
Farmers' Party (*Christlich-
Nationale Bauern-und
Landvolkpartei*)

CSVD
Christian-Social People's Service
(*Christlich-Sozialer Volksdienst*)

DDP
German Democratic Party
(*Deutsche Demokratische Partei*)

DKP
German Conservative Party
(*Deutschkonservative Partei*)

DNVP
German National People's Party
(*Deutschnationale Volkspartei*)

DStP
German State Party (*Deutsche
Staatspartei*)

DVLP
German Fatherland Party
(*Deutsche Vaterlandspartei*)

DVP
German People's Party (*Deutsche
Volkspartei*)

FVP
Progressive People's Party
(*Fortschrittliche Volkspartei*)

KPD
Communist Party of Germany
(*Kommunistische Partei
Deutschlands*)

KVP
Conservative People's Party
(*Konservative Volkspartei*)

MSPD
Majority Social Democratic Party
(*Mehrheitssozialdemokratische
Partei Deutschlands*)

NLP
National Liberal Party
(*Nationalliberale Partei*)

NSDAP
National Socialist German
Workers' Party
(*Nationalsozialistische Deutsche
Arbeiterspartei*)

SPD
Social Democratic Party
(*Sozialdemokratische Partei
Deutschlands*)

USPD
Independent Social Democratic
Party (*Unabhängige
Sozialdemokratische Partei
Deutschlands*)

VPR
People's Justice Party
(*Volksrechtspartei*)

WP
Reich Party of the German
Middle Class (*Wirtschaftspartei des
deutschen Mittelstandes*)

Zentrum
Centre Party (*Deutsche
Zentrumpartei*)

I DEFEAT AND REVOLUTION

1 For a useful overview see K. Hoyer, *Blood and Iron: The Rise and Fall of the German Empire* (Cheltenham: History Press, 2021).

2 R. Evans, *The Coming of the Third Reich* (Penguin, 2004), p.9.

3 The name Kaiser derives from the Latin name for the Roman emperors, *Caesar*.

4 Hoyer, *Blood and Iron*, p.203.

5 S. Gross, 'Confidence and Gold: German War Finance 1914–1918', *Central European History*, Vol. 42 (2009), pp. 223–252.

6 Evans, *Coming of the Third Reich*, p.20. See also A. Milward and S. Saul, *The Development of the Economies of Continental Europe, 1850–1914* (Allen & Unwin, 1977), pp. 18–22.

7 For a detailed analysis see M. Kitchen, *The Silent Dictatorship: The Politics of the German High Command under Hindenburg and Ludendorff 1916–1918* (Abingdon: Routledge, 2019).

8 D. Steffen, 'The Holtzendorff Memorandum of 22 December and Germany's Declaration of Unrestricted U-boat Warfare', *Journal of Military History*, Vol. 68 (2004), pp. 215–24.

9 A. Ryder, *The German Revolution of 1918: A Study of Socialism in War and Revolt* (Cambridge: Cambridge University Press, 1967), pp. 87–93.

10 M. Balfour, *The Kaiser and His Times* (Penguin, 1969), pp. 380–382.

11 For a detailed analysis see J. Wheeler-Bennet, *Brest-Litovsk: The Forgotten Peace, March 1918* (Macmillan, 1938).

12 R. Gerwarth, *November 1918: The German Revolution* (Oxford: Oxford University Press, 2020), pp. 1–19.

13 E. Ludendorff, *Ludendorff's Own Story*, Vol 1 (New York: Harper and Brothers, 1919), p.326.

14 R. Evans, *The Hitler Conspiracies: The Third Reich and the Paranoid Imagination* (Penguin, 2021), p. 49.

15 Quoted in E. Sass, 'WWI Centennial: The Black Day of the German Army', available online at www.mentalfloss.com/article/554193/wwi-centennial-black-day-german-army.

16 For details of these discussions see P. Liddle and H. Cecil (eds), *At the Eleventh Hour: Reflections, Hopes and Anxieties at the Closing of the Great War, 1918* (Barnsley: Pen & Sword, 1998).

17 J. Snell, 'Wilson on Germany and the Fourteen Points', *Journal of Modern History*, Vol. 26 (1964), pp. 364–9.

18 E. Eyck, *A History of the Weimar Republic*, Vol. 1: *From the Collapse of the Empire to Hindenburg's Election* (New York: Atheneum, 1970), p. 32.

19 J. Wheeler-Bennet, *Hindenburg: The Wooden Titan* (Macmillan, 1967), pp. 162–3.

20 J. Röhl, *William II: Into the Abyss of War and Exile* (Cambridge: Cambridge University Press, 2014), pp. 1164–87.

21 L. Machtan, *Prinz Max von Baden: Der letzte Kanzler des Kaisers, Eine Biographie* (Berlin: Suhrkamp, 2013), pp. 244–53.

22 K. Epstein, 'Wrong Man in a Maelstrom: The Government of Max of Baden', *Review of Politics*, Vol. 26 (1964), pp. 215–43.

23 Wheeler-Bennett, *Hindenburg*, p.165.

24 For details see W. Mühlhausen, *Friedrich Ebert 1871–1925: Reichspräsident der Weimarer Republik* (Bonn: Deitz, 2006).

25 P. Bookbinder, *Weimar Germany: The Republic of the Reasonable* (Manchester: Manchester University Press, 1996), p.17.

26 For details see C. Gellinek, *Philipp Scheidemann: Gedächtnis und Errinnerung* (Berlin: Waxmann, 2006).

27 For the role of the USPD see D. Morgan, *The Socialist Left and the German Revolution: A History of the German Independent Social Democratic Party* (Ithaca: Cornell University Press, 1975).

28 For a detailed analysis of the Social Democrats see L. Guttmann, *The German Social Democratic Party, 1875–1933: From Ghetto to Government* (Routledge, 1981).

29 German High Command's Recommendation of Peace to the Reichstag, 2 October 1918, quoted in www.firstworldwar.com/source/germancollapse_bussche.html.

30 Wheeler-Bennet, *Hindenburg*, p. 168.

31 Paul von Hindenburg's Appeal for Peace Negotiations, 3 October 1918, quoted in www.firstworldwar.com/source/germancollapse_hindenburg.html.

32 United States National Archives (USNA), telegraph from Prince Max of Baden to President Woodrow Wilson, 4 October 1918, FO 608/148.

33 *The Times*, 6 October 1918.

34 R. Lutz, *The German Revolution, 1918–1919* (Cambridge: Cambridge University Press, 1922), pp. 130–4.

35 Papers relating to the Foreign Relations of the USA, 1918, Vol. 1, United States Printing Office, 1933 (FRUS): Wilson to German Government, 8 October 1918, File No. 763.72119/2113.

36 For details see P. Lecane, *Torpedoed!: The RMS Leinster Disaster* (Penzance: Periscope, 2005).

37 FRUS: German Secretary of State (Solf) to Wilson, 12 October 1918, File No.763.72119/2313.

38   FRUS: Wilson to German Government, 14 October 1918, file No. 763.72119/2313.

39   FRUS: German Government to President Wilson, 20 October 1918, File No. 763.72119/2377a.

40   FRUS: Wilson to German Government 23 October 1918, File No 763.72119/2377a.

41   For the full text of Hindenburg's memorandum see *United States Army in the World War: The Armistice Agreement and Related Documents*, Vol. 10, part 1 (Washington DC: Center of Military History United States Army, 1991), p.19.

42   W. Gorlitz (ed.), *The Kaiser and his Court: The Diaries, Notebooks and Letters of Admiral Georg Alexander von Müller, Chief of the Naval Cabinet, 1914–1916*, trans. M. Savill (Macdonald, p.413).

43   Wheeler-Bennet, *Hindenburg*, pp. 180–3.

44   For the full text of the law see 'Gesetz zur Abänderung der Reichsverfassung', Deutsches, available online at documentArchiv.de - Gesetz zur Abänderung der Reichsverfassung/ksr1918/reichsverfassung-aenderung_ges02.html.

45   See 'Correspondence Between the United States and Germany Regarding an Armistice', *American Journal of International Law*, Vol. 13 (1919), pp. 85–96.

46   N. Ashton and D. Hellema, 'Hanging the Kaiser: Anglo-Dutch Relations and the Fate of Wilhelm, 1918-20', *Diplomacy and Statecraft*, Vol. 11 (2000), pp. 53–78.

47   Quoted in Gerwarth, *November 1918*, p. 102.

48   Wheeler Bennet, *Hindenburg*, pp. 184–6.

49   FRUS: Wilson to German Government 5 November 1918, File No 763.72119/3813k.

50   E. Weitz, *Creating German Communism, 1890–1990: From Popular Protests to Socialist State* (Princeton, NJ: Princeton University Press, 1997), pp. 88–92.

51   For details see E. Burns, *Karl Liebknecht* (Martin Lawrence, 1934).

52   See L. Basso, *Rosa Luxemburg* (Andre Deutsch, 1975).

53   Gerwarth, *November 1918*, pp. 142–3.

54   For details see R. Hoffrogge, *Working Class Politics in the German Revolution: Richard Müller, the Revolutionary Stewards and the Origins of the Council Movement* (Leiden: Brill, 2014).

55   L. Heid, *Oskar Cohn: ein Sozialist und Zionist im Kaiserreich und in der Weimarer Republik* (Frankfurt am Main: Campus, 2002), p. 238.

56   For details see D. Dähnhardt, *Revolution in Keil: Der Übergang vom Kaiserreich zur Weimarer Republik 1918-19* (Neümunster: K. Wacholtz, 1984).

57   Bundesarchiv Marburg (BA-MA): Rm 31/v.2373, Police Report of 2 November 1918.

58   M. Baden, *Erinnerungen and Dokumente* (Munich: Deutsche Verlags-Anstalt, 1927), p. 599.

59   For details on his life see B. Grau, *Kurt Eisner, 1867–1919* (Munich: C.H. Beck, 2001).

60   Wheeler-Bennet, *Hindenburg*, pp. 188–9.

61   A. Niemann, *Kaiser and Revolution: Die entscheidenden Ereignisse im Grossen Hauptquartier im Herbst 1918* (Berlin: Verlag für Kulturpolitik, 1928), p. 134.

62   W. Groener, *Lebenserinnerungen: Jugend, Generalstab, Weltkrieg* (Göttingen: Vandenhoeck and Ruprecht, 1957), pp. 457–578.

63   Gerwarth, *November 1918*, p. 124.

64   For Erzberger's own account see M. Erzberger, *Erlebnisse im Weltkrieg* (Berlin: Deutsche Verlags Anstalt, 1920), pp. 330–3.

65   Prince Max von Baden's Announcement of Kaiser Wilhelm's Abdication, 9 November, quoted in www.firstworldwar.com/source/abdication_maxvonbaden.htm.

66   Wheeler-Bennet, *Hindenburg*, pp. 199–206.

67   Quoted in Gerwarth, *November 1918*, p. 116.

68   *Vorwärts*, 9 November 1918.

69   A. Kaes, M. Jay and E. Dimenberg (eds), *The Weimar Republic Sourcebook* (Berkeley: University of California Press, 1994): Bernhard Prince von Bulow, 'Revolution in Berlin, November 1918', p. 47.

70   M. Jessen-Klingenberg, 'Die Ausrufung der Republik durch Philipp Scheidemann am 9 November 1918', *Geschichte in Wissenschaft und Unterricht*, Vol. 19 (1968), pp. 649–56. See also Gerwarth, *November 1918*, p. 118.

71   P. Scheidemann, *Der Zusammenbruch* (Norderstedt: Vero, 2013), p. 173.

72   See R. Rurup, 'Problems of the German Revolution 1918-19', *Journal of Contemporary History*, Vol. 3 (1968), pp. 109–35.

73   See H. Frambach, 'The First Socialization Debate of 1918: Was the Socialization Commission Doomed to Failure from the Start?' in J. Backhaus, G. Chaloupek and H. Frambach (eds), *The First Socialization Debate (1918) and Early Efforts Towards Socialization* (New York: Springer, 2019), pp. 1–16.

74   D. Buse, 'Ebert and the German Crisis, 1917–1920, *Central European History*, Vol. 5 (1972), pp. 234–55.

75　For a detailed account see H. Rudin, *Armistice 1918* (Ann Arbor, MI: University of Michigan Press). See also Gerwarth, *November 1918*, pp. 126–8.

76　See G. Vascik and M. Sadler (eds), *The Stab-in-the-Back Myth and the Fall of the Weimar Republic: A History in Documents and Visual Sources* (Bloomsbury, 2016).

77　For details see G. Kuo, 'Explaining Historical Employer Coordination: Evidence from Germany', *Comparative Politics*, Vol. 48 (2015), pp. 87–106.

78　C. Seidl, 'The Bauer-Schumpeter Controversy on Socialization', *History of Economic Ideas*, Vol. 2 (1994), pp. 41–69.

79　Bundesarchiv Berlin (BAB): Stenographic Report of Congress of the Workers' and Soldiers' Councils, 16–21 December 1918, R201/3.

80　For details see M. Jones, *Founding Weimar: Violence and the German Revolution of 1918–1918* (Cambridge: Cambridge University Press, 2016); also Gerwarth, *November 1918*, p. 146.

81　For the discussions at the Congress on the need for violence to overthrow the Ebert government, see H. Ludewig, *Arbeiterbewegung und Aufstand: Eine Untersuchung zum Verhalten der Arbeiterparteien in den Aufstandsbewegungen der frühen Weimarer Republik, 1920–1923* (Hasum: Mattheissen, 1978), pp. 34–8.

2　THE JANUARY UPRISING, THE VERSAILLES TREATY, AND THE CONSTITUTION

1　For the text of Hirch's letter of dismissal to Eichhorn see E. Bernstein, *Die Deutsche Revolution* (Berlin: Verlag fuer Gesellschaft und Erziehung, 1921), p. 133.

2　See Eugen Ernst's interview with the *Manchester Guardian*, quoted in W. Astrow, A.Slepkow and J.Thomas (eds) *Illustrierte Geschichte der Russischen Revolution* (Berlin, Neuer Deutscher Verlag, 1928), pp. 271, 273.

3　*Die Rote Fahn (The Red Flag)*, 5 January 1918.

4　R. Müller, *Der Bürgerkrieg in Deutschland: Geburstswehen der Republik* (Berlin, Phoebus-Verlag, 1925), pp. 32, 35.

5　Bernstein, *Die Deutsche Revolution*, p. 138.

6　G. Noske, *Von Kiel bis Kapp: Zur Geschichte der deutschen Revolution* (Berlin, Verlag fuer Politik und Wirtschaft, 1920), pp. 69–70.

7　Müller, *Der Bürgerkrieg*, pp. 254–5.

8　Gerwarth, *November 1918*, p. 149.

9　Müller, *Der Bürgerkrieg*, p. 75.

10　Astrow, Slepkow and Thomas, *Illustrierte Geschichte*, p.277.

11　Gerwarth, *November 1918*, pp. 154–6; M. Jones, *Founding Weimar* (Cambridge, Cambridge University Press, 2016), p. 197.

12　R. Luxemburg, *Die Ordnung herrscht in Berlin* in Luxemburg, *Ausgewaehlte Reden und Schriften*, Vol. 2 (Berlin, Dietz Verlag, 1951), pp. 709–11; K. Liebknecht, 'Trotz alledem' in K. Liebknecht, *Ausgwaehlte Reden, Briefe und Aufsaetze* (Berlin, Dietz Verlag, 1952), pp. 526–30.

13　W. Wette, *The Wehrmacht: History, Myth, Reality* (Cambridge, MA: Harvard University Press, 2006), p.44.

14　See L. Feigel, 'The Murder of Rosa Luxemburg – Tragedy and Farce', *The Guardian*, 9 January 2019.

15　See 'Berlin Authorities Seize Corpse for Pre-Burial Autopsy', *Der Spiegel* online, 17 December 2009.

16　Astrow, Slepkow and Thomas, *Illustrierte Geschichte*, p. 298.

17　For details see A. Berlau, *German Social Democratic Party, 1914–1921* (New York: Columbia University Press, 1949).

18　For an interesting micro-study of the fluctuating electoral fortunes of the DDP in the early Weimar era, see A. Burkhardt, 'A Republican Potential: The Rise and Fall of the German Democratic Party in Hof-an-der-Saale, 1918–1920', *Central European History*, Vol. 50 (2017), pp. 471–92.

19　D. Walker, 'The German Nationalist People's Party: The Conservative Dilemma in the Weimar Republic', *Journal of Contemporary History*, Vol. 14 (1979), pp. 627–47.

20　For the debate on the role of the Centre Party in Weimar see J. Zeender, 'Recent Literature on the German Centre Party', *Catholic Historical Review*, Vol. 70 (1984), pp. 428–41.

21　For details see L. Hertzman, 'The Founding of the German National People's Party (DNVP), November 1918–January 1919', *Journal of Modern History*, Vol. 30 (1958), pp. 24–36.

22　For the full detailed results see D. Nohlen and P. Stöver, *Elections in Europe: A Data Handbook* (Baden-Baden and Nomos: Verlagsgesellschaft, 2010), p. 762.

23　Ebert's Speech to the National Assembly, 7 February 1919, quoted in www.firstworldwar.com/source/germanassembly_ebert1.htm.

24　Kolb, Weimar Republic, p.226.

25　Ebert's speech to the National Assembly, 11 February 1919; for full text see www.ebert-gedenkstaette.de/ebert_dok_wahl.html.

26　For the details of Scheidemann's cabinet meetings see H. Schulze (ed.), *Das Kabinett Scheidemann* (Berlin, Walter de Gruyter, 1971).

27　See W. Hubatsch, 'The Scheidemann Cabinet, February 13, 1919, to June 20, 1919', *Philosophy and History*, Vol. 5 (1972), pp. 100–2.

28 V. Weidermann, *Dreamers: When the Writers Took Power: Germany, 1919* (Pushkin Press, 2019), pp. 101–2.

29 Arco-Valley became a committed supporter of the Bavarian People's Party but was never a member of the Nazi party. On 29 June 1945 he was killed in a car accident in Salzburg.

30 See http://www.muenchner-stadtmuseum.de/en/revolutionary-and-state-premier-kurt-eisner-1867-1919/chapter-10-kurt-eisners-assassination.

31 For an overview of Eisner's government see A. Mitchell, *Revolution in Bavaria: The Eisner Regime and the Soviet Republic* (Princeton, NJ, Princeton University Press, 1965).

32 For a contemporary report see F. Moore, 'Eisner: A Great Loss', *New York Tribune*, 25 February 1919.

33 Evans, *The Coming of the Third Reich*, pp. 158-161; for Toller's own interesting account see E. Toller, *I Was a German* (Bodley Head, 1934).

34 Noske, *Von Kiel bis Kapp*, p.136.

35 Weidermann, *Dreamers*, pp. 152–4.

36 For details see E. Hooglund, *The Munich Soviet Republic of April, 1919* (Orno, ME: University of Maine, 1966).

37 For details see R. Phelps, '"Before Hitler Came": Thule Society and Germanen Orden', *Journal of Modern History*, Vol. 35 (1963), pp. 245–61.

38 Weidermann, *Dreamers*, p. 249.

39 For a detailed account of the Munich revolt see G. Kuhn (ed. and trans.), *All Power to the Councils: A Documentary History of the German Revolution of 1918–1919* (Oakland, CA: PM Press, 2012).

40 For a detailed examination of Hitler's early life see V. Ullrich, *Hitler*, Vol 1: *Ascent*, trans. J. Chase (Bodley Head, 2016), pp. 13–29

(original German edition, 2013); I. Kershaw, *Hitler*, Vol 1: *1889–1936* (Penguin, 2001), pp. 1–69; A. Bullock, *Stalin and Hitler: Parallel Lives* (Harper Collins, 1991), pp. 5–12.

41 R. Waite, *The Psychopathic God: Adolf Hitler* (New York, Basic Books, 1977), p. 137.

42 Kershaw, *Hitler*, Vol 1, p.12.

43 See A. Kubizek, *The Hitler I Knew: The Memoirs of Hitler's Childhood Friend* (Frontline, revised edn, 2011).

44 Ullrich, *Hitler*, Vol. 1, pp. 23–6.

45 A. Hitler, *Mein Kampf* (Paternoster, 1936), p.20.

46 Ullrich, *Hitler*, Vol. 1, pp. 26–7.

47 The best study of Hitler's Vienna period is B. Haman, *Hitler's Vienna: A Dictator's Apprenticeship: A. Portrait of the Tyrant as a Young Man* (Taurus Parke, 2010).

48 L. Machtan, *The Hidden Hitler* (Perseus Press, 2001), p. 41.

49 Ullrich, *Hitler*, Vol. 1, p. 40.

50 W. Shirer, *The Rise and Fall of The Third Reich* (Arrow, 1991), p. 17.

51 Kershaw, *Hitler*, Vol. 1, pp. 53–4.

52 Ullrich, *Hitler*, Vol. 1, p.40.

53 Shirer, *Third Reich*, pp. 21–8.

54 Ullrich, *Hitler*, Vol. 1, pp. 48–9

55 A. Bullock, *Hitler: A Study in Tyranny* (Penguin, 1962), p. 48.

56 Ullrich, *Hitler*, Vol. 1, p. 53.

57 Bullock, *Stalin and Hitler*, p. 50.

58 Bullock, *Stalin and Hitler*, p. 49.

59 Ullrich, *Hitler*, Vol. 1, p. 61.

60 Quoted in Ullrich, *Hitler*, Vol. 1, p. 59.

61 J. Fest, *Hitler* (Weidenfeld and Nicolson, 1974), p. 69.

62 For the full details of the evidence of Hans Mend, see Machtan, *The Hidden Hitler*, pp. 65–104.

63 Ullrich, *Hitler*, Vol. 1, p.62.

64 Shirer, *Third Reich*, p.29.

65 Ernst Schmidt was discharged from the army on 12 April 1919.

66 T. Weber, *Becoming Hitler: The Making of a Nazi* (Oxford, Oxford University Press, 2017), p. 25.

67 Ullrich, *Hitler*, Vol. 1, p. 75.

68 Weber, *Becoming Hitler*, pp. 39-40.

69 Ullrich, *Hitler*, Vol. 1, p. 79.

70 Machtan, *The Hidden Hitler*, p. 94.

71 Kershaw, *Hitler*, Vol 1, p. 122.

72 Interview by Mayr in *Münchener Post*, 13 November 1928.

73 Ullrich, *Hitler*, Vol. 1, p.81.

74 Kershaw, *Hitler*, Vol 1, p.123.

75 Eyck, *Weimar Republic*, Vol. 1, p. 94.

76 See D. van der Vat, *The Great Scuttle: The Sinking of the Fleet at Scapa Flow in 1919* (Edinburgh: Birlinn, 2007).

77 For the full text of the Treaty of Versailles see *The Treaty of Peace between the Allied and Associated Powers and Germany*, HMSO, 1920.

78 *New York Times*, 13 May 1919.

79 Wheeler-Bennett, *Hindenburg*, p. 217.

80 For the details of Bauer's cabinet meetings see A. Golecki (ed.), *Das Kabinett Bauer* (Berlin: Walter de Gruyter, 1996).

81 For detailed studies on the negotiations, signing and consequences of the Versailles Treaty see M. Macmillan, *Paris 1919: Six Months That Changed the World* (New York, Random House, 2001); A. Sharp, *Versailles 1919: A Centennial Perspective* (Haus, 2018); A. Adelman, *A Shattered Peace: Versailles 1919 and the Price We Pay Today* (Chichester: John Wiley, 2008).

82 For details see C. Wolff, *Magnus Hirschfeld: A Portrait of a Pioneer in Sexology* (Quartet Books,

1986); W. Robinson, 'The Institute of Social Science', *Medical Critic and Guide*, Vol. 25 (1925), pp. 391–6.

83 R. Bleachey, *Gay Berlin: Birthplace of Modern Identity* (New York, Vintage Books, 2014), p. 163.

84 See J. Steakley, 'Cinema and Censorship in the Weimar Republic: The Case of Anders als Die Andens', *Film History*, Vol. 11 (1999), pp. 181–203.

85 Bleachey, *Gay Berlin*, p. 170.

86 Bleachey, *Gay Berlin*, p. 179.

87 See S. Bach, '100 years of the Modern German Tax System: Foundation, Reforms and Challenges', *Deutsches Institut für Wirtschaftsforschung*, Vol. 9 (2019), pp. 407–13.

88 The term 'Länder' translates into English most appropriately as 'States'.

89 For details on the electoral system in Weimar see F. Hermens, 'Proportional Representation and the Breakdown of German Democracy', *Social Research*, Vol. 3 (1936), pp. 411–33.

90 For a discussion on the use of Article 48 during the Weimar era see M. De Wilde, 'The State of Emergency in the Weimar Republic: Legal Disputes over Article 48 of the Weimar Constitution', *Legal History Review*, Vol. 78 (2010), pp. 135–58.

91 For the full text of the Weimar Constitution and a commentary on all its articles see R. Brunet, *The New German Constitution – with Text* (New York: Knopf, 1923). See also the definitive German account of the Weimar Constitution: E. Huber, *Deutsche Verfassungsgeschichte seit 1789*, Bd. 5: *Weltkrieg, Revolution und Reichserneuerung, 1914–1919* (Stuttgart: Kohlhammer, 1978).

92 See N. Rossol, 'Visualizing the Republic: State Representation and Public Ritual in Weimar Germany', in J. Williams (ed.),

Weimar Culture Revisited (Basingstoke: Palgrave Macmillan, 2011), pp. 139–59.

93 Ullrich, *Hitler*, Vol.1, p. 82.

94 Weber, *Becoming Hitler*, p. 111.

95 F. Mayer-Hartmann and A. Dresler (eds), *Dokumente der Zeitgeschichte* (Munich: Franz Eher Nachfolger, 1938), p. 85.

96 E. Piper, *Kurze Geschichte des Nationalsozialismus von 1919 bis Heute Zeitgeschichte* (Hamburg: Hoffmann und Kampf, 2007), p. 15.

97 Ullrich, *Hitler*, Vol. 1, p.87.

98 Kershaw, *Hitler*, Vol. 1, p.137.

99 Fest, *Hitler*, p.11.

100 F. McDonough (with J. Cochrane), *The Holocaust* (Basingstoke: Palgrave Macmillan, 2008), p. 16.

101 Adolf Hitler to Adolf Gemlich, 16 September 1919, quoted in E. Jäckel and A. Kuhn (eds), *Hitler: Sämtliche Aufzeichnungen, 1905–1924* (Stuttgart: Deutsche Verlags-Anstalt, 1980), pp. 88–90.

102 *Communist World*, 15 November 1919.

103 Wheeler-Bennett, *Hindenburg*, p. 238.

104 See R. Hunt, 'Myths, Guilt and Shame in Pre-Nazi Germany', *Virginia Quarterly Review*, Vol. 34 (1958), pp. 355–71.

105 See J. Keynes, *The Economic Consequences of the Peace* (Macmillan, 1919). The term 'Carthaginian peace' derived from the terms imposed by the Roman Empire on the Carthaginian Empire after the Second Punic War (218–201 BC), which was intended to permanently cripple the losing side.

106 For excellent contemporary reviews of the book see C. Day, 'Keynes' Economic Consequences of the Peace', *American History Review*, Vol 10 (1920), pp. 299–312; F. Taussig, 'Review: Keynes, The

Economic Consequences of the Peace', *Quarterly Journal of Economics*. Vol. 34 (1920), pp. 381–87.

3 FAILED REVOLT FROM THE RIGHT

1 *Manchester Guardian*, 12 January 1920.

2 For details see G. Hankel, *The Leipzig Trials: German War Crimes and Their Legal Consequences after World War I* (Dordrecht, Netherlands: Republic of Letters, 2014).

3 See R. Butler, J. Bury and M. Lambert (eds), *Documents on British Foreign Policy, 1919–1939* (DBFP), First Series, Vol. IX, *German Affairs, 1920* (HMSO, 1960), No. 571, pp. 621–4: Sir R. Graham to Earl Curzon, 30 January 1920.

4 See J. Yarnall, *Barbed Wire Disease: British and German Prisoners of War, 1914–1918* (Stroud: Spellmount, 2011), pp. 183–96.

5 'Arnold Brecht on Matthias Erzberger's Libel Suit against Karl Helfferich in 1920', German History in Documents and Images (GHDI), German Historical Institute, Washington DC, available online at www.ghdi-dc.org.

6 H. Winkler, *Weimar 1918–1933: Die Geschichte der ersten Deutschen Demokratie* (Frankfurt am Main: Beck, 1993), p. 117.

7 Eyck, *Weimar Republic*, Vol.1, p. 145.

8 N. Wachsmann, *Hitler's Prisons: Legal Terror in Nazi Germany* (New Haven, CT, Yale University Press, 2004), p. 37.

9 E. Kolb, *The Weimar Republic* (trans. P. Fall) (Routledge, 1988), p. 37.

10 For the role of Noske see U. Czisnik, *Gustav Noske: Ein sozialdemokratischer Staatsmann* (Gottingen, Mustarschmidt Verlag, 1969).

11 J. Erger, *Der Kapp-Lüttwitz-Putsch: Ein Beitrag zur deutschen Innenpolitik 1919–1920* (Düsseldorf: Droste, 1967), pp. 17‒28.

12 Erger, *Der Kapp-Lüttwitz-Putsch*, pp. 121–2.

13 F. Carsten, *The Reichswehr and Politics, 1918–1933* (Oxford, Clarendon Press, 1966), pp. 78–9.

14 Erger, *Der Kapp-Lüttwitz-Putsch*, pp. 139–43.

15 The Kapp Proclamation, March 1920, quoted in www.alphahistory.com/weimarrepublic/proclamation-kapp-putsch-1920/

16 Quoted in W. Pelz, *A People's History of the German Revolution* (Pluto Press, 2018), p.123.

17 Butler, Bury and Lambert, DBFP, First Series, Vol IX, No. 119, pp. 148–39: Lord Kilmarnock (Berlin) to Lord Curzon, 15 March 1920.

18 H. Heiber, *The Weimar Republic* (Oxford, Blackwell, 1993), p. 53.

19 Carsten, *Reichswehr and Politics*, pp. 93–9.

20 For details of the first Müller cabinet see M. Vogt (ed.), *Das Kabinett Müller I* (Boppard am Rhein: Boldt, 1970).

21 Lutz, *The German Revolution*, p. 243.

22 See R. Koepp, 'Gustav von Kahr and the Emergence of the Radical Right in Bavaria', *Historian*, Vol.77 (2015), pp. 740–63.

23 For details see H. Stern, 'The Organisation Consul', *Journal of Modern History*, Vol. 35 (1963), pp. 20–33.

24 The 25 Points of the Nazi Party (NSDAP) Programme, 24 February 1920, available online at www.alphahistory.com/nazigermany/nazi-party-25-points-1920/.

25 Ullrich, *Hitler*, Vol.1, p. 91.

26 For a detailed overview of the Ruhr Uprising see D. Schumann, *Political Violence in the Weimar Republic, 1918–1933* (Oxford, Berghahn, 2009), pp. 25–53.

27 P. Fritsche, *Rehearsals for Fascism: Populism and Political Mobilization in Weimar Germany* (New York, Oxford University Press, 1990), pp. 56–65.

28 For how the German government handled the Ruhr Uprising see W. Angress, 'Weimar Coalition and Ruhr Insurrection, March–April 1920', *Journal of Modern History*, Vol. 29 (1957), pp. 1–20.

29 H. Winkler, *Germany: The Long Road West*, Vol. 2: *1933–1990* (Oxford: Oxford University Press, 2006), p. 371.

30 For details see R. Waite, *Vanguard of Nazism: The Free Corps Movement in Post War Germany, 1918–1923* (Cambridge, MA: Harvard University Press, 1952).

31 Kolb, *Weimar Republic*, p. 96.

32 C. Rogowski (ed.), *The Many Faces of Weimar Cinema: Rediscovering Germany's Filmic Legacy* (Rochester, NY: Camden House 2010), p. 4.

33 S. Kracauer, *From Caligari to Hitler: A Psychological History of German Film*, revised edn (Princeton, NJ: Princeton University Press, 2004), pp. 61–76.

34 D. Robinson, *Das Cabinet des Dr. Caligari* (British Film Institute, 1997), p. 33.

35 H. Janowitz, 'Caligari – The Story of a Famous Story (Excerpts)', in M. Budd (ed.), *In The Cabinet of Dr. Caligari: Texts, Contexts, Histories* (New Brunswick, NJ: Rutgers University Press, 1990), pp. 224–5.

36 For full results of the Reichstag election of 6 June 1920 see Nohlen and Stöver, *Elections in Europe*, p.762.

37 For details of Fehrenbach's cabinet meetings see P. Wulf (ed.), *Das Kabinett Fehrenbach* (Oldenburg: Wissenschaftsverlag, 1972).

38 For the text of the coal agreement see 'Protocol of Spa Conference Respecting Coal', *American Journal of International Law*, Vol. 16 (1922), pp. 205–7.

39 *The Mercury*, Hobart, Australia, 29 July 1920.

40 T. Nakagaki, *The Buddhist Swastika and Hitler's Cross: Rescuing a Symbol of Peace from the Forces of Hate* (Berkeley, CA: Stone Bridge Press, 2018), p. 89.

41 Butler, Bury and Lambert, DBFP, First Series, Vol. X (HMSO, 1960), No. 219, pp. 309–12: Robert Smallbones to Lord Curzon, 28 September 1920.

42 For a good overview of the development of Communism in Germany see D. Priestland, *Red Flag: A History of Communism* (New York: Grove, 2009).

43 For details on the split of the USPD see D. Morril, 'The Comintern and the German Independent Social Democratic Party', *The Historian*, Vol. 31 (1970), pp. 191–209.

44 Butler, Bury and Lambert, DBFP, First Series, Vol. X, No. 233, pp. 329–330: Lord D'Abernon to Lord Curzon, 8 November 1920.

45 Butler, Bury and Lambert, DBFP, First Series, Vol. X, No. 352, pp. 479–94: Report by Marshal Foch, President of the Allied Military Committee of Versailles to the President of the Conference of Ambassadors, 28 December 1920. See also *New York Times*, 1 January 1921.

4 MAKE GERMANY PAY

1 H. Harmer, *Friedrich Ebert* (Haus, 2008), pp. 131–2.

2 *American Review of Reviews*, February 1921.

3   See J. Bois, 'Aristide Briand: Member of Twenty-One French Cabinets', *Current History*, Vol. 31 (1929), pp. 529–35.

4   For details of the reparations saga see S. Marks, 'The Myths of Reparations', *Central European History*, Vol. 11 (1978), pp. 231–55.

5   *New York Times*, 27 January 1921.

6   *New York Times*, 2 February 1921.

7   Butler, Bury and Lambert, DBFP, First Series, Vol. XVI, No. 434, pp. 454–7: Lord Kilmarnock to Lord Curzon, 1 February 1921.

8   *Minneapolis Morning Tribune*, 12 February 1921.

9   Butler, Bury and Lambert, DBFP, First Series, Vol. XVI, No. 444, p. 467: Lord D'Abernon to Lord Curzon, 24 February 1921.

10   Eyck, *The Weimar Republic*, Vol 1, p.174.

11   House of Commons Debates (HCD) , cols 2015–17: Lloyd George speech, 3 May 1921.

12   *New York Times*, 17 March 1921, 19 March 1921; American Review of Reviews, May 1921.

13   C. Harman, *The Lost Revolution: Germany 1918–1923* (Bookmarks, 1982), pp. 199–200.

14   For details of the 'March action' see W. Angress, *Stillborn Revolution: The Communist Bid for Power in Germany, 1921–1923* (Princeton, NJ, Princeton University Press, 1963).

15   P. Lesniewski, 'Three Insurrections: Upper Silesia, 1919–1921', in P. Stachura (ed.), *Poland Between the Wars, 1918–1939* (New York: St. Martin's Press, 1998), pp. 13–42.

16   For the French approach to Eastern Europe in the period 1918 to 1926 see P. Wandycz, *France and Her Eastern Allies: French-Czechoslovak–Polish Relations from the Paris Peace Conference to Locarno* (Minneapolis: University of Minnesota Press, 1962).

17   For details see T. Tooley, 'German Political Violence and the Border Plebiscite in Upper Silesia, 1919–1921', *Central European History*, Vol. 21 (1988), pp. 56–98; F. Campbell, 'The Struggle for Upper Silesia, 1919–1922', *Journal of Modern History*, Vol. 42 (1970), pp. 361–85.

18   Butler, Bury and Lambert, DBFP, First Series, Vol. XVI. No. 484, pp. 521–2: Lord D'Abernon to Lord Curzon, 30 March 1921.

19   Butler, Bury and Lambert, DBFP, First Series, Vol. XVI. No. 510, pp. 546–7: Lord D'Abernon to Lord Curzon, 18 March 1921.

20   Butler, Bury and Lambert, DBFP, First Series, Vol. XVI, No. 535, p. 570: A Geddes to Lord Geddes, 25 April 1921.

21   Marks, 'The Myths of Reparations', p.236.

22   Butler, Bury and Lambert, DBFP, First Series, Vol. XVI, No. 545, pp. 582–3: Lord Kilmarnock to Lord Curzon, 29 April 1921.

23   *New York Times*, 5 May 1921, 6 May 1921.

24   For the meetings of the first Wirth cabinet see I. Schulz-Bidlingmaier (ed.), *Die Kabinette Wirth I und II* (Boppard am Rhein: Boldt, 1973).

25   *New York Times*, 11 May 1921, 12 May 1921, 31 May 1921.

26   W. Rathenau, *An Deutschlands Jugend* (Berlin: Fischer, 1918), p.9.

27   See E. Kollman, 'Walter Rathenau and German Foreign Policy: Thoughts and Actions', *Journal of Modern History*, Vol.24 (1952), pp. 127–42.

28   Butler, Bury and Lambert, DBFP, First Series, Vol. XVI. No. 623, pp. 674–5: Lord D'Abernon to Lord Curzon, 19 May 1921.

29   D. Jablonsky, *The Nazi Party in Dissolution: Hitler and the Verbotzeit, 1923–1925* (Routledge, 2013), pp. 8–9. See also D. Large, 'The Politics of Law and Order: A History of the Bavarian

Einwohnerwehr, 1918-1921', *Transactions of the American Philosophical Society*, Vol. 70 (1980), pp. 1–87.

30   Kershaw, *Hitler*, Vol. 1, p. 161.

31   See R. Griffin (ed.), *Fascism* (New York: Oxford University Press, 1995), pp. 105–6.

32   Ullrich, *Hitler*, Vol. 1, pp. 110–11.

33   Kershaw, *Hitler*, Vol. 1, p. 164.

34   E. Deuerlein (ed.), *Der Aufstieg der NSDAP in Augenzeugenberichten* (Düsseldorf: E. Rauch, 1968), pp. 136–41. After the left-wing *Münchner Post* reprinted the leaflet, Hitler sued the newspaper for libel and received a settlement of 600 marks, in December 1921. It was never discovered who the author of the leaflet was.

35   Kershaw, *Hitler*, Vol. 1, pp. 169–170.

36   Ullrich, *Hitler*, Vol. 1, pp. 113–15.

37   *Washington Post*, 19 September 1921.

38   R. Wetzell, *Crime and Criminal Justice in Modern Germany* (Berghahn, 2014), p. 222.

39   For details see T. Lessing, 'Haarmann: The Story of a Werewolf', in T. Lessing, K. Berg and G. Goodwin (eds), *Monsters of Weimar* (Nemesis, 1993).

40   N. Wachsmann, *Hitler's Prisons*, p. 19.

41   See M. Wolfgang, 'Cesare Lombroso', in H. Mannheim (ed.), *Pioneers in Criminology* (Stevens, 1960), pp. 168–227.

42   F. Wetzell, *Inventing the Criminal: A History of The German Criminal, 1880–1945* (Chapel Hill: University of Carolina Press, 2000), p. 107.

43   Wetzell, *Inventing the Criminal*, p. 121.

44   Waite, *Vanguard of Nazism*, pp. 200–15.

45 For relevant documents on the case see R. Lanzenauer, *Der Mord an Matthias Erzberger* (Karlsruhe, Verlag der Gesellschaft für Kulturhistorische Dokumentation, 2008).

46 *New York Times*, 27 August 1921.

47 Schumann, *Political Violence*, p.98.

48 H. Turner, *Stresemann and the Politics of the Weimar Republic* (Princeton, NJ: Princeton University Press, 1963), p.91.

49 *New York Times*, 31 August 1921.

50 *American Review of Reviews*, November 1921.

51 S. Payne, *The Life and Death of Adolf Hitler* (New York: Popular Library, 1973), p. 160.

52 The incident was not forgotten by Hitler. During the notorious Night of the Long Knives in 1934, Ballerstedt was murdered.

53 Wachsmann, *Hitler's Prisons*, p. 37

54 *New York Times*, 23 October 1921.

55 Butler, Bury and Lambert, DBFP, First Series, Vol. XVI, No. 357, p. 375: Lord D'Abernon to Lord Curzon, 27 October 1921.

56 *New York Times*, 27 October 1921. For the meetings of the second Wirth cabinet, see Schulz-Bidlingmaier, *Kabinette Wirth I und II.*

57 *American Review of Reviews*, January 1922, December 1921.

58 Butler, Bury and Lambert, DBFP, First Series, Vol. XVI, No. 735, pp. 808–9: Memorandum on German Financial Position by Lord D'Abernon, Berlin, 15 November 1921.

59 *American Review of Reviews*, January 1922.

60 A. Fergusson, *When Money Dies: The Nightmare of the Weimar Hyper-Inflation* (William Kimber, 1975), p. 65.

61 Butler, Bury and Lambert, DBFP, First Series, Vol. XVI, No. 761, pp. 851–2: German Ambassador to Lord Curzon, 15 December 1921.

62 Fergusson, *When Money Dies*, p. 66.

63 For details see H. James, 'The Weimar Economy', in A. McElligott (ed.), *Weimar Germany* (Oxford: Oxford University Press, 2009), pp. 102–26.

64 For a detailed study on the collapse of the mark and hyperinflation see A. Fergusson, *When Money Dies*, pp. 52–66.

---

5 REPARATIONS DIFFICULTIES

1 For details of the Lloyd George–Briand relationship in this period see H. Hall, 'Lloyd George, Briand and the Failure of the Anglo-French Entente', *Journal of Modern History*, Vol. 50 (1978), pp. 1121–38.

2 DPFP, First Series, Vol XX, Her Majesty's Stationery Office 1976, Document No.1, pp. 1–3: Memorandum by Ralph Wigram on the position of negotiations at the end of the Cannes Conference, 19 January 1922.

3 See C. Fink, *The Genoa Conference: European Diplomacy, 1921–1922* (Chapel Hill: University of North Carolina Press), 1984.

4 *New York Times*, 16 January 1922.

5 Ferguson, *When Money Dies*, p.67.

6 See Eyck, *Weimar Republic*, Vol. I, p.200.

7 Quoted by Guido Westerwelle, German Foreign Minister, in a speech in Berlin, 24 June 2012, commemorating the 90th anniversary of Rathenau's death; see www.auswaertiges-amt.de/en/newsroom/news/120624-bm-gedenkveranstaltung-rathenau/250600.

8 J. Wheeler-Bennet, *The Nemesis of Power: German Army in Politics, 1918–1945* (New York: Palgrave Macmillan, 2005), pp. 133–8.

9 For details on Seeckt's role see H. Meier-Welcker, *Seeckt* (Frankfurt am Main: Bernard Verlag für Wehrwesen, 1967), pp. 524–58.

10 For Maltzan's key role see P. Shekarloo, *Maltzan, The Architect of Rapallo: Weimar Foreign Policy, German-Soviet Relations, and the Treaty of Versailles, 1920–1922* (Munich: Grin, 2010).

11 R. Himmer, 'Rathenau, Russia and Rapallo', *Central European History*, Vol. 9 (1976), pp. 146–83.

12 *New York Times*, 23 March 1922.

13 F. Taylor, *The Downfall of Money: Germany's Hyperinflation and the Destruction of the Middle Class* (Bloomsbury, 2013), p. 184.

14 J. Mills, *Genoa Conference* (Hutchinson, 1922), p.10.

15 *Manchester Guardian*, 17 April 1922.

16 Eyck, *Weimar Republic*, Vol. I, p.206.

17 L.Kochan, 'The Russian Road to Rapallo', *Soviet Studies*, Vol. 2 (1950), pp. 109–17.

18 For details see G. Mueller, 'Rapallo Re-examined: A New Look at Germany's Secret Military Collaboration with Russia in 1922', *Military Affairs*, Vol. 40 (1976), pp. 109–17.

19 *Chicago Daily Tribune*, 25 April 1922.

20 Taylor, *Downfall of Money*, p.106.

21 For details see B. Carrol, 'Germany Disarmed and Rearming, 1925–1935', *Journal of Peace Research*, Vol. 3 (1966), pp. 114–24.

22 Eyck, *Weimar Republic*, Vol. I, p.210.

23 *New York Times*, 1 June 1922.

24 Kolb, *Weimar Republic*, p.44.

25 *Chicago Daily Tribune*, 23 July 1922.

26 Taylor, *Downfall of Money*, pp. 188-189.

27 M. Sabrow, *Der Rathenaumord: Rekonstruktion einer Verschwörung gegen die Republik von Weimar*, (Munich: Oldenburg, 1994), pp. 86-8.

28 Taylor, *Downfall of Money*, pp. 199-200.

29 Sabrow, *Der Rathenaumord*, pp. 91-103.

30 For details see N. Cohn, *Warrant for Genocide: The Myth of the Jewish World Conspiracy and the Protocols of the Elders of Zion* (New York, Harper & Row), pp. 145-6.

31 See R. Evans, 'Prophet in a Tuxedo', *London Review of Books* (November 2012).

32 Sabrow, *Der Rathenaumord*, pp. 149-51.

33 H. Kippers, *Joseph Wirth: Parlamentarier, Minister Und Kanzler der Weimarer Republik* (Stuttgart: Franz Steiner Verlag, 1997), p.189.

34 N. Rossol, 'Visualizing the Republic', p. 147.

35 For full text see GHDI, Law for the Protection of the Republic, 1922.

36 For details see C. Landauer, 'The Bavarian Problem in the Weimar Republic, Part 2', *Journal of Modern History*, Vol. 16 (1944), pp. 205-23.

37 Taylor, *Downfall of Money*, p. 20.

38 Fergusson, *When Money Dies*, p. 111, p. 90.

39 *Brooklyn Daily Eagle*, 12 July 1922.

40 Butler, Bury and Lambert, DBFP, Vol. XVI, No. 45, pp. 99-101: Earl of Balfour to Count de Saint Auclaire, 1 August 1922.

41 B. Rhodes, *United States Foreign Policy in the Interwar Period: The Golden Age of American Diplomatic and Military Complacency* (Westport, CT, Praeger, 2001), p.50.

42 Butler, Bury and Lambert, DBFP, Vol. XVI, No. 50, pp. 112-14: German Chancellor [Wirth] to David Lloyd George, 5 August 1922 [Appendix].

43 Butler, Bury and Lambert, DBFP, Vol. XVI, No. 51, pp. 114-25: Notes of Allied Conference, 10 Downing Street, 7 August 1922.

44 Butler, Bury and Lambert, DBFP, Vol. XVI, No. 54, pp. 129-45: Notes of Allied Conference, 10 Downing Street, 7 August 1922.

45 *Chicago Daily Tribune*, 16 August 1922, 1 September 1922.

46 For the details on the negotiations leading to the merger see H. Winkler, *Von der Revolution zur Stabilisierung: Arbeiter und Arbeiterbewegung in der Weimarer Republik, 1918–1924* (Berlin: J.W. Deitz Nachf, 1984), pp. 487-501.

47 H. Herzfeld (ed.), *Geschichte in Gestalten: Ein Biographisches Lexikon – A-E* (Frankfurt am Main: Fischer, 1981), pp. 335-6.

48 For details see G. Bennett, *Foreign Policy During the Curzon Period, 1919–1924* (Basingstoke: Palgrave Macmillan, 1995).

49 A. Lyttelton, *The Seizure of Power: Fascism in Italy, 1919–1929* (New York: Routledge, 2008), pp. 74-8.

50 Kershaw, *Hitler*, Vol. 1, p.180.

51 *New York Times*, 21 November 1922.

52 Butler, Bury and Lambert, DBFP, Vol. XVI, No. 73, p. 241: Lord D'Abernon to Lord Curzon, 24 August 1922; Butler, Bury and Lambert, DBFP, Vol. XVI, No. 97, pp. 265-71: Sir John Bradbury to the Treasury, 6 October 1922.

53 *Chicago Daily Tribune*, 4 November 1922, 9 November 1922.

54 Butler, Bury and Lambert, DBFP, Vol. XVI, No. 110, pp. 288-9: Lord D'Abernon to Lord Curzon, 11 November 1922; Butler, Bury and Lambert, DBFP, Vol. XVI, No. 113, pp. 291-3: Lord D'Abernon to Lord Curzon, 19 November 1922.

55 *Chicago Daily Tribune*, 17 November 1922.

56 For the meetings of the Cuno Cabinet see K. Harbeck (ed.), *Das Kabinett Cuno* (Boppard am Rhein: Boldt, 1968).

57 *New York Times*, 24 November 1922.

58 For details see J. Keiger, *Raymond Poincaré and the Ruhr Crisis* (Routledge, 1998).

59 Butler, Bury and Lambert, DBFP, Vol. XVI, No. 131, pp. 315-6: Draft Note from German Chancellor [Wilhelm Cuno], 9 December 1922. See also A. Cornebise, 'Cuno, Germany and the Coming of the Ruhr Occupation: A Study in German–West European Relations', *Proceedings of the American Philosophical Society*, Vol. 116 (1972), pp. 502-31.

60 Butler, Bury and Lambert, DBFP, Vol. XVI, No. 133, pp. 317-18: Sir E. Crowe to Lord Curzon, 10 December 1922.

61 HCD, cols 3221-30: Bonar Law speech, 14 December 1922.

62 Butler, Bury and Lambert, DBFP, Vol. XVI, No. 148, pp. 344-6: Memorandum by Ralph Wigram on the legal position under the Treaty of Versailles, in the event of a default by the German government in the payment of reparations, 18 December 1922.

63 Butler, Bury and Lambert, DBFP, Vol. XVI, No. 146, pp. 340-2: Record by Sir Eyre Crowe of a Conversation with the German Ambassador [Friedrich Sthamer], 18 December 1922.

64 Butler, Bury and Lambert, DBFP, Vol. XVI, No. 152, pp. 354-5: Sir John Bradbury to the Treasury, 26 December 1922.

65 *Chicago Daily Tribune*, 27 December 1922.

66 Butler, Bury and Lambert, DBPF, Vol. XVI, No. 163, p. 369: Lord D'Abernon to Lord Curzon, 31 December 1922.

---

6 RUHR OCCUPATION, HYPERINFLATION AND REVOLT

1 British Parliamentary Papers, 1923 (BPP), available online at www.archives.parliament.uk/online-resources/parliamentary-papers, Vol.XXIV: Command Paper No. 1812, ICP 258, Minutes of Meeting in Paris, 2 January 1923.

2 National Archives (NA), FO 371/8626, C287/1/18: Telegram from Lord Crewe, enclosing a message from Bonar Law, 3 January 1923.

3 BPP, Vol. XXIV: Command Paper 1812, ICP 259, Minutes of Meeting in Paris, 3 January.

4 NA, FO 801/9: Minutes of the Reparations Commission, 9 January 1923.

5 NA, CAB 24/158: Communication from Paris to German Embassy, 10 January 1923.

6 For details see D. Williamson, 'Great Britain and the Ruhr Crisis, 1923–1924', *British Journal of International Studies*, Vol.3 (1977), pp. 70–91.

7 As reported in the *Chicago Daily Tribune*, 13 January 1923.

8 Taylor, *Downfall of Money*, p. 234.

9 *Chicago Daily Tribune*, 13 January 1923; E. Sutton (ed. and trans.), *Gustav Stresemann, His Diaries, Letters and Papers*, 3 vols (Macmillan, 1937): Vol. 1, p. 36.

10 Ulrich, *Hitler*, Vol. 1, p. 132.

11 Eyck, *Weimar Republic*, Vol. 1, p. 236.

12 *Chicago Daily Tribune*, 20 January 1922.

13 For details see C. Fischer, *The Ruhr Crisis, 1923–1924* (Oxford, Oxford University Press, 2003).

14 SPD, Vol. 1, pp. 44 5.

15 Fergusson, *When Money Dies*, p.130.

16 *Chicago Daily Tribune*, 25 January 1922, 1 February 1922.

17 For the full text of the proceedings see A. Krupp von Bohlen and F. Halbach-Stiftung, *The Krupp Trial before French Court Martial* (Munich: Sueddeutsche Monatshefte, 1923).

18 SPD, Vol. 1, p. 62; House of Lords Debates (HLD), Vol. 54, cols 2-4: Statement by Lord Curzon, 8 May 1923; G. Feldman, *The Great Disorder: Politics, Economics and Society in the Great Inflation, 1914-1924* (Oxford, Oxford University Press, 1993), pp. 662–4.

19 Ullrich, *Hitler*, Vol. 1, p. 139; Taylor, *Downfall of Money*, pp. 246–8.

20 Fergusson, *When Money Dies*, pp. 139–40, 142. For details on the hyperinflation, see F. Ringer (ed.), *The German Inflation of 1923* (Oxford, Oxford University Press, 1969), which includes valuable accounts of personal experiences of hyperinflation.

21 K. Wallach, *Passing Illusions: Jewish Visibility in Weimar Germany* (Ann Arbor: University of Michigan Press, 2017), p. 100.

22 *Manchester Guardian*, 7 November 1923. See also S. Seal, 'Transnational Press Discourses on German Antisemitism during the Weimar Republic: The Riots in Berlin's Scheunenviertel, 1923', *The Leo Boeck Institute Yearbook*, Vol. 59 (2014), pp. 91–120.

23 Jewish Telegraphic Agency report, reproduced in *The Jewish Press*, Omaha, Nebraska, 22 November 1923.

24 Feldman, *The Great Disorder*, pp. 663–8.

25 *Chicago Daily Tribune*, 28 June 1922, 30 June 1922.

26 HCD, Vol. 166, cols 1585–1890: Stanley Baldwin Statement, 12 July 1923.

27 *Chicago Daily Tribune*, 16 July 1923.

28 SPD, Vol. 1, p. 76.

29 HCD, Vol. 167, cols 1769–1822: Speech by Ramsay MacDonald, 2 August 1923.

30 *The Times*, 13 August 1923.

31 'Reply of French government to the Note of British government of 11 August 1923, 20 August 1923', Ministère des Affairs étrangères, Paris, Imprimerie National, 1923, available online at www.gsc.contentdm.oclc.org/digital/collection/p4013coll7/id/860/.

32 *Chicago Daily Tribune*, 11 August 1922.

33 H. Winkler, *Weimar 1918–1933: Die Geschichte der Ersten Deutschen Demokratie* (Munich: Beck, 1998), pp. 200–2.

34 *Chicago Daily Tribune*, 12 August 1922.

35 Taylor, *Downfall of Money*, p.287.

36 See H. Turner, 'Continuity in German Foreign Policy? The Case of Stresemann', *International History Review*, Vol. 1 (1979), pp. 509–21.

37 For details of the proceedings of the two Stresemann cabinets of 1923 see K. Erdmann and M. Vogt (eds), *Die Kabinette Stresemann I und II* (Boppard am Rhein: Boldt, 1978).

38 SPD, Vol. 1, pp. 89–90.

39 See S. Lauryssens, *The Man Who Invented the Third Reich* (Cheltenham: History Press, 2010).

40 *The Times*, 20 September 1923.

41 SPD, Vol. 1, pp. 131–2.

42 SPD, Vol. 1, p. 133.

43 Harman, *Lost Revolution*, p. 279.

44 *Chicago Daily Tribune*, 27 September 1922.

45 SPD, Vol. 1, pp. 129–31.

46 *Chicago Daily Tribune*, 30 September 1922.

47 For details see J. Dernberg, *Munich 1923: Hitler's First Bid for Power* (New York: Harper, and Row, 1982).

48 SPD, Vol. 1, pp. 148–9.

49 SPD, Vol. 1, p. 145.

50 Fergusson, *When Money Dies*, p.191.

51 For details see A. Kunz, *Civil Servants and the Politics of Inflation, 1914–1924* (New York: Walter de Gruyter, 1986).

52 E. O'Riordan, 'British Foreign Policy and the Ruhr Occupation Crisis', University of London PhD thesis, January 1998, p. 208.

53 See W. Fischer, *German Hyperinflation 1922–23: A Law and Economics Approach* (Cologne: Josef Eul, 2010).

54 Harman, *Lost Revolution*, pp. 273–6

55 Schumann, *Political Violence*, pp. 128–34.

56 Harman, *Lost Revolution*, p. 286.

57 R. Lemmons, *Hitler's Rival: Ernst Thälman in Myth and Memory* (Lexington: University of Kentucky Press, 2013), p. 36.

58 SPD, Vol. 1, p. 183.

59 For details see D. Pryce, 'The Reich Government versus Saxony, 1923: The Decision to Intervene', *Central European History*, Vol. 10 (1977), pp. 112–47.

60 Eyck, *Weimar Republic*, Vol.1, pp. 270–271.

61 *Chicago Daily Tribune*, 3 November 1922.

62 Ullrich, *Hitler*, Vol. 1, p. 145.

63 Weber, *Becoming Hitler*, pp. 302–3.

64 Ullrich, *Hitler*, Vol.1, p. 148.

65 P. Longerich, *Hitler* (Oxford: Oxford University Press, 2019), p. 118.

66 Ullrich, *Hitler*, Vol.1, p.149.

67 SPD, Vol. 1, p. 199.

68 A. Hitler, *Mein Kampf* (New York: Houghton Mifflin, 1999 edn), p. v.

69 M. Hauner, *Hitler: A Chronology of His Life and Times* (Basingstoke: Palgrave Macmillan, 1983), p. 46.

70 Weber, *Becoming Hitler*, p. 307.

71 For greater detail see H. Gordon, *Hitler and the Beer Hall Putsch* (Princeton, NJ: Princeton University Press, 1972). For succinct summaries see Ullrich, *Hitler*, Vol. 1, pp. 131–64; Evans, *The Coming of the Third Reich*, pp. 189–94; Kershaw, *Hitler*, Vol. 1, pp. 200–12; Weber, *Becoming Hitler*, pp. 293–312.

72 SPD, Vol. 1, pp. 203–7.

73 See H. Dorten, 'The Rhineland Movement', *Foreign Affairs*, Vol. 3 (1925), pp. 399–410.

74 For details of French policy see W. McDougall, *France's Rhineland Policy, 1914–1924: The Last Bid for a Balance of Power in Europe* (Princeton NJ: Princeton University Press, 2015).

75 Eyck, *Weimar Republic*, Vol. 1, pp. 249–51.

76 NA, FO 371/8663 C22416/1/18: Communication from Reparations Committee, 26 December 1923, giving details on the composition and aims of the two committees.

77 SPD, Vol. 1, p. 243.

78 For details of the proceedings of the first two Marx cabinets from 1923 to 1925 see G. Abramowski (ed.) *Die Kabinette Marx I and II*, 2 vols (Boppard am Rhein: Boldt, 1973).

79 *Chicago Daily Tribune*, 25 December 1923.

80 F. Ambler, *The Story of the Bauhaus* (Ilex, 1918), p. 23.

81 For detailed studies on the Bauhaus movement see G. Naylor, *The Bauhaus Reassessed* (New York: Dutton, 1985); M. Droste, *Bauhaus, 1918–1933* (Berlin: Taschen, 2002); F. Whitford (ed.), *The Bauhaus: Masters and Students by Themselves* (Conran Octopus, 1992).

7 THE DAWES PLAN, HITLER ON TRIAL, AND MEIN KAMPF

1 SPD, Vol. 1, pp. 263–5.

2 R. Dawes, *The Dawes Plan in the Making* (Indianapolis: Bobbs-Merrill, 1925), pp. 37–40.

3 Dawes, *Dawes Plan in the Making*, p. 145.

4 Eyck, *Weimar Republic*, Vol. 1, pp. 304–6.

5 *Chicago Daily Tribune*, 20 February 1924.

6 Dawes, *Dawes Plan in the Making*, p. 177.

7 For details see C. Kitching, 'Prime Minister and Foreign Secretary: The Dual Role of James Ramsay MacDonald', *Review of International Studies*, Vol. 37 (2011), pp. 1403–22.

8 Ullrich, *Hitler*, Vol. 1, pp. 157–8.

9 P. Range, *1924: The Year That Made Hitler* (Little Brown, 2016), p.131.

10 For detail on the trial, see the trial transcript, L. Gruchmann and R. Weber (eds), *Der Hitler-Prozess* (Munich: K.G. Saur, 1997). There are also two studies that cover the trial in detail: Range, *1924*; and D. King, *The Trial of Adolf Hitler: The Beer Hall Putsch and the Rise of Nazi Germany* (Pan, 2018).

11 *The Times* report on 27 February 1924 suggests Hitler spoke for 'up to four hours', but the trial transcript indicates about three hours.

12 *The Times*, 1 March 1924.

13 King, *Trial of Adolf Hitler*, pp. 224–9.

14 *The Times*, 13 March 1924.

15 Range, *1924*, pp. 161–4.

16 Range, *1924*, pp. 279–85.

17 King, *Trial of Adolf Hitler*, p. 297.

18 King, *Trial of Adolf Hitler*, pp. 293–4.

19 Range, *1924*, p. 295.

20 Weber, *Becoming Hitler*, p. 311.

21 For the full text of the Dawes Report see Dawes, *Dawes Plan in the Making*, pp. 285–509. The quotation is from p. 303.

22 S. Parker Gilbert died of a sudden heart attack on 23 February 1938.

23 Dawes, *The Dawes Plan in the Making*, p. 360.

24 SPD, Vol. 1, p. 331.

25 SPD, Vol. 1, pp. 332–3.

26 *Chicago Daily Tribune*, 14 March 1924.

27 SPD, Vol.1, p. 338.

28 Turner, *Stresemann*, p. 165.

29 For full results of the 4 May 1924 German election see Nohlen and Stöver (eds), *Elections in Europe*, pp. 762, 777, 790.

30 *Chicago Daily Tribune*, 7 June 1924.

31 For details see J. Leopold, *Alfred Hugenberg: The Radical Nationalist Campaign against the Weimar Republic* (New Haven, CT, Yale University Press, 1977).

32 SPD, Vol. 1, p. 351.

33 T. Abel, *Why Hitler Came to Power* (Cambridge, MA: Harvard University Press, 1986), p. 72.

34 See later in the chapter for details on the change from Rentenmarks to Reichsmarks.

35 Shirer, *Third Reich*, pp. 80–1.

36 Range, *1924*, p. 217.

37 O. Lurker, *Hitler hinter Festungsmauern: Ein Bild aus Trüben Tagen* (Berlin, Mittler, 1933), p.56.

38 Quoted in Ullrich, *Hitler*, Vol 1, p. 174.

39 Longerich, *Hitler*, p.135.

40 Longerich, *Hitler*, p.140.

41 H. Heske, 'Karl Haushofer: his role in German politics and in Nazi politics', *Political Geography*, Vol.6 (1987), pp. 135–44.

42 D. Smith, 'Friedrich Ratzal and the Origins of Lebensraum', *German Studies Review*, Vol.3 (1980), pp. 51–68.

43 The analysis of *Mein Kampf* offered here draws on the following full editions of the whole book: A. Hitler, *Mein Kampf* (Mariner Books, 1998) and C. Hartmann et al. (eds), *Hitler, Mein Kampf: Eine Kritische Edition* (Munich: Institut für Zeitgeschichte, 2016). See also: Range, *1924*, pp. 214-38; Weber, *Becoming Hitler*, pp. 313-27; Ullrich, *Hitler*, Vol.1, pp. 165–84; Kershaw, *Hitler*, Vol.1, pp. 250–252 and Longerich, *Hitler*, pp. 133–40.

44 This section was based on the detailed proceedings of the London Conference, outlined in SPD, Vol.1, pp. 369–406. See also G. Finch, 'The London Conference on the Application of the Dawes Plan', *American Journal of International Law*, Vol. 18 (1924), pp. 707–19.

45 *Chicago Daily Tribune*, 25 July 1924.

46 *Kreuzzeitung*, 30 August 1924.

47 Eyck, *Weimar Republic*, Vol. 1, p. 315.

48 *Chicago Daily Tribune*, 30 August 1924.

49 *The Argus*, Melbourne, 8 September 1924.

50 For details see R. Yee, 'Reparations Revisited: The Role of Economic Advisers in Reforming German Central Banking and Public Finance', *Financial History Review*, Vol. 27 (2020), pp. 45–72.

51 C.Patterson, 'The Admission of Germany to the League of Nations and its Probable Significance', *Southwestern Political Science Quarterly*, Vol. 7 (1926), p. 221.

52 SPD, Vol. 1, pp. 293–92.

53 NA, FO 371/9749. C10810/70/18: Minutes of meetings at Chequers between Ramsay MacDonald and Édouard Herriot, 21–22 June 1924.

54 J. Fox, 'Britain and the Allied Military Commission of Control, 1925–26', *Journal of Contemporary History*, Vol. 4 (1969), pp. 143–64.

55 Fergusson, *When Money Dies*, p.229.

56 *Chicago Daily Tribune*, 21 October 1924, 22 October 1924.

57 For the full results of the 7 December 1924 election see Nohlen and Stöver, *Elections in Europe*, pp. 762, 777, 790.

58 O. Gessler, *Reichswehr Politics in the Weimar Period* (Stuttgart: Sendtner, 1958), pp. 498–500 (German edition, *Reichswehrpolitik in der Weimarer Zeit* published by Deutsche Verlags-Anstalt, 1958).

59 Ullrich, *Hitler*, Vol.1, p.183

60 *New York Times*, 21 December 1924.

61 Eyck, *Weimar Republic*, Vol.1, p. 330.

62 Harmer, *Ebert*, p.1 45.

63 Eyck, *Weimar Republic*, Vol.1, p. 330.

8 DIPLOMATIC TRIUMPH AT LOCARNO

1 For details of the first Luther cabinet see K.-H. Minuth (ed.), *Die Kabinette Luther I und II* (Boppard am Rhein: Vandenhoeck und Ruprecht, 1977), Vol. 1.

2 *Chicago Daily Tribune*, 20 January 1925.

3 Turner, *Stresemann*, p. 186. See also F. Stambrook, '"Das Kind": Lord D'Abernon and the Origins of the Locarno Pact', *Central European History*, Vol. 1 (1968), 233–63.

4 For the full text of the Stresemann memorandum of 20 January 1925 see *An Ambassador of Peace: Lord D'Abernon's Diary*, Vol. 3: *Years of Recovery* (Hodder & Stoughton, 1930), pp. 276–9.

5 C. Petrie, *The Life and Letters of the Right Hon. Sir Austen Chamberlain*, Vol. 2 (Cassel, 1940), p. 27.

6 See J. Williams, 'The Geneva Protocol of 1924 for the Pacific Settlement of International Disputes', *Journal of the British Institute of International Affairs*, Vol. 3 (1924), pp. 288–304.

7 C. Elcock, *Could the Versailles System Have Worked?* (Basingstoke: Palgrave Macmillan, 2018), p. 103.

8 SPD, Vol. 2, pp. 503–5.

9 *New York Times*, 7 February 1925. Bauer would later regain admission to the SPD and would represent the party again in the Reichstag.

10 For details of the scandal see M. Geyer, 'Contested Narratives of the Weimar Republic: The Case of the Kutisker-Barmat Scandal' in K. Canning, K. Barndt and K. McGuire (eds), *Weimar Publics/Weimar Subjects: Rethinking the Political Culture of Germany in the 1920s* (Oxford: Berghahn, 2010), pp. 211–35.

11 *Evening Record* (Ellensburg, WA), 24 February 1925; Harmer, *Ebert*, p. 146.

12 Turner, *Stresemann*, p. 191.

13 *New York Times*, 5 March 1925.

14 Rossol, 'Visualizing the Republic', pp. 147–9.

15 Nohlen and Stöver, *Elections in Europe*, p.762.

16 A. Dorpalen, *Hindenburg and the Weimar Republic* (Princeton, NJ: Princeton University Press, 1964), p. 71.

17 Ullrich, *Hitler*, Vol.1, p.191.

18 W. Pyta, *Hindenburg: Herrschaft zwischen Hohenzollern und Hitler* (Munich: Siedler, 2007), pp. 39–40.

19 For detailed insights on Marx's campaign see J. Zeender, 'The German Catholics and the Presidential Election of 1925', *Journal of Modern History*, Vol. 25 (1963), pp. 266–381.

20 For detailed discussion of the two rounds of the 1925 presidential elections see J. Falter, 'The Two Hindenburg Elections of 1925 and 1932: A Total Reversal of Voter Coalitions', *Historical Social Research*, Supplement, No. 2 (2013), pp. 217–32; N. Clay, 'The Making of the Reich President, 1925: German Conservatism and the Nomination of Paul von Hindenburg', *Central European History*, Vol. 23 (1990), pp. 179–204; P. Fritzsche, 'Presidential Victory and Popular Festivity in Weimar Germany: Hindenburg's 1925 Election', *Central European History*, Vol. 23 (1990), pp. 205–24.

21 Sutton, *Stresemann*, Vol.2, p. 54.

22 *Chicago Daily Tribune*, 13 May 1925.

23 SPD, Vol. 2, p. 57.

24 *Weimar Republic Sourcebook*: G. Hartlaub, 'Introduction to "New Objectivity"', pp. 491–3.

25 The analysis of New Objectivity offered here draws on the following works: W. Schmied, *Neue Sachlichkeit and German Realism in the Twenties* (Arts Council of Great Britain, 1979); J. Willet, *Art and Politics in the Weimar Period: The New Sobriety 1917–1933* (Thames and Hudson, 1978), pp. 111–17; S. Becker, *Neue Sachlichkeit* (Cologne: Böhlau, 2000); D. Crockett, *German Post-Expressionism: The Art of the Great Disorder* (Philadephia, PA: Penn State University Press), 1999.

26 P. Gay, *Weimar Culture: The Outsider as Insider*, (W.W. Norton, 2001), p. 106.

27 For details see S. Lackner, *Max Beckmann* (Thames and Hudson, 2001).

28 See E. Karcher, *Otto Dix, 1891–1969: His Life and Works* (Cologne, B.Taschen, 1988).

29 See I. Kranzfelder, *George Grosz* (Cologne, B. Taschen, 2005).

30 Wallach, *Passing Illusions*, pp. 97–8; *Israelitisches Familienblatt*, 10 December 1925.

31 SPD, Vol. 2, p. 88.

32 E. Eyck, *A History of the Weimar Republic*, Vol. 2: *From the Locarno Conference to Hitler's Seizure of Power* (Cambridge, MA: Harvard University Press, 1967), pp. 10–11.

33 NA, Command Paper, 2468, 1925: Reply of the German government to the Note handed to Herr Stresemann by the Ambassador at Berlin on 16 June 1925, Respecting the Proposals for a Pact of Security.

34 SPD, Vol. 2, p. 94.

35 S. Marks, *The Illusion of Peace: International Relations in Europe 1918–1933* (Macmillan, 1976), pp. 67–8.

36 Quoted in the *Chicago Daily Tribune*, 30 September 1925.

37 Eyck, *Weimar Republic*, Vol. 2, pp. 23–7.

38 SPD, Vol. 2, p. 171.

39 Eyck, *Weimar Republic*, Vol. 2, pp. 31–2.

40 SPD, Vol.2, p. 176.

41 Marks, *Illusion of Peace*, p. 68.

42 S. Marks, 'Mussolini and Locarno: Mussolini's Foreign Policy in Microcosm', *Journal of Contemporary History*, Vol. 14 (1979), pp. 423–39.

43 Avalon Project, 'Treaty of Mutual Guarantee between Germany, Belgium, France, Great Britain, and Italy, 16 October 1925', available online at: www.avalon. law.yale.edu/20th_century/locarno_001.asp.

44 For the full text of the arbitration treaties see *Advocate of Peace Through Justice*, Vol. 78 (1925), pp. 685–692.

45 For details on the negotiations at Locarno see the following: J. Wright, 'Stresemann and Locarno', *Contemporary European History*, Vol. 4 (1995), pp. 109–31; J. Wright and J. Wright, 'One Mind at Locarno? Aristide Briand and Gustav Stresemann', in S. Casey and J. Wright (eds), *Mental Maps in the Era of Two World Wars* (Basingstoke: Palgrave Macmillan, 2008), pp. 58–76; M. Enssle, 'Stresemann's Diplomacy Fifty Years After Locarno: Some Recent Perspectives', *Historical Journal*, Vol. 20 (1977), pp. 937–48.

46 Kolb, *Weimar Republic*, p. 64.

47 Sutton, *Stresemann*, Vol. 2, p. 191.

48 Eyck, *Weimar Republic*, Vol. 2, p. 38.

49 L. Jones, *The German Right 1918–1930: Political Parties, Organized Interests and Patriotic Associations in the Struggle against Weimar Germany* (Cambridge: Cambridge University Press, 2021), p. 325.

50 Minuth, (ed.), *Kabinette Luther I*, pp. 780–9.

51 Jones, *German Right*, p. 326.

52 Turner, *Stresemann*, p. 214.

53 BA-MA, Freiburg, NL Tirpitz 176/33-36: Tirpitz to Hindenburg, 26 October 1925; BA-MA, NL Tirpitz 176/37, 3 November 1925.

54 Turner, *Stresemann*, p. 217.

55 SPD, Vol. 2, p. 230.

56 Eyck, *Weimar Republic*, Vol. 2, pp. 41–3.

57 SPD, Vol 2, pp. 234–40.

58 L. Jones, *German Liberalism and the Dissolution of the Weimar Party System, 1918–1933* (Chapel Hill: University of North Carolina Press, 1988), pp. 247–8.

9 GERMANY JOINS THE LEAGUE OF NATIONS

1 For details of the first Luther cabinet see Minuth, *Kabinette Luther I*.

2 Jones, *German Right*, pp. 333–5.

3 Eyck, *Weimar Republic*, Vol. 2, pp. 52–4.

4 SPD, Vol 2, p. 506.

5 *Chicago Daily Tribune*, 3 March 1926.

6 SPD, Vol. 2, p. 507.

7 Eyck, *Weimar Republic*, Vol. 2, pp. 56–67.

8 J. Smith, *Unequal Giants: Diplomatic Relations between the United States and Brazil, 1890–1930* (Pittsburgh: PA, University of Pittsburgh Press, 1977), p. 171.

9 SPD, Vol. 2, p. 508.

10 Eyck, *Weimar Republic*, Vol. 2, p. 59.

11 For details see R. Lemmons, *Goebbels und Der Angriff* (Lexington: University of Kentucky Press, 1994).

12 Ullrich, *Hitler*, Vol. 1, p.193.

13 BAB, NS, 26/896: Otto Strasser's Draft Programme, 24 January 1926.

14 Institut für Zeigeschichte, Munich, ED 874: Gottfried Feder Diaries, Vol 8, Entry for 14 February 1924.

15 E. Hanfstaengl, *15 Jahre mit Hitler: Zwischen Weissem und Braunem Haus* (Munich: Piper, 1980), p. 190.

16 A. Read, *The Devil's Disciples: Hitler's Inner Circle* (W.W. Norton 2004), p. 148.

17 Kershaw, *Hitler*, Vol. 1, p.257.

18 Ullrich, *Hitler*, Vol. 1, p. 197.

19 Kershaw, *Hitler*, Vol. 1, p. 277. See also J. Noakes, 'Conflict and Development in the NSDAP', *Journal of Contemporary History*, Vol. 1 (1966), pp. 3–36.

20 Eyck, *Weimar Republic*, Vol. 2, p. 60.

21 League of Nations Treaty Series, Vol. 53, pp. 388–96, League of Nations, Geneva, 1926, available online at https://treaties.un.org/doc/Publication/UNTS/LON/Volume%2053/v53.pdf.

22 Marks, *Illusion of Peace*, p. 79.

23 SPD, Vol. 2, p. 489.

24 P. Wandycz, *Twilight of French Eastern Alliances, 1926–1936: French-Czechoslovak-Polish Relations from Locarno to the Remilitarization of the Rhineland* (2nd edn, Princeton, NJ: Princeton University Press, 2014), pp. 40–2.

25 SPD, Vol.2, p.490.

26 D. Orlow, *Weimar Prussia, 1925-1933: The Illusion of Strength* (Pittsburgh, PA: University of Pittsburgh Press, 1991), pp. 111–12.

27 SPD, Vol 2, p.372.

28 F. West, *A Crisis of the Weimar Republic: The Referendum of 20 June 1926* (Philadelphia, PA: American Philosophical Society, 1985), p. 228.

29 Eyck, *Weimar Republic*, Vol. 2, p. 67.

30 E. Clingan, *The Lives of Hans Luther, 1879–1962: German Chancellor, Reichsbank President, and Hitler's Ambassador* (Plymouth: Lexington Books, 2010), p.5.

31 SPD, Vol 2, pp. 375-376.

32 For details of the third Marx cabinet see Abramowski (ed.), *Die Kabinette Marx III und IV*.

33 W. Kaufmann, *Monarchism in the Weimar Republic* (New York: Octogan Books, 1973), p. 160.

34 Wheeler-Bennet, *Hindenburg*, p. 306.

35 R. Freyh, 'Stärken und Schwächen der Weimarer Republik', in T. Walter (ed.), *Die Weimarer Republik* (Hanover: Fackelträger), p. 147.

36 *Vorwärts*, 13 June 1926; *Die Rote Fahne*, 29 May 1926.

37 U. Schüren, *Der Volksentscheid zur Fürstenenteignung, 1926* (Düsseldorf: Drost, 1978), pp. 206, 208.

38 *Die Rote Fahne*, 22 June 1926.

39 West, *Referendum of 20 June 1926*, p. 11. See also H. Gosnell, 'The German Referendum on the Princes' Property', *American Political Science Review*, Vol. 21 (1927), pp. 119–23.

40 See Patterson, 'Admission of Germany to the League of Nations', pp. 215–37.

41 Sutton, *Stresemann*, Vol. 2, p. 531.

42 Marks, *Illusion of Peace*, p. 80.

43 SPD, Vol. 2, pp. 522–3.

44 Marks, *Diplomacy of Illusion*, p. 80.

45 See SPD, Vol. 3, pp. 17–27; G. Suarez (ed.), *Briand*, Vol. 6: *L'Artisan de la Paix, 1923–1932* (Paris: Plon, 1940), p. 218.

46 Eyck, *Weimar Republic*, Vol. 2, p. 73.

47 For details see J. Jacobson, 'The Impulse for a Franco-German Entente: The Origins of the Thoiry Conference, 1926', *Journal of Contemporary History*, Vol. 10 (1975), pp. 157–81.

48 SPD, Vol. 3, pp. 27–8.

49 SPD, Vol. 3, pp. 29–33.

50 Eyck, *Weimar Republic*, Vol. 2, pp. 78–9, 80.

51 Carsten, *Reichswehr and Politics*, pp. 245–6.

52 F. Rabenau (ed.), *Seeckt: Aus Seinem Leben,1918–1936* (Leipzig: Hase and Kohler, 1940), p. 542.

53 See H. Gordon, 'The Character of Hans von Seeckt', *Military Affairs*, Vol. 20 (1956), pp. 94–101.

54 Dorpalen, *Hindenburg and the Weimar Republic*, pp. 111–12; Carsten, *Reichswehr and Politics*, p. 248.

55 Eyck. *Weimar Republic*, Vol. 2, p.88.

56 Carsten, *Reichswehr and Politics*, p. 246.

57 *Chicago Daily Tribune*, 8 October 1926.

58 Carsten, *Reichswehr and Politics*, p. 246.

59 Rabenau, *Seeckt*, p. 558.

60 *Tägliche Rundschau*, 15 October 1926.

61 The section on the Bauhaus draws on the following sources: K. Baumann, *Bauhaus Dessau: Architektur– Gestaltung– Idee* (Jovis: Berlin, 2007) and C. Irrgang and I. Kern (ed.), *Neue Meisterhäuser in Dessau 1925–2014* (Leipzig: Spector Books, 2017).

62 E. Weitz, *Weimar Germany: Promise and Tragedy* (Princeton, NJ: Princeton University Press, 1967), p. 201. In October 1931, when Hitler's NSDAP took control of the local government in Dessau, funding was withdrawn from the Bauhaus school, and on 22 August 1932, the National Socialists decided to close the building. The school was fully restored in the 1990s, and since 1996, Bauhaus Dessau has been listed as a UNESCO World Heritage Site.

63 *New York Times*, 12 December 1926.

64 *Manchester Guardian*, 3 December 1926, 6 December 1926.

65 Eyck, *Weimar Republic*, Vol. 2, p.95.

66 *Vorwärts*, 17 December 1926.

67 *Chicago Daily Tribune*, 18 December 1926.

10 METROPOLIS AND MARX'S SOCIAL REFORMS

1 M. Minden and H. Bachmann, *Fritz Lang's* Metropolis*: Cinematic Versions of Technology and Fear* (New York: Camden House, 2002), p. 4.

2 After 1933, Lang left for exile in Hollywood, but his former wife became a committed member of the National Socialist Party.

3 See www.encyclopedia.com and iMDb.com for more explanation of the Schüfftan Process.

4 For a succinct summary of the film see T. Elsaesser, *Metropolis* (British Film Institute, 2012).

5 *Weimar Republic Sourcebook*: Review by W. Haas, *Film Kurier*, 11 January 1927, pp. 623–5; Wells quoted in Elsaesser, *Metropolis*, p. 59; *New York Times*, 7 March 1927.

6 Elsaesser, *Metropolis*, p. 58.

7 Jones, *German Right*, p. 293.

8 Wheeler-Bennet, *Hindenburg*, p. 309.

9 Eyck, *Weimar Republic*, Vol. 2, p. 103.

10 Jones, *German Right*, p. 363.

11 Kolb, *Weimar Republic*, p. 78.

12 For details of the fourth Marx cabinet see G. Abramowski (ed.), *Die Kabinette Marx III and IV* (Boppard am Rhein: Boldt, 1988).

13 SPD, Vol. 3, p. 114.

14 Eyck, *Weimar Republic*, Vol.2 , pp. 104–5.

15 Wallach, *Passing Illusions*, pp. 100–1.

16 Jones, *German Right*, p. 366.

17 T. Childers, *The Nazi Voter: The Social Foundations of Fascism in Germany, 1919–1933* (Chapel Hill: University of North Carolina Press, 1983), pp. 144–5.

18 For details see F. Wunderlich, 'The German Unemployment Insurance Act of 1927', *Quarterly Journal of Economics*, Vol. 42 (1928), pp. 278–306.

19 For details see J. Bähr, *Staatliche Schlichtung in der Weimarer Republik: Tarifpolitik, Korporatismus und Industrieller Konflikt zwischen Inflation und Deflation, 1919–1932* (Berlin: Colloquium, 1989).

20 Jones, *German Right*, pp. 370–1.

21 Ullrich, *Hitler*, Vol. 1, pp. 210–12.

22 Förster was a longstanding critic of German militarism and published a book in 1920 called: *Mein Kampf gegen das militarische*

nationalistische Deutschland (*My Struggle against Militaristic and Nationalist Germany*).

23 SPD, Vol. 3, pp. 234–5, 236.

24 Eyck, *Weimar Republic*, Vol. 2, p. 132.

25 Wheeler-Bennet, *Hindenburg*, p. 318.

26 *Time*, 3 October 1927.

27 Eyck, *Weimar Republic*, Vol. 2, pp. 129–30.

28 SPD, Vol. 3, pp. 212–14.

29 Wheeler-Bennet, *Hindenburg*, pp. 315–16.

30 Ruttmann went on to become the assistant director on Leni Riefenstahl's 1935 National Socialist propaganda film, *The Triumph of the Will*.

31 The section on *Berlin: Symphony of a City* draws on the following sources: Internet Archive: *Berlin: Symphony of a City, 1927*, available online at: archive.org/details/Berlin Symphony of a GreatCity; S.Jacobs, E. Hielscher and A. Kinik (eds), *The City Symphony Phenomenon: Cinema, Art, and Urban Modernity Between the Wars* (New York: Routledge, 2019); M. Cowan, *W. Ruttmann and the Cinema of Multiplicity: Avant-garde film – Advertising – Modernity* (Amsterdam: Amsterdam University Press, 2014); J. Goergen, *Walter Ruttmann: Eine Dokumentation* (Berlin: Freunde der deutschen Kinemathek, 1989).

32 Jones, *German Right*, pp. 379–81.

33 SPD, Vol. 3, p. 279.

34 Eyck, *Weimar Republic*, Vol. 2, pp. 135–8.

35 SPD, Vol. 3, pp. 264–9.

11 THE SOCIAL DEMOCRATS RETURN TO POWER

1 K. Kreimeier, *The UFA Story: A History of Germany's Greatest Film Company, 1918–1945* (Berkeley: University of California Press, 1999), pp. 166–7.

2 Carsten, *Reichswehr and Politics*, pp. 285–6.

3 O. Gessler, *Reichswehr Politics in the Weimar Period* (Stuttgart, Kurt Sendtner, 1958), p.446.

4 Eyck, *Weimar Republic*, Vol. 2, p. 145.

5 Carsten, *Reichswehr and Politics*, p. 286.

6 Jones, *German Right*, p. 282.

7 For details see E. Sieche, 'Germany', in R. Gardiner and R. Chesneau (eds), *Conway's All the World's Fighting Ships, 1922-1946* (Conway Maritime Press, 1992), pp. 218–54.

8 For details on how these splinter parties affected the traditional parties of the Right see B. Lieberman, 'Turning against the Weimar Right: Landlords, the Economic Party and the DNVP', *German History*, Vol. 15 (1997), pp. 56–79.

9 Jones, *German Liberalism*, p. 299.

10 For details of Stalin's influence on the KPD from 1928 see B. Hoppe, *In Stalins Gefolgschaft: Moskow und die KPD 1928–1932* (Oldenburg: Wissenschaftsverlag, 2011).

11 M. Kater, *The Nazi Party: A Social Profile of Members and Leaders, 1919-1945* (Oxford: Blackwell, 1983), p. 35.

12 *Völkischer Beobachter*, 19 April 1928.

13 SPD, Vol. 3, pp. 314–16.

14 Eyck, *Weimar Republic*, Vol. 2, p. 157.

15 Sutton, *Stresemann*, Vol. 3, pp. 316–18.

16 Nohlen and Stöver, *Elections in Europe*, p. 777.

17 Guttsmann, *German Social Democratic Party*, pp. 116–22.

18 Jones, *German Right*, pp. 409–12. For a detailed analysis see D. Walker, 'The German National People's Party: The Conservative Dilemma in the Weimar Republic', *Journal of Contemporary History* Vol. 14 (1979), pp. 627–47.

19 Jones, *German Liberalism*, p. 302.

20 Kershaw, *Hitler*, Vol. 1, p. 303.

21 B. Hett, *The Death of Democracy: Hitler's Rise to Power and the Downfall of the Weimar Republic* (New York: St.Martin's Griffin, 2019), p. 117.

22 *Völkischer Beobachter*, 31 May 1928.

23 V. Ullrich, *Hitler*, Vol 2: *Downfall*, trans. J. Chase (Bodley Head, 2020), p. 213.

24 Kolb, *Weimar Republic*, p. 80; Eyck, *Weimar Republic*, Vol. 2, p.161.

25 This became known as 'The shot from Bühlerhöhe', which was the location of Stresemann's health sanitorium.

26 SPD, Vol. 3, p. 325.

27 For details of the second Müller cabinet see M. Vogt (ed.), *Das Kabinett Müller II* (Boppard am Rhein: Walter de Gruyter, 1996).

28 Eyck, *Weimar Republic*, Vol. 2, p. 162.

29 Eyck, *Weimar Republic*, Vol. 2, pp. 162–166.

30 Ullrich, *Hitler*, Vol. 1, p. 215.

31 For details see G. Weinberg, *Hitler's Second Book: The Unpublished Sequel to Mein Kampf* (New York: Enigma Books, 2003). See also E. Jäckel, *Hitler's World View: A Blueprint for World Power* (Cambridge, MA: Harvard University Press, 1981) and B. Simms, *Hitler: Only the World Was Enough* (Allen Lane, 2019).

32 For a detailed study of Kellogg's role see E. Ellis, *Frank B. Kellogg and American Foreign*

Relations 1925-1929 (New Brunswick, NJ: Rutgers University Press, 1961). For details on the negotiations leading to the signing of the Kellogg–Briand Pact see R. Ferrel, *Peace in Their Time: The Origins of the Kellogg–Briand Pact* (New Haven, CT: Yale University Press, 1952). See also J. Bunck and M. Fowler, 'The Kellogg-Briand Pact: A Reappraisal', *Tuland Journal of International and Comparative Law*, Vol. 27 (2018), pp. 229–76; M. Carrol, 'War and Peace and International Law: The Kellogg-Briand Peace Pact Reconsidered', *Canadian Journal of History*, Vol. 53 (2018), pp. 86–96.

33   SPD, Vol. 3, p. 379.

34   AP-IMT: Full text of the Kellogg–Briand Pact, 27 August 1928.

35   K. Askin, *War Crimes Against Women: Prosecution in the International War Crimes* (Leiden: Martinus Nijhoff, 1997), p. 46.

36   Eyck, *Weimar Republic*, Vol 2, p. 176.

37   SPD, Vol. 3, pp. 383–92.

38   For details see B. Brecht, *The Threepenny Opera* (Methuen Drama, 1979); S. Hinton (ed.), *Kurt Weill: The Threepenny Opera* (Cambridge: Cambridge University Press, 1990); P. Thompson and G. Sacks (eds), *The Cambridge Companion to Brecht* (Cambridge: Cambridge University Press, 1994); D. Zoob, *Brecht: A Political Handbook* (Nick Hern Books, 2018).

39   SPD, Vol. 3, pp. 395–6.

40   Eyck, *Weimar Republic*, Vol. 2, pp. 178–81.

41   SPD, Vol. 3, p. 398.

42   For details see J. Wilson, *Hitler's Alpine Retreat* (Barnsley: Pen & Sword, 2005).

43   Quoted in Ullrich, *Hitler*, Vol. I, p. 214.

44   Simms, *Hitler*, p. 137.

45   J. Toland, *Adolf Hitler: The Definitive Biography* (New York: Bantam Doubleday Dell, 1991), p. 229.

46   See L. Jones, 'German Conservatism at the Crossroads: Count Kuno von Westarp and the Struggle for the Control of the DNVP, 1928-1930', *Contemporary European History*, Vol. 18 (2009), pp. 147–77; Jones, *German Right*, pp. 425–31.

47   Eyck, *Weimar Republic*, Vol. 2, pp. 192–5.

48   Kolb, *Weimar Republic*, pp. 83–4.

49   SPD, Vol. 3, pp. 403–10.

50   U. Hehl, *Wilhelm Marx 1863-1946: Eine Politische Biographie* (Mainz: Matthias-Grünewald, 1987), pp. 455–62.

51   For further detailed insight on Kaas see M. Menke, 'Ludwig Kaas and the end of the German Centre Party' in H. Beck and L. Jones (eds), *From Weimar to Hitler: Studies in the Dissolution of the Weimar Republic and the Establishment of the Third Reich, 1932–1934* (Oxford: Berghahn, 2019), pp. 79–110.

52   Jones, *German Right*, pp. 437–44.

53   SPD, Vol. 3, pp. 417–19.

54   See G. Finch, 'The Settlement of the Reparation Problem', *American Journal of International Law*, Vol. 24 (1930), pp. 339–50.

55   For details on the role of Owen Young see J. Case and E. Case, *Owen D. Young and American Enterprise: A Biography* (Boston, MA: David R. Godine, 1982).

56   SPD, Vol. 3, p. 419.

12 THE END OF THE STRESEMANN ERA

1   *Chicago Daily Tribune*, 2 January 1929.

2   SPD, Vol. 3, pp. 458–9.

3   M. Eksteins, 'All Quiet on the Western Front and the Fate of War', *Journal of Contemporary History*, Vol. 15 (1980), p. 353.

4   For details see M. Taylor, *The Life and writings of Erich Maria Remarque* (New York: Fales Library, New York University, 2011).

5   The preceding analysis of *All Quiet on the Western Front* draws on the following: E. Remarque, *All Quiet on the Western Front* (Putnam, 1929); B. Murdoch, 'Innocent Killing: Erich Maria Remarque and the Weimar Anti-War Novels', in K. Leydecker, *German Novelists of the Weimar Republic: Intersections of Literature and Politics* (Rochester, NY: Camden House, 2006), pp. 141–68.

6   Kaes, Jay and Dimenberg, *The Weimar Republic Sourcebook*: Elsa Herrmann, 'This is the New Woman', pp. 206–8. For the full text of the book see E. Hermann, *So ist die neue Frau* (Hellerau: Avalun, 1929). See also A. Grossmann, 'The New Woman and the Rationalization of Sexuality in the Weimar Republic', in A. Snitow, C. Stansell and S. Thompson (eds), *Desire: The Politics of Sexuality* (Virago, 1984), pp. 190–208.

7   Weitz, *Weimar Germany*, pp. 305–7.

8   For an excellent and detailed analysis see H. Boak, *Women in the Weimar Republic* (Manchester: Manchester University Press, 2013), pp. 134–99. See also H. Boak, 'The State as an Employer of Women in the Weimar Republic', in W. Lee and E. Rosenhaft (eds), *The State and Social Change in Germany, 1880–1980* (Oxford: Berg, 1990), pp. 61–98; C. Usborne, 'The New Woman and Generational Conflict: Perceptions of Young Women's Sexual Mores in the Weimar Republic', in M. Roseman (ed.), *Generations in Conflict: Youth Revolt and Generational Formation in Germany, 1770–1968* (Cambridge: Cambridge University Press, 1995),

pp. 137–63; G. Bry, *Wages in Germany, 1871–1945* (Princeton, NJ: Princeton University Press, 1960); K. Ankum (ed.), *Women in the Metropolis: Gender and Modernity in Weimar Republic* (Berkeley, CA: University of California Press, 1997).

9   SPD, Vol. 3, pp. 436–7.

10   A. Dunlap, *Charles Gates Dawes: A Life* (Evanston, IL: Northwestern University Press, 2016), p. 215.

11   Kolb, *Weimar Republic*, p.66.

12   W. Medlicott, D. Dakin and M. Lambert (eds), Documents on British Foreign Policy, Series 1A, Vol.VI, No.183 (HMSO, 1975), pp. 349–52: Memorandum by E.H. Carr on Bank for International Settlements, 17 June 1929.

13   SPD, Vol. 3, pp. 437–8.

14   Eyck, *Weimar Republic*, Vol. 2, p. 204.

15   SPD, Vol. 3, p. 438.

16   Quoted in the *Chicago Daily Tribune*, 28 June 1929.

17   Leopold, *Hugenberg*, p. 61.

18   Jones, *German Right*, pp. 463–6.

19   BAB, NS 26/863: Adolf Hitler to Stahlhelm Leadership, April 1929.

20   Ullrich, , Vol.1, p.220.

21   Medlicott, Dakin and Lambert, DBFP, Vol. VI, No. 290, pp. 481–2: A. Henderson to Sir R. Lindsay, 6 August 1929.

22   Quoted in Eyck, *Weimar Republic*, Vol. 2, p. 205.

23   SPD, Vol. 3, p. 583.

24   SPD, Vol. 3, p. 599.

25   Medlicott, Dakin and Lambert, DBFP, Vol. VI, No. 294, pp. 488–90: Mr Nicolson to Mr Sargent, 7 August 1929.

26   SPD, Vol. 3, p. 485; Eyck, *Weimar Republic*, Vol. 2, p. 206.

27   Medlicott, Dakin and Lambert, DBFP, Vol. VI, No. 351, pp. 618–21: Protocol of the Hague Conference, 31 August 1929; Eyck, *Weimar Republic*, Vol. 2, p. 210.

28   SPD, Vol. 3, pp. 611–20.

29   Eyck, *Weimar Republic*, Vol. 2, p. 212.

30   SPD, Vol. 3, p. 603.

31   *Berlin Lokal-Anzeiger*, 2 September 1929.

32   Jones, *German Right*, p. 472.

33   SPD, Vol. 3, pp. 623–4.

34   W. Medlicott, D. Dakin and M. Lambert (eds), *Documents on British Foreign Policy, 1919–1939*, Series IA, Vol. VII (HMSO, 1975), No. 22, pp. 41–44: Sir H. Rumbold to A Henderson, 10 October 1929.

35   *Sun Herald* (Auckland), 4 October 1929.

36   Rossol, 'Visualizing the Republic', p. 149.

37   For details on the early debate on Stresemann see H. Gatzke, 'Gustav Stresemann: A Bibliographical Article, *Journal of Modern History*, Vol. 36 (1964), pp. 113.

38   Kolb, *Weimar Republic*, p. 199.

39   For details see G. Axon, *The Stock Market Crash of 1929* (Mason and Lipscomb, 1974); M. Klein, *Rainbow's End: The Crash of 1929* (New York: Oxford University Press, 2001); T. Shachtman, *The Day America Crashed: A Narrative Account of the Great Stock Market Crash of October 24, 1929* (New York: G.P. Putnam, 1979).

40   *Sydney Morning Herald*, 30 October 1929.

41   Jones, *German Right*, p. 491.

42   *Chicago Daily Tribune*, 30 November 1929.

43   W. Ribhegge, *Preussen im Westen: Kampf um Parlamentarismus in Rheinland und Westfalen 1789-1947* (Munster: Richter Ludwig, 2008), p. 453.

44   Eyck, *Weimar Republic*, Vol. 2, pp. 222–3.

45   Eyck, *Weimar Republic*, Vol. 2, pp. 229–32.

46   Medlicott, Dakin and Lambert, DBFP, Vol. VII, No. 112, pp. 227–8: Mr Nicholson to A Henderson, 6 December 1929.

47   Kolb, *Weimar Republic*, p.84.

48   W. Patch, *Heinrich Brüning and the Dissolution of the Weimar Republic* (Cambridge: Cambridge University Press, 1998), p. 57.

49   After Hitler came to power, Hilferding went into exile in Paris, but he was arrested by the Gestapo on 9 February 1941, and after being tortured during interrogation, he died in custody on 11 February 1941, most probably killed by the Gestapo.

50   Müller died on 20 March 1931, aged 51, shortly after an operation to remove his gallbladder.

51   Kershaw, *Hitler*, Vol. 1, pp. 323–4.

52   P. Walther, *Darkness Falling: The Strange Death of the Weimar Republic, 1930-1933*, trans. P. Lewis (Head of Zeus, 2021), p. 143.

53   H. Brüning, *Memoiren* (Stuttgart: Deutsche Verlags-Anstalt, 1970), pp. 143–7.

54   G. Treviranus, *Das Ende von Weimar: Heinrich Brüning und seine Zeit* (Düsseldorf: Econ Verlag, 1968), pp. 114–15; Wheeler-Bennett, *Hindenburg*, pp. 328–30.

55   Kershaw, *Hitler*, Vol.1, p. 318.

56   Jones, *German Liberalism*, p. 330.

57   Ullrich, *Hitler*, Vol. 1, p. 221.

58   Medlicott, Dakin and Lambert, DBFP, Vol. VII, No.142, pp. 258–61: Sir Rumbold to A. Henderson, 17 December 1929.

---

13 HINDENBURG'S PRESIDENTIAL RULE AND HITLER'S ELECTION BREAKTHROUGH

1   Eyck, *Weimar Republic*, Vol. 2, p. 237.

2   Marks, *Illusion of Peace*, p. 106.

3 Wheeler-Bennet, *Hindenburg*, pp. 334–5.

4 See D. Petzina, 'Germany and the Great Depression', *Journal of Contemporary History*, Vol. 4 (1969), pp. 59–74 and S. Berman, 'Civil Society and the Collapse of the Weimar Republic', *World Politics*, Vol. 49 (1997), pp. 401–29.

5 Wheeler-Bennet, *Hindenburg*, p. 347. For the cabinet discussion on 27 March 1929 see Vogt (ed.), *Kabinett Müller II*, pp. 1608–10.

6 Eyck, *Weimar Republic*, Vol. 2, p. 248.

7 Brüning, *Memoiren*, pp. 157–8.

8 For a discussion of the dangers of Hindenburg's presidential cabinets see D. Dyzenhaus, 'Legal Theory in the Collapse of Weimar: Contemporary Lessons', *American Science Review*, Vol. 91 (1997), pp. 121–34.

9 Wheeler-Bennet, *Hindenburg*, p. 346.

10 Eyck, *Weimar Republic*, Vol. 2, p. 254.

11 Patch, *Brüning*, p. 78.

12 Brüning was Chancellor for 2 years and 61 days, the longest continuous period of any German Chancellor during the Weimar years.

13 For details of the first Brüning presidential cabinet, see T. Koops (ed.), *Die Kabinette Brüning I and II*, 3 vols (Boppard am Rhein: Boldt, 1982–1990).

14 Jones, *German Right*, pp. 535–6.

15 *Chicago Daily Tribune*, 1 April 1930.

16 Eyck, *Weimar Republic*, Vol. 2, pp. 258–9.

17 Jones, *German Right*, p. 532.

18 Patch, *Brüning*, p. 84.

19 Koops (ed.), *Kabinette Brüning*, Vol. 1, pp. 186–8.

20 Koops (ed.), *Kabinette Brüning*, Vol. 1, pp. 209–14.

21 Ullrich, *Hitler*, Vol. 2, p. 229.

22 Marks, *Illusion of Peace*, p.106.

23 Eyck, *Weimar Republic*, Vol. 2, p. 263.

24 Koops (ed.), *Kabinette Brüning*, Vol. 1, pp. 284–6.

25 Brüning, *Memoiren*, pp. 469–70.

26 Patch, *Brüning*, p. 93.

27 Patch, *Brüning*, p. 94.

28 J. Curtius, *Sechs Jahre Minister der deutschen Republik* (Heidelberg: Carl Winter, 1948), p. 165.

29 L. Maltin (ed.), *Leonard Martin's 2005 Movie Guide* (Plume, 2005), p. 151.

30 Kracauer, *From Caligari to Hitler*, p. 217.

31 W. Sudendorf, *Marlene Dietrich* (Berlin: DTV Deutscher Taschenbuch Verlag, 1980), pp. 71–2.

32 See J. Mayne, 'Marlene Dietrich, The Blue Angel and Female Performance', in D. Hunter (ed.), *Seduction and Theory: Readings of Gender, Representation and Rhetoric* (Urbana: University of Illinois Press, 1989), pp. 28–46.

33 For details see D. Imhoof, 'Blue Angel, Brown Culture: The Politics of Film Reception in Göttingen', in Williams (ed.), *Weimar Culture Revisited*, pp. 50–72, and J. Baxter, *The Cinema of Josef von Sternberg* (A. Zwemmer, 1971).

34 The Catacomb Club was closed on 10 May 1935 on the orders of Joseph Goebbels, the Propaganda Minister.

35 S. Funkenstein, 'Anita Berber: Imaging a Weimar Performance Artist', *Women's Art Journal*, Vol. 26 (2005), pp. 26–31.

36 Quoted in A. Jonge, *The Weimar Chronicle: Prelude to Hitler* (Paddington Press, 1978), p. 161.

37 Patch, *Brüning*, p. 98.

38 Leopold, *Hugenberg*, pp. 84, 81.

39 Jones, *German Right*, pp. 566–7.

40 Jones, *German Liberalism*, pp. 366–77.

41 Childers, *The Nazi Voter*, p. 183.

42 Childers, *The Nazi Voter*, p. 182.

43 Ullrich, *Hitler*, Vol. 1, p. 222.

44 Childers, *Third Reich*, pp. 110–12, 115; *Völkischer Beobachter*, 18 August 1930.

45 Longerich, *Hitler*, p. 202.

46 Longerich, *Hitler*, p. 201.

47 Ullrich, *Hitler*, Vol. 2, pp. 229–31.

48 Ullrich, *Hitler*, Vol. 2, p. 233.

49 For a discussion of why voters surged to the KPD at the 1930 German national election see C. Stogbauer, 'The radicalisation of the German Electorate: Swinging to the Right and the Left in the twilight of the Weimar Republic', *European Review of Economic History*, Vol. 5 (2001), pp. 251–80.

50 T. Fandel, *Konfession und Nationalsozialismus: Evangelische und Katholische Pfarrer in der Pfalz, 1930–1939* (Paderborn: Schöningh, 1997), p. 35.

51 Jones, *German Right*, p. 591.

52 See J. Pollock, 'The German Reichstag Elections of 1930', *American Political Science Review*, Vol. 24 (1930), pp. 989–95.

53 Ullrich, *Hitler*, Vol. 1, p. 233.

54 Jewish Telegraphic Agency, 19 September 1930.

55 The most extensive analysis of why people voted for Hitler in 1930 is J. Falter, *Hitler's Wähler* (Munich: C.H. Beck, 1991). See also K. O'Lessker, 'Who Voted for Hitler? A New Look at the Class Basis of Nazism', *American Journal of Sociology*, Vol. 74 (1968), pp. 63–9.

56 For details see J. O'Loughlin, C. Flint and L. Anselin, 'The Geography of the Nazi Vote: Context, Confession and Class in the Reichstag Election of 1930', *Annals of the Association of American Geographers*, Vol. 84 (1994), pp. 351–80.

57 S. Fritz, 'The NSDAP as Volkspartei? A Look at the Social Bases of the Nazi Voter', *The History Teacher*, Vol. 20 (1987), pp. 379–99.

58 J. Falter and R. Zintl, 'The Economic Crisis of the 1930s and the Nazi vote', *Journal of Interdisciplinary History*, Vol. 19 (1988), pp. 55–85.

59 Ullrich, *Hitler*, Vol. 1, p. 234.

60 Eyck, *Weimar Republic*, Vol. 2, p. 283.

61 *The Times*, 16 September 1930.

62 Kershaw, *Hitler*, Vol. 1, pp. 336–7.

63 Kershaw, *Hitler*, Vol. 1, pp. 337–8.

64 Longerich, *Hitler*, p. 210.

65 Ullrich, *Hitler*, Vol. 1, p. 236.

66 Kershaw, *Hitler*, Vol. 1, p. 339.

67 Patch, *Brüning*, p. 136

68 Patch, *Brüning*, p.107.

69 Longerich, *Hitler*, p. 211.

70 See Koops, *Kabinette Brüning*, Vol. 1, pp. 469–75, 480–4.

71 Eyck, *Weimar Republic*, Vol. 2, pp. 290–3.

72 Eyck, *Weimar Republic*, Vol. 2, pp. 294–5.

73 Patch, *Brüning*, p. 115.

74 Longerich, *Hitler*, p. 124.

75 Ullrich, *Hitler*, Vol. 2, p. 243.

76 *New York Times*, 12 December 1930.

77 *Manchester Guardian*, 12 December 1930; Ullrich, *Hitler*, Vol. 1, p. 243.

14 BRÜNING'S AGE OF AUSTERITY

1 *Chicago Daily Tribune*, 9 January 1931.

2 Jones, *German Liberalism*, pp. 408–10.

3 Ullrich, *Hitler*, Vol. 1, p. 247.

4 Fest, *Hitler*, p. 306.

5 C. Zentner and F. Bedürftig, *The Encyclopedia of the Third Reich* (New York: Macmillan, 1991), p. 116.

6 For details see A. Heusler, *Das Braune Haus* (Munich: Deutche Verlags-Ansalt, 2008), pp. 136–7. The building was largely destroyed by an Allied bombing raid in October 1943, but the Munich Documentation Centre for the History of National Socialism is now located on the site.

7 H. Schacht, *My First Seventy-Six Years* (Allan Wingate, 1955), pp. 279–80.

8 For a detailed study of Röhm's role in the SA see T. Atcherley and M. Carey, *Hitler's Gay Traitor: The Story of Ernst Röhm, Chief of Staff of the SA* (Manchester: Trafford, 2007).

9 C. Fischer, *The Rise of the Nazis* (Manchester: Manchester University Press, 2002), p. 85.

10 After Stennes re-ignited the SA conflict with Hitler in the spring of 1931, he was expelled from the party on 1 April 1931. It has subsequently come to light that Brüning secretly supported the Stennes revolt, in order to split the National Socialist movement. See Patch, *Brüning*, pp. 148–9.

11 Fest, *Hitler*, p. 294.

12 *Chicago Daily Tribune*, 24 January 1930; Brüning, *Memoiren*, pp. 242–4.

13 *Zentralblatt der Christlichen Gewerkschaften*, 1 February 1931.

14 *Chicago Daily Tribune*, 26 January 1931.

15 Brüning, *Memoiren*, pp. 255–6.

16 Patch, *Brüning*, p. 147.

17 V. Berghahn, *Der Stahlhelm: Bund der Frontsoldaten, 1918–1935* (Düsseldorf: Droste, 1966), pp. 164–75; *Chicago Daily Tribune*, 31 March 1931.

18 See cabinet meetings of 16 and 18 March 1931 in Koops (ed.), *Kabinette Brüning*, Vol. 2, pp. 952–5, 969–71; Brüning, *Memoiren*, pp. 263–4.

19 See A. Orde, 'The Origins of the German Austrian Customs Union Affair of 1931', *Central European History*, Vol. 13 (1980), pp. 34–59.

20 M. Newman, 'Britain and the German-Austrian Customs Union Proposal of 1931', *European History Quarterly*, Vol. 6 (1976), pp. 449–72.

21 M. Hudson, 'The World Court and The Austro-German Customs Regime', *American Bar Association Journal*, Vol. 17 (1931), pp. 791–3.

22 For details on the Austrian banking crisis see I. Aguado, 'The Creditanstalt Crisis of 1931 and the Failure of the Austria-German Customs Project', *Historical Journal*, Vol. 44 (2001), pp. 199–221, and A. Schubert, 'The Credit-Anstalt Crisis of 1931: A Financial Crisis Revisited', *Journal of Economic History*, Vol. 47 (1987), pp. 495–7.

23 Longerich, *Hitler*, p. 224.

24 Brüning, *Memoiren*, pp. 278–9.

25 Patch, *Brüning*, p. 161.

26 Just prior to Hoover's announcement, President Hindenburg had sent a letter to the US President, pleading with him to intervene in Europe's economic problems. On the French rejection of Hoover's proposal, see S. Banholzer and T. Straumann, 'Why the French said: "Non": A New Perspective on the Hoover Moratorium of June 1931', *Journal of Contemporary History*, Vol. 55 (2020), pp. 11–17.

27 I. Schnabel, 'The German Twin Crisis of 1931', *Journal of Economic History*, Vol. 64 (2004), pp. 822–71.

28 K. Born, *Die Deutsche Bankenkrise 1931: Finanzen and Politik* (Munich: Piper 1967), pp. 91–7.

29 See T. Balderston, 'German Banking between the Wars: The Crisis of the Credit Banks', *Business History Review*, Vol. 65 (1991), pp. 554–605.

30 For details see P. Termin, 'The German Crisis of 1931', *Clionetrica*, Vol. 2 (2007), pp. 5–17.

31 Eyck, *Weimar Republic*, Vol. 2, pp. 321–3; Patch, *Brüning*, p. 170.

32 Patch, *Brüning*, p. 163.

33 A. Clifford, *Hindenburg, Ludendorff and Hitler: Germany's Generals and the Rise of the Nazis* (Barnsley: Pen & Sword, 2021), p. 154.

34 Leopold, *Hugenberg*, p. 92–3.

35 Eyck, *Weimar Republic*, Vol. 2, p. 297.

36 Hanfstaengl, *15 Jahre*, p. 233; C. Schroeder, *Er War Mein Chef: aus dem Nachlass der Sekretärin von Adolf Hitler* (Munich: Langen, Müller, 1985), p. 153.

37 Machtan, *Hidden Hitler*, p. 162.

38 A. Sigmund, *Die Frauen der Nazis* (Munich: Heyne, 2005), p. 148.

39 Ullrich, *Hitler*, Vol. 1, p. 281.

40 Ullrich, *Hitler*, Vol. 1, p. 281.

41 *Münchener Post*, 21 September 1931; Ullrich, *Hitler*, Vol. 2, p. 282.

42 *Münchener Post*, 22 September 1931.

43 For full details on the death of Geli Raubel see R. Hayman, *Hitler and Geli* (Bloomsbury, 1997); R. Rosenbaum, 'Hitler's Doomed Angel', *Vanity Fair*, April 1992; Ullrich, *Hitler*, Vol. 1, pp. 276–85; Kershaw, *Hitler*, Vol. 1, pp. 351–5.

44 Clifford, *Hindenburg, Ludendorff and Hitler*, p. 153.

45 F. Plehwe, *Reichskanzler Kurt von Schleicher: Weimars letzte Chance gegen Hitler* (Esslingen; Bechtle, 1983), pp. 138–9; Brüning, *Memoiren*, pp. 379–85.

46 Patch, *Brüning*, p. 190; L. Jones, 'Taming the Beast: Kurt von Schleicher and the End of the Weimar Republic', in H. Beck and L. Jones (eds), *From Weimar to Hitler: Studies in the Dissolution of the Weimar Republic and the Establishment of the Third Reich 1932–1934* (Oxford: Berghahn, 2019), pp. 24–6; Brüning, *Memoiren*, pp. 399–400.

47 Walther, *Darkness Falling*, p. 121.

48 Walther, *Darkness Falling*, p. 128.

49 Patch, *Brüning*, pp. 225–6.

50 Longerich, *Hitler*, p. 227.

51 Patch, *Brüning*, p. 193.

52 *Chicago Daily Tribune*, 7 October 1931; Eyck, *Weimar Republic*, Vol. 2, p. 329.

53 Clifford, *Hindenburg, Ludendorff and Hitler*, p. 249.

54 Shirer, *Third Reich*, pp. 153–4.

55 Ullrich, *Hitler*, Vol. 1, pp. 258–9.

56 Patch, *Brüning*, pp. 195, 198.

57 For detailed discussion of the 'Harzburg Front' see L. Jones, 'Nationalists, Nazis and the Assault against Weimar: Revisiting the Harzburg Rally of October 1931', *German Studies Review*, Vol. 29 (2006), pp. 483–94.

58 Eyck, *Weimar Republic*, Vol. 1, pp. 333–4.

59 Simms, *Hitler*, p. 161.

60 *Chicago Daily Tribune*, 17 October 1931.

61 *Welt am Montag*, 12 October 1931.

62 Schumann, *Political Violence*, pp. 250–61.

63 D. Siemens, *The Making of a Nazi Hero: The Murder and Myth of Horst Wessel* (I.B.Taurus, 2013), p. 3.

64 Childers, *Third Reich*, pp. 124–6.

65 Quoted in Fest, *Hitler*, p. 295.

66 Ullrich, *Hitler*, Vol. 2, pp. 255–6.

67 *Chicago Daily Tribune*, 26 November 1931. On 30 November 1931, legal proceedings were started against Dr Werner Best for high treason, but they were quietly dropped, without charge, in October 1932.

68 *Chicago Daily Tribune*, 5 December 1931; *The Times*, 5 December 1931; Simms, *Hitler*, p. 163.

69 *Völkischer Beobachter*, 13–14 December 1931.

70 *Chicago Daily Tribune*, 9 December 1931. See also Patch, *Brüning*, pp. 210–13.

71 Quoted in Eyck, *Weimar Republic*, Vol. 2, p. 341.

72 *Chicago Daily Tribune*, 1 January 1932.

15 DIGGING WEIMAR'S GRAVE

1 Dorpalen, *Hindenburg and the Weimar Republic*, pp. 255–61.

2 Brüning, *Memoiren*, p. 504.

3 Ullrich, *Hitler*, Vol. 1, p. 294.

4 Longerich, *Hitler*, pp. 236–7.

5 For details see G. Hallgarten, 'Adolf Hitler and Heavy Industry, 1931-1933', *Journal of Economic History*, Vol. 12 (1952), pp. 222–46.

6 GHDI: Hitler speech to the Industry Club, Düsseldorf, 26 January 1932.

7 For details see M. Borg, 'Reducing Offensive Capabilities - the Attempt of 1932', *Journal of Peace Research*, Vol. 29 (1992), pp. 145–60.

8 Eyck, *Weimar Republic*, Vol. 2, p. 357.

9 Eyck, *Weimar Republic*, Vol. 2, p. 357.

10 *Chicago Daily Tribune*, 26 February 1932.

11 For a thorough analysis see L. Jones, *Hitler versus Hindenburg: The 1932 Presidential Elections and the End of the Weimar Republic* (Cambridge: Cambridge University Press, 2015).

12 Eyck, *Weimar Republic*, Vol. 2, p. 355.

13 Clifford, *Hindenburg, Ludendorff and Hitler*, p. 168.

14 Patch, *Brüning*, p. 241.

15 Childers, *Third Reich*, pp. 144–5.

16 Clifford, *Hindenburg, Ludendorff and Hitler*, pp. 171–2.

17 Jewish Telegraphic Agency, 7 September 1932.

18 R. Lemmons, '"Germany's Eternal Son": The Genesis of the Ernst Thälmann Myth, 1930–1950', *German Studies Review*, Vol. 32 (2009), pp. 343–56.

19 Simms, *Hitler*, p. 168.

20 W. Chrystal, 'Nazi Party Election Films, 1927-1938', Cinema Journal, Vol. 15 (1975), pp. 29–47.

21 Childers, *Third Reich*, pp. 144–7.

22 Longerich, *Hitler*, p. 237.

23 Simms, *Hitler*, p. 169.

24 *New York Daily News*, 15 March 1932.

25 Ullrich, *Hitler*, Vol. 1, p. 299.

26 Clifford, *Hindenburg, Ludendorff and Hitler*, p. 173.

27 Childers, *Third Reich*, pp. 150–2.

28 Jones, *Hitler versus Hindenburg*, pp. 247, 298–300.

29 See Falter, 'The Two Hindenburg Elections of 1925 and 1932', pp. 225–41.

30 O. Braun, *Von Weimar zu Hitler* (New York: Europa, 1941), p. 373.

31 Patch, *Brüning*, p. 247.

32 Brüning, *Memoiren*, pp. 538–54.

33 Patch, *Brüning*, p. 250.

34 Patch, *Brüning*, pp. 251–2.

35 Childers, *Third Reich*, p. 155.

36 Kershaw, *Hitler*, Vol. 1, p. 363.

37 Ullrich, *Hitler*, Vol. 1, p. 304.

38 Childers, *The Nazi Voter*, p. 201.

39 Eyck, *Weimar Republic*, Vol. 2, p. 388.

40 Ullrich, *Hitler*, Vol. 1, pp. 306–7.

41 Longerich, *Hitler*, p. 243.

42 Eyck, *Weimar Republic*, Vol. 2, pp. 374–5.

43 Patch, *Brüning*, p. 255.

44 *Chicago Daily Tribune*, 13 May 1932.

45 Brüning, *Memoiren*, pp. 597–600.

46 See L. Jones, 'Franz von Papen, the German Centre Party and the failure of Catholic Conservatism in the Weimar Republic', *Central European History*, Vol. 38 (2005), pp. 191–217; L. Jones, 'Franz von Papen and the Establishment of the Third Reich', *Journal of Modern History*, Vol. 83 (2011), pp. 272–318.

47 This section draws on Papen's own account of how he became Chancellor. See F. Papen, *Memoirs*, trans. B. Connell (Andre Deutsch, 1952), pp. 146–56.

48 J. Petzold, *Franz von Papen: Eine Deutsches Verhängnis* (Munich: Buchverlag Union, 1995), pp. 60–1.

49 Clifford, *Hindenburg, Ludendorff and Hitler*, p. 186.

50 Papen, *Memoirs*, p. 158.

51 Interestingly, Hitler retained five members of Papen's cabinet when he was appointed Chancellor. For details on the Papen Cabinet see K. Minuth (ed.), *Das Kabinett von Papen*, 2 vols (Boppard and Rhein: Boldt, 1989).

52 Eyck, *Weimar Republic*, Vol. 2, p. 397.

53 *Chicago Daily Tribune*, 15 June 1932.

54 *Chicago Daily Tribune*, 10 July 1932.

55 Kershaw, *Hitler*, Vol, 1, p. 368.

56 For details see L. Schirmann, *Justizmanipulationen: Der Altonaer Blutsonntag und die Altonaer bzw Hamburger Justiz 1932–1994* (Berlin: Typographica Mitte, 1995).

57 Longerich, *Hitler*, p. 252.

58 Hett, *Death of Democracy*, p. 148.

59 *Chicago Daily Tribune*, 26 October 1932.

60 Ullrich, *Hitler*, Vol. 1, p.3 15.

61 For detailed election results see J. Kerwin, 'The German Reichstag Elections of July 31, 1932', *American Political Science Review*, Vol. 26 (1932), pp. 921–6.

62 Longerich, *Hitler*, pp. 252–3.

63 For greater detail on reasons for middle-class and working-class support for the NSDAP in the July 1932 election see Childers, *The Nazi Voter*, pp. 211–61.

64 G. King et al., 'Ordinary Economic Voting Behaviour in the Extraordinary Election of Adolf Hitler', *Journal of Economic History*, Vol. 68 (2008), pp. 951–96.

65 See C. Stogbauer, 'The Radicalization of the German Electorate: Swinging to the Right and to the Left in the twilight of the Weimar Republic', *European Review of Economic History*, Vol. 5 (2000), pp. 251–80.

66 O. Heilbronner, 'The Failure That Succeeded: Nazi Party Activity in a Catholic Region in Germany, 1929-32', *Journal of Contemporary History*, Vol. 27 (1992), pp. 531–49.

67 Jones, *German Liberalism*, pp. 448–61.

68 Kershaw, *Hitler*, Vol. 1, pp. 370–1.

69 Fest, *Hitler*, p. 341.

70 Kolb, *Weimar Republic*, p. 128.

71 Patch, *Brüning*, p. 280.

72 Ullrich, *Hitler*, Vol. 1, p. 319.

73 Fest, *Hitler*, p. 341.

74 Longerich, *Hitler*, pp. 255–6.

75 Papen, *Memoirs*, p. 197.

76 Ullrich, *Hitler*, Vol. 1, p. 320.

77 Clifford, *Hindenburg, Ludendorff and Hitler*, p. 193.

78 Fest, *Hitler*, p. 342.

79 Ullrich, *Hitler*, Vol. 1, p. 324.

80 *Chicago Daily Tribune*, 9 August 1932.

81 For details see R. Bessel, 'The Potempa Murder', *Central European History*, Vol. 10 (1977) pp. 241–54.

82 Quoted in Bessel, 'Potempa Murder'.

83 Quoted in Eyck, *Weimar Republic*, Vol. 2, p. 421.

84 *The West Australian*, 3 September 1932.

85 Papen, *Memoirs*, p. 207.

86 Eyck, *Weimar Republic*, Vol. 2, p. 428.

87 Ullrich, *Hitler*, Vol. 1, p. 326.

88 See G. Colm, 'Why the "Papen Plan" for Economic Recovery Failed', *Social Research*, Vol. 1 (1934), pp. 83–96.

89 Papen, *Memoirs*, pp. 208, 209.

90 Ullrich, *Hitler*, Vol. 1, p. 328.

91 Ullrich, *Hitler*, Vol. 1, pp. 329–30.

92 *Chicago Daily Tribune*, 13 October 1932.

93 Eyck, *Weimar Republic*, Vol. 2, pp. 433–4. The Transport Strike ended on 7 November 1932, when the strikers returned to work and accepted the original arbitration settlement.

94 Childers, *Third Reich*, pp. 190–1.

95 For the full results of the 6 November 1932 elections see Nohlen and Stöver, *Elections in Europe*, p. 762.

96 Ullrich, *Hitler*, Vol. 1, p. 352.

97 Kershaw, *Hitler*, Vol. 1, pp. 392–4.

98 Ullrich, *Hitler*, Vol. 1, p. 335.

99 Kershaw, *Hitler*, Vol. 1, p. 395.

100 For Papen's account of this meeting on 1 December 1932 see Papen, *Memoirs*, pp. 216–17.

101 Hett, *Death of Democracy*, pp. 158–9.

102 Ullrich, *Hitler*, Vol. 1, p. 338.

103 Papen, *Memoirs*, p. 217.

104 Papen, *Memoirs*, p. 223.

105 Eyck, *Weimar Republic*, Vol. 2, p. 447.

106 For details on the Schleicher cabinet see A. Golecki (ed.), *Das Kabinett von Schleicher* (Boppard am Rhein: Boldt, 1986).

107 Ullrich, *Hitler*, Vol. 1, p. 342.

108 Quoted in Clifford, *Hindenburg, Ludendorff and Hitler*, p. 210.

109 Eyck, *Weimar Republic*, Vol. 2, p.452–3.

110 Ullrich, *Hitler*, Vol.1, p. 342.

111 For the full story see H. Turner, 'The Myth of Chancellor von Schleicher's Querfront Strategy', *Central European History*, Vol. 41 (2008), pp. 673–81.

112 Eyck, *Weimar Republic*, Vol. 2, 459–60.

113 Hett, *Death of Democracy*, pp. 170–1.

114 Ullrich, *Hitler*, Vol. 1, p. 350.

115 Papen, *Memoirs*, pp. 226–7.

POSTSCRIPT: THE MONTH OF JANUARY 1933

1 Toland, *Hitler*, p. 283; Papen, *Memoirs*, p. 227.

2 AP-IMT: Testimony of Franz Von Papen, 18 June 1946; H. Turner, *Hitler's Thirty Days to Power: January 1933* (Basic Books, 1997), p.44; Ullrich, *Hitler*, Vol. 1, p. 351.

3 Institut für Zeitgeschichte, Munich, ZS/557: Kurt Schröder Interrogation, 18 June 1947; Papen, *Memoirs*, pp. 227–8; Ullrich, *Hitler*, Vol. 1, p.352.

4 Toland, *Hitler*, p.284.

5 *Frankfurter Zeitung*, 7 January 1933; Ullrich, *Hitler*, Vol. 1, p. 352.

6 Ullrich, *Hitler*, Vol. 1, p. 356.

7 Toland, *Hitler*, p. 284.

8 Hett, *Death of Democracy*, p. 174.

9 Toland, *Hitler*, p. 285.

10 J. Noakes and G. Pridham, *Documents on Nazism* (Jonathan Cape, 1974), Vol. 1, p. 117: Testimony of Otto Meissner at Nuremberg Trial; p.118: Ribbentrop Diary Notes, 18 January 1933; Ullrich, *Hitler*, Vol. 1, p. 359.

11 Papen, *Memoirs*, p. 235

12 Noakes and Pridham, *Documents on Nazism*, Vol. 1, pp. 116–17: Testimony of Otto Meissner at Nuremberg Trial.

13 Toland, *Hitler*, pp. 285–6.

14 Kershaw, Hitler, Vol. 1, p. 418.

15 Toland, Hitler, p. 286.

16 Noakes and Pridham, *Documents on Nazism*, Vol. 1, p. 118: Testimony of Otto Meissner at Nuremberg Trial; p.117: Ribbentrop Diary Notes, 22 January 1933; Papen, *Memoirs*, pp. 235–6.

17 Papen, *Memoirs*, p. 237; Noakes and Pridham, *Documents on Nazism*, Vol. 1, p.117: Testimony of Otto Meissner at Nuremberg Trial.

18 Fest, *Hitler*, p. 361.

19 Toland, *Hitler*, p. 286.

20 Frankfurter *Zeitung*, 28 January 1933

21 Fest, *Hitler*, pp. 361–2, 120.

22 Golecki, *Das Kabinett von Schleicher*, pp. 306–10.

23 Toland, *Hitler*, p. 287.

24 Noakes and Pridham, *Documents on Nazism*, Vol. 1, p. 117: Testimony of Otto Meissner at Nuremberg Trial.

25 Papen, *Memoirs*, p. 240; Noakes and Pridham, *Documents on Nazism*, Vol. 1, p. 121.

26 Papen, *Memoirs*, p. 244.

27 Toland, *Hitler*, p. 290.

BIBLIOGRAPHY

Place of publication is London unless otherwise stated.

Abel, T. *Why Hitler Came to Power* (Cambridge, MA: Harvard University Press, 1986)

Abramowski, G. (ed.) *Die Kabinette Marx I and II*, 2 vols (Boppard am Rhein: Boldt, 1973)

_____ (ed.) *Die Kabinette Marx III and IV* (Boppard am Rhein: Boldt, 1988)

Adelman, A. *A Shattered Peace: Versailles 1919 and the Price We Pay Today* (Chichester: John Wiley, 2008)

Aguado, I. 'The Creditanstalt Crisis of 1931 and the Failure of the Austria-German Customs Project', *Historical Journal*, Vol. 44 (2001), pp.199–221

Ambler, F. *The Story of the Bauhaus* (Ilex, 1918)

Angress, W. 'Weimar Coalition and Ruhr Insurrection, March–April 1920', *Journal of Modern History*, Vol. 29 (1957), pp.1–20

_____ *Stillborn Revolution: The Communist Bid for Power in Germany, 1921–1923* (Princeton,
NJ: Princeton University Press, 1963)

Ankum, K. (ed.) *Women in the Metropolis: Gender and Modernity in Weimar Culture* (Berkeley: University of California Press, 1997)

Askin, K. *War Crimes Against Women: Prosecution in the International War Crimes Tribunals* (The Hague: Martinus Nijhoff, 1997)

Astrow, W., Sleopkow, A. and Thomas, J. (eds) *Illustrierte Geschichte der Russischen Revolution* (Berlin: Neuer Deutscher Verlag, 1928)

Atcherley, T. and Carey, M. *Hitler's Gay Traitor: The Story of Ernst Röhm, Chief of Staff of the SA* (Manchester: Trafford, 2007)

Avalon Project. 'Treaty of Mutual Guarantee between Germany, Belgium, France, Great Britain, and Italy, 16 October 1925', available online at: https://avalon.law.yale.edu/20th_century/locarno_001.asp

Axon, G. *The Stock Market Crash of 1929* (Mason & Lipscomb, 1974)
Bach, S. '100 years of the Modern German Tax System: Foundation, Reforms and Challenges', Deutsches Institut für Wirtschaftsforschung *Weekly Report*, Vol. 9 (2019), pp.407–13

Baden, M. *Erinnerungen and Dokumente* (Munich: Deutsche Verlags-Anstalt, 1927)

Bähr, J. *Staatliche Schlichtung in der Weimarer Republik: Tarifpolitik, Korporatismus und Industrieller Konflikt zwischen Inflation and Deflation, 1919–1932* (Berlin: Colloquium, 1989)

Balderston, T. 'German Banking between the Wars: The Crisis of the Credit Banks', *Business History Review*, Vol. 65 (1991), pp.554–605

Balfour, M. *The Kaiser and His Times* (Penguin, 1969)

Banholzer, S. and Straumann, T. 'Why the French said: "Non": A New Perspective on the Hoover Moratorium of June 1931', *Journal of Contemporary History*, Vol. 55 (2020), pp.11–17

Baumann, K. *Bauhaus Dessau: Architektur– Gestaltung– Idee* (Berlin: Jovis, 2007)

Baxter, J. *The Cinema of Josef von Sternberg* (Zwemmer, 1971)

Bennett, G. *Foreign Policy During the Curzon Period, 1919–1924* (Basingstoke: Macmillan Press, 1995)

Berghahn, V. *Der Stahlhelm: Bund der Frontsoldaten, 1918–1935* (Düsseldorf: Droste, 1966)

Berlau, A. *German Social Democratic Party, 1914–1921* (New York: Columbia University Press, 1949)

Berman, S. 'Civil Society and the Collapse of the Weimar Republic', *World Politics*, Vol. 49 (1997), pp.401–29

Bessel, R. 'The Potempa Murder', *Central European History*, Vol. 10 (1977) pp.241–54

Bleachey, R. *Gay Berlin: Birthplace of Modern Identity* (New York: Vintage, 2014)

Boak, H. 'The State as an Employer of Women in the Weimar Republic', in W. Lee and E. Rosenhaft (eds) *The State and Social Change in Germany, 1880–1980* (Oxford: Berg, 1990), pp.61–98

_____ *Women in the Weimar Republic* (Manchester: Manchester University Press, 2013)

Bois, J. 'Aristide Briand: Member of Twenty-One French Cabinets', *Current History*, Vol. 31 (1929), pp.529–35

Bookbinder, P. *Weimar Germany: The Republic of the Reasonable* (Manchester: Manchester University Press, 1996)

Borg, M. 'Reducing Offensive Capabilities – the Attempt of 1932', *Journal of Peace Research*, Vol. 29 (1992), pp.145–60

Born, K. *Die Deutsche Bankenkrise 1931: Finanzen und Politik* (Munich: Piper, 1967)

Braun, O. *Von Weimar zu Hitler* (New York: Europa, 1941)

Brunet, R. *The New German Constitution – with Text* (New York: Knopf, 1923)

Brüning, H. *Memoiren* (Stuttgart: Deutsche Verlags-Anstalt, 1970)

Bry, G. *Wages in Germany, 1871–1945* (Princeton, NJ: Princeton University Press, 1960)

Bullock, A. *Hitler: A Study in Tyranny* (Penguin, 1962)

_____ *Stalin and Hitler: Parallel Lives* (HarperCollins, 1991)

Bunck, J. and Fowler, M. 'The Kellogg–Briand Pact: A Reappraisal', *Tuland Journal of International and Comparative Law*, Vol. 27 (2018), pp.229–76

Burkhardt, A. 'A Republican Potential: The Rise and Fall of the German Democratic Party in Hof-an-der-Saale, 1918–1920', *Central European History*, Vol. 50 (2017), pp.471–92

Burns, E. *Karl Liebknecht* (Martin Lawrence, 1934)

Buse, D. 'Ebert and the German Crisis, 1917–1920, *Central European History*, Vol. 5 (1972), pp.234–55

Butler, R., Bury, J. and Lambert, M. (eds) *Documents on British Foreign Policy, 1919–1939*, First Series, Vols IX and X (HMSO, 1960)

Campbell, F. 'The Struggle for Upper Silesia, 1919–1922', *Journal of Modern History*, Vol. 42 (1970), pp.361–85

Canning, K., Barndt, K. and McGuire, K. (eds) *Weimar Publics/Weimar Subjects: Rethinking the Political Culture of Germany in the 1920s* (Oxford: Berghahn, 2010)

Carrol, M. 'War and Peace and International Law: The Kellogg-Briand Peace Pact Reconsidered', *Canadian Journal of History*, Vol. 53 (2018), pp.86–96

Carsten, F. *The Reichswehr and Politics, 1918–1933* (Oxford: Clarendon Press, 1966)

Case, J. and Case, E. *Owen D. Young and American Enterprise: A Biography* (Boston, MA: David R. Godine, 1982)

Childers, T. *The Nazi Voter: The Social Foundations of Fascism in Germany, 1919–1933* (Chapel Hill: University of North Carolina Press, 1983)

Chrystal, W. 'Nazi Party Election Films, 1927–1938', *Cinema Journal*, Vol. 15 (1975), pp.29–47

Clay, N. 'The Making of the Reich President, 1925: German Conservatism and the Nomination of Paul von Hindenburg', *Central European History*, Vol. 23 (1990), pp.179–204

Clifford, A. *Hindenburg, Ludendorff and Hitler: Germany's Generals and the Rise of the Nazis* (Barnsley: Pen & Sword, 2021)

Clingan, E. *The Lives of Hans Luther, 1879–1962* (Plymouth: Lexington Books, 2010)

Cohn, N. *Warrant for Genocide: The Myth of the Jewish World Conspiracy and the Protocols of the Elders of Zion* (New York: Harper & Row, 1966)

Colm, G. 'Why the "Papen Plan" for Economic Recovery Failed', *Social Research*, Vol. 1 (1934), pp.83–96

Cornebise, A. 'Cuno, Germany and the Coming of the Ruhr Occupation: A Study in German–West European Relations, *Proceedings of the American Philosophical Society*, Vol. 116 (1972), pp.502–31

Cowan, M. *W. Ruttmann and the Cinema of Multiplicity: Avant-garde film – Advertising – Modernity* (Amsterdam: Amsterdam University Press, 2014)

Crockett, D. *German Post-Expressionism: The Art of the*

Great Disorder (Philadephia, PA: Penn State University Press, 1999)

Curtius, J. *Sechs Jahre Minister der deutschen Republik* (Heidelberg: Carl Winter, 1948)

Czisnik, U. *Gustav Noske: Ein sozialdemokratischer Staatsmann* (Göttingen: Mustarschmidt, 1969)

D'Abernon, Viscount E. *An Ambassador of Peace: Lord D'Abernon's Diary, Vol 3: Years of Recovery* (Hodder & Stoughton, 1930)

Dähnhardt, D. *Revolution in Kiel: Der Übergang vom Kaiserreich zur Weimarer Republik 1918–19* (Neümunster: K. Wacholtz, 1984)

Dawes, R. *The Dawes Plan in the Making* (Indianapolis: Bobbs-Merrill, 1925)

De Wilde, M. 'The State of Emergency in the Weimar Republic: Legal Disputes over Article 48 of the Weimar Constitution', *Legal History Review*, Vol. 78 (2010), pp.135–58

Dernberg, J. *Munich 1923: Hitler's First Bid for Power* (New York: Harper & Row, 1982)

Deuerlein, E. (ed.) *Der Aufstieg der NSDAP in Augenzeugenberichten* (Düsseldorf: K. Rauch, 1968)

Dorpalen, A. *Hindenburg and the Weimar Republic* (Princeton, NJ: Princeton University Press, 1964)

Dorten, H. 'The Rhineland Movement', *Foreign Affairs*, Vol. 3 (1925), pp.399–410

Droste, M. *Bauhaus, 1918–1933* (Berlin: Taschen, 2002)

Dunlap, A. *Charles Gates Dawes: A Life* (Evanston, IL: Northwestern University Press, 2016)

Dyzenhaus, D. 'Legal Theory in the Collapse of Weimar: Contemporary Lessons', *American Science Review*, Vol. 91 (1997), pp.121–34

Eksteins, M. 'All Quiet on the Western Front and the Fate of War', *Journal of Contemporary History*, Vol. 15 (1980), pp.345–66

Elcock, C. *Could the Versailles System Have Worked?* (Basingstoke: Palgrave Macmillan, 2018)

Ellis, E. *Frank B. Kellogg and American Foreign Relations 1925–1929* (New Brunswick, NJ: Rutgers University Press, 1961)

Elsaesser, T. *Metropolis* (British Film Institute, 2012)

Enssle, M. 'Stresemann's Diplomacy Fifty Years After Locarno: Some Recent Perspectives', *Historical Journal*, Vol. 20 (1977), pp.937–48

Epstein, K. 'Wrong Man in a Maelstrom: The Government of Max of Baden', *Review of Politics*, Vol. 26 (1964), pp.215–43

Erdmann, K. and Vogt, M. (eds) *Die Kabinette Stresemann I und I* (Boppard am Rhein: Boldt, 1978)

Erger, J. *Der Kapp-Lüttwitz-Putsch: Ein Beitrag zur deutschen Innenpolitik 1919–1920* (Düsselfdorf: Droste, 1967)

Erzberger, M. *Erlebnisse im Weltkrieg* (Berlin: Deutsche Verlags-Anstalt, 1920)

Evans, R. *The Coming of the Third Reich* (Penguin, 2004)

_____ 'Prophet in a Tuxedo', *London Review of Books* (November 2012)

_____ *The Hitler Conspiracies: The Third Reich and the Paranoid Imagination* (Penguin, 2021)

Eyck, E. *A History of the Weimar Republic, Vol. 2: From the Locarno Conference to Hitler's Seizure of Power* (Cambridge, MA: Harvard University Press, 1967)

_____ *A History of the Weimar Republic, Vol. 1: From the Collapse of the Empire to Hindenburg's Election* (New York: Atheneum, 1970)

Falter, J. *Hitler's Wähler* (Munich: C.H. Beck, 1991)

_____ 'The Two Hindenburg Elections of 1925 and 1932: A Total Reversal of Voter Coalitions', *Historical Social Research*, Supplement, No. 2 (2013), pp. 217–32

_____ and Gruner, W. 'The Economic Crisis of the 1930s and the Nazi vote', *Journal of Interdisciplinary History*, Vol. 21(1988), pp.55–85

Fandel, T. *Konfession and Nationalsozialismus: Evangelische und Katholische Pfarrer in der Pfalz, 1930–1939* (Paderborn: Schöningh, 1997)

Feldman, G. *The Great Disorder: Politics, Economics and Society in the Great Inflation, 1914–1924* (Oxford: Oxford University Press, 1993)

Fergusson, A. *When Money Dies: The Nightmare of the Weimar Hyper-Inflation* (William Kimber, 1975)

Ferrel, R. *Peace in Their Time: The Origins of the Kellogg–Briand Pact* (New Haven: Yale University Press, 1952)

Fest, J. *Hitler* (Weidenfeld & Nicolson, 1974)

Finch, G. 'The London Conference on the Application of the Dawes Plan', *American Journal of International Law*, Vol. 18 (1924), pp.707–19

_____ 'The Settlement of the Reparation Problem', *American Journal of International Law*, Vol. 24 (1930), pp.339–50

Fink, C. *The Genoa Conference, European Diplomacy, 1921–1922* (Chapel Hill: University of North Carolina Press, 1984)

Fischer, C. *The Rise of the Nazis* (Manchester: Manchester University Press, 2002)

_____ *The Ruhr Crisis, 1923–1924* (Oxford: Oxford University Press, 2003)

Fischer, W. *German Hyperinflation 1922–23: A Law and Economics Approach* (Cologne: Josef Eul, 2010)

Fox, J. 'Britain and the Allied Military Commission of Control, 1925–26', *Journal of Contemporary History*, Vol. 4 (1969), pp.143–64

Frambach, H. 'The First Socialization Debate of 1918: Was the Socialization Commission Doomed to Failure from the Start?' in J. Backhaus, G. Chaloupek and H. Frambach (eds) *The First Socialization Debate (1918) and Early Efforts Towards Socialization* (New York: Springer, 2019), pp.1–16

Freyh, R. 'Stärke und Schwäche der Weimarer Republik', in W. Tormin (ed.) *Die Weimarer Republik* (Hanover: Fackeltäge,1962), pp.137-187.

Fritz, S. 'The NSDAP as Volkspartei? A Look at the Social Bases of the Nazi Voter', *The History Teacher*, Vol. 20 (1987), pp.379–99

Fritzsche, P. 'Presidential Victory and Popular Festivity in Weimar Germany: Hindenburg's 1925 Election, *Central European History*, Vol. 23 (1990), pp.205–24

_____ *Rehearsals for Fascism: Populism and Political Mobilization in Weimar Germany* (New York: Oxford University Press, 1990)

Funkenstein, S. 'Anita Berber: Imaging a Weimar Performance Artist', *Women's*

Art Journal, Vol. 26 (2005), pp.26–31

Gatzke, H. 'Gustav Stresemann: A Bibliographical Article', *Journal of Modern History*, Vol. 36 (1964), pp.1–13

Gay, P. *Weimar Culture: The Outsider as Insider* (W.W. Norton, 2001)

Gellinek, C. *Philipp Scheidemann: Gedächtnis und Erinnerung* (Berlin: Waxmann, 2006)

Gerwarth, R. *November 1918: The German Revolution* (Oxford: Oxford University Press, 2020)

Gessler, O. *Reichswehr Politics in the Weimar Period* (Stuttgart: Kurt Sendtner, 1958)

Geyer, M. 'Contested Narratives of the Weimar Republic: The Case of the Kutisker-Barmat Scandal' in K. Canning, K. Barndt and K. McGuire (eds) *Weimar Publics/Weimar Subjects: Rethinking the Political Culture of Germany in the 1920s* (Oxford: Berghahn, 2010)

Goergen, J. *Walter Ruttmann: Eine Dokumentation* (Berlin: Freunde der deutschen Kinemathek, 1989)

Golecki, A. (ed.) *Das Kabinett von Schleicher* (Boppard am Rhein: Boldt, 1986)

_____ (ed.) *Das Kabinett Bauer (1919/1920)* (Berlin: De Gruyter, 1996)

Gordon, H. 'The Character of Hans von Seeckt', *Military Affairs*, Vol. 20 (1956), pp.94–101

_____ *Hitler and the Beer Hall Putsch* (Princeton, NJ: Princeton University Press, 1972)

Gosnell, H. 'The German Referendum on the Princes' Property', *American Political Science Review*, Vol. 21 (1927), pp.119–23

Grau, B. *Kurt Eisner, 1867–1919* (Munich: C.H. Beck, 2001)

Griffin, R. (ed.) *Fascism* (New York: Oxford University Press, 1995)

Groener, W. *Lebenserinnerungen: Jugend, Generalstab, Weltkrieg* (Göttingen: Vandenhoeck & Ruprecht, 1957)

Gross, S. 'Confidence and Gold: German War Finance 1914–1918', *Central European History*, Vol. 42 (2009), pp.223–52

Grossmann, A. 'The New Woman and the Rationalization of Sexuality in the Weimar Republic', in A. Snitow, C. Stansell and S. Thompson (eds) *Desire: The Politics of Sexuality* (Virago, 1984), pp.190–208

Gruchmann, L. and Weber, R. (eds) *Der Hitler-Prozess* (Munich: K.G. Saur, 1997)

Guttmann, W. *The German Social Democratic Party, 1875–1933* (George Allen and Unwin, 1981)

Hall, H. 'Lloyd George, Briand and the Failure of the Anglo-French Entente', *Journal of Modern History*, Vol. 50 (1978), pp.1121–38

Hallgarten, G. 'Adolf Hitler and Heavy Industry, 1931–1933', *Journal of Economic History*, Vol. 12 (1952), pp.222–46

Haman, B. *Hitler's Vienna: A Dictator's Apprenticeship: A Portrait of the Tyrant as a Young Man*, 2nd edn (Taurus & Parke, 2010)

Hanfstaengl, E. *15 Jahre mit Hitler: Zwischen Weissem und Braunem Haus* (Munich: R. Piper, 1980)

Hankel, G. *The Leipzig Trials: German War Crimes and Their Legal Consequences after World War I* (Dordrecht, Netherlands: Republic of Letters, 2014)

Harbeck, K. (ed.) *Das Kabinett Cuno* (Boppard: H. Boldt, 1968)

Harman, C. *The Lost Revolution: Germany 1918–1923* (Bookmarks, 1982)

Harmer, H. *Friedrich Ebert* (Haus, 2008)

Hartmann, C., Plöckinger, O., Töppel, R. and Vordermayer, T. (eds) *Hitler, Mein Kampf: Eine Kritische Edition* (Munich: Institut für Zeitgeschichte, 2016)

Hauner, M. *Hitler: A Chronology of His Life and Times* (Basingstoke: Palgrave Macmillan, 2005)

Hayman, R. *Hitler and Geli* (Bloomsbury, 1997)

Hehl, U. *Wilhelm Marx 1863–1946; Eine Politische Biographie* (Mainz: Matthias-Grünewald, 1987)

Heiber, H. *The Weimar Republic* (Oxford: Blackwell, 1993)

Heid, L. *Oskar Cohn: ein Sozialist und Zionist im Kaiserreich und in der Weimarer Republik* (Frankfurt am Mein: Campus, 2002)

Heilbronner, O. 'The Failure That Succeeded: Nazi Party Activity in a Catholic Region in Germany, 1929–32', *Journal of Contemporary History*, Vol. 27 (1992), pp.531–49

Hermann, E. *So Ist die neue Frau* (Hellerau: Avalun, 1929)

Hermens, F. 'Proportional Representation and the Breakdown of German Democracy', *Social Research*, Vol. 3 (1936), pp.411–33

Hertzman, L. 'The Founding of the German National People's Party (DNVP), November 1918–January 1919', *Journal of Modern History*, Vol. 30 (1958), pp.24–36

Herzfeld, H. (ed.) *Geschichte in Gestalten: Ein Biographisches Lexikon – A–E* (Frankfurt am Main: Fischer, 1981)

Heske, H. 'Karl Haushofer: His Role in German Politics and in Nazi Politics', *Political Geography*, Vol. 6 (1987), pp.135–44

Hett, B. *The Death of Democracy: Hitler's Rise to Power and the Downfall of the Weimar Republic* (New York: St. Martin's Griffin, 2019)

Heusler, A. *Das Braune Haus* (Munich: Deutsche Verlags-Anstalt, 2008)

Himmer, R. 'Rathenau, Russia and Rapallo', *Central European History*, Vol. 9 (1976), pp.146–83

Hinton, S. (ed.) *Kurt Weill: The Threepenny Opera* (Cambridge: Cambridge University Press, 1990)

Hoffrogge, R. *Working Class Politics in the German Revolution: Richard Müller, the Revolutionary Stewards and the Origins of the Council Movement* (Leiden: Brill, 2014)

Hooglund, E. *The Munich Soviet Republic of April, 1919* (Orno: University of Maine, 1966)

Hoppe, B. *In Stalins Gefolgschaft: Moskow und die KPD 1928–1932* (Oldenburg: Wissenschaftsverlag, 2011)

Hoyer, K. *Blood and Iron: The Rise and Fall of the German Empire* (Cheltenham: History Press, 2021)

Hubatsch, W. 'The Scheidemann Cabinet, February 13, 1919, to June 20, 1919', *Philosophy and History*, Vol. 5 (1972), pp.100–2

Huber, E. *Deutsche Verfassungsgeschichte seit 1789*, Bd. 5: *Weltkrieg, Revolution and Reichserneuerung, 1914–1919* (Stuttgart: Kohlhammer, 1978)

Hudson, M. 'The World Court and the Austro-German Customs Regime', *American Bar Association Journal*, Vol. 17 (1931), pp.791–3

Hunt, R. 'Myths, Guilt and Shame in Pre-Nazi Germany', *Virginia Quarterly Review*, Vol. 34 (1958), pp.355–71

Hunter, D. (ed.) *Seduction and Theory: Readings of Gender, Representation and Rhetoric* (Urbana: University of Illinois Press, 1989)

Imhoof, D. 'Blue Angel, Brown Culture: The Politics of Film Reception in Göttingen', in J. Williams (ed.) *Weimar Culture Revisited* (Basingstoke: Palgrave Macmillan, 2011), pp.50–72

Irrgang, C. and Kern, I. (ed.) *Neue Meisterhäuser in Dessau 1925–2014* (Leipzig: Spector Books, 2013)

Jablonsky, D. *The Nazi Party in Dissolution: Hitler and the Verbotzeit, 1923–1925* (Routledge, 2013)

Jäckel, E. *Hitler's World View: A Blueprint for World Power* (Cambridge, MA: Harvard University Press, 1981)

_____ and Kuhn, A. (eds) *Hitler: Sämtliche Aufzeichnungen, 1905–1924* (Stuttgart: Deutsche Verlags-Anstalt, 1980)

Jacobs, S., Hielscher, E. and Kinik, A. (eds) *The City Symphony Phenomenon: Cinema, Art, and Urban Modernity Between the Wars* (New York: Routledge, 2019)

Jacobson, J. 'The Impulse for a Franco-German Entente: The Origins of the Thoiry Conference, 1926', *Journal of Contemporary History*, Vol. 10 (1975), pp.157–81

Jessen-Klingenberg, M. 'Die Ausrufung der Republik durch Philipp Scheidemann am 9 November 1918', *Geschichte in Wissenschaft und Unterricht*, Vol. 19 (1968), pp.649–56

Jones, L. *German Liberalism and the Dissolution of the Weimar Party System, 1918–1933* (Chapel Hill: University of North Carolina Press, 1988)

_____ 'Franz von Papen, the German Centre Party and the failure of Catholic Conservatism in the Weimar Republic', *Central European History*, Vol. 38 (2005), pp.191–217

_____ 'Nationalists, Nazis and the Assault against Weimar: Revisiting the Harzburg Rally of October 1931', *German Studies Review*, Vol. 29 (2006), pp.483–94

_____ 'German Conservatism at the Crossroads: Count Kuno von Westarp and the Struggle for the Control of the DNVP, 1928–1930', *Contemporary European History*, Vol. 18 (2009), pp.147–77

_____'Franz von Papen and the Establishment of the Third Reich', *Journal of Modern History*, Vol. 83 (2011), pp.272–318

_____*Hitler versus Hindenburg: The 1932 Presidential Elections and the End of the Weimar Republic* (Cambridge: Cambridge University Press, 2015)

_____ 'Taming the Beast: Kurt von Schleicher and the End of the Weimar Republic', in H. Beck and L. Jones (eds) *From Weimar to Hitler: Studies in the Dissolution of the Weimar Republic and the Establishment of the Third Reich 1932–1934* (Oxford: Berghahn, 2019), pp.24–6

_____*The German Right, 1918–1930: Political Parties, Organized Interests and Patriotic Associations in the Struggle against Weimar Germany* (Cambridge: Cambridge University Press, 2021)

Jones, M. *Founding Weimar: Violence and the German Revolution of 1918–1919* (Cambridge: Cambridge University Press, 2016)

Jonge, A. *The Weimar Chronicle: Prelude to Hitler* (Paddington Press, 1978)

Kaes, A., Jay, M. and Dimenberg, E. (eds) *The Weimar Republic Sourcebook* (Berkeley: University of California Press, 1994)

Karcher, E. *Otto Dix; 1891–1969: His Life and Works* (Cologne: Benedikt Taschen, 1988)

Kater, M. *The Nazi Party: A Social Profile of Members and Leaders, 1919–1945* (Oxford: Blackwell, 1983)

Kaufmann, W. *Monarchism in the Weimar Republic* (New York: Octogan Books, 1973)

Keiger, J. *Raymond Poincaré and the Ruhr Crisis* (Routledge, 1998)

Kershaw, I. *Hitler, Vol 1: 1889–1936* (Penguin, 2001)

Kerwin, J. 'The German Reichstag Elections of July 31, 1932', *American Political Science Review*, Vol. 26 (1932), pp.921–6

Keynes, J. *The Economic Consequences of the Peace* (Macmillan, 1919)

King, D. *The Trial of Adolf Hitler: The Beer Hall Putsch and the Rise of Nazi Germany* (Pan, 2018)

King, G., Rosen, O., Tanner, M. and Wagner, A. 'Ordinary Economic Voting Behaviour in the Extraordinary Election of Adolf Hitler', *Journal of Economic History*, Vol. 68 (2008), pp.951–96

Kippers, H. *Joseph Wirth: Parlamentarier, Minister und Kanzler der Weimarer Republik* (Stuttgart: Franz Steiner, 1997)

Kitchen, M. *The Silent Dictatorship: The Politics of the German High Command under Hindenburg and Ludendorff 1916–1918* (Routledge, 2019)

Kitching, C. 'Prime Minister and Foreign Secretary: The Dual

Role of James Ramsay MacDonald', *Review of International Studies*, Vol. 37 (2011), pp.1403–22

Klein, M. *Rainbow's End: The Crash of 1929* (New York: Oxford University Press, 2001)

Kochan, L. 'The Russian Road to Rapallo', *Soviet Studies*, Vol. 2 (1950), pp.109–17

Koepp, R. 'Gustav von Kahr and the Emergence of the Radical Right in Bavaria', *The Historian*, Vol. 77 (2015), pp.740–3

Kolb, E. *The Weimar Republic*, trans. P. Fall (Routledge, 1988)

Kollman, E. 'Walter Rathenau and German Foreign Policy: Thoughts and Actions', *Journal of Modern History*, Vol. 24 (1952), pp.127–42

Koops, T. (ed.) *Die Kabinette Brüning I and II*, 3 vols (Boppard am Rhein: Boldt, 1982–1990)

Kracauer, S. *From Caligari to Hitler: A Psychological History of German Film*, revised edn (Princeton, NJ: Princeton University Press, 2004)

Kranzfelder, I. *George Grosz* (Cologne: Benedikt Taschen, 2005)

Kreimeier, K. *The UFA Story: A History of Germany's Greatest Film Company, 1918–1945* (Berkeley: University of California Press, 1999)

Krupp von Bohlen, A. and Halbach-Stiftung, F. *The Krupp Trial before French Court Martial* (Munich: Sueddeutsche Monatshefte, 1923)

Kubizek, A. *The Hitler I Knew: The Memoirs of Hitler's Childhood Friend*, revised edn (Frontline, 2011)

Kuhn, G. (ed. and trans.) *All Power to the Councils: A Documentary History of the German Revolution of 1918–1919*

(Oakland, CA: PM Press, 2012)

Kunz, A. *Civil Servants and the Politics of Inflation, 1914–1924* (New York: De Gruyter, 1986)

Kuo, G. 'Explaining Historical Employer Coordination: Evidence from Germany', *Comparative Politics*, Vol. 48 (2015), pp.87–106

Lackner, S. *Max Beckmann* (Thames & Hudson, 2001)

Landauer, C. 'The Bavarian Problem in the Weimar Republic, Part 2', *Journal of Modern History*, Vol. 16 (1944), pp.205–23

Large, D. 'The Politics of Law and Order: A History of the Bavarian Einwohnerwehr, 1918–1921', *Transactions of the American Philosophical Society*, Vol. 70 (1980), pp.1–87

Lauryssens, S. *The Man Who Invented the Third Reich* (Cheltenham: History Press, 2010)

Lecane, P. *Torpedoed!: The RMS Leinster Disaster* (Penzance: Persicope, 2005)

Lemmons, R. *Goebbels and Der Angriff* (Lexington: University of Kentucky Press, 1994)

_____ '"Germany's Eternal Son": The Genesis of the Ernst Thälmann Myth, 1930–1950', *German Studies Review*, Vol. 32 (2009), pp.343–56

_____ *Hitler's Rival: Ernst Thälmann in Myth and Memory* (Lexington: University of Kentucky Press, 2013)

Leopold, J. *Alfred Hugenberg: The Radical Nationalist Campaign against the Weimar Republic* (New Haven, CT: Yale University Press, 1977)

Lesniewski, P. 'Three Insurrections: Upper Silesia, 1919–1921', in P. Stachura (ed.) *Poland Between the Wars, 1918–1939* (New York: St. Martin's Press, 1998), pp.13–42

Lessing, T., Berg, K. and Goodwin, G. (eds) *Monsters of Weimar* (Nemesis, 1993)

Liddle, P. and Cecil, H. (eds) *At the Eleventh Hour: Reflections, Hopes and Anxieties at the Closing of the Great War, 1918* (Barnsley: Pen & Sword, 1998)

Lieberman, B. 'Turning against the Weimar Right: Landlords, the Economic Party and the DNVP', *German History*, Vol. 15 (1997), pp.56–79

Longerich, P. *Hitler* (Oxford: Oxford University Press, 2019)

Ludendorff, E. *Ludendorff's Own Story*, Vol.1 (New York: Harper & Brothers, 1919)

Ludewig, H. *Arbeiterbewegung und Aufstand: Eine Untersuchung zum Verhalten der Arbeiterparteien in den Aufstandsbewegungen der frühen Weimarer Republik, 1920–1923* (Hasum: Matthiesen, 1978)

Lurker, O. *Hitler hinter Festungsmauern: Ein Bild aus Trüben Tagen* (Berlin: Mittler, 1933)

Lutz, R. *The German Revolution, 1918–1919* (Cambridge: Cambridge University Press, 1922)

Luxemburg, R. 'Die Ordnung herrscht in Berlin', in R. Luxemburg, *Ausgewaehlte Reden und Schriften*, Vol. 2 (Berlin: Dietz, 1951)

Lyttelton, A. *The Seizure of Power: Fascism in Italy, 1919–1929* (New York: Routledge, 2008)

Machtan, L. *The Hidden Hitler* (Perseus Press, 2001)

_____ *Prinz Max von Baden: Der letzte Kanzler des Kaisers* (Berlin: Theiss, 2013)

Malin, L. (ed.) *Leonard Martin's 2005 Movie Guide* (Plume, 2005)

Marks, S. *The Illusion of Peace: International Relations in Europe 1918–1933* (Macmillan, 1976)

_____ 'The Myths of Reparations', *Central European History*, Vol. 11 (1978), pp.231–55

_____ 'Mussolini and Locarno: Mussolini's Foreign Policy in Microcosm', *Journal of Contemporary History*, Vol. 14 (1979), pp.423–39

Mayer-Hartmann, F. and Dresler, A. (eds) *Dokumente der Zeitgeschichte* (Munich: Franz Eher Nachfolger, 1938)

Mayne, J. 'Marlene Dietrich, The Blue Angel and Female Performance', in D. Hunter (ed.) *Seduction and Theory: Readings of Gender, Representation and Rhetoric* (Urbana: University of Illinois Press, 1989), pp.28–46

McDonough, F., with Cochrane, J. *The Holocaust* (Basingstoke: Palgrave Macmillan, 2008)

McDougall, W. *France's Rhineland Policy, 1914–1924: The Last Bid for a Balance of Power in Europe* (Princeton, NJ: Princeton University Press, 2015)

McElligott, A. (ed.) *Weimar Germany* (Oxford: Oxford University Press, 2009)

Medlicott, W., Dakin, D. and Lambert, M. (eds) *Documents on British Foreign Policy, 1919–1939*, First Series, Vol. XVI (HMSO, 1966)

_____ (eds) *Documents on British Foreign Policy, 1919–1939*, Series IA, Vols VI, VII (HMSO, 1975)

_____ (eds) *Documents on British Foreign Policy, 1919–1939*, First Series, Vol. XX (HMSO, 1976)

Meier-Welcker, H. *Seeckt* (Frankfurt am Main: Bernard Verlag für Wehrwesen, 1967)

Menke, M. 'Ludwig Kaas and the end of the German Centre Party', in H. Beck and L. Jones (eds) *From Weimar to Hitler:*

Studies in the Dissolution of the Weimar Republic and the Establishment of the Third Reich, 1932–1934 (Oxford: Berghahn, 2019), pp.79–110

Mills, J. *Genoa Conference* (Hutchinson, 1922)

Milward, A. and Saul, S. *The Development of the Economies of Continental Europe, 1850–1914* (Allen & Unwin, 1977)

Minden, M. and Bachmann, H. *Fritz Lang's Metropolis: Cinematic Versions of Technology and Fear* (New York: Camden House, 2002)

Minuth, K. (ed.) *Die Kabinette Luther I und II*, 2 vols (Boppard am Rhein: Vandenhoeck und Ruprecht, 1977)

_____(ed.) *Das Kabinett von Papen*, 2 vols (Boppard am Rhein: Boldt, 1989)

Mitchell, A. *Revolution in Bavaria: The Eisner Regime and the Soviet Republic* (Princeton, NJ: Princeton University Press, 1965)

Moore, F. 'Eisner: A Great Loss', *New York Tribune*, 25 February 1919

Morgan, D. *The Socialist Left and the German Revolution: A History of the German Independent Social Democratic Party* (Ithaca, NY: Cornell University Press, 1975)

Morril, D. 'The Comintern and the German Independent Social Democratic Party', *The Historian*, Vol. 31 (1970), pp.191–209

Mueller, G. 'Rapallo Re-examined: A New Look at Germany's Secret Military Collaboration with Russia in 1922', *Military Affairs*, Vol. 40 (1976), pp.109–17

Mühlhausen, W. *Friedrich Ebert 1871–1925, Reichspräsident der Weimarer Republik* (Bonn: Deitz, 2006)

Murdoch, B. 'Innocent Killing: Erich Maria Remarque and the Weimar Anti-War Novels', in K. Leydecker, *German Novelists of the Weimar Republic: Intersections of Literature and Politics* (Rochester, NY: Camden House, 2006), pp.141–68

Nakagaki, T. *The Buddhist Swastika and Hitler's Cross: Rescuing a Symbol of Peace from the Forces of Hate* (Berkeley, CA: Stone Bridge Press, 2018)

Naylor, G. *The Bauhaus Reassessed* (New York: Dutton, 1985)

Newman, M. 'Britain and the German–Austrian Customs Union Proposal of 1931', *European History Quarterly*, Vol. 6 (1976), pp.449–72

Niemann, A. *Kaiser und Revolution: Die entscheidenden Ereignisse im Grossen Hauptquartier im Herbst 1918* (Berlin: Verlag fur Kulturpolitik, 1928)

Noakes, J. 'Conflict and Development in the NSDAP', *Journal of Contemporary History*, Vol. 1 (1966), pp.3–36

_____ and G. Pridham (eds) *Nazism, 1919–1945: A Documentary Reader*, Vol 1: *The Rise to Power* (Exeter: Exeter University Press, 1983)

Nohlen, D. and Stöver, P. (eds) *Elections in Europe: A Data Handbook* (Baden-Baden: Nomos, 2010)

Noske, G. *Von Kiel bis Kapp: Zur Geschichte der deutschen Revolution* (Berlin: Verlag für Politik und Wirtschaft, 1920)

O'Lessker, K. 'Who Voted for Hitler? A New Look at the Class Basis of Nazism', *American Journal of Sociology*, Vol. 74 (1968), pp.63–9

O'Loughlin, J., Flint, C. and Anselin, L. 'The Geography of the Nazi Vote: Context, Confession and Class in the Reichstag Election of 1930',

Annals of the Association of American Geographers, Vol. 84 (1994), pp.351–80

O'Riordan, E. 'British Foreign Policy and the Ruhr Occupation Crisis' (University of London PhD thesis, January 1998)

Orde, A. 'The Origins of the German–Austrian Customs Union Affair of 1931', *Central European History*, Vol. 13 (1980), pp.34–59

Orlow, D. *Weimar Prussia, 1925–1933: The Illusion of Strength* (Pittsburgh, PA: University of Pittsburgh Press, 1991)

Papen, F. *Memoirs*, trans. B. Connell (Andre Deutsch, 1952)

Patch, W. *Heinrich Brüning and the Dissolution of the Weimar Republic* (Cambridge: Cambridge University Press, 1998)

Patterson, C. 'The Admission of Germany to the League of Nations and its Probable Significance', *Southwestern Political and Social Science Quarterly*, Vol. 7 (1926), pp.215–37

Payne, S. *The Life and Death of Adolf Hitler* (New York: Popular Library, 1973)

Pelz, W. *A People's History of the German Revolution* (Pluto Press, 2018)

Petrie, C. *The Life and Letters of the Right Hon. Sir Austen Chamberlain*, Vol. 2 (Cassel, 1940)

Petzina, D. 'Germany and the Great Depression', *Journal of Contemporary History*, Vol. 4 (1969), pp.59–74

Petzold, J. *Franz von Papen: Ein Deutsches Verhängnis* (Munich: Buchverlag Union, 1995)

Phelps, R. '"Before Hitler Came": Thule Society and Germanen Orden', *Journal of Modern*

History, Vol. 35 (1963), pp. 245–61

Piper, E. *Kurze Geschichte des Nationalsozialismus von 1919 bis Heute (Zeitgeschite)* (Hamburg: Hoffmann & Kampf, 2007)

Plehwe, F. *Reichskanzler Kurt von Schleicher: Weimars letzte Chance gegen Hitler* (Esslingen: Bechtle, 1983)

Pollock, J. 'The German Reichstag Elections of 1930', *American Political Science Review*, Vol. 24 (1930), pp. 989–95

Priestland, D. *Red Flag: A History of Communism* (New York: Grove, 2009)

Pryce, D. 'The Reich Government versus Saxony, 1923: The Decision to Intervene', *Central European History*, Vol. 10 (1977), pp. 112–47

Pyta, W. *Hindenburg; Herrschaft zwischen Hohenzollern und Hitler* (Munich: Siedler, 2007)

Rabenau, F. (ed.) *Seeckt: Aus Seinem Leben, 1918–1936* (Leipzig: Hase & Kohler, 1940)

Range, P. *1924: The Year That Made Hitler* (Little Brown, 2016)

Rathenau, W. *An Deutschlands Jugend* (Berlin: Fischer, 1918)

Read, A. *The Devil's Disciples: Hitler's Inner Circle* (W.W. Norton 2004)

Remarque, E. *All Quiet on the Western Front* (Putnam, 1929)

Rhodes, B. *United States Foreign Policy in the Interwar Period: The Golden Age of American Diplomatic and Military Complacency* (Westport, CT: Praeger, 2001)

Ribhegge, W. *Preussen im Westen: Kampf um Parlamentarismus in Rheinland und Westfalen 1789–1947* (Münster: Richter Ludwig, 2008)

Ringer, F. (ed.) *The German Inflation of 1923* (Oxford: Oxford University Press, 1969)

Rogowski, C. (ed.) *The Many Faces of Weimar Cinema: Rediscovering Germany's Filmic Legacy* (Rochester, NY: Camden House 2010)

Röhl, J. *Wilhelm II*, Vol. 3: *Into the Abyss of War and Exile, 1900–1941*, trans. S. de Bellaigue and F. Bridge (Cambridge: Cambridge University Press, 2014)

Rosenbaum, R. 'Hitler's Doomed Angel', *Vanity Fair*, April 1992

Rurup, R. 'Problems of the German Revolution 1918-19', *Journal of Contemporary History*, Vol. 3 (1968), pp. 109–35

Ryder, A. *The German Revolution of 1918: A Study of Socialism in War and Revolt* (Cambridge: Cambridge University Press, 1967)

Sass, E. 'WWI Centennial: The Black Day of the German Army', available online at www.mentalfloss.com/article/554193/wwi-centennial-black-day-german-army

Schacht, H. *My First Seventy-Six Years* (Allan Wingate, 1955)

Scheidemann, P. *Der Zusammenbruch* (Norderstedt: Vero, 2013)

Schirmann, L. *Justizmanipulationen Der Altonaer Blutsonntag und die Altonaer bzw Hamburger Justiz 1932–1994* (Berlin: Typographica Mitte, 1995)

Schmied, W. *Neue Sachlichkeit and German Realism in the Twenties* (Arts Council of Great Britain, 1979)

Schnabel, I. 'The German Twin Crisis of 1931', *Journal of Economic History*, Vol. 64 (2004), pp. 822–71

Schroeder, C. *Er War Mein Chef: Aus den Nachlass der Sekretärin von Adolf Hitler* (Munich: Langen Müller, 1985)

Schulz-Bidlingmaier, I. (ed.) *Die Kabinette Wirth I und II* (Boppard am Rhein: H. Boldt, 1973)

Schulze, H. (ed.) *Das Kabinett Scheidemann* (Berlin: De Gruyter, 1971)

Schumann, D. *Political Violence in the Weimar Republic, 1918–1933* (Oxford: Berghahn, 2009)

Schüren, U. *Der Volksentscheid zur Fürstenenteignung, 1926* (Düsseldorf: Drost, 1978)

Seal, S. 'Transnational Press Discourses on German Antisemitism during the Weimar Republic: The Riots in Berlin's Scheunenviertel, 1923', *The Leo Boeck Institute Yearbook*, Vol. 59 (2014), pp. 91–120

Sebrow, M. *Der Rathenaumord: Rekonstruktion einer Verschwörung gegen die Republik von Weimar* (Munich: Oldenburg, 1994)

Seidl, C. 'The Bauer-Schumpeter Controversy on Socialization', *History of Economic Ideas*, Vol. 2 (1994), pp 41–69

Seul, S. 'Transnational Press Discourses on German Antisemitism during the Weimar Republic: The Riots in Berlin's Scheunenviertel, 1923', *Leo Baeck Institute Yearbook*, Vol. 59 (2014), pp. 91–120

Shachtman, T. *The Day America Crashed: A Narrative Account of the Great Stock Market Crash of October 24, 1929* (New York: Putnam, 1979)

Sharp, A. *Versailles 1919: A Centennial Perspective* (Haus, 2018)

Shekarloo, P. *Maltzan, the Architect of Rapallo: Weimar Foreign Policy, German-Soviet Relations, and the Treaty of Versailles, 1920–1922* (Munich: Grin, 2010)

Shirer, W. *The Rise and Fall of The Third Reich* (Arrow, 1991)

Sieche, E. 'Germany', in R. Gardiner and R. Chesneau (eds) *Conway's All the World's Fighting Ships, 1922–1946* (Conway Maritime Press, 1992), pp.218–54

Siemens, D. *The Making of a Nazi Hero: The Murder and Myth of Horst Wessel* (I.B.Taurus, 2013)

Sigmund, A. *Die Frauen der Nazis* (Munich: Heyne, 2005)

Simms, B. *Hitler: Only the World Was Enough* (Allen Lane, 2019)

Smith, D. 'Friedrich Ratzal and the Origins of Lebensraum', *German Studies Review*, Vol. 3 (1980), pp.51–68

Smith, J. *Unequal Giants: Diplomatic Relations between the United States and Brazil, 1890–1930* (Pittsburgh, PA: University of Pittsburgh Press, 1977)

Snell, J. 'Wilson on Germany and the Fourteen Points', *Journal of Modern History*, Vol. 26 (1964), pp.364–9

Stambrook, F. '"Das Kind": Lord D'Abernon and the Origins of the Locarno Pact', *Central European History*, Vol. 1 (1968), pp.233–63

Stern, H. 'The Organisation Consul', *Journal of Modern History*, Vol. 35 (1963), pp.20–33

Stogbauer, C. 'The radicalisation of the German Electorate: Swinging to the Right and the Left in the twilight of the Weimar Republic', *European Review of Economic History*, Vol. 5 (2001), pp.251–80

Suarez, G. (ed.) *Briand*, Vol. 6: *L'Artisan de la Paix, 1923–1932* (Paris: Plon, 1940)

Sudendorf, W. *Marlene Dietrich* (Berlin: DTV Deutscher Taschenbuch, 1980)

Sutton, E. (ed.) *Gustav Stresemann, His Diaries, Letters and Papers*, 3 vols (Macmillan, 1935, 1937, 1940)

Taylor, F. *The Downfall of Money: Germany's Hyperinflation and the Destruction of the Middle Class* (Bloomsbury, 2013)

Taylor, M. *The Life and Writings of Erich Maria Remarque* (Fales Library, New York University, 2011)

Termin, P. 'The German Crisis of 1931', *Clionetrica*, Vol. 2 (2007), pp.5–17

Thompson, P. and Sacks, G. (eds) *The Cambridge Companion to Brecht* (Cambridge: Cambridge University Press, 1994)

Toland, J. *Adolf Hitler: The Definitive Biography* (New York: Bantam Doubleday Dell, 1991)

Toller, E. *I Was a German*, trans. E. Crankshaw (Bodley Head, 1934)

Tooley, T. 'German Political Violence and the Border Plebiscite in Upper Silesia, 1919–1921', *Central European History*, Vol. 21 (1988), pp.56–98

Treviranus, G. *Das Ende von Weimar: Heinrich Brüning und seine Zeit* (Düsseldorf: Econ Verlag, 1968)

Turner, H. *Stresemann and The Politics of the Weimar Republic* (Princeton, NJ: Princeton University Press, 1963)

_____ 'Continuity in German Foreign Policy? The Case of Stresemann', *International History Review*, Vol. 1 (1979), pp.509–21

_____ *Hitler's Thirty Days to Power: January 1933* (Basic Books, 1997)

_____ 'The Myth of Chancellor von Schleicher's Querfront Strategy', *Central European History*, Vol. 41 (2008), pp.673–81

Ullrich, V. *Hitler*: Vol. 1: *Ascent* (Bodley Head, 2013)

_____ *Hitler*, Vol. 2: *Downfall* (Bodley Head, 2020)

Usborne, C. 'The New Woman and Generational Conflict: Perceptions of Young Women's Sexual Mores in the Weimar Republic', in M. Roseman (ed.) *Generations in Conflict: Youth Revolt and Generational Formation in Germany, 1770–1968* (Cambridge: Cambridge University Press, 1995), pp.137–63

van der Vat, D. *The Great Scuttle: The Sinking of the Fleet at Scapa Flow in 1919* (Edinburgh: Birlinn, 2007)

Vascik, G. and Sadler, M. (eds) *The Stab-in-the-Back Myth and the Fall of the Weimar Republic: A History in Documents and Visual Sources* (London: Bloomsbury, 2016)

Vogt, M. (ed.) *Das Kabinett Müller I* (Boppard am Rhein: Boldt, 1970)

_____ (ed.) *Das Kabinett Müller II* (Berlin: De Gruyter, 1996)

Wachsmann, N. *Hitler's Prisons: Legal terror in Nazi Germany* (New Haven: Yale University Press, 2004)

Waite, R. *Vanguard of Nazism: The Free Corps Movement in Post War Germany, 1918–1923* (Cambridge, MA: Harvard University Press, 1952)

_____ *The Psychopathic God: Adolf Hitler* (New York: Basic Books, 1977)

Walker, D. 'The German National People's Party: The Conservative Dilemma in the Weimar Republic', *Journal of Contemporary History*, Vol. 14 (1979), pp.627–47

Wallach, K. *Passing Illusions: Jewish Visibility in Weimar Germany* (Ann Arbor: University of Michigan Press, 2017)

Walter, T. (ed.) *Die Weimarer Republik* (Hanover, Fackeltäger, 1973)

Walther, P. *Darkness Falling: The Strange Death of the Weimar*

Republic, 1930–1933 (Head of Zeus, 2021)

Wandycz, P. *France and Her Eastern Allies 1919–1925: French–Czechoslovak–Polish Relations from the Paris Peace Conference to Locarno* (Minneapolis: University of Minnesota Press, 1962)

_____ *Twilight of French Eastern Alliances, 1926–1936: French–Czechoslovak–Polish Relations from Locarno to the Remilitarization of the Rhineland*, 2nd edn (Princeton, NJ: Princeton University Press, 2014)

Weber, T. *Becoming Hitler: The Making of a Nazi* (Oxford: Oxford University Press, 2017)

Weidermann, V. *Dreamers: When the Writers Took Power: Germany, 1919* (Pushkin Press, 2019)

Weinberg, G. *Hitler's Second Book: The Unpublished Sequel to Mein Kampf* (New York: Enigma Books, 2003)

Weitz, E. *Creating German Communism, 1890–1990: From Popular Protests to Socialist State* (Princeton, NJ: Princeton University Press, 1997)

_____ *Weimar Germany: Promise and Tragedy* (Princeton, NJ: Princeton University Press, 2007)

West, F. *A Crisis of the Weimar Republic: The Referendum of 20 June 1926* (Philadelphia, PA: American Philosophical Society, 1985)

Wette, W. *The Wehrmacht: History, Myth, Reality* (Cambridge, MA: Harvard University Press, 2006)

Wetzell, F. *Inventing the Criminal: A History of the German Criminal, 1880–1945* (Chapel Hill: University of Carolina Press, 2000)

_____ *Crime and Criminal Justice in Modern Germany* (Oxford: Berghahn, 2014)

Wheeler-Bennett, J. *Brest-Litovsk: The Forgotten Peace, March 1918* (Macmillan, 1938)

_____ *Hindenburg: The Wooden Titan* (Macmillan, 1967)

_____ *The Nemesis of Power: German Army in Politics, 1918–1945*, 2nd edn (New York: Palgrave Macmillan, 2005)

Whitford, F. (ed.) *The Bauhaus: Masters and Students by Themselves* (Conran Octopus, 1992)

Wilde, M. 'The State of Emergency in the Weimar Republic: Legal Disputes over Article 48 of the Weimar Constitution', *Legal History Review*, Vol. 78 (2010), pp.135–58

Willet, J. *Art and Politics in the Weimar Period: The New Sobriety 1917–1933* (Thames & Hudson, 1978)

Williams, J. 'The Geneva Protocol of 1924 for the Pacific Settlement of International Disputes', *Journal of the British Institute of International Affairs*, Vol. 3 (1924), pp.288–304

Williamson, D. 'Great Britain and the Ruhr Crisis, 1923-1924', *British Journal of International Studies*, Vol. 3 (1977), pp.70–91

Wilson, J. *Hitler's Alpine Retreat* (Barnsley: Pen & Sword, 2005)

Winkler, H. *Von der Revolution zur Stabilisierung: Arbeiter und Arbeiterbewegung in der Weimarer Republik, 1918–1924* (Berlin: J.W. Deitz Nachf, 1984)

_____ *Weimar 1918–1933: Die Geschichte der Ersten Deutschen Demokratie* (Munich: C.H. Beck, 1998)

_____ *Germany: The Long Road West*, Vol. 2: *1933–1990* (Oxford: Oxford University Press, 2006)

Wolff, C. *Magnus Hirschfeld: A Portrait of a Pioneer in Sexology* (Quartet Books, 1986)

Wolfgang, M. 'Cesare Lombroso', in H. Mannheim (ed.) *Pioneers in Criminology* (Stevens, 1960), pp.168–227

Wright, J. 'Stresemann and Locarno', *Contemporary European History*, Vol. 4 (1995), pp.109–31

_____ and Wright, J. 'One Mind at Locarno? Aristide Briand and Gustav Stresemann', in S. Casey and J. Wright (eds) *Mental Maps in the Era of Two World Wars* (Basingstoke: Palgrave Macmillan, 2008), pp.58–76

Wulf, P. (ed.) *Das Kabinett Fehrenbach* (Oldenburg: Wissenschaftsverlag, 1972)

Wunderlich, F. 'The German Unemployment Insurance Act of 1927', *Quarterly Journal of Economics*, Vol. 42 (1928), pp.278–306

Yarnall, J. *Barbed Wire Disease: British and German Prisoners of War, 1914–1918* (Stroud: Spellmount, 2011)

Yee, R. 'Reparations Revisited: The Role of Economic Advisers in Reforming German Central Banking and Public Finance', *Financial History Review*, Vol. 27 (2020), pp.45–72

Zeender, J. 'The German Catholics and the Presidential Election of 1925', *Journal of Modern History*, Vol. 25 (1963), pp.266–381

_____ 'Recent Literature on the German Centre Party', *Catholic Historical Review*, Vol. 70 (1984), pp.428–41

Zentner, C. and Bedürftig, F. *The Encyclopedia of the Third Reich* (New York: Macmillan, 1991)

Zoob, D. *Brecht: A Political Handbook* (Nick Hern Books, 2018)

IMAGE CREDITS

INDEX

Goebbels, Joseph, 254, 311, 314, 344,
363, 434–6, 440, 444–5, 450, 476,
484, 487, 495, 498, 509, 517, 524–5,
530
Golem, Der, 338
Goltz, Count Rüdiger von der, 117,
394
Göring, Hermann, 363, 449, 470,
477, 509, 512–13, 524, 531, 533–4
Gotheim, Georg, 74, 101
Gothein, Eberhard, 117–18
Gradnauer, Georg, 158
Gray, Joel, 428
Great Depression, 13, 403–4, 537
Gröber, Adolf, 27, 31, 70
Groener, Wilhelm, 23, 35–7, 47, 53,
58, 104, 143, 158, 170, 198, 359, 366,
408, 411, 419, 445, 470, 491–2
Gropius, Walter, 14, 239, 326
Grossman, Karl (the 'Berlin
Butcher'), 163
Grosz, George, 14, 291
Guard Cavalry Rifle Division, 65
Guérard, Theodor von, 359, 365, 386,
419, 470
Guide to Depraved Berlin, 428
Gürtner, Franz, 499
Gutmann, Hugo, 92
Gutt, Camille, 383

H

Haarmann, Fritz (the 'Vampire of
Hanover'), 163–4
Haas, Willy, 340
Haase, Hugo, 30, 32, 53, 56, 58–9, 69,
117
Habsburg Empire, 27, 88
Hague Conferences, 395–6, 407, 416
Hall, Mordaunt, 342
Hamburg American Line
(HAPAG), 198, 348
Hamburg revolt, 225
Hamburger Nachrichten, 124
Hameister, Willy, 139
Hamm, Eduard, 236
Hammerstein-Equord, Kurt von,
492
Hanfstaengl, Ernst ('Putzi'), 232,
462
Hanisch, Reinhold, 87–8
Harbou, Thea von, 338
Harden, Sylvia von, 291
Harding, William, 156
Harrer, Karl, 113, 115–16

Hartlaub, Gustav, 288
Hartwig, Josef, 242
Harzburg Front, 471
Haslinde, Heinrich, 308
Hauptmann, Elisabeth, 372
Haushofer, Karl, 264
Häusler, Rudolf, 89–90
Haussmann, Conrad, 31
Heartfield, John, 14
Heidler, Johann Georg, 81
Heidler, Johann Nepomuk, 81
Heinz, Rudolf, 70, 143, 198, 225
Held, Heinrich, 284–5
Helfferich, Karl, 123–5, 164, 178
Hellmann, Ernst, 282
Hellpach, Willy, 284–5
Helm, Brigitte, 338
Henderson, Arthur, 395, 412, 422
Henning, Wilhelm, 308
Hergt, Oskar, 126, 142, 269, 300, 343
Hermes, Andreas, 143, 158, 170, 198
Herrenvolk, 262
Herriot, Édouard, 247, 259, 265,
267–9, 271, 280, 292
Herrmann, Elsa, 388
Hertling, Georg von, 27–8, 31
Hesnard, Oswald, 322
Hess, Rudolf, 260, 367, 463–4
Hesse, Fritz, 326
Hesse, Hermann Karl, 291
Heye, Wilhelm, 324
Heyne, Karl, 123
High Seas Fleet, 42, 48, 98, 152
Hilferding, Rudolf, 55, 216, 222, 365,
396, 407–8
Hindenburg, Oskar von, 343, 408,
468, 492, 495, 532–4
Hindenburg, Paul von, 13, 17, 23,
25–31, 35, 37, 46–7, 49, 54, 109, 195,
274
and Boxheim Papers, 477
and Brüning government, 408,
418–19, 422–3, 440, 444, 454,
458, 466, 469–71, 483, 492,
495–7
and collapse of Weimar
democracy, 537, 539–41
and Crown Prince Wilhelm,
325–6
and 'Day of Liberation', 422
'Easter Message', 286
and elections (1928), 360, 364
and expropriation, 318–20
and Flag Decree, 316–17
and Hitler's appointment as
Chancellor, 527, 530, 532–5
and Luther government, 304–5,
308–9, 316–17

and Marx government, 317, 331,
342–3, 359–60
meetings with Hitler, 470,
510–11, 519
and Müller government, 407–8,
418
and Papen government,
498–500, 510, 513, 516, 518–21
presidential election (1925),
285–8, 320
presidential election (1932),
482–5, 487–9, 491
radio broadcast, 478–9
and Rhineland occupation, 386
and Schleicher government, 521,
530
supports Locarno accords, 301,
304
Tannenberg speech and 80th
birthday, 349–51
and Versailles Treaty, 101, 104,
117–18, 394
and Young Plan, 417
Hindenburg Fund, 351
Hindenburg Programme, 23
Hintze, Paul von, 26, 28
Hirsch, Paul, 62
Hirschfeld, Dr Magnus, 104–6
Hirschfeld, Oltwig von, 124
Hitler, Adolf, 12–13, 15–17, 80–96
'Adolf Hitler – Traitor?'
pamphlet, 162
air tours, 489, 493, 516
and America, 367, 370
antisemitism, 87, 89, 116–17, 146,
196, 263–4, 347
appointed Chancellor, 530–5
and army treason trial, 439
avoids conscription, 90
awarded Iron Cross, 91–2
and Beer Hall Putsch, 226–7,
230, 232–3, 261, 265
and Boxheim Papers, 477
and Brown House, 448–9
and business community, 347
buys Berghof, 377
and *The Blue Angel*, 428
and Brüning government, 420,
451, 454
and *The Cabinet of Dr Caligari*,
141
childhood, 81–3
and collapse of Weimar
democracy, 537–41
compared with Stresemann, 401
cryptorchidism, 232
designs NSDAP flag, 146
Düsseldorf speech, 483
elections (1928), 361, 363–4

M

M – Eine Stadt sucht einen Mörder, 164
MacDonald, Ramsay, 214, 247, 265–9, 271, 395, 400, 457
Macedonian Front, 26
McKenna, Reginald, 235
Magdeburgische Zeitung, 165
Majority Social Democratic Party (MSPD), 29–30, 32, 43, 48–51, 53, 56–8
    declare 'People's Republic of Bavaria', 76
Maltzan, Baron Adolf von, 179, 181
Manchester Guardian, 211, 330, 445
Mann, Ernst Karl August Klemens von, 31
Mann, Heinrich, 426
March Action, 153–4
'March on Berlin', 221, 226–7, 248–9, 252
March on Rome, 195, 221
Marie Louise of Hanover and Cumberland, Princess, 29
Marne, Battle of the, 22–3
Marx, Karl, 39, 55, 261
Marx, Wilhelm, 236, 239, 255–8, 267–73, 275, 308, 317, 342–6, 353–4, 359, 362–4, 378–9
    and Hindenburg's speech and 80th birthday, 349–51
    and presidential election (1925), 284–7
    and secret rearmament, 330–1
Maslow, Arkadi, 224
Matsui, Keishiro, 122
Matthes, Joseph, 234
Matzelberger, Franziska ('Fanni'), 82
Max von Baden, Prince, 28–37, 40, 43, 46, 48–50
May, Karl, 82
Mayer, Carl, 140–1
Mayer, Wilhelm, 101, 132
Mayr, Karl, 95–6, 113, 115–16
Meissner, Otto, 408, 411, 418, 495, 510, 532–4
Mellon, Andrew, 192
Mend, Hans, 92
Mendelsohn, Erich, 14
Menschheit, Die, 348–9
Merkle, Benno, 74
Métivier, Jean, 448
Metropolis, 14, 291, 334, 338–40, 342, 351
Meyer, Carl, 351
Michaelis, Georg, 25
Milestone, Lewis, 388

Millerand, Alexandre, 144–5, 177
Minnelli, Liza, 428
Mitteldeutsche Zeitung, 274
Moeller van den Bruck, Arthur, 218–19
Möhl, Arnold von, 95, 134
Moholy-Nagy, László, 240
Moldenhauer, Paul, 407, 416–17, 419, 421
Moreau, Émile, 383
Moreck, Curt, 428
Morgan, J. P., 255, 383
Morgan, John, 383
Mori, Kengo, 383
Mosconi, Antonio, 395
Mozart, Wolfgang Amadeus, 284
MSPD, *see* Majority Social Democratic Party
Muche, Georg, 242
Mühsam, Erich, 80
Müller, Adolf, 274
Müller, Alfred, 224–5
Müller, Hermann, 101, 104, 123, 132, 136, 142, 194, 215, 364–7, 376–7, 379, 386, 399–400, 405, 407–8, 417–18, 432, 441, 538
Müller, Karl von, 96
Müller, Richard, 40, 57
Müller-Meiningen, Ernst, 134
Münchener Beobachter, 80
Münchener Post, 464–5
Munich Beer Hall Putsch, 13, 226–7, 230, 232–3, 257, 261, 265, 450
    trial, 247–9, 252–4
Munich Revolt, 77, 80, 93–4, 126
Murnau, F. W., 427
Mussolini, Benito, 195–6, 199–200, 219, 221, 252, 265, 297–8, 304, 363–4, 440, 448

N

Nagel, Fritz, 26
National Association of Industry, 379
National Congress of Workers' and Soldiers' Councils, 56
National Economic Council, 111
National Liberal Party (NLP), 20, 31, 70
'National Opposition', 466, 471
National Socialist Freedom Party (NSFP), 257, 273, 310

National Socialist German Workers' Party (NSDAP), 12, 15, 17
    acquires Brown House, 448–9
    adopts swastika symbol, 145–6
    and *All Quiet on the Western Front*, 444–5
    alliance with DNVP, 405
    antisemitic attacks, 344
    ban on SA and SS, 492, 495, 497, 500
    bans on, 208, 230, 257
    and Beer Hall Putsch, 230, 232
    Boxheim Papers, 477
    and Brüning government, 420, 422, 440–1, 444, 462, 466, 469, 474
    and business community, 347, 483
    and cabarets, 428
    elections (1928), 361, 363–4
    elections (1930), 433–9, 448
    elections (1932), 504, 508–9, 517–18
    electoral successes, 412–13, 422–3, 477, 493–4, 532, 537, 540
    founding, 134–5, 260
    and Freedom Law referendum, 398, 412
    and Harzburg Front, 471
    Hitler gains control, 160, 162–3, 310–11, 313–14
    and Hitler's appointment as Chancellor, 530–3, 541
    and Luther government, 309
    membership, 221
    oppose Locarno accords, 300, 304
    oppose Young Plan, 394–5, 435
    organisational changes, 471, 474
    and Papen government, 510–12, 516–17, 520–1
    and presidential election, 482, 484, 487–9
    and Prussian referendum, 462
    Röhm returns to leadership, 450–1
    and Ruhr occupation, 208, 211
    and Schleicher government, 524–7, 533
    split with German Party, 310
    and Strasser split, 520, 524–5
    and Versailles anniversary, 394
    violent clashes with Communists, 474–6, 489, 500–1
Working Community, 311, 313
National-Social Association, 262